SOLZHENITSYN

200 Years Together
Volume 2
The Jews in the Soviet Union

Aleksandr Solzhenitsyn
(1918-2008)

Aleksandr Solzhenitsyn was a Russian novelist, historian, and outspoken critic of Soviet totalitarianism. He is remembered as one of the most important writers and dissidents of the 20th century. His works provided a powerful and damning account of the Soviet Union's repressive system and have had a lasting impact on both literature and political thought. He was awarded the Nobel Prize in Literature in 1970 for the ethical force with which he pursued the indispensable traditions of Russian literature.

Two Hundred Years Together
Volume 2 – The Jews in the Soviet Union

Двести лет вместе, *Dvesti let vmeste - 2001-2002*

Translated and published by
Omnia Veritas Limited

www.omnia-veritas.com

© Omnia Veritas Ltd - 2024

All rights reserved. No part of this publication may be reproduced, distributed, or transmitted in any form or by any means, including photocopying, recording, or other electronic or mechanical methods, without the prior written permission of the publisher, except in the case of brief quotations embodied in critical reviews and certain other noncommercial uses permitted by copyright law.

CHAPTER 13	**11**
THE FEBRUARY REVOLUTION	11
CHAPTER 14	**26**
DURING 1917	26
CHAPTER 15	**54**
ALONGSIDE THE BOLSHEVIKS	54
CHAPTER 16	**96**
DURING THE CIVIL WAR	96
CHAPTER 17	**132**
EMIGRATION BETWEEN THE TWO WORLD WARS	132
CHAPTER 18	**164**
IN THE 1920S	164
CHAPTER 19	**227**
IN THE 1930S	227
CHAPTER 20	**274**
IN THE CAMPS OF GULAG	274
CHAPTER 21	**286**
DURING THE SOVIET-GERMAN WAR	286
CHAPTER 22	**327**
FROM THE END OF THE WAR TO STALIN'S DEATH	327
CHAPTER 23	**345**
BEFORE THE SIX-DAY WAR	345
CHAPTER 24	**366**
BREAKING AWAY FROM BOLSHEVISM	366
CHAPTER 25	**382**
ACCUSING RUSSIA	382
CHAPTER 26	**401**
THE BEGINNING OF EXODUS	401
CHAPTER 27	**421**
ABOUT THE ASSIMILATION	421

Author's afterword 441
OTHER TITLES 443

"A great disaster had befallen Russia: Men have forgotten God; that's why all this has happened."

Chapter 13

The February Revolution

The 123-year-old history of unequal citizenship of the Jewish people in Russia, from the Act of Catherine the Great of 1791, ended with the February Revolution.

It bears looking into the atmosphere of those February days; what was the state of society by the moment of emancipation?

There were no newspapers during the first week of the Revolutionary events in Petrograd. And then they began trumpeting, not looking for the ways to rebuild the state but vying with each other in denouncing all the things of the past. In an unprecedented gesture, the newspaper of the Constitutional Democrats (Kadets), *Rech*, announced that from now on "all Russian life must be rebuilt from the roots."[1646] (A thousand-year life! — why, all of a sudden from "the roots"?) And the *Stock-Market News* announced a program of action:

"Yank, yank all these weed-roots out! No need to worry that there might be some useful plants among them — it's better to weed them all even at the price of unavoidable innocent victims."[1647] (Was this really March 1917 or March 1937?) The new Minister of Foreign Affairs Milyukov bowed and scraped: "Up to now we blushed in front of our allies because of our government…. Russia was a dead weight for our allies."[1648]

Rarely in those beginning days was it possible to hear reasonable suggestions about rebuilding Russia. The streets of Petrograd were in chaos, the police were non-functional and all over the city there was continuous disorderly gunfire. But everything poured into a general rejoicing, though for every concrete question, there was a mess of thoughts and opinions, a cacophony of debating pens. All the press and society agreed on one thing — the immediate legislative enactment of Jewish equality. Fyodor Sologub eloquently wrote in the *Birzheviye Vedomosti*:

[1646] *Rech*, 1917, March 17.
[1647] Birzhevye Vedomosti, 1917, March 8 (here and further, the morning edition).
[1648] ibid, March 10, page 6.

"The most essential beginning of the civil freedom, without which our land cannot be blessed, the people cannot be righteous, national achievements would not be sanctified ... — is the repeal of all religious and racial restrictions."

The equality of Jews advanced very quickly. The 1st of March [old calendar style], one day before the abdication, a few hours before the infamous "Order No. 1," which pushed the army to collapse, V. Makhlakov and M. Adzhemov, two commissars of the Duma Committee delegated to the Ministry of Justice, had issued an internal Ministry of Justice directive, ordering to enlist all Jewish-assistants to attorneys-at-law into the Guild of Judicial Attorneys. "Already by the 3rd of March ... the Chairman of the State Duma, M. Rodzianko, and the Prime Minister of the Provisional Government, Prince G. Lvov, signed a declaration which stated that one of the main goals of the new government is a repeal of all restrictions based upon religion, nationality and social class.'"[1649]

Then, on the 4th of March, the Defense Minister Guchkov proposed to open a path for the Jews to become military officers, and the Minister of Education Manuelov proposed to repeal the percentage quotas on the Jews. Both proposals were accepted without obstacles. On the 6th of March the Minister of Trade and Manufacturing, Konovalov, started to eliminate "national restrictions in corporative legislation," that is, a repeal of the law forbidding purchase of land by companies with Jewish executives.

These measures were quickly put into practice. By the 8th of March in Moscow, 110 Jewish "assistants" were raised to the status of attorneys-at-law; by March 9th in Petrograd — 124 such Jews[1650]; by the 8th of March in Odessa— 60.[1651] On the 9th of March the City Duma of Kiev, not waiting for the upcoming elections, included in its body five Jews with voting power.[1652]

And here — on March 20 the Provisional Government made a resolution, prepared by the Minister of Justice, A. Kerensky, with the participation of members of the political bureau of Jewish deputies in the 4th State Duma ... legislated an act, published on March 22, that repealed "all restrictions on the rights of Russian citizens, regardless of religious creed, dogma or nationality."

[1649] Abridged Jewish Encyclopedia, (heretofore AJE) Jerusalem: Society for the Research of Jewish Community, 1994, Volume 7, Page 377.
[1650] Rech', March 9, 1917 Page 4: March 10, Page 5, et. al.
[1651] Birzheviye Vedomosti, March 9, 1917, Page 2.
[1652] Ibid, March 10, Page 2.

This was, in essence, the first broad legislative act of the Provisional Government. "At the request of the political bureaus (of Jewish deputies), the Jews were not specifically mentioned in the resolution."[1653]

But in order to "repeal all the restrictions on Jews in all of our laws, in order to uproot ... completely the inequality of Jews," G.B. Sliozberg recalls, "it was necessary to make a complete list of all the restrictions ... and the collation of the list of laws to be repealed required great thoroughness and experience."

(This task was undertaken by Sliozberg and L.M. Bramson.)[1654] *The Jewish Encyclopedia* says: "The Act listed the statutes of Russian law that were being abolished by the Act — almost all those statutes (there were nearly 150) contained some or other anti-Jewish restrictions. Subject to repeal were, in part, all proscriptions connected to the Pale of Settlement; thereby its factual liquidation in 1915 was legally validated.[1655] The restrictions were removed layer by layer: travel, habitation, educational institutions, participation in local self-government, the right to acquire property anywhere in Russia, participation in government contracts, from stock exchanges, hiring servants, workers and stewards of a different religion, the right to occupy high positions in the government and military service, guardianship and trusteeship. Recalling a cancellation of an agreement with the United States, they repealed similar restrictions on "foreigners who are not at war with the Russian government," mainly in reference to Jews coming from the United States.

The promulgation of the Act inspired many emotional speeches. Deputy Freedman of the State Duma asserted: "For the past thirty-five years the Jews have been subjected to oppression and humiliation, unheard of and unprecedented even in the history of our long suffering people.... All of it ... was the result of state-sponsored anti-Semitism."[1656] Attorney O.O. Gruzenberg stated: "If the pre-Revolution Russian government was a vast and monstrous prison, ... then its most stinking, terrible cell, its torture chamber was carted away for us, the six-million Jewish people. And for the first time the Jewish child learned ... about this usurious term ìnterestín the state school.... Like hard labor camp prisoners on their way to camp, all Jews were chained together as despised aliens.... The drops of blood of our fathers and mothers, the drops of blood of our sisters and brothers fell on

---

[1653] AJE, Volume 7, Page 377.
[1654] G.B. Sliozberg, Dela Minuvshikh Dney: Zapiski Russkovo Yevreya: Paris, 1933-1934, Volume 3, Page 360.
[1655] AJE, Volume 7, Page 377.
[1656] Rech', March 25, 1917, Page 6.

our souls, there igniting and enlivening the unextinguishable Revolutionary fire."[1657]

Rosa Georgievna, the wife of Vinaver, recalls: "The events (of the March 1917 Revolution) coincided with the Jewish Passover. It looked like this was a second escape from Egypt. Such a long, long path of suffering and struggle has passed, and how quickly everything had happened. A large Jewish meeting was called," at which Milyukov spoke: "At last, a shameful spot has been washed away from Russia, which can now bravely step into the ranks of civilized nations." Vinaver "proposed to the gathering to build a large Jewish public house in Petrograd in memory of the meeting, which will be called "The House of Freedom."[1658]

Three members of the State Duma, M. Bomash, E. Gurevich and N. Freedman published an "open letter to the Jewish people": that now "our military misfortunes could deal grave damage to the still infirm free Russia. Free Jewish warriors ... will draw new strength for the ongoing struggle, with the tenfold energy extending the great feat of arms." And here was the natural plan: "The Jewish people should quickly re-organize their society. The long-obsolete forms of our communal life must be renewed on the free, democratic principles."[1659]

The author-journalist David Eisman responded to the Act with an outcry: "Our Motherland! Our Fatherland! They are in trouble! With all our hearts ... we will defend our land.... Not since the defense of the Temple has there been such a sacred feat of arms."

And from the memoirs of Sliozberg: "The great fortune to have lived to see the day of the declaration of emancipation of Jews in Russia and the elimination of our lack of rights — everything I have fought for with all my strength over the course of three decades — did not fill me with the joy as it should had been," because the collapse had begun right away.[1660]

And seventy years later one Jewish author expressed doubts too: "Did that formal legislative Act really change the situation in the country, where all legal norms were precipitously losing their power?"[1661]

[1657] Ibid.
[1658] R.G. Vinaver, Memoirs (New York, 1944) // Hraneniye Guverskovo Instituta Voyni, Revolutsiyi I Mira – Stanford, California, Mashinopis', Page 92.
[1659] Russkaya Volya, March 29, Page 5.
[1660] G.B. Slyozberg, Dela Minuvshikh Dney, Volume 3, Page 360.
[1661] B. Orlov, Rossiya byez Yevreev (Russia without Jews) // "22": Obshestvenno-politicheskiy a literaturniy zhurnal yevreyskoy inteligentsi'I iz SSSR v Izrayelye. Tel-Aviv, 1988, No. 60, Page 157.

We answer: in hindsight, from great distance, one should not downplay the significance of what was achieved. Then, the Act suddenly and dramatically improved the situation of the Jews. As for the rest of the country, falling, with all its peoples, into an abyss — that was the unpredictable way of the history.

The most abrupt and notable change occurred in the judiciary. If earlier, the Batyushin's commission on bribery investigated the business of the obvious crook D. Rubinstein, now the situation became reversed: the case against Rubinstein was dropped, and Rubinstein paid a visit to the Extraordinary Investigatory Commission in the Winter Palace and successfully demanded prosecution of the Batyushin's commission itself. Indeed, in March 1917 they arrested General Batyushin, Colonel Rezanov, and other investigators. The investigation of activities of that commission began in April, and, as it turned out, the extortion of bribes from the bankers and sugar factory owners by them was apparently significant. Then the safes of Volga-Kama, Siberian, and Junker banks, previously sealed up by Batyushin, were unsealed and all the documents returned to the banks. (Semanovich and Manus were not so lucky. When Simanovich was arrested as secretary to Rasputin, he offered 15,000 rubles to the prison convoy guards, if they would let him make a phone call, yet "the request was, of course, turned down."[1662] As for Manus, suspected of being involved in shady dealings with the German agent Kolyshko, he battled the counterintelligence agents who came for him by shooting through his apartment's door. After his arrest, he fled the country). The situation in the Extraordinary Investigatory Commission of the Provisional Government can be manifestly traced by records of interrogations in late March. Protopopov was asked how he came to be appointed to the Ministry of Internal Affairs, and in response he mentioned the directive issued by him: "the residence rights of the Jews were significantly expanded" in Moscow. Asked about the priorities of his Ministry, he first recalled the foodstuffs affair, and, after then the progressive issue — the Jewish question...." The director of the Department of Police, A.T. Vasilyev didn't miss an opportunity to inform the interrogators that he helped defend the sugar factory owners (Jews): "Gruzenberg called me in the morning in my apartment and thanked me for my cooperation"; "Rosenberg ... visited me to thank me for my efforts on his behalf."[1663] In this way, the accused tried to get some leniency for themselves.

[1662] Rech', March 17, 1917, Page 5.
[1663] Padeniye Tsarskovo Rezhima (Fall of the Tsarist Regime): Stenographicheskiye otchyoti doprosov a pokazani'I, dannikh v. 1917 g. v Chryezvichaynoy Sledstvennoy Kommissi'I Vremennovo Pravityelstva. L.: GUZ, 1924, T.1. Pages 119-121, 429.

A notable aspect of the weeks of March was an energetic pursuit of known or suspected Judeophobes. The first one arrested, on February 27, was the Minister of Justice Scheglovitov. He was accused of personally giving the order to unjustly pursue the case against Beilis. In subsequent days, the Beilis's accusers, the prosecutor Vipper and Senator Chaplinsky, were also arrested.

(However, they were not charged with anything specific, and in May 1917 Vipper was merely dismissed from his position as the chief prosecutor of the Criminal Department of the Senate; his fate was sealed later, by the Bolsheviks). The court investigator Mashkevich was ordered to resign — for during the Beilis trial he had sanctioned not only expert witness testimony against the argument on the ritual murder, but he also allowed a second expert testimony arguing for the case of such murder. The Minister of Justice Kerensky requested transfer of all materials of the Beilis case from the Kiev Regional Court,[1664] planning a loud re-trial, but during the stormy course of 1917 that didn't happen. The chairman of the "Union of the Russian People," Dmitry Dubrovin, was arrested and his archive was seized; the publishers of the far-right newspapers Glinka-Yanchevsky and Poluboyarinova were arrested too; the bookstores of the Monarchist Union were simply burned down.

For two weeks, they hunted for the fugitives N. Markov and Zamyslovsky, doing nightly searches for two weeks in St. Petersburg, Kiev and Kursk.

Zamislovsky was hunted for his participation in the case against Beilis, and Markov, obviously, for his speeches in the State Duma. At the same time, they didn't touch Purishkevich, one assumes, because of his Revolutionary speeches in the Duma and his participation in the murder of Rasputin. An ugly rumor arose that Stolypin took part in the murder of Iollos, and in Kremenchuk, a street that had previously been named after Stolypin was renamed after Iollos.

Over all of Russia there were hundreds of arrests, either because of their former positions or even because of their former attitudes.

It should be noted that the announcement of Jewish equality did not cause a single pogrom. It is worth noticing not only for the comparison to 1905, but also because, all through March and April, all major newspapers were constantly reporting the preparation of pogroms, and that somewhere, the pogroms had already supposedly begun.

Rumors started on March 5, that somewhere either in Kiev or Poltava Province, Jewish pogroms were brewing, and someone in Petrograd put up a hand-written anti-Jewish flyer. As a result, the Executive Committee of

---

[1664] Russkaya Volya (Russian Will), April 21, 1917, Page 4.

Soviet Workers and Soldiers' Deputies formed a special "visiting commission ... led by Rafes, Aleksandrovich, and Sukhanov." Their task was to "delegate commissars to various towns, with the first priority to go into the regions where the Black Hundreds, the servants of the old regime, are trying to sow ethnic antagonism among the population."[1665] In the newspaper *Izvestia SRSD* [Soviet Workers and Soldiers' Deputies] there was an article *Incitement to Pogrom*: "It would be a huge mistake, tantamount to a crime, to close our eyes to a new attempt of the overthrown dynasty..." — because it is them [translator's note — the Monarchists] who organize the trouble.... "In Kiev and Poltava provinces, among the underdeveloped, backwards classes of the population at this moment there is incitement against Jews.... Jews are blamed for the defeats of our Army, for the revolutionary movement in Russia, and for the fall of the monarchy....

It's an old trick, ... but all the more dangerous because of its timing.... It is necessary to quickly take decisive measures against the pogrom instigators."[1666] After this the commander of the Kiev Military District General Khodorovich issued an order: all military units are to be on high alert and be ready to prevent possible anti-Jewish riots.

Long after this, but still in April, in various newspapers, every two or three days they published rumors of preparations for Jewish pogroms,[1667] or at the very least, about moving of piles of "pogrom literature" by railroads. Yet the most stubborn rumors circulated about a coming pogrom in Kishinev — that was to happen at the end of March, right between the Jewish and (Russian) Orthodox Passovers, as happened in 1903.

And there were many more such alarming press reports (one even said that the police in Mogilev was preparing a pogrom near the Headquarters of Supreme High Command). Not one of these proved true.

One need only get acquainted with the facts of those months, to immerse oneself in the whole "February" atmosphere — of the defeated Right and the triumphant Left, of the stupor and confusion of the common folk — to dismiss outright any realistic possibility of anti-Jewish pogroms. But how could ordinary Jewish residents of Kiev or Odessa forget those horrible days twelve years before? Their apprehension, their wary caution to any motion in that direction was absolutely understandable.

[1665] Izvestiya Petrogradskovo Sovieta Rabochikh I Soldatskikh Deputatov, (heretofore "Izvestiya), March 6, 1917, Page 4.
[1666] Izvestiya, March 6, Page 2.
[1667] For example: Birzheviye Vedomosti, April 8 and 12, 1917; Russkaya Volya, April 9, 1917; Izvestiya, April 15, and 28, 1917; et. al.

The well-informed newspapers were a different story. The alarms raised by the newspapers, by enlightened leaders of the liberal camp, and half-baked socialist intellectuals — one cannot call this anything except political provocation. Provocation, however, that fortunately didn't work.

One actual episode occurred at the Bessarabian bazaar in Kiev, on April 28: a girl stole a piece of ribbon in a Jewish shop and ran away; the store clerk caught up to her and began to beat her. A crowd rushed to lynch the clerk and the store owner, but the police defended them. In another incident, in the Rogachevsky district, people, angered by exorbitant prices, smashed the stores — including Jewish ones.

Where and by whom was the Jewish emancipation met with hostility?

Those were our legendary revolutionary Finland, and our "powerful" ally, Romania. In Finland (as we learned in Chapter 10 from Jabotinsky) the Jews were forbidden to reside permanently, and since 1858, only descendants of "Jewish soldiers who served here" (in Finland, during the Crimean War) were allowed to settle. "The passport law of 1862 ... confirmed that Jews were forbidden entry into Finland," and "temporary habitation [was permitted] at the discretion of a local governor"; the Jews could not become Finnish citizens; in order to get married, a Jew had to go to Russia; the rights of Jews to testify in Finnish courts were restricted. Several attempts to mitigate the restriction of the civil rights of the Jews in Finland were not successful.[1668] And now, with the advent of Jewish equal rights in Russia, Finland, not having yet announced its complete independence (from Russia), did not legislate Jewish equality.

Moreover, they were deporting Jews who had illegally moved to Finland, and not in a day, but in an hour, on the next train out. (One such case on March 16 caused quite a splash in the Russian press.) But Finland was always extolled for helping the revolutionaries, and liberals and socialists stopped short of criticizing her. Only the Bund sent a wire to very influential Finnish socialists, reprimanding them that this "medieval" law was still not repealed. The Bund, "the party of the Jewish proletariat, expresses strong certainty that you will take out that shameful stain from free Finland."[1669] However, in this certainty, the Bund was mistaken.

And a huge alarm was raised in the post-February press about the persecution of Jews in Romania. They wrote that in Jassy it was even forbidden to speak Yiddish at public meetings. The All-Russian Zionist Student Congress "Gekhover" proposed "to passionately protest this civil

---

[1668] Yevreyskaya Encyclopedia (Jewish Encyclopedia): Volume 16 SPB: Obshestvo dlya Nauchnikh Yevreskikh Izdanni'I I Izd-Vo Brokaw-Yefron, 1906-1913. Volume 15, Page 281-284.
[1669] Izvyestiya, March 26, 1917 Page 2.

inequality of Jews in Romania and Finland, which is humiliating to the world Jewry and demeaning to worldwide democracy."[1670] At that time Romania was weakened by major military defeats. So the Prime Minister Bratianu was making excuses in Petrograd in April saying that "most of the Jews in Romania ... migrated there from Russia," and in particular that "prompted Romanian government to limit the political rights of the Jews"; he promised equality soon.[1671] However, in May we read: "In fact, nothing is happening in that direction."[1672] (In May, the Romanian communist Rakovsky reported that "the situation of the Jews in Romania is ... unbearable"; the Jews were blamed for the military defeat of the country; they were accused of "fraternizing" with Germans in the occupied parts of the country. "If the Romanian government was not afraid [to anger their allies in the Entente], then one would fear for the very lives of the Jews.")[1673]

The worldwide response among the allies of the February Revolution was expressed in a tone of deep satisfaction, even ecstasy among many, but in this response there was also a short-sighted calculation: that now Russia will become invincible in war. In Great Britain and the USA there were large meetings in support of the Revolution and the rights of the Jews. (I wrote about some of these responses in *March 1917* in Chapters 510 and 621). From America they offered to send a copy of the Statue of Liberty to Russia. (Yet as the situation in Russia continued to deteriorate, they never got around to the Statue). On March 9 in the House of Commons of the British Parliament the Minister of Foreign Affairs was asked a question about the situation of the Jews in Russia: does he plan to consult with the Russian government regarding guarantees to the Russian Jews for the future and reparations for the past? The answer showed the full trust that the British government had for the new Russian government.[1674] From Paris, the president of the International Jewish Union congratulated [Russian Prime Minister] Prince Lvov, and Lvov answered: "From today onward liberated Russia will be able to respect the faiths and customs of all of its peoples forever bound by a common religion of love of their homeland." The newspapers *Birzhevka*, *Rech* and many others reported on the sympathies of Jacob Schiff, "a well known leader of North American circles that are hostile to Russia." He wrote: "I was always the enemy of Russian absolutism, which mercilessly persecuted my co-religionists. Now let me congratulate ... the Russian people for this great act which they

---

[1670] Russkaya Volya, April 15, 1917, Page 4.
[1671] Birzheviye Vedomosti, April 23, 1917, Page 3.
[1672] ibid, May 19, Page 1.
[1673] Dyen' (Day), May 10, 1917.
[1674] Birzheviye Vedomosti, March 11, 1917, Page 2.

committed so perfectly."[1675] And now he "invites the new Russia to conduct broad credit operations in America."[1676] Indeed, "at the time he provided substantial credit to the Kerensky government."[1677] Later in emigration, the exiled Russian right-wing press published investigative reports attempting to show that Schiff actively financed the Revolution itself. Perhaps Schiff shared the short-sighted Western hope that the liberal revolution in Russia would strengthen Russia in the war. Still, the known and public acts of Schiff, who had always been hostile to Russian absolutism, had even greater effect than any possible secret assistance to such a revolution.

The February Revolution itself often consciously appealed for support to Jews, an entire nation enslaved. Eye-witness testimonies that Russian Jews were very ecstatic about the February Revolution are rife.

Yet there are counter-witnesses too, such as Gregory Aronson, who formed and led the Soviet of Workers' Deputies of Vitebsk (which later had as a member Y.V. Tarle, a future historian). He wrote that on the very first day, when news of the Revolution reached Vitebsk, the newly formed Security Council met in the city Duma, and immediately afterwards Aronson was invited to a meeting of representatives of the Jewish community (clearly, not rank and file, but leaders). "Apparently, there was a need to consult with me as a representative of the new dawning era, what to do further.... I felt alienation from these people, from the circle of their interests and from the tense atmosphere, which was at that meeting.... I had a sense that this society belonged mostly to the old world, which was retreating into the past."[1678] "We were not able to eliminate a certain mutual chill that had come from somewhere. The faces of the people I was working with, displayed no uplift or faith. At times, it appeared that these selfless social activists perceived themselves as elements of the old order."[1679]

That is a precise witness account. Such bewilderment, caution and wavering predominated among religiously conservative Jews, one assumes, not only in Vitebsk. The sensible old Jewry, carrying a sense of many centuries of experience of hard ordeals, was apparently shocked by the sudden overthrow of the monarchy and had serious misgivings.

[1675] Birzheviye Vedomosti, March 10, 1917, Page 6.
[1676] Rech', March 10, 1917, Page 3.
[1677] *Encyclopedia Judaica*, Jerusalem, Keter Publishing House, 1971, Volume 14, Page 961.
[1678] G.Y. Aronson, Intervyu Radiostantsi'I "Svoboda" // Vospominaniya o revolutsi'I 1917 goda, Intervyu No. 66, Munchen, 1966, Page 13-14.
[1679] G. Aronson, Revolutsionnaya Yunost': Vospominaniya, 1903-1917 // Inter-University Project on the History of the Menshevik Movement, Paper No. 6, New York, August 1961, Page 33.

Yet, in the spirit of the 20th century, the dynamic masses of every nation, including Jews, were already secular, not chained to traditions and very eager to build "the happy new world."

The Jewish Encyclopedia notes "a sharp intensification of the political activity of Jewry, noticeable even against a background of stormy social uplift that gripped Russia after February 1917."[1680]

Myself, having worked for many years on the "February" press and memoirs of the contemporaries of the February, could not fail to noticed this "sharp strengthening," this gusting. In those materials, from the most varied witnesses and participants of those events, there are so many Jewish names, and the Jewish theme is very loud and persistent. From the memories of Rodzyanko, from the town governor Balk, from General Globachyov and many others, from the first days of the Revolution in the depths of the Tavrichesky Palace, the numbers of Jews jumped out at me — among the members of the commandants office, the interrogation commissions, the pamphlet-merchants and so on. V.D. Nabokov, who was well disposed towards Jews, wrote that on

March 2 at the entrance to the Tavrichesky mini-park in front of the Duma building, there was "an unbelievable crush of people and shouting; at the entrance of the gates some young, Jewish-looking men were questioning the bypassers."[1681] According to Balk, the crowd that went on the rampage at the "Astoria" [an elite hotel in St. Petersburg] on the night of February 28, consisted of armed ... soldiers, sailors and Jews.[1682] I would indulge some emigrant irritability here as they used to say "well, that's all the Jews"; yet the same was witnessed by another neutral observer, the Methodist pastor Dr. Simons, an American who had already been in Petrograd for ten years and knew it well. He was debriefed by a commission of the American Senate in 1919:

"Soon after the March Revolution of 1917, everywhere in Petrograd you could see groups of Jews, standing on benches, soap boxes and such, making speeches.... There had been restrictions on the rights of Jews to live in Petrograd, but after the Revolution they came in droves, and the majority of agitators were Jews ... they were apostate Jews.[1683]

[1680] AJE, T. 7, Page 378.
[1681] V. Nabokov, Vremennoye Pravitelstvo // Arkhiv Russkoy Revolutsi'I, izdavaemiy I.V. Gessenom. Berlin: Slovo, 1922-1937, Vol. 1, Page 15.
[1682] A. Balk, Posledniye pyat' dney tsarskovo Petrograda (23-28 Fevralya 1917) Dnevnik poslednevo Petrogradskovo Gradonachal'nika // Khranenie Guverskovo Instituta, Mashinopis', Page 16.
[1683] Oktyabrskaya revolutsiya pered sudom amerikanskikh senatorov: Ofitsialniy otchyot "overmenskoy kommissi'I" Senata. M.;L.; GIZ, 1927 Page 5.

A certain "Student Hanokh" came to Kronstadt a few days before a planned massacre of sixty officers, who were named on a hit-list; he became the founder and chairman of the Kronstadt's "Committee of the Revolutionary Movement."

(The order of the Committee was to arrest and try each and all officers.

"Somebody had carefully prepared and disseminated false information," triggering massacres first in Kronstadt, then in Sveaborg; it was "because of the uncertainty of the situation, when every fabrication was taken for a hard fact."[1684]) The baton of the bloody Kronstadt affair was carried by the drop-out psychoneurologist "Dr. Roshal." (Later, after the October coup, S.G. Roshal was appointed the Commandant of the Gatchina, and from November he was the commissar of the whole Romanian Front, where he was killed upon arrival.[1685])

A certain Solomon and a Kaplun spoke on behalf of the newly-formed revolutionary militia of the Vasilievsky Island (in the future, the latter would become the bloody henchman of Zinoviev).

The Petrograd Bar created a special "Commission for the examination of the justice of imprisoning persons arrested during the time of the Revolution" (thousands were arrested during this time in Petrograd) — that is, to virtually decide their fate without due process (and that of all the former gendarmes and police). This commission was headed by the barrister Goldstein. Yet, the unique story of the petty officer Timofey Kirpichnikov, who triggered the street Revolution, was written in March 1917 and preserved for us by the Jew Jacob Markovich Fishman — a curious historical figure. (I with gratitude relied on this story in *The Red Wheel*.)

The Jewish Encyclopedia concludes: "Jews for the first time in Russian history had occupied posts in the central and regional administrations."[1686]

On the very heights, in the Executive Committee of the Soviets of Workers' and Soldiers' Deputies, invisibly ruling the country in those months, two leaders distinguished themselves: Nakhamkis-Steklov and Gummer-Sukhanov. On the night of March 1st to March 2nd they dictated to the complacently-blind Provisional Government a program which preemptively destroyed its power for the entire period of its existence.

[1684] D.O. Zaslavskiy, Vl. A. Kantorovich. Khronika Fevralskoy revolutsi'I, Pg.: Biloye, 1924. Volume 1, Page 63, 65.

[1685] Rosskiskaya Yevreyskaya Encyclopedia, 2-e izd., ispr. I dop. M., 1995, Volume 2, Page 502.

[1686] AJE, Volume 7, Page 381.

Reflective contemporary G.A. Landau thus explains the active participation of the Jews in the revolution: "The misfortune of Russia, and the misfortune of the Russian Jewry, is that the results of the first Revolution [1905] were still not processed, not transformed into a new social fabric; no new generation was born, when a great and back-breaking war broke out. And when the hour of disintegration came, it came upon the generation that from the very beginning was a kind of exhausted remnant of the previous revolution; it found the inertia of depleted spirituality, lacking an organic connection to the situation, and chained by spiritual stagnation to the ten-years-ago-bygone period. And so the organic Revolutionism of the beginning of the 20th century [of the First Russian Revolution of 1905] had turned into the mechanical 'permanent Revolutionóf the wartime era."[1687]

Through many years of detailed studies I have spent much time trying to comprehend the essence of the February Revolution and the Jewish role in it. I came to this conclusion and can now repeat: no, the February Revolution was not something the Jews did to the Russians, but rather it was done by the Russians themselves, which I believe I amply demonstrated in *The Red Wheel*.

We committed this downfall ourselves: our anointed Tsar, the court circles, the hapless high-ranking generals, obtuse administrators, and their enemies — the elite intelligentsia, the Octobrist Party, the Zemstvo, the Kadets, the Revolutionary Democrats, socialists and revolutionaries, and along with them, a bandit element of army reservists, distressingly confined to the Petersburg's barracks. And *this* is precisely why we perished. True, there were already many Jews among the intelligentsia by that time, yet that is in no way a basis to call it a Jewish revolution.

One may classify revolutions by their main animating forces, and then the February Revolution must be seen as a Russian national Revolution, or more precisely, a Russian ethnic Revolution. Though if one would judge it using the methodology of materialistic sociologists — asking who benefited the most, or benefited most quickly, or the most solidly and in the long term from the Revolution, — then it could be called otherwise, Jewish, for example. But then again why not German? After all, Kaiser Wilhelm initially benefited from it. But the remaining Russian population got nothing but harm and destruction; however, that doesn't make the Revolution "non-Russian." The Jewish society got everything it fought for from the Revolution, and the October Revolution was altogether

---

[1687] G.A. Landau, Revolutsionniye idyee v Yevreyskoy obshestvennosti // Rossi'I I every: Sb. 1 / Otechestvennoye ob'yedinennie russkikh yevreyev za granitsyey. Paris: YMCA – Press, 1978, Page 116 [1-e izd. – Berlin: Osnova, 1924].

unnecessary for them, except for a small slice of young cutthroat Jews, who with their Russian internationalist brothers accumulated an explosive charge of hate for the Russian governing class and burst forth to "deepen" the Revolution.

So how, having understood this, was I to move through *March 1917* and then *April 1917*? Describing the Revolution literally hour by hour, I frequently found the many episodes in the sources that had a Jewish theme. Yet would it be right to simply pour all that on the pages of *March 1917*? Then that easy and piquant temptation — to put all the blame on Jews, on their ideas and actions, to see them as the main reason for these events — would easily skew the book and overcome the readers, and divert the research away from the truly main causes of the Revolution.

And so in order to avoid the self-deception of the Russians, I persistently and purposely downplayed the Jewish theme in *The Red Wheel*, relative to its actual coverage in the press and on the streets in those days.

The February Revolution was carried out by Russian hands and Russian foolishness. Yet at the same time, its ideology was permeated and dominated by the intransigent hostility to the historical Russian state that ordinary Russians didn't have, but the Jews — had. So the Russian intelligentsia too had adopted this view. (This was discussed in Chapter 11). This intransigent hostility grew especially sharp after the trial of Beilis, and then after the mass expulsion of Jews in 1915. And so this intransigence overcame the moderation.

Yet the Executive Committee of Workers' and Soldiers' Deputies, which was formed within *hours* of the Revolution, appears very different. This Executive Committee was in fact a tough shadow government that deprived the liberal Provisional Government of any real power, while at the same time, criminally refused to accept responsibility for its power openly. By its "Order No. 1," the Executive Committee wrested the power from the military and created support for itself in the demoralized garrison of Petrograd. It was precisely this Executive Committee, and not the judiciary, not the timber industrialists, not the bankers, which fast-tracked the country to her doom. In the summer of 1917, Joseph Goldenberg, a member of the Executive Committee explained to the French Diplomat Claude Anet: "The Order No. 1 was not a mistake; it was a necessity…. On the day we executed the Revolution, we realized that if we did not destroy the old army, it would crush the Revolution. We had to choose between the army and the Revolution, and we did not waver: we chose the latter … [and we inflicted,] I dare say, a brilliant blow."[1688] So there you have it. The

---

[1688] Claude Anet, *La révolution russe*: Juin-Novembre 1917. Paris: Payot et C-ie, 1918, Page 61.

Executive Committee quite purposely destroyed the army in the middle of the war.

Is it legitimate to ask who were those successful and fatal-for-Russia leaders of the Executive Committee? Yes, it is legitimate, when actions of such leaders abruptly change the course of history. And it must be said that the composition of the Executive Committee greatly concerned the public and the newspapers in 1917, during which time many members of the Committee concealed themselves behind pseudonyms from the public eye: who was ruling Russia? No one knew.

Then, as it turned out, there was a dozen of soldiers, who were there just for show and weren't very bright, they were kept out of any real power or decision making. From the other thirty, though, of those who actually wielded power, more than half were Jewish socialists. There were also Russians, Caucasians, Latvians and Poles. Less than a quarter were Russians.

The moderate socialist V.B. Stankevich noted: "What really stuck out in the composition of the Committee was the large foreign element ... totally out of proportion to their part of the population in Petrograd or the country in general."

Stankevich asks, "Was this the unhealthy scum of Russian society? Or was this the consequence of the sins of the old regime, which by its actions violently pushed the foreign element into the Leftist parties? Or was that simply the result of free competition?" And then, "there remains an open question — who bears more guilt for this — the foreign born, who were there, or the Russians who could have been there but weren't?"[1689]

For a socialist that might be a case to look for a *guilty* party. Yet wouldn't it better for all — for us, for you, for them — to avoid sinking into that mad dirty torrent altogether?

[1689] V.B. Stankevich, Vospominaniya, 1914-1919, Berlin: Izd-vo I.P. Ladizhnikova, 1920, Page 86.

Chapter 14

During 1917

In the beginning of April 1917 the Provisional Government had discovered to its surprise that Russian finances, already for some time in quite bad shape, were on the brink of complete collapse. In an attempt to mend the situation, and stir enthusiastic patriotism, the government loudly, announced the issuance of domestic Freedom Loan bonds.

Rumors about the loan had began circulating as early as March and Minister of Finance Tereshchenko informed the press that there were already multi-million pledges from bankers to buy bonds, "mainly from the Jewish bankers, which is undoubtedly related to the abolition of religious and national restrictions."[1690] Indeed, as soon as the loan was officially announced, names of large Jewish subscribers began appearing in newspapers, accompanied by prominent front-page appeals: "Jewish citizens! Subscribe to the Freedom Loan!" and "Every Jew must have the Freedom Loan bonds!"[1691] In a single subscription drive in a Moscow synagogue 22 million rubles was collected.

During the first two days, Jews in Tiflis subscribed to 1.5 million rubles of bonds; Jews in Minsk – to half a million in the first week; the Saratov community – to 800 thousand rubles of bonds. In Kiev, the heirs of Brodsky and Klara Ginzburg each spent one million. The Jews abroad came forward as well: Jacob Schiff, 1 million; Rothschild in London, 1 million; in Paris, on the initiative of Baron Ginzburg, Russian Jews participated actively and subscribed to several million worth of bonds.[1692] At the same time, the Jewish Committee in Support for Freedom Loan was established and appealed to public.[1693]

However, the government was very disappointed with the overall result of the first month of the subscription. For encouragement, the lists of major

---

[1690] *Delo Naroda*, March 25, 1917, p. 3.
[1691] *Russkaya Volya*, April 14, 1917, p. 1; April 20, p. 1. See also *Rech*, April 16, 1917, p. 1; April 20, p. 1.
[1692] *Russkaya Volya*, April 23, 1917, p. 4.
[1693] *Birzhevye Vedomosti*, May 24, 1917, p. 2.

subscribers (who purchased bonds on 25 thousand rubles or more) were published several times: in the beginning of May, in the beginning of June and in the end of July. "The rich who did not subscribe"[1694] were shamed. What is most striking is not the sheer number of Jewish names on the lists (assimilated Russian-Germans with their precarious situation during the Russo-German War were in the second place among bond-holders) but the near absence of the top Russian bourgeoisie, apart from a handful of prominent Moscow entrepreneurs.

In politics, "left and center parties burgeoned and many Jews had became politically active." [1695] From the very first days after the February Revolution, central newspapers published an enormous number of announcements about private meetings, assemblies and sessions of various Jewish parties, initially mostly the Bund, but later Poale Zion, Zionists, Socialist Zionists, Territorialist Zionists, and the Socialist Jewish Workers' Party (SJWP). By March 7 we already read about an oncoming assembly of the All-Russian Jewish Congress – finally, the pre-revolutionary idea of Dubnov had become widely accepted.

However, "because of sharp differences between Zionists and Bundists," the Congress did not materialize in 1917 (nor did it occur in 1918 either "because of the Civil War and antagonism of Bolshevik authorities").[1696] "In Petrograd, Jewish People's Group was re-established with M. Vinaver at the helm."[1697]

They were liberals, not socialists; initially, they hoped to establish an alliance with Jewish socialists. Vinaver declared: "we applaud the Bund – the vanguard of the revolutionary movement." [1698] Yet the socialists stubbornly rejected all gestures of rapprochement.

The rallying of Jewish parties in Petrograd had indirectly indicated that by the time of revolution the Jewish population there was already substantial and energetic. Surprisingly, despite the fact that almost no "Jewish proletariat"

[1694] See, for instance, *Russkaya Volya,* May 10, 1917, p. 5; *Birzhevye Vedomosti*, May 9, 1917, p. 5; *Birzhevye Vedomosti*, June 1, 1917, p. 6; *Rech*, July 29, 1917, p. 6.
[1695] *Kratkaya Evreiskaya Entsiklopediya* [*The Short Jewish Encyclopedia* (henceforth—SJE)]. Jerusalem, 1994. v. 7, p. 399.
[1696] Ibid., p. 380-381.
[1697] Ibid., p. 379.
[1698] G. Aronson. *Evreyskaya obshchestvennost v Rossii v 1917-1918* [The Jewish Public in Russia in 1917-1918] // *Kniga o russkom evreystve: 1917-1967* [The Book of Russian Jewry: 1917-1967 (henceforth — BRJ-2)]. New York: Association of Russian Jews, 1968, p. 6.

existed in Petrograd, the Bund was very successful there. It was extraordinarily active in Petrograd, arranging a number of meetings of local organization (in the lawyer's club and then on April 1 in the Tenishev's school); there was a meeting with a concert in the Mikhailovsky Theatre; then on April 14-19 "the All-Russian Conference of the Bund took place, at which a demand to establish a national and cultural Jewish autonomy in Russia was brought forward again."[1699] ("After conclusion of speeches, all the conference participants had sung the Bund's anthem *Oath, The Internationale,* and *La Marseillaise.*"[1700])

And, as in past, Bund had to balance its national and revolutionary platforms: in 1903 it struggled for the independence from the Russian Social Democratic Labor Party, and yet in 1905 it rushed headlong into the All-Russian revolution.

Likewise, now, in 1917, the Bund's representatives occupied prominent positions in the Executive Committee of the Soviet of Workers' and Soldiers' Deputies [a Soviet is the Russian term used for an elected (at least in theory) council] and later among the Social Democrats of Kiev. "By the end of 1917 the Bund had nearly 400 sections countrywide, totaling around 40,000 members."[1701]

Developments in Poale Zion were no less amazing. In the beginning of April they also held their All-Russian Conference in Moscow. Among its resolutions we see on the one hand a motion to organize the All-Russian Jewish Congress and discuss the problem of emigration to Palestine. On the other hand, the Poale Zion Conference in Odessa had simultaneously announced the party's uncompromising program of class warfare: "Through the efforts of Jewish revolutionary democracy the power over destinies of the Jewish nation was ... wrested from the dirty grasp of 'wealthy and settled' Jews despite all the resistance of bourgeoisie to the right and the Bund to the left.... Do not allow the bourgeois parties to bring in the garbage of the old order.... Do not let the hypocrites speak – they did not fight but sweated out the rights for our people on their bended knees in the offices of anti-Semitic ministers; ... they did not believe in the revolutionary action of the masses." Then, in April 1917, when the party had split the "Radical Socialist" Poale Zion moved toward the Zionists, breaking away from the main "Social Democratic" Poale Zion,[1702] which later would join the Third International.[1703]

[1699] SJE, v.7, p. 378.
[1700] *Izvestiya,* April 9, 1917, p. 4.
[1701] SJE, v.7, p. 378-379.
[1702] SJE, v.7, p. 378.
[1703] *Izvestiya,* September 15, 1917, p. 2.

Like the two above-mentioned parties, the SJWP also held its statewide conference at which it had merged with the Socialist Zionists, forming the United Jewish Socialist Workers' Party (Fareynikte) and parting with the idea "of any extraterritorial Jewish nation" with its own parliament and national autonomy. "Fareynikte appealed to the Provisional Government asking it to declare equality of languages and to establish a council on the affairs of nationalities" which would specifically "fund Jewish schools and public agencies." At the same time, Fareynikte closely collaborated with the Socialist Revolutionaries.[1704]

However, it was Zionism that became the most influential political force in the Jewish milieu.[1705] As early as the beginning of March, the resolution of Petrograd's Zionist Assembly contained the following wording: "The Russian Jewry is called upon to support the Provisional Government in every possible way, to enthusiastic work, to national consolidation and organization for the sake of the prosperity of Jewish national life in Russia and the national and political renaissance of Jewish nation in Palestine." And what an inspiring historical moment it was – March 1917 – with the British troops closing on Jerusalem right at that time! Already on March 19 the proclamation of Odessa's Zionists stated: "today is the time when states rearrange themselves on national foundations. Woe to us if we miss this historic opportunity." In April, the Zionist movement was strongly reinforced by the public announcement of Jacob Schiff, who had decided to join Zionists "because of fear of Jewish assimilation as a result of Jewish civil equality in Russia. He believes that Palestine could become the center to spread ideals of Jewish culture all over the world."[1706] In the beginning of May, Zionists held a large meeting in the building of Petrograd Stock Exchange, with Zionist hymns performed several times. In the end of May the All-Russian Zionist Conference was held in the Petrograd Conservatory. It outlined major Zionist objectives: cultural revival of the Jewish nation, "social revolution in the economic structure of Jewish society to transform the 'nation of merchants and artisans into the nation of farmers and workers,' an increase in emigration to Palestine and 'mobilization of Jewish capital to finance the Jewish settlers'." Both Jabotinsky's plan on creation of a Jewish legion in the British Army and the I. Trumpeldorf's plan for the "formation of a Jewish army in Russia which would cross the Caucasus and liberate *Eretz Yisrael* [The land of Israel] from Turkish occupation have been discussed and rejected on the basis of the neutrality of Zionists in the World War I."[1707]

[1704] SJE, v.6, p. 85; v.7, p. 379.
[1705] SJE, v.7, p. 378.
[1706] *Birzhevye Vedomosti*, April 12, 1917, p. 4.
[1707] SJE, v.6, p. 463, 464.

The Zionist Conference decreed to vote during the oncoming local elections for the parties "not farther to the right than the People's Socialists," and even to refuse to support Constitutional Democrats like D. Pasmanik, who later complained: "It was absolutely meaningless – it looked like the entire Russian Jewry, with its petty and large bourgeoisie, are socialists."[1708] His bewilderment was not unfounded.

The congress of student Zionist organization, Gekhover, with delegates from 25 cities and all Russian universities, had taken place in the beginning of April in Petrograd. Their resolution stated that the Jews were suffering not for the sake of equality in Russia but for the rebirth of Jewish nation in the native Palestine. They decided to form legions in Russia to conquer Palestine. Overall, "during the summer and fall of 1917 Zionism in Russia continued to gain strength: by September its members numbered 300,000."[1709]

It is less known that in 1917 Jewish "orthodox movements enjoyed substantial popularity second only to the Zionists and ahead of the socialist parties" (as illustrated by their success "during elections of the leadership of reorganized Jewish communities").[1710]

There were rallies ("The Jews are together with the democratic Russia in both love and hatred!"), public lectures ("The Jewish Question and the Russian Revolution"), city-wide "assemblies of Jewish high school students" in Petrograd and other cities (aside from general student meetings). In Petrograd, the Central Organ of Jewish Students was established, though not recognized by the Bund and other leftist parties. While many provincial committees for the assistance to the "victims of the war" (i.e., to Jewish refugees and deportees) ceased to exist because at this time "democratic forces needed to engage in broader social activities," and so the Central Jewish Committee for providing such aid was formed by April. In May the Jewish People's Union was established to facilitate consolidation of all Jewish forces, to prepare for the convocation of the All-Russian Jewish Union and to get ready for the oncoming elections to the Constituent Assembly. In the end of May there was another attempt of unification: the steering committee of the Jewish Democratic Alliance convened the conference of all Jewish democratic organizations in Russia. Meanwhile, lively public discussion went on regarding convocation of the All-Russian Jewish Congress: the Bund rejected it as inconsistent with

---

[1708] D. Pasmanik. *Chego zhe my dobivaemsya?* [What are we struggling for?] // Rossiya i evrei: Otechestvennoe objedinenie russkikh evreev za granitsei [Russia and Jews: Expatriate Society of Russian Jews in Exile (henceforth— *RJ*)]. Paris, YMCA-Press, 1978, p. 211 [The 1st Edition: Berlin, Osnova, 1924].
[1709] SJE, v.7, p. 378.
[1710] Ibid., p. 379.

their plans; the Zionists demanded the Congress include on their agenda the question of Palestine – and were themselves rejected by the rest; in July the All-Russian Conference on the Jewish Congress preparation took place in Petrograd.[1711]

Because of social enthusiasm, Vinaver was able to declare there that the idea of united Jewish nation, dispersed among different countries, is ripe, and that from now on the Russian Jews may not be indifferent to the situation of Jews in other countries, such as Romania or Poland. The Congress date was set for December.

What an upsurge of Jewish national energy it was! Even amid the upheavals of 1917, Jewish social and political activities stood out in their diversity, vigor and organization.

The "period between February and November 1917 was the time of blossoming" of Jewish culture and healthcare. In addition to the Petrograd publication *The Jews of Russia*, the publisher of *The Jewish Week* had moved to Petrograd; publication of the *Petrograd-Torgblat* in Yiddish had begun; similar publications were started in other cities. The Tarbut and Culture League [a network of secular, Hebrew-language schools] had established "dozens of kindergartens, secondary and high schools and pedagogic colleges" teaching both in Yiddish and in Hebrew. A Jewish grammar school was founded in Kiev.

In April, the first All-Russian Congress on Jewish Culture and Education was held in Moscow. It requested state funding for Jewish schools A conference of the Society of Admirers of Jewish Language and Culture took place. The Habima Theatre, "the first professional theatre in Hebrew in the world,"[1712] opened in Moscow. There were an exposition of Jewish artists and a conference of the Society on Jewish Health Care in April in Moscow.

These Jewish activities are all the more amazing given the state of general governmental, administrative and cultural confusion in Russia 1917. A major event in the Jewish life of the time was the granting of official permission for Jewish youth to enlist as officers in the Russian Army. It was a large-scale move: in April, the headquarters of the Petrograd military district had issued an order to the commanders of Guards military units to immediately post *all* Jewish students to the training battalion at Nizhny Novgorod with the purpose of their further assignment to military academies[1713] – that is virtually mass-scale promotion of young Jews into

---

[1711] Ibid., p. 380-381.
[1712] Ibid., p. 379.
[1713] *Rech*, April 27, 1917, p. 3.

the officer ranks. "Already in the beginning of June 1917, 131 Jews graduated from the accelerated military courses at the Konstantinovsky military academy in Kiev as officers; in the summer 1917 Odessa, 160 Jewish cadets were promoted into officers."[1714] In June 2600 Jews were promoted to warrant-officer rank all over Russia.

There is evidence that in some military academies Junkers [used in Tsarist Russia for cadets and young officers] met Jewish newcomers unkindly, as it was in the Alexandrovsky military academy after more than 300 Jews had been posted to it. In the Mikhailovsky military academy a group of Junkers proposed a resolution that: "Although we are not against the Jews in general, we consider it inconceivable to let them into the command ranks of the Russian Army." The officers of the academy dissociated themselves from this statement and a group of socialist Junkers (141-strong) had expressed their disapproval, "finding anti-Jewish protests shameful for the revolutionary army,"[1715] and the resolution did not pass. When Jewish warrant officers arrived to their regiments, they often encountered mistrust and enmity on the part of soldiers for whom having Jews as officers was extremely unusual and strange. (Yet the newly-minted officers who adopted new revolutionary style of behavior gained popularity lightning-fast.)

On the other hand, the way Jewish Junkers from the military academy in Odessa behaved was simply striking. In the end of March, 240 Jews had been accepted into the academy. Barely three weeks later, on April 18 old style, there was a First of May parade in Odessa and the Jewish Junkers marched ostentatiously singing ancient Jewish songs. Did they not understand that Russian soldiers would hardly follow such officers? What kind of officers were they going to become? It would be fine if they were being prepared for the separate Jewish battalions. Yet according to General Denikin, the year 1917 saw successful formation of all kinds of national regiments – Polish, Ukrainian, Transcaucasian (the Latvian units were already in place for a while) – except the Jewish ones: it was "the only nationality not demanding national self-determination in military. And every time, when in response to complaints about bad acceptance of Jewish officers in army formation of separate Jewish regiments was suggested, such a proposal was met with a storm of indignation on the part of Jews and the Left and with accusations of a spiteful provocation." [1716] (Newspapers had reported that Germans also planned to form separate

---

[1714] SJE, v.7, p. 378.
[1715] *Russkaya Volya*, April 25, 1917, p. 5.
[1716] A. I. *Denikin*. Ocherki russkoi smuty. *V1* : Krushenie vlasti I armii, fevral-sentyabr 1917 [Russian Turmoil. Memoirs. V1: Collapse of Authority and Army]. Paris, 1922, p. 129-130.

Jewish regiments but the project was dismissed.) It appears, though, that new Jewish officers still wanted some national organization in the military.

In Odessa on August 18, the convention of Jewish officers decided to establish a section which would be responsible for connections between different fronts "to report on the situation of Jewish officers in the field." In August, "unions of Jewish warriors appeared; by October such unions were present at all fronts and in many garrisons. During the October 10-15, 1917 conference in Kiev, the All-Russian Union of Jewish Warriors was founded."[1717] (Although it was a new 'revolutionary army', some reporters still harbored hostility toward officer corps in general and to officer's epaulettes in particular; for instance, A. Alperovich whipped up emotions against officers in general in *Birzhevye Vedomosti* [*Stock Exchange News*] as late as May 5.)[1718]

Various sources indicate that Jews were not eager to be drafted as common soldiers even in 1917; apparently, there were instances when to avoid the draft sick individuals passed off as genuine conscripts at the medical examining boards, and, as a result, some district draft commissions began demanding photo-IDs from Jewish conscripts (an unusual practice in those simple times). It immediately triggered angry protests that such a requirement goes against the repulsion of national restrictions, and the Ministry of Internal Affairs forbade asking for such IDs.

In the beginning of April the Provisional Government issued an order by telegraph to free without individual investigation all Jews previously exiled as suspects of espionage. Some of them resided in the now-occupied territories, while others could safely return home, and yet many deportees asked for permission to reside in the cities of the European part of Russia. There was a flow of Jews into Petrograd (Jewish population of 50,000 in 1917)[1719] and a sharp increase of Jewish population in Moscow (60,000).[1720]

Russian Jews received less numerous, but highly energetic reinforcement from abroad. Take those two famous trains that crossed hostile Germany without hindrance and brought to Russia nearly 200 prominent individuals, 30 in Lenin's and 160 in Natanson-Martov's train, with Jews comprising an absolute majority (the lists of passengers of the 'exterritorial trains' were for the first time published by V. Burtsev).[1721] They represented almost all

---

[1717] SJE, v.7, p. 379.
[1718] *Birzhevye Vedomosti*, May 5, 1917, p. 2.
[1719] SJE, v.4, p. 775.
[1720] SJE, v.5, p. 475.
[1721] *Obshchee delo*, October 14 and 16, 1917.

Jewish parties, and virtually all of them would play a substantial role in the future events in Russia.

Hundreds of Jews returned from the United States: former emigrants, revolutionaries, and draft escapees – now they all were the 'revolutionary fighters' and 'victims of Tsarism'. By order of Kerensky, the Russian embassy in the USA issued Russian passports to anyone who could provide just two witnesses (to testify to identity) literally from the street. (The situation around Trotsky's group was peculiar. They were apprehended in Canada on suspicion of connections with Germany. The investigation found that Trotsky travelled not with flimsy Russian papers, but with a solid American passport, inexplicably granted to him despite his short stay in the USA, and with a substantial sum of money, the source of which remained a mystery.[1722]) On June 26 at the exalted "Russian rally in New York City" (directed by P. Rutenberg, one-time friend and then a murderer of Gapon), Abraham Kagan, the editor of Jewish newspaper *Forwards*, addressed Russian ambassador Bakhmetev "on behalf of two million Russian Jews residing in the United States of America": "We have always loved our motherland; we have always sensed the links of brotherhood with the entire Russian nation.... Our hearts are loyal to the red banner of the Russian liberation and to the national tricolor of the free Russia." He had also claimed that the self-sacrifice of the members of Narodnaya Volya [literally, The People's Will, a terrorist leftwing revolutionary group in Tsarist Russia, best known for its assassination of Tsar Alexander II, known as 'the Tsar Liberator for ending serfdom] "was directly connected to the fact of increased persecution of the Jews" and that "people like Zundelevich, Deich, Gershuni, Liber and Abramovich were among the bravest."[1723]

And so they had begun coming back, and not just from New York, judging by the official introduction of discounted railroad fare for 'political emigrants' travelling from Vladivostok. At the late July rally in Whitechapel, London, "it was found that in London alone 10,000 Jews declared their willingness to return to Russia"; the final resolution had expressed pleasure that "Jews would go back to struggle for the new social and democratic Russia."[1724]

Destinies of many returnees, hurrying to participate in the revolution and jumping headlong into the thick of things, were outstanding. Among the returnees were the famous V. Volodarsky, M. Uritsky, and Yu. Larin, the

---

[1722] A. Sutton. *Wall Street and the Bolshevik Revolution*. Translation from English, Moscow, 1998, p. 14-36.
[1723] *Rech*, June 27, 1917, p. 3; June 28, p. 2-3.
[1724] *Rech*, August 2, 1917, p. 3.

latter was the author of the 'War Communism economy' program. It is less known that Yakov Sverdlov's brother, Veniamin, was also among the returnees. Still, he would not manage to rise higher than the deputy Narkom [People's Commissar] of Communications and a member of Board of the Supreme Soviet of the National Economy. Moisei Kharitonov, Lenin's associate in emigration who returned to Russia in the same train with him, quickly gained notoriety by assisting the anarchists in their famous robbery in April; later he was the secretary of Perm, Saratov and Sverdlov gubkoms [guberniya's Party committee], and the secretary of Urals Bureau of the Central Committee.

Semyon Dimanshtein, a member of a Bolshevik group in Paris, would become the head of the Jewish Commissariat at the People's Commissariat of Nationalities, and later the head of YevSek [Jewish Section] at the All-Russian Central Executive Committee; he would in fact supervise the entire Jewish life.

Amazingly, at the age of 18 he managed "to pass qualification test to become a rabbi" and became a member of the Russian Social Democratic Workers' Party – all this in course of one year.[1725] Similarly, members of the Trotsky's group had also fared well: the jeweler G. Melnichansky, the accountant Friman, the typographer A. Minkin-Menson, and the decorator Gomberg-Zorin had respectively headed Soviet trade unions, *Pravda*, the dispatch office of bank notes and securities, and the Petrograd Revolutionary Tribunal.

Names of other returnees after the February Revolution are now completely forgotten, yet wrongly so, as they played important roles in the revolutionary events. For example, the Doctor of Biology Ivan Zalkind had actively participated in the October coup and then in fact ran Trotsky's People's Commissariat of Internal Affairs. Semyon Kogan-Semkov became the "political commissar of Izhevsk weapons and steel factories" in November 1918; that is he was in charge of the vindictive actions during suppression of major uprising of Izhevsk workers[1726] known for its large, in many thousands, victim's toll; in a single incident on the Sobornaya Square in Izhevsk 400 workers were gunned down.[1727] Tobinson-

---

[1725] *Russkaya Evreiskaya Entsiklopediya* [*The Russian Jewish Encyclopedia* (henceforth—RJE)]. 2nd edition, Moscow, 1994 – 1997. v. 1, p. 240, 427; v. 2, p. 124; v. 3, p. 29, 179, 280.
[1726] RJE, v. 1, p. 473; v. 3, p. 41.
[1727] *Narodnoe soprotivlenie kommunismu v Rossii: Ural i Prikamye. Noyabr 1917 – yanvar 1919* [People's Resistance to Communism: Urals and Prikamye. November 1917 – January 1919. Redactor M. Bernshtam. Paris: YMCA-Press, 1982, p. 356. Volume 3 of the series *Issledovaniya Noveishei Russkoi istorii* [Studies of Modern Russian History].

Krasnoshchekov later headed the entire Far East as the secretary of the Far East Bureau and the head of local government. Girshfeld-Stashevsky under the pseudonym "Verkhovsky" was in command of a squad of German POWs and turncoats, that is, he laid foundation for the Bolshevik international squads; in 1920 he was the head of clandestine intelligence at the Western front; later, in peacetime, "he, on orders of Cheka Presidium, had organized intelligence network in the Western Europe"; he was awarded the title of "Honorary Chekist."[1728]

Among returnees were many who did not share Bolshevik views (at least at the time of arrival) but they were nevertheless welcomed into the ranks of Lenin's and Trotsky's party. For instance, although Yakov Fishman, a member of the Military Revolutionary Committee of the October coup, had deviated from the Bolshevik mainstream by participating in the Left Socialist Revolutionary insurrection in July 1918, he was later accepted into the Russian Communist party of Bolsheviks (RCPB) and entrusted with a post in the Military Intelligence Administration of the Red Army. Or take Yefim Yarchuk, who had returned as an Anarchist Syndicalist, but was delegated by the Petrograd Soviet to reinforce the Kronstadt Soviet; during the October coup he had brought a squad of sailors to Petrograd to storm the Winter Palace. The returnee Vsevolod Volin-Eikhenbaum (the brother of the literary scholar) was a consistent supporter of anarchism and the ideologist of Makhno [a Ukrainian separatist-anarchist] movement; he was the head of the Revolutionary Military Soviet in the Makhno army. We know that Makno was more of an advantage than a detriment to Bolsheviks and as a result Volin was later merely forced to emigrate together with a dozen of other anarchists.[1729]

The expectations of returnees were not unfounded: those were the months marked by a notable rise to prominence for many Jews in Russia. "The Jewish Question exists no longer in Russia."[1730] (Still, in the newspaper essay by D. Aizman, Sura Alperovich, the wife of a merchant who moved from Minsk to Petrograd, had expressed her doubts: "So there is no more slavery and that's it?"

So what about the things "that 'Nicholas of yesterday' did to us in Kishinev [in regard to the Kishinev pogrom]?"[1731]) In another article David Aizman thus elaborated his thought: "Jews must secure the gains of revolution by any means... without any qualms. Any necessary sacrifice must be made. Everything is on the stake here and all will be lost if we hesitate.... Even

---

[1728] RJE, v. 2, p. 85; v. 3, p. 106.
[1729] RJE, v. 3, p. 224, 505; v. 1, p. 239.
[1730] *Rech*, June 28, 1917, p. 2.
[1731] *Russkaya Volya*, April 13, 1917, p. 3.

the most backward parts of Jewish mass understand this." "No one questions what would happen to Jews if the counter-revolution prevails." He was absolutely confident that if that happens there would be mass executions of Jews. Therefore, "the filthy scum must be crushed even before it had any chance to develop, in embryo. Their very seed must be destroyed.... Jews will be able to defend their freedom."[1732]

Crushed in embryo.... And even *their very seed....* It was already pretty much the Bolshevik program, though expressed in the words of Old Testament.

Yet whose seed must be destroyed? Monarchists'? But they were already breathless; all their activists could be counted on fingers. So it could only be those who had taken a stand against the unbridled, running wild soviets, against all kinds of committees and mad crowds; those, who wished to halt the breakdown of life in the country – prudent ordinary people, former government officials, and first of all officers and very soon the soldier-general Kornilov.

There were Jews among those counter-revolutionaries, but overall that movement was the Russian national one.

What about press? In 1917, the influence of print media grew; the number of periodicals and associated journalists and staff was rising. Before the revolution, only a limited number of media workers qualified for draft deferral, and only those who were associated with newspapers and printing offices which were established in the pre-war years. (They were classified as 'defense enterprises' despite their desperate fight against governmental and military censorship.) But now, from April, on the insistence of the publishers, press privileges were expanded with respect to the number of workers exempt from military service; newly founded political newspapers were henceforth also covered by the exemption (sometimes fraudulently as the only thing needed to qualify was maintaining a circulation of 30,000 for at least two weeks). Draft privileges were introduced on the basis of youth, for the 'political emigrants' and those 'released from exile' – everything that favored employment of new arrivals in the leftist newspapers. At the same time, rightist newspapers were being closed: *Malenkaya Gazeta* [*Small Newspaper*] and *Narodnaya Gazeta* [*People's Newspaper*] were shut down for accusing Bolsheviks of having links with Germans. When many newspapers published the telegrams fraudulently attributed to the Empress and the fake was exposed (it was "an innocent joke of a telegraph operator lady," for which, of course, she was never disciplined) and so they had to retract their pieces, *Birzhevye Vedomosti*, for instance, had produced such texts: "It turned out that neither the special

---

[1732] *Russkaya Volya*, April 9, 1917, p. 3.

archive at the Main Department of Post and Telegraph, where the royal telegrams were stored, nor the head office of telegraph contain any evidence of this correspondence."[1733]

See, they presented it as if the telegrams were real but all traces of their existence had been skillfully erased. What a brave free press!

As early as in the beginning of March the prudent Vinaver had warned the Jewish public: "Apart from love for freedom, self-control is needed.... It is better for us to avoid highly visible and prominent posts.... Do not hurry to practice our rights."[1734] We know that Vinaver (and also Dan, Liber and Branson) "at different times have been offered minister posts, but all of them refused, believing that Jews should not be present in Russian Government." The attorney Vinaver could not, of course, reject his sensational appointment to the Senate, where he became one of four Jewish Senators (together with G. Blumenfeld, O. Gruzenberg, and I. Gurevich).[1735] There were no Jews among the ministers but four influential Jews occupied posts of deputy ministers: V. Gurevich was a deputy to Avksentiev, the Minister of Internal Affairs; S. Lurie was in the Ministry of Trade and Industry; S. Schwartz and A. Ginzburg-Naumov – in the ministry of Labor; and P. Rutenberg should be mentioned here too. From July, A. Galpern became the chief of the administration of the Provisional Government (after V. Nabokov)[1736]; the director of 1st Department in the Ministry of Foreign Affairs was A. N. Mandelshtam. The assistant to the head of the Moscow military district was Second Lieutenant Sher (since July 1917); from May, the head of foreign supply department at General Staff was A. Mikhelson; the commissar of the Provisional Government in the field construction office was Naum Glazberg; several Jews were incorporated by Chernov into the Central Land Committee responsible for everything related to allotting land to peasants. Of course, most of those were not key posts, having negligibly small influence when compared to the principal role of the Executive Committee, whose ethnic composition would soon become a hotly debated public worry.

At the August Government Conference dedicated to the disturbing situation in the country, apart from the representatives of soviets, parties, and guilds, a separate representation was granted to the ethnic groups of Russia, with Jews represented by eight delegates, including G. Sliozberg, M. Liber, N. Fridman, G. Landau, and O. Gruzenberg.

[1733] *Birzhevye vedomosti*, May 7, 1917, p. 3.
[1734] G. Aronson. *Evreyskaya obshchestvennost v Rossii v 1917-1918* [The Jewish Public in Russia in 1917-1918]. // *BRJ*- 2, p. 7.
[1735] RJE, v. 7, p. 381.
[1736] Ibid.

The favorite slogan of 1917 was "Expand the Revolution!" All socialist parties worked to implement it. I. O. Levin writes: "There is no doubt that Jewish representation in the Bolshevik and other parties which facilitated "expanding of revolution" – Mensheviks, Socialist Revolutionaries, etc. – with respect to both general Jewish membership and Jewish presence among the leaders, greatly exceeds the Jewish share in the population of Russia. This is an indisputable fact; while its reasons should be debated, its factual veracity is unchallengeable and its denial is pointless"; and "a certainly convincing explanation of this phenomenon by Jewish inequality before the March revolution ... is still not sufficiently exhaustive."[1737] Members of central committees of the socialist parties are known. Interestingly, Jewish representation in the leadership of Mensheviks, the Right and the Left Socialist Revolutionaries, and the Anarchists was much greater than among the Bolshevik leaders. At the Socialist Revolutionary Congress, which took place in the end of May and beginning of June 1917, 39 out of 318 delegates were Jewish, and out of 20 members of the Central Committee of the party elected during the Congress, 7 were Jewish. A. Gotz was one of the leaders of the right wing faction and M. Natanson was among the leaders of the left Socialist Revolutionaries."[1738] (What a despicable role awaited Natanson, "the wise Mark," one of the founder of Russian Narodnichestvo ["Populism"]! During the war, living abroad, he was receiving financial aid from Germany. In May 1917 he returned in Russia in one of the 'extraterritorial trains' across Germany; in Russia, he had immediately endorsed Lenin and threw his weight in support of the latter's goal of dissolving the Constituent Assembly; actually, it was he who had voiced this idea first, though Lenin, of course, needed no such nudge.) Local government elections took place in the summer. Overall, socialist parties were victorious, and "Jews actively participated in the local and municipal work in a number of cities and towns outside of the [former] Pale of Settlement." For instance, Socialist Revolutionary O. Minor.became head of the Moscow City Duma; member of the Central Committee of the Bund, A. Vainshtein (Rakhmiel),of the Minsk Duma; Menshevik I. Polonsky, of the Ekaterinoslav Duma, Bundist D. Chertkov, of the Saratov Duma." G. Shreider had become the mayor of Petrograd, and A. Ginzburg-Naumov was elected a deputy mayor in Kiev."[1739]

But most of these persons were gone with the October coup and it was not they who shaped the subsequent developments in Russia. It would become the lot of those who now occupied much lower posts, mostly in the soviets;

[1737] I. O. Levin. *Evrei v revolutsii* [The Jews in the Revolution]. // RJ, p. 124.
[1738] RJE, v. 7, p. 399.
[1739] G. Aronson. *Evreyskaya obshchestvennost v Rossii v 1917-1918* [The Jewish Public in Russia in 1917-1918] // BRJ-2, p. 10. RJE, v. 7, p. 381.

they were numerous and spread all over the country: take, for instance, Khinchuk, head of the Moscow Soviet of Workers' Deputies, or Nasimovich and M. Trilisser of the Irkutsk Soviet (the latter would later serve in the Central Executive Committee of the Soviets of Siberia and become a famous Chekist).[1740]

All over the provinces "Jewish socialist parties enjoyed large representation in the Soviets of Workers' and Soldiers' Deputies."[1741] They were also prominently presented at the All-Russian Democratic Conference in September 1917, which annoyed Lenin so much that he had even demanded surrounding the Alexandrinsky Theater with troops and arresting the entire assembly. (The theater's superintendent, comrade Nashatyr, would have to act on the order, but Trotsky had dissuaded Lenin.) And even after the October coup, the Moscow Soviet of *Soldiers'* Deputies had among its members, according to Bukharin, "dentists, pharmacists, etc., – representatives of trades as close to the soldier's profession as to that of the Chinese Emperor."[1742]

But above all of that, above all of Russia, from the spring to the autumn of 1917, stood the power of one body – and it was not the Provisional Government. It was the powerful and insular Executive Committee of the Petrograd Soviet, and later, after June, the successor to its power, the All-Russian Central Executive Committee (CEC) – it was they who had in fact ruled over Russia. While appearing solid and determined from outside, in reality they were being torn apart by internal contradictions and interfactional ideological confusion. Initially, the Executive Committee of the Petrograd Soviet of Workers' and Soldiers' Deputies unanimously approved the Order No. 1, but later was doubtful about the war – whether to continue destroying army or to strengthen it. (Quite unexpectedly, they declared their support for the Freedom Loan; thus they had incensed the Bolsheviks but agreed with the public opinion on this issue, including the attitudes of liberal Jews.) The Presidium of the first All-Russian CEC of the Soviet of Workers' and Soldiers' Deputies (the first governing Soviet body) consisted of nine men.

Among them were the Social Revolutionaries (SRs) A. Gots and M. Gendelman, the Menshevik, F. Dan, and the member of Bund, M. Liber. (In March at the All-Russian Conference of the Soviets, Gendelman and Steklov had demanded stricter conditions be imposed on the Tsar's family, which was under house arrest, and also insisted on the arrest of all crown

---

[1740] RJE, v. 3, p. 162, 293.
[1741] G. Aronson. *Evreyskaya obshchestvennost v Rossii v 1917-1918* [The Jewish Public in Russia in 1917-1918] // *BRJ-2*, p. 7.
[1742] *Izvestiya*, November 8, 1917, p. 5.

princes – this is how confident they were in their power.) The prominent Bolshevik, L. Kamenev, was among the members of that Presidium. It also included the Georgian, Chkheidze; the Armenian, Saakjan; one Krushinsky, most likely a Pole; and Nikolsky, likely a Russian – quite an impudent [ethnic] composition for the governing organ of Russia in such a critical time.

Apart from the CEC of the Soviet of Workers' and Soldiers' Deputies, there was also the All-Russian Executive Committee of the Soviet of Peasants' Deputies, elected in the end of May. Of its 30 members, there were only *three* actual peasants – an already habitual sham of the pre-Bolshevik regime. Of those thirty, D. Pasmanik identified seven Jews: "a sad thing it was, especially considering Jewish interests"; and "they had become an eyesore to everybody."[1743] Then this *peasant* organ put forward a list of its candidates for the future Constituent Assembly. Apart from Kerensky, the list contained several Jews, such as the boisterous Ilya Rubanovich, who had just arrived from Paris, the terrorist Abram Gots, and the little-known Gurevich...[1744] (In the same article, there was a report on the arrest for desertion of warrant officer M. Golman, the head of the Mogilev Guberniya, a *Peasant* Soviet.[1745])

Of course, the actions of the executive committees could not be solely explained by their ethnic composition – not at all! (Many of those personalities irreversibly distanced themselves from their native communities and had even forgotten the way to their shtetls.) All of them sincerely believed that because of their talents and revolutionary spirit, they would have no problem arranging workers', soldiers' and peasants' matters in the best way possible. They would manage it better simply because of being more educated and smarter than all this clumsy hoi polloi.

Yet for many Russians, from commoner toa general, this sudden, eye-striking transformation in the appearance among the directors and orators at rallies and meetings, in command and in government, was overwhelming.

V. Stankevich, the only officer-socialist in the Executive Committee, provided an example: "this fact [of the abundance of Jews in the Committee] alone had enormous influence on the public opinion and sympathies....

[1743] D. S. Pasmanik. *Russkaya revolutsia i evreistvo: (Bolshevism i iudaizm)* [Russian Revolution and Jewry: Bolshevism and Judaism]. Paris, 1923, p. 153-154.
[1744] *Rech*, July 28, 1917, p. 3.
[1745] Ibid.; see also G. Lelevich. *Oktyabr v stavke* [The October in the general Headquarters]. Gomel, 1922, p. 13, 66-67.

Noteworthy, when Kornilov met with the Committee for the first time, he had accidently sat in the midst of Jews; in front of him sat two insignificant and plain members of the Committee, whom I remember merely because of their grotesquely Jewish facial features. Who knows how that affected Kornilov's attitudes toward Russian revolution?"[1746]

Yet the treatment of all things Russian by the new regime was very taletelling. Here is an example from the "days of Kornilov" in the end of August 1918. Russia was visibly dying, losing the war, with its army corrupted and the rear in collapse. General Kornilov, cunningly deceived by Kerensky, artlessly appealed to the people, almost howling with pain: "Russian people! Our great Motherland is dying. The hour of her death is nigh.... All, whose bosoms harbor a beating Russian heart, go to the temples and pray to God to grant us the greatest miracle of salvation for our beloved country!"[1747] In response to that the ideologist of the February Revolution and one of the leading members of the Executive Committee, Gimmer-Sukhanov, chuckled in amusement: "What an awkward, silly, clueless, politically illiterate call ... what a lowbrow imitation of Suzdalshchina ['Suzdalshchina' refers to resistance in Suzdal to the Mongol invaders]!"[1748]

Yes, it sounded pompously and awkwardly, without a clear political position. Indeed, Kornilov was not a politician but his heart ached. And what about Sukhanov's heart – did he feel any pain at all? He did not have any sense of the living land and culture, nor he had any urge to preserve them – he served to his ideology only, the International, seeing in Kornilov's words a total lack of ideological content. Yes, his response was caustic. But note that he had not only labeled Kornilov's appeal an 'imitation', he had also derogatorily referred to 'Suzdalshchina,' to Russian history, ancient art and sanctity. And with such disdain to the entire Russian historical heritage, all that internationalist ilk – Sukhanov and his henchmen from the malicious Executive Committee, steered the February Revolution.

And it was not the ethnic origin of Sukhanov and the rest; it was their antinational, anti-Russian and anti-conservative attitudes. We have seen similar attitudes on the part of the Provisional Government too, with its task of governing the entire Russia and its quite Russian ethnic

---

[1746] V. B. Stankevich. *Vospominaniya, 1914-1919* [Memoirs, 1914-1919]. Berlin, publishing house of I. P. Ladyzhnikov, 1920, p. 86-87.
[1747] A. I. Denikin. *Ocherki russkoi smuty. V1 : Krushenie vlasti I armii, fevral-sentyabr 1917* [Russian Turmoil. Memoirs. V1: Collapse of Authority and Army]. Paris, 1922, p. 216.
[1748] Nik Sukhanov. *Zapiski o revolutsii* [Memoirs of the Revolution]. Berlin, Publishing House of Z. I. Grzhebin, 1923, v.5, p. 287.

composition. Yet did it display a Russian worldview or represent Russian interests if only a little? Not at all! The Government's most consistent and 'patriotic' activity was to guide the already unraveling country (the 'Kronstadt Republic' was not the only place which had "seceded from Russia" by that time) to the victory in war! To the victory at any cost! With loyalty to the allies! (Sure, the allies, their governments, public and financers, put pressure on Russia. For instance, in May, Russian newspapers cited *The Morning Post* from Washington: "America made it clear to the Russian government" that if [Russia] makes a separate peace [with Germany], the United States would "annul all financial agreements with Russia."[1749] Prince Lvov [Prince Georgi Lvov, led the Russian Provisional Government during the Russian revolution's initial phase, from March 1917 until he relinquished control to Alexander Kerensky in July 1917] upheld the sentiment: "The country must determinately send its army to battle."[1750]) They had no concern about consequences of the ongoing war for Russia. And this mismatch, this loss of sense of national self-preservation, could be observed almost at every meeting of the Provisional Government cabinet, almost in every discussion.

There were simply ridiculous incidents. Throwing millions of rubles left and right and always keenly supporting "cultural needs of ethnic minorities," the Provisional Government at its April 6 meeting had rejected the request of the long-established "Great Russian Orchestra of V. V. Andreev" to continue getting paid as before, "from the funds of the former His Majesty's Personal Chancellery" (the funds were confiscated by the Provisional Government itself).

The petition was turned down despite the fact that the requested sum, 30 thousand rubles per year, was equivalent to the annual pay of just three minister assistants. "Deny!" (Why not disband your so-called "Great Russian" orchestra? – What kind of name is that?) Taken aback and believing that it was just a misunderstanding, Andreev petitioned again. Yet with an unusual for this torpid government determination, he was refused a second time too, at the April 27 meeting.[1751]

Milyukov, a Russian historian and minister of the Provisional Government, did not utter a single specifically Russian sentiment during that year. Similarly, "the key figure of the revolution," Alexander Kerensky, could not be at any stage accused of possessing an ethnic Russian consciousness. Yet at the same time the government demonstrated constant anxious bias

---

[1749] *Russkaya Volya*, May 7, 1917, p. 4.
[1750] Ibid., p. 6.
[1751] *Zhurnaly zasedanii Vremennogo Pravitelstva* [Minutes of the meetings of the Provisional Government]. Petrograd, 1917. V1: March-May; April 6 meeting (book 44, p. 5) and April 27 meeting (book 64, p. 4).

against any conservative circles, and especially – against Russian conservatives. Even during his last speech in the Council of the Russian Republic (Pre-Parliament) on October 24, when Trotsky's troops were already seizing Petrograd building after building, Kerensky emphatically argued that the Bolshevik newspaper *Rabochy Put* (*Worker's Way*) and the right-wing *Novaya Rus* (*New Russia*) – both of which Kerensky had just shut down – shared similar political views....

The "darned incognito" of the members of the Executive Committee was, of course, noticed by the public. Initially it was the educated society of Petrograd that was obsessed with this question, which several times surfaced in newspapers. For two months, the Committee tried to keep the secret, but by May they had no other choice but reveal themselves and had published the actual names of most of the pseudonym-holders (except for Steklov-Nakhamkis and Boris Osipovich Bogdanov, the energetic permanent chair of the council; they had managed to keep their identities secret for a while; the latter's name confused the public by similarity with another personality, Bogdanov-Malinovsky). This odd secrecy irritated the public, and even ordinary citizens began asking questions. It was already typical in May that if, during a plenary meeting of the Soviet, someone proposed Zinoviev or Kamenev for something, the public shouted from the auditorium demanding their true names.

Concealing true names was incomprehensible to the ordinary man of that time: only thieves hide and change their names. Why is Boris Katz ashamed of his name, and instead calling himself "Kamkov"? Why does Lurie hide under the alias of "Larin"? Why does Mandelshtam use the pseudonym "Lyadov"?

Many of these had aliases that originated out of necessity in their past underground life, but what had compelled the likes of Shotman, the Socialist Revolutionary from Tomsk, (and not him alone) to become "Danilov" in 1917?

Certainly, the goal of a revolutionary, hiding behind a pseudonym, is to outsmart someone, and that may include not only the police and government. In this way, ordinary people as well are unable to figure out who their new leaders are.

Intoxicated by the freedom of the first months of the February Revolution, many Jewish activists and orators failed to notice that their constant fussing around presidiums and rallies produced certain bewilderment and wry glances.

By the time of the February Revolution there was no "popular anti-Semitism" in the internal regions of Russia, it was confined exclusively to the areas of the Pale of Settlement. (For instance, Abraham Cogan had even stated in 1917: "We loved Russia despite all the oppression from the previous regime because we knew that it was not the Russian people" behind it but Tsarism.[1752]) But after just a few months following the February Revolution, resentment against Jews had suddenly flared up among the masses of people and spread over Russia, growing stronger with each passing month. And even the official newspapers reported, for instance, on the exasperation in the waiting lines in the cities.

"Everything has been changed in that twinkle of the eye that created a chasm between the old and the new Russia. But it is queues that have changed the most. Strangely, while everything has moved to the left, the food lines have moved to the right. If you ... would like to hear Black Hundred propaganda ... then go and spend some time in a waiting line." Among other things you will find out that "there are virtually no Jews in the lines, they don't need it as they have enough bread hoarded." The same "gossip about Jews who tuck away bread" rolls from another end of the line as well; "the waiting lines is the most dangerous source of counterrevolution."[1753] The author Ivan Nazhivin noted that in the autumn in Moscow anti-Semitic propaganda fell on ready ears in the hungry revolutionary queues: "What rascals! ... They wormed themselves onto the very top! ... See, how proudly they ride in their cars.... Sure, not a single Yid can be found in the lines here.... Just you wait!"[1754]

Any revolution releases a flood of obscenity, envy, and anger from the people. The same happened among the Russian people, with their weakened Christian spirituality. And so the Jews – many of whom had ascended to the top, to visibility, and, what is more, who had not concealed their revolutionary jubilation, nor waited in the miserable lines – increasingly became a target of popular resentment.

Many instances of such resentment were documented in 1917 newspapers. Below are several examples. When, at the Apraksin market on Sennaya Square, a hoard of goods was discovered in possession of Jewish merchants, "people began shout ... 'plunder Jewish shops!', because 'Yids are responsible for all the troubles' ... and this word 'Yid' is on everyone's lips."[1755] A stockpile of flour and bacon was found in the store of a merchant (likely a Jew) in Poltava.

The crowd started plundering his shop and then began calling for a Jewish pogrom. Later, several members of the Soviet of Workers' Deputies, including Drobnis, arrived and attempted to appease the crowd; as a result,

---

[1752] *Rech*, June 28, 1917, p. 2.
[1753] *Rech*, May 3, 1917, p. 6.
[1754] Ivan Nazhivin. *Zapiski o revolutsii* [Notes about Revolution]. Vienna, 1921, p. 28.
[1755] *Rech*, June 17, 1917, evening issue, p. 4.

Drobnis was beaten.[1756] In October in Ekaterinoslav soldiers trashed small shops, shouting "Smash the bourgeois! Smash the Yids!" In Kiev at the Vladimirsky market a boy had hit a woman, who tried to buy flour out her turn on the head Instantly, the crowd started yelling "the Yids are beating the Russians!" and a brawl ensued. (Note that it had happened in the same Kiev where one could already see the streamers "Long live free Ukraine without Yids and Poles!") By that time "Smash the Yids!" could be heard in almost every street brawl, even in Petrograd, and often completely without foundation. For instance, in a Petrograd streetcar two women "called for disbanding of the Soviet of Workers' and Soldiers' Deputies, filled, according to them, exclusively by 'Germans and Yids'. Both were arrested and called to account."[1757]

Newspaper *Russkaya Volya* (*Russian Freedom*) reported: "Right in front of our eyes, anti-Semitism, in its most primitive form … re-arises and spreads…. It is enough to hear to conversations in streetcars [in Petrograd] or in waiting lines to various shops, or in the countless fleeting rallies at every corner and crossroad … they accuse Jews of political stranglehold, of seizing parties and soviets, and even of ruining the army … of looting and hoarding goods."[1758]

Many Jewish socialists, agitators in the front units, enjoyed unlimited success during the spring months when calls for a "democratic peace" were tolerated and fighting was not required. Then nobody blamed them for being Jewish. But in June when the policy of the Executive Committee had changed toward support and even propaganda for the offensive, calls of "smash the Yids!" began appearing and those Jewish persuaders suffered battering by unruly soldiers time and time again.

Rumors were spreading that the Executive Committee in Petrograd was "seized by Yids." By June this belief had taken root in the Petrograd garrison and factories; this is exactly what soldiers shouted to the member of the Committee Voitinsky who had visited an infantry regiment to dissuade the troops from the looming demonstration conceived by Bolsheviks on June 10.

V. D. Nabokov, hardly known for anti-Semitism, joked that the meeting of the foremen of the Pre-Parliament in October 1917 "could be safely called a Sanhedrin": its majority was Jewish; of Russians, there were only

---

[1756] *Rech*, September 9, 1917, p. 3.
[1757] *Rech*, August 8, 1917, p. 5.
[1758] *Russkaya Volya*, June 17, 1917, evening issue, p. 4.

Avksentiev, me, Peshekhonov, and Chaikovsky...." His attention was drawn to that fact by Mark Vishnyak who was present there also.[1759]

By autumn, the activity of Jews in power had created such an effect that even *Iskry* (*Sparks*), the illustrated supplement to the surpassingly gentle *Russkoe Slovo* (*Russian Word*) that would until then never dare defying public opinion in such a way, had published an abrasive anti-Jewish caricature in the October 29 issue, that is, already during fights of the October coup in Moscow.

The Executive Committee of the Soviet of Workers' and Soldiers' Deputies actively fought against anti-Semitism. (I cannot rule out that the harsh refusal to accept the well-deserved Plekhanov into the CEC in April 1917 was a kind of revenge for his anti-Bund referral to the "tribe of Gad," which was mentioned in Lenin's publications.[1760] Indeed, I cannot provide any other explanation.) On July 21 the 1st All-Russian Congress of Soviets had issued a proclamation about a struggle against anti-Semitism ("about the only resolution approved by the Congress unanimously, without any objections or arguments"[1761]). When in the end of June (28th and 29th) the re-elected Bureau of the CEC had assembled, they had heard a report on "the rise of anti-Semitic agitation ... mainly in the northwestern and southwestern" guberniyas; a decision was made immediately to send a delegation of 15 members of the CEC with special powers there[1762], subordinating them to the direction of the "Department on the Struggle against Counter-Revolution."

On the other hand, Bolsheviks, who advanced their agenda under the slogan "Down with the ministers-capitalists!" not only did nothing to alleviate this problem, they even fanned its flames (along with the anarchists, despite the fact that the latter were headed by one Bleikhman). They claimed that the Executive Committee was so exceptionally lenient toward the government only because capitalists and Jews control everything (isn't that reminiscent of Narodnaya Volya [the People's Will terrorist organization] of 1881?).

And when the Bolshevik uprising of July 3-4 broke out (it was in fact targeted not against the already impotent Provisional Government but against the Bolshevik's true competitor – Executive Committee), the

---

[1759] V. Nabokov. *Vremennoye pravitelstvo* [The Provisional Government] // Archive of Russian Revolution, published by Gessen. Berlin: Slovo, 1922, v. 1, p. 80.

[1760] V. I. Lenin. *Sochineniya* [Works]. In 45 volumes, 4th Edition (henceforth — Lenin, 4th edition). Moscow, Gospolitizdat, 1941-1967, v. 4, p. 311.

[1761] *Izvestiya*, June 28, 1917, p. 5.

[1762] *Izvestiya*, June 30, 1917, p. 10.

Bolsheviks slyly exploited the anger of soldiers toward Jews by pointing them to that very body – see, there they are!

But when the Bolsheviks had lost their uprising, the CEC had conducted an official investigation and many members of the commission of inquiry were Jews from the presidium of the CEC. And because of their "socialist conscience" they dared not call the Bolshevik uprising a crime and deal with it accordingly. So the commission had yielded no result and was soon liquidated.

During the garrison meeting, arranged by the CEC on October 19, just before the decisive Bolshevik uprising, "one of representatives of 176th Infantry Regiment, a Jew," warned that "those people down on the streets scream that Jews are responsible for all the wrongs."[1763] At the CEC meeting during the night of October 25, Gendelman reported that when he was giving a speech in the Peter and Paul Fortress earlier that afternoon he was taunted: "You are Gendelman! That is you are a Yid and a Rightist!"[1764] When on October 27 Gotz and his delegation to Kerensky tried to depart to Gatchina from the Baltiysky Rail Terminal, he was nearly killed by sailors who screamed that "the soviets are controlled by Yids."[1765] And during the 'wine pogroms' on the eve of the 'glorious Bolshevik victory,' the calls "Slaughter Yids!" were heard also.

And yet there was not a single *Jewish* pogrom over the whole year of 1917. The infamous outrageous pogroms in Kalusha and Ternopol were in fact the work of frenzied drunken revolutionary soldiers, retreating in disorder. They smashed everything on their way, all shops and stores; and because most of those were Jewish-owned, the word spread about 'Jewish pogroms'. A similar pogrom took place in Stanislavov, with its much smaller Jewish population, and quite reasonably it was not labeled a 'Jewish' pogrom.

Already by the mid-summer of 1917 the Jews felt threatened by the embittered population (or drunken soldiers), but the ongoing collapse of the state was fraught with incomparably greater dangers. Amazingly, it seems that both the Jewish community and the press, the latter to a large extent identified with the former, learned nothing from the formidable experiences of 1917 in general, but narrowly looked at the "isolated manifestations of pogroms." And so time after time they missed the real danger. The executive power behaved similarly. When the Germans breached the front at Ternopol in the night of July 10, the desperate joint

---

[1763] *Rech*, October 20, 1917, p. 3.
[1764] *Izvestiya*, October 26, 1917, p. 2.
[1765] *Delo Naroda*, October 29, 1917, p. 1.

meeting of the CEC of the Soviet of Workers' and Soldiers' Deputies and the Executive Committee of the Soviet of Peasants'

Deputies had taken place. They had acknowledged that should the revolution perish, the country crumbles down (in that exact order), and then named Provisional Government a "Government for Salvation of the Revolution," and noted in their appeal to the people that "dark forces are again prepared to torment our longsuffering Motherland. They are setting backward masses upon the Jews."[1766]

On July 18 at a panel session of the State Duma, in an extremely small circle, Rep. Maslennikov spoke against the Executive Committee and among other things spelled out the real names of its members. On the very same evening at the factional meeting of the CEC they beat an alarm: "This is a case of *counterrevolution*, it must be dealt with according to the recently issued decree of the Minister of Internal Affairs Tsereteli on suppression of counterrevolution! (The decree was issued in response to the Bolshevik uprising, though it was never used against Bolsheviks.) In two days Maslennikov made excuses in an article in the newspaper *Rech* [*Speech*]: indeed, he named Steklov, Kamenev, and Trotsky but never intended to incite anger against the entire Jewish people, and "anyway, attacking them, I had absolutely no wish to make Jewish people responsible for the actions of these individuals."[1767]

Then, in mid-September, when the all gains of the February Revolution were already irreversibly ruined, on the eve of the by now imminent Bolshevik coup, Ya. Kantorovich warned in *Rech* about the danger that: "The dark forces and evil geniuses of Russia will soon emerge from their dens to jubilantly perform Black Masses...." Indeed, it will happen soon. Yet what kind of Black masses? – "...Of bestial patriotism and pogrom-loving 'truly-Russian' national identity."[1768] In October in Petrograd I. Trumpeldor had organized Jewish self-defense forces for protection against pogroms, but they were never needed.

Indeed, Russian minds were confused, and so were Jewish ones. Several years after the revolution, G. Landau, looking back with sadness, wrote: "Jewish participation in the Russian turmoil had astonishingly suicidal overtones in it; I am referring not only to their role in Bolshevism, but to their involvement in the whole thing. And it is not just about the huge number of politically active people, socialists and revolutionaries, who have joined the revolution; I am talking mainly about the broad sympathy of the masses it was met with.... Although many harbored pessimistic

---

[1766] *Rech*, July 11, 1917, p. 3.
[1767] *Rech*, July 21, 1917, p. 4.
[1768] *Rech*, September 16, 1917, p. 3.

expectations, in particular, an anticipation of pogroms, they were still able to reconcile such a foreboding with an acceptance of turmoil which unleashed countless miseries and pogroms. It resembled the fatal attraction of butterflies to fire, to the annihilating fire.... It is certain there were some strong motives pushing the Jews into that direction, and yet those were clearly suicidal.... Granted, Jews were not different in that from the rest of Russian intelligentsia and from the Russian society.... Yet we *had to* be different ... we, the ancient people of city-dwellers, merchants, artisans, intellectuals ... we had to be different from the people of land and power, from peasants, landowners, officials."[1769]

And let's not forget those who were different. We must always remember that Jewry was and is very heterogeneous, that attitudes and actions vary greatly among the Jews. So it was with the Russian Jewry in 1917: in provinces and even in the capital there were circles with reasonable views and they were growing as October was getting closer.

The Jewish stance toward Russian unity during the months when Russia was pulled apart not only by other nations, but even by Siberians, was remarkable. "All over the course of revolution Jews, together with Great Russians, were among the most ardent champions of the idea of Great Russia."[1770] Now, when Jews had gotten their equal rights, what could they have in common with different peoples on the periphery of the former empire? And yet the disintegration of a united country would fracture Jewry. In July at the 9th Congress of Constitutional Democrats, Vinaver and Nolde openly argued against territorial partition of peoples and in favor of Russian unity.[1771] Also in September, in the national section of the Democratic Conference, the Jewish socialists spoke *against* any federalization of Russia (in that they had joined the Centralists). Today they write in an Israeli magazine that Trumpeldor's Jewish detachments "backed the Provisional Government and had even foiled the Kornilov's mutiny."[1772] Perhaps. However, in rigorously studying events of 1917, I did not encounter any such information. But I am aware of opposite instances: in early May 1917 in the thundering patriotic and essentially

---

[1769] G. A. Landau. *Revolutsionnye idei v evreiskoi obchshestvennosti* [Revolutionary ideas in Jewish society] // *RJ*, p. 105, 106.

[1770] D. S. Pasmanik. *Russkaya revolutsia i evreistvo: (Bolshevism i iudaizm)* [Russian Revolution and Jewry: Bolshevism and Judaism]. Paris, 1923, p. 245.

[1771] *Rech*, July 26, 1917, p. 3.

[1772] I. Eldad. *Tak kto zhe nasledniki Zhabotinskogo?* [So Who Are the Heirs of Jabotinsky?] // *"22"*: Obshchestvenno-politicheskiy i literaturniy zhurnal evreyskoy intelligentsii iz SSSR *v Izraile [*Social, Political and Literary Journal of the Jewish Intelligentsia from the USSR *in Israel* (henceforth – *"22"*)]. Tel-Aviv, 1980, (16), p. 120.

counterrevolutionary "Black Sea Delegation," the most successful orator calling for the defense of Russia was Jewish sailor Batkin.

D. Pasmanik had published the letters of millionaire steamship owner Shulim Bespalov to the Minister of Trade and Industry Shakhovsky dated as early as September 1915: "Excessive profits made by all industrialists and traders lead our Motherland to the imminent wreck." He had donated half a million rubles to the state and proposed to establish a law limiting all profits by 15%. Unfortunately, these self-restricting measures were not introduced as 'rush to freedom' *progressives,* such as Konovalov and Ryabushinsky, did not mind making 100% war profits. When Konovalov himself became the Minister of Trade and Industry, Shulim Bespalov wrote to him on July 5, 1917: "Excessive profits of industrialists are ruining our country, now we must take 50% of the value of their capitals and property," and added that he is ready to part with 50% of his own assets. Konovalov paid no heed.[1773]

In August, at the Moscow All-Russian State Conference, O. O. Gruzenberg (a future member of the Constituent Assembly) stated: "These days the Jewish people ... are united in their allegiance to our Motherland, in unanimous aspiration to defend her integrity and achievements of democracy" and were prepared to give for her defense "all their material and intellectual assets, to part with everything precious, with the flower of their people, all their young."[1774]

These words reflected the realization that the February regime was the best for the Russian Jewry, promising economic progress as well as political and cultural prosperity. And that realization was adequate.

The closer it got to October coup and the more apparent the Bolshevik threat, the wider this realization spread among Jews, leading them to oppose Bolshevism. It was taking root even among socialist parties and during the October coup many Jewish socialists were actively against it. Yet they were debilitated by their socialist views and their opposition was limited by negotiations and newspaper articles – until the Bolsheviks shut down those newspapers.

It is necessary to state explicitly that the October coup was not carried by Jews (though it was under the general command of Trotsky and with energetic actions of young Grigory Chudnovsky during the arrest of Provisional Government and the massacre of the defenders of the Winter Palace). Broadly speaking, the common rebuke, that the 170-million-

---

[1773] D. S. Pasmanik. *Russkaya revolutsia i evreistvo: (Bolshevism i iudaizm)* [Russian Revolution and Jewry: Bolshevism and Judaism]. Paris, 1923, p. 179-181.
[1774] *Rech,* August 16, 1917, p. 3.

people could not be pushed into Bolshevism by a small Jewish minority, is justified. Indeed, we had ourselves sealed our fate in 1917, through our foolishness from February to October-December.

The October coup proved a devastating lot for Russia. Yet the state of affairs even *before* it promised little good to the people. We had already lost responsible statesmanship and the events of 1917 had proved it in excess. The best Russia could expect was an inept, feeble, and disorderly pseudo-democracy, unable to rely on enough citizens with developed legal consciousness and economic independence.

After October fights in Moscow, representatives of the Bund and Poale-Zion had taken part in the peace negotiations – not in alliance with the Junkers or the Bolsheviks — but as a third independent party. There were many Jews among Junkers of the Engineers School who defended the Winter Palace on October 25: in the memoirs of Sinegub, a palace defender, Jewish names appear regularly; I personally knew one such engineer from my prison experience. And during the Odessa City Duma elections the Jewish block had opposed the Bolsheviks and won, though only marginally.

During the Constituent Assembly elections "more than 80% of Jewish population in Russia had voted" for Zionist parties.[1775] Lenin wrote that 550 thousands voted for Jewish nationalists.[1776] "Most Jewish parties have formed a united national list of candidates; seven deputies were elected from that list – six Zionists" and Gruzenberg. The success of Zionists was facilitated by the recently published declaration of British Minister of Foreign Affairs Balfour on the establishment of 'Jewish national home' in Palestine, which was "met with enthusiasm by the majority of Russian Jewry (celebratory demonstrations, rallies and worship services took place in Moscow, Petrograd, Odessa, Kiev and many other cities)."[1777]

Prior to the October coup, Bolshevism was not very influential among Jews. But just before the uprising, Natanson, Kamkov, and Shteinberg on behalf of the left Socialist Revolutionaries had signed a combat pact with Bolsheviks Trotsky and Kamenev.[1778] And some Jews distinguished themselves among the Bolsheviks in their very first victories and some even became famous. The commissar of the famed Latvian regiments of the 12th Army, which did so much for the success of Bolshevik coup, was

---

[1775] V. Boguslavsky. V sachshitu Kunyaeva [In Defense of Kunyaev] // "22", 1980, (16), p. 169.
[1776] Lenin, 4th edition, v. 30, p. 231.
[1777] SJE, v.7, p. 381.
[1778] Kh. M. Astrakhan. *Bolsheviki i ikh politicheskie protivniki v 1917 godu* [The Bolsheviks and Their Political Adversaries in 1917]. Leningrad, 1973, p. 407.

Semyon Nakhimson. "Jewish soldiers played a notable role during preparation and execution of the armed uprising of October 1917 in Petrograd and other cities, and also during suppression of mutinies and armed resurrections against the new Soviet regime."[1779]

It is widely known that during the 'historical' session of the Congress of Soviets on October 27 two acts, the 'Decree on Land' and the 'Decree on Peace', were passed. But it didn't leave a mark in history that after the 'Decree on Peace' but before the 'Decree on Land' another resolution was passed. It declared it "a matter of honor for local soviets to prevent Jewish and any other pogroms by dark forces."[1780] (Pogroms by 'Red forces of light' were not anticipated.)

So even here, at the Congress of Workers' and Peasants' Deputies, the Jewish question was put ahead of the peasant one.

[1779] Aron Abramovich. *V reshayuchshey voine: Uchastie i rol evreev SSSR v voine protiv natsisma* [In the Deciding War: Participation and Role of Jews in the USSR in the War Against Nazism] 2nd Edition, Tel Aviv, 1982, v. 1, p. 45, 46.

[1780] L. Trotsky. *Istoriya russkoi revolutsii. T. 2: Oktyabrskaya revolutsia* [The History of Russian Revolution]. Berlin, Granit, 1933, v. 2: October Revolution, Part 2, p. 361.

Chapter 15

Alongside the Bolsheviks

This theme—the Jews alongside the Bolsheviks—is not new, far from it. How many pages already written on the subject! The one who wants to demonstrate that the revolution was "anything but Russian", "foreign by nature", invokes Jewish surnames and pseudonyms, thus claiming to exonerate the Russians from all responsibility in the revolution of seventeen. As for the Jewish authors, those who denied the Jews' share in the revolution as well as those who have always recognised it, all agree that these Jews were not Jews *by spirit*, they were *renegades*.

We also agree on that. We must judge people for their *spirit*. Yes, they were renegades.

But the Russian leaders of the Bolshevik Party were also not Russians by the spirit; they were very anti-Russian, and certainly anti-Orthodox. With them, the great Russian culture, reduced to a doctrine and to political calculations, was distorted.

The question should be asked in another way, namely: how many scattered renegades should be brought together to form a homogeneous political current?

What proportion of nationals? As far as the Russian renegades are concerned, the answer is known: alongside the Bolsheviks there were enormous numbers, an unforgivable number. But for the Jewish renegades, what was, by the enrolment and by the energy deployed, their share in the establishment of Bolshevik power?

Another question concerns the attitude of the nation towards its own renegades. However, the latter was contrasted, ranging from abomination to admiration, from mistrust to adherence. It has manifested itself in the very reactions of the popular masses, whether Russian, Jewish, or Lithuanian, in life itself much more than in the briefings of historians.

And finally: can nations deny their renegades? Is there any sense in this denial? Should a nation remember or not remember them? Can it forget the monster they have begotten? To this question the answer is no doubt: it is necessary to remember. Every people must remember its own renegades, remember them as *their own*—to that, there is no escape.

And then, deep down, is there an example of renegade more striking than Lenin himself? However, Lenin was Russian, there is no point in denying it.

Yes, he loathed, he detested everything that had to do with ancient Russia, all Russian history and *a fortiori* Orthodoxy. From Russian literature he had retained only Chernyshevsky and Saltykov-Shchedrin; Turgenev, with his liberal spirit, amused him, and Tolstoy the accuser, too. He never showed the least feeling of affection for anything, not even for the river, the Volga, on whose banks his childhood took place (and did he not instigate a lawsuit against his peasants for damage to his lands?). Moreover: it was he who pitilessly delivered the whole region to the appalling famine of 1921. Yes, all this is true. But it was we, the Russians, who created the climate in which Lenin grew up and filled him with hatred. It is in *us* that the Orthodox faith has lost its vigour, this faith in which he could have grown instead of declaring it a merciless war. How can one not see in him a renegade? And yet, he is Russian, and we Russians, we answer for him. His ethnic origins are sometimes invoked. Lenin was a mestizo issued from different races: his paternal grandfather, Nikolai Vasilyevich, was of Kalmyk and Chuvash blood, his grandmother, Anna Aleksievna Smirnova, was a Kalmyk, his other grandfather, Israel (Alexander of his name of baptism) Davidovitch Blank, was a Jew, his other grandmother, Anna Iohannovna (Ivanovna) Groschopf, was the daughter of a German and a Swede, Anna Beata Estedt. But that does not change the case. For nothing of this makes it possible to exclude him from the Russian people: we must recognise in him a *Russian* phenomenon on the one hand, for all the ethnic groups which gave him birth have been implicated in the history of the Russian Empire, and, on the other hand, a *Russian* phenomenon, the fruit of the country we have built, we Russians, and its social climate—even if he appears to us, because of his spirit always indifferent to Russia, or even completely anti-Russian, as a phenomenon completely foreign to us. We cannot, in spite of everything, disown him.

What about the Jewish renegades? As we have seen, during the year 1917, there was no particular attraction for the Bolsheviks that manifested among the Jews. But their activism has played its part in the revolutionary upheavals. At the last Congress of the Russian Social-Democratic Labour Party (RSDLP) (London, 1907), which was, it is true, common with the Mensheviks, of 302-305 delegates, 160 were Jews, more than half—it was promising. Then, after the April 1917 Conference, just after the announcement of the explosive *April Theses* of Lenin, among the nine members of the new Central Committee were G. Zinoviev, L. Kamenev,

Ia. Sverdlov. At the VIth summer Congress of the RKP (b) (the Russian Communist Party of the Bolsheviks, the new name of the RSDLP), eleven members were elected to the Central Committee, including Zinoviev, Sverdlov, Trotsky, Uritsky.[1781] Then, at the "historic meeting" in Karpovka Street, in the apartment of Himmer and Flaksermann, on 10 October 1917, when the decision to launch the Bolshevik coup was taken, among the twelve participants were Trotsky, Zinoviev, Kamenev, Sverdlov, Uritsky, Sokolnikov. It was there that was elected the first "Politburo" which was to have such a brilliant future, and among its seven members, always the same: Trotsky, Zinoviev, Kamenev, Sokolnikov. Which is already a lot. D. S. Pasmanik clearly states: "There is no doubt that the Jewish renegades outnumbered the normal percentage...; they occupied too great a place among the Bolshevik commissioners."[1782]

Of course, all this was happening in the governing spheres of Bolshevism and in no way foreshadowed a mass movement of Jews. Moreover, the Jewish members of the Politburo did not act as a constituted group. Thus Kamenev and Zinoviev were against a hasty coup. The only master of the work, the genius of October's *coup de force*, was in fact Trotsky: he did not exaggerate his role in his *Lessons of October*. This cowardly Lenin, who, he, had been hiding out, made no substantial contribution to the putsch.

Basically, because of his internationalism and following his dispute with the Bund in 1903, Lenin adhered to the opinion that there was not and never would be such a thing as a "Jewish nationality"; that this was a reactionary action which disunited the revolutionary forces. (In agreement with him, Stalin held the Jews for a "paper nation", and considered their assimilation inevitable.) Lenin therefore saw anti-Semitism as a manœuvre of capitalism, an easy weapon in the hands of counter-revolution, something that was not natural. He understood very well, however, what mobilising force the Jewish question represented in the ideological struggle in general. And to exploit, for the good of the revolution, the feeling of bitterness particularly prevalent among the Jews, Lenin was always ready to do so.

From the first days of the revolution, however, this appeal proved to be oh so necessary! Lenin clung to it. He, who had not foreseen everything on the plane of the state, had not yet perceived how much the cultivated layer of the Jewish nation, and even more so its semi-cultivated layer, which, as a result of the war, was found scattered throughout the whole of Russia, was going to save the day throughout decisive months and years. To begin

---

[1781] SJE, t. 7, p. 399.
[1782] *D. S. Pasmanik*, Rousskaia revolioutsiia i evreistvo (Bolchevism i ioudaism) [The Russian Revolution and the Jews {Bolshevism and Judaism}], Paris, 1923, p. 155.

with, it was going to take the place of the Russian officials massively determined to boycott the Bolshevik power. This population was composed of border residents who had been driven out of their villages and who had not returned there after the end of the war. (For example, Jews expelled from Lithuania during the war had not all returned after the revolution: only the small rural people had returned, while the "urban contingent" of the Jews of Lithuania and "the young had stayed to live in the big cities of Russia."[1783])

And it was precisely "after the abolition of the Pale of Settlement in 1917 that the great exodus of Jews from its boundaries into the interior of the country ensued."[1784] This exodus is no longer that of refugees or expellees, but indeed of new settlers. Information from a Soviet source for the year 1920 testifies: "In the city of Samara, in recent years, tens of thousands of Jewish refugees and expellees have established themselves"; in Irkutsk, "the Jewish population has increased, reaching fifteen thousand people; important Jewish settlements were formed in Central Russia as well as on the banks of the Volga and the Urals."

However, "the majority continue to live on subsidies from social welfare and other philanthropic organisations." And here are the *Izvestia* calling for "the Party organisations, the Jewish sections and the departments of the National Commissariat to organise a vast campaign for the non-return to the 'tombs of the ancestors' and for the participation in the work of production in Soviet Russia."[1785]

But put yourself in the place of the Bolsheviks: they were only a small handful that had seized power, a power that was so fragile: in whom, great gods, could one have confidence? Who could be called to the rescue? Simon (Shimon) Dimantstein, a Bolshevik from the very beginning and who, since January 1918, was at the head of a European Committee specially created within the Commissariat of Nationalities, gives us the thought of Lenin on this subject: "the fact that a large part of the middle Jewish intelligentsia settled in Russian cities has rendered a proud service to the revolution. They defeated the vast sabotage enterprise we faced after the October Revolution, which was a great danger to us. They were numerous—not all, of course, far from it—to sabotage this sabotage, and it was they who, at that fateful hour, saved the revolution." Lenin considered it "inappropriate to emphasise this episode in the press…", but he remarked that "if we succeeded in seizing and restructuring the State

---

[1783] S. *Gringaouz*, Evreiskaya natsionalnaia avtonomiia v Litve i drougikh stranakh Pribaltiki [Jewish national self-government in Lithuania and the other Baltic countries]—BJWR-2, p. 46.
[1784] SJE, t. 2, p. 312.
[1785] Izvestia, 12 Oct. 1920, p. 1.

apparatus, it was exclusively thanks to this pool of new civil servants—lucid, educated, and reasonably competent."[1786]

The Bolsheviks thus *appealed* to the Jews from the very first hours of their takeover, offering to some executive positions, to others tasks of execution within the Soviet State apparatus. And many, many, answered the call, and immediately entered. The new power was in desperate need of executors who were faithful in every way—and there were many of them among the young secularised Jews, who thus mingled with their colleagues, Slavs and others.

These were not necessarily "renegades": there were among them some without political party affiliations, persons outside the revolution, who had hitherto remained indifferent to politics. For some, this approach was not ideological; it could be dictated only by personal interest. It was a mass phenomenon. And from that time the Jews no longer sought to settle in the forbidden countryside, they endeavoured to reach the capitals: "Thousands of Jews joined the Bolsheviks in crowds, seeing them as the most fierce defenders of the revolution and the most reliable internationalists... The Jews abounded in the lower levels of the Party apparatus."[1787]

"The Jew, who obviously could not have come from the nobility, the clergy, or the civil service, found himself among the ranks of the personalities of the future of the new clan."[1788] In order to promote the Jews' commitment to Bolshevism, "at the end of 1917, while the Bolsheviks were still sketching out their institutions, a Jewish department within the Commissariat of Nationalities began to function."[1789] This department was, since 1918, transformed into a separate European Commissariat. And in March 1919, at the VIIIth Congress of the RKP (b), the Communist European Union of Soviet Russia was to be proclaimed as an integral but autonomous part of the RKP (b). (The intention was to integrate this Union into the Comintern and thereby permanently undermine the Bund). A special European section within the Russian Telegraph Agency was also created (ROSTA).

D. Schub justifies these initiatives by saying that "large contingents of the Jewish youth joined the Communist Party" following the pogroms in the

---

[1786] V. Lenin, O evreiskom voprosis v Rossii [On the Jewish Question in Russia]. Preface by S. Dimanstein, M., Proletarii, 1924, pp. 17-18.

[1787] *Leonard Schapiro*, The Role of the Jews in the Russian Revolutionary Movement, in The Slavonic and East European Review, vol. 40, London, Athlone Press, 1961-62, p. 164.

[1788] *M. Kheifets*, Nashi obschiie ouroki [Our lessons]—"22", no. 14, p. 62.

[1789] *Jewish Tribune, Weekly*, Number dedicated to the interests of Russian Jews, Paris, 1923, September 7, p. 1.

territories occupied by the Whites[1790] (i.e. from 1919 onwards). But this explanation does not hold the road. For the massive entry of the Jews into the Soviet apparatus occurred towards the end of the year 1917 and during 1918.

There is no doubt that the events of 1919 (see *infra*, chapter 16) strengthened the link between the Jewish elites and the Bolsheviks, but they in no way provoked it. Another author, a communist, explains "the particularly important role of the Jewish revolutionary in our labour movement" by the fact that we can observe with the Jewish workers, "highly developed, the traits of character required of any leading role," traits which are still in draft form among the Russian workers: an exceptional energy, a sense of solidarity, a systematic mind.[1791]

Few authors deny the role of organisers that was that of the Jews in Bolshevism. D. S. Pasmanik points out: "The appearance of Bolshevism is linked to the peculiarities of Russian history... But its excellent organisation, Bolshevism, is due in part to the action of the Jewish commissioners."[1792] The active role of the Jews in Bolshevism did not escape the notice of observers, notably in America: "The Russian revolution rapidly moved from the destructive phase to the constructive phase, and this is clearly attributable to the edifying genius inherent to Jewish dissatisfaction."[1793] In the midst of the euphoria of October, how many were not, the Jews themselves admit it, with their heads held high, their action within Bolshevism!

Let us remember: just as, before the revolution, the revolutionaries and liberal radicals had been quick to exploit for political purposes—and not for charity—the restrictions imposed on Jews, likewise, in the months and years that followed October, the Bolsheviks, with the utmost complaisance, used the Jews within the State apparatus and the Party, too, not because of sympathy, but because they found their interest in the competence, intelligence and the particularism of the Jews towards the Russian population. On the spot they used Latvians, Hungarians, Chinese: these were not going to be sentimental...

The Jewish population in its mass showed a suspicious, even hostile attitude towards the Bolsheviks. But when, as a result of the revolution, it

---

[1790] *D. Schub*, Evrei vrusskoï revolioutsii [The Jews in the Russian Revolution]—BJWR-2, p. 142.

[1791] *Iou. Larine*, Evrei i antisemitizn v SSSR [The Jews and anti-Semitism in the USSR], M., L., *Giz*, 1929, pp. 260-262.

[1792] *D. S. Pasmanik*, Tchevo my dobyvaemsia? [What are we looking for?]—RaJ, p. 212.

[1793] *American Hebrew*, Sept. 10, 1920, p. 507.

had acquired complete freedom which fostered a real expansion of Jewish activity in the political, social and cultural spheres—a well-organised activity to boot—it did nothing to prevent the Bolshevik Jews from occupying the key positions, and these made an exceedingly cruel use of this new power fallen into their hands.

From the 40s of the twentieth century onwards, after Communist rule broke with international Judaism, Jews and communists became embarrassed and afraid, and they preferred to stay quiet and conceal the strong participation of Jews in the communist revolution, however the inclinations to remember and name the phenomenon were described by the Jews themselves as purely anti-Semitic intentions.

In the 1970s and 1980s, under the pressure of new revelations, the vision of the revolutionary years was adjusted. A considerable number of voices were heard publicly. Thus the poet Nahum Korzhavin wrote: "If we make the participation of the Jews in the revolution a taboo subject, we can no longer talk about the revolution at all. There was a time when the pride of this participation was even prized... The Jews took part in the revolution, and in abnormally high proportions."[1794] M. Agursky wrote on his part: "The participation of the Jews in the revolution and the civil war has not been limited to a very active engagement in the State apparatus; it has been infinitely wider." [1795] Similarly, the Israeli Socialist S. Tsyroulnikov asserts: "At the beginning of the revolution, the Jews... served as the foundation of the new regime."[1796]

But there are also many Jewish writers who, up to this day, either deny the Jews' contribution to Bolshevism, or even reject the idea rashly, or—this is the most frequent—consider it only reluctantly.

However the fact is proven: Jewish *renegades* have long been *leaders* in the Bolshevik Party, heading the Red Army (Trotsky), the VTsIK (Sverdlov), the two capitals (Zinoviev and Kamenev), the Comintern (Zinoviev), the Profintern (Dridzo-Lozovski) and the Komsomol (Oscar Ryvkin, and later Lazar Shatskin, who also headed the International Communist Youth).

"It is true that in the first Sovnarkom there was only one Jew, but that one was Trotsky, the number two, behind Lenin, whose authority surpassed that of all the others."[1797] And from November 1917 to the summer of 1918, the

---

[1794] Literatournyi kourier [The Literary Courier], quarterly, USA, 1985, no. 11, p. 67.
[1795] M. *Agursky*, Ideologuia natsional-bolchevisma [The ideology of National-Bolshevism], Paris, YMCA Press, 1980, p. 264.
[1796] S. *Tsyroulnikov*, SSSR, evrei i Israil [The USSR, the Jews, and Israel]—TN, no. 96, p. 155.
[1797] L. *Schapiro, op. cit.*, pp. 164-165.

real organ of government was not the Sovnarkom, but what was called the "Little Sovnarkom": Lenin, Trotsky, Stalin, Kareline, Prochian. After October, the VTsIK Presidium was of equal importance to that of the Sovnarkom, and among its six members were Sverdlov, Kamenev, Volodarski, Svetlov-Nakhamkis.

M. Agursky rightly points out: for a country where it was not customary to see Jews in power, what a contrast! "A Jew in the presidency of the country... a Jew in the Ministry of War... There was there something to which the ethnic population of Russia could hardly accustom itself to."[1798] Yes, what a contrast!

Especially when one knows of *what* president, of *what* minister it was! The first major action of the Bolsheviks was, by signing the peace separated from Brest-Litovsk, to cede to Germany an enormous portion of the Russian territory, in order to assert their power over the remaining part. The head of the signatory delegation was Ioffe; the head of foreign policy, Trotsky. His secretary and attorney, I. Zalkin, had occupied the cabinet of comrade Neratov at the ministry and purged the old apparatus to create a new organisation, the Commissariat for Foreign Affairs.

During the auditions held in 1919 in the American Senate and quoted above, the doctor A. Simons, who from 1907 to 1918 had been the dean of the Methodist Episcopal Church of Petrograd, made an interesting remark: "While they did not mince their words to criticise the Allies, Lenin, Trotsky, and their followers never expressed—at least I have never heard—the slightest blame on Germany." And at the same time, when I spoke with official representatives of the Soviet government, I discovered that they had a desire to preserve friendly relations with America as far as possible. This desire was interpreted by the allied chancelleries as an attempt to detach America from its partners.

Moreover, if the Soviet regime collapsed, they expected our country [the United States] to serve as a refuge for the Bolshevik demons who could thus save their skin."[1799]

The calculation is plausible. Is it not even... certain? It may be supposed that Trotsky himself, strengthened by his recent experience in America, comforted his companions with this hope.

[1798] *M. Agursky*, p. 264.
[1799] Oktiabrskaïa revolioutsiia pered soudom amcrikanskikh senatorov [The October Revolution in front of the tribunal of American Senators], Official Report of the Overmen's Committee of the Senate, M. L., *GIZ*, 1927, p. 7.

But where the calculation of the Bolshevik leaders was more ambitious and well-founded, it was when it dealt with the use of the great American financiers.

Trotsky himself was an incontestable internationalist, and one can believe him when he declares emphatically that he rejects for himself all belonging to Jewishness. But judging by the choices he made in his appointments, we see that the renegade Jews were closer to him than the renegade Russians. (His two closest assistants were Glazman and Sermuks, the head of his personal guard, Dreitser.[1800]) Thus, when it became necessary to find an authoritative and ruthless substitute to occupy this post at the War Commissariat—judge the lack! —, Trotsky named without flinching Ephraim Sklyansky, a doctor who had nothing of a soldier or a commissar. And this Sklyansky, as vice-president of the Revolutionary Council of War, would add his signature above the one of the Supreme Commander, the General S. S. Kamenev!

Trotsky did not think for a moment of the impression that the appointment of a doctor or the extraordinary promotion of a Sklyansky would make on the non-commissioned members: he could not care less. And yet, it was he who once declared: "Russia has not reached the maturity necessary to tolerate a Jew at its head"; this famous sentence shows that the question concerned him all the same when it was formulated about him…

There was also this well-known scene: the inaugural session of the Constituent Assembly is opened on 5 January 1918 by the Dean of Deputies, S. P. Chevtsov, but Sverdlov, with utter imprudence, snatches the bell from him, chases him from the tribune, and resumes the meeting. This Constituent Assembly, so long awaited, so ardently desired, that sacred sun that was about to pour happiness onto Russia—it only takes a few hours for Sverdlov and the sailor Jelezniakov to wring its neck!

The pan-Russian Commission for the election of the Constituent Assembly had previously been dissolved, and its organisation had been entrusted to a private person, the young Brodsky. As for the Assembly—so ardently desired—its management was handed to Uritsky, who was assisted by Drabkin, who was to set up a new chancellery. It was thus, by this kind of operation, that the new type of—Jewish—government was sketched. Other preliminary actions: eminent members of the Constituent Assembly, personalities known to the whole of Russia, such as the Countess Panina, an immense benefactress, were arrested by an obscure personage, a certain Gordon. (According to the newspaper *Den* [The Day], Gordon was the author of some wicked patriotic articles that appeared in *Petrogradski*

[1800] *Roheri Conquest*, Bolshoi terror [The Great Terror], trans. from English "The Great Terror", London, 1968, French trans., Paris, 1968.

Kourier [The Courier of Petrograd], then went on to trade in cabbage and chemical fertilisers—before finally becoming Bolshevik.[1801])

Another thing not to be forgotten: the new masters of the country did not neglect their personal interest. In other words: they plundered honest people.

"Stolen money is usually converted into diamonds... In Moscow, Sklyansky is said to be 'the first diamond buyer'"; he was caught in Lithuania, during the baggage verification of Zinoviev's wife, Zlata Bernstein-Lilina—"jewelery was found, worth several tens of millions of rubles."[1802] (And to say that we believed in the *legend* that the first revolutionary leaders were disinterested idealists!) In the Cheka, a trustworthy witness tells us, himself having passed in its clutches in 1920, the chiefs of the prisons were usually Poles or Latvians, while "the section in charge of the fight against traffickers, the least dangerous and the most lucrative, was in the hands of Jews."[1803]

Other than the positions at the front of the stage, there existed in the structure of Lenin's power, as in any other conspiracy, silent and invisible figures destined to never write their names in any chronicle: from Ganetski, that adventurer Lenin liked, up to all the disturbing figures gravitating in the orbit of Parvus. (This Evgeniya Sumenson, for example, who surfaced for a short time during the summer of 1917, who was even arrested for financial manipulation with Germany and who remained in liaison with the Bolshevik leaders, although she never appeared on the lists of leaders of the apparatus) After the "days of July", *Russkaya Volio* published raw documents on the clandestine activity of Parvus and his closest collaborator, Zurabov, who "occupies today, in the social democratic circles of Petrograd, a well-placed position"; "were also found in Petrograd Misters Binstock, Levin, Perazich and a few others."[1804]

Or also: Samuel Zaks, the brother-in-law of Zinoviev (his sister's husband), the boss of the subsidiary of the Parvus pharmacy in Petrograd and the son of a wealthy maker of the city, who had given the Bolsheviks, in 1917, a whole printing house. Or, belonging to the Parvus team itself,

---

[1801] Den, 1917, December 5, p. 2.
[1802] S. S. *Maslov*, Rossiia posle tchetyriokh let revolioutsii (Russia after four years of revolution), Paris, Rousskaya petchat, 1922, book 2, p. 190
[1803] S. E. *Troubetskoi*, Minovchee [The Past], Paris, YMCA Press, 1989, pp. 195-196, coll. The Library of Russian Memoirs (LRM); Series: Our recent past, fasc. 10.
[1804] Ruskaya Uolia [The Russian Will], 1917, 8 July, evening delivery, p. 4.

Samuel Pikker (Alexander Martynov[1805], whom had formerly polemicised Lenin on theoretical questions—but now the time had come to serve the Party and Martynov had gone into hiding).

Let us mention some other striking figures. The most illustrious (for massacres in Crimea) Rosalia Zalkind-Zemlyachka, a real fury of terror: she was in 1917 1920, long before Kaganovich, secretary of the Committee of the Bolsheviks of Moscow along with V. Zagorsky, I. Zelensky, I. Piatnitsky.[1806]

When one knows that the Jews constituted more than a third of the population of Odessa, it is not surprising to learn that "in the revolutionary institutions of Odessa there were a great number of Jews". The President of the Revolutionary War Council, and later of the Sovnarkom of Odessa, was V. Yudovsky; the chairman of the Provincial Party Committee, the Gamarnik.[1807] The latter would soon rise in Kiev to be the chairman of the provincial committees—Revolutionary Committee, Party Executive Committee, then Chairman of the Regional Committees, and finally Secretary of the Central Committee of Belarus, member of the Military Region Revolutionary War Council of Belarus.[1808] And what about the rising star, Lazar Kaganovich, the president of the Provincial Committee Party of Nizhny Novgorod in 1918? In August-September, the reports of mass terror operations in the province all begin with the words: "In the presence of Kaganovich", "Kaganovitch being present"[1809]—and with what vigilance!... There is a photo, which was inadvertently published and which bears this caption: "Photograph of the Presidium of one of the meetings of the Leningrad Committee, that is to say of the Petrograd Soviet after the October Revolution. The absolute majority at the presidium table is constituted of Jews."[1810]

Reviewing all the names of those who have held important positions, and often even key positions, is beyond the reach of anyone. We will cite for illustrative purposes a few names, trying to attach them with a few details.— Here is Arkady Rosengoltz among the actors of the October coup in Moscow; he was afterwards a member of the Revolutionary War

---

[1805] Bolsheviki: Dokoumenty po istorii bolchevizma s 1903 in 1916 god byvch. Moskovskogo Okhrannogo Otdeleniia [The Bolsheviks: Materials for the history of Bolshevism from 1903 to 1916 from the former Moscow Okhrana]. Presented by M. A. Tsiavlovski, supplemented by A. M. Serebriannikov, New York, Telex, 1990, p. 318.
[1806] SJE, t. 5, p. 476.
[1807] SJE, t. 6, p. 124.
[1808] RJE (2nd edition revised and completed), t. 1, p. 267.
[1809] Nijegorodski Partarkhiv [Archives of the Nizhny Novgorod Party], f. 1, op. 1, file 66, leaflets 3, 12, etc.
[1810] *Larine*, p. 258.

Councils of several army corps, then of the Republic; he was Trotsky's "closest assistant"; he then occupied a number of important posts: the Commissariat of Finance, the Workers' and Peasants' Inspectorate (an organ of inquisition), and finally the Commissariat for Foreign Trade for seven years.—Semyon Nakhimson, who, on the eve of October, was commissioner of the notorious Latvian skirmishers, was the fierce commissioner of the military region of Yaroslav (he was killed during an insurrection in the city).—Samuel Zwilling, who, after his victory over the Orenburg ataman, Dutov, took the head of the Orenburg District Executive Committee (he was killed shortly thereafter).—Zorakh Grindberg, Commissioner for Instruction and Fine Arts of the Northern Commune, who took a stand against the teaching of Hebrew, the "right arm" of Lunacharsky.—Here is Yevgeniya Kogan, wife of Kuybyshev: she was already in 1917 secretary of the Party Committee of the region of Samara; in 1918-19 she became a member of the Volga Military Revolutionary Tribunal; in 1920 she met at the Tashkent City Committee, then in 1921 in Moscow, where she became Secretary of the City Committee and then Secretary of the National Committee in the 1930s.—And here is the secretary of Kuybyshev, Semyon Zhukovsky: he goes from political sections to political sections of the armies; he is sometimes found in the Propaganda Department of the Central Committee of Turkestan, sometimes the political leader of the Baltic Fleet (for the Bolsheviks, everything is at hand...), and, finally, at the Central Committee.—

Or there are the Bielienki brothers: Abram, at the head of the personal guard of Lenin during the last five years of his life; Grigori, who moved from the Krasnaya Presnia District Committee to the position of head of the agitprop at the Comintern; finally, he is found at the Higher Council of the National Economy, the Workers' and Peasants' Inspectorate (RKI), at the Commissariat of Finances.—Dimanstein, after passing through the European Commission and the European Section, is at the Central Committee of Lithuania–Belarus, at the Commissariat of Instruction of Turkestan, then Head of the Political Propaganda of Ukraine.—Or Samuel Filler, an apothecary apprentice from the province of Kherson, who hoisted himself up to the presidium of the Cheka of Moscow and then of the RKI.—Anatoly (Isaac) Koltun ("deserted and emigrated immediately after", then returned in 1917): he is found both as a senior officer in the Central Control Commission of the VKP (b) and in charge of the Party of Kazakhstan, then in Yaroslavl, in Ivanovo, then back to the Control Commission, and then to the Moscow Court—and suddenly he is in Scientific Research![1811] The role of the Jews is particularly visible in the

---

[1811] Bolchevki [The Bolsheviks], 1903-1916, p. 340; RJE, t. 1, pp. 100, 101, 376, 427, 465-466; t. 2, pp. 51, 61, 321, 482; t. 3, p. 306.

RSFSR organs responsible for what constitutes the crucial problem of those years, the years of war communism: *supplies*. Let's just look at the key positions.—Moisei Frumkin: from 1918 to 1922, member of the college of the Commissariat of Supply of the RSFSR, and from 1921—in full famine—Deputy Commissioner: he is also Chairman of the Board of Trustees of the Food Fund (Glavprodukt) and has as his assistant I. Rafailov.—Iakov Brandenbourgski–Goldzinski, returning from Paris in 1917 and immediately becoming a member of the Petrograd Supply Committee and from 1918 onwards a member of the Commissariat; during the civil war, with extraordinary powers in the VTsIK for requisition operations in several provinces.—Isaak Zelensky: in 1918-20 in the supply section of the Moscow Soviet, then member of the college of the RSFSR Supply Commissariat; Later in the Secretariat of the Central Committee and Secretary for Central Asia.— Semyon Voskov (arrived from America in 1917, actor of the October coup in Petrograd): in 1918, commissioner of supply for the immense region of the North.—Miron Vladimirov–Cheinfinkel: since October 1917 as head of the supply service for the city of Petrograd, then member of the college of the Supply Commission of the RSFSR; in 1921: commissioner for the Supply for Ukraine, then for Agriculture. —Grigori Zusmanovich, commissioner in 1918 at the Supply of the Army in Ukraine.—Moisei Kalmanovitch: late 1917, commissioner of the Supply of the Western Front; In 1919-1920, commissioner of the supply of the Byelorussian SSR, then of the Lithuania–Belarus SSR, and chairman of a special commission for the supply of the Western Front (at the summit of his career: president of the Administration Council of the Central Bank of the USSR).[1812]

Recently published documents inform us of the way in which the great peasant revolt of 1921 in Western Siberia broke out, the insurrection of Ichim.

After the fierce requisitions of 1920, when the region had, on 1 January 1921, fulfilled the required requisition plan by 102%, the Supply Commissioner of the Tyumen Province, Indenbaum, instituted an additional week to "finalise" it, the 1st to 7th January, i.e. the week before Christmas.[1813] The commissioner of requisitions at Ichim received, as did the others, the official direction: "Requisitions must be carried out without taking into account the consequences, confiscating, if necessary, *all the grain in the villages* (emphasised by me—A. S.) and leaving the producer only a ration of famine." In a telegram signed by his hand, Indenbaum demanded "the most merciless repression and systematic confiscation of

---

[1812] RJE, t. 1, pp. 160, 250, 234, 483, 502, 533; t. 3, p. 260.
[1813] According to the Julian calendar still in force in the Orthodox Church. Christmas is celebrated on January 7th.

the wheat that might still be there." In order to form the brigades of requisition, were recruited, not with the consent of Ingenbaum, thugs, and sub-proletarians who had no scruples in bludgeoning the peasants. The Latvian Matvei Lauris, a member of the Provincial Commissariat of Supply, used his power for his personal enrichment and pleasure: having taken up his quarters in a village, he had thirty-one women brought in for himself and his squad. At the Xth Congress of the RKP (b), the delegation of Tyumen reported that "the peasants who refused to give their wheat were placed in pits, watered, and died frozen."[1814]

The existence of some individuals was only learned a few years later thanks to obituaries published in the Izvestia. Thus: "comrade Isaac Samoylovich Kizelstein died of tuberculosis"; he had been an agent of the Cheka College, then a member of the Revolutionary War Council of the 5th and 14th Armies, "always devoted to the Party and to the working class".[1815] And oh how many of these "obscure workers" of all nationalities were found among the stranglers of Russia!

Bolshevik Jews often had, in addition to their surname as underground revolutionaries, pseudonyms, or modified surnames. Example: in an obituary of 1928, the death of a Bolshevik of the first hour, Lev Mikhailovich Mikhailov, who was known to the Party as Politikus, in other words by a nickname; his real name, Elinson, he carried it to the grave.[1816] What prompted an Aron Rupelevich to take the Ukrainian surname of Taratut? Was Aronovitch Tarchis ashamed of his name or did he want to gain more weight by taking the name of Piatnitsky?

And what about the Gontcharovs, Vassilenko, and others...? Were they considered in their own families as traitors or simply as cowards?

Observations made on the spot have remained. I. F. Najivin records the impressions he received at the very beginning of Soviet power: in the Kremlin, in the administration of the Sovnarkom, "reigns disorder and chaos. We see only Latvians and even more Latvians, Jews and even more Jews. I have never been an anti-Semite, but there were so many it could not escape your attention, and each one was younger than the last."[1817]

Korolenko himself, as liberal and extremely tolerant as he was, he who was deeply sympathetic to the Jews who had been victims of the pogroms, noted in his Notebooks in the spring of 1919: "Among the Bolsheviks there are a great number of Jews, men and women. Their lack of tact, their

---

[1814] Zemlia sibirskaia, dalnievostotchnaia [Siberian Land, Far East], Omsk, 1993, nos. 5-6 (May-June), pp. 35-37.
[1815] Izvestia, 1931, 7 April, p. 2.
[1816] Izvestia, 1928, 6 March, p. 5; RJE, t. 2, pp. 295, 296.
[1817] *Iv. Najivine*, Zapiski o revolioutsii [Notes on the Revolution]. Vienna, 1921, p. 93.

assurance are striking and irritating," "Bolshevism has already exhausted itself in Ukraine, the 'Commune' encounters only hatred on its way. One sees constantly emerge among the Bolsheviks—and especially the Cheka—Jewish physiognomies, and this exacerbates the traditional feelings, still very virulent, of Judæophobia."[1818]

From the early years of Soviet rule, the Jews were not only superior in number in the upper echelons of the Party, but also, more remarkably and more sensitively for the population, to local administrations, provinces and townships, to inferior spheres, where the anonymous mass of the *Streitbrecher* had come to the rescue of the new and still fragile power which had consolidated it, saved it. The author of the *Book of the Jews of Russia* writes: "One cannot fail to evoke the action of the many Jewish Bolsheviks who worked in the localities as subordinate agents of the dictatorship and who caused innumerable ills to the population of the country"—and he adds: "including the Jewish population."[1819]

The omnipresence of the Jews alongside the Bolsheviks had, during these terrible days and months, the most atrocious consequences. Among them is the assassination of the Imperial family, of which, today, everybody speaks, and where the Russians now exaggerate the share of the Jews, who find in this heart-wrenching thought an evil enjoyment. As it should, the most dynamic Jews (and they are many) were at the height of events and often at the command posts. Thus, for the assassination of the Tsar's family: the guards (the assassins) were Latvians, Russians, and Magyars, but two characters played a decisive role: Philip Goloshchekin and Yakov Yurovsky (who had received baptism).

The final decision belonged to Lenin. If he dared to decide in favour of the assassination (when his power was still fragile), it was because he had foreseen both the total indifference of the Allies (the King of England, cousin of the tsar, had he not already, in the spring of 1918, refused asylum to Nicholas II?) And the fatal weakness of the conservative strata of the Russian people.

Goloshchekin, who had been exiled to Tobolsk in 1912 for four years, and who in 1917 was in the Urals, was in perfect agreement with Sverdlov: their telephone conversations between Yekaterinburg and Moscow revealed that 1918 they were on first-name basis. As early as 1912 (following the example of Sverdlov), Goloshchekin was a member of the

---

[1818] P. I. Negretov, V. G. Korolenko; Letopis jizni i tvortchestva [V. G. Korolenko: Chronicle of Life and Work, 1917-1921] under publ. of A. V. Khrabrovitski, Moskva: Kniga, 1990, p. 97, 106.

[1819] G. Aronson, Evreiskaya obschestvennost v Rossii v 1917-1918 gg. [The Jewish Public Opinion in Russia in 1917-1918], SJE-2, 1968, p. 16.

Central Committee of the Bolshevik Party. After the coup of October, he became secretary of the Provincial Committee of Perm and Yekaterinburg, and later of the Ural Region Committee, in other words he had become the absolute master of the region.[1820]

The project of assassination of the imperial family was ripening in the brains of Lenin and his acolytes—while, on their side, the two patrons of the Urals, Goloshchekin and Bieloborodov (president of the Ural Soviet), simmered their own machinations. It is now known that at the beginning of July 1918 Goloshchekin went to Moscow in order to convince Lenin that letting the tsar and his family "flee" was a bad solution, that they had to be openly executed, and then announce the matter publicly. Convincing Lenin that the tsar and his family should be suppressed was not necessary, he himself did not doubt it for a moment. What he feared was the reaction of the Russian people and the West.

There were, however, already indications that the thing would pass without making waves. (The decision would also depend, of course, on Trotsky, Kamenev, Zinoviev, Bukharin—but they were for the time absent from Moscow, and their mentality, with the possible exception, possibly, of that of Kamenev, allowed to suppose none of them would have anything to say about it. Trotsky, as we know, approved of this without feeling any emotion. In his diary of 1935, he says that on his arrival in Moscow he had a conversation with Sverdlov. "I asked incidentally: 'By the way, where is the tsar?'—'It's done, he replied. Executed.'—'and the family?'—'the family as well, with him.'—'all of them?' I asked with a touch of astonishment. 'All of them! replied Sverdlov... so what?' He was waiting for a reaction from me. I did not answer anything.

'And who decided it?' I asked.—'All of us, here'—I did not ask any more questions, I forgot about it... Basically, this decision was more than reasonable, it was necessary—not merely in order to frighten, to scare the enemy, to make him lose all hope, but in order to electrify our own ranks, to make us understand that there was no turning back, that we had before us only an undivided victory or certain death."[1821]

M. Heifets sought out who was able to attend this last council chaired by Lenin; without a doubt: Sverdlov, Dzerzhinsky; probably: Petrovsky and Vladimirski (of the Cheka), Stutchka (of the Commissariat for Justice); Perhaps: V. Schmidt. Such was the tribunal that condemned the tsar. As for Goloshchekin, he had returned to Yekaterinburg on 12 July, awaiting the last signal sent from Moscow. It was Sverdlov who transmitted Lenin's last instruction. And Yakov Yurovsky, a watchmaker, the son of a criminal who

---

[1820] Bolshevik, 1903-1916, p. 13, pp. 283-284.
[1821] *Lev Trogski*, Dnevniki i pisma [Newspapers and Letters], Ermitage, 1986, p. 101.

had been deported to Siberia—where was born the offspring—had been placed in July 1918 at the head of the Ipatiev house. This Yurovsky was manœuvring the operation and reflecting on the concrete means of carrying it out (with the help of Magyars and Russians, including Pavel Medvedev, Piotr Ermakov), as well as the best way of making the bodies disappear.[1822] (Let us point out here the assistance provided by P. L. Voïkov, the regional supply commissioner, who supplied barrels of gasoline and sulphuric acid to destroy the corpses.) How the deadly salvos succeeded each other in the basement of the Ipatiev house, which of these shots were mortal, who were the shooters, nobody later could specify, not even the executants. Afterwards, "Yurovsky boasted of being the best: 'It was the bullet from my colt that killed Nicholas'." But this honour also fell to Ermakov and his "comrade Mauser".[1823]

Goloshchekin did not seek glory, and it is this idiot of Bieloborodov who beat him. In the 1920s, everyone knew it was him, the tsar's number one killer.

In 1936, during a tour in Rostov-on-Don, during a Party Conference, he still boasted of it from the rostrum—just a year before being himself executed. In 1941 it was Goloshchekin's turn to be executed. As for Yurovsky, after the assassination of the tsar, he joined Moscow, "worked" there for a year alongside Dzerzhinsky (thus shedding blood) and died of natural death.[1824]

In fact, the question of the ethnic origin of the actors has constantly cast a shadow over the revolution as a whole and on each of its events. All the participations and complicities, since the assassination of Stolypin, necessarily collided with the feelings of the Russians. Yes, but what about the assassination of the tsar's brother, Grand Duke Mikhail Alexandrovich? Who were his assassins? Andrei Markov, Gavril Myasnikov, Nikolai Zhukov, Ivan Kolpaschikov—clearly, all of them Russians.

Here, everyone must—oh how much!—ask themselves the question: have I enlightened my people with a little ray of good, or have I obscured it with all the darkness of evil?

So that is that when it comes to the executioners of the revolution. And what about the victims? Hostages and prisoners by entire batches— shot, drowned on crowded barges: the officers—Russians; the nobles—mostly Russians; the priests— Russians; members of the Zemstvos—Russians;

[1822] *Mikhail Heifets*, Tsareoubiistvo v 1918 godou [The Assassination of the Tsar in 1918], Moscow-Jerusalem, 1991, pp. 246-247, 258, 268-271.
[1823] *Ibidem*, p. 355.
[1824] *Ibidem*, pp. 246, 378-380.

and the peasants fleeing enlistment in the Red Army, taken up in the forests—all Russians. And this Russian intelligentsia of high moral, anti-anti-Semitic—for it also, it was bad deaths and bloody basements. If names and lists of all those who had been shot and drowned in the first years of Soviet power could be found today, from September 1918 onwards, if statistics were available, it would be surprising to find that the revolution in no way manifested its international character, but indeed its anti-Slavic character (in accordance, moreover, with the dreams of Marx and Engels).

And it is this that has imprinted this deep and cruel mark on the face of the revolution, which defines it best: *who* has it exterminated, carrying away its dead forever, without return, far from this sordid revolution and this unfortunate country, the body of this poor, misguided people?

During all those months, Lenin was very much occupied with the climate of tension that had arisen around the Jewish question. As early as April 1918, the Council of the People's Commissars of Moscow and the Moscow region published in the *Izvestia*[1825] (thus for a wider audience than the region of Moscow alone) a circular addressed to the Soviets "on the question of the anti-Semitic propaganda of the pogroms", which evoked "events having occurred in the region of Moscow that recalled anti-Jewish pogroms" (no city was named); it stressed the need to organise "special sessions among the Soviets on the Jewish question and the fight against anti-Semitism", as well as "meetings and conferences", in short, a whole propaganda campaign. But who, by the way, was the number one culprit, who had to have his bones broken? But the Orthodox priests, of course! The first point prescribed: "Pay the utmost attention to the anti-Semitic propaganda carried out by the clergy; take the most radical measures to stop the counter-revolution and the propaganda of the priests" (we do not ask ourselves at this moment what measures these were... but, in reality, who knows them better than we do?). Then point number two recommended "to recognise the necessity to not create a separate Jewish fighting organisation" (at the time a Jewish guard was being considered). The point number four entrusted the Office of Jewish Affairs and the War Commissariat with the task of taking "preventive measures to combat anti-Jewish pogroms".

At the height of the same year 1918, Lenin recorded on gramophone a "special discourse on anti-Semitism and the Jews". He there denounced "the cursed tsarist autocracy which had always launched uneducated workers and peasants against the Jews. The tsarist police, assisted by landowners and capitalists, perpetrated anti-Jewish pogroms. Hostility towards the Jews is perennial only where the capitalist cabal has definitely

---

[1825] Izvestia, 1918, 28 April, p. 4.

obscured the minds of the workers and the peasants... There are among the Jews workmen, men of labour, they are the majority. They are our brothers, oppressed as we are by capitalism, they are our comrades who struggle with us for socialism... Shame on the cursed tsarism!... Shame on those who sow hostility towards the Jews!"—"Recordings of this speech were carried all the way to the front, transported through towns and villages aboard special propaganda trains which criss-crossed the country. Gramophones spread this discourse in clubs, meetings, assemblies. Soldiers, workers and peasants listened to their leader's harangue and began to understand what this was all about."[1826] But this speech, at the time, was not published (... by intentional omission?); it only was so in 1926 (in the book of Agursky senior).

On 27 July 1918 (just after the execution of the imperial family), the Sovnarkom promulgated a special law on anti-Semitism: "The Soviet of the People's Commissars declares that any anti-Semitic movement is a danger to the cause of the Revolution of the workers and peasants." In conclusion (from Lenin's own hand, Lunacharsky tells us): "The Sovnarkom directed all Soviet deputations to take radical measures to eradicate anti-Semitism. The inciters of pogroms, those who propagate them, will be declared outlaws." Signed: VI. Ulyanov (Lenin).[1827]

If the meaning of the word "outlaw" may have escaped some at the time, in the months of the Red Terror it would appear clearly, ten years later, in a sentence of a communist militant—Larine—who was himself, for a while, the commissar of the people and even the promoter of "war communism": "to 'outlaw' the active anti-Semites was to shoot them."[1828]

And then there is Lenin's famous reply to Dimanstein in 1919. Dimanstein "wished to obtain from Lenin that be retained the distribution of Gorky's tract containing such praises to the address of the Jews that it could create 'the impression that the revolution was based only on the Jews and especially on the individuals from the middle class'." Lenin replied—as we have already said—that, immediately after October, it was the Jews who had saved the revolution by defeating the resistance of the civil servants, and consequently "Gorky's opinion was perfectly correct."[1829] The *Jewish Encyclopædia* does not doubt it either: "Lenin refused to sweep under the

---

[1826] Iou. Larine, Evrei i antisemitism v SSSR* [The Jews and anti-Semitism in the USSR], pp. 7-8 (with a reference to S. Agursky, Evreiskii rabotchii v kommounistitcheskom dvijenii [The Jewish Worker in the Communist Movement], Minsk GIZ, 1926, p. 155.
[1827] Izvestia, 1918, 27 July, p. 4.
[1828] Iou. Larine, p. 259.
[1829] V. I. Lenin, O evreiskom voprose v Rossii [On the Jewish Question in Russia], preface by S. Dimanstein. M., Proletarii, 1924, 3 July.

carpet the extremely pro-Semite proclamation of M. Gorky, and it was disseminated in great circulation during the civil war, in spite of the fact that it risked becoming an asset in the hands of the anti-Semites who were enemies of the revolution."[1830]

And it became so, of course, for the *Whites* who saw two images merge, that of Judaism and that of Bolshevism.

The surprising (short-sighted!) indifference of the Bolshevik leaders to the popular sentiment and the growing irritation of the population is blatant when we see how much Jews were involved in repression directed against the Orthodox clergy: it was in summer 1918 that was initiated the assault on the Orthodox churches in central Russia and especially in the Moscow region (which included several provinces), an assault which only ceased thanks to the wave of rebellions in the parishes.

In January 1918, the workers who were building the fortress of Kronstadt rebelled and protested: the executive committee of the Party, composed "exclusively of non-natives", had designated for guard duty, instead of militia...

Orthodox priests, while "not a Jewish rabbi, not a Moslem mullah, not a Catholic pastor, not a Protestant pastor, was put to use."[1831] (Let us note in passing that even on this small, fortified island of the "prison of the peoples" there were places of worship for all the confessions...)

A text entitled "Charge on the Jews!" appeared even all the way to the *Pravda*, a call from the workers of Arkangelsk "to Russian workers and peasants conscious of their fate", in which they read: "are profaned, defiled, plundered"—"exclusively Orthodox churches, never synagogues... Death by hunger and disease carries hundreds of thousands of innocent lives among the Russians," while "the Jews do not die of hunger or disease."[1832] (There was also, during the summer 1918, "a criminal case of anti-Semitism in the church of Basil the Blissful, in Moscow...").

What madness on the part of the Jewish militants to have mingled with the ferocious repression exerted by the Bolsheviks against Orthodoxy, even more fierce than against the other confessions, with this persecution of priests, with this outburst in the press of sarcasms aimed at the Christ! The Russian pens also zealously attacked Demian Bedny (Efim Pridvorov), for example, and he was not the only one. Yes, the Jews should have stayed out of it.

[1830] SJE, t. 4, p. 766.
[1831] Tserkovnye Vedomosti [News of the Church], 1918, no. 1 (quoted according to M. Agursky, p. 10)
[1832] *Pravda*, 1919, 3 July.

On 9 August 1919, Patriarch Tikhon wrote to the president of the VTsIK Kalinin (with a copy to the Sovnarkom president, Ulyanov–Lenin) to demand the dismissal of the investigating magistrate Chpitsberg, in charge of the "affairs" of the Church: "a man who publicly outrages the religious beliefs of people, who openly mocks ritual gestures, who, in the preface to the book *The Religious Plague* (1919), gave Jesus Christ abominable names and thus profoundly upset my religious feeling."[1833] The text was transmitted to the Small Sovnarkom, from which came the reply on 3 September: "classify the complaint of citizen Belavine (Patriarch Tikhon) without follow-up."[1834] But Kalinin changed his mind and addressed a secret letter to the Justice Commissioner, Krasikov, saying that he believed that "for practical and political considerations... replace Chpitsberg with someone else", given that "the audience in the court is probably in its majority Orthodox" and that it is therefore necessary "to deprive the religious circles... of their main reason for ethnic revenge."[1835]

And what about the profanation of relics? How could the masses understand such an obvious outrage, so provocative? "'Could the Russians, the Orthodox have done such things?' they asked each other across Russia. 'All that, it is the Jews who have plotted it. It makes no difference, to those who crucified Christ'."[1836]—And who is responsible for this state of mind, if not the Bolshevik power, by offering to the people spectacles of such savagery?

S. Bulgakov, who followed closely what happened to Orthodoxy under the Bolsheviks, wrote in 1941: "In the USSR, the persecution of Christians "surpassed in violence and amplitude all previous persecutions known throughout History. Of course, we should not blame everything on the Jews, but we should not downplay their influence."[1837]—"Were manifested in Bolshevism, above all, the force of will and the energy of Judaism."—"The part played by the Jews in Bolshevism is, alas, disproportionately great. And it is above all *the sin of Judaism against Ben–Israel*... And it is not the 'sacred Israel', but the strong will of Judaism that, in power, manifested itself in Bolshevism and the crushing of the Russian people."—"Although it derived from the ideological and practical programme of Bolshevism, without distinction of nationality, the persecution of

---

[1833] Sledstvennoe delo Patriarkha Tikhona [The instruction of Patriarch Tikhon], rec. of documents from the materials of the Central Archives, M., 2000, doc. no. 58, pp. 600-604.

[1834] GARF, f. 130, op. 4, ed. Khr. 94, l. 1, Minutes of the meeting of the Small Council of 2 Sept. 1920, no. 546.

[1835] GARF, f. 1235, op. 56, d. 26, l. 43.

[1836] *S. S. Maslov*, p. 43.

[1837] Arch. Sergui Bulgakov Khristianstvo i evreiskii vopros [Christianity and the Jewish Question], rec, Paris, YMCA Press, 1991, p. 76.

Christians found its most zealous actors among Jewish 'commissioners' of militant atheism," and to have put a Goubelman–Iaroslavski at the head of the Union of the Godless was to commit "in the face of all the Russian Orthodox people an act... of religious effrontery."[1838]

Another very ostensible effrontery: this way of rechristening cities and places. Custom, in fact, less Jewish than typically Soviet. But can we affirm that for the inhabitants of Gatchina, the new name of their city—Trotsk—did not have a foreign resonance? Likewise for Pavlosk, now Slutsk... Uritsky gives its name to the square of the Palace, Vorovski to the Saint-Isaac Plaza, Volodarski to the Prospect of the Founders, Nakhimson to the Saint Vladimir Prospect, Rochal to the barge of the Admiralty, and the second-class painter Isaak Brodsky gives his name to the so beautiful Saint Michael street...

They could no longer stand each other, their heads were turning. Through the immensity of Russia, it flashes by: Elisabethgrad becomes Zinovievsk... and let's go boldly! The city where the tsar was assassinated takes the name of the assassin: Sverdlovsk.

It is obvious that was present in the Russian national consciousness, as early as 1920, the idea of a national revenge on the part of Bolshevik Jews, since it even appeared in the papers of the Soviet government (it served as an argument to Kalinin).

Of course, Pasmanik's refutation was right: "For the wicked and narrow-minded, everything could not be explained more simply—the Jewish *Kahal*[1839] has decided to seize Russia; or: it is the revengeful Judaism that settles its accounts with Russia for the humiliations undergone in the past."[1840] Of course, we cannot explain the victory and the maintenance of the Bolsheviks.—But: if the pogrom of 1905 burns in the memory of your family, and if, in 1915, were driven out of the western territories, with the strikes of a whip, your brothers by blood, you can very well, three or four years later, want to avenge yourself in your turn with a whip or a revolver bullet. We are not going to ask whether Communist Jews consciously wanted to take revenge on Russia by destroying, by breaking the Russian heritage, but totally denying this spirit of vengeance would be denying any relationship between the inequality in rights under the tsar and the participation of Jews in Bolshevism, a relationship that is constantly evoked.

[1838] *Ibidem*, pp. 98, 121, 124.
[1839] Former governing body of the Jewish Community.
[1840] *D. S. Pasmanik*, Rousskaia revolioutsiia i evreistvo [The Russian Revolution and the Jews], p. 156.

And this is how I. M. Biekerman, confronted with "the fact of the disproportionate participation of the Jews in the work of barbaric destruction", to those who recognise the right of the Jews to avenge past persecutions, refutes this right: "the destructive zeal of our co-religionists is blamed on the State, who, by its vexations and persecutions, would have pushed the Jews into the revolution"; well no, he says, for "it is to the manner in which an individual reacts to the evil suffered that he is distinguished from another, and the same is true of a community of men."[1841]

Later, in 1939, taking in the destiny of Judaism under the black cloud of the coming new era, the same Biekerman wrote: "The great difference between the Jews and the world around them was that they could only be the anvil, and never the hammer."[1842]

I do not intend to dig here, in this limited work, the great historical destinies, but I am expressing a categorical reservation on this point: perhaps this was so since the beginning of time, but, as of 1918, in Russia, and for another fifteen years, the Jews who joined the revolution *also* served as *hammer*—at least a large part of them.

Here, in our review, comes the voice of Boris Pasternak. In his *Doctor Zhivago*, he writes, it is true, after the Second World War, thus after the Cataclysm which came down, crushing and sinister, over the Jews of Europe and which overturned our entire vision of the world—but, in the novel itself, is discussed the years of the revolution—, he speaks of "this modest, sacrificial way of remaining aloof, which only engenders misfortune," of "their [i.e. the Jews'] fragility and their inability to strike back."

Yet, did we not both have before us the same country—at different ages, certainly, but where we lived the same 20s and 30s? The contemporary of those years remains mute with astonishment: Pasternak would thus not have seen (I believe) what was happening?—His parents, his painter father, his pianist mother, belonged to a highly cultivated Jewish milieu, living in perfect harmony with the Russian intelligentsia; he himself grew up in a tradition already quite rich, a tradition that led the Rubinstein brothers, the moving Levitan, the subtle Guerchenson, the philosophers Frank and Chestov, to give themselves to Russia and Russian culture… It is probable that this unambiguous choice, that perfect equilibrium between life and

---

[1841] *I. M. Biekerman*, Rossiia i rousskoie evrcistvo [Russia and the Russian Jews], RaJ, p. 25.
[1842] Id, K samosoznaniou evreia tchem my byli. Tchem my doljny, byt [For the self-consciousness of the Jew: who have we been, who we must become], Paris, 1930, p. 42.

service, which was theirs, appeared to Pasternak as *the norm*, while the monstrous gaps, frightening relative to this norm, did not reach the retina of his eye.

On the other hand, these differences penetrated the field of view of thousands of others. Thus, witness of these years, Biekerman writes: "The too visible participation of the Jews in the Bolshevik saturnalia attracts the eyes of the Russians and those of the whole world."[1843]

No, the Jews were not the great driving force of the October coup. The latter, moreover, brought them nothing, since the February revolution had already granted them full and complete freedom. But, after the *coup de force* took place, it was then that the younger laic generation quickly changed horses and launched themselves with no less assurance into the infernal gallop of Bolshevism.

Obviously, it was not the melamedes [1844] that produced this. But the reasonable part of the Jewish people let itself be overwhelmed by hotheads. And thus an almost entire generation became *renegade*. And the race was launched.

G. Landau looked for the *motives* that led the younger generation to join the camp of the new victors. He writes: "Here was the rancour with regard to the old world, and the exclusion of political life and Russian life in general, as well as a certain rationalism peculiar to the Jewish people," and "willpower which, in mediocre beings, can take the form of insolence and ruthless ambition."[1845]

Some people seek an apology by way of explanations: "The material conditions of life after the October coup created a climate such that the Jews were forced to join the Bolsheviks." [1846] This explanation is widespread: "42% of the Jewish population of Russia were engaged in commercial activity"; they lost it; they found themselves in a dead-end situation—where to go? "In order not to die of hunger, they were forced to take service with the government, without paying too much attention to the kind of work they were asked to do." It was necessary to enter the Soviet apparatus where "the number of Jewish officials, from the beginning of the October Revolution, was very high."[1847]

[1843] *I. M. Biekerman*, RaJ, pp. 14 15.

[1844] Those who teach Jewish law privately.

[1845] *G. A. Landau*, Revolioutsionnye idei v evreiskoi obschestvennosti [The Revolutionary Ideas in Jewish Public Opinion], RaJ, p. 117.

[1846] *D. S. Pasmanik*, Rousskaia revolioutsiia i evreistvo [The Russian Revolution and the Jews], p. 156.

[1847] *D. S. Pasmanik*, p. 157.

They had no *way out*? Did the tens of thousands of Russian officials who refused to serve Bolshevism have somewhere to go?—To starve? But how were living the others? Especially since they were receiving food aid from organisations such as the Joint, the ORT[1848], financed by wealthy Jews from the West. Enlisting in the Cheka was never the *only* way out. There was at least another: not to do it, to resist.

The result, Pasmanik concludes, is that "Bolshevism became, for the hungry Jews of cities, a trade equal to the previous trades—tailor, broker, or apothecary."[1849]

But if this is so, it may be said, seventy years later, in good conscience: for those "who did not want to immigrate to the United States and become American, who did not want to immigrate to Palestine to remain Jews, for those, the only issue was communism"?[1850] Again—the *only* way out!?

It is precisely *this* that is called renouncing one's historical responsibility!

Other arguments have more substance and weight: "A people that has suffered such persecution"—and this, throughout its history—"could not, in its great majority, not become bearers of the revolutionary doctrine and internationalism of socialism," for it "gave its Jewish followers the hope of never again being pariahs" on this very earth, and not "in the chimerical Palestine of the great ancestors." Further on: "During the civil war already, and immediately afterwards, they were stronger in competition with the newcomers from the ethnic population, and they filled many of the voids that the revolution had created in society... In doing so, they had for the most part broken with their national and spiritual tradition," after which "all those who wanted to assimilate, especially the first generation and at the time of their massive apparition, took root in the relatively superficial layers of a culture that was new to them."[1851]

One wonders, however, how it is possible that "the centuries-old traditions of this ancient culture have proved powerless to counteract the infatuation with the barbaric slogans of the Bolshevik revolutionaries."[1852] When "socialism, the companion of the revolution, melted onto Russia, not only were these Jews, numerous and dynamic, brought to life on the crest of the

---

[1848] Obchtchestvo Pemeslennogo Troude welded evreiev: Association for craftwork among Jews.
[1849] D. *Choub*, Evrei v rousskoi revolioutsii [The Jews in the Russian Revolution], BJWR-2, p. 143.
[1850] *Chlomo Avineri*, Vozvraschenie v istoriiou [Back to the story]—"22", 1990, no. 73, p. 112.
[1851] D. *Chiurmann*, O natsionalnykh fobiiakh [On national phobias],—"22", 1989, no. 68, pp. 149-150.
[1852] I. O. *Levine*, Evrei v revolioutsii [The Jews in the Revolution], RaJ, p. 127.

devastating wave, but the rest of the Jewish people found itself deprived of any idea of resistance and was invited to look at what was happening with a perplexed sympathy, wondering, impotent, what was going to result from it."[1853] How is it that "in every circle of Jewish society the revolution was welcomed with enthusiasm, an inexplicable enthusiasm when one knows of what disillusionments composed the history of this people"? How could "the Jewish people, rationalist and lucid, allow itself to indulge in the intoxication of revolutionary phraseology"[1854]?

D. S. Pasmanik evokes in 1924 "those Jews who proclaimed loudly and clearly the genetic link between Bolshevism and Judaism, who openly boasted about the sentiments of sympathy which the mass of the Jewish people nourished towards the power of the commissioners."[1855] At the same time, Pasmanik himself pointed out "the points which may at first be the foundation of a rapprochement between Bolshevism and Judaism... These are: the concern for *happiness on earth* and that of *social justice*... Judaism was the first to put forward these two great principles."[1856]

We read in an issue of the London newspaper *Jewish Chronicle* of 1919 (when the revolution had not yet cooled down) an interesting debate on the issue. The permanent correspondent of this paper, a certain Mentor, writes that it is not fitting for the Jews to pretend that they have no connection with the Bolsheviks. Thus, in America, the Rabbi and Doctor Judah Magnes supported the Bolsheviks, which means that he did not regard Bolshevism as incompatible with Judaism.[1857] He writes again the following week: Bolshevism is in itself a great evil, but, paradoxically, it also represents the hope of humanity. Was the French Revolution not bloody, it as well, and yet it was justified by History. The Jew is idealistic by nature and it is not surprising, it is even logical that he believed the promises of Bolshevism. "There is much room for reflection in the very fact of Bolshevism, in the adherence of many Jews to Bolshevism, in the fact that the ideals of Bolshevism in many respects join those of Judaism— a great number of which have been taken up by the founder of Christianity. The Jews who think must examine all this carefully. One must be foolish to see in Bolshevism only its off-putting aspects..."[1858]

[1853] *Landau*, RaJ, p. 109.

[1854] D. O. *Linski*, O natsionalnom samosoznanii rousskogo evreia [The National Consciousness of the Russian Jew], RaJ, pp. 145, 146.

[1855] D. S. *Pasmanik*, RaJ, p. 225.

[1856] D. S. *Pasmanik*, Rousskaia revolioutsiia i evreistvo [The Russian Revolution and Judaism], p. 129.

[1857] Jewish Chronicle, 28 March 1919, p. 10.

[1858] *Ibidem*, 4 April 1919, p. 7.

All the same, is not Judaism above all the recognition of the one God? But, this in itself is enough to make it incompatible with Bolshevism, the denier of God!

Still on the search for the motives for such a broad participation of the Jews in the Bolshevik adventure, I. Biekerman writes: "We might, before of the facts, despair of the future of our people—if we did not know that, of all the contagions, the worst is that of words. Why was the Jewish consciousness so receptive to this infection, the question would be too long to develop here." The causes reside "not only in the circumstances of yesterday," but also "in the ideas inherited from ancient times, which predispose Jews to be contaminated by ideology, even if it is null and subversive."[1859]

S. Bulgakov also writes: "The face that Judaism shows in Russian Bolshevism is by no means the true face of Israel... It reflects, even within Israel, a state of terrible spiritual crisis, which can lead to bestiality."[1860]

As for the argument that the Jews of Russia have thrown themselves into the arms of the Bolsheviks because of the vexations they have suffered in the past, it must be confronted with the two other communist shows of strength that occurred at the same time as that of Lenin, in Bavaria and in Hungary. We read in I. Levin: "The number of Jews serving the Bolshevik regime is, in these two countries, very high. In Bavaria, we find among the commissaries the Jews E. Levine, M. Levin, Axelrod, the anarchist ideologist Landauer, Ernst Toller."

"The proportion of Jews who took the lead of the Bolshevik movement in Hungary is of 95%.... However, the situation of the Jews in terms of civic rights was excellent in Hungary, where there had not been any limitation for a long time already; in the cultural and economic sphere, the Jews occupied such a position that the anti-Semites could even speak of a hold of the Jews."[1861] We may add here the remark of an eminent Jewish publisher of America; he writes that the Jews of Germany "have prospered and gained a high position in society."[1862] Let us not forget in this connection that the ferment of rebellion that was at the origin of the *coups de force*—of which we shall speak again in chapter 16—had been introduced by the Bolsheviks through the intermediary of "repatriated prisoners" stuffed with propaganda.

[1859] *Biekerman*, RaJ, p. 34.
[1860] Arch. Sergui Bulgakov, Khristianstvo i evreiskii vopros [Christianity and the Jewish Question], pp. 124-125.
[1861] *Levine*, RaJ, pp. 125, 126.
[1862] *Norman Podgorets*, Evrei v sovremennom mire [The Jews in the Modern World] (Int.) BM, no. 86, p. 113.

What brought all these rebels together—and, later, beyond the seas—, was a flurry of unbridled revolutionary internationalism, an impulse towards revolution, a revolution that was global and "permanent". The rapid success of the Jews in the Bolshevik administration could not be ignored in Europe and the United States. Even worse: they were admired there! At the time of the passage from February to October, Jewish public opinion in America did not mute its sympathies for the Russian revolution.

Meanwhile, the Bolsheviks were conducting their financial operations diligently abroad, mainly via Stockholm. Since Lenin's return to Russia, secret supplies had come to them, of German provenance, through the Nia Banken of Olof Aschberg. This did not exclude the financial support of certain Russian bankers, those who, fleeing the revolution, had sought refuge abroad but had transformed there into volunteer support of the Bolsheviks. An American researcher, Anthony Sutton, has found (with half a century of delay) archival documents; he tells us that, if we are to believe a report sent in 1918 to the State Department by the U.S. Ambassador in Stockholm, "among these 'Bolshevik bankers' is the infamous Dmitri Rubinstein that the revolution of February had gotten out of prison, who had reached Stockholm and made himself the financial agent of the Bolsheviks"; "we also find Abram Jivotovski, a relative of Trostky and Lev Kamenev." Among the syndicates were "Denisov of the ex-Bank of Siberia, Kamenka of the Bank Azov-Don, and Davidov of the Bank for Foreign Trade.

Other 'Bolshevik bankers': Grigori Lessine, Shtifter, Iakov Berline, and their agent Isidore Kohn."[1863]

These had left Russia. Others, in the opposite direction, left America to return. They were the *revenants*, all of them "revolutionaries" (some from long ago, others of recent date) who dreamed of finally building and consolidating the New World of Universal Happiness. We talked about it in Chapter 14. They were flocking across the oceans from the port of New York to the East or from the port of San Francisco in direction of the West, some former subjects of the Russian Empire, others purely and simply American citizens, enthusiasts who even did not know the Russian language.

In 1919, A. V. Tyrkova–Williams wrote in a book published then in England: "There are few Russians among the Bolshevik leaders, few men imbued with Russian culture and concerned with the interests of the Russian people… In addition to foreign citizens, Bolshevism recruited immigrants who had spent many years outside the borders. Some had never

---

[1863] A. Sutton, Orol strit i bolshevitskaya revolioutsiia, [Wall Street and the Bolshevik Revolution], trans. from the English, M., 1998, pp. 141-142.

been to Russia before. There were many Jews among them. They spoke Russian badly. The nation of which they had become masters was foreign to them and, moreover, they behaved like invaders in a conquered country." And if, in tsarist Russia,

"Jews were excluded from all official posts, if schools and State service were closed to them, on the other hand, in the Soviet Republic all committees and commissariats were filled with Jews. Often, they exchanged their Jewish name for a Russian name... but this masquerade did not deceive anyone."[1864]

That same year, 1919, at the Senate Hearings of the Overmen Commission, an Illinois university professor, P. B. Dennis, who arrived in Russia in 1917, declared that in his opinion—"an opinion that matched that of other Americans, Englishmen, Frenchmen...—, these people deployed in Russia an extreme cruelty and ferocity in their repression against the *bourgeoisie*" (the word is used here without any pejorative nuance in its primary sense: the inhabitants of the boroughs). Or: "Among those who carried out 'murderous propaganda' in the trenches and in the rear, there were those who, one or two years before [i.e. in 1917 1918], still lived New York."[1865]

In February 1920, Winston Churchill spoke in the pages of the *Sunday Herald*. In an article entitled "Zionism Against Bolshevism: Struggle for the Soul of the Jewish People", he wrote: "Today we see this company of outstanding personalities, emerging from clandestinity, from the basements of the great cities of Europe and America, who grabbed by the hair and seized by the throat the Russian people, and established itself as the undisputed mistress of the immense Russian Empire."[1866]

There are many known names among these people who have returned from beyond the ocean. Here is M. M. Gruzenberg: he had previously lived in England (where he had met Sun Yat–sen), then lived for a long time in the United States, in Chicago where he had "organised a school for the immigrants", and we find him in 1919 general consul of the RSFSR in Mexico (a country on which the revolutionaries founded great hopes: Trotsky would turn up there...), then, in the same year, he sat in the central organs of the Comintern. He took service in Scandinavia, Sweden; he was arrested in Scotland. He resurfaced in China in 1923 under the name of Borodin[1867] with a whole squad of spies: he was the "principal political

---

[1864] *Ariadna Tyrkova-Williams*, From Liberty to Brest–Litovsk London, Macmillan and Co., 1919, pp. 297-299.
[1865] *Overmen*, pp. 22-23, 26-27.
[1866] Jerry Muller, Dialektika traguedii antisemitizm i kommounizm v Tsentralnoï i Vostotchnoï Evrope, Evreiskaya Tribouna* (The Jewish Tribune), 1920, no. 10, p. 3.
[1867] This is the character of *Man's Fate* by Andre Malraux.

adviser to the Executive Committee of the Kuomintang", a role which enabled him to promote the career of Mao Tse–tung and of Zhou Enlai. However, having suspected Borodin–Gruzenberg of engaging in subversive work, Chiang Kai–shek expelled him from China in 1927. Returning to the USSR, he passed unharmed the year 1937; during the war with Germany, we find him editor-in-chief of the Soviet Information Office alongside Dridzo–Lozovsky. He will be executed in 1951.[1868]

(About the Bolshevik Jews executed in the 1930s, see *infra*, chapter 19.) Among them also, Samuel Agursky, who became one of the leaders of Belarus; arrested in 1938, he served a sentence of deportation. (He is the father of the late M. Agursky, who prematurely disappeared, and who did not follow the same path as his progenitor, far from it![1869] [1870]—Let us also mention Solomon Slepak, an influential member of the Comintern, he returned to Russia by Vladivostok where he took part in assassinations; he then went to China to try to attract Sun Yat–sen in an alliance with communism; his son Vladimir would have to tear himself, not without a clash, from the trap into which his father had fallen in his quest for the radiant future of communism.[1871] Stories like this, and some even more paradoxical, there are hundreds of them.

Demolishers of the "*bourgeois*" Jewish culture also turned up. Among them, the collaborators of S. Dimanstein in the European Commissariat: the S.–R. Dobkovski, Agursky (already mentioned), and also "Kantor, Shapiro, Kaplan, former emigrant anarchists who had returned from London and New York". The objective of the Commissariat was to create a "Centre for the Jewish Communist Movement". In August 1918, the new Communist newspaper in Yiddish *Emes* (the Truth) announced: "The proletarian revolution began in the street of the Jews"; a campaign was immediately launched against the *Heders* and the "Talmud-Torah"... In June 1919, countersigned by S. Agursky and Stalin, the dissolution of the Central Bureau of the Jewish Communities was proclaimed,[1872] which represented the conservative fraction of Judaism, the one that had not sided with the Bolsheviks.

It is nonetheless true that the socialist Jews were not attracted primarily to the Bolsheviks. Now however: where were the other parties, what had

---

[1868] RJE, t. 1, p. 154.
[1869] Collaborator of the collection *From Under the Rubble*, published by Aleksandr Solzhenitsyn in 1974.
[1870] *Ibidem*, p. 22.
[1871] *Chaim Potok*, The Gates of November, Chronicles of the Slepak Family, New York, Alfred A. Knopf, 1996, pp. 37, 44-45.
[1872] *G. Aronson*, Evreiski vopros v epokhou Stalina [The Jewish Question in Stalin's Era], BJWR, pp. 133-134.

become of them? What allowed the Bolshevik Party to occupy an exclusive position was the disintegration of the old Jewish political parties. The Bund, the Zionist Socialists and the Zionists of the Poalei had split up and their leaders had joined the victors' camp by denying the ideals of democratic socialism—such as M. Raies, M. Froumkina-Ester, A. Weinstein, M. Litvanov.[1873]

Is it possible? Even the Bund, this extremely belligerent organisation to which even Lenin's positions were not suitable, which showed itself so intransigent on the principle of the cultural and national autonomy of the Jews?

Well yes, even the Bund! "After the establishment of Soviet power, the leadership of the Bund in Russia split into two groups (1920): the right, which in its majority, emigrated, and the left which liquidated the Bund (1921) and adhered in large part to the Bolshevik Party."[1874] Among the former members of the Bund, we can cite the irremovable David Zaslavski, the one who for decades would put his pen at the service of Stalin (he would be responsible for stigmatising Mandelstam and Pasternak). Also: the Leplevski brothers, Israel and Grigori (one, from the outset, would become an agent of the Cheka and stay there for the rest of his life, the other would occupy a high position in the NKVD in 1920, then would be Deputy Commissar of the People, President of the Small Sovnarkom of the RSFSR, then Deputy Attorney General of the USSR (1934-39); he would be a victim of repression in 1939. Solomon Kotliar, immediately promoted First Secretary of Orthbourg, of Vologda, of Tver, of the regional Committee of Orel. Or also Abram Heifets: he returned to Russia after February 1917, joined the Presidium of the Bund's Main Committee in Ukraine, was a member of the Central Committee of the Bund; in October 1917, he was already for the Bolsheviks and, in 1919, he figured in the leading group of the Comintern.[1875]

To the leftists of the Bund joined the left of the Zionist Socialists and the SERP[1876]; those entered the Communist Party as early as 1919. The left wing of the Poalei–Tsion did the same in 1921.[1877] In 1926, according to an internal census, there were up to 2,500 former members of the Bund in the Party. It goes without saying that many, later on, fell under the blade:

[1873] *Ibidem*, pp. 135-136.
[1874] SJE, t. 1, p. 560.
[1875] RJE, t. 1, p. 478; t. 2, pp. 78, 163; t.3, p. 286.
[1876] Sotsial–evreiskaya raborchaya partia: Jewish Social Workers Party.
[1877] S. Dimanstein, Revolioutsionnie dvijenie sredi evreev [The revolutionary movement among the Jews] in The Revolutionaries through several essays, ed. of M. N. Pokrovski, t. 3, b. I, M-L, GJZ, p. 215.

"Under Stalin, the majority of them were victims of ferocious persecutions."[1878]

Biekerman exclaims: "The Bund, which had assumed the role of representative of the Jewish working masses, joined the Bolsheviks in its most important and active part."[1879]

In his memoirs, David Azbel tries to explain the reasons for this accession by reflecting on the example of his uncle, Aron Isaakievich Weinstein, an influential member of the Bund that we mentioned above: "He had understood before all others that his Party, as well as the other socialist parties, were condemned... He had understood also another thing: to survive and continue to defend the interests of the Jews would be possible only by joining the Bolsheviks."[1880]

For how many of them the reasons 1) survive, 2) continue to defend the interests of the Jews, were decisive? Tentatively, both objectives were achieved.

It will note also that after October the other socialist parties, the S.–R. and the Mensheviks, who, as we know, had a large number of Jews in their ranks and at their heads, did not stand up against Bolshevism either. Scarcely aware of the fact that the Bolsheviks had dismissed this Constituent Assembly which they had called for, they withdrew, hesitated, divided themselves in their turn, sometimes proclaiming their neutrality in the civil war, other times their intention to temporise. As for the S.–R., they downright opened to the Bolsheviks a portion of the Eastern front and tried to demoralise the rear of the Whites.

But we also find Jews among the leaders of the resistance to the Bolsheviks in 1918: out of the twenty-six signatures of the "Open Letter of Prisoners on the Affair of the Workers' Congress" written at Taganka Prison, no less of a quarter are Jewish.[1881] The Bolsheviks were pitiless towards the Mensheviks of this kind. In the summer of 1918, R. Abramovich, an important Menshevik leader, avoided execution only by means of a letter addressed to Lenin from an Austrian prison by Friedrich Adler, the one who had shot down the Austrian Prime Minister in 1916 and who had been

---

[1878] SJE, t. 1, p. 560.
[1879] *I. M. Biekerman*, RaJ, p. 44.
[1880] *D. Azbel*, Do, vo vremia i posle [Avant, pendant et après], VM, 1989, no. 104, p. 231.
[1881] Nezavisimoie rabotcheie dvijeniie v 1918 godou: Dokumenty i materialy [The independent workers' movement], established by M. Bernstam, Paris, YMCA Press, 1981, pp. 291-293, in Research on Contemporary Russian History.

reprieved. Others, too, were stoic: Grigori Binshtok, Semyon Weinstein; arrested several times, they were eventually expelled from the country.[1882]

In February 1921, in Petrograd, the Mensheviks certainly supported the deceived and hungry workers, they pushed them to protest and strike—but without any real conviction. And they lacked audacity to take the lead of the Kronstadt insurrection. However, this did not in any way protect them from repression.

We also know a lot of Mensheviks who joined the Bolsheviks, who exchanged one party label for another. They were: Boris Maguidov (he became head of the political section in the 10th Army, then Donbass, secretary of the provincial committees of Poltava, Samara, instructor on the Central Committee): Abram Deborine, a true defector (he rapidly climbed the echelons of a career of "red professor", stuffing our heads with Dialectical Materialism and Historical Materialism…); Alexander Goikhbarg (member of the Soviet Revolutionary Committee, public prosecutor at the trial of the ministers of Kolchak, member of the college of the Commissariat for Justice, then president of the Little Sovnarkom). Some of them held out for some time until their arrest, such as I. Liakhovetski–Maïski[1883]; the others, in great numbers, were reduced very early to silence, from the trial of the imaginary "Unified Menshevik Bureau" of 1931 (where we find Guimmer–Sukhanov who was the designer of the tactics of the Executive Committee in March 1917.) A huge raid was organised throughout the Union to apprehend them.

There were defectors in the S.–R.: Lakov Lifchitz, for example, vice-president of the Chernigov Cheka in 1919, then Kharkov, then president of the Kiev Cheka and, at the height of a rapid career, vice-president of the Ukrainian GPU. There was anarchist communists, the most famous being Lazar Kogan (Special Section of the Armies, Assistant to the Chief of the Army of the Vecheka in 1930—senior official of the Gulag and, in 1931, chief of the White Sea shipyard of the NKVD). There are extremely sinuous biographies: Ilya Kit–Viitenko, a lieutenant in the Austrian army, taken prisoner by the Russians, and from the moment the Bolsheviks are in power, takes his ranks at the Cheka–Guepeou and then in the army and, in the 1930s, was one of the reformers of the Red Army. And then in the hole for twenty years![1884]

And what about the Zionists? Let us remember: in 1906 they had posited and proclaimed that they could not stay away from the Russians' fight against the yoke of the Autocracy, and they had actively engaged in the

---

[1882] RJE, t. 1, pp. 135 136, 199-200.
[1883] RJE, t. 1, pp. 331, 419; t. 2, pp. 221, 222, 230.
[1884] RJE, t. 2, pp. 36, 51-52, 176.

said battle. This did not prevent them, in May 1918 (when the yoke still weighed so heavily), to declare that, in matters of Russian domestic policy, they would henceforth be neutral, "very obviously in the hope of avoiding the risk" that the Bolsheviks "would accuse them of being counter-revolutionaries."[1885] And at first—it worked. Throughout the year 1918 and during the first six months of 1919, the Bolsheviks left them alone: in the summer of 1918 they were able to hold the All-Russian Congress of Jewish Communities in Moscow, and hundreds of these Communities had their "Palestinian Week"; their newspapers appeared freely and a youth club, the "Heraluts"[1886], was created.—But in the spring of 1919 local authorities undertook to ban the Zionist press here and there, and in the autumn of 1919 a few prominent figures were accused of "espionage for the benefit of England". In the spring of 1920, the Zionists organised a Pan-Russian Conference in Moscow. Result: all the participants (90 people) were interned in the Butyrka prison; some were condemned, but the penalty was not applied, following the intervention of a delegation of Jewish syndicates from America.

"The Vecheka presidium declared that the Zionist organisation was counterrevolutionary, and its activity was now forbidden in Soviet Russia... From this moment began the era of clandestinity for the Zionists."[1887]

M. Heifets, who is a thoughtful man, reminds us very well of this: did the October coup not coincide exactly with the Balfour declaration which laid the foundations of an independent Jewish state? Well, what happened?: "A part of the new Jewish generation followed the path of Herzl and Jabotinsky, while the other [let us precise: the biggest] yielded to temptation and swelled the ranks of the Lenin–Trotsky–Stalin band." (Exactly what Churchill feared.) "Herzl's way then appeared distant, unreal, while that of Trotsky and Bagritsky enabled the Jews to gain immediate stature and immediately become a nation in Russia, equal in right and even privileged."[1888]

Also defector, of course, and not least, Lev Mekhlis, of the Poalei–Tsion. His career is well known: in Stalin's secretariat, in the editorial board of the *Pravda*, at the head of the Red Army's political sector, in the State Defence Commissariat and Commissioner of State Control. It was he who made our landing in Crimea in 1942 fail. At the height of his career: in the

---

[1885] *I. B. Shekhtman*, Sovetskaia Rossiia, Sionizm i Izrail [Soviet Russia, Zionism, and Israel], BJWR-2, p. 31.
[1886] *Ibidem*, p. 315.
[1887] *S. Hepshtein*, Rousskie sionisty v barbe za Palestinou [The Russian Zionists in the Fight for Palestine], BJWR-2, pp. 390-392.
[1888] *Heifets*, "22", 1980, no. 14, p. 162.

Orgburo of the Central Committee. His ashes are sealed in the wall of the Kremlin.[1889]

Of course, there was an important part of the Jews of Russia who did not adhere to Bolshevism: neither the rabbis, the lecturers, nor the great doctors, nor a whole mass of good people, fell into the arms of the Bolsheviks. Tyrkova writes in the same passage in her book, a few lines later: "This predominance of the Jews among the Soviet leaders put to despair those of the Russian Jews who, despite the cruel iniquities suffered under the tsarist regime, regarded Russia as the Motherland and led the common life of all Russian intelligentsia, refusing, in communion with her, any collaboration with the Bolsheviks."[1890]—

But at the time they had no opportunity of making themselves heard publicly, and these pages are naturally filled not with their names, but with those of the conquerors, those who have bridled the course of events.

Two illustrious terrorist acts perpetrated by Jewish arms against the Bolsheviks in 1918 occupy a special place: the assassination of Uritsky by Leonid Kannegisser, and the attack on Lenin by Fanny Kaplan. Here too, though the other way around, was expressed the vocation of the Jewish people to be always among the first. Perhaps the blows fired at Lenin were rather the result of S.–R. intentions[1891]. But, as for Kannegisser (born of hereditary nobility by his grandfather, he entered the School of Officer Cadets in 1917; by the way, he was in friendly relations with Sergei Yesenin), I admit full well Mark Aldanov's explanation: in the face of the Russian people and History, he was moved by the desire to oppose the names of Uritsky and Zinoviev with another Jewish name.

This is the feeling he expresses in a note transmitted to his sister on the eve of the attack, in which he says he wants to avenge the peace of Brest-Litovsk, that he is ashamed to see the Jews contribute to install the Bolsheviks in power, and also avenge the execution of his companion of the School of artillery at the Cheka of Petrograd.

It should be noted, however, that recent studies have revealed that these two attacks were perpetrated under suspicious circumstances.[1892] There is strong presumption that Fanny Kaplan did not shoot Lenin at all, but was apprehended "to close the case": a convenient culprit, by chance. There is also a hypothesis that the Bolshevik authorities themselves would have created the necessary conditions for Kannegisser to fire his shot. This I

[1889] RJE, t. 2, pp. 276-277.
[1890] Ariadna Tyrkova-Williams, op. cit., *p. 299.*
[1891] Party of Socialists Revolutionaries (S–R.).
[1892] *B. Orlov,* Mif o Fanni Kaplan [The Myth of Fanny Kaplan], ME, 1975, no. 2; G. Nilov. Ouritski, Voldarski, and others, Strana i Mir, Munich, 1989, no. 6.

strongly doubt: for what provocation would the Bolsheviks have sacrificed their beloved child, president of the Cheka? One thing, however, is troubling: how is it that later, in full Red Terror, when was attained by force of arms, through the entire country, thousands of innocent hostages, totally unconnected with the affair, the whole Kannegisser family was freed from prison and allowed to emigrate... We do not recognise here the Bolshevik claw! Or would it be the intervention of a very long arm to the highest ranking Soviet instances?—A recent publication tells us that the relatives and friends of L. Kannegisser had even drawn up an armed attack plan against the Cheka of Petrograd to free their prisoner, and that all, as soon as they were arrested, were released and remained in Petrograd without being disturbed. Such clemency on the part of the Bolshevik authorities may be explained by their concern to avoid ill feelings with the influential Jewish circles in Petrograd. The Kannegisser family had kept its Judaic faith and Leonid's mother, Rosalia Edouardovna, declared during an interrogation that her son had fired on Uritsky because he "had turned away from Judaism."[1893]

But here is a Jewish name that has not yet obtained the deserved celebrity: Alexander Abramovich Vilenkin, hero of the clandestine struggle against the Bolsheviks. He was a volunteer in the hussars at the age of seventeen, in 1914, he was decorated four times with the Cross of Saint George, promoted to officer, then, on the eve of the revolution, he became captain of cavalry; in 1918, he joined the clandestine organisation Union for the Defence of the Homeland and of Liberty; he was apprehended by the Cheka at the time when, as the organisation had been discovered, he was delaying the destruction of compromising documents. Focused, intelligent, energetic, uncompromising towards the Bolsheviks, he infused in others the spirit of resistance. Executed by the Bolsheviks—it goes without saying. (The information about him came to us from his comrade-in-arms in the underground in 1918, and also from his cellmate in 1919, Vasily Fyodorovich Klementiev, captain in the Russian army.[1894])

These fighters against Bolshevism, whatever their motivations, we venerate their memory as Jews. We regret that they were so few, as were too few the White forces during the civil war.

A very prosaic and entirely new phenomenon reinforced the victory of the Bolsheviks. These occupied important positions, from which many advantages resulted, notably the enjoyment in both capitals of "vacant"

[1893] *Nikolaï Koniaev*, On oubival, slovno pisal stikhotvorenie [He killed as he would have written verses], Don, pp. 241, 250-252.
[1894] *V. F. Klementiev*, V bolchevitskoï Moskve: 1918-1920 [In the Moscow of the Bolsheviks], M., Rousski Pout (Russian Memories, series: Our close past, book 3).

apartments freed by their owners, "former aristocrats", now on the run. In these apartments could live a whole tributary flock of the former Pale of Settlement. This was a real "exodus"! G. A. Landau writes: "The Jews have climbed the stairs of power and occupied a few 'summits'... From there, it is normal that they brought (as they do everywhere, in any environment) their relatives, friends, companions from their youth... A perfectly natural process: the granting of functions to people who are known, trusted, protected, or simply begging for your favours. This process multiplied the number of Jews in the Soviet state apparatus."[1895] We will not say how many Zinoviev's wife, Lilina, thus brought parents and relatives, nor how Zinoviev distributed positions to his 'own'. They are the focus, but the influx, not to have been noticed at the moment, was enormous and concerns tens of thousands of people. The people transmigrated en masse from Odessa to Moscow. (Is it known that Trotsky himself gratified his father, whom he moderately loved, of a Sovkhoz in the suburbs of Moscow?)

These migrations can be followed throughout biographies. So that of David (not to be confused with Mark) Azbel. In 1919, still a kid, he left Chemigov where he was born to come to Moscow where his two aunts already lived. He first lived in the house of one of them, Ida, "a wealthy merchant of the First Guild", whose husband had returned from America, and then with the other, Liolia, who was housed in the First House of the Soviets (The National) with all the best of the Soviet Union. Their neighbour Ulrich, who would later become famous, said jokingly: "Why don't we open a synagogue in the National where only Jews live?" A whole Soviet elite then left Saint Petersburg to settle in the Second House of the Soviets (the Metropolis), in the Third (the Seminary, Bojedomski Street), in the Fourth (Mokhovaya / Vozdvijenka street) and in the Fifth (Cheremetievski street). These tenants received from a special distribution centre abundant parcels: "Caviar, cheese, butter, smoked sturgeon were never lacking on their table" (we are in 1920). "Everything was special, designed especially for the new elite: kindergartens, schools, clubs, libraries." (In 1921-22, the year of the murderous famine on the Volga and the help of TARA[1896], in their "model school, the canteen was fed by the ARA foundation and served American breakfasts: rice pudding, hot chocolate, white bread, and fried eggs.") And "no one remembered that, the day before, it was vociferated in the classrooms that the *bourgeois* should be hung high on the lantern." "The children of the neighbouring houses hated those of the 'Soviet Houses' and, at the first opportunity, went after them."

[1895] *Landau*, RaJ, p. 110.
[1896] American Relief Administration (1919-1923) the Hoover commission rescued the victims of the 1922 famine in Russia.

The NEP came. The tenants of the National then moved into cosy apartments or pavilions that had previously belonged to aristocrats or *bourgeois*.

In 1921: "spend the summer in Moscow, where you suffocate?", no, you are invited to an old mansion, now confiscated, in the outskirts of Moscow. There, "everything is in the state, as in the days of the former owners"... except that high fences are erected around these houses, that guards are posted at the entrance... Wives of the commissioners began to frequent the best spas of the West. We see the development, owed to the scarcity of food, of misery and the concealment of foodstuffs, a second-hand trade and a whole traffic of goods.

"Having bought for peanuts an entire lot of commodities from emigrating merchants, Aunt Ida and Uncle Micha sold them under the table" and thus became "probably the richest people in all of Moscow."—However, in 1926 they were sentenced to five years' imprisonment for "economic counterrevolution", to which were added, at the end of the NEP, ten years of camp.[1897]

Let us also quote: "When the Bolsheviks became 'the government', all sorts of individuals from the Jewish sub-proletariat joined them, wishing to get their share."[1898]—And as free trade and private enterprise were forbidden, many Jewish families saw their daily lives greatly modified: "The middle-aged people were mostly deprived, while the younger ones, rid of all spiritual 'ballast', by having social careers, were able to maintain their elders... Hence the excessive number of Jews in the Soviet state apparatus." Note: the author does not justify this process by calling it a "unique issue", but he notes with grief the aspect that counts: "This destructive process did not meet the resistance it would have required in the Jewish milieu," on the contrary, it found there "voluntary executants and a climate of sympathy."[1899]

It is thus that many Jews entered the Soviet ruling class. But could this process, however occult as it was, go unnoticed by the disadvantaged Russian social strata?

And how could the man in the street react? Either by jeers: "Rosa of the Sovnarkhoz", "the husband of Khaïka of the Cheka". Or by funny stories, from those that flooded Russia as early as 1918: "Vyssotski tea, Brodsky sugar, Trotsky Russia." And, in Ukraine, it gave: "Hop! Harvest Workers

---

[1897] D. Azbel, ME, 1989, no. 104, pp. 192-196, 199, 203, 209, 223, 225 226.
[1898] V. S. Mandel, RaJ, p. 200.
[1899] Landau, RaJ, pp. 111-112.

/ All Jews are bosses!" And they began to whisper a new slogan: "The Soviets without the Jews!"

The co-authors of the book of *Russia and the Jews* became alarmed in 1924: it is clear that "not all Jews are Bolsheviks and all Bolsheviks are not Jews, but there is no need today to prove the zealous participation of the Jews in the martyrdom imposed on an exsanguinate Russia by the Bolsheviks. What we must, on the contrary, is try to elucidate in a calm manner how this work of destruction was refracted in the consciousness of the Russian people. The Russians had never seen any Jews in command before."[1900]

They now saw them today at every step. Invested with a ferocious and unlimited power.

"To answer the question of Judaism's responsibility in the emergence of Bolshevik Jews, we must first consider the psychology of non-Jews, that of all these Russians who suffer directly from the atrocities committed... The Jewish actors of public life who wish to prevent any new bloody tragedy, to save the Jews of Russia from new pogroms, must take account of this fact."[1901] We must "understand the psychology of the Russians who suddenly found themselves under the authority of an evil, arrogant, rude, self-confident and impudent brood."[1902]

It is not for the purpose of settling accounts that we must remember History. Nor to reassume mutual accusations. But to understand how, for example, it was possible for important layers of a perfectly correct Jewish society to have tolerated an enormous participation of Jews in the rise (1918) of a State that was not only insensitive to the Russian people, foreign to Russian history, but which, moreover, inflicted on the population all the outbursts of *terror*.

The presence of Jews alongside the Bolsheviks raises questions *not because* it would induce a foreign origin to this power. When we speak of the abundance of Jewish names in revolutionary Russia, we paint a picture of nothing new: how many Germanic and Baltic names have figured, for a century and a half to two centuries, in The tsarist administration? The real question is: in what direction did this power work?

D. S. Pasmanik, however, gives us this reflection: "Let all the Russians who are capable of reflecting ask themselves whether Bolshevism, even with Lenin at its head, would have triumphed if there had been in Soviet

---

[1900] *I. M. Biekerman*, RaJ, p. 22.
[1901] *D. S. Pasmanik*, RaJ, p. 212.
[1902] *D. S. Pasmanik*, Rousskaia revolioutsia i evreistvo [The Russian Revolution and Judaism], p. 200.

Russia a satisfied and educated peasantry owning land? Could all the 'Sages of Zion' gathered together, even with a Trotsky at their head, be able to bring about the great chaos in Russia?"[1903] He is right: they could never have done so.

But the first to ask the question should be the Jews more than the Russians.

This episode of History should call out to them today. The question of the mass participation of the Jews in the Bolshevik administration and the atrocities committed by the Jews should be elucidated in a spirit of far-sighted analysis of History. It is not admissible to evade the question by saying: it was the scum, the renegades of Judaism, we do not have to answer for them.

D. S. Chturmann is right to remind me of my own remarks about the communist leaders of any nation: "they have all turned away from their people and poured into the inhuman."[1904] I believe it. But Pasmanik, was right to write in the 20s: "We cannot confine ourselves to saying that the Jewish people do not answer for the acts committed by one or the other of its members. We answer for Trotsky as long as we have not dissociated ourselves from him."[1905] Now, to dissociate oneself does not mean to turn away, on the contrary, it means rejecting *actions*, to the end, and learning from them.

I have studied Trotsky's biography extensively, and I agree that he did not have any specifically Jewish attachments, but was rather a fanatical internationalist. Does this mean that a compatriot like him is easier to incriminate than the others? But as soon as his star rose, in the autumn of 1917, Trotsky became, for far too many people, a subject of pride, and for the radical left of the Jews of America, a true idol.

What can I say of America? But of everywhere else as well! There was a young man in the camp where I was interned in the 50s, Vladimir Gershuni, a fervent socialist, an internationalist, who had kept a full conscience of his Jewishness; I saw him again in the 60s after our release, and he gave me his notes. I read there that Trotsky was the Prometheus of October for the sole reason that he was Jewish: "He was a Prometheus not because he was born such, but because he was a child of the Prometheus-people, this people, who, if it was not attached to the rock of obtuse wickedness by the

---

[1903] *Ibidem*, p. 157.
[1904] *Dora Chturmann*, Gorodou i mirou [Urbi and orbi], Paris–New York, Third Wave, 1988, p. 357.
[1905] *D. S. Pasmanik*, Rousskaia revolioutsia i evreistvo [The Russian Revolution and Judaism], p. 11.

chains of a patent and latent hostility, would have done much more than he did for the good of humanity."

"All historians who deny the participation of Jews in the revolution tend not to recognise in these Jews their national character. Those, on the contrary, and especially Israeli historians, who see Jewish hegemony as a victory of the Judaic spirit, those ones exalt their belonging to Jewishness."[1906]

It was as early as the 20s, when the civil war ended, that arguments were made to exonerate the Jews. I. O. Levin reviews them in the collection *Russia and the Jews* (the Bolshevik Jews were not so numerous as that... there is no reason why a whole people should respond to the acts of a few..., The Jews were persecuted in tsarist Russia..., during the civil war the Jews had to flee the pogroms by seeking refuge with the Bolsheviks, etc.), and he rejected them by arguing that it was not a matter of criminal responsibility, which is always individual, but a *moral* responsibility.[1907]

Pasmanik thought it impossible to be relieved of a moral responsibility, but he consoled himself by saying: "Why should the mass of the Jewish people answer for the turpitudes of certain commissioners? It is profoundly unjust.

However, to admit that there is a collective responsibility for the Jews is to recognise the existence of a Jewish nation of its own. From the moment when the Jews cease to be a nation, from the day when they are Russians, Germans, Englishmen of Judaic confession, it is then that they will shake off the shackles of collective responsibility."[1908]

Now, the twentieth century has rightly taught us to recognise the Hebrew nation as such, with its anchorage in Israel. And the collective responsibility of a people (of the Russian people too, of course) is inseparable from its capacity to build a morally worthy life.

Yes, they are abounding, the arguments that explain why the Jews stood by the Bolsheviks (and we will discuss others, very solid, when we talk about the civil war). Nevertheless, if the Jews of Russia remember this period only to justify themselves, it will mean that the level of their national consciousness has fallen, that this consciousness will have lost itself.

The Germans could also challenge their responsibility for the Nazi period by saying: they were not real Germans, they were the dregs of society, they did not ask for our opinion... But this people answers for its past even in

---

[1906] Sonja Margolina. Das Ende der Lügen: Russland und die Juden im 20 Jahrhundert [The End of Lies: Russia and the Jews in the 20th Century], Berlin, Siedler Verlag, 1992, pp. 99-100.
[1907] *I. O. Levine*, RaJ, p. 123.
[1908] *D. S. Pasmanik*, p. 198.

its ignominious periods. How to respond? By endeavouring to conscientise it, to understand it: how did such a thing happen? Where lies *our* fault? Is there a danger that this will happen again?

It is in this spirit that the Jewish people must respond to their revolutionary assassins as well as the columns of well-disposed individuals who put themselves at their service. It is not a question here of answering before other peoples, but before oneself, before one's conscience and before God. As we Russians must answer, both for the pogroms, and our incendiary peasants, insensible to all pity, and for our red soldiers who have fallen into madness, and our sailors transformed into wild beasts. (I have spoken of them with enough depth, I believe, in *The Red Wheel*, and I will add an example here: the Red Guard A. R. Bassov, in charge of escorting Shingaryov[1909]—this man passionate of justice, a popular intercessor—, began by collecting money from the sister of the prisoner—as a tip and to finance his transfer from the Peter and Paul fortress to the Mariinski hospital—and a few hours later, in the same night, he leads to the hospital some sailors who coldly shoot down Shingaryov and Kokochkine.[1910] In this individual—so many homegrown traits!!) Answer, yes, as one answers for a member of one's family.[1911]

For if we are absolved of all responsibility for the actions of our compatriots, it is the very notion of nation which then loses all true meaning.

[1909] 1869-1918; Publicist, physician, one of the cadet leaders (K.D.). Deputy in the Duma in 1917, shot dead by the terrorists.

[1910] 1871-1918, jurist, leader of the Cadet party, deputy in the Duma in 1917, also shot down by the terrorists.

[1911] A. I. *Chingariova*, postface to Dnevnik A. Chingariova. Kak eto bylo: Petropavloskaia krepost [Journal of the fortress Peter and Paul, 27 Nov. 1917-5 Jan. 1918], 2nd ed., M., 1918, pp. 66-68.

Chapter 16

During the Civil War

Trotsky once boasted that during the Civil War, "even" traveling in his special Revvoyensovet's [Revolutionary Military Council] railroad coach, he was able to find time to acquaint himself with the latest works of French literature.

Not that he realized exactly *what* he said. He acknowledged that he was able to find not just time, but room in his heart between appeals to the "revolutionary sailors," forcibly mobilized units of Red Army, and a thrown order to execute every tenth soldier in a unit that wavered in battle. Well, he usually did not stay around to supervise *carrying out* such orders.

Orchestrating a bloody war on the vast plains of Russia, he was absolutely untouched by the unprecedented sufferings of her inhabitants, by her pain. He soared aloft, above it all, on the wings of the international intoxication of the Revolution.

The February Revolution was a *Russian* revolution: no matter how headlong, erroneous and pernicious it was, it did not aspire to *burn down* the entire pre-existing life, to annihilate the whole pre-revolutionary Russia. Yet immediately after the October [Bolshevik revolution], the Revolution spilled abroad and became an *international* and devastating plague, feeding itself by devouring and destroying social order wherever it spread — everything built was to be annihilated; everything cultivated — to be confiscated; whoever resisted — to be shot. The Reds were exclusively preoccupied with their grand social experiment, predestined to be repeated, expanded and implemented all over the world.

From an easy, quick blow, the October coup snowballed into a fierce three-year-long Civil War, which brought countless bloody calamities to all the peoples of Russia.

The multinationality of the former Empire and the cannon recoil from the Great War complicated both the inhumane Bolshevik plot and its implementation. Unlike the French Revolution, which unfolded on the territory of mono-national France and did not see much foreign intervention apart from a short incursion of hostile troops, and with all its horrors being a national affair from beginning to end, the Russian Revolution was horribly aggravated by its multinational madness. It saw the strong participation of Red Latvians (then Russian subjects), former German and Austrian prisoners of war (organized into full-blown regiments like the Hungarians), and even large numbers of Chinese.

No doubt the brunt of the fighting for the Reds was carried out by Russians; some of them were drafted on pain of death while others volunteered in a mad belief they would be fighting for a happy future for themselves. Yet the Russian Jews were not lost in all that diversity.

The politically active part of Russian Jewry, which backed the Bolshevik civic regime in 1917, now just as boldly stepped into the military structures of Bolsheviks. During the first years after the October Revolution in the midst of the internationalist frenzy, the power over this enormous land was effortlessly slipping into the hands of those clinging to the Bolsheviks. And they were overwhelmed by the newfound immensity of that power. They immediately began using it without a backward glance or any fear of control — some, without doubt, in the name of higher ideals, while others — in the name of lower ones ("obstinacy of fanaticism in some and ability to adapt in others"[1912]).

At that time, nobody could imagine that the Civil War would ignite enormous Jewish pogroms, unprecedented in their atrocity and bloodshed, all over the South of Russia.

We can judge the true nature of the multi-ethnic war from the Red pogrom during the suppression of the Kronstadt Uprising in March 1921. A well-known socialist-revolutionary and sociologist Pitrim Sorokin writes: "For three days, Latvian, Bashkir, Hungarian, Tatar, Russian, Jewish and international rabble, crazed by alcohol and the smell of blood, raped and killed without restraint."[1913]

Or here is another recollection from ordinary witnesses. During the feast of the Epiphany in 1918, an Orthodox Sacred Procession stirred forth from the gates of the Kremlin in Tula — and an "international squad" gunned it down.

Even with the ruthless international squads, the force of the "Red Guard" alone was no longer sufficient. The Bolshevik regime needed a regular army. In 1918, "Lev Trotsky, with the help of Sklyansky and Jacov

---

[1912] Г.А. Ландау. Революционные идеи в еврейской общественности // Россия и евреи: Сб. 1 (далее — РиЕ) / Отечественное объединение русских евреев за границей. Париж: YMCA-Press, 1978, с. 117 [1-е изд. — Берлин: Основа, 1924].
[1913] *Pitirim Sorokin.* Leaves from a Russian Diary. New York: E.F.Button & Co., 1925, p. 267.

Sverdlov, created the Red Army." "Many Jews were fighting in its ranks. Some units were entirely Jewish, like, for example, the brigade of Josef Furman."[1914] The Jewish share in the command corps the Red Army become large and influential and this trend continued for many years even after the end of the Civil War. This Jewish involvement has been researched by several Jewish authors and encyclopedias.

In the 1980s, Israeli scholar Aaron Abramovich used many Soviet sources (including *The Fifty-Year Anniversary of the Soviet Armed Forces*, *The Soviet Historical Encyclopedia*, volumes of *Directives of the Front Command of the Red Army*) to compile detailed nominal rosters of highly ranked Jewish commanders (exclusively Jewish ones) in the Red Army during the period from the Civil War up to the aftermath of Second World War.

Let's skim through the pages allocated to the Civil War.[1915] This is a very extensive roster; it begins with the Revvoyensoviet, where Abramovich lists L. Trotsky, E. Sklyansky, A. Rosengoltz, and Y. Drabkin-Gusev. Trotsky ordered the "establishment of fronts with headquarters, and formation of new armies," and "Jews were present in almost all the revvoyensoviets of the fronts and armies." (Abramovich lists the most prominent individuals: D. Vayman, E. Pyatnitsky, L. Glezarov, L. Pechyorsky, I. Slavin, M. Lisovsky, G. Bitker, Bela Kun, Brilliant-Sokolnikov, I. Khodorovsky). Earlier, at the onset of the Civil War, the Extraordinary Command Staff of the Petrograd Military District was headed by Uritsky, and among the members of the Petrograd Committee of Revolutionary Defense were Sverdlov (the chairman), Volodarsky, Drabkin-Gusev, Ya. Fishman (a leftist Socialist Revolutionary) and G. Chudnovsky. In May 1918 there were two Jews among the eleven commissars of military districts: E. Yaroslavsky-Gubelman (Moscow District) and S. Nakhimson (Yaroslavsky District). During the war, several Jews were in charge of armies: M. Lashevich was in charge of the 3rd — and later, of the 7th Army of Eastern Front; V. Lazarevich was in charge of the 3rd Army of the Western Front, G. Sokolnikov led the 8th Army of the Southern Front, N. Sorkin — the 9th, and I. Yakir — the 14th Army. Abramovich painstakingly lists numerous Jewish heads of staff and members of the revvoyensoviets in each of the twenty armies; then the commanders, heads of staff and military commissars of divisions (the list of the latter, i.e., those in charge of the ideological branch of command, was three-times longer than the list of Jewish commanders of divisions). In

---

[1914] Краткая Еврейская Энциклопедия (далее — КЕЭ). Иерусалим: Кетер, 1976. Т. 1, с. 686.

[1915] *Арон Абрамович*. В решающей войне: Участие и роль евреев СССР в войне против нацизма. 2-е изд. Тель-Авив, 1982. Т. 1, с. 45-61.

this manner Abramovich describes brigades, regiments and separate detachments. He lists Jewish heads of political administrations and revolutionary military tribunals at all levels, noting that "especially large percentage of Jews can be found among political officers at all levels of the Red Army...." "Jews played an important role in the provision and supply services. Let's name some of them...." "Jews occupied important positions in military medicine as well: heads of sanitary administrations of the fronts and armies, senior doctors of units and bodies of troops...." "Many Jews — commanders of large units and detachments — were distinguished for their courage, heroism and generalship" but "due to the synoptic character of this chapter we cannot provide detailed descriptions of the accomplishments of Jewish Red Army soldiers, commanders and political officers." (Meticulously listing the commanders of armies, the researcher misses another Jew, Tikhon Khvesin, who happened to be in charge of the 4th Army of the Eastern Front, then — of the 8th Army of the Southern Front, and later of the 1st Army of the Turkestan Front.[1916])

The *Russian Jewish Encyclopedia* provides additional information about some commanders. (Here I would like to commend this encyclopedia (1994), for in our new free times its authors performed an honest choice — writing frankly about everything, including less than honorable things.)

Drabkin-Gusev became the Head of Political Administration of the Red Army and the Chief of the entire Red Army in 1921. Later he was the head of IstPart (Commission on the History of October Revolution and Bolshevist Party) and a big figure in the Comintern, and was buried in the Kremlin wall [in Moscow].

Mikhail Gaskovich-Lashkevich was a member of many revvoyensoviets, and later he was in charge of the Siberian Military District, and even later — the First Deputy Chairman of the Revvoyensoviet of the USSR (yet he was buried merely on the Field of Mars [in St. Petersburg]).

Israel Razgon was the military commissar of the Headquarters of Petrograd Military District and participated in the suppression of the Kronstadt Uprising; later, he was in charge of the Red Army of Bukhara, suppressing the uprising in Central Asia; still later he worked in the Headquarters of the Black See Fleet.

Boris Goldberg was Military Commissar of the Tomskaya Guberniya, later of the Permskaya Guberniya, still later of the Privolzhskiy Military District, and even later he was in charge of the Reserve Army and was acknowledged as one of the founders of Soviet Civil Aviation.

[1916] Российская Еврейская Энциклопедия (далее — РЕЭ). 2-е изд., испр. и доп. М., 1997. Т. 3, с. 285.

Modest Rubenstein was Deputy Head of the Revvoyensoviet of the Special Army, and later he was head of political administration of an army group.

Boris Hippo was the Head of Political Administration of the Black Sea Fleet. (Later he worked in the political administrations of the Baltic Sea Fleet, the Turkestan Front, was the Head of Political Administration of the Central-Asian Military District, and later of the Caucasian Army.)

Michail Landa was a head of the political division of an army, later — Deputy Head of Political Administration of the entire Red Army, and still later Head of Political Administration of the Byelorussian and then of the Siberian Military Districts.

Lev Berlin was Commissar of the Volga Military Flotilla and later worked in the Political Administration of the Crimean Army and still later in that of the Baltic Fleet.[1917]

Yet how many outstanding characters acted at lower levels?

Boris Skundin, previously a lowly apprentice of clockmaker Sverdlov, Sr., successively evolved into the military commissar of a division, commissar of army headquarters, political inspector of front, and, finally, into Deputy Head of Political Administration of the 1st Cavalry Army.

Avenir Khanukaev was commander of a guerilla band who later was tried before the revolutionary tribunal for crimes during the capture of Ashgabat and acquitted, and in the same year of 1919 was made into political plenipotentiary of the TurkCommission of the All-Russian Central Executive Committee of the Soviet of People's Commissars on Kashgar, Bukhara and Khiva.

Moses Vinnitsky ("Mishka-Yaponchik") was a member of the Jewish militia squad in Odessa 1905, and later a gang-leader; he was freed from a hard labor camp by the February Revolution and became a commander of a Jewish fighting brigade in Odessa, simultaneously managing the entire criminal underworld of Odessa. In 1919 he was a commander of a special battalion and later he was in charge of an infantry regiment in the Red Army. His unit was "composed of anarchists and criminals." In the end he was shot by his own side.

Military commissar Isaiah Tzalkovich was in command of a composite company of the [Red] cadets during the suppression of the Kronstadt Uprising.[1918]

[1917] РЕЭ, т. 1, с. 122, 340, 404, 515; т. 2, с. 120, 126, 434, 511.
[1918] РЕЭ, т. 3, с. 61, 278, 305, 503.

We can see extraordinary Jewish women in the higher Bolshevik ranks as well.

Nadezda Ostrovskaya rose from the Head of Gubkom [Party Committee of a Guberniya, the highest executive authority in a guberniya] of Vladimir Guberniya to the post of the Head of Political Administration of the entire 10th Army.

Revekka Plastinina headed Gubrevkom and later the Gubkom of Archangel Guberniya.

Is it proper to mention here Cecilia Zelikson-Bobrovskaya, who was a seamstress in her youth, and became the Head of the *Military* Department of the Moscow Committee of the All-Russian Communist Party of Bolsheviks?[1919] Or take one of the Furies of the Revolution Eugenia Bosh (or her sister Elena Rozmirovich)?

Or another thing — the Soviets used the phrase "Corps of Red Cossacks."

Yet those were not Cossacks who embraced communist ideology but plain bandits (who occasionally disguised themselves as Whites for deception). Those "Cossack Corps" were made of all nationalities from Romanians to Chinese with a full-blown Latvian cavalry regiment. A Russian, Vitaly Primakov, was in command and its Political Department was headed by I. I. Minz (by Isaac Greenberg in the Second Division) and S. Turovskiy was head of the Headquarters. A. Shilman was the head of operative section of the staff, S. Davidson managed the division newspaper, and Ya. Rubinov was in charge of the administrative section of the staff.[1920]

Since we began particularizing let's look at the famous leaders of the Red Army, at those never-fading names: Vladimir Antonov-Ovseyenko, Vasily Blucher, Semyon Budyonny, Klim Voroshilov, Boris Dumenko, Pavel Dybenko, Aleksa Dundich, Dmitry Zhloba, Vasily Kikvidze, Epifan Kovtukh, Grigory Kotovsky, Philip Mironov, Mikhail Muravyov, Vitaly Primakov, Ivan Sorokin, Semyon Timoshenko, Mikhail Tukhachevsky, Ieronim Uborevich, Mikhail Frunze, Vasily Chapaev, Yefim Shchadenko, Nikolay Shchors. Why, couldn't they pull it off without Jews?

Or take hundreds and thousands of *Russian* generals and officers of the former Imperial Army, who served in the Red Army, though not in the political sections (they were not invited there), but in other significant posts. True, they had a commissar with a gun behind them, and many served on pain of execution of their hostage families especially in case of military failures. Yet they gave an invaluable advantage to the Reds, which

---

[1919] РЕЭ, т. 1, с. 144; т. 2, с. 354, 388-389.
[1920] Червонное казачество: воспоминания ветеранов: [Сб.] М.: Воениздат, 1969.

actually might have been crucial for the eventual victory of Bolsheviks. Why, "just about half of the officers of the General Staff worked for the Bolsheviks."[1921]

And we should not forget that initial and fatal susceptibility of many Russian peasants (by no means all of them, of course) to Bolshevik propaganda.

Shulgin flatly noted: "Death to the Bourgeois" was so successful in Russia because the smell of blood inebriates, alas, so many Russians; and they get into a frenzy like wild beasts."[1922]

Yet let's avoid going into another unreasonable extreme, such as the following: "The most zealous executioners in Cheka were not at all the 'notorious Jews,' but the recent minions of the throne, generals and officers."[1923]

As though they would be tolerated in there, in the Cheka! They were invited there with the only one purpose — to be executed. Yet why such a quick-temper? Those Jews, who worked in the Cheka, were, of course, not the "notorious Jews," but quite young and "committed" ones, with revolutionary garbage filling their heads. And I deem that they served not as *executioners* but mostly as interrogators.

The Cheka ("Extraordinary Commission," *Che-Ka*) was established in December 1917. It instantly gained strength and by the beginning of 1918 it was already filling the entire populace with mortal fear. In fact, it was the *Cheka* that started the *"Red Terror"* long before its beginning was officially announced on September 5, 1918. The Cheka practiced terror from the moment of its inception and continued it long after the end of the Civil War. By January of 1918, the Cheka was "enforcing the death penalty *on the spot* without investigation and trial." Then the country saw the snatching of hundreds and later thousands of absolutely innocent *hostages*, their mass executions at night or mass drowning in whole barges. Historian S. P. Melgunov, who himself happened to experience perilous incarceration in Cheka prisons, unforgettably reflected upon the whole epic story of the "Red Terror" in his famous book *"Red Terror" in Russia 1918-1923.*

"There was not a single town or a district without an office of the omnipotent All-Russian Extraordinary Commission [that is, the Cheka],

---

[1921] В.В. Шульгин. «Что нам в них не нравится…»: Об Антисемитизме в России [далее — В.В. Шульгин]. Париж, 1929, с. 145.
[1922] Там же, с. 157.
[1923] Б. Мирский. Чёрная сотня // Еврейская трибуна: Еженедельник, посвящённый интересам русских евреев. Париж, 1924, 1 февраля, с. 3.

which from now on becomes the main nerve of state governance and absorbs the last vestiges of law"; "there was not a single place (in the RSFSR [Russian Federation]) without ongoing executions"; "a single verbal order of one man (Dzerzhinsky) doomed to immediate death many thousand people." And even when investigation took place, the Chekists [members of the Cheka] followed their official instructions: "Do not look for evidence incriminating a suspect in hostile speech or action against Soviet power. The very first question you should ask him is about the social class he belongs to, and what is his descent, upbringing, education and profession. It is these questions that should determine the suspect's fate (the words of M. Latsis in the bulletin *Red Terror* on November 1, 1918 and in *Pravda* on December 25, 1918)." Melgunov notes:

"Latsis was not original here, he simply rephrased the words of Robespierre in Convent about the mass terror: 'To execute the enemies of the Fatherland, it is sufficient to establish their identities. Not punishment but elimination is required'." Directives from the center are picked up and distributed all over Russia by the *Cheka Weekly* and Melgunov cites the periodical profusely: "*Red Sword* is published in Kiev ... in an editorial by Lev Krainy we read: Old foundations of morality and humanity invented by the bourgeoisie do not and cannot exist for us'.... A. certain Schwartz follows: 'The proclaimed Red Terror should be implemented in a proletarian way... If physical extermination of all servants of Tsarism and capitalism is the prerequisite for the establishment of the worldwide dictatorship of proletariat, then it wouldn't stop us.'"[1924]

It was a *targeted*, pre-designed and long-term Terror. Melgunov also provides estimates of the body count of that "unheard-of swing of murders" (precise numbers were practically not available then). "Yet, I suppose these horrors ... pale into insignificance with respect to the number of victims if compared to what happened in the South after the end of the Civil War.

Denikin's [the general of the White army in command of the South Russian front] rule was crumbling. New power was ascending, accompanied by a bloody reign of vengeful terror, of mere retaliation. At this point it was not a civil war, it was physical liquidation of a former adversary." There were waves and waves of raids, searches, new raids and arrests. "Entire wards of prisoners are escorted out and every last man is executed. Because of the large number of victims, a machine-gun is used"; "they execute 15-16-years-old children and 60-years-old elders." The following is a quote from a Cheka announcement in the Kuban region: "Cossack villages and settlements, which give shelter to Whites and Greens [Ukrainian

---

[1924] С.П. Мельгунов. «Красный Террор» в России, 1918-1923. 2-е изд. доп. Берлин: Ватага, 1924, с. 43, 48, 57, 70-71, 72-73.

nationalists], will be destroyed, the entire adult population — executed, and all property — confiscated." After Wrangel [another White general] left, "Crimea was dubbed the Àll-Russian Cemetery'" (different estimates suggest the number of murdered as between 120,000 and 150,000).

"In Sevastopol people were not just shot but hanged, hanged by dozens and even by hundreds," Nakhimov Prospect [a major street] was lined with the corpses of the hanged ... people arrested on the streets and hastily executed without trial." Terror in the Crimea continued through 1921.[1925]

But no matter how deep we dig into the history of Cheka, special departments, special squads, too many deeds and names will remain unknown, covered by the decomposed remnants of witnesses and the ash of incinerated Bolshevik documents. Yet even the remaining documents are overly eloquent.

Here is a copy of a secret "Extract from the protocol of a meeting of the Political Bureau of the Central Committee of the All-Russian Communist Party of Bolsheviks" dated by April 18, 1919, obtained from the Trotsky archive at Columbia University.

"Attended cc.[comrades] Lenin, Krestinsky, Stalin, Trotsky.

Heard: ...3. Statement of c. Trotsky that Jews and Latvians constitute a huge percentage of officials in the front-line Chekas, front-line and rear area executive commissions and central Soviet agencies, and that their percentage in the front-line troops is relatively small, and that because of this, strong chauvinist agitation is conducted among the Red Army soldiers with certain success, and that, according to c. Trotsky's opinion, it is necessary to redistribute the Party personnel to achieve a more uniform representation of officials of all nationalities between front-line and rear areas.

Decided: To propose cc. Trotsky and Smilga to draft an appropriate Directive of the Central Committee to the commissions responsible for the allotment of cadres between the central and local Soviet organizations and the front."[1926]

Yet it is hard to believe that the meeting produced the intended effect. A contemporary researcher, the first who approached "the problem of the role and place of Jews (and other ethnic minorities) in Soviet machinery," studied declassified archive documents and concluded that "at the initial stage of activity of the punitive agencies, during thèRed Terror, national

---

[1925] Там же, с. 50, 99, 100, 105, 109, 113.
[1926] Columbia University, New York, Trotsky's Archive, bMs Russ 13 T-160, Дело: «Партийная переписка № 9 за 1919 г.», с. 9.

minorities constituted approximately 50% of the central Cheka apparatus, with their representation on the major posts reaching 70%."[1927] The author provides September 25, 1918 statistical data: among the ethnic minorities — numerous Latvians and fairly numerous Poles "– the Jews are quite noticeable, especially among "major and active Cheka officials," i.e., commissars and investigators.

For instance, among the "investigators of the Department of Counter Revolutionary Activities — the most important Cheka department — half were Jews."[1928]

Below are the service records of several Chekists of the very first call (from the *Russian Jewish Encyclopedia*).[1929]

Veniamin Gerson was in the Cheka from 1918, and from 1920 he was a personal referent to Dzerzhinsky.

Israel Leplevsky, a former member of Bund, joined the Bolsheviks in 1917 and worked in the Cheka from 1918; he was the head of the State Political Directorate [formed from the Cheka in 1922] of the Podolsk Guberniya and later of the Special Department of Odessa. And he climbed all the way up to the post of head of the OGPU [Joint State Political Directorate, the successor to the Cheka] of USSR! Later he occupied posts of Narkom of Internal Affairs of Byelorussia and Uzbekistan.

Zinovy Katznelson became a Chekist immediately after the October Revolution; later he was a head of special departments in several armies, and then of the entire Southern Front. Still later we can see him in the highest ranks in the Cheka headquarters, and even later at different times he was in charge of the Cheka of the Archangel Guberniya, the Transcaucasian Cheka, the North Caucasus GPU, the Kharkov GPU [another Cheka-successor secret police organization]; he also was deputy to the Narkom of Internal Affairs of Ukraine and deputy head of the entire GULag [that is, the government agency that administered the main Soviet penal labor camp systems].

Solomon Mogilevsky was chair of the Ivano-Voznesensk tribunal in 1917, then in charge of Cheka in Saratov. Later we find him again in an army tribunal; and after that he was in succession: deputy head of the Bureau of

---

[1927] *Л.Ю. Кричевский*. Евреи в аппарате ВЧК-ОГПУ в 20-е годы // Евреи и русская революция: Материалы и исследования / Ред.-сост. О.В. Будницкий. Москва; Иерусалим: Гешарим, 1999, с. 321, 344.

[1928] *Л.Ю. Кричевский*. Евреи в аппарате ВЧК-ОГПУ в 20-е годы // Евреи и русская революция, с. 327-329.

[1929] РЭЕ, т. 1, с. 106, 124, 223, 288; т. 2, с. 22, 176, 302, 350, 393; т. 3, с. 374, 473.

Investigations of the Moscow Cheka, head of Foreign Affairs Department of Cheka headquarters, and head of the Cheka of Transcaucasia.

Did Ignaty Vizner contemplate the scale of his actions when he investigated the case of Nicolay Gumilev? Not likely — he was too busy. He served in the Special Section at the Presidium of Cheka headquarters, he was the founder of the Bryansk Cheka, and later he was an investigator in the case of the Kronstadt Uprising and a special plenipotentiary of the Presidium of the Cheka-GPU on cases of special importance.

Lev Levin-Velsky, former member of the Bund [a Jewish socialist labor organization], was in charge of the Cheka of the Simbirsk Guberniya in 1918-1919, later of the Special Department of the 8th Army, still later of the Cheka of the Astrakhan Guberniya. Beginning in 1921, he was an envoy plenipotentiary of the central Cheka in the Far East, and later, from 1923, an envoy plenipotentiary of the OGPU in Central Asia. Still later, from the beginning of 1930, he worked in the Moscow OGPU. (And even later in his career he was deputy Narkom of Internal Affairs of the USSR.)

Or consider Nahum (Leonid) Etington: active in the Cheka beginning in 1919, later head of the Cheka of the Smolensk Guberniya; still later he worked in the GPU of Bashkiria; it was he who orchestrated the assassination of Trotsky.

Isaak (Semyon) Schwartz: in 1918-1919 he was the very first chair of the All-Ukranian Cheka. He was succeeded by Yakov Lifshitz who beginning in 1919 was the head of the Secret Operations Division and simultaneously a deputy head of the Cheka of the Kiev Guberniya; later he was deputy head of the Cheka of the Chernigov Guberniya, and still later — of the Kharkov Guberniya; and even later he was in charge of the Operative Headquarters of the

All-Ukrainian Cheka; still later, in 1921-1922, he ran the Cheka of the Kiev Guberniya.

Let's look at the famous Matvei Berman. He began his career in a district Cheka in the North Urals; in 1919 he was assigned as deputy dead of the Cheka of the Yekaterinburg Guberniya, from 1920 — head of Cheka of Tomsk Guberniya, from 1923 — of the Buryat-Mongolian Guberniya, from 1924 — Deputy Head of the OGPU of all of Central Asia, from 1928 — head of the OGPU of Vladivostok, from 1932 — head of the entire GULag and simultaneously a deputy Narkom of the NKVD [a successor organization to the Cheka, GPU and OGPU] (from 1936). (His brother Boris was in the State Intelligence Organs since 1920; in 1936 he served as deputy head of foreign intelligence section in the NKVD.) Boris Pozern, a commissar of the Petrograd Commune, substantially contributed to matching images of a Jew and that of a Chekist in people's minds; on

September 2, 1918, he co-signed the proclamation on "Red Terror" with Zinoviev and Dzerzhinsky. (The *Encyclopedia* missed one Aleksandr Ioselevich, secretary of the Petrograd Cheka, who had co-signed the Red Terror execution lists with Gleb Bokiy in September, 1918.)

Yet there were others, even more famous individuals. For instance, Yakov Agranov, a Chekist, phenomenally successful in conducting repressions; he invented "Tagantzev's Conspiracy" (through which he had killed Gumilev); he directed "cruel interrogations of participants of the Kronstadt Uprising." Or take notorious Yakov Blumkin, who participated in the assassination of the German ambassador in 1918; he was arrested and later amnestied, and then served in Trotsky's secretariat, and later — in Mongolia, Transcaucasia, the Middle East, and was shot in 1929.

And there were numerous personnel behind every Cheka organizer.... And hundreds and thousands of innocents met them during interrogations, in basements and during the executions.

There were Jews among the victims too. Those who suffered from the massive communist onslaught on the "bourgeoisie" were mostly merchants. "In the Maloarkhangelsk District, a merchant (Yushkevich) was placed on a red-hot cast-iron stove by members of a communist squad for failure to pay taxes."

(From the same source: some peasants, who defaulted on the surplus appropriation system, were lowered on ropes into water wells to simulate drowning; or, during the winter, they froze people into ice pillars for failure to pay revolutionary taxes. The particular sort of punishment depended on the imagination of the executioners.[1930]) Similarly, Korolenko described how two millers, named Aronov and Mirkin, were extrajudicially shot for not complying with absurd communist-mandated prices on flour.[1931] Or here is another example. In 1913, former Kiev Governor Sukovkin advocated innocence of Beilis [during Beilis' Trial]. When the Reds came, he was arrested. Thousands of Jews in Kiev signed a petition on his behalf, yet the Cheka had shot him nevertheless.

How then can we explain that the Russian populace generally regarded the new terror as "Jewish terror"? Look how many innocent Jews were accused of that. Why was the perception that Chekists and Jews were all but the same so widespread among both the Reds and the Whites alike and among the people in general? Who is responsible for that? Many. And the White Army is also responsible as we discuss below. Yet not the least among

---

[1930] С.С. *Мослов*. Россия после четырёх лет революции (далее *С.С.Маслов*). Париж: Русская печать, 1922. Кн. 2, с. 193.

[1931] *П.И. Негретов*. В.Г. Короленко: Летопись жизни и творчества, 1917-1921 / Под ред. А.В. Храбровицкого. Москва: Книга, 1990, с. 151-154, 232-236.

these reasons is because of the Chekists themselves, who facilitated this identification by their ardent service on the highest posts in Cheka.

Today we hear bitter complaints that it was not only Jews who clung to the power, and why any particular clemency should be expected from the Jewish Chekists? True. These objections, however, cannot alter the harsh certitude: the incredibly enormous power on an unimaginable scale had come into the hands of those Jewish Chekists, who at that time were *supreme*, by status and rank, representatives of Russian Jewry (no matter how horribly it sounds). And those representatives (again, *not elected* by their own people) were not capable of finding enough self-restraint and self-scrutinizing sobriety to come around, check themselves, and opt out. It is like the Russian cautionary proverb: "Ah, do not hurry to grab, first blow on your fingers" And the Jewish people (who did not elect those Chekists as their representatives), that already numerous and active city-dwelling community (weren't there prudent elders among them?) also failed to stop them: be careful, we are a small minority in this country! (Yet who listened to elders in that age?)

G. Landau writes: "Loss of affiliation with a social class overthrew the fine structure of Jewish society and destroyed the inner forces of resistance and even that of stability, sending even them under the chariot of triumphant Bolshevism." He finds that apart from the ideas of socialism, separatist nationalism, and permanent revolution, "we were astonished to find among the Jews what we never expected from them — cruelty, sadism, unbridled violence — everything that seemed so alien to a people so detached from physical activity; those who yesterday couldn't handle a rifle, today were among the vicious cutthroats."[1932]

Here is more about the aforementioned Revekka Plastinina-Maizel from the Archangel Guberniya Cheka: "Infamous for her cruelty all over the north of Russia..., [she] voluntarily 'perforated napes and foreheads'... and personally shot more than one hundred men." Or "about one Baka who was nicknamed à bloody boy' for his youth and cruelty" — first "in Tomsk and then as the head of the Cheka" of the Irkutsk Guberniya.[1933] (Plastinina's career carried her up right to a seat in the Supreme Court of RSFSR which she occupied in 1940s.[1934])

Some may recall the punitive squad of Mandelbaum in Archangel in the north of Russia, others — the squad of "Mishka-Yaponchik" in Ukraine....

[1932] Г.А. *Ландау*. Революционные идеи в еврейской общественности // РиЕ, с. 117-118.
[1933] *С.С. Маслов*, с. 196.
[1934] РЕЭ, т. 2, с. 388-389.

What would you expect from peasants in the Tambov Guberniya if, during the heat of the suppression of the great peasant uprising in this Central-Russian black-earth region, the dismal den of the Tambov Gubcom was inhabited by masterminds of grain allotments, secretaries of Gubcom P. Raivid and Pinson and by the head of the propaganda department, Eidman? (A. G. Shlikhter, whom we remember from Kiev in 1905, was there as well, this time as the chairman of the Executive Committee of the guberniya.) Y. Goldin was the Foodstuffs Commissar of the Tambov Guberniya; it was he who triggered the uprising by exorbitant confiscations of grain, whereas one N. Margolin, commander of a grain confiscation squad, was famous for *whipping* the peasants who failed to provide grain. (And he murdered them too.) According to Kakurin, who was the chief of staff to Tukhachevsky, a plenipotentiary representative of the Cheka headquarters in the Tambov Guberniya during that period was Lev Levin. Of course, not only Jews were in it! However, when Moscow took the suppression of the uprising into her own hands in February 1921, the supreme command of the operation was assigned to Efraim Sklyansky, the head of "Interdepartmental Anti-Banditry Commission," — and so the peasants, notified about that with leaflets, were able to draw their own conclusions.

And what should we say about the genocide on the river Don, when hundreds of thousands of the flower of Don Cossacks were murdered? What should we expect from the Cossack memories when we take into consideration all those unsettled accounts between a revolutionary Jew and a Don Cossack?

In August 1919, the Volunteer Army took Kiev and opened several Chekas and found the bodies of those recently executed; Shulgin[1935] composed nominal lists of victims using funeral announcements published in the reopened *Kievlyanin*; one can't help noticing that almost all names were Slavic ... it was the "chosen Russians" who were shot. Materials produced by the *Special Investigative Commission in the South of Russia* provide insights into the Kiev Cheka and its command personnel (based on the testimony of a captured Cheka interrogator)[1936]: "The headcount of thèChekastaff varied between 150 and 300 ... percentage-wise, there was 75% Jews and 25% others, and those in charge were almost exclusively Jews." Out of twenty members of the Commission, i.e., the top brass who determined people's destinies, fourteen were Jews. "All detained were kept either in thèCheka' building or in the Lukyanov's prison.... A special shed was fitted for executions in the building on Institutskaya St. 40, on the

---

[1935] В.В. Шульгин, Приложения, с. 313-318.
[1936] Чекист о ЧК (Из архива «Особой Следств. Комиссии на Юге России») // На чужой стороне: Историко-литературные сборники / Под ред. С.П. Мельгунова. Берлин: Ватага; Прага: Пламя, 1925. Т. 9, с. 111-141.

corner with Levashovskaya St., where the main 'Chekaóffice of the guberniya had moved from Ekaterininskaya St. An executioner (and sometimes àmateurChekists) escorted a completely naked victim into a shed and ordered the victim to fall facedown on the ground. Then he finished the victim with a shot in the back of the head. Executions were performed using revolvers (typically Colts). Usually because of the short distance, the skull of the executed person exploded into fragments.... The next victim was similarly escorted inside and laid down nearby.... When number of victims was exceeding ... the capacity of the shed, new victims were laid down right upon the dead or were shot at the entrance of the shed.... Usually the victims went to their execution without resistance."

This is what the "people were whispering about." Or take another incident, witnessed by Remizov (whom it is hard to suspect of anti-Semitism given his revolutionary-democratic past): "Recently there was a military training nearby, at the Academy, and one Red Army soldier said: 'Comrades, lets not go to the front, it is all because of Yids that we fight! And someone with a brief-case asked him: 'Which regiment are you from? And the soldier again: 'Comrades, let's not go to the front, it is all because of Yids!Ánd that one with a briefcase ordered: 'Shoot him!' Then two other Red Army soldiers came out and the first one tried to flee. But he didn't make it to the corner as others got him and shot him — his brain spilled over and there was a pool of blood."[1937]

The Kronstadt Uprising had distinctly anti-Jewish character (and so all the more was it doomed): they destroyed portraits of Trotsky and Zinoviev [both Jewish], but not those of Lenin. And Zinoviev didn't have guts to go to negotiate with the rebels — he would be torn into pieces. So they sent Kalinin [Russian].

There were labor strikes in Moscow in February 1921 that had the slogan: "Down with Communists and Jews!"

We have already mentioned that during the Civil War the majority of Russian socialists (and there were numerous Jews among them) were, of course, on Lenin's side, not on Admiral Kolchak's and some of them actually fought for the Bolsheviks. (For example, consider Bund member Solomon Schwartz: during the period of the provisional government, he was a director of a department in a ministry; during the Civil War he volunteered to the Red Army though he did not indicate his rank; later he emigrated abroad where he published two books about the Jewish situation in the USSR; we will cite him below.)

[1937] Алексей Ремизов. Взвихренная Русь. London: Overseas Publications, 1979, с. 376-377.

Thus it *looked* as though not only Bolshevik Jews, but all of Jewry had decided to take the Red side in the Civil War. Could we claim that their choice was completely deliberate? No. Could we claim that they didn't have any other choice? Again, no.

Shulgin describes the enormous exodus from Kiev on October 1, 1919 as the city was to be surrendered to Bolsheviks. It was an entirely Russian exodus, people were leaving on foot with knapsacks, across the bridges over Dnepr river; he estimated their numbers at around 60,000. "There were no Jews in this exodus: they were not noticeable among those many thousands of Russians (men, women and children), with bundles in their hands streaming across the beautiful Chain Bridge under a sorrowful net of rain." There were more than 100,000 Jews in Kiev at that time, Shulgin writes. And all of those rich and very rich Jews — they didn't leave, they chose to stay and wait for arrival of Bolsheviks. "The Jews decided not to share their fate with us. And with that they carved a new and possibly the deepest divide between us."[1938]

So it was in many other places. According to the testimony of socialist-revolutionary S. Maslov: "It is a fact that in towns and cities of southern Russia, especially in cities to the west of the Dnepr that changed hands repeatedly, the arrival of Soviets was most celebrated and the most of hollow sympathy was expressed in the Jewish quarters, and not infrequently only in those alone."[1939]

A contemporary American historian (Bruce Lincoln, author of a big treatise about our Civil War) "said that the entire Ukrainian Cheka was composed of almost 80% by Jews," that "can be explained by the fact that, prior to arrival of the Reds, cruel pogroms went on non-stop; indeed those were the bloodiest pogroms since the times of Bogdan Khmelnytsky [leader of the Cossack rebellion in Ukraine in 1648-1657]."[1940] We will discuss the pogroms soon, though it should be noted that the time sequence was actually the opposite: those 80% [Jews] were already staffing the Cheka in 1918, whereas the Petliura's [a Ukrainian publicist, writer, journalist who was head of state during the Ukrainian independence of 1918-1920] pogroms only gathered momentum during 1919 (the pogroms by White Army troops began in the fall of 1919).

Yet it is impossible to answer the eternal question who is the guilty party, who pushed it into abyss. Of course, it is incorrect to say that the Kiev

---

[1938] *В.В. Шульгин*, с. 95-96.
[1939] *С.С. Маслов*, с. 44.
[1940] Изложение беседы с Б.Линкольном см.: *В.Любарский*. Что делать, а не кто виноват // Время и мы: Международный журнал литературы и общественных проблем. Нью-Йорк, 1990, № 109, с. 134.

Cheka did what it did because it was three-quarters Jewish. Still, this is something that Jewish people should remember and reflect upon.

And yes, there were Jews then who appealed to their compatriots looking back on the tragedy that had befallen both Russia and Russian Jewry. In their proclamation *To the Jews of all countries!*, this group wrote in 1923 that "overly zealous participation of Jewish Bolsheviks in the oppression and destruction of Russia ... is blamed upon all of us ... the Soviet rule is identified with Jewish rule, and fierce hatred of Bolsheviks turns into the equally fierce hatred of Jews.... [We] firmly believe that Bolshevism is *the worst* of all evils possible for the Jews and all other peoples of Russia, and that to fight tooth and nail against the rule of that international rabble over Russia is our sacred duty before humankind, culture, before our Motherland and the Jewish people." [1941] Yet the Jewish community "reacted to these declarations with great indignation."[1942] (We will discuss it in the next chapter.)

The Civil War spilled over Russia's borders. Let's review that briefly (though the events in Europe are outside of the scope of this book).

The Bolsheviks invaded Poland in 1920. (At this point they had recalled and adroitly used the Russian "national longing and national enthusiasm" — as Nahamkis-Steklov put it in an *Izvestia* editorial.[1943]) And it appears that Polish Jews met the Red Army very warmly. According to a Soviet source, whole battalions of Jewish workers participated in the fighting at Minsk. [1944] Reading from the *Jewish Encyclopedia*: "on numerous occasions, Poles accused Jews of supporting the enemy, of ànti-Polish', 'pro-Bolshevistánd even 'pro-Ukrainianáttitudes." During the Soviet-Polish war many Jews "were killed [by Polish Army] on charges of spying for the Red Army." [1945] However, we should be wary of possible exaggerations here as we remember similar accusations in espionage made by Russian military authorities during the war, in 1915.

The Soviets quickly formed a revolutionary "government" for Poland headed by F. Dzerzhinsky. In it were Y. Markhlevsky and F. Kon. Of course, they were surrounded by "blood work" specialists and ardent propagandists.

(Among the latter we see a former pharmacist from Mogilev A. I. Rotenberg. Soon after the aborted Red revolution in Poland, he, together

---

[1941] РиЕ, с. 6, 7.
[1942] *Г.А. Ландау*. Революционные идеи в еврейской общественности // РиЕ, с. 100.
[1943] *Ю. Стеклов*. Народная оборона — национальная оборона // Известия, 1920, 18 мая, с. 1.
[1944] *Ю. Ларин*. Евреи и антисемитизм в СССР. М.; Л.: ГИЗ, 1929, с.31.
[1945] КЕЭ, т 6, с.646; т. 1, с. 326.

with Bela Kun and Zalkind-Zemlyachka, went on to conduct the deadly "cleansing" of the Crimea. In 1921 he participated in that glorious work again — this time "purging" Georgia, again under the direct command of Dzerzhinsky. At the end of 1920s Rotenberg was in charge of the Moscow NKVD.)

Not only Poland but Hungary and Germany as well were affected by the Red Revolution. An American researcher writes: "the intensity and tenacity of anti-Semitic prejudice in both the east and the center of Europe was significantly influenced by Jewish participation in the revolutionary movement." "In the beginning of 1919, the Soviets, under predominantly Jewish leadership, started revolutions in Berlin and Munich," and "the share of activist Jews was" disproportionately high in the German Communist Party of that period," though "that party's support in the Jewish community at large was not significant." Four out of eleven members of the Central Committee were Jews with a university education." In December 1918, one of them, Rosa Luxemburg, wrote: "In the name of the greatest aspirations of humankind, our motto when we deal with our enemies is: "Finger into the eye, knee on the chest!" Rebellion in Munich was led by a theater critic, Kurt Eisner, a Jew of "bohemian appearance." He was killed, but the power in conservative and Catholic Bavaria was seized by "a new government made up of leftist intellectual Jews, who proclaimed thèBavarian Soviet Republic'"(G. Landauer, E. Toller, E. Muhsam, O. Neurath) In a week the republic "was overthrown by an even more radical group," which declared the "Second Bavarian Soviet Republic" with Eugen Levine at the helm.[1946] Let's read an article about him in the *Encyclopedia*: born into merchant Jewish family, he used to be a socialist-revolutionary; he participated in the [Russian] revolution of 1905, later became German national, joined the "Spartacist movement" of R. Luxemburg and K. Liebknecht, and now he became the head of the Communist government in Bavaria, which also included the abovementioned E. Muhsam, E. Toller and a native of Russia, M. Levin.[1947] The uprising was defeated in May 1919. "The fact that the leaders of the suppressed Communist revolts were Jews was one of the most important reasons for the resurrection of political antiSemitism in contemporary Germany."[1948]

[1946] *Дж. Мюллер.* Диалектика трагедии: антисемитизм и коммунизм в Центральной и Восточной Европе // "22": Общественно-политический и литературный журнал еврейской интеллигенции из СССР в Израиле. Тель-Авив, 1990, № 73, с. 96, 99-100.
[1947] КЕЭ, т. 4, с. 733-734.
[1948] *Дж. Мюллер.* Диалектика трагедии... // "22", 1990, № 73, с. 99.

"While Jews played a "quite conspicuous" role in the Russian and German communist revolutions, their role in Hungary became central.... Out of 49 People's Commissars there, 31 were Jews," Bela Kun being the most prominent of them; "the foreign minister (de-facto head of government)," he would orchestrate a bloodbath in the Crimea half a year later. Here we find Matyas Rakosi, Tibor Szamuely, Gyorgy Lukacs. "Granted, the prime-minister was a gentile, Sandor Garbai, but Rakosi later joked that Garbai was elected because someone had to sign execution orders on Sabbath days." "Statues of Hungarian kings and heroes were knocked off their pedestals, the national anthem outlawed, and wearing the national colors criminalized." "The tragedy of the situation was escalated by the fact that historically Hungarian Jews were much wealthier than their Eastern-European countrymen and were much more successful in Hungarian society."[1949]

The direct relation between the Hungarian Soviet Republic and our Civil War becomes more clear by the virtue of the fact that special Red Army Corps were being prepared to go to the rescue of the Hungarian Soviet Republic, but they couldn't manage it in time and the Republic fell (in August 1919).

The breakdown of the universally hated Russian Empire cost all involved dearly, including the Jews. G. Landau writes: "In general, revolution is gruesome, risky and dangerous business. It is especially gruesome and dangerous for a minority, which in many ways is alien to the bulk of population.... To secure their wellbeing, such minority should unwaveringly cling to law and rely on unshakable continuity of social order and on the inertia of statutory power. Forces of revolutionary misalignment and permissiveness hit such a minority particularly hard."[1950]

It was looming — straight forward, into the so promising future! Yet in the near future, during the Civil War, there was no law and Jewry was hit by pillages and pogroms on the scale not even close to anything they experienced in days of the Tsar. And those pogroms were launched not by the White side.

Because of the density of the Jewish population in Ukraine, it was inevitable that a third force, apart from the Reds and Whites, would interfere in the Jewish destinies — that of Ukrainian separatism.

In April 1917, when the Ukrainian Rada [upper house of parliament] assembled for the first time, "Jewry ... did not yet believe in the victory of Ukrainian Nationalism," and that was manifested in the character of their

---

[1949] Там же, с. 100-101.
[1950] *Г.А. Ландау.* Революционные идеи в еврейской общественности // РиЕ, с. 115.

voting during municipal summer elections: Jews did not have "any reason" to vote for Ukrainian separatists.[1951] But already in June, when something resembling real independent Ukrainian governance was taking shape — under which apparently the Jews would have to live from now on — the Jewish representatives entered the Lesser [lower] Rada, and a Vice-Secretariat on Jewish nationality ("Jewish Ministry") was established. The latter worked on the long-cherished project of "Jewish National Autonomy" (according to which every nationality and now — the Jewish one, creates its own national union, which can legislate according to the needs and interests of their nation and for that it receives financial support from the treasury, and a representative of the union becomes a member of the cabinet). Initially, the formative Ukrainian government was generally benevolent toward Jews, but by the end of 1917 the mood changed, and the bill on autonomy was met in the Rada with laughter and contempt; nevertheless, in January 1918, it was passed, though with difficulties. For their part, the Jews reluctantly accepted "the Third Universal" (November 9, 1917, the initiation of Ukrainian independence from Russia) as now they feared anarchy, traditionally dangerous for Jewish populations, and were afraid of a split within Russian Jewry. Still, Jewish philistines were making fun of the Ukrainian language and shop-signs, were afraid of Ukrainian nationalism, and believed in the Russian state and Russian culture.[1952] Lenin wrote: Jews, like Great Russians, "ignore the significance of the national question in Ukraine."[1953]

However, everything pointed toward secession and the Jewish delegates in the Rada did not dare to vote against the Fourth Universal (January 11, 1918, on complete secession of Ukraine). Immediately thereafter, the Bolsheviks began an offensive against Ukraine. The first "Ukrainian" Central Committee of the Ukrainian Communist Party of Bolsheviks was formed in Moscow and later moved to Kharkov; it was headed by Georgiy Pyatakov and among its members were Semyon Schwartz and Serafima Gopner. When by the end of January 1918 they moved to Kiev, Grigory Chudnovsky took the post of the Commissar of Kiev, Kreitzberg became a commissar of finances, D. Raikhstein " press commissar, Shapiro — commissar of the army. "There was no shortage of Jewish names among the top Bolsheviks ... in such centers as Odessa and Ekaterinoslav. That was sufficient to fuel talks about "Bolshevik Jews" and "Jewish Bolsheviks" among the troops loyal to the Rada. Verbal cursing about

---

[1951] И.Б. Шехтман. Еврейская общественность на Украине (1917-1919) //Книга о русском еврействе*, 1917-1967 (далее — КРЕ-2). Нью-Йорк: Союз Русских Евреев, 1968, с. 22.
[1952] Там же, с. 29, 30, 35.
[1953] В.И. Ленин. Сочинения: В 45 т. 4-е изд. М.: Госполитиздат, 1941-1967. Т. 30, с. 246.

"traitorous Jews" became almost commonplace"; "in the very midst of street fighting [for Kiev], the Zionist fraction produced an official inquiry on the matter of anti-Jewish excesses." The question turned into a "verbal skirmish between Ukrainian delegates and representatives of national minorities."[1954]

Thus enmity split apart the Jews and the Ukrainian separatists.

"The Ukrainian government and the leaders of Ukrainian parties were evacuated to Zhitomir, but the Jewish representatives did not follow them," they remained under the Bolsheviks. And in addition, the Bolsheviks in Kiev were "supported by a sizable group of Jewish workers, who returned from England after the [February, Kerensky] revolution" and who now wholly siding with the Soviet regime ... took up the posts of commissars and ... officials," and created a "special Jewish squad of Red Guards."[1955]

Yet soon after the conclusion of the Treaty of Brest-Litovsk [in which the Soviets ceded Ukraine to the Central Powers] as the government of independent Ukraine returned to Kiev under the aegis of Austrian and German bayonets in the beginning of February of 1918, the "haidamakas" [spontaneous, popular uprisings against Polish rule that took place in Ukraine in the 18th century] and "free Cossacks" began snatching and shooting any former "Jewish commissars," they could find. Yet those were not actual Jewish pogroms, and very soon Petliura's government was replaced by the Hetman government of [Cossack leader] Skoropadsky for the next seven months. "The command of the units of the German Army that had occupied Kiev in the spring, treated the needs of Jewish population with understanding." (And that population was not-insubstantial: in 1919, 21% of Kiev's inhabitants were Jewish.[1956]) A Jewish Kadet [a member of Russian Constitutional Democrat Party] Sergei Gutnik became the Minister of Trade and Industry in the Hetman government.[1957] Under the Hetmanate, Zionists acted without hindrance, and an independent Jewish Provisional National Assembly and a Jewish National Secretariat were elected.

Yet Hetmanate fell and in December 1918 Kiev came under the control of the Directorate of Ukraine led by Petliura and Vynnychenko. The Bund and Poale-Zion [a movement of Marxist Jewish workers] did their best to help their fellow socialists of the Directorate and Jewish Secretariat and also made conciliatory moves. But Petliura saw it differently. His mouthpiece, the newspaper *Vidrodzhennya* wrote: "The birth of the

---

[1954] *И.Б. Шехтман*. Еврейская общественность... // КРЕ-2, с. 33-34.
[1955] *И.Б. Шехтман*. Еврейская общественность... // КРЕ-2, с. 35-37.
[1956] КЕЭ, т. 4, с. 256.
[1957] РЕЭ, т. 1, с. 407.

Ukrainian State was not expected by the Jews. The Jews did not anticipate it despite having an extraordinary ability of getting the wind of any news. They ... emphasize their knowledge of Russian language and ignore the fact of Ukrainian statehood ...

Jewry again has joined the side of our enemy."[1958] Jews were blamed for all the Bolshevik victories in Ukraine. In Kiev, the Sich Riflemen plundered apartments of wealthy people which *in masse* came over to the capital while the military and atamans [originally Cossack commanders, then used by the Ukrainian National Army] robbed smaller towns and shtetls. That year, a regiment named after Petliura inaugurated mass pogroms by pillaging the town of Sarny.

A Jewish deputy from the Lesser Rada attempted to ward off the growing tendency toward pogroms among Petliura's troops: "We need to warn Ukrainians that you cannot found your state on anti-Semitism. Leaders of the Directorate should remember that they are dealing with the world's people, which outlived many of its enemies" and threatened to start a struggle against such government.[1959] Jewish parties quickly began to radicalize toward the Left, thus inevitably turning their sympathies to Bolshevism.

Arnold Margolin, then Deputy Minister of Foreign Affairs of Ukraine, said that the situation in Ukraine was reminiscent of the worst times of Khmelnytsky and Gonta [Cossack leader against Polish occupation of Ukraine].[1960] D. Pasmanik bitterly noted that Zionists and Jewish nationalists supported the Directorate's government for a while even when anti-Jewish pogroms raged across Ukraine[1961] : "How could Jewish socialists forget about the pogromist attitudes of Petliura and other heroes of the Ukrainian Revolution".. How could they forget about the Jewish blood shed by the descendants and disciples of Khmelnytsky, Gonta and Zalizniak"[1962] "Between December 1918 and August 1919, Petliura's troops carried out dozens of pogroms, killing, according to the Commission of International Red Cross, around 50,000 Jews. The largest pogrom happened on February 15, 1919, in Proskurov after a failed Bolshevik coup attempt."[1963] "Jewish pogroms that went on non-stop from the very moment of Ukrainian independence became particularly ferocious during

---

[1958] И.М. Троцкий. Еврейские погромы на Украине и в Белоруссии 1918-1920 гг. // КРЕ-2*, с. 59.
[1959] Там же, с. 62.
[1960] Там же.
[1961] Д.С. Пасманик. Чего же мы добиваемся? // РиЕ, с. 211.
[1962] И.М. Бикерман. Россия и русское еврейство // РиЕ, с. 66-67.
[1963] КЕЭ, т. 6, с. 570.

the period of the so-called Directorate and kept going until the Ukrainian armed forces existed."[1964]

S. Maslov writes: "True, in the Tsar's times Jews were killed during pogroms but they have never had been killed in such numbers as now and with such callous indifference"; "sometimes during anti-Jewish pogroms by rebellious peasant bands the *entire* shtetls were exterminated with indiscriminate slaughter of children, women and elders."[1965] After the pogromists finished with their business, peasants from surrounding villages usually arrived on wagons to join in looting commercial goods often stored in large amounts in the towns because of the unsettled times.[1966] "All over Ukraine rebels attacked passenger trains and often commanded 'communists and Jews to get out of the coach and those who did were shot right on the spot"; or, checking papers of passengers, "suspected Jews were ordered to pronounce kukuruza [corn]) and those who spoke with an accent were escorted out and executed."[1967]

American scholar Muller thinks that "the mass extermination of Jews in Ukraine and Byelorussia during the Civil War was by no means a result of articulated policy but rather a common peasant reaction."[1968]

Independent rebellious bands of Grigoriev, Zelyony, Sokolovsky, Struk, Angel, Tyutyunik, Yatzeiko, Volynetz and Kozyr-Zirka were particularly uncontrolled and because of this acted with extreme atrocity. However, Nestor Makhno was different.

The raging Civil War provided fertile soil for the self-realization of Makhno's criminal and rebellious personality. We are not going to recount his villainous and clinically-mad deeds in this work, yet it should be noted that he did not harbor anti-Jewish attitudes and that his anarchist-communist followers loudly proclaimed their "implacable hostility toward any form of antiSemitism." At different times, a certain Aaron Baron was his Chief of Staff, Lev Zadov-Zenkovsky was his head of counter-intelligence, Volin-Eikhenbaum was head of Makhno's agitprop, Arshinov was his close adviser, and one Kogan headed Administration of Huliaipole [his "capital"]. There was even a 300-strong separate Jewish company among his troops, led by Taranovsky, and though at one point they betrayed Makhno, nevertheless Taranovsky was later pardoned and even made the Makhno's Chief of Staff. "The Jewish poor joined Makhno's army in masses" and allegedly Makhno trapped and executed ataman Grigoriev for

---

[1964] И.М. Бикерман. Россия и русское еврейство // РиЕ, с. 65.
[1965] С.С. Мослов, с. 25, 26.
[1966] Ю. Ларин. Евреи и антисемитизм в СССР, с. 40, 41.
[1967] С.С. Маслов, с. 40.
[1968] Дж. Мюллер. Диалектика трагедии... // "22", 1990, № 73, с. 97.

the latter's anti-Semitism. In March 1919 Makhno executed peasants from Uspenovka village for a pogrom in the Jewish agricultural colony Gorkoye. However, despite his indisputable pro-Jewish stance (later in emigration in Paris "he was always in a Jewish milieu" until his death), his often uncontrollable troops carried out several Jewish pogroms, for instance, in 1918 near Ekaterinoslav[1969] or in the summer of 1919 in Aleksandrovsk, though Makhno and his officers rigorously protected Jewish populations and punished pogromists with death."[1970]

To examine the anti-Jewish pogroms during the Russian Civil War, we consult a large volume *Jewish Pogroms: 1918-1921* compiled by Jewish Public Committee for Aid to Victims of Pogroms in 1923 and published later in 1926.[1971] (The year of publication explains why we find nothing about pogroms by the Reds — the book "aims to examine the roles of Petliura's troops, the Volunteer [White] Army, and Poles in the carnage of pogroms in the described period.")

Regular troops participated in pogroms in larger cities and towns as they marched, whereas independent bands acted in the hinterlands, thus effectively denying the Jews safety anywhere.

Pogroms by Petliura's troops were particularly atrocious and systematic and sometimes even without looting, such as, for example, pogroms in Proskurov, Felsztyn and Zhytomir in February of 1919, Ovruch in March, Trostyanets, Uman and Novomirgorod in May 1919. The worst pogroms by bands were in Smila (March 1919), Elisavetgrad, Radomyshl, Vapniarka and Slovechno in May 1919, in Dubovka (June 1919); by Denikin's troops — in Fastov (September 1919) and Kiev (October 1919). In Byelorussia, there were pogroms by Polish troops, for example, in Borisov and in the Bobruisk District, and by Polish-supported troops of Bulak-Balachowicz in Mazyr, Turov, Petrakov, Kapatkevitchy, Kovchitsy and Gorodyatitchy (in 1919, 1920, and 1921).

Ukrainian Jewry was horrified by the murderous wave of pogroms. During brief periods of respite, the Jewish population fled *en masse* from already pillaged or threatened places. There was indeed a mass exodus of Jews from shtetls and small towns into larger cities nearby or toward the border with Romania in a foolish hope to find aid there, or they simply "aimlessly fled in panic" as they did from Tetiiv and Radomyshl. "The most populous and flourishing communities were turned into deserts. Jewish towns and

---

[1969] В. Литвинов. Махно и евреи // "22", 1983, № 28, с. 191-206.

[1970] КЕЭ, т. 6, с. 574.

[1971] Еврейские погромы, 1918-1921 / Сост. З.С. Островский. М.: Акц. об-во «Школа и книга», 1926.

shtetls looked like gloomy cemeteries — homes burnt and streets dead and desolated.

Several Jewish townships were completely wrecked and turned into ashes — Volodarka, Boguslav, Borshchagovka, Znamenka, Fastov, Tefiapol, Kutuzovka and other places."[1972]

Let us now examine the White side. At first glance it may appear counter-intuitive that Jews did not support the anti-Bolshevik movement. After all, the White forces were substantially more pro-democratic then Bolsheviks (as it was with [White generals] Denikin and Wrangel) and included not only monarchists and all kinds of nationalists but also many liberal groups and all varieties of anti-Bolshevik socialists. So why didn't we see Jews who shared the same political views and sympathies there?

Fateful events irredeemably separated the Jews from the White movement. The *Jewish Encyclopedia* informs us that "initially many Jews of Rostov supported the White movement. On December 13, 1917 a merchant prince, A. Alperin, gave 800,000 rubles collected by the Jews of Rostov to A. Kaledin, the leader of Don Cossacks, 'to organize anti-Bolshevik Cossack troops."[1973] Yet when General Alekseev [another White commander] was mustering his first squadron in December 1917 in the same city of Rostov and needed funds and asked (note — asked and did not impress) the Rostov-Nakhichevan bourgeoisie (mainly Jewish and Armenian) for money, they refused and he collected just a dab of money and was forced to march out into the winter with unequipped troops — into his Ice March. And later "all appeals by the Volunteer Army were mostly ignored, yet whenever the Bolsheviks showed up and demanded money and valuables, the population obediently handed over millions of rubles and whole stores of goods."[1974] When former Russian prime minister (of the Provisional Government) prince G. E. Lvov, begging for aid abroad, visited New York and Washington in 1918, he met a delegation of American Jews who heard him out but offered no aid.[1975]

However, Pasmanik quotes a letter saying that by the end of 1918 "more than three and half millions rubles ... were being collected in the exclusive Jewish circle" with accompanying "promises and reassurances" of goodwill toward Jews from the White authorities. Despite that, Jews were officially prohibited to buy land in the Chernomorskaya Guberniya because

---

[1972] Еврейские погромы, 1918-1921, с. 73-74.
[1973] КЕЭ, т. 7, с, 403.
[1974] *Д.С. Пасманик*. Русская революция и еврейство: (Большевизм и иудаизм). Париж, 1923, с. 169.
[1975] *Т.И. Полнер*. Жизненный путь Князя Георгия Евгениевича Львова. Париж, 1932, с. 274.

of "vicious speculations by several Jews," though the order was revoked soon afterwards.[1976]

Here is another example from my own sources: again in Rostov in February 1918 when the White movement was merely nascent and seemed almost hopeless, an elderly Jewish engineer and manufacturer A. I. Arkhangorodsky, who sincerely considered himself a Russian patriot, literally pushed his reluctant student son into joining the White youth marching out into the night [February 22], embarking on their Ice March (however, his sister didn't let him go). The *Jewish Encyclopedia* also tells us that the "Jews of Rostov were joining Cossack guerilla squadrons and the student's battalion of [White] general L. Kornilov's army."[1977]

In Paris in 1975, Col. Levitin, the last surviving commander of the Kornilov Regiment, told me that quite a few Jewish warrant officers, who were commissioned in Kerensky's times, were loyal to Kornilov during the so-called "days of Kornilov" in August 1917. He recalled one Katzman, a holder of the Order of St. George from the First Kutepov Division.

Yet we know that many Whites rejected sympathetic or neutral Jews — because of the prominent involvement of *other* Jews on the Red side, mistrust and anger was bred among the White forces. A modern study suggests that "during the first year of its existence, the White movement was virtually free of anti-Semitism at least in terms of major incidents and Jews were actually serving in the Volunteer Army. However ... the situation dramatically changed by 1919. First, after the Allied victory [in WWI], the widespread conviction among the Whites that Germans helped Bolsheviks was displaced by a mythos about Jews being the backbone of Bolshevism. On the other hand, after the White troops occupied Ukraine, they came under influence of obsessive local anti-Semitism that facilitated their espousal of anti-Jewish actions."[1978]

The White Army "was hypnotized by Trotsky and Nakhamkis [an agent of the Bolshevik Central Committee] and that caused the identification of Bolshevism with Jewry and led to pogroms."[1979] The Whites perceived Russia as occupied by Jewish commissars — and they marched to liberate her. And given considerable unaccountability of separate units of that nascent and poorly organized army strewn over the vast Russian territories and the general lack of central authority in that war, it is not surprising that, unfortunately, some White troops carried out pogroms. "A. I. Denikin ...,

---

[1976] Д.С. *Пасманик*. Русская революция и еврейство, с. 176-177.
[1977] КЕЭ, т. 7, с. 403.
[1978] Г.В. *Костырченко*. Тайная политика Сталина: Власть и антисемитизм. М.: Международные отношения, 2001, с. 56-57.
[1979] Д.С. *Пасманик*. Чего же мы добиваемся? // РиЕ, с. 216.

like some other leaders of the South Army (e.g., V. Z. Mai-Mayevsky), endorsed Kadet [the Constitutional Democratic Party] and Socialist Revolutionary views and sought to stop the outrages perpetrated by his troops. Yet those efforts were not effective."[1980]

Naturally, many Jews were driven by survival instinct and even if they initially expected goodwill on the part of the Volunteer Army, after pogroms by Denikin's troops they lost any inclination to support the White movement.

Pasmanik provides a lively case. "Aleksandrovsk was taken by the Volunteers from the Bolsheviks. They were met by unanimous sincere joy of the citizenry.... Overnight half of the town was sacked and filled by the screaming and moaning of distressed Jews.... Wives were raped ... men beaten and murdered, Jewish homes were totally ransacked. The pogrom continued for three days and three nights. Post-executive Cossack cornet Sliva dismissed complaints of the Public Administration saying it is always like that: we take a city and it belongs to the troops for three days.'"[1981] It is impossible to explain all this plunder and violence by soldiers of the Volunteer Army by actions of Jewish commissars.

A top White general, A. von Lampe, claims that rumors about *Jewish pogroms* by the Whites are "tendentiously exaggerated", that these pillaging "requisitions" were unavoidable actions of an army without quartermaster services or regular supplies from the rear areas. He says that Jews were not targeted deliberately but that all citizens suffered and that Jews "suffered more" because they were "numerous and rich." "I am absolutely confident that in the operational theaters of the White armies there were no Jewish *pogroms*, i.e., no organized extermination and pillaging of Jews. There were robberies and even murders ... which were purposefully overblown and misrepresented as anti-Jewish pogroms by special press.... Because of these accidents, the Second Kuban Infantry Brigade and the Ossetian Cavalry Regiment were disbanded....

All the people, be they Christian or Jewish, suffered in disorderly areas."[1982]

There were executions (on tip offs by locals) of those unfortunate commissars and Chekists who did not manage to escape and there were quite a few Jews among them.

[1980] *Г.В. Костырченко*. Тайная политика Сталина, с. 56.
[1981] *Д.С. Пасманик*. Русская революция и еврейство, с. 185.
[1982] *Ген. А. фон Лампе*. Причины неудачи вооружённого выступления белых // Посев, 1981, № 3, с. 38-39 (перепечатка из: Русский колокол, 1929, № 6-7).

Events in Fastov in September 1919 appear differently. According to the *Jewish Encyclopedia*, Cossacks "behaved outrageously ... they killed, raped and flouted Jewish religious feelings (they had broken into a synagogue during Yom Kippur, beat up the whole congregation, raped the women and tore apart the Torah scrolls.) About one thousand were killed."[1983] A methodical quarter-by-quarter pillaging of Jews in Kiev after a brief return of the White troops in the end of October 1919 was dubbed the "quiet pogrom." Shulgin writes: "The commanders strictly prohibited 'pogroms.' Yet the "Yids" were really an annoyance and, secondly, thèheroes' were hungry.... In general, the Volunteers in large cities were starving." There were nights of plunder but without murder and rape. It was "the end of Denikin's period ... and the beginning of the agony of the Volunteer Army."[1984]

"By the route of its offensive and, particularly, its retreat," during its last brutal retreat in November-December of 1919, the White Army carried out "a large number of Jewish pogroms" (acknowledged by Denikin), apparently not only for plunder but also for revenge. However, Bikerman says that "murders, pillage and rape of women were not faithful companions of the White Army, unlike what is claimed by our [Jewish] National Socialists who exaggerate the horrible events to advance their own agenda."[1985]

Shulgin agrees: "For a true White, a massacre of unarmed civilians, the murder of women and children, and robbing someone's property are absolutely impossible things to do." Thus, the "true Whites" in this case are guilty of *negligence*. They were not sufficiently rigorous in checking the scum adhering to the White movement."[1986]

Pasmanik concurred that "everybody understands that General Denikin did not want pogroms but when I was in Novorossiysk and Ekaterinodar in April-May 1919, i.e., before the march to the north, I could sense a thickened and pervasive atmosphere of anti-Semitism everywhere."[1987] Whatever it was — negligence or revenge — it served well to ignite the "White" pogroms of 1919.

Still, "by unanimous testimony of those unlucky enough to experience both types of pogroms [those by Petliura's troops and those by White Army], it

---

[1983] КЕЭ, т. 6, с. 572.
[1984] В.В. Шульгин, с. 97-98.
[1985] И.М. Бикерман. Россия и русское еврейство // РиЕ, с. 64.
[1986] В.В. Шульгин. *с. 86.*
[1987] Д.С. Пасманик. Русская революция и еврейство, с. 186-187.

was predominantly Petliura's troops who went for Jewish life and soul — they did the most killing."[1988]

"It was not the Volunteer Army that initiated Jewish pogroms in the new Russia. They began in the "reborn" Poland the day after she become a free and independent state. While in Russia itself they were started by the Ukrainian troops of the Democrat Petliura and the Socialist Vynnychenko.... The Ukrainians turned pogroms into an everyday event."[1989].

The Volunteer Army did not start the pogroms but it carried on with them, being fueled by a false conviction that *all* Jews were for Bolsheviks. "The name of L. Trotsky was particularly hated among the Whites and Petliura's soldiers and almost every pogrom went under a slogan 'This is what you get for Trotsky.'" And even "the Kadets who in the past always denounced any expression of anti-Semitism, and all the more so the pogroms ... during their November 1919 conference in Kharkov ... demanded that Jews 'declare relentless war against those elements of Jewry who actively participate in the Bolshevist movement.'"

At the same time the Kadets "emphasized ... that the White authorities do everything possible to stop pogroms," namely that since the beginning of October 1919 "the leadership of the [Volunteer] Army began punishing pogromists with many measures including execution" and as a result "pogroms stopped for a while." Yet "during the December 1919-March 1920 retreat of the Volunteer Army from Ukraine the pogroms become particularly violent" and the Jews were accused "of shooting the retreating Whites in the back." (Importantly, "there were no pogroms in Siberia by A. Kolchak's troops," as "Kolchak did not tolerate pogroms."[1990])

D.O. Linsky, himself a former White Guard, emphatically writes: "Jewry was possibly given a unique chance to fight so hard for the Russian land, that the slanderous claim, that for Jews Russia is just geography and not Fatherland, would disappear once and for all." Actually, "there was and is no alternative: the victory of anti-Bolshevik forces will lead from suffering to revival of the whole country and of the Jewish people in particular.... Jewry should devote itself to the Russian Cause entirely, to sacrifice their lives and wealth.... Through the dark stains on the White chasubles one should perceive the pure soul of the White Movement.... In an army where many Jewish youths were enlisted, in an army relying on extensive material support from Jewish population, antiSemitism would suffocate and any pogromist movement would be countered and checked by internal forces.

[1988] Я.М. Бикерман. Россия и русское еврейство // РиЕ, с. 65-66.
[1989] Д.С. Пасманик. Русская революция и еврейство, с. 173-174.
[1990] КЕЭ, т. 6, с. 572-574.

Jewry should have supported the Russian Army which went on in an immortal struggle for the Russian land.... Jewry was pushed from the Russian Cause, yet Jewry had to push away the pushers." He writes all this "after having painful personal experience of participation in the White movement. Despite all those dark and serious problems that surfaced in the White movement, we delightfully and with great reverence bow our uncovered heads before this one and only commendable fact of the struggle against the ignominy of Russian history, the so-called Russian Revolution." It was "a great movement for the unfading values of [upholding] the human spirit."[1991]

Yet the White Army did not support even those Jews who volunteered for service in it. What a humiliation people like doctor Pasmanik had to go through (many Jews were outraged after finding him "among the pogromists")! "The Volunteer Army persistently refused to accept Jewish petty officers and cadets, even those who in October 1917 bravely fought against Bolsheviks. It was a huge moral blow to Russian Jewry." "I will never forget," he writes, "how eleven Jewish petty officers came to me in Simferopol complaining that they were expelled from fighting units and posted as ... cooks in the rear."[1992]

Shulgin writes: "If only as many Jews participated in the White Movement as did in the revolutionary democracy or in 'constitutional democracy' before that...." Yet only a tiny part of Jewry joined the White Guards ... only very few individuals, whose dedication could not be overvalued as the anti-Semitism [among the Whites] was already clearly obvious by that time. Meanwhile, there were many Jews among the Reds..., there, most importantly, they often occupied the top command positions'.... Aren't we really aware of the bitter tragedy of those few Jews who joined the Volunteer Army" The lives of those Jewish Volunteers were as endangered by the enemy's bullets as they were by the heroes of the rear' who tried to solve the Jewish question in their own manner."[1993]

Yet it was not all about the "heroes of the rear." And anti-Semitic feelings had burst into flames among the young White officers from the intellectual families — despite all their education, tradition, and upbringing.

And this all the more doomed the White Army to isolation and perdition.

Linsky tells us that on the territories controlled by the Volunteer Army, the Jews were not employable in the government services or in the OsvAg ("Information-Propaganda Agency," an intelligence and counter-

---

[1991] Д.О. Линский. О национальном самосознании русского еврея // РиЕ, с. 149-151.
[1992] Д.С. Пасманик. Русская революция и еврейство, с. 183.
[1993] В.В. Шульгин, с. 55, 81, 82.

intelligence agency, established in the White Army by General A.M. Dragomirov). Yet he refutes the claim that publications of OsvAg contained anti-Semitic propaganda and that pogromists were not punished. No, "the command did not want Jewish pogroms, yet ... it could not act against the pogromist attitudes of their troops... it psychologically couldn't use severe measures.... The army was not as it used to be, and requirements of the regular wartime or peacetime military charters could not be fully applied to it," as the minds of all soldiers were already battle-scarred by the Civil War.[1994] "Although they didn't want pogroms, Denikin's government didn't dare to denounce anti-Semitic propaganda loudly," despite the fact that the pogroms inflicted great harm on Denikin's army.

Pasmanik concludes: the Volunteer Army "generally assumed a hostile attitude toward the entire Russian Jewry."[1995] But I. Levin disagrees, saying that "the views of only one part of the movement, those of the active pogromists, are now attributed to the whole movement," while in reality "the White Movement was quite complex, it was composed of different factions ... with often opposite views."[1996] Yet to bet on Bolsheviks, to walk in their shadows because of fear of pogroms, is ... obvious and evident madness.... A Jew says: either the Bolsheviks or the pogroms, whereas he should have been saying: the longer the Bolsheviks hold power, the closer we are to certain death."[1997] Yet the "Judeo-Communists" were, in the parlance of the Whites, agitators as well.

All this was resolutely stopped by Wrangel in Crimea, where there was nothing like what was described above. (Wrangel even personally ordered Rev. Vladimir Vostokov to stop his public anti-Jewish sermons.)

In July 1920, Shulim Bezpalov, the aforementioned Jewish millionaire, wrote from Paris to Wrangel in the Crimea: "We must save our Motherland. She will be saved by the children of the soil and industrialists. We must give away 75% of our revenue until the value of ruble has recovered and normal life rebuilt."[1998]

Yet it was already too late....

Still, a part of the Jewish population of the Crimea chose to evacuate with Wrangel's army.[1999]

[1994] *Д.О. Линский.* О национальном самосознании русского еврея // РиЕ, с. 157, 160-161.
[1995] *Д.С. Пасманик.* Русская революция и еврейство, с. 181, 187.
[1996] *И.О. Левин.* Евреи в революции // РиЕ, с. 136.
[1997] *И.М. Бикерман.* Россия и русское еврейство // РиЕ, с. 81,82.
[1998] *Д.С. Пасманик.* Русская революция и еврейство, с. 181.
[1999] КЕЭ, т. 4, с. 598.

True, the White Movement was in desperate need of the support by the Western public opinion, which in turn largely depended on the fate of Russian Jewry. It needed that support, yet, as we saw, it had fatally and unavoidably developed a hostility toward the Jews and later it was not able to prevent pogroms. As Secretary of State for War, Winston Churchill "was the major advocate of the Allied intervention in Russia and military aid to the White armies." Because of the pogroms, Churchill appealed directly to Denikin: "my goal of securing the support in the Parliament for the Russian national movement will be incomparably more difficult," if the pogroms are not stopped.

"Churchill also feared the reaction of powerful Jewish circles among the British elite."[2000] Jewish circles in the USA held similar opinions [on the situation in Russia].

However, the pogroms were not stopped, which largely explains the extremely weak and reluctant assistance given by the Western powers to the White armies. And calculations by Wall Street naturally led it to support Bolsheviks as the more likely future rulers over Russia's riches. Moreover, the climate in the US and Europe was permeated by sympathy toward those who claimed to be builders of a New World, with their grandiose plans and great social objective.

And yet, the behavior of the former Entente of Western nations during the entire Civil War is striking by its greed and blind indifference toward the White Movement — the successor of their wartime ally, Imperial Russia. They even demanded that the Whites join the Bolshevik delegation at the Versailles Peace Conference; then there was that delirious idea of peace negotiations with the Bolsheviks on the Princes' Islands. The Entente, which did not recognize any of the White governments officially, was hastily recognizing all those new national states emerging on the periphery of Russia — thus unambiguously betraying the desire for its dismemberment. The British hurried to occupy the oil-rich region of Baku; the Japanese claimed parts of the Far East and the Kamchatka Peninsula. The American troops in Siberia were more of hindrance than a help and actually facilitated the capture of Primorye by the Bolsheviks. The Allies even extorted payments for any aid they provided — in gold from Kolchak; in the South of Russia, in the form of Black Sea vessels, concessions and future obligations. (There were truly shameful episodes: when the British were leaving the Archangel region in the Russian north, they took with them some of the Tsar's military equipment and ammunition. They gave some of what they couldn't take to the Reds and sunk the rest in the sea —

[2000] *Michael J. Cohen.* Churchill and the Jews. London; Totowa, NJ: Frank Cass, 1985, p. 56, 57.

to prevent it from getting into the hands of the Whites!) In the spring of 1920, the Entente put forward an ultimatum to the White Generals Denikin and Wrangel demanding an end to their struggle against the Bolsheviks. (In the summer of 1920 France provided some material aid to Wrangel so that he could help Poland. Yet only six months later they were parsimoniously deducting Wrangel's military equipment as payment for feeding of those Russian soldiers who retreated to Gallipoli.)

We can judge about the actions of the few occupational forces actually sent by the Entente from a testimonial by Prince Grigory Trubetskoy, a serious diplomat, who observed the French Army during its occupation of Odessa in 1919: "French policies in the South of Russia in general and their treatment of issues of Russian statehood in particular were strikingly confused, revealing their gross misunderstanding of the situation."[2001]

The black streak of Jewish pogroms in Ukraine ran through the whole of 1919 and the beginning of 1920. By their scope, scale and atrocity, these pogroms immeasurably exceeded all the previous historical instances discussed in this book — the pogroms of 1881-1882, 1903, and 1905. Yu. Larin, a high-placed Soviet functionary, wrote in the 1920s that during the Civil War Ukraine saw "a very large number of massive Jewish pogroms far exceeding anything from the past with respect to the number of victims and *number of perpetrators*."

Vynnychenko allegedly said that "the pogroms would stop only when the Jews would stop being communists."[2002]

There is no precise estimate of the number of victims of those pogroms. Of course, no reliable count could be performed in that situation, neither during the events, nor immediately afterwards. In the book, *Jewish Pogroms*, we read: "The number of murdered in Ukraine and Byelorussia between 1917 and 1921 is approximately 180,000-200,000.... The number of orphans alone, 300,000, bespeaks of the enormous scale of the catastrophe." [2003] The first Soviet Encyclopedia proposes the same number.[2004] The present-day *Jewish Encyclopedia* tells us that "by different estimates, from 70,000 to 180,000-200,000 Jews were killed."[2005]

Compiling data from different Jewish sources, a modern historian comes up with 900 *mass* pogroms, of which: 40% by Petliura's Ukrainian

---

[2001] *Кн. Гр. Н. Трубецкой*. Очерк взаимоотношений Вооружённых Сил Юга России и Представителей Французского Командования. Екатеринодар, 1919 // Кн. Гр. Н.Трубецкой. Годы смут и надежд. Монреаль, 1981, с. 202.
[2002] *Ю. Ларин*. Евреи и антисемитизм в СССР, с. 38.
[2003] Еврейские погромы, 1918-1921, с. 74.
[2004] Большая Советская Энциклопедия. 1-е изд. М., 1932. Т. 24, с. 148.
[2005] КЕЭ, т. 6, с. 569.

Directorate troops; 25% by the squads of the various Ukrainian "atamans"; 17% by Denikin's White Army troops; and 8.5% by the First Cavalry Army of Budyonny and other Red Army troops.[2006]

Yet how many butchered lives are behind these figures!

Already during the Civil War, national and socialist Jewish parties began merging with the Reds. The "Fareynikte" [the United Jewish Socialist Worker's Party] turned into the "ComFareynikte" [Communist Jewish Socialist Worker's Party] and "adopted the communist program and together with the communist wing of the Bund formed the [All-Russian] "ComBund" in June 1920; in Ukraine, associates and members of the Fareynikte together with the Ukrainian ComBund formed the "ComFarband" (the Jewish Communist Union) which later joined the All-Russian Communist Party of Bolsheviks.[2007] In 1919 in Kiev, the official Soviet press provided texts in three languages — Russian, Ukrainian and Yiddish.

"The Bolsheviks used these pogroms [in Ukraine] to their enormous advantage, they extremely skillfully exploited the pogroms in order to influence public opinion in Russia and abroad ... in many Jewish and non-Jewish circles in Europe and America."[2008]

Yet the Reds had the finger in the pie as well — and they were actually first ones. "In the spring of 1918, units of the Red Army, retreating from Ukraine, perpetrated pogroms using the slogan 'Strike the Yids and the bourgeoisie '"; "the most atrocious pogroms were carried out by the First Cavalry Army during its retreat from Poland in the end of August 1920."[2009] Yet historical awareness of the pogroms carried out by the Red Army during the Civil War has been rather glossed over. Only a few condemning voices have spoken on the topic. Pasmanik wrote: "During the first winter of Bolshevik rule, the Red troops fighting under the red banner carried out several bloody pogroms, most notable of which were pogroms in Glukhov and Novgorod-Siverskiy. By number of victims, deliberate brutality, torture and abuse, those two had eclipsed even the Kalush massacre. Retreating before the advancing Germans, the Red troops were destroying Jewish settlements on their route."[2010]

S. Maslov is also quite clear: "The march of the Budyonny's Cavalry Army during its relocation from the Polish to the Crimean Front was marked by

---

[2006] *Г.В. Костырченко*. Тайная политика Сталина, с. 56.
[2007] *И.Б. Шехтман*. Советская Россия, сионизм и Израиль // КРЕ-2, с. 321; КЕЭ, т. 6, с. 85; т. 1, с. 560.
[2008] *И.О. Левин*. Евреи в революции // РиЕ, с. 134.
[2009] КЕЭ, т. 6, 570, 574.
[2010] *И.М. Бикерман*. Россия и русское еврейство // РиЕ, с. 63.

thousands of murdered Jews, thousands of raped women and dozens of utterly razed and looted Jewish settlements.... In Zhytomyr, each new authority inaugurated its rule with a pogrom, and often repeatedly after each time the city changed hands again. The feature of all those pogroms — by Petliura's troops, the Poles, or the Soviets — was the large number of killed."[2011] The Bogunskiy and Taraschanskiy regiments stood out in particular (though those two having came over to Budyonny from the Directorate); allegedly, those regiments were disarmed because of the pogroms and the instigators were hanged.

The above-cited socialist S. Schwartz concludes from his historical standpoint (1952): "During the revolutionary period, particularly during the Civil War, ... anti-Semitism has grown extraordinarily ... and, especially in the South, spread extensively in the broad masses of the urban and rural population."[2012]

Alas, the resistance of the Russian population to the Bolsheviks (without which we wouldn't have a right to call ourselves a people) had faltered and took wrong turns in many ways, including on the Jewish issue. Meanwhile the Bolshevik regime was touting the Jews and they were joining it, and the Civil War was more and more broadening that chasm between Reds and Whites.

"If the revolution in general has cleared Jewry of suspicion in counterrevolutionary attitude, the counter-revolution has suspected all Jewry of being pro-revolutionary." And thus, "the Civil War became an unbearable torment for Jewry, further consolidating them on the wrong revolutionary positions," and so "they failed to recognize the genuine redemptive essence of the White armies."[2013]

Let's not overlook the general situation during the Civil War. "It was literally a chaos which released unbridled anarchy across Russia.... Anybody who wanted and was able to rob and kill was robbing and killing whoever he wanted.... Officers of the Russian Army were massacred in the hundreds and thousands by bands of mutinous rabble. Entire families of landowners were murdered ..., estates ... were burned; valuable pieces of art were pilfered and destroyed ... in some places in manors all living things including livestock were exterminated. Mob rule spread terror ... on the streets of cities. Owners of plants and factories were driven out of their enterprises and dwellings.... Tens of thousands people all over Russia were

---

[2011] *С.С. Маслов*, с. 26.

[2012] *С.М. Шварц*. Антисемитизм в Советском Союзе. Нью-Йорк: Изд-во им. Чехова, 1952, с. 14.

[2013] *Д.О. Линский*. О национальном самосознании русского еврея // РиЕ, с. 147, 148, 149.

shot for the glory of the proletarian revolution ...; others ... rotted in stinking and vermin-infested prisons as hostages.... It was not a crime or personal actions that put a man under the axe but his affiliation with a certain social stratum or class. It would be an absolute miracle if, under conditions when whole human groups were designated for extermination, the group named 'Jews remained exempt.... The curse of the time was that ... it was possible to declare an entire class or a tribe evil... So, condemning an entire social class to destruction ... is called revolution, yet to kill and rob Jews is called a pogrom? ... The Jewish pogrom in the South of Russia was a component of the All-Russian pogrom."[2014]

Such was the woeful acquisition of all the peoples of Russia, including the Jews, after the successful attainment of equal rights, after the splendid Revolution of March, 1917, that both the general sympathy of Russian Jews toward the Bolsheviks and the developed attitude of the White forces toward Jews eclipsed and erased the most important benefit of a possible White victory — the sane evolution of the Russian state.

[2014] И.М. Бикерман. Россия и русское еврейство // РиЕ, с. 58-60.

Chapter 17

Emigration between the two World Wars

As a result of the October coup and the subsequent Civil War, hundreds of thousands Russian citizens emigrated abroad, some retreating in battles, others simply fleeing. Among those emigrants were the entire surviving combat personnel of the White Army, and many Cossacks. They were joined by the old nobility, who were so strikingly passive during the fateful revolutionary years, although their wealth was precisely in land or estates. Many former landowners, who failed to take their valuables with them, upon arrival to Europe had to become taxi drivers or waiters. There were merchants, industrialists, financiers, quite a few of whom had money safely deposited abroad, and ordinary citizens too, of whom not all were well-educated, but who could not bear to stay under Bolshevism.

Many emigrants were Russian Jews. "Of more than 2 million emigrants from the Soviet republics in 1918-1922 more than 200,000 were Jews. Most of them crossed the Polish and Romanian borders, and later emigrated to the USA, Canada, and the countries of South America and Western Europe. Many repatriated to Palestine."[2015] The newly formed independent Poland played an important role. It had a large Jewish population of its own before the revolution, and now a part of those who left Poland during the war were returning there too.

"Poles estimate that after the Bolshevik revolution" 200-300 thousand Jews "arrived in Poland from Russia."[2016] (This figure could be explained not only by increased emigration, but also by the re-arrangement of the Russian-Polish border). However "the majority of the Jews who left Russia in the first years after the revolution settled in Western Europe. For

---

[2015] *Kratkaja Evreiskaja Entsiklopedija* [*The Short Jewish Encyclopedia* (henceforth—SJE)]. Jerusalem, 1996. v. 8, p. 294.
[2016] James Parkes. The Jew and his Neighbour: a Study of the Causes of Antisemitism. *Paris: YMCA-Press, 1932, p. 44.*

example, around 100,000 Russian Jews had gathered in Germany by the end of World War I."[2017]

"While Paris was, from the beginning, the political centre and unofficial capital of Russia-in-Exile., The second, so to say cultural capital of Russian emigration in Europe from the end of 1920 until the beginning of 1924, was Berlin (there was also an intense cultural life in the 1920s in the Russian quarters of Prague, which became ... Russia-in-Exile's main university city)."[2018] It was "easier to settle" in Berlin because of inflation. "On the streets of Berlin" you could see "former major industrialists and merchants, bankers and manufacturers,"[2019] and many émigrés had capital there. Compared to other emigrants from Russia, Jewish emigrants had fewer problems with integration into the Diaspora life, and felt more confident there. Jewish emigrants were more active than Russians and generally avoided humiliating jobs. Mihkail Levitov, the commander of the Kornilov Regiment who had experienced all sorts of unskilled labour after emigration, told me: "Who paid us decently in Paris? Jews. Russian multi-millionaires treated their own miserably."

Both in Berlin and in Paris "the Jewish intelligentsia was prominent – lawyers, book publishers, social and political activists, scholars, writers and journalists"[2020]; many of them were deeply assimilated, while Russian emigrants "from the capitals [Moscow and St. Petersburg]" mostly had liberal opinions which facilitated mutual amity between the two groups (unlike the feeling between Jews and the Russian monarchist emigrants). The influence of Russian Jews in the entire cultural atmosphere of Russia-in-Exile between the two world wars was more than palpable. (Here it is proper to mention a very interesting series of collections, *Jews in the Culture of Russia-in-Exile*, published in Israel in 1990s and still

---

[2017] D. Kharuv. *Evreiskaja emigratsija iz Rossiiskoj imperii i Sovetskogo Sojuza: statisticheskij aspect* [Jewish Emigration from the Russian Empire and Soviet Union: statistical aspect] // *Russkoe evreistvo v zarubezhje: Statji, publikatsii, memuary i esse* [Russian Jewry in Exile: Articles, Publications, Memoires, and Essays]. Jerusalem, 1998, v. 1 (6), p. 352.

[2018] Gleb Struve. *Russkaja literatura v izgnanii* [Russian Literature in Exile]. The 2nd edition. Paris, YMCA-Press, 1984, p. 24.

[2019] A. Sedykh. *Russkie evrei v emigrantskoj literature* [Russian Jews in the émigré Literature] // *Kniga o russkom evrejstve: 1917-1967* [The Book of Russian Jewry: 1917-1967 (henceforth — BRJ-2)]. New York: Association of Russian Jews, 1968, p. 426-427.

[2020] Ibid., p. 426.

continuing.[2021]) Some Jewish families with a comfortable income opened Russian artistic salons, clearly demonstrating Jewish attachment to and immersion in Russian culture. There was a famously generous house of the Tsetlins in Paris. Many others, I. V. Gessen's (in Berlin), I. I. Fondaminsky-Bunakov (tireless in his "endless, selfless cares for Russian culture abroad"[2022]),

Sofia Pregel, Sonya Delone, Alexander and Salomeia Galpern, were constantly engaged in the burdensome business of providing assistance for impoverished writers and artists. They helped many, and not just the famous, such as Bunin, Remizov, Balmont, Teffi, but also unknown young poets and painters.

(However, this help did not extend to "White" and monarchist emigrants, with whom there was mutual antagonism). Overall, among all the emigrants, Russian Jews proved themselves the most active in all forms of cultural and social enterprise. This was so striking that it was reflected in Mihail Osorgin's article, Osorgin wrote: "In Russia, there was not this 'Russian loneliness' neither in the social nor the revolutionary movement (I mean the depths and not just the surface); the most prominent figures who gave specific flavour to the whole movement ... were Slavic Russians." But after emigration "where there is a refined spirituality, where there is deep interest in thought and art, where the calibre of man is higher, there a Russian feels national loneliness; on the other hand, where there are more of his kin, he feels cultural solitude. I call this tragedy the *Russian loneliness*. I am not at all an anti-Semite, but I am primarily a Russian Slav... My people, Russians, are much closer to me in spirit, in language and speech, in their specific national strengths and weaknesses. For me, it is precious to have them as my fellow thinkers and peers, or perhaps it is just more comfortable and pleasant. Although I can respect the Jew, the Tatar, the Pole in the multi-ethnic and not at all "Russian" Russia, and recognise each as possessing the same right to Russia, our collective mother, as I have; yet I myself belong to the Russian group, to that spiritually influential group which has shaped the Russian culture." But now "Russians abroad have faded and given up and surrendered the positions of power to another tribe's energy. Jews adapt easier – and good

---

[2021] *Evrei v culture Russkogo Zarubezhja: Statji, publikatsii, memuary i esse* [*Jews in the Culture of Russia-in-Exile*: Articles, Publications, Memoires, and Essays]. In 5 volumes, Jerusalem, 1992-1996, complied by M. Parkhomovskij. See also *Russkoe evreistvo v zarubezhje: Statji, publikatsii, memuary i esse* [Russian Jewry in Exile: Articles, Publications, Memoires, and Essays]. Jerusalem, 1998, compiled and edited by M. Parkhomovskij.

[2022] Roman Gul. *Ya unes Rossiju* [I Have Carried Russia with Me]. New York, Most, 1984, v. 2: Russia in France, p. 99. *Russian Loneliness*, printed in the Russian Zionist magazine *Rassvet* [*Dawn*], re-established abroad by V. Jabotinsky.

for them! I am not envious, I am happy for them. I am equally willing to step aside and grant them the honour of leadership in various social movements and enterprises abroad.... But there is one area where this 'Jewish empowerment' strikes me at the heart – charity. I do not know who has more money and diamonds, rich Jews or rich Russians. But I know for certain that all large charitable organizations in Paris and Berlin can help poor *Russian* emigrants only because they collect the money needed from generous Jewry. My experience of organizing soirées, concerts, meetings with authors has proven that appealing to rich Russians is a pointless and humiliating waste of time....

Just to soften the tone of such an 'anti-Semitic' article, I will add that, in my opinion, the nationally-sensitive Jew can often mistake national sensitivity of a Slav for a spectre of anti-Semitism."[2023]

Osorgin's article was accompanied by the editorial (most likely written by the editor-in-chief Jabotinsky based on the ideas expressed and with a similar style) to the effect that M.A. Osorgin "has no reason to fear that the reader of *Rassvet* would find anti-Semitic tendencies [in his article]. There was once a generation that shuddered at the word 'Jew' on the lips of a non-Jew. One of the foreign leaders of that generation said: 'The best favour the major press can give us is to not mention us.' He was listened to, and for a long time in progressive circles in Russia and Europe the word 'Jew' was regarded as an unprintable obscenity. Thank God, that time is over." We can assure Osorgin "of our understanding and sympathy.... However, we disagree with him on one point. He gives too much importance to the role of Jews in charity among refugees. First, this prominent role is natural. Unlike Russians, we were learning the art of living in Diaspora for a long time.... But there is a deeper explanation.... We have received much that is precious from the Russian culture; we will use it even in our future independent national art.... We, Russian Jews, are in debt to Russian culture; we have not come close to repaying that debt. Those of us that do what they can to help it survive during these hard times are doing what is right and, we hope, will continue doing so."[2024]

However let us return to the years immediately after the revolution.

"Political passions were still running high among Russian emigrants, and there was a desire to comprehend what had happened in Russia.

[2023] M. Osorgin. *Russkoe odinochestvo* [Russian Loneliness]. Publication of A. Razgon. // *Jews in the Culture of Russia-in-Exile: Articles, Publications, Memoires, and Essays.* V. 1, p. 15-17. (Reprinted from *Rassvet*. Paris, January 15, 1925 (7)).

[2024] M. Osorgin. *Russkoe odinochestvo* [Russian Solitude]. // *Jews in the Culture of Russia-in-Exile.* V. 1, p. 18-19.

Newspapers, magazines, book publishers sprung up."[2025] Some rich men, usually Jews, financed this new liberal and more left-of-center Russian emigrant press. There were many Jews among journalists, newspaper and magazine editors, book publishers. A detailed record of their contribution can be found in *The Book of Russian Jewry* (now also in *Jews in the Culture of Russia-in-Exile*).

Of significant historical value among these are the twenty two volumes of I. V. Gessen's *Archive of the Russian Revolution*. Gessen himself, along with A. I. Kaminkov and V. D. Nabokov (and G. A. Landau after the latter's death), published a prominent Berlin newspaper *Rul* [*Steering Wheel*], "a kind of emigrant version of *Rech* [*Speech*]," but unlike Milyukov's brainchild, Josef Gessen's position was consistently patriotic. *Rul* often published articles by G. A. Landau and I. O. Levin, whom I have amply cited, and also articles by the famous literary critic U. I. Aikhenvald. The political spectrum of Berlin papers ranged from *Rul* on the right to the socialists on the left. A. F. Kerensky published *Dni* [*Days*], which provided a platform for such personalities as A. M. Kulisher-Yunius (author "of a number of sociological works" and a Zionist from Jabotinsky's circle), S. M. Soloveichik, the famous former Socialist Revolutionary O. C. Minor (he also wrote for the Prague *Volya Rossii* [*Russia's Will*]), and the former secretary of the Constituent Assembly M. V. Vishnyak. In 1921 U. O. Martov and R. A. Abramovich founded the *Socialist Gerald* in Berlin (it later moved to Paris and then New York). F. I. Dan, D. U. Dalin, P. A. Garvi, and G. Y. Aranson worked on it among others.

V. E. Jabotinsky, whose arrival in Berlin (after three years in Jerusalem) coincided with the first wave of emigration, re-established *Rassvet*, first in Berlin and then in Paris, and also published his own novels. In addition "many Russian Jewish journalists lived in Berlin in 1920-1923, working in the local and international emigrant press." There we could find I. M. Trotsky from the defunct *Russkoe Slovo* [*Russian Word*], N. M. Volkovyssky, P. I. Zvezdich (who died at the hands of Nazis during the World War II), the Menshevik S. O. Portugeis from the St. Petersburg *Den* [*Day*] (he wrote under the pseudonym S. Ivanovich), the playwriter Osip Dymov-Perelman, and the novelist V. Y. Iretsky.[2026]

Berlin also became the capital of Russian book publishing: "In 1922 all these Russian publishers released more Russian books and publications than there were German books published in the whole of Germany. Most

---

[2025] A. Sedykh. *Russkie evrei v emigrantskoj literature* [Russian Jews in the émigré Literature] // *BRJ-2*, p. 427.
[2026] Ibid., 429, 430.

of these publishers and booksellers were Jewish."[2027] Most notable were the publishing houses of I. P. Ladyzhnikov, owned since the war by B. N. Rubinstein (classical, modern and popular scientific literature), of Z. I. Grzhebin (which had links to the Soviets, and so sold some of his works in the USSR), the publishing house, *Word*, established as early as 1919 and run by I. V. Gessen and A. I. Kaminka (collections of Russian classics, emigrant writers and philosophers, valuable historical and biographical works), and the artistically superb issues of *Zhar-Ptitsa* run by A. E. Kogan. Also there was *Edges* of A. Tsatskis, *Petropolis* of Y. N. Blokh, *Obelisk* of A. S. Kagan, *Helicon* of A.G. Vishnyak, and *Scythians* of I. Shteinberg. S. Dubnov's *World History of the Jewish People* was also published in Berlin in ten German volumes, and during the 1930s in Russian in Riga.

Riga and other cities in the once again independent Baltic countries (with their substantial Jewish populations) became major destinations of Jewish emigration. Moreover, "the only common language that Latvians, Estonians and Lithuanians shared was Russian," and so the Riga newspaper *Segodnya* [*Today*] (publishers Ya. I. Brams and B. Yu. Polyak) became "highly influential." "A large number of Russian-Jewish journalists" worked there: the editor M. I. Ganfman, and after his death M. S. Milrud; *Segodnya Vecherom* [*Today Evening*] was edited by B. I. Khariton (the latter two were arrested by the NKVD in 1940 and died in Soviet camps). V. Ziv, an economist, and M. K. Aizenshtadt (under the pen names of first Zheleznov, then Argus) wrote for the newspaper. Gershon Svet wrote from Berlin. Andrei Sedykh (Y. M. Tsvibak) was its Paris correspondent, Volkovyssky reported from Berlin, and L. M. Nemanov from Geneva.[2028]

From the late 1920s, Berlin started to lose its position as the centre of emigrant culture because of the economic instability and the rise of Nazism. *Rul* had to close in 1931. Emigrants had dispersed with the "main wave going to France," especially to Paris which was already a major centre of emigration.

In Paris the main emigrant newspaper was *Poslednie Novosti* [*Breaking News*], founded " at the beginning of 1920 by the St. Petersburg barrister M. L. Goldstein. It was financed by M. S. Zalshupin," and in a year the newspaper was bought by "P. N. Milyukov.... While it was in a precarious position, the paper was significantly financially supported by M. M. Vinaver." "Milyukov's right hand" was A. A. Polyakov. Editorials and

---

[2027] I. Levitan. *Russkie izdatelstva v 20-kh gg. v Berline* [Russian Publishing Houses in Berlin in 1920s]. // *BRJ-2*, p. 448.

[2028] A. Sedykh. *Russkie evrei v emigrantskoj literature* [Russian Jews in the émigré Literature] // *BRJ-2*, p. 431, 432.

political articles were written by Kulisher-Yunius (who was arrested in 1942 in France and died in a concentration camp). The international news section was run by M. Yu. Berkhin-Benedictov, an acquaintance of Jabotinsky. The staff included the acerbic publicist S. L. Polyakov-Litovtsev (who had only learnt "to speak and write Russian at fifteen"), B. S. Mirkin-Getsevich (who wrote as Boris Mirsky), the noted Kadet [Constitutional Democrat] publicist Pyotr Ryss and others.

Poslednie Novosti published the satirical articles of I. V. Dioneo-Shklovsky and the popular science of Yu. Delevsky (Ya. L. Yudelevsky). The best humorists were V. Azov (V. A. Ashkenazi), Sasha Cherny (A. M. Gliksberg), the "king of humour" Don-Aminado (Shpolyansky). *Poslednie Novosti* had the widest circulation of all emigrant newspapers.[2029] Shulgin called it "the citadel of political Jewishness and philo-Semitic Russians."[2030] Sedykh regarded this opinion as an "obvious exaggeration." The political tension around the paper also stemmed from the fact that immediately after the Civil War it was dedicated to "disclosure" and sometimes outright condemnation of the Volunteer Army. Sedykh noted that in Paris "there was not only a political divide, but also a national one"; "Milyukov's editorial team included many Russian-Jewish journalists," while "Jewish names virtually never appeared on the pages of the right-wing *Vozrozhdenie* [*Rebirth*] (with the exception of I. M. Bikerman).[2031] (*Vozrozhdenie* was founded later than the other papers and ceased operation in 1927, when its benefactor Gukasov fired the main editor P. B. Struve.)

The leading literary-political magazine Sovremennye Zapiski [*Contemporary Notes*], published in Paris from 1920 to 1940, was established and run by Socialist Revolutionaries, N. D. Avksentiev, I. I. Fondaminsky-Bunakov, V. V. Rudnev, M. V. Vishnyak and A. I. Gukovsky. Sedykh noted that "out of [its] five editors ... three were Jews. In 70 volumes of the *Sovremennye Zapiski* we see fiction, articles on various topics and the memoirs of a large number of Jewish authors." *Illyustrirovannaya Rossia* [*Illustrated Russia*] was published by the St. Petersburg journalist M. P. Mironov, and later by B. A. Gordon (earlier the owner of *Priazovsky Krai*).[2032] Its weekly supplement "gave the readers 52 pieces of classic or contemporary emigrant literature each year."

[2029] Ibid., p. 431, 432-434.
[2030] V. V. Shulgin. "*Chto nam v nikh ne nravitsya...: ob antisemitizme v Rossii*" [What we don't like about them: on Anti-Semitism in Russia (henceforth – V. V. Shulgin]. Paris, 1929, p. 210.
[2031] A. Sedykh. *Russkie evrei v emigrantskoj literature* [Russian Jews in the émigré Literature] // *BRJ-2*, p. 432, 434.
[2032] Ibid., p. 435-436.

(The literary emigrant world also included many prominent Russian Jews, such as Mark Aldanov, Semyon Yushkevich, the already mentioned Jabotinsky and Yuly Aikhenvald, M. O. Tsetlin (Amari). However, the topic of Russian emigrant literature cannot be examined in any detail here due to its immenseness.)

Here I would like to address the life of Ilya Fondaminsky (born in 1880). Himself from a prosperous merchant family and married in his youth to the granddaughter of the millionaire tea trader V. Y. Vysotsky, he nonetheless joined the Socialist Revolutionaries (SRs) and "sacrificed a large part of his wealth and his wife's inheritance to the revolution"[2033] by buying weaponry. He worked towards the outbreak of the All-Russian political strike in 1905 and during the uprising he served in the headquarters of the SRs. He emigrated from Russia to Paris in 1906, where he became close to D. Merezhkovsky and Z. Gippius and developed an interest in Christianity. He returned to St. Petersburg in April 1917. In the summer of 1917 he was the commissar of the Black Sea Fleet, and later a delegate in the Constituent Assembly, fleeing after it was disbanded.

From 1919 he lived in Paris, France, during the period under discussion. He devoted much time and effort to *Sovremennye Zapiski*, including publication of a series of articles titled *The Ways of Russia*. He played an active role in emigrant cultural life and provided all possible support to Russian writers and poets. For a while he even managed to maintain a Russian theatre in Paris. "His passion, many-sidedness, energy and selflessness ... were without parallel among emigrants."[2034] He estranged himself from the SRs and joined Christian Democrats. Along with the like-minded G. P. Fedotov and F. A. Stepun he began to publish the Christian Democratic *Novy Grad [New City]*. "He grew ever closer to Orthodoxy during these years."[2035] "In June 1940 he fled Paris from the advancing German forces," but came back and was arrested in July 1941and sent to Compiegne camp near Paris; "by some accounts, he converted to Christianity there. In 1942 he was deported to Auschwitz and killed."[2036]

Between 1920 and 1924, the most important forum for purely Jewish issues was the Paris weekly, *Jewish Tribune*, published in both French and Russian with the prominent participation of M. M. Vinaver and S. B.

[2033] SJE, v.9, p. 253.
[2034] Roman Gul. *Ya unes Rossiju* [I Have Carried Russia with Me]. New York, Most, 1984, v. 2: Russia in France, p. 100.
[2035] Gleb Struve. *Russkaja literatura v izgnanii* [Russian Literature in Exile]. The 2nd edition. Paris, YMCA-Press, 1984, p. 230.
[2036] SJE, v.9, p. 255.

Pozner. It published articles by many of the aforementioned journalists from other newspapers.

Novoe Russkoe Slovo [*New Russian Word*] was founded in 1910 in the United States and added its voice from across the ocean. Its publisher from 1920 was V. I. Shimkin and the main editor (from 1922) was M. E. Veinbaum.

Veinbaum remembered: "The newspaper was often criticised, and not without reason. But gradually it earned the reader's confidence."[2037] (Its masthead now proudly boasts: "the oldest Russian newspaper in the world"; it is even two years older than *Pravda*. All the others have died out at various times, for various reasons.)

Right-wing or nationalist Russian newspapers appeared in Sofia, Prague, and even Suvorin's *Novoe Vremya* [*New Times*] continued in Belgrade as *Vechernee Vremya* [*Evening Times*], but they all either collapsed or withered away without leaving a lasting contribution. (The publisher of *Rus* in Sofia was killed.) The Paris *Vozrozhdenie* of Yu. Semenov "did not shirk from anti-Semitic outbursts"[2038] (but not under Struve's short reign).

Those who left soon after the Bolshevik victory could not even imagine the scale of inferno that broke out in Russia. It was impossible to believe in rumours. Testimonies from the White camp were mostly ignored. This changed when several Russian democratic journalists (the Constitutional Democrat (Kadet) A. V. Tyrkova-Williams, the socialist E. D. Kuskova (exiled from the USSR in 1922), and the escaped SR S. S. Maslov began to inform the stunned emigrant public about rapid growth of grass-root anti-Semitism in Soviet Russia: "Judeophobia is one of the most acrid features of modern Russia. Perhaps even the most acrid. Judeophobia is everywhere: North, South, East, and West. It is shared regardless of intellect, party membership, tribe, age.... Even some Jews share it."[2039]

These claims were at first met with suspicion by Jews who had emigrated earlier – what's the reason for this anti-Semitism? *The Jewish Tribune* initially rejected these claims: "generally, Russian Jewry suffered from Bolshevism perhaps more than any other ethnic group in Russia"; as to the "familiar identification of Jews and commissars" – we all know that it is the work of the [anti-Semitic] "Black Hundreds." The old view, that anti-Semitism resides not in the people but in Tsarism, began to transform into another, that the Russian people are themselves its carriers. Therefore,

---

[2037] A. Sedykh. *Russkie evrei v emigrantskoj literature* [Russian Jews in the émigré Literature] // *BRJ-2*, p. 443.

[2038] Ibid., p. 432.

[2039] S. S. Moslov. *Rossija posle chetyrekh let revolutsii* [Russia After Four Years of Revolution]. Paris: Russkaya Pechat [Russian Press], 1922, v. 2, p. 37.

Bolsheviks should be credited for the suppression of popular "Black Hundred" attitudes in Russia. (Others began to excuse even their capitulation at Brest [at which Russia ceded large amounts of territory to the Kaiser's German military]. The Jewish Tribune in 1924 dusted off even such argument: "the Russian revolution of 1917, when it reached Brest-Litovsk, prevented the much greater and more fateful betrayal planned by Tsarist Russia."[2040])

Yet the information was gradually confirmed; moreover, anti-Jewish sentiments spread over a large segment of Russian emigration. The Union for Russian Salvation (dedicated to crown prince Nikolai Nikolaevich) produced leaflets for distribution in the USSR in a manner like this: "To the Red Army. The Jews have ruled Great Russia for seven years...." "To Russian workers. You were assured that you would be the masters of the country; that it will be the 'dictatorship of the proletariat.' Where is it then? Who is in power in all the cities of the republic?" Of course, these leaflets did not reach the USSR, but they scared and offended Jewish emigrants.

S. Litovtsev wrote: "In the beginning of 1920s, anti-Semitism among emigrants became almost an illness, a sort of delirium tremens."[2041] But it was a broader attitude as many in Europe during the first years after the Bolshevik victory rejected and damned the Jews, so that "the identification of Bolshevism with Judaism became a widespread part of European thought. It is ridiculous to assert that it is only anti-Semites preach this social-political heresy."[2042] But could it be that the conclusions of Dr. Pasmanik were somehow premature? Yet this is what he wrote in 1922: "In the whole civilised world, among all nations and social classes and political parties, it is the established opinion now that Jews played the crucial role in the appearance and in all the manifestations of Bolshevism. Personal experience tells that this is the opinion not only of downright anti-Semites, but also ... that representatives of the democratic public ... reference these claims, i.e., to the role of Jews not only in Russian Bolshevism, but also in Hungary, Germany and everywhere else it has appeared.

At the same time, the downright anti-Semites care little for truth. For them all Bolsheviks are Jews, and all Jews are Bolsheviks."[2043]

[2040] B. Mirsky. *Chernaja sotnya* [The Black Hundred]. // *Evreiskaja tribuna: Ezhenedelnik, posvyashchenny interesam russkikh evreev* [The Jewish Tribune: A Weekly Dedicated to the Interests of Russian Jews]. Paris, February 1, 1924, p. 3.
[2041] S. Litovtsev. *Disput ob antisemitizme* [Debate on Anti-Semitism]. // *Poslednie Novosti*, May 29, 1928, p. 2.
[2042] D. S. Pasmanik. *Russkaja revolutsia i evreistvo: (Bolshevism i iudaizm)* [Russian Revolution and Jewry: Bolshevism and Judaism]. Paris, 1923, p. 9.
[2043] Ibid.

Bikerman wrote a year later: "Waves of Judeophobia now roll over nations and peoples, with no end in sight"; "not just in Bavaria or Hungary ... not only in the nations formed from the ruins of the once great Russia ... but also in countries separated from Russia by continents and oceans and untouched by the turmoil.... Japanese academics came to Germany to get acquainted with anti-Semitic literature: there is interest in us even on distant islands where almost no Jews live.... It is precisely Judeophobia – the fear of the Jew-destroyer. Russia's miserable fate serves as the material evidence to frighten and enrage."[2044]

In the collective declaration *To the Jews of the World!* the authors warn: "Never have so many clouds gathered above the Jewish people."[2045]

Should we conclude that these authors exaggerated, that they were too sensitive? That they imagined a non-existent threat? Yet doesn't the abovementioned warning about "anti-Semitic literature in Germany" sound very scary – in retrospect, from our historical perspective?

"The opinion that Jews created Bolshevism" was already so widespread in Europe (this was the "*average* opinion of French and English philistines," Pasmanik notes) that it was supported even by Plekhanov's son-in-law, George Bato, who claims in his book [2046] that Jews are inherently revolutionaries: "as Judaism preaches an ideal of social justice on earth ... it has to support revolution." Pasmanik cites Bato: "Over the centuries ... Jews have always been against the established order.... This does not mean that Jews carried out all revolutions, or that they were always the sole or even main instigators; they help the revolutions and participate in them"; "One can responsibly claim, as many Russian patriots, often from very progressive circles, do, that Russia now agonizes under the power of Jewish dictatorship and Jewish terror"; "Impartial analysis of the worldwide situation shows the rebirth of anti-Semitism, not so much against Jews as individuals, as against the manifestations of the Jewish spirit."[2047] The Englishman Hilaire Belloc[2048] similarly wrote about "the Jewish character of Bolshevik revolution," or simply: "the Jewish revolution in Russia." Pasmanik adds that "anyone who has lived in England recently knows that Belloc's opinion is not marginal." The books

---

[2044] I. M. Bikerman. *Rossija i russkoe evreistvo* [Russia and Russian Jewry]. // Rossiya i evrei: Otechestvennoe objedinenie russkikh evreev za granitsei [Russia and Jews: Expatriate Society of Russian Jews in Exile (henceforth— *RJ*)]. Paris, YMCA-Press, 1978, p. 11-12 [The 1st Edition: Berlin, Osnova, 1924].
[2045] *To the Jews of the World!* // RJ, p. 6.
[2046] Georges Batault. Le problème juif. Sedition, Paris, 1921.
[2047] D. S. Pasmanik. *Russkaja revolutsia i evreistvo: (Bolshevism i iudaizm)* [Russian Revolution and Jewry: Bolshevism and Judaism]. Paris, 1923, p. 15-16, 95.
[2048] Hilaire Belloc. The Jews. London, 1922.

of both authors (Bato and Belloc) "are enormously popular with the public"; "journalists all over the world argue that all the destructive ideas of the past hundred years are spread by Jews, through precisely Judaism."[2049]

"We must defend ourselves," Pasmanik writes, "because we cannot deny obvious facts.... We cannot just declare that the Jewish people are not to blame for the acts of this or that individual Jew.... Our goal ... is not only an argument with anti-Semites, but also a struggle with Bolshevism ... not only to parry blows, but to inflict them on those proclaiming the Kingdom of Ham.... To fight against Ham is the duty of Japheth and Shem, and of Helenes, and Hebrews." Where should we look for the real roots of Bolshevism?

"Bolshevism is primarily an anti-cultural force ... it is both a Russian and a global problem, and not the machination of the notorious 'Elders of Zion.'"[2050]

The Jews acutely realized the need to "defend themselves" in part because the post-war Europe and America were flooded with *Protocols of the Elders of Zion*, suddenly and virtually instantly. These were five editions in England in 1920, several editions in both Germany and France; half a million copies in America were printed by Henry Ford. "The unheard-of success of the *Protocols*, which were translated into several languages, showed how much the Bolshevik revolution was believed to be Jewish.[2051]" English researcher Norman Cohn wrote: "in the years immediately after the World War I, when the *Protocols* entered mainstream and thundered across the world, many otherwise entirely sensible people took them completely seriously."[2052] The London *Times* and *Morning Post* of that time vouched for their authenticity, although by August 1921 the *Times* published a series of articles from its Istanbul correspondent, Philipp Greaves, who sensationally demonstrated the extensive borrowing of the text in the *Protocols* from Maurice Jolie's anti-Napoleon III pamphlets (*The Dialogue in Hell between Machiavelli and Montesquieu*, 1864). At that time the French police managed to confiscate every single copy of the infamous pamphlet.

[2049] D. S. Pasmanik. *Russkaja revolutsia i evreistvo: (Bolshevism i iudaizm)* [Russian Revolution and Jewry: Bolshevism and Judaism]. Paris, 1923, p. 16, 78.
[2050] Ibid., p. 11-13.
[2051] M. Daursky. *Ideologiya national-bolshevizma* [Ideology of National Bolshevism]. Paris. YMCA-Press, 1980, p. 195.
[2052] Norman Cohn. *Warrant for Genocide: The Myth of the Jewish World Conspiracy and the "Protocols of the Elders of Zion"*. Russian translation. Moscow, Progress, 1990, p. 24.

The *Protocols* came to the West from a Russia overtaken by the Civil War.

A journalistic fraud produced in the early 20th century (in 1900 or 1901), the *Protocols* were first published in 1903 in St. Petersburg. The mastermind behind them is thought to be P. I. Rachkovsky, the 1884-1902 head of the Foreign Intelligence unit of the Police Department; their production is attributed to Matvei Golovinsky, a secret agent from 1892 and son of V. A. Golovinsky, who was a member of Petrashevsky Circle. [The latter was a Russian literary discussion group of progressive-minded commoner-intellectuals in St. Petersburg organized by Mikhail Petrashevsky, a follower of the French utopian socialist Charles Fourier. Among the members were writers, teachers, students, minor government officials, army officers. While differing in political views, most of them were opponents of the Tsarist autocracy and the Russian serfdom.

Among those connected to the circle were writers Dostoyevsky]. (Still, new theories about the origin of the *Protocols* appear all the time). Although the *Protocols* were published and re-published in 1905, 1906, 1911, they had little success in pre-revolutionary Russia: "they did not find broad support in Russian society.... The Court did not give support to distribution either."[2053] After many failed attempts, the *Protocols* were finally presented to Nicholas II in 1906 and he was very impressed. His notes on the margins of the book included: "What a foresight!', 'What precise execution!', "It is definitely them who orchestrated the [revolutionary] events of 1905!', 'There can be no doubt about their authenticity.' But when the right-wing activists suggested using the *Protocols* for the defence of the monarchy, Prime Minister P. A. Stolypin ordered a secret investigation into their origins. It showed they were a definite fabrication. The monarch was shocked by Stolypin's report, but wrote firmly: "remove the *Protocols* from circulation. You cannot defend a noble cause with dirty means."[2054] And since then "Russia's rulers' dismissal of the *Protocols of the Elders of Zion* came into force: no reference to the 'Protocols' was allowed ...even during the Beilis Trial."[2055]

[2053] SJE, v.6, p. 846.
[2054] This information was obtained by V. L. Burtsev in 1934 from General K. I. Globachev, the former head of St. Petersburg Guard Department (from February 1915 until March 1917). Burtsev published this information in 1938 in Paris in his study of the *Protocols of the Elders of* Zion. See V. L. Burtsev. *V pogone za provokatorami.* "Protokoly sionskikh mudretsov" – *dokazanny podlog* [Chasing the Provocateurs. Protocols of the Elders of Z ion is a proven forgery]. Foreword by Yu. V. Davydov, annotation by L. G. Aronov. Moscow, 1991.
[2055] SJE, v.6, p. 847.

However "1918 changed everything for the *Protocols*.[2056]" After the Bolsheviks seized power, after the murder of the royal family and the beginning of the Civil War, the popularity of the *Protocols* surged. They were printed and re-printed by the OsvAg [White Army counter-intelligence agency in the South of Russia] in Novocherkassk, Kharkov, Rostov-on-Don, Omsk, Khabarovsk, Vladivostok, and were widely circulated among both the Volunteer Army and the population (and later Russian emigrants, especially in Sofia and Belgrade).

"After the Bolshevik victory the selling of *Protocols* was banned in Russia" and become a criminal offence, but "in Europe the *Protocols* brought in by the White emigration played an ominous role in the development of right-wing ideology, especially National Socialism in Germany."[2057]

Exposure of the *Protocols* as forgery, and general denial of identity between Bolsheviks and Jews constituted a major share of liberal emigrant journalism of the 1920s and 1930s. We see several prominent Russians there: Milyukov, Rodichev, Burtsev and Kartashev.

A.V. Kartashev, historian of religion, Orthodox theologian and at the same time, a public figure, wrote about the unacceptability of anti-Semitism for a Christian in the pre-revolutionary collection *Shchit* [Shield],[2058] which I have often cited. In 1922, in emigration, he wrote the foreword to Yu. Delevsky's book on the *Protocols*.[2059] In 1937 Burtsev too asked him to write a foreword for his book. Kartashev wrote in it: "A man with common sense, good will and a little scientific discipline cannot even discuss the authenticity of this police and journalistic forgery, though certainly a talented forgery, able to infect the ignorant.... It's unfair to continue supporting this obvious deceit after it has been so unambiguously exposed. Yet it is equally unfair to do the opposite, to exploit the easy victory over the *Protocols* authenticity to dismiss legitimate concerns.... A half-truth is a lie. The whole truth is that the Jewish question is posed before the world as one of the tragic questions of history. And it cannot be resolved either by savage pogroms, or by libel and lies, but only by honest and open efforts of all mankind. Pogroms and slander make a sensible and honest raising of the question more difficult, degrading it to outright stupidity and absurdity. They confuse the Jews themselves, who constantly emphasize their

---

[2056] Ibid.
[2057] SJE, v.6, p. 848.
[2058] A. V. Kartashev. *Izbrannye i pomilovannye* [The Chosen and the Pardoned]. // *Sheet: Literaturny sbornik* [Shield: Literary Collection]. Edited by L. Andreev, M. Gorky and F. Sologub. The 3rd Enlarged Edition. Moscow, Russian Society on Study of Jewish Life, 1916, p. 110-115.
[2059] *Yu. Delevsky. Protokoly sionskikh mudretsov: istorija odnogo podloga [Protocols of the Elders of Z ion: the History of a Forgery]. Berlin, 1923.*

'oppressed innocence' and expect from everybody else nothing but sympathy and some sort of obligatory Judeophilia." Kartashev certainly regarded debunking of this "sensational apocrypha" as a "moral duty," but also thought that "in washing out the dust of *Protocols* from the eyes of the ignorant, it is unacceptable to impair their vision anew by pretending that this obliterates the Jewish question itself."[2060]

Indeed, the "Jewish question" cannot be removed by either books or articles. Consider the new reality faced in the 1920s by Jews in the Baltic countries and Poland. In Baltics, although "Jews managed to maintain for a while their influential position in trade and industry"[2061] they felt social pressure.

"A good half of Russian Jewry lived in the newly independent states.... New states trumpet their nationalism all the louder the less secure they feel."[2062]

There "Jews feel themselves besieged by a hostile, energetic and restless popular environment. One day, it is demanded that there be no more Jews percentage-wise in the institutions of higher learning than in the army ... the next, the air of everyday life becomes so tense and stressful that Jews can no longer breathe.... In the self-determined nations, the war against Jews is waged by the society itself: by students, military, political parties, and ordinary people." I. Bikerman concluded that "in leading the charge for self-determination, Jews were preparing the ground for their own oppression by virtue of higher dependence on the alien society."[2063] "The situation of Jews in Latvia, Estonia and Lithuania is literally tragic. Yesterday's oppressed are today's oppressors, what is more – extremely uncouth oppressors, entirely unashamed of their lack of culture."[2064]

So it transpired "that the breakup of Russia also meant the breakup of Russian Jewry" as the history paradoxically showed that the Jews were

---

[2060] State Archive of the Russian Federation, fonds 5802, catalog 1, file 31, p. 417-421. The foreword by A. V. Kartashev was not published by V. L. Burtsev in 1938 but was preserved among his papers. We discovered the fact of existence of this foreword from the article of O. Budnitsky *"Evreiskij vopros" v emigranskoj publitsistike 1920-1930-kh* ["The Jewish Question" in Emigrant Journalism of 1920-1930s]. // *Evrei i russkaja revolutsia: Materialy i issledovanija* [Jews and the Russian Revolution: Materials and Studies]. Edited by O. V. Budnitsky; Moscow, Jerusalem. Gesharim, 1999.

[2061] I. Gar. *Evrei v Pribaltijskikh stranakh pod nemetskoj okkupatsiej* [Jews in the Baltic countries under German Occupation]. // *BRJ-2*, p. 95.

[2062] To the Jews of the World! // *RJ*, p. 6.

[2063] I. M. Bikerman. *Rossija i russkoe evreistvo* [Russia and Russian Jewry]. // *RJ*, p. 87-89.

[2064] D. S. Pasmanik. *Chego zhe my dobivaemsya* [What Do We Want to Achieve?]. // *RJ*, p. 219.

better off in the united Russian Empire despite all the oppression. So now in these splintered border countries "Jews became the faithful guardians of the Russian language, Russian culture, impatiently waiting for the restoration of the great Russia. Schools that still teach in Russian became filled with Jewish children," to the exclusion of learning the languages of the newly-formed states. "In these tiny countries, the Russian Jew, accustomed to life in the open swathes of a great empire, feels uncomfortable, squeezed and diminished in his social status, despite all the civil rights and autonomy.... Indeed our people's fate is bound up with the fate of the great Russia."[2065]

Still, the position of Jewry in the circles of international post-war politics was strong, especially in Paris, and in particular regarding Zionism. "In July 1922 the League of Nations recognised the World Zionist Organization as the 'Jewish Agency,'" which first and foremost represented the interests of Zionists, and secondly of non-Zionists, and also provided support to the European Jews.[2066]

Bikerman accused the Zionists of seeing a "fragmented Russia ... as an ideal. This is why the organization of Russian Zionists calls itself not Russian, but Russo-Ukrainian. This is why the Zionists and related Jewish groups so assiduously fraternized with the Ukrainian separatists."[2067]

After the Civil War, Soviet Russia sank into a heavy silence. From this point and for decades to follow, all independent voices were squashed and only the official line could be heard. And the less was heard from Russia, the louder was the voice of emigration. All of them, from anarchists to monarchists, looked back in pain and argued intensely: who and to what extent was to blame for what had happened? Discussion developed within emigrant Jewry as well.

In 1923 Bikerman noted: "Jews answer everything with a familiar gesture and familiar words: we know, we're to blame; whenever something goes wrong, you'll look for a Jew and find one. Ninety percents of what is written in the contemporary Jewish press about Jews in Russia is just a paraphrase of this stereotype. And because it's impossible that we're always to blame for everything, Jews take from this the flattering and at first glance quite convenient conclusion that we're always and everywhere in the right."[2068]

[2065] I. M. Bikerman. *Rossija i russkoe evreistvo* [Russia and Russian Jewry]. // *RJ*, p. 84, 89.
[2066] S JE, v.7, p. 890.
[2067] I. M. Bikerman. *Rossija i russkoe evreistvo* [Russia and Russian Jewry]. // *RJ*, p. 40.
[2068] Ibid., p. 12.

However, consider: "Before the revolution, the Jewish society passionately argued that a revolution would save the Jews, and we still ardently adhere to this position." When the Jewish organizations gather resources in the West to aid their co-ethnics, suffering in the USSR, they "denounce, belittle, and slander everything about pre-revolutionary Russia, including the most positive and constructive things; See, "the Bolshevik Russia has now become the Promised Land," egalitarian and socialist. Many Jews who emigrated from Russia settled in the United States, and "pro-Bolshevik attitudes spread quickly among them."[2069] The general Jewish mood was that Bolshevism was better than restoration of monarchy. It was widely believed "that the fall of Bolshevism in Russia would inevitably engender a new wave of bloody Jewish pogroms and mass extermination.... And it is on this basis that Bolshevism is preferred as the lesser evil."[2070]

Then, as if to confirm that Bolsheviks are changing for the better, that they can learn, the NEP came! They've loosened their suffocating grip on the economy, and that made them all the more acceptable. "First NEP, then some concessions – hopefully, it'll all work out for us."[2071]

We cannot call the entire Jewish emigration pro-Bolshevik. Yet they did not see the Bolshevik state as their main enemy, and many still sympathized with it.

Yet a noteworthy incident, mockingly described in *Izvestiya*, happened to Goryansky, a Jewish emigrant writer.[2072] In 1928, the already famous Babel (and already well-known for his links to the Cheka) was "temporarily residing" in Paris to muster creative inspiration. While in the Cafe Rotonda he noticed his "old acquaintance," probably from Odessa, who magnanimously offered his hand to him: "Greetings, Goryansky." But Goryansky stood up and contemptuously turned away from the offered hand.

Rise of Hitlerism in Germany naturally and for a long time reinforced the preference for Bolshevism in the social mind of the European Jewry.

The First International Jewish Congress took place in Vienna in August 1936. M. Vishnyak disapprovingly suggested that the collective attitude toward the Bolshevik regime was perfectly exemplified by the opinion of N. Goldman: if all sorts of freedom-loving governments and organizations

---

[2069] Ibid., p. 47, 48, 72.
[2070] Yu. Delevsky. *Menshee li zlo bolsheviki?* [Are Bolsheviks the Lesser Evil?] // *The Jewish Tribune*, September 19, 1922, p. 2.
[2071] D. S. Pasmanik. *Chego zhe my dobivaemsya* [What Do We Want to Achieve?]. // *RJ*, p. 221.
[2072] G. Ryklin. *Sluchai s babelem* [An Incident with Babel]. // *Izvestiya*, March 16, 1928, p. 5.

"flatter and even fawn before the Bolsheviks ... why shouldn't supporters of Jewish ethnic and cultural independence follow the same path? ... Only Moscow's open support for anti-Jewish violence in Palestine slightly cooled the Congress leaders' disposition toward the Soviet state. Even then ... they only protested the banning of Hebrew ... and the banning of emigration from the USSR to Palestine, and, finally, they objected to the continuing suffering of Zionists in political prisons and concentration camps. Here N. Goldman found both the necessary words and inspiration."[2073] In 1939 on the eve of the World War II, S. Ivanovich noted: "It cannot be denied that among emigrant Russian Jews" the mood was to "rely on the perseverance of the Soviet dictatorship" if only to prevent pogroms.[2074]

What of Jewish Bolsheviks? I. Bikerman: "Prowess doesn't taint – that is our attitude to Bolsheviks who were raised among us and to their satanic evil.

Or the modern version: Jews have the right to have their own Bolsheviks"; "I have heard this declaration a thousand times"; at a meeting of Jewish emigrants in Berlin "one after the other, a respected Kadet, a Democrat, a Zionist ascended the podium" and each "proclaimed this right of Jews to have their own Bolsheviks ... their right to monstrosity."[2075]

"Here are the consequences of these words: Jewish opinion across the world turned away from Russia and accepted the Bolsheviks"; "when a famous, old, and well respected Jewish public figure – a white crow – suggested to a high Jewish dignitary in one of the European capitals organizing a protest against the executions of Orthodox priests in Russia [i.e. in the USSR], the latter, after reflecting on the idea, said that it would mean struggling against Bolshevism, which he considers an impossible thing to do because the collapse of Bolshevik regime would lead to anti-Jewish pogroms."[2076]

But if they can live with Bolsheviks, what do they think of the White movement? When Josef Bikerman spoke in Berlin in November 1922 at the fifth anniversary of the founding of the White Army, Jewish society in general was offended and took this as a slight against them.

Meanwhile, Dr. D. S. Pasmanik (who fought on the German front until February 1917, then in the White Army until May 1919, when he left Russia) had already finished and in 1923 published in Paris his book

---

[2073] *Poslednie Novosti*. August 13, 1936.
[2074] S. Ivanovich. *Evrei i sovetskaya diktatura* [Jews and the Soviet Dictatorship].
[2075] I. M. Bikerman. *Rossija i russkoe evreistvo* [Russia and Russian Jewry]. // *RJ*, p. 23-24.
[2076] Ibid., p. 54-55.

Russian Revolution and Jewry: Bolshevism and Judaism (I cited it here), where he passionately argued against the commonplace explanation that Bolshevism originated from the Jewish religion. "The identification of Judaism with Bolshevism is a grave global danger." In 1923, together with I. M. Bikerman, G. A. Landau, I. O. Levin, D. O. Linsky (also an ex-member of the White Army) and V. C. Mandel, Pasmanik founded the National Union of Russian Jews Abroad. This group published an appeal *To the Jews of the World!* in the same year, and soon after published a collection *Russia and the Jews* in Berlin.

Here is how they describe the task they undertook and their feelings.

Pasmanik said: "The unspeakable pain of the Jew and the unending sorrow of the Russian citizen" motivated this work. "Because of the dark events of the recent years, it was difficult to find a balanced point of view on both Russian and Jewish questions. We ... attempted to merge the interests of the renewed Russia and of the afflicted Russian Jewry." [2077] Linsky: "Unfathomed sorrow" dwells in the souls of those who "realize their Jewishness while similarly identifying as Russians." It is much easier when "one of the two streams of your national consciousness dries up, leaving you only a Jew or only a Russian, thus simplifying your position toward Russia's tragic experience....The villainous years of the revolution killed ... the shoots of hope" for rapprochement between Jews and Russians that had appeared just before the war; now "we witness active ... Russo-Jewish divergence."[2078] Levin: "It is our duty to honestly and objectively examine the causes of and the extent of Jewish involvement in the revolution. This ... might have certain effect on future relations between Russians and Jews."[2079] The co-authors of the collection rightly warned Russians not to mix up the meaning of the February Revolution and Jewish involvement in it. Bikerman if anything minimised this involvement (the power balance between the Executive Committee of the Soviet of Soldiers' and Workers' Deputies and the Provisional Government was for the most part unclear to contemporaries). However he thought that after the October Bolshevik coup "the Jewish right to have their Bolsheviks implies a duty to have also their right-wingers and extreme right-wingers, the polar opposites of the Bolsheviks." [2080] Pasmanik: "In all its varieties and forms, Bolshevik communism ... is an evil and true foe of Jewry, as it is first of all the enemy

---

[2077] D. S. Pasmanik. *Russkaja revolutsia i evreistvo: (Bolshevism i iudaizm)* [Russian Revolution and Jewry: Bolshevism and Judaism]. Paris, 1923, p. 7, 14.

[2078] D. O. Linsky. *O natsionalnom samosoznanii russkogo evreja* [On the National Consciousness of the Russian Jew]. // *RJ*, p. 141, 144-145.

[2079] I. O. Levin. *Evrei v revolutsii* [The Jews in the Revolution]. // *RJ*, p. 124.

[2080] I. M. Bikerman. *Rossija i russkoe evreistvo* [Russia and Russian Jewry]. // *RJ*, p. 24.

of personal identity in general and of cultural identity in particular."[2081] "Bound by a plethora of intimate connections to our motherland, to its political system, economy and culture, we cannot flourish while the country disintegrates around us."[2082]

Obviously, these authors were fully aware of the significance of the Russian catastrophe. In describing those years, I heavily relied on the work of these people with the hope that their bitter, but not at all "self-hating," reflections can finally be understood and comprehended in their entirety.

Their 1923 Proclamation stated: "The National Union of Russian Jews Abroad firmly believes that the Bolsheviks epitomize the *greatest* evil for the Jews as well as for all other peoples of Russia…. It is time for the Jew to stop tremble at the thought of going against the revolution…. Rather, the Jew should fear going against his motherland [Russia] and his people [Jewish]."[2083]

However, the authors of *Russia and the Jews* saw the Jewish national consciousness of the early 1920s as something very different from what they've thought it should have been. "Almost all circles and classes of Russian society are now engaged in grievous self-reflections, trying to comprehend what has happened….Whether these self-accusations and admissions of guilt are fair or not, they at least reveal the work of thought, conscience, and aching hearts….

But it would be no exaggeration to claim that such spiritual work is the least noticeable among the Jewish intelligentsia, which is no doubt a symptom of certain morbidity…. For an outsider it appears that a typical Jewish intellectual has no concerns."[2084] For this intellectual "everyone else is to blame – the government, the generals, the peasants, etc. He has nothing to do with all this….

In no way did he forge his own destiny and the destinies of those around him; he is just a passersby, hit on the head by a falling brick"; "so they were complicit in destroying [the world around them], but after it was finished they became unaware of their role in it."[2085]

Jewish Bolsheviks was a particular pain for the authors. "A sin that carries the seed of its own nemesis, … what greater affliction is there for a people

---

[2081] D. S. Pasmanik. *Chego zhe my dobivaemsya* [What Do We Want to Achieve?]. // *RJ*, p. 215.
[2082] To the Jews of the World! // *RJ*, p. 5.
[2083] Ibid., p. 7-8.
[2084] G. A. Landau. *Revolutsionnye idei v evreiskoi obshchestvennosti* [Revolutionary Ideas in Jewish Society]. // *RJ*, p. 100.
[2085] Ibid., p. 104.

than to see its sons debauched?"²⁰⁸⁶ "It is not just that the Russian upheaval needed people of a certain sort for its perpetuation, or that the Jewish society provided this sort of people; what is most important is that they were not rebuffed, did not meet enough opposition from within their own society."²⁰⁸⁷ "It is our duty to shoulder the struggle specifically against the Jewish Bolsheviks, against all kinds of YevSeks [the 'Jewish Section,' the name given to officials appointed by the Soviets to deal with Jewish affairs], and against Jewish commissars in general."²⁰⁸⁸

It should be noted that these authors were not alone in arguing that Russian (and now emigrant) Jews should fight against the Bolsheviks. From the pages of the *Jewish Tribune*: "If Bolshevism was swept from power in Russia by a wave of popular wrath, Jewry might be held, in the eyes of the masses, responsible for prolonging Bolshevism's lifespan.... Only active participation in the struggle to liquidate Bolshevism can secure Jews a safe position in the common cause of saving Russia."²⁰⁸⁹

Bikerman warned: if we support the Bolsheviks "on the principle that your own shirt is closer to the body" then "we should not forget that we thus allow the Russian to take care of his own shirt that is closer to his body; that it justifies the call, 'Slaughter Yids, Save Russia.'"²⁰⁹⁰

What of the Jewish attitudes toward the White Army? "This unworthy attitude that Jews have towards people who have taken upon their shoulders the endlessly difficult task of fighting for Russia, for the millions of the sheepish and weak-willed, points out to the complete moral disintegration, to a sort of perversion of mind...." While "all of us, Jews and non-Jews alike, placed ourselves obediently under the communist yoke and our backs under the whip, there were some Russians, courageous and proud, who overcame all obstacles, gathered from what remained of the breached and ripped apart fronts [of World War I], consolidated and raised the banner of resistance.... Just that they were willing to fight under these circumstances alone immortalizes them for the history. And these people became an object for abuse" on the side of so many Jews, "libeled by every loquacious tongue"; so "instead of appreciation the tragedy, we see epidemic mindlessness, endless laxity of speech, and triumphant superficiality." And

---

²⁰⁸⁶ To the Jews of the World! // RJ, p. 6.
²⁰⁸⁷ G. A. Landau. *Revolutsionnye idei v evreiskoi obshchestvennosti* [Revolutionary Ideas in Jewish Society]. // RJ, p. 118.
²⁰⁸⁸ D. S. Pasmanik. *Chego zhe my dobivaemsya* [What Do We Want to Achieve?]. // RJ, p. 225.
²⁰⁸⁹ Yu. Delevsky. *Menshee li zlo bolsheviki?* [Are Bolsheviks the Lesser Evil?] // The Jewish Tribune, September 19, 1922, p. 3.
²⁰⁹⁰ I. M. Bikerman. *Rossija i russkoe evreistvo* [Russia and Russian Jewry]. // RJ, p. 78.

yet "the Russia for which the Whites fought is not alien to us; it is 'our shirt' too."[2091] "Jewry should have fought for the White cause as for the cause of Jewish salvation, for ... only in the restoration and swift rescue of Russian statehood can Jews find salvation from that death that has never been as close as in these days." [2092] (Death was indeed approaching, although from another direction).

Who would deny these conclusions today, after decades of Soviet regime? But at that time, only few authors, Jewish or Russian, could see so far ahead.

The Jewish emigrant community as a whole rejected these thoughts. And thus they had failed the test of history. It might be objected that it did not cause Jewry a noticeable, significant harm, and certainly it was not the Holocaust brought by Hitlerism. Yes, it did not bring commeasurable physical harm, but, historically, its spiritual harm was noticeable; take, for instance, the success of Bolshevism in the expulsion of the Jewish religion from the country where it had once deeply spread its sacred roots. And there was more – the Jews, by "betting on Bolshevism" influenced the overall course of events in Europe.

The authors of the *Russia and the Jews* appealed in vain: "In the many centuries of Jewish dispersion ... there has not been a political catastrophe as deeply threatening to our national existence as the breaking of the Russian Power, for never have the vital forces of the Jewish people been as united as in the bygone, living Russia. Even the breakup of the Caliphate can scarcely compare with the current disaster." [2093] "*For the united Russian Jewry* the breakup of Russia into separate sovereign states is a *national calamity.*"[2094] "If there is no place for the Jews in the great spaces of the Russian land, in the boundlessness of the Russian soul, then there is no space [for Jews] anywhere in the world.... Woe to us, if we do not wise up."[2095]

Of course, by the very end of the 20th century we can easily reject these grim prophecies, if only as a matter of fact – just as enough space has been found on earth for formerly Russian Jews, so a Jewish state has been

---

[2091] Ibid., p. 52, 53-54.
[2092] D. O. Linsky. *O natsionalnom samosoznanii russkogo evreja* [On the National Consciousness of the Russian Jew]. // *RJ*, p. 149.
[2093] I. M. Bikerman. *Rossija i russkoe evreistvo* [Russia and Russian Jewry]. // *RJ*, p. 92.
[2094] V. S. Mandel. Konservativnye i razrushitelnye elementy v evreisve [Conservative and Subversive Forces among Jewry]. // *RJ*, p. 202.
[2095] D. O. Linsky. *O natsionalnom samosoznanii russkogo evreja* [On the National Consciousness of the Russian Jew]. // *RJ*, p. 153, 154.

founded and secured itself, while Russia still lies in ruin, so powerless and humiliated.

The warnings of the authors on how Russia should be treated already appear a great exaggeration, a failed prophecy. And now we can reflect on these words only in regard of the spiritual chord that so unexpectedly bound the two our peoples together in History.

"If Russia is not our motherland, then we are foreigners and have no right to interfere in her national life."[2096] "Russia will survive; her renaissance must become our national concern, the concern of the entire ... Russian Jewry."[2097]

And in conclusion: *"The fate of Russian Jewry is inextricably linked to the fate of Russia; we must save Russia, if we want to save Jewry .... The Jews must fight the molesters of the great country shoulder to shoulder with all other anti-Bolshevik forces; a consolidated struggle against the common enemy will heal the rifts and substantially reduce the current dramatic and ubiquitous growth of anti-Semitism; only by saving Russia, can we prevent a Jewish catastrophe."*[2098]

Catastrophe! – this was said ten years before Hitler's ascension to power, eighteen years before his stunning sweep across the USSR and before the start of his program of Jewish extermination. Would it have been possible for Hitler to preach hatred of "Jews and communists" in Germany so easily and successfully, to claim Jews and communists are the same, if the Jews were among the most prominent and persistent opponents of the Soviet regime? The spiritual search of the authors of *Russia and the Jews* led them to prophetically sense the shadow of the impending Jewish Catastrophe, though erring in its geographical origin and failing to predict other fateful developments. Yet their dreadful warning remained unheard.

I am not aware of anything else close to *Russia and the Jews* in the history of Russian-Jewish relations. It shook the Jewish emigration. Imagine how hurtful it was to hear such things coming from Jewish lips, from within Jewry itself.

On the part of Russians, we must learn a lesson from this story as well. We should take *Russia and the Jews* as an example of how to love our own people and at the same time be able to speak about our mistakes, and to do

---

[2096] D. S. Pasmanik. *Chego zhe my dobivaemsya* [What Do We Want to Achieve?]. // *RJ*, p. 227-228.
[2097] I. M. Bikerman. *Rossija i russkoe evreistvo* [Russia and Russian Jewry]. // *RJ*, p. 93.
[2098] D. S. Pasmanik. *Chego zhe my dobivaemsya* [What Do We Want to Achieve?]. // *RJ*, p. 217-218.

so mercilessly if necessary. And in doing that, we should never alienate or separate ourselves from our people. The surest path to social truth is for each to admit their *own* mistakes, from each, from every side.

Having devoted much time and thought to these authors (and having dragged the reader along with me), I would like here to leave a brief record of their lives.

Josef Menassievich Bikerman (1867-1942) came from a poor petty bourgeois family. He attended a cheder, then a yeshiva, provided for himself from the age of fifteen; educated himself under difficult circumstances. In 1903 he graduated from the historical-philological faculty of the Imperial Novorossiya University (after a two-year-exclusion gap for participation in student unrest). He opposed Zionism as, in his opinion, an illusory and reactionary idea. He called on Jews to unite, without relinquishing their spiritual identity, with progressive forces in Russia to fight for the good of the common motherland. His first article was a large tract on Zionism published in the *Russkoe Bogatstvo* [Russian Treasure] (1902, issue 7), which was noticed and debated even abroad. In 1905 he was deeply involved into the Liberation movement. He worked in several periodicals: *Syn Otechestva* [Son of the Fatherland], *Russkoe Bogatstvo*, *Nash Den* [Our day], *Bodroe Slovo* [Buoyant Word]. As an emigrant he was printed in the Paris *Vozrozhdenie*, when it was run by P. B. Struve.

Daniil Samoilovich Pasmanik (1869-1930) was a son of Melamed (a teacher in a cheder). In 1923 he graduated from the medical faculty of Zurich University and then practiced medicine in Bulgaria for seven years. In 1899-1905 he was the freelance lecturer in the medical faculty at Geneva University.

He joined Zionist movement in 1900 and became one of its leading theorists and publicists. He returned to Russia in 1905 and passed the medical license exam. He participated in the struggle for civil rights for Jews; he opposed the Bund and worked on the program for Poale-Zion; in 1906-1917 he was a member of the Central Committee of the Russian Zionist organization. He was a member of editorial boards of *Evreiskaya Zhizn* [Jewish Life], and then of *Rassvet*. He wrote many articles for *Evreisky Mir* [Jewish *World*] and the *Jewish Encyclopaedia*. He published his medical works in specialized journals in German and French. Pasmanik was in Vienna when the WWI broke out in 1914, from where he with great difficulty managed to return to Russia; he joined the army and served in field hospitals until February 1917. He joined the Kadets after the February Revolution; he supported General Kornilov and the White movement; in 1918-1919 he was involved in the White government of the Crimea, was elected chairman of the Union of the Jewish Communities of the Crimea.

In 1919 he emigrated from Russia to France. In 1920-1922 in Paris he together with V. L. Burtsev edited the White émigré newspaper *Obshchee Delo* [*The Common Cause*]. Overall, he authored hundreds of articles and tens of books; the most notable of them include Wandering Israel: The Psychology of Jewry in Dispersion *(1910)*, Fates of the Jewish People: The Problems of Jewish Society *(1917)*, The Russian Revolution and Jewry: Bolshevism and Judaism *(1923)* The Revolutionary Years in Crimea *(1926)*, What Is Judaism? (French edition, 1930).

Isaak Osipovich Levin (1876-1944) was a historian and publicist. Before the revolution, he worked as a foreign affairs commentator for *Russkie Vedomosti* [Russian Journal] and for the P. B. Struve's magazine, *Russkaya Mysl* [*Russian Thought*]. He emigrated first to Berlin. He was a member of the Russian Institute of Science, worked in the *Rul, Russkie Zapiski* and in the historical-literary almanac *Na Chuzhoi Storone* [*In the Foreign Land*]; he regularly gave presentations (in particular on the topic of the rise of German anti-Semitism). He moved to Paris in 1931 or 1932. He was widowed and lived in poverty. Among his works are *Emigration during the French Revolution* and a book in French about Mongolia. During the German occupation he registered according to his "racial origins" as was required by authorities; he was arrested in the early 1943, for a short time was held in a concentration camp near Paris, then deported; he died in a Nazi concentration camp in 1944.

Grigory (Gavriel) Adolfovich Landau (1877-1941) was son of the well-known publicist and publisher A. E. Landau. He graduated from the law faculty of the St. Petersburg University in 1902. He wrote for periodicals from 1903 *(the newspapers* Voskhod *[Sunrise],* Nash Den, Evreiskoe Obozrenie *[Jewish Observer], the magazines* Bodroe Slovo, Evreisky Mir, Vestnik Evropy

[European Herald], *Sovremennik, Severnye Zapiski* [Northern Notes], the yearly almanac *Logos*). He was one of the founders of the Jewish Democratic Group in 1904 and the Union for Equal Rights for Jews in Russia in 1905. He was an outstanding Kadet, member of the Central Committee of the Kadet Party. In August 1917 he participated in the Government Conference in Moscow; from December 1917 he was a member of the Executive Committee of the Jewish Community of Petrograd. He emigrated to Germany in 1919; from 1922 to 1931 he was I. V. Gessen's deputy at *Rul*. Apart from *Rul*, he also wrote for the magazine, *Russkaya Mysl*, the weekly, *Russia and the Slavs*, the collection *Chisla* [*Dates*], etc. He often lectured at émigré evenings (in 1927 in the talk titled *The Eurasian Delusion* he criticised "eurasianism" as the movement contrary to the values of Russian history and leading to ideological Bolshevism). From Nazi Germany he fled for Latvia, where he worked for the Riga newspaper *Segodnya* [Today]. He was arrested by the NKVD in June 1941 and died in the Usollag camp (near Solikamsk) in November.[2099] Among his works the most influential were *Clownish Culture* (in *Nash Den*, 1908), the article *Twilight of Europe* (*Severnye Zapiski*, 1914, issue 12), which antedated "much of what would later bestow worldwide fame on Oswald Spengler"[2100] (and later a book with the same title (Berlin, 1923)), *Polish-Jewish Relations* (1915), *On Overcoming Evil* (in the collection book *The Works of Russian Scholars Abroad*, Berlin, 1923), *The Byzantine and the Hebrew* (*Russkaya Mysl*, 1923, issues 1 and 2), *Theses Against Dostoevsky* (*Chisla*, volume 6, Paris, 1932), *Epigraphs* (Berlin, 1927). Much of what he wrote was dismissed by contemporaries. He was too conservative in spirit to be accepted by progressive public. He was a sagacious thinker.

We could not find any substantial information about D. O. Linsky (he served in the White Army during the Civil War) or V. C. Mandel (active participant in Russian political life 1907-1918, he emigrated to Berlin and died in 1931).

In *Russia and the Jews* the behavior of Jewish emigrants during 1920s was explicitly and harshly admonished. The authors called on their co-ethnics to "admit their own mistakes and not to judge the Great Russia in which they had lived and which they had made a home for hundreds of years"; "remember how they demanded justice for themselves and how upset they are when they are collectively accused for the acts of some individuals"[2101]; Jews should not be afraid "to acknowledge *some* responsibility for all that has happened."[2102] "First of all we must determine precisely our *share* of responsibility and so counter anti-Semitic slander....This is absolutely not about becoming accustomed to anti-Semitism, as claimed by some Jewish demagogues.... This admission is vital for us, it is our moral duty."[2103] "Jewry has to pick righteous path worthy of the great wisdom of our religious teachings which will lead us to brotherly reconciliation with the

---

[2099] The information about G. A. Landau's arrest and death was taken from V. Gessen. *Iosif Gessen: jurist, politik i zhurnalist* [Josef Gessen: an attorney, politician and journalist]. // Jews in the Culture of Russia-in-Exile: Articles, Publications, Memoires, and Essays. Jerusalem, 1993, v. 2, p. 543.

[2100] Fyodor Stepun. *Byvshee i nesbyvsheesja* [What Have Been and What Might-have-been]. The 2nd Edition. London, Overseas Publications, 1990, v. 1, p. 301.

[2101] V. S. Mandel. Konservativnye i razrushitelnye elementy v evreisve [Conservative and Subversive Forces among Jewry]. // *RJ*, p. 204.

[2102] D. S. Pasmanik. *Chego zhe my dobivaemsya* [What Do We Want to Achieve?]. // *RJ*, p. 210.

[2103] Ibid., p. 212, 213.

Russian people.... to build the Russian house and the Jewish home so they might stand for centuries to come."[2104]

But "we spread storms and thunder and expect to be cradled by gentle zephyrs.... I know you will shriek that I am justifying pogroms! ... I know how much these people are worth, who think themselves salt of the earth, the arbiters of fate, and at the very least the beacons of Israel.... They, whose every whisper is about Black Hundreds and Black Hundreders, they themselves are dark people, their essence is black, *viri obscure* indeed, they were never able to comprehend ... the power of creativity in human history...." It is imperative for us "to make less of a display of our pain, to shout less about *our* losses. It is time we understood that crying and wailing ... is mostly [evidence] of emotional infirmity, of a lack of culture of the soul.... You are not alone in this world, and your sorrow cannot fill the entire universe ... when you put on a display only your own grief, only your own pain it shows ... disrespect to others' grief, to others' sufferings."[2105]

It could have been said today, and to all of us. These words cannot be obviated either by the millions lost in the prisons and camps of the GULag, nor by the millions exterminated in the Nazi death camps.

The lectures of the authors of *Russia and the Jews* at that year's National Union of Jews "were met with great indignation" on the part of emigrant Jewry.

"Even when explicitly or tacitly accepting the truth of the facts and the analysis, many expressed indignation or surprise that anyone dared to bring these into the open. See, it was not the right time to speak of Jews, to criticise them, to determine their revolutionary misdeeds and responsibility, when Jewry has just suffered so much and may suffer even more in the future."[2106] The collection's authors "were almost declared 'enemies of the [Jewish] people,' the abetters of reaction and allies of the pogromists."[2107]

The *Jewish Tribune* replied them from Paris a few months later: "The question of 'Jewish responsibility for the Russian revolution' has hitherto only been posed by anti-Semites." But now "there is a whole penitent and

---

[2104] D. O. Linsky. *O natsionalnom samosoznanii russkogo evreja* [On the National Consciousness of the Russian Jew]. // *RJ*, p. 152.

[2105] I. M. Bikerman. *Rossija i russkoe evreistvo* [Russia and Russian Jewry]. // *RJ*, p. 74-75.

[2106] G. A. Landau. *Revolutsionnye idei v evreiskoi obshchestvennosti* [Revolutionary Ideas in Jewish Society]. // *RJ*, p. 100-101.

[2107] D. S. Pasmanik. *Chego zhe my dobivaemsya* [What Do We Want to Achieve?]. // *RJ*, p. 226.

accusative movement," apparently "we have to 'not only blame others, but also admit our own faults'"; yet there is nothing new apart from "the same old boring 'name counting' [of Jews among Bolsheviks]." "Too late ... did Mr. Landau come to love" "the old 'statehood'"; "'penitent' Jews turned reactionaries"; their "words are incompatible with the dignity of the Jewish people ... and are completely irresponsible."[2108] Especially offensive was this attempt to "separate the 'popular' anti-Semitism from the 'official' one", attempting to prove that "the people, the society, the country – the entire populace hates the Jews and considers them the true culprit responsible for all national woes"; just like those who connived the pogroms, they repeat "the old canard about the 'popular anger.'"[2109] Sometimes it descended into the outright abuse: "this group of Berlin journalists and activists, which has nearly disappeared from the Jewish public life by now ... craves to put themselves into limelight again ... and for that they could think of no better way than to attack their own compatriots, Russian Jews"; this "tiny group of loyalists Jews ... are blinded by a desire to turn the wheel of history backwards," they write "indecencies," give "comical advice," take on themselves the "ridiculous role of healers to cure national wounds." They should remember that "sometimes it is better to stay quiet."[2110]

One sophisticated modern critic could find a better assessment for that collection than a "severe hysteria." Both that attempt "and their later journey are genuine tragedies," in his opinion, and he explains this tragedy as a "self-hatred complex."[2111]

Yet was Bikerman hateful when he wrote, on his "later tragic journey," that: "The Jewish people ... is not a sect, not an order, but a whole people, dispersed over the world but united in itself; it has raised up the banner of peaceful labour and has gathered around this banner, as around the symbol of godly order"?[2112]

However it is not true that European or émigré Jews did not at all hark to such explanations or warnings. A similar discussion had taken place a little

---

[2108] A. Kulisher. *Ob otvetstvennosti i bezotvetstvennosti* [On Responsibility and Irresponsibility]. // *The Jewish Tribune*, April 6, 1923, p. 3-4.

[2109] B. Mirsky. *"16 punktov"* ["16 Points"]. // *The Jewish Tribune*, April 7, 1924, p. 2.

[2110] S. Pozner. V chem zhe delo? [So What's the problem?] // *The Jewish Tribune*, April 7, 1924, p. 1-2.

[2111] Sh. Markish. O evreiskoj nenavisti k Rossii [On the Jewish Hatred Toward Russia]. // *"22":* Obshchestvenno-politichesky i literaturny zhurnal evreyskoj intelligentsii iz SSSR v Izraile [*Social, Political and Literary Journal of the Jewish Intelligentsia from the USSR in Israel*]. Tel-Aviv, 1984, (38), p. 218.

[2112] I. M. Bikerman. *K samopoznaniju evreya: chem. my byli, chem. my stali, chem. my dolzhny stat* [On the Self-knowledge of the Jew: Who We Were, Who We Are, Who We Must Become]. Paris, 1939, p. 25.

earlier, in 1922. In the re-established Zionist publication *Rassvet* the nationalist G. I. Shekhtman expressed his incomprehension at how the intelligentsia of other nationalities could be anything other than nationalistic. An intelligentsia is invariably connected to *its own* nationality and feels its pains. A Jew cannot be a "Russian democrat", but naturally a "Jewish democrat." "I do not recognise dual national or democratic loyalties." And if the Russian intelligentsia "does not identify with its nationality" (Herzen), it is simply because until now it "has not had the opportunity or need to feel sharp pains over its national identity, to worry about it. But that has changed now." Now the Russian intelligentsia "has to cast aside its aspirations to be a universal All-Russian intelligentsia, and instead to regard itself as the *Great Russian* democracy."[2113]

It was difficult to counter. The gauntlet was picked up by P. N. Milyukov, though not very confidently. We remember (see Chapter 11) that back in 1909 he had also expressed horror at the unveiling of this stinging, unpleasant national question "who benefits?" But now this new awkward situation (and not a change in Milyukov's views), when so many Russian intellectuals in emigration suddenly realized that they lost their Russia, forced Milyukov to amend his previous position. He replied to Shekhtman, though in a rather ambiguous manner and not in his own (highly popular) *Poslednie Novosti*, but in the *Jewish Tribune* with much smaller circulation, to the effect that a Russian Jew could and had to be a "Russian democrat." Milyukov treaded carefully: "but when this demand ... is fulfilled, and there appears a 'new national face' of Russian Democracy (the Great Russian)," well, wouldn't Shekhtman be first to get scared at the prospect of "empowerment of ethnically conscious Great Russian Democracy with imperial ambitions." Do we then need these phantoms? Is this what we wish to ruin our relations over?[2114]

The émigrés lived in an atmosphere of not just verbal tension. There was a sensational murder trial in Paris in 1927 of a clock-maker Samuel Shvartsbard, who lost his whole family in the pogroms in Ukraine, and who killed Petliura with five bullets.[2115] (*Izvestiya* sympathetically reported on the case and printed Shvartsbard's portrait.[2116]) The defence raised the stakes claiming that the murder was a justified revenge for Petliura's pogroms: "The defendant wished and felt a duty to raise the issue of anti-Semitism before the world's conscience."[2117] The defence called many

---

[2113] P. N. Milyukov. *Natsionalnost i natsia* [Ethnicity and Nation]. // *The Jewish Tribune,* September 1, 1922, p. 1-2.
[2114] Ibid.
[2115] *Poslednie Novosti*. October 14, 1927, p. 2; October 19, 1927, p. 1-2.
[2116] *Izvestiya*, October 21, p. 3.
[2117] *Izvestiya*, October 22, p. 1.

witnesses to testify that during the Civil War Petliura had been personally responsible for pogroms in Ukraine. The prosecution suggested that the murder had been ordered by Cheka.

"Shvartsbard, agitated, called out from his place: '[the witness] doesn't want to admit that I acted as a Jew, and so claims I'm a Bolshevik.'"[2118] Shvartsbard was acquitted by the French court. Denikin [a leading White general during the Civil War] was mentioned at that trial, and Shvartsbard's lawyer proclaimed: "If you wish to bring Denikin to trial, I am with you"; "I would have defended the one who would have taken revenge upon Denikin with the same passionate commitment as I am here defending the man who had taken revenge upon Petliura."[2119] And as Denikin lived in Paris without guards, anyone wishing to take revenge upon him had an open road. However Denikin was never put on trial. (A similar murder happened later in Moscow in 1929, when Lazar Kolenberg shot the former White general Slashchev, [who after the Civil War returned to Russia and served in Soviet military], for doing nothing to stop pogroms in Nikolayev. "During the investigation, the accused was found to be mentally incompetent to stand trial and released."[2120]) During Shvartsbard's trial the prosecutor drew a parallel to another notorious case (that of Boris Koverda): for Petliura had previously lived in Poland, but "you [speaking to Shvartsbard] did not attempt to kill him there, as you knew that in Poland you would be tried by military tribunal."[2121] In 1929, a young man, Boris Koverda, also "wishing to present a problem before the world's conscience," had killed the Bolshevik sadist Voikov; he was sentenced to ten years in jail and served his full term.

A White émigré from Revolutionary Terrorist Boris Savinkov's group, Captain V. F. Klementiev, told me that in Warsaw at that time former Russian officers were abused as "White-Guard rascals" and that they were not served in Jewish-owned shops. Such was the hostility, and not just in Warsaw.

Russian émigrés all over Europe were flattened by scarcity, poverty, hardship, and they quickly tired of the showdown over "who is more to blame?"

Anti-Jewish sentiments among them abated in the second half of the 1920s.

During these years Vasily Shulgin wrote: "Are not our 'visa ordeals' remarkably similar to the oppression experienced by Jews in the Pale of

---

[2118] *Izvestiya*, October 23, p. 1.
[2119] *Poslednie Novosti*. October 25, 1927, p. 2; October 26, 1927, p. 1.
[2120] Russian Jewish Encyclopedia. The 2nd Revised and Enlarged Edition. Moscow, 1995, v. 2, p. 59.
[2121] *Poslednie Novosti*. October 23, 1927, p. 1.

Settlement? Aren't our Nansen passports [internationally recognized identity cards first issued by the League of Nations to stateless refugees], which are a sort of wolf ticket obstructing movement, reminiscent of the 'Jewish religion' label, which we stamped in Jewish passports in Russia, thereby closing many doors to them? Do we not resort to all kinds of middleman jobs when we are unable to attain, because of our peculiar position, a civil servant post or a certain profession? ...

Are we not gradually learning to 'work around' laws that are inconvenient for us, precisely as Jews did with our laws, and for which we criticized them?"[2122]

Yet during these same years anti-Jewish sentiments were on the rise in the USSR and were even reported in the Soviet press, causing distress among Jewish émigrés. So in May 1928 a public "debate on anti-Semitism" was organized in Paris among them. A report of it was placed in the Milyukov's newspaper.[2123] (Bikerman's and Pasmanik's group, already non-active, did not participate.)

The formal reason for the debate was "a strong rise of Judeophobia in Russia, a phenomenon that periodically occurs there." The Socialist Revolutionary N. D. Avksentiev chaired the debate, and there were "more Russians than Jews" among the public. Mark Slonim explained that "the long oppressed Russian Jewry, having finally attained freedom, has dashed to secure formerly prohibited positions," and this annoys Russians. "In essence, the past fatefully determined the present." "Bad things" of the past (Tsarist times) "resulted in bad consequences." S. Ivanovich stated that Jews were now tormented in the USSR, because it has become impossible to torment "the bourgeois" thanks to the NEP. But what is worrying is that the Russian intelligentsia in the USSR, although neutral on the Jewish question, now takes the liberty to think: good, "it will begin with anti-Semitism, and lead to the Russian freedom. What a dangerous and foolish illusion."

Such apologetic ideas outraged the next orator, V. Grosman: "It is as if Jewry stands accused!" The question needs to be considered more deeply: "There is no reason to distinguish Soviet anti-Semitism from the anti-Semitism of old Russia," that is to say there is still the same Black Hundredism so dear to Russian hearts. "This is not a Jewish question, but a Russian one, a question of Russian culture."

(But if it is so quintessentially Russian, entirely Russian, inherently Russian problem, then what can be done? What need then for a mutual

---

[2122] V. V. Shulgin, p. 156.
[2123] *Poslednie Novosti*. May 29, 1928.

dialogue?) The author of the debate report, S. Litovtsev, regretted *post factum* that it was necessary to find for the debate "several honest people, brave enough to acknowledge their anti-Semitism and frankly explain why they are anti-Semites... Who would say simply, without evasiveness: 'I don't like this and that about Jews...' Alongside there should have been several equally candid Jews who would say: 'and we don't like this and that about you...' Rest assured, such an honest and open exchange of opinions, with goodwill and a desire for mutual comprehension, would be really beneficial for both Jews and Russians – and for Russia...."[2124]

Shulgin replied to this: "Now, among Russian émigrés, surely one needs more bravery to declare oneself a philo-Semite." He extended his answer into a whole book, inserting Litovtsev's question into the title, *What we don't like about them*.[2125]

Shulgin's book was regarded as anti-Semitic, and the proposed "interexchange of views" never took place. Anyway, the impending Catastrophe, coming from Germany, soon took the issue of any debate off the table.

A Union of Russian-Jewish Intelligentsia was created in Paris as if in the attempt to preserve a link between the two cultures. Yet it soon transpired that "life in exile had created a chasm between fathers and sons, and the latter no longer understand what a "Russian-Jewish intelligentsia" is.[2126] So the fathers sadly acknowledged that "the Russian Jews, who used to lead global Jewry in spiritual art and in the nation building, now virtually quit the stage."[2127] Before the war, the Union had managed to publish only the first issue of collection *Jewish world*. During the war, those who could, fled across the ocean and untiringly created the Union of Russian Jews in New York City, and published the second issue of the *Jewish World*. In the 1960s, they published the *Book of Russian Jewry* in two volumes, about pre- and post-revolutionary Jewish life in Russia. The bygone life in the bygone Russia still attracted their minds.

In this work I cite all these books with gratitude and respect.

[2124] S. Litovtsev. *Disput ob antisemitizme* [Debate on Anti-Semitism]. // *Poslednie Novosti*, May 29, 1928, p. 2.
[2125] V. V. Shulgin, p. 11.
[2126] S. M. Ginzburg. O russko-evreiskoi intelligentsia [On Russian Jewish Intelligentsia]. // *JW-1*, p. 33.
[2127] Foreword // *JW-1*, p. 7.

Chapter 18

In the 1920s

The twenties in the Soviet Union was an epoch with a unique atmosphere – a grand social experiment which intoxicated world liberal opinion for decades.

And in some places this intoxication still persists. However, almost no one remains of those who drank deeply of its poisonous spirit.

The uniqueness of that spirit was manifested in the ferocity of class antagonism, in the promise of a never-before-seen new society, in the novelty of new forms of human relationships, in the breakdown of the nation's economy, daily life and family structure. The social and demographic changes were, in fact, colossal.

The "great exodus" of the Jewish population to the capitals began, for many reasons, during the first years of communist power. Some Jewish writers are categorical in their description: "Thousands of Jews left their settlements and a handful of southern towns for Moscow, Leningrad and Kiev to find 'real life'."[2128]

Beginning in 1917, "Jews flooded into Leningrad and Moscow".[2129] According to the *Jewish Encyclopedia*, "hundreds of thousands of Jews moved to Moscow, Leningrad and other major centers",[2130] "in 1920, 28,000 Jews lived in Moscow – by 1923, about 86,000; according to 1926 USSR census, 131,000 and in 1933, 226,500."[2131] "Moscow became fashionable," they used to say half-seriously in Odessa.

Lurie-Larin, a fanatical and zealous Bolshevik leader during "War Communism" writes that in the first years not less than a million Jews left their settlements; in 1923 about half of Ukraine's Jews lived in large cities,

---

[2128] М. Поповский. О нас — со всей искренностью // Новый американец, Нью-Йорк, 1981, 20-26 сентября (№ 84), с. 7.
[2129] А. Львов. Где ты, Адам // Новая газета, Нью-Йорк, 1981, 28 ноября-4 декабря (№ 82), с. 4.
[2130] Краткая Еврейская Энциклопедия (далее — КЕЭ). Иерусалим, 1976. Т. 1, с. 235.
[2131] Там же, т. 5, с. 477-478.

pouring as well into parts of Russia formerly off-limits to Jews (so called "prohibited provinces") from Ukraine and Byelorussia, into Transcaucasia and Central Asia.

The magnitude of this flow was half a million, and four-fifth of them settled in RSFSR. One in five of the Jewish migrants went to Moscow.[2132]

M. Agursky considers Larin's numbers to be substantially undercounted and points out that this demographic change affected interests important to the Russian population.[2133]

During "War Communism" with its ban on private trade and limitations on craftsmen and on those of certain "social origins" there arose a new social category – the "deprived" (deprived of civil rights). "Many Jews were deprived of civil rights and numbered among the "deprived"." Still, the "migration of the Jewish population from Byelorussia into the interior of the USSR, mainly to Moscow and Leningrad" did not slow.[2134] The new arrivals joined relatives or co-ethnics who offered communal support.

According to the 1926 USSR census, 2,211,000 or 83% of the Jewish population lived in cities and towns. 467,000 lived in rural districts. Another 300,000 did not identify themselves as Jews and these were practically all city dwellers. About five out of six Jews in the USSR were urban dwellers, constituting up to 23% and 40% of the urban population in Ukraine and Byelorussia respectively.[2135]

Most striking in the provincial capitals and major cities was the flow of Jews into the apparatus of the Soviet government. Ordzhonikidze in 1927 at the 15th Communist Party Congress reported on the "national make up of our party". By his statistics Jews constituted 11.8% of the Soviet government of Moscow; 22.6% in Ukraine (30.3% in Kharkov, the capital); 30.6% in Byelorussia (38.3% in Minsk).[2136] If true, then the percentage of Jews in urban areas about equaled that of Jews in the government.

Solomon Schwartz, using data from the work of Lev Singer maintained that the percentage of Jews in the Soviet government was about the same as their percentage of the urban population (and it was significantly lower

---

[2132] Ю. Ларин. Евреи и антисемитизм в СССР (далее — Ю. Ларин). М.;Л.: ГИЗ, 1929, с. 58-60.
[2133] М. Агурский. Идеология национал-большевизма. Париж: YMCA-Press, 1980, с. 265.
[2134] КЕЭ, т. 1, с. 326.
[2135] Ю. Ларин, с. 63-64, 74.
[2136] Izvestia, 1927, 11 déc.. p. 1.

in the Bolshevik party itself).[2137] Using Ordzhonikidze's data, Jews at 1.82% of the population by 1926 were represented in the Apparatus at about 6.5 times their proportion in the *population at large*.

Its easy to underestimate the impact of the sudden freedom from pre-revolutionary limits on civil rights: "Earlier, power was not accessible to Jews at all and now they had more access to power than anyone else" according to I. Bikerman.[2138] This sudden change provoked a varied reaction in all strata of society. S. Schwartz writes "from the mid-twenties there arose a new wave of anti-Semitism" which was "not related to the old anti-Semitism, nor a legacy of the past"". "It is an extreme exaggeration to explain it as originating with backwards workers from rural areas as anti-Semitism generally was not a fact of life in the Russian countryside." No, "It was a much more dangerous phenomenon." It arose in the middle strata of urban society and reached the highest levels of the working class which, before the revolution, had remained practically untouched by the phenomenon. "It reached students and members of the communist party and the Komsomol and, even earlier, local government in smaller provincial towns" where "an aggressive and active anti-Semitism took hold".[2139]

The *Jewish Encyclopedia* writes that from the beginning of the 20th century "though official Soviet propaganda writes that anti-Semitism in the latter part of the 20?s was a "legacy of the past", "the facts show that, it arose mainly as a result of colliding social forces in large cities." It was fanned by the "widely held opinion that power in the country had been seized by Jews who formed the nucleus of the Bolsheviks.[2140]" Bikerman wrote with evident concern in 1923 that "the Jew is in all corners and on all levels of power." "The Russian sees him as a ruler of Moscow, at the head of the capital on Neva [Petrograd], and at the head of the Red Army, a perfected death machine. He sees that St. Vladimir Prospect has been renamed Nakhimson Prospect... The Russian sees the Jew as judge and hangman; he sees Jews at every turn, not only among the communists, but among people like himself, everywhere doing the bidding of Soviet power" not surprising, the Russian, comparing present with past, is confirmed in his

---

[2137] С.М. Шварц. Антисемитизм в Советском Союзе. Нью-Йорк: Изд-во им. Чехова, 1952, с. 44-46, 48-49 (со ссылкой на: Л. Зингер. Материалы и исследования Объединённой статистико-экономической комиссии при ЦК ОРТа. М., 1927. Вып. 1; Еврейское население в СССР (статистико-экономический обзор) М.; Л.: Соцэгиз, 1932).

[2138] И.М. Бикерман. Россия и русское еврейство // Россия и евреи: Сб. 1 (далее — РиЕ) / Отечественное объединение русских евреев заграницей. Париж: YMCA-Press, 1978, с. 28 [1-е изд. — Берлин: Основа, 1924].

[2139] С.М. Шварц. Антисемитизм..., с. 7, 17, 25, 29, 39.

[2140] PEJ. t. 8, pp. 161-162.

idea that power is Jewish power, that it exists for Jews and does the bidding of Jews".[2141]

No less visible than Jewish participation in government was the suddenly created new order in culture and education.

The new societal inequality was not so much along the lines of nationality as it was a matter of town versus country. The Russian reader needs no explanation of the advantages bestowed by Soviet power from the 20's to the 80's on capital cities when compared to the rest of the country. One of the main advantages was the level of education and range of opportunities for higher learning. Those established during the early years of Soviet power in capital cities assured for their children and grandchildren future decades of advantages, vis a vis those in the country. The enhanced opportunities in post-secondary education and graduate education meant increased access to the educated elite.

Meanwhile, from 1918 the ethnic Russian intelligentsia was being pushed to the margins.

In the 20's students already enrolled in institutions of higher learning were *expelled* based on social origins policy. Children of the nobility, the clergy, government bureaucrats, military officers, merchants, even children of petty shop keepers were expelled. Applicants from these classes and children of the intelligentsia were denied entry to institutions of higher learning in the years that followed. As a "nationality repressed by the Tsar's regime," Jews did not receive this treatment. Despite "bourgeois origin," the Jewish youth was freely accepted in institutions of higher learning. Jews were forgiven for *not being proletarian.*

According to the *Jewish Encyclopedia*, "with the absence of limitations based upon nationality for entry to institutions of higher learning, Jews came to make up 15.4% of all university students in the USSR, almost twice their proportion of the urban population at large.[2142] Further, Jews "owing to a high level of motivation" quickly bypassed the unprepared "proletarian" factory workers who had been pushed forward in the education system, and proceeded unhindered into graduate school. In the 20's and 30's and for a long time after, Jews were a disproportionately large part of the intelligentsia.

According to G. Aronson, wide access to higher and specialized education led to the formation of cadres of doctors, teachers and particularly engineers and technical workers among Jews, which naturally led to

---

[2141] И.М. Бикерман. Россия и русское еврейство // РиЕ, с. 22-23.
[2142] КЕЭ, т. 8, с. 186.

university faculty posts in the expanding system of higher education[2143] and in the widely proliferating research institutions. In the beginning of 1920's, the post of "the State Chair of Science" was occupied not by a scientist but a Bolshevik official, Mandelshtam-Lyadov.[2144]

Even sharper changes gripped the economic life of the country. Bukharin publicly announced at a Communist Party conference in 1927 that "during War Communism, we purged the Russian petty and middle bourgeoisie along with leading capitalists." When the economy was later opened up to free trade "petty and middle Jewish bourgeoisie took the place of the Russian bourgeoisie... and roughly the same happened with our Russian intelligentsia which bucked and sabotaged our efforts... Its place has been taken in some areas by the Jewish intelligentsia". Moreover, Jewish bourgeousie and intelligentsia are concentrated in our central regions and cities, where they moved in from western provinces and southern towns." Here "even in the Party ranks one often encounters anti-Semitic tendencies." "Comrades, we must wage a fierce battle against anti-Semitism".[2145]

Bukharin described a situation that was obvious to all. Unlike Russian bourgeosie, the Jewish bourgeoisie was not destroyed. The Jewish merchant, much less likely to be damned as a "man of the past," found defenders.

Relatives or sympathizers in the Soviet Apparatus... warned about pending arrests or seizures. And if he lost anything – it was just capital, not life.

Cooperation was quasi-official through the Jewish Commissariat at the Sovnarkom. The Jews until now had been "a repressed people" and that meant, naturally, they needed help. Larin explained the destruction of the "Russian bourgeoisie" as a "correction of the injustice that existed under the Tsars before the Revolution".[2146]

When NEP (New Economic Policy) was crushed, the blow fell with less force against Jewish NEPmen owing to connections in Soviet ruling circles.

Bukharin had been speaking in answer to a remarkable speech by Prof. Y.V. Klyutchnikov, a publicist and a former Kadet. In December 1926, the

---

[2143] Г. Аронсон. Еврейский вопрос в эпоху Сталина // Книга о русском еврействе, 1917-1967 (далее — КРЕ-2). Нью-Йорк: Союз Русских Евреев, 1968, с. 137.
[2144] Российская Еврейская Энциклопедия (далее — РЕЭ). 2-е изд., испр. и доп. М., 1995. Т. 2, с. 218.
[2145] Н. Бухарин. [Доклад на XXIV Ленинградской губпартконференции] // Правда, 1927, 2 февраля, с. 4.
[2146] Ю. Ларин, с. 86.

professor spoke at a "meeting on the Jewish question" at the Moscow Conservatory. "We have isolated expressions of hooliganism... Its source is the hurt national feelings of Russians. The February Revolution established the equality of all citizens of Russia, including Jews. The October Revolution went further with the Russian nation proclaiming self-renunciation. A certain imbalance has developed with respect to the proportion of the Jewish population in the country as a whole and the positions they have temporarily occupied in the cities. We are in our own cities and they arrive and squeeze us out. When Russians see Russian women, elders and children freezing on the street 9 to 11 hours a day, getting soaked by the rain in their tents at the market and when they see relatively warm covered Jewish kiosks with bread and sausage they are not happy. These phenomena are catastrophic... and must be considered... There is a terrible disproportion in the government structure, in daily life and in other areas... We have a housing crisis in Moscow – masses of people are crowding into areas not fit for habitation and at the same time people see others pouring in from other parts of the country taking up housing. These arrivals are Jews. A national dissatisfaction is rising and a defensiveness and fear of other nationalities. We must not close our eyes to that. A Russian speaking to a Russian will say things that he will not say to a Jew. Many are saying that there are too many Jews in Moscow. This must be dealt with, but don't call it anti-Semitism".[2147]

But Larin regarded Klyutchnikov's speech as a manifestation of antiSemitism, saying "this speech serves as an example of the good nature of Soviet power in its battle against anti-Semitism because Klyutchnikov was roundly criticized by speakers who followed at the same meeting, but no "administrative measures" were taken against him".[2148] (Here it is, the frustration of the communist activist!) Agursky writes: "one would expect repression to swiftly follow for such a speech in the 20's and 30's," but Klyutchnikov got off. Maybe he received secret support from some quarters?[2149] (But why look for secret causes? It would have been too much of a scandal to punish such a famous publicist, who just returned from abroad and could have harmed a reverse migration that was so important for Soviet authorities [Translator's note: "reverse migration" – return of people who emigrated from Russia during previous period of revolutions and Civil War].)

The 20's were spoken of as the "conquest" by the Jews of Russian capital cities and industrial centers where conditions were better. As well, there

---

[2147] Ю. Ларин*, с. 124-125 (со ссылкой на стенограмму речи Ключникова и указанием, что часть её была напечатана в «Рабочей Москве» 7 дек. 1926).
[2148] Там же, с. 127.
[2149] М. Агурский. Идеология национал-большевизма, с. 223.

was a migration to the better areas within the cities. G. Fedotov describes Moscow at that time: "The revolution deformed its soul, turning it inside out, emptying out its mansions, and filling them with a foreign and alien people".[2150] A Jewish joke from the era: "Even from Berdichev and even the very old come to Moscow: they want to die in a Jewish city".[2151]

In a private letter V.I. Vernadsky, a prominent Russian polymath, in 1927 writes: "Moscow now is like Berdichev; the power of Jewry is enormous – and anti-Semitism (including in communist circles) is growing unabated".[2152]

Larin: "We do not hide figures that demonstrate growth of the Jewish population in urban centers," it is completely unavoidable and will continue into the future." He forecasted the migration from Ukraine and Byelorussia of an additional 600,000 Jews. "We can't look upon this as something shameful, that the party would silence… we must create a spirit in the working class so that anyone who gives a speech against the arrival of Jews in Moscow would be considered a counter-revolutionary".[2153]

And for *counter-revolutionaries* there is nine grams of lead[2154] – that much is clear.

But, what to do about "anti-Semitic tendencies" even in "our party circles" was a concern in the upper levels of the party.

According to official data reported in *Pravda* in 1922, Jews made up 5.2% of the party.[2155] M. Agursky: "But their actual influence was considerably more.

In that same year at the 11th Communist Party Congress Jews made up 14.6% of the voting delegates, 18.3% of the non-voting delegates and 26% of those elected to the Central Committee at the conference". [2156] (Sometimes one accidentally comes upon such data: a taciturn memoirist from Moscow opens *Pravda* in July, 1930 and notes: "The portrait of the 25-member Presidium of the Communist Party included 11 Russians, 8

[2150] Г.П. Федотов. Лицо России: Сб. статей (1918-1931). Париж: YMCA-Press, 1967, с, 57.
[2151] Г. Симон. Евреи царствуют в России: Из воспоминаний американца. Париж: Родник, 1929, с. 50.
[2152] Письмо В.И. Вернадского И.И. Петрункевичу от 14 июня 1927 // Новый мир, 1989, №12, с. 219.
[2153] Ю. Ларин, с. 61-63, 86.
[2154] Там же, с. 259.
[2155] Е.С. О национальном составе РКП // Правда, 1923, 21 августа, с. 5.
[2156] М. Агурский. Идеология национал-большевизма, с. 264.

Jews, 3 from the Caucasus, and 3 Latvians".[2157]) In the large cities, close to areas of the former Pale of Settlement, the following data: In the early 20's party organizations in Minsk, Gomel and Vitebsk in 1922 were, respectively, 35.8%, 21.1%, and 16.6% Jewish, respectively.[2158] Larin notes: "Jewish revolutionaries play a bigger part than any others in revolutionary activity" thanks to their qualities, Jewish workers often find it easier to rise to positions of local leadership".[2159]

In the same issue of *Pravda*, it is noted that Jews at 5.2% of the Party were in the third place after Russians (72%) and Ukrainians (5.9%), followed by Latvians (2.5%) and then Georgians, Tatars, Poles and Byelorussians. Jews had the highest rate of per capita party membership – 7.2% of Jews were in the party versus 3.8% for Great Russians.[2160]

M. Agursky correctly notes that in absolute numbers the majority of communists were, of course, Russians, but "the unusual role of Jews in leadership was dawning on the Russians".[2161] It was just too obvious.

For instance, Zinoviev "gathered many Jews around himself in the Petersburg leadership." (Agursky suggests this was what Larin was referring to in his discussion of the photograph of the Presidium of Petrograd Soviet in 1918 in his book[2162]). By 1921 the preponderance of Jews in Petrograd CP organization... "was apparently so odious that the Politburo, reflecting on the lessons of Kronshtadt and the anti-Semitic mood of Petrograd, decided to send several ethnic Russian communists to Petrograd, though entirely for publicity purposes." So Uglanov took the place of Zorin-Homberg as head of Gubkom; Komarov replaced Trilisser and Semyonov went to the Cheka. But Zinoviev "objected to the decision of Politboro and fought the new group" – and as a result Uglanov was recalled from Petrograd and "a purely Russian opposition group formed spontaneously in the Petrograd organization," a group, "forced to counter the rest of the organization whose tone was set by Jews".[2163]

But not only in Petrograd – at the 12th Communist Party Congress (1923) three out of six Politburo members were Jewish. Three out of seven were Jews in the leadership of the Komsomol and in the Presidium of the all-

---

[2157] И.И. Шитц. Дневник «Великого перелома» (март 1928 — август 1931). Париж: YMCA-Press, 1991, с. 202.
[2158] Евреи в коммунистической партии // Еврейская трибуна, 1923, 1 июня(№ 164).
[2159] Ю. Ларин, с. 257, 268.
[2160] Е.С. О национальном составе РКП // Правда, 1923, 21 августа, с. 5.
[2161] М. Агурский. Идеология национал-большевизма, с. 303.
[2162] Ю. Ларин, с. 258.
[2163] М. Агурский. Идеология национал-большевизма, с. 238-239.

Russia Conference in 1922.[2164] This was not tolerable to other leading communists and, apparently, preparations were begun for an anti-Jewish revolt at the 13th Party Congress (May 1924)."There is evidence that a group of members of CK was planning to drive leading Jews from the Politburo, replacing them with Nogin, Troyanovsky and others and that only the death of Nogin interrupted the plot."

His death, "literally on the eve of the Congress", resulted from an "unsuccessful and unnecessary operation for a stomach ulcer by the same surgeon who dispatched Frunze with an equally unneeded operation a year and a half later".[2165]

The Cheka-GPU had second place in terms of real power after the Party. A researcher of archival material, whom we quoted in Chapter 16, reports interesting statistics on the composition of the Cheka in 1920, 1922, 1923, 1924, 1925 and 1927.[2166] He concludes that the proportion of national minorities in the apparatus gradually fell towards the mid-20's. "In the OGPU as a whole, the proportion of personnel from a national minority fell to 30-35% and to 40-45% for those in leadership." (These figures contrast with 50% and 70% respectively during the "Red Terror.") However, "we observe a decline in the percentage of Latvians and an increase in the percentage of Jews". The 20's was a period of significant influx of Jewish cadres into the organs of the OGPU".

The author explains this: "Jews strived to utilize capabilities not needed in the pre-revolutionary period. With the increasing professionalism and need for organization, Jews, better than others, were able to meet the needs of OGPU and the new conditions." For example, three of Dzerzhinsky's four assistants were Jews – G. Yagoda, V.L. Gerson, and M.M. Lutsky.[2167]

In the 20's and 30's, the leading Chekists circled over the land like birds of prey flying quickly from cliff to cliff. From the top ranks of the Central Asian GPU off to Byelorussia and from Western Siberia to the North Caucasus, from Kharkov to Orenburg and from Orel to Vinnitza – there was a perpetual whirlwind of movement and change. And the lonely voices of those surviving witnesses could only speak much later, without precise

---

[2164] Известия, 1922, 17 мая, с. 4.
[2165] Большевики: Документы по истории большевизма с 1903 по 1916 год бывш. Московского Охранного Отделения / Сост. М.А. Цявловский, с дополн. Справками А.М. Серебренникова. Нью-Йорк: Телекс, 1990, с. 316.
[2166] Л.Ю. Кричевский. Евреи в аппарате ВЧК-ОГПУ в 20-е годы // Евреи и русская революция: Материалы и исследования / Ред.-сост. О.В. Будницкий. Москва, Иерусалим: Гешарим, 1999, с. 330-336.
[2167] Там же, с. 340, 344-345.

reference to time, of the executioners whose names flashed by them. The personnel, the deeds and the power of the Cheka were completely secret.

For the 10th anniversary of the glorious Cheka we read in a newspaper a formal order signed by the omnipresent Unshlicht (from 1921 – deputy head of Cheka, from 1923 – member of Revvoensovet, from 1925 – Deputy Narkom of the Navy[2168]). In it, Yagoda was rewarded for "particularly valuable service... for sacrifice in the battle with counter revolution"; also given awards were M. Trilisser (distinguished for his "devotion to the revolution and untiring persecution of its enemies") as well as 32 Chekists who had not been before the public until then. Each of them with the flick of a finger could destroy anyone of us! Among them were Jakov Agranov (for the work on all important political trials – and in the future he will orchestrate the trials of Zinoviev, Kamenev, the "Industrial Party Trial," and others[2169]), Zinovy Katznelson, Matvey Berman (transferred from Central Asia to the Far East) and Lev Belsky (transferred from the Far East to Central Asia).

There were several new names: Lev Zalin, Lev Meyer, Leonid Bull (dubbed "warden of Solovki"), Simeon Gendin, Karl Pauker. Some were already known to only a few, but now the people would get to know them. In this jubilee newspaper[2170] issue we can find a large image of slick Menzhinsky with his faithful deputy Yagoda and a photograph of Trilisser. Shortly afterward, another twenty Chekists were awarded with the order of the Red Banner, and again we see a motley company of Russians, Latvians, and Jews, the latter in the same proportions – around one-third.

Some of them were avoiding publicity. Simeon Schwartz was director of the Ukrainian Cheka. A colleague of his, Yevsei Shirvindt directed the transport of prisoners and convoys throughout the USSR. Naturally, such Chekists as Grimmeril Heifetz (a spy from the end of the Civil War to the end of WWII) and Sergei Spigelglas (a Chekist from 1917 who, through his work as a spy, rose to become director of the Foreign Department of the NKVD and a two-time recipient of the honorary title of "distinguished chekist") worked out of the public eye. Careers of others, like Albert Stromin-Stroyev, were less impressive (he "conducted interrogations of scientists during the "Academy trial" in 1929-31"[2171]).

David Azbel remembers the Nakhamkins, a family of Hasidic Jews from Gomel. (Azbel himself was imprisoned because of snitching by the younger family member, Lev.) "The revolution threw the Nakhamkins onto

---

[2168] РЭЭ, т. 3, с. 178.
[2169] РЭЭ, т.1. с. 21.
[2170] Известия, 1927, 18 дек., с. 1, 3, 4.
[2171] РЭЭ, т. 3, с. 115-116, 286, 374, 394, 414.

the crest of a wave. They thirsted for the revenge on everyone – aristocrats, the wealthy, Russians, few were left out. This was their path to self-realization. It was no accident that fate led the offspring of this glorious clan to the Cheka, GPU, NKVD and the prosecutor's office. To fulfill their plans, the Bolsheviks needed "rabid" people and this is what they got with the Nakhamkins. One member of this family, Roginsky, achieved "brilliant heights" as Deputy Prosecutor for the USSR "but during the Stalinist purges was imprisoned, as were many, and became a cheap stool pigeon... the others were not so well known. They changed their last name to one more familiar to the Russian ear and occupied high places in the Organs".[2172] Unshlict did not change his name to one "more familiar to the Russian ear."

See, this Slavic brother became truly a "father of Russians": a warplane built with funds of farmer mutual aid societies (that is, – on the last dabs of money extorted from peasants) was named after him. No doubt, farmers could not even pronounce his name and likely thought that this Pole was a Jew. Indeed, this reminds us that the Jewish issue does not explain the devastation of revolution, albeit it places a heavy hue on it. As it was also hued by many other unpronounceable names – from Polish Dzerzhinsky and Eismont to Latvian Vatsetis. And what if we looked into the Latvian issue? Apart from those soldiers who forced the dissolution of the Russian Constituent Assembly and who later provided security for the Bolshevik leaders during the entire Civil War, we find many high-placed Latvian Bolsheviks. Gekker suppressed the uprising in Yaroslavl Guberniya. Among others, there were Rudzutak, Eikhe, Eikhmans from Solovki, M. Karklin, A. Kaktyn, R. Kisis, V. Knorin, A. Skundre (one of those who suppressed the Tambov Uprising); Chekists Petere, Latsis, and an "honorary Chekist" Lithuanian I. Yusis. This thread can lead directly to 1991 (Pugo...) And what if we separate Ukrainians from Russians (as demanded by the Ukrainians these days)? We will find dozens of them at the highest posts of Bolshevik hierarchy, from its conception to the very end.

No, power was not Jewish power then. Political power was internationalist – and its ranks were to the large extent Russian. But under its multi-hued internationalism it united in an *anti-Russian* front against a Russian state and Russian traditions.

In view of the anti-Russian orientation of power and the multinational makeup of the executioners, why, in Ukraine, Central Asia and the Baltics

---

[2172] Д. Азбель. До, во время и после // Время и мы (далее — ВМ): Международный журнал литературы и общественных проблем. Нью-Йорк, 1989, № 105, с. 204-205.

did the people think it was Russians who had enslaved them? Because they were alien. A destroyer from one's own nation is much closer than a destroyer from an alien tribe. And while it is a mistake to attribute the ruin and destruction to nationalist chauvinism, at the same time in Russia in the 20's the inevitable question hanged in the air that was posed many year later by Leonard Schapiro: why was it "highly likely that anyone unfortunate enough to fall into the hands of the Cheka would go before a Jewish interrogator or be shot by a Jew."[2173]?

Yet the majority of modern writers fail to even acknowledge these questions. Often Jewish authors thoughtlessly and meticulously comply and publish vast lists of Jewish leadership of the time. For example, see how proudly the article "Jews in Kremlin",[2174] published in journal *Alef*, provides a list of the highest Soviet officials – Jews for 1925. It listed eight out of twelve directors of Gosbank. The same level of Jewish representation was found among top trade union leaders. And it comments: "We do not fear accusations.

Quite opposite – it is active Jewish participation in governing the state that helps to understand why state affairs were better then than now, when Jews at top positions are as rare as hen's teeth. Unbelievably, that was written in 1989.

Regarding the army, one Israeli scholar[2175] painstakingly researched and proudly published a long list of Jewish commanders of the Red Army, during and after the Civil War. Another Israeli researcher published statistics obtained from the 1926 census to the effect that while Jews made up 1.7% of the male population in the USSR, they comprised 2.1% of the combat officers, 4.4% of the command staff, 10.3% of the political leadership and 18.6% of military doctors.[2176]

And what did the West see? If the government apparatus could operate in secret under the communist party, which maintained its conspiratorial secrecy even after coming to power, diplomats were on view everywhere in the world.

[2173] Leonard Schapiro. The Role of the Jews in the Russian Revolutionary Movement // The Slavonic and East European Review, vol. 40, London: Athlone Press, 1961-62, p. 165.
[2174] М. Зарубежный. Евреи в Кремле // Алеф, Тель-Авив, 1989, Февраль (№ 263), с. 24-28.
[2175] Арон Абрамович. В решающей войне: Участие и роль евреев СССР в войне против нацизма. 2-е изд. Тель-Авив, 1982. Т. 1.
[2176] Ицхак Арад. Холокауст: Катастрофа европейского еврейства (1933-1945). Иерусалим, 1990, с. 96.

At the first diplomatic conferences with Soviets in Geneva and the Hague in 1922, Europe could not help but notice that Soviet delegations and their staff were mostly Jewish.[2177] Due to the injustice of history, a long and successful career of Boris Yefimovich Stern is now completely forgotten (he wasn't even mentioned in the Great Soviet Encyclopedia (GSE) of 1971). Yet he was the second most important assistant to Chicherin during Genoa Conference, and later at Hague Conference, and still later he led Soviet delegation during longstanding demilitarization negotiations. He was also a member of Soviet delegation at League of Nations. Stern was ambassador in Italy and Finland and conducted delicate negotiations with the Finns before the Soviet-Finnish war.

Finally, from 1946 to 1948 he was the head of the Soviet delegation at UN. And he used to be a longstanding lecturer at the High Diplomatic School (at one point during "anti-cosmopolitan" purges he was fired but in 1953 he was restored at that position).

An associate of Chicherin, Leon Haikis worked for many years in the Narkomat of the Foreign Affairs (NKID). In 1937 he was sent to a warmer place as ambassador to the embattled Republican government of Spain (where he directed the Republican side during the Civil War), but was arrested and removed. Fyodor Rotshtein founded the communist party in Great Britain in 1920 and in that very year he was a member of the Soviet delegation in negotiations with England! Two years later he represented RSFSR at the Hague conference.[2178] (As Litvinov's right hand man he independently negotiated with ambassadors to Russia in important matters; until 1930 he was in the Presidium of NKID and for 30 years before his death, a professor at the Moscow State University.)

And on the other side of the globe, in southern China, M. Gruzenberg-Borodin had served for 5 years when the December 1927 Canton Rebellion against the Kuomintang broke out. It is now recognized that the revolt was prepared by our Vice Consul, Abram Hassis, who, at age of 33 was killed by Chinese soldiers. *Izvestia* ran several articles with the obituaries and the photographs of "comrades in arms" under Kuibishev, comparing the fallen comrade with highly distinguished communists like Furmanov and Frunze.[2179]

In 1922 Gorky told the academic Ipatiev that 98% of the Soviet trade mission in Berlin was Jewish[2180] and this probably was not much of an

---

[2177] Об этом, в частности, см.: Д.С. Пасманик. Русская революция и еврейство: (Большевизм и иудаизм). Париж, 1923, с. 148.
[2178] РЕЭ, т. 2, с. 499-500, т. 3, с. 273, 422.
[2179] Известия, 1927, 22 декабря, с. 1.
[2180] Vladimir N. Ipatieff. The Life of a Chemist. Stanford, 1946, p. 377.

exaggeration. A similar picture would be found in other Western capitals where the Soviets were ensconced. The "work" that was performed in early Soviet trade missions is colorfully described in a book by G.A. Solomon,[2181] the first Soviet trade representative in Tallinn, Estonia – the first European capital to recognize the Bolsheviks. There are simply no words to describe the boundless theft by the early Bolsheviks in Russia (along with covert actions against the West) and the corruption of soul these activities brought to their effecters.

Shortly after Gorky's conversation with Ipatiev he "was criticized in the Soviet press for an article where he reproached the Soviet government for its placement of so many Jews in positions of responsibility in government and industry. He had nothing against Jews per se, but, departing from views he expressed in 1918, he thought that Russians should be in charge".[2182]

And *Pravda*'s twin publication *Dar Amos* (*Pravda* in Yiddish) objected strongly: Do they (i.e. Gorky and Shalom Ash, the interviewer) really want for Jews to refuse to serve in any government position? For them to get out of the way? That kind of decision could only be made by counter-revolutionaries or cowards".[2183]

In *Jews in the Kremlin*, the author, using the 1925 Annual Report of NKID, introduces leading figures and positions in the central apparatus. "In the publishing arm there is not one non-Jew" and further, with evident pride, the author "examines the staff in the Soviet consulates around the world and finds there is not one country in the world where the Kremlin has not placed a trusted Jew".[2184]

If he was interested, the author of *Alef* could find no small number of Jews in the Supreme Court of RSFSR of 1920's,[2185] in the Procurator's office and RKI. Here we can find already familiar A. Goikhbarg, who, after chairing the Lesser Sovnarcom, worked out the legal system for the NEP era, supervised development of Civil Code of RSFSR and was director of the Institute of Soviet Law.[2186]

It is much harder to examine lower, provincial level authorities, and not only because of their lower exposure to the press but also due to their rapid fluidity, and frequent turnover of cadres from post to post, from region to region. This amazing early Soviet shuffling of personnel might have been caused either by an acute deficit of reliable men as in in the Lenin's era or

---

[2181] Г.А. Соломон. Среди красных вождей. Париж: Мишень, 1930. 4.2.
[2182] Vladimir N. Ipatieff. The Life of a Chemist, p. 377.
[2183] Еврейская трибуна*, 1922, 6 июля (№ 130), с. 6.
[2184] М. Зарубежный. Евреи в Кремле // Алеф, 1989, Февраль, с. 26-27.
[2185] Izvestia. 1927, 25 août, p. 2.
[2186] РЕЭ, т. 1, с. 331.

by mistrust (and the "tearing" of a functionary from the developed connections) in Stalin's times. Here are several such career "trajectories".

Lev Maryasin was Secretary of Gubkom of Orel Guberniya, later – chair of Sovnarkhoz of Tatar Republic, later – head of a department of CK of Ukraine, later – chair of board of directors of Gosbank of USSR, and later – Deputy Narkom of Finances of USSR. Moris Belotsky was head of Politotdel of the First Cavalry Army (a very powerful position), participated in suppression of the Kronshtadt Uprising, later – in NKID, then later – the First Secretary of North Ossetian Obkom, and even later was First Secretary of CK of Kyrgyzstan.

A versatile functionary Grigory Kaminsky was Secretary of Gubkom of Tula Guberniya, later – Secretary of CK of Azerbaijan, later – chair of Kolkhozcenter, and later – Narkom of Health Care Service.

Abram Kamensky was Narkom of State Control Commission of Donetsk-Krivoy Rog Republic, later – Deputy Narkom of Nationalities of RSFSR, later – Secretary of Gubkom of Donetsk, later served in Narkomat of Agriculture, then – director of Industrial Academy, and still later he served in the Narkomat of Finances.[2187] There were many Jewish leaders of the Komsomol.

Ascendant career of Efim Tzetlin began with the post of the First Chairman of CK RKSM (fall of 1918); after the Civil War he become Secretary of CK and Moscow Committee of RKSM, since 1922 – a member of executive committee of KIM (Young Communist International), in 1923-24 – a spy in Germany, later he worked in Secretariat of Executive Committee of Communist International, still later – in editorial office of *Pravda*, and even later he was head of Bukharin's secretariat, where this latter post eventually proved fatal for him.[2188]

The career of Isaiah Khurgin was truly amazing. In 1917 he was a member of Ukrainian Rada [Parliament], served both in the Central and the Lesser chambers and worked on the draft of legislation on Jewish autonomy in Ukraine. Since 1920 we see him as a member VKPb, in 1921 – he was the Trade Commissioner of Ukraine in Poland, in 1923 he represented German-American Transport Society in USA, serving as a de facto Soviet plenipotentiary. He founded and chaired Amtorg (American Trading Corporation). His future seemed incredibly bright but alas at the age of 38 (in 1925) he was drowned in a lake in USA.[2189] What a life he had!

[2187] Там же, с. 105, 536, 538, т. 2, с. 256.
[2188] РЕЭ. т. 3, с. 311-312.
[2189] РЕЭ, т. 3, с. 302.

Let's glance at the economy. Moses Rukhimovitch was Deputy Chair of Supreme Soviet of the National Economy. Ruvim Levin was a member of Presidium of Gosplan (Ministry of Economic Planning) of USSR and Chair of Gosplan of RSFSR (later – Deputy Narkom of Finances of USSR). Zakhary Katzenelenbaum was inventor of the governmental "Loan for Industrialization"

in 1927 (and, therefore, of all subsequent "loans"). He also was one of the founders of Soviet Gosbank. Moses Frumkin was Deputy Narkom of Foreign Trade from 1922 but in fact he was in charge of the entire Narkomat. He and A. I. Vainstein were long-serving members of the panel of Narkomat of Finances of USSR. Vladimirov-Sheinfinkel was Narkom of Provand of Ukraine, later – Narkom of Agriculture of Ukraine, and even later he served as Narkom of Finances of RSFSR and Deputy Narkom of Finances of USSR.[2190]

If you are building a mill, you are responsible for possible flood. A newspaper article by Z. Zangvil describes celebratory jubilee meeting of the Gosbank board of directors in 1927 (five years after introduction of chervonets [a former currency of the Russian Empire and Soviet Union] and explains the importance of chervonets and displays a group photograph. The article lauds Sheinman, the chairman of the board, and Katzenelenbaum, a member of the board.[2191] Sheinman's signature was reproduced on every Soviet chervonets and he simultaneously held the post of Narkom of Domestic Commerce (from 1924). And hold your breath, my reader! He didn't return from a foreign visit in 1929![2192] He preferred to live in bloody capitalism!

Speaking of mid-level Soviet institutions, the well-known economist and professor B. D. Brutskus asks: "Did not the revolution open up new opportunities for the Jewish population?" Among these opportunities would be government service. "…more than anything it is obvious the large numbers of Jews in government, particularly in higher posts," and "most of the Jewish government employees come from the higher classes not the Jewish masses."

But, upperclass Jews, required to serve the Soviet government did not gain, but lost in comparison with what they would have had in their own businesses or freely pursuing professions. As well, those who moved through the Soviet hierarchy had to display the utmost of tact to avoid arousing jealousy and dissatisfaction. A large number of Jewish public servants, regardless of talent and qualities, would not lessen anti-Semitism,

---

[2190] РЕЭ, т. 1, с. 197-198, 234, 275-276, т. 2, с. 18, 140 518 т. 3, с. 260.
[2191] Известия, 1927, 27 ноября, с. 4.
[2192] РЕЭ, т. 3, с. 383.

but would strengthen it among other workers and among the intelligentsia." He maintained "there are many Jewish public servants particularly in the commissariats devoted to economic functions".[2193]

Larin put it more simply: "the Jewish intelligentsia in large numbers served the victorious revolution readily" realizing "access to previously denied government service".[2194]

G. Pomerantz, speaking 50 years later justified this: "history dragged Jews into the government apparatus," ... Jews had nowhere else to go besides to government institutions," including the Cheka [2195] as we commented earlier. The Bolsheviks also "had no other place to go – the Jewish Tribune from Paris explains "there were so many Jews in various Soviet functions" because of the need for literate, sober bureaucrats".[2196]

However one can read in *Jewish World*, a Parisian publication, that: "there is no denying that a large percentage of Jewish youth from lower social elements — some completely hopeless failures, were drawn to Bolshevism by the sudden prospect of power; for others it was the 'world proletarian revolution' and for still others it was a mixture of adventurous idealism and practical utilitarianism.[2197]

Of course not all were "drawn to Bolshevism." There were large numbers of peaceful Jews whom the revolution crushed. However, the life in the towns of the former Pale of Settlement was not visible to ordinary non-Jewish person.

Instead the average person saw, as described by M. Heifetz, "arrogant, self-confident and self-satisfied adult Jews at ease on 'red holidays' and 'red weddings'... 'We now sit where Tsars and generals once sat, and they sit beneath us'".[2198]

These were not unwaveringly ideological Bolsheviks. The invitation to power was extended to "millions of residents from rotting shtetls, to pawn brokers, tavern owners, contrabandists, seltzer water salesmen and those who sharpened their wills in the fight for survival and their minds in

---

[2193] Б. Бруцкус. Еврейское население под коммунистической властью // Современные записки, Париж, 1928, кн. 36, с. 519-521.
[2194] Ю. Ларин, с. 73.
[2195] Г. Померанц. Сон о справедливом возмездии // Синтаксис: Публицистика, критика, полемика. Париж, 1980, № 6, с. 52-53, 68.
[2196] В. Мирский. Чёрная сотня // Еврейская трибуна, 1924, 1 февраля (№ 58), с. 3.
[2197] Ст. Иванович. Евреи и советская диктатура // Еврейский мир: Ежегодник на 1939г. (далее — ЕМ-1). Париж: Объединение русско-еврейской интеллигенции, с. 47.
[2198] Михаил Хейфец. Место и время (еврейские заметки). Париж: Третья волна, 1978, с. 43.

evening study of the Torah and the Talmud. The authorities invited them to Moscow, Petrograd and Kiev to take into their quick nervous hands that which was falling from the soft, pampered hands of the hereditary intelligentsia – everything from the finances of a great power, nuclear physics and the secret police.

They couldn't resist the temptation of Esau, the less so since, in addition to a bowl of potage, they were offered the chance to build the promised land, that is, communism".[2199] There was "a Jewish illusion that this was their country".[2200]

Many Jews did not enter the whirlwind of revolution and didn't automatically join the Bolsheviks, but the general national inclination was one of sympathy for the Bolshevik cause and a feeling that life would now be incomparably better. "The majority of Jews met the revolution, not with fear, but with welcome arms".[2201] In the early 20's the Jews of Byelorussia and Ukraine were a "significant source of support for the centralization of power in Moscow over and against the influence of regional power".[2202] Evidence of Jewish attitudes in 1923 showed the overwhelming majority considered Bolshevism to be a lesser evil and that if the Bolsheviks lost power it would be worse for them.[2203]

"Now, a Jew can command an army!... These gifts alone were enough to bring Jewish support for the communists... The disorder of the Bolshevism seemed like a brilliant victory for justice and no one noticed the complete suppression of freedom".[2204] Large number of Jews who did not leave after the revolution failed to foresee the bloodthirstiness of the new government, though the persecution, even of socialists, was well underway. The Soviet government was as unjust and cruel then as it was to be in '37 and in 1950. But in the 20's it did not raise alarm or resistance in the wider Jewish population since its force was aimed not at Jewry.

When Leskov, in a report for the Palensky Commission - a pre-revolution government commission, one by one refuted all the presumed consequences for Russians from the removal of restrictions on Jewish settlement in Russia he couldn't have foreseen the great degree to which

---

[2199] Там же, с. 44-45.

[2200] В. Богуславский. В защиту Куняева // "22": Общественно-политический и литературный журнал еврейской интеллигенции из СССР в Израиле. Тель-Авив, 1980, № 16, с. 174.

[2201] R. Rutman. Solzhenitsyn and the Jewish Question // Soviet Jewish Affairs, 1974, Vol. 4, № 2, p. 7.

[2202] М. Агурский. Идеология национал-большевизма, с. 150.

[2203] К евреям всех стран! // РиЕ, с. 7.

[2204] И.М. Бикерман. К самопознанию еврея: Чем мы были, чем мы стали, чем мы должны быть. Париж, 1939, с. 70.

Jews would be participating in governing the country and the economy in the 20's.

The revolution changed the entire course of events and we don't know how things would have developed without it.

When in 1920, Solomon Luria aka Lurie, a professor of ancient history in Petrograd, found that in Soviet, internationalist and communist Russia anti-Semitism was again on the rise, he was not surprised.

On the contrary, "events substantiated the correctness of [his] earlier conclusions" that the "cause of anti-Semitism lies with the Jews themselves" and currently "with or in spite of the complete absence of legal restrictions on Jews, anti-Semitism has erupted with a new strength and reached a pitch that could never have been imagined in the old regime".[2205]

Russian (more precisely Little Russian) anti-Semitism of past centuries and the early 20th century was blown away with its seeds by the winds of the October revolution. Those who joined the Union of the Russian People, those who marched with their religious standards to smash Jewish shops, those who demanded the execution of Beilis, those who defended the royal throne, the urban middle class and those who were with them or who resembled them or who were suspected to be like them were rounded up by the thousands and shot or imprisoned.

Among Russian *workers* and *peasants* there was no anti-Semitism before the revolution – this is attested to by leaders of the revolution themselves. The Russian *intelligentsia* was actively sympathetic to the cause of the oppressed Jews and children of the post-revolution years were raised only in the internationalist spirit.

Stripped of any strength, discredited and crushed completely, where did anti-Semitism come from?

We already described how surprising it was for Jewish-Russian émigrés to learn that anti-Semitism had not died. They followed the phenomenon in writings of socialists E.D. Kuskova and S.S. Maslov, who came from Russia in 1922.

In an article in the *Jewish Tribune*, Kuskova states that anti-Semitism in the USSR is not a figment of the imagination and that "in Russia, Bolshevism is now blending with Judaism — this cannot be doubted." She even met highly cultured Jews who were anti-Semites of the new "Soviet type." A Jewish doctor told her: "Jewish Bolshevik administrators ruined the excellent relations he had with the local population." A teacher said

---

[2205] С.Я. Лурье. Антисемитизм в древнем мире. Тель-Авив: Сова, 1976, с. 8 [1-е изд. — Пг.: Былое, 1922].

"children tell me that I teach in a Jewish school" because we have "forbidden the teaching of The Ten Commandments and driven off the priest." "There are only Jews in the Narkomat of Education. In high school circles ('from radical families') there is talk about the predominance of the Jews." "Young people, in general are more anti-Semitic than the older generation... and one hears everywhere 'they showed their true colors and tortured us'." "Russian life is full of this stuff today. But if you ask me who they are, these anti-Semites, they are most of the society." "So widespread is this thinking that the political administration distributed a proclamation explaining why there are so many Jews in it: 'When the Russian proletariat needed its own new intelligentsia, mid-level intelligentsia, technical workers and administrative workers, not surprisingly, Jews, who, before had been in the opposition, came forward to meet them... the occupation by Jews of administrative posts in the new Russia is historically inevitable and would have been the natural outcome, regardless of whether the new Russia had become KD (Constitutional Democrat), SR (Socialist Revolutionary) or proletarian. Any problems with having Aaron Moiseevich Tankelevich sitting in the place of Ivan Petrovich Ivanov need to be 'cured'."

Kuskova parries "in a Constitutional Democratic or SR Russia many administrative posts would have been occupied by Jews.... but neither the Kadets nor SR's would have forbidden teaching the Ten Commandments and wouldn't have chopped off heads... Stop Tankelevich from doing evil and there will be no microbe of anti-Semitism".[2206]

The Jewish émigré community was chilled by Maslov's findings. Here was a tested SR with an unassailable reputation who lived through the first four years of Soviet power. "Judeophobia is everywhere in Russia today. It has swept areas where Jews were never before seen and where the Jewish question never occurred to anyone. The same hatred for Jews is found in Vologda, Archangel, in the towns of Siberia and the Urals".[2207] He recounts several episodes affecting the perception of the simple Russian peasants such as the Tyumen Produce Commissar Indenbaum's order to shear sheep for the second time in the season, "because the Republic needs wool." (This was prior to collectivization, no less; these actions of this commissar caused the Ishim peasant uprising.) The problem arose because it was late in the fall and the sheep would die without their coats from the coming winter cold. Maslov does not name the commissars who ordered the planting of *millet* and *fried sun-flower seeds* or issued a prohibition on

---

[2206] Е. Кускова. Кто они и как быть? // Еврейская трибуна, 1922, 19 октября (№ 144), с. 1-2.
[2207] С.С. Маслов. Россия после четырёх лет революции. Париж: Русская печать, 1922. Кн. 2, с. 41.

planting malt, but one can conclude they did not come from ordinary Russian folk or from the Russian aristocracy or from "yesterday's men." From all this, the peasantry could only conclude that the power over them was "Jewish." So too did the workers. Several workers' resolutions from the Urals in Feb and March of 1921 sent to the Kremlin "complained with outrage of the dominance of the Jews in central and local government." "The intelligentsia, of course does not think that Soviet power is Jewish, but it has noted the vastly disproportionate role of Jews in authority" when compared to their numbers in the population.

"And if a Jew approaches a group of non-Jews who are freely discussing Soviet reality, they almost always change the topic of conversation even if the new arrival is a personal acquaintance".[2208]

Maslov tries to understand "the cause of the widespread and bitter hatred of Jews in modern Russia" and it seems to him to be the "identification throughout society of Soviet power and Jewish power."

"The expression 'Yid Power' is often used in Russia and particularly in Ukraine and in the former Pale of Settlement not as a polemic, but as a completely objective definition of power, its content and its politics." "Soviet power in the first place answers the wishes and interests of Jews and they are its ardent supporters and in the second place, power resides in Jewish hands."

Among the causes of Judeophobia Maslov notes the "tightly welded ethnic cohesion they have formed as a result of their difficult thousands year old history". "This is particularly noticeable when it comes to selecting staff at institutions – if the selection process is in the hands of Jews, you can bet that the entire staff of responsible positions will go to Jews, even if it means removing the existing staff." And often that "preference for *their own* is displayed in a sharp, discourteous manner which is offensive to others." In the Jewish bureaucrat, Soviet power manifests more obviously its negative features… the intoxicating wine of power is stronger for Jews and goes to their head… I don't know where this comes from," perhaps because of the low cultural level of the former pharmacists and shopkeepers. Maybe from living earlier without full civil rights?".[2209]

The Parisian Zionist journal *Sunrise* wrote in 1922 that Gorky essentially said that "*the growth of anti-Semitism is aided by the tactless behavior of the Jewish Bolsheviks themselves* in many situations."

That is the blessed truth! And Gorky wasn't speaking of Trotsky, Zinoviev and Kamenev – he was speaking of the typical Jewish communist who

---

[2208] Там же, с. 41,42,43, 155, 176-177.
[2209] Там же, с. 42,44-45.

occupies a position in the collegia, presidia and petty and mid-level Soviet institutions where he comes into contact with large swaths of the population. Such individuals occupy leading front-line positions which naturally multiplies their number in the mind of the public.[2210]

D. Pasmanik comments: "we must admit that many Jews through their own actions provoke acute anti-Semitism... all the impudent Jews filling the communist ranks – these pharmacists, shopkeepers, peddlers, dropouts and pseudo intellectuals are indeed causing much evil to Russia and Jewry".[2211]

"Hardly ever before inside of Russia or outside of Russia have Jews been the subject of such an active and concentrated hostility — it has never reached such an intensity nor been so widespread. This elemental hostility has been fed by the open and undeniable participation of Jews in destructive processes underway in Europe as well as by the tales and exaggerations about such participation".[2212] "A terrible anti-Semitic mood is taking hold, fed exclusively by Bolshevism which continues to be identified with Jewry".[2213]

In 1927 Mikhail Kozakov (shot in 1930 after the "food workers' trial") wrote in a private letter to his brother overseas about the "Judeophobic mood of the masses (among non-party and party members)... it is no secret that the mass of workers do not love the Jews".[2214]

And Shulgin, after his "secret" trip to the USSR in 1928 says: No one says anymore that anti-Semitism is propaganda planted by the "Tsar's government" or an infection limited to the "dregs of society"... Geographically it spreads wider each day threatening to engulf all of Russia. The main center today seems to be Moscow... anti-Semitism is a new phenomenon in Great Russia," but is much more serious than old anti-Semitism in the South (anti-Semitism of the South of Russia was traditionally humorous and mitigated by anecdotes about Jews[2215]).

Larin brings up an anti-Jewish slogan allegedly used for propaganda purposes by the White Guards — "Russians are sent to Narym - a locale in the far north and Jews to the Crimea": a vacation spot.[2216]

[2210] Д.С. Пасманик. Русская революция и еврейство*, с. 198-199.
[2211] Д.С. Пасманик. Русская революция и еврейство, с. 198, 200.
[2212] Г.А. Ландау. Революционные идеи в еврейской общественности // РиЕ, с. 101.
[2213] Д.С. Пасманик. Чего же мы добиваемся? // РиЕ, с. 217.
[2214] М. Козаков. [Письмо] // Библиотека-фонд «Русское Зарубежье» (БФРЗ). Ф. 1, Е-60, с. 1.
[2215] В.В. Шульгин. «Что нам в них не нравится...»: Об Антисемитизме в России. Париж, 1929, с. 41-43.
[2216] Ю. Ларин, с. 254.

The Soviet authorities eventually became seriously concerned with the rise of anti-Semitism. In 1923 the *Jewish Tribune* writes, albeit with skepticism, "the Commissariat of Internal Affairs has established a commission to study the question of 'protecting the Jews from dark forces'".[2217]

In 1926 Kalinin (and other functionaries) received many questions about Jews in letters and at meetings. As a result, Larin undertook a study of the problem in a book *Jews and anti-Semitism in the USSR*. From his own reports, queries and interviews (taken, we can presume, from communists or communist sympathizers) he enumerates 66 questions from those the authorities received, recording them without editing the language. Among these questions:[2218]

- *Where are the Jews in Moscow coming from?*
- *Why is authority predominantly Jewish?*
- *How come Jews don't wait in line?*
- *How do Jews arriving from Berdichev and other cities immediately receive apartments?* (There is a joke that the last Jew left Berdichev and gave the keys to the city to Kalinin.)
- *Why do Jews have money and own their own bakeries, etc?*
- *Why are Jews drawn to light work and not to physical labor?*
- *Why do Jews in government service and in professions stick together and help each other while Russians do not?*
- *They do not want to work at everyday jobs, but are concerned only with their careers.*
- *Why do they not farm even though it is now allowed them?*
- *Why are Jews given good land in the Crimea while Russians are given inferior land?*
- *Why is party opposition 76% Jewish?*
- *Why did anti-Semitism develop only against Jews and not against other nationalities?*
- *What should a group agitprop leader do when he tries to counter anti-Semitic tendencies in his group and no one supports him?*

[2217] Г. Римский. Правительственный антисемитизм в Советской России // Еврейская трибуна, 1923, 7 сент. (№ 170), с. 3.
[2218] Ю. Ларин, с. 240-244.

Larin suspects that these questions were dreamed up and spread among the masses by an underground organization of counter-revolutionaries![2219] As we will see later, this is where some official explanations came from. But he fixates on the unexpected phenomenon and tries to address scientifically the question "How could anti-Semitism take hold in the USSR in those strata of society — [factory workers, students], where, before the revolution, it was little noted?"[2220]

His findings were:

Anti-Semitism among the intelligentsia.

"Among the intelligentsia anti-Semitism is more developed than in any other group." However, he maintains that "dissatisfaction rises not from the large number of Jews, but from the fact that Jews presumed to enter into competition with the Russian intelligentsia for government jobs."

"The obvious development of anti-Semitic attitudes among city clerks and workers by 1928 cannot be explained by excessive numbers of Jews claiming jobs". "Among the intellectual professions, anti-Semitic tendencies are felt in the medical sphere and in engineering... The army has "good political training" and there is no anti-Semitism there, even though the command staff of the Red Army has a significantly higher percentage of Jews than are present in the country as a whole".[2221]

Anti-Semitism among the urban bourgeoisie.

"The root of anti-Semitism is found in urban bourgeois philistinism." But, "the battle against anti-Semitism among the bourgeoisie...it is mixed in with the question of the destruction of the bourgeoisie in general... The antiSemitism of the bourgeoisie will disappear when the bourgeoisie disappears".[2222]

Anti-Semitism in the countryside.

"We have almost completely pushed out the private trader of the peasant's grain, therefore among the peasant masses anti-Semitism is not showing itself and has even weakened against its pre-war levels." Now it appears only in those areas where Jews have been resettled on the land, allegedly from Kulaks and former landowners.[2223]

Anti-Semitism among the working class.

[2219] Ю. Ларин, с. 244.
[2220] Там же, с. 47.
[2221] Там же, с. 35, 86, 102, 108-110, 120.
[2222] Там же, с. 121, 134, 135.
[2223] Там же, с. 144, 145, 148-149.

"Anti-Semitism among the workers has grown noticeably stronger in recent years." By 1929 there could be no doubt of its existence. Now it occurs with more frequency and intensity than a few years ago. It is particularly strong among the "backwards parts of the working class" — women and seasonal workers. However, an anti-Semitic mood can be observed among a broad spectrum of workers," not only among the "corrupted fringe." And here economic competition is not a factor — it arises even where there is no such competition; Jews make up only make "only 2.7%" of the working class. In the lower level professional organizations they tried to paint over anti-Semitism.

Difficulties arise because attempts to "hide anti-Semitism" come from the "active proletariat" itself; indeed, anti-Semitism originates from the "active proletariat." "In many cases Party members and members of Komsomol demonstrate anti-Semitism. Talk of Jewish dominance is particularly widespread, and in meetings one hears complaints that the Soviet authority limits itself to battle with the Orthodox religion alone."

What savagery — anti-Semitism among the proletariat?!! How could this occur in the most progressive and politically aware class in the world?! Larin finds that it arose because "no other means remained for the White Guard to influence the masses besides anti-Semitism." Its plan of action moves along "the rails of anti-Semitism".[2224] This was a theory that was to have frightening consequences.

Larin's views on the anti-Semitism of the time were to find echoes later in other authors. S. Shwartz provides his own variant on anti-Semitism as being the result of a "vulgar perception of Jews as the main carriers of the New Economic Policy (NEP)." But he agrees: "The Soviet government, not without basis, saw in antiSemitism a possible tool of the counter-revolution".[2225]

In 1968 the author adds: "After the civil war, anti-Semitism began to spread, gripping layers of society which were free of this tendency before the revolution".[2226]

Against this it was necessary to engage not in academic discussion but to act energetically and forcefully. In May, 1928 the CK of the VKPb issued an Agitprop communication about "measures to be taken in the battle with antiSemitism." (As was often the case in implementation of party directives, related documents were not publicized, but circulated among party organizations.) The battle to create an atmosphere of intolerance of

---

[2224] Ю. Ларин, с. 238-240, 244-245, 247, 248.
[2225] С.М. Шварц. Антисемитизм..., с. 8, 39.
[2226] В. Александрова. Евреи в советской литературе // КРЕ-2, с. 290.

anti-Semitism was to be taken up in educational programs, public reports, lectures, the press, radio and school textbooks and finally, authorities were "to apply the strictest disciplinary measures to those found guilty of anti-Semitic practices".[2227] Sharp newspaper articles followed. In *Pravda's* article by a highly connected Lev Sosnovsky, he incriminates all kinds of party and educational officials in anti-Semitism: an official in Kiev "openly fires Jews" with "the connivance of the local district party committee"; defamatory anti-Jewish graffiti is widespread etc. From a newspaper article: "with the growing battle against anti-Semitism there are demands to solve the problem by increasing repression on those carriers of antiSemitism and on those who protect them." Clearly it was the GPU speaking through the language of a newspaper article.[2228]

After Larin's report, the issue of anti-Semitism was included into various educational curricula, while Larin himself continued to research the ways to overcome anti-Semitism decisively. "Until now we were too soft... allowing propaganda to spread... Locally officials often do not deal with anti-Semitism as rigorously as they should." Newspapers "should not fear to point attention to "the Jewish issue" (to avoid dissemination of anti-Semitism) as it only interferes with the fight against counter revolutionary sabotage." "AntiSemitism is a social pathology like alcoholism or vagrancy. Too often when dealing with communists we let them off with mere censure. If a person goes to church and gets married, then we exclude him without discussion — antiSemitism is no less an evil."

"As the USSR develops towards socialism, the prognosis is good that 'Soviet' anti-Semitism and the legacy of pre-Soviet relationships will be torn out by the roots. Nevertheless, it is absolutely necessary to impose severe controls on intellectual anti-Semitism especially in the teaching profession and civil service".[2229]

But the very spirit of the brave Twenties demands stronger language. "The nature of modern-day anti-Jewish agitation in the USSR is *political* and *not nationalistic.*" Agitation against the Jews is directed not just against Jews, but indirectly against the Soviet power." Or maybe not so indirect: "anti-Semitism is a means of mobilization against Soviet power." And "those against the position of Soviet authorities on the Jewish question are *against the working class and for the capitalists.*" Any talk of " 'Jewish dominance' will be regarded as counterrevolutionary activity against the very foundation of the nationalities policy of the proletarian revolution...

[2227] С.М. Шварц. Антисемитизм..., с. 83-84.
[2228] Л.С. На борьбу с пособниками контрреволюции // Правда, 1928, 17мая, с. 4.
[2229] Ю. Ларин, с. 9, 119-120, 269-270, 276-277, 280-282.

Parts of the intelligentsia, and sometimes the White Guards are using anti-Semitism to transmit bourgeois ideology."

Yes, that's it – a White Guard whispering campaign, clearly there is "planned... agitation by secret White Guard organizations." Behind "the philistine anti-Jewish agitation, secret monarchist organizations are leading a battle against Soviet power..." And from "the central organs of anti-Soviet emigration (including Jewish bankers and Tsarist generals) an ideology is transmitted right into our factories proving that anti-Jewish agitation in the USSR is class-based, not nationality-based... It is necessary to explain to the masses that encouragement of anti-Jewish feelings in essence is an attempt to lay the groundwork for counter-revolution. *The masses must regard anyone who shows sympathy to anti-Semitism* as a secret counter-revolutionary or the mouthpiece of a secret monarchist organization." (There are conspiracies everywhere!) "The term 'anti-Semite' must take on the same meaning in the public mind as the term 'counter-revolutionary' ".[2230]

The authorities had seen through everything and named everything for what it was: counter-revolution, White Guards, monarchists, White generals and "anyone suspected of being any of the above..."

For the thickheaded, the revolutionary orator elaborates: "The methods to fight anti-Semitism are clear." At a minimum, to conduct open investigations and sessions of "people's tribunal against anti-Semitism" at local levels under the motto "explanations for the backward workers" and "repressions for the malicious." "There is no reason why "Lenin's decree" should not apply")[2231]

Under "Lenin's decree" (that from July 27, 1918) active anti-Semites were to be placed *outside of the law* — that is, to be shot even for agitating for a pogrom, not just for participating in one.[2232] The law encouraged each Jew to register a complaint about any ethnic insult visited upon him.

Now some later author will object that the "July 27 Act" was ultimately not included in the law and was not part of the criminal code of 1922. Though the criminal code of 1926 did include an article about the "instigation of ethnic hostility and dissension," there were "no specific articles about acts of antiSemitism." This is not convincing. Article 59-7 of the Criminal Code ("propaganda or agitation intended to incite national or religious hatred or dissension") was sufficient to send one to prison and the article provided for confiscation of the property of perpetrators of

---

[2230] Ю. Ларин, с. 27, 45-46, 106, 116, 252, 254, 255, 257.
[2231] Там же, с. 138, 283, 288.
[2232] Там же, с. 259, 278.

"widespread disturbances" and, under aggravated circumstances (for instance, class origin) – death. Article 59-7 was based on the "RSFSR Penal Code" of Feb 26, 1927, which widened the definition of "instigation of national hatred" making it equal in seriousness to "dissemination or preparation and storing of literature".[2233]

Storing books! How familiar is that proscription, contained in the related law 58-10! [Translator's note: infamous **Article 58** of the Penal Code of RSFSR dealt with so-called counter-revolutionary and anti-Soviet activities.]

Many brochures on anti-Semitism were published and "finally, Feb 19, 1929 *Pravda* devoted its lead article to the matter: 'Attention to the battle with anti-Semitism' ".[2234] A 1929 resolution of CK of Communist Party of Byelorussia stated that "counter-revolutionary nature of anti-Semitic incidents is often ignored" and that organs of justice should "intensify the fight, prosecuting both perpetrators of the law and those who inspire them".[2235]

The secretary of the CK of Komsomol said "most dangerous in our conditions are secret anti-Semites who hide their anti-Semitic attitudes".[2236]

Those who are familiar with Soviet language understand: it is necessary to cut off suspected ways of thinking. (This recalls Grigory Landau, speaking of Jewish opponents: "They suspect or accuse other groups around them of antiSemitism... Anyone who voices a negative opinion about Jews is accused of being an open anti-Semite and others are called secret anti-Semites".[2237]

In 1929, a certain I. Zilberman in *Daily Soviet Jurisprudence* (no. 4) writes that there were too few court trials relating to anti-Semitism in Moscow Province. In the city of Moscow alone for the year there were only 34 cases (that is, every 10 days there was a trial for anti-Semitism somewhere in Moscow). The *Journal of Narkomyust* was read as an instruction manual for bringing such cases.

Could the most evil anti-Semite have thought up a better way to identify Jews with Soviet power in the opinion of the people?

It went so far that in 1930 the Supreme Court of RSFSR ruled that Article 59-7 "should not be used by members of national minorities seeking

---

[2233] С.М. Шварц. Антисемитизм..., с. 72-73.
[2234] Там же*, с. 32.
[2235] С.М. Шварц. Антисемитизм... *, с. 88-89.
[2236] Там же*, с. 90-91.
[2237] Г.А. Ландау. Революционные идеи в еврейской общественности // РиЕ, с. 101.

redress in conflicts of a personal nature".[2238] In other words the judicial juggernaut had already been wound up and was running at full speed.

If we look at life of regular, not "commanding", Jewish folk, we see desolation and despair in formerly vibrant and thriving shtetls. *Jewish Tribune* reproduced report by a special official who inspected towns and shtetls in the south-west of Russia in 1923, indicating that as the most active inhabitants moved into cities, the remaining population of elders and families with many children lived to large extent by relying on humanitarian and financial aid from America.[2239]

Indeed, by the end of the period of "War Communism" (1918-1920) when all trade, or any buying and selling, were prohibited under threat of property confiscation and fines, the Jews were helped by Jewish charities like Joint through the all-Russian Public Committee for "assistance to victims of pogroms and destitute Jews". Several other charities protected the Jewish population later at different times, such as the SC (Society of Craftsmen, which after the revolution moved abroad), EKOPO (the Jewish committee for assistance to victims of war) and EKO (the Jewish colonizing society). In 1921-22, Soviet-based Jewish charities functioned in Moscow and St. Petersburg.

Despite intervention and obstacles from YevSeks (Jewish communist organizations), "Joint provided Soviet Jews with extensive financial and other assistance", whereas SC "was dedicated to establishment and development of Jewish industry and agriculture in the south of Ukraine" during first half of 1920's.[2240]

The first Soviet census provides insight into Jewish life during the liberalized NEP period. Forty percent of Jews were classified as "active" (not dependents). Of those, 28% were public servants, 21% – craftsmen, 19% – industry workers (including apprentices), 12% – merchants, 9% – peasants, 1% – military men, and 10% were classified as "others". Among public servants, Jews were well represented in trade-related occupations. For instance, in Moscow business organizations 16% of the clerks were Jews, in credit and trade organizations – 13% (30% according to the *Jewish Encyclopedia*)[2241], in public organizations – 19%, in fiscal organizations – 9%, in Sovdeps – 10%, with virtually no presence in police force. The percentages were correspondingly higher in the former Pale of Settlement areas, up to 62% in the state trade of Byelorussia, 44% – in Ukraine (77% in category of "private state servants").

[2238] С.М. Шварц. Антисемитизм…*, с. 73, 74.
[2239] НЭП и евреи // Еврейская трибуна, 1923, 21 сентября (№ 171), с. 3-4.
[2240] КЕЭ, т. 8, с. 170, 171.
[2241] КЕЭ, т. 8, с. 186.

The flow of Jewish workers into industry was much slower than government wished. There were almost no Jews among railroad men and miners' they rather preferred the professions of tailor, tanner, typographer, woodworker and food-related specialties and other fields of consumer industry. To recruit Jewish workers into industry, special professional schools were created with predominantly foreign funding from Jewish organizations abroad.[2242]

It was the time of NEP, which "improved economic conditions of Jewish population within a new, Soviet framework".[2243] In 1924 Moscow 75% of the perfume and pharmaceutical trade was in Jewish hands, as well as 55% of the manufactured goods trade, 49% of the jewelry trade, 39% of the small ware trade, and 36% of the wood-depots. "Starting business in a new place, a Jew usually run down prices in private sector to attract clientele".[2244] The first and most prominent NEPmen often were Jews. To large extent, anger against them stemmed from the fact that they utilized the Soviet as well as the market systems: their commerce was routinely facilitated by their links and pulls in the Soviet apparatus. Sometimes such connections were exposed by authorities as in the case of famous "Paraffin Affair" (1922). During 1920's, there were abundant opportunities to buy up belongings of oppressed and persecuted "former" people, especially high quality or rare furniture. S. Ettinger noted that Jews made a majority of NEPmen and new-riches,[2245] which was supported by impressive list of individuals who "failed to pay state taxes and dues" in *Izvestia* in 1929.[2246]

However, at the end of NEP, authorities launched "anti-capitalist" assault against financiers, merchants and manufacturers, many of whom were Jewish.

As a result, many Jews turned into "Soviet trade servants" and continued working in the same spheres of finance, credit and commerce. A steamroller of merchandise and property confiscations, outright state robbery and social ostracizing (outclassing people into disenfranchised "lishenets" category) was advancing on private commerce. "Some Jewish merchants, attempting to avoid discriminating and endlessly increasing taxation, declared themselves as having no occupation during the census".[2247] Nevertheless "virtually the entire Jewish male population in towns and shtetls… passed through the torture chambers of GPU" during

---

[2242] Ю. Ларин, с. 75, 77-80, 107.
[2243] Г. Аронсон. Еврейский вопрос в эпоху Сталина // КРЕ-2,
[2244] Ю. Ларин* с. 121-122.
[2245] Samuel Ettinger. Russian Society and the Jews // Bulletin on Soviet and East European Jewish Affairs, 1970, № 5, p. 38-39.
[2246] Известия, 1928, 22 апреля, с. 7.
[2247] КЕЭ. т. 8, с. 187.

the campaign of gold and jewelry extortion in the beginning of 1930's.[2248] Such things would be regarded as an impossible nightmare in Czar's Russia. Many Jewish families, to avoid the stigma of being "lishenets", moved into large cities. In the end, "only one-fifth of Soviet Jews lived in the traditional Jewish settlements by 1930's".[2249]

"Socioeconomic experiments by the Soviet authorities including all kinds of nationalization and socialization had not only devastated the middle classes, but also hit badly the small merchants and craftsmen".[2250] "Due to general lack of merchandise and solvent customers as well as low liquidity and exorbitant taxes, many shtetl merchants had no other choice but to close down their shops" and while the "most active left for cities", the remaining populace has nothing else to do but "aimlessly roam decrepit streets, loudly complaining about their fate, people and God". It is apparent that Jewish masses have completely lost their economic foundations".[2251] It was really like that in many shtetls at that time. To address the problem, even special resolution of Sovnarkom was issued in 1929.

G. Simon, a former emigrant, came to USSR in the end of 1920's as an American businessman with a mission "to investigate shortages of Jewish craftsmen in tools". Later, in Paris, he published a book with an emotional and ironic title *Jews Rule Over Russia*. Describing the situation with Jewish manufacturing and trade, its oppression and destruction by Soviets, he also shares his impressions. Quoting many conversations, the general mood of populace is pretty gloomy. "Many bad things, many crimes happen in Russia these days but it's better to suppress that blinding hatred"; "they often fear that the revolution will inevitably end in the Russian manner, i.e. by mass-murder of Jews". A local Bolshevik-Jew suggests that "it's only the revolution that stands between the Jews and those wishing to aggrandize Russia by the rape of Jewish women and spilling the blood of Jewish children".[2252]

A well-known economist B. D. Brutskus, who in 1920 provided a damning analysis of the socialist economy (he was expelled from the country in 1922 by Lenin), published an extensive article "Jewish population under Communist power" in *Contemporary Notes* in 1928, chronicling the NEP in the former Pale of Settlement areas of Ukraine and Byelorussia.

The relative importance of private enterprise was declining as even the smallest merchants were deprived of their political rights (they became

---

[2248] Там же, с. 161.
[2249] Там же, с. 188.
[2250] Г. Аронсон. Еврейский вопрос в эпоху Сталина // КРЕ-2, с. 136.
[2251] НЭП и евреи // Еврейская трибуна, 1923, 21 сентября (№ 171)-с. 3-4.
[2252] Г. Симон. Евреи царствуют в России, с. 22, 159, 192, 217, 237.

disenfranchised "lishenets" and couldn't vote in Soviet elections), and, thus, their civil rights. (In contrast, handcraftsmen still enjoyed a certain semblance of rights.) "The fight of Soviet authorities against private enterprise and entrepreneurs is in large part a fight against Jewish populace." Because in those days "not only almost the entire private city enterprise in Ukraine and Byelorussia was represented by Jews, but the Jewish participation in the small capitalist upperclass in capital cities of Moscow, St. Petersburg and Kharkov had also became very substantial".[2253]

Brutskus distinguished three periods during the NEP: 1921-23, 1923-25 and 1925-27. "Development of private enterprise was least impeded by communists during first two and half years when Bolsheviks were still overwhelmed by their economic debacles". "The first communist reaction followed between the end of 1923 and the spring of 1925." Wholesale and shop trade in the former Pale of Settlement was destroyed, with only small flea market trade still permitted." Crafts were "burdened by taxation. Artisans lost their last tools and materials (the latter often belonged to their peasant customers) to confiscations." "The concept of Jewish equality virtually turned into fiction as two-thirds of Jews lost their voting rights."

Because YevSek (Jewish section of the communist party) "inherited specific hatred toward petty Jewish bourgeoisie cultivated by earlier Jewish socialist parties and saw their own purpose in fighting it, its policy in the beginning of NEP was substantially different from the general party line".

During the second part of NEP, the "YevSek attempted to complete the dismantling of Jewish bourgeoisie, which began with "War Communism".

However, information about bleak life of Jewish population in USSR was leaking out into Jewish press abroad. "YevSeks attempted to blame that on the Czar's regime which allegedly obstructed Jewish participation in productive labor, that is by communist definition, in physical labor. And since Jews still prefer "unproductive labor", they inevitably suffer. Soviet authorities has nothing to do with it".

But Brutskus objected claiming that in reality it was opposite. "The class of Jewish craftsmen nearly disappeared with the annihilation of petty Jewish manufacture... Indeed, professional the Jewish classes grew and become diversified while excessive numbers of petty Jewish middlemen slowly decreased under the Tsar because of the gradual development of ethnic Russian enterprise and deepening business connections between the

---

[2253] Б. Бруцкус. Еврейское население под коммунистической властью // Современные записки, 1928, кн. 36, с. 511-512.

Pale of Settlement and inner Russia. But now the Jewish population again was turned into a mass of petty middlemen".

During the third period of NEP, from spring of 1925 to autumn of 1926, large tax remissions were made for craftsmen and street vendors and village fairs were relieved of taxation while activities of state financial inspectors supervising large businesses were brought "under the law". The economy and well-being of the Jewish population started to recover rapidly. It was a boom for Jewish craftsmen and merchants specializing in agriculture. Petty manufacturing grew and "successfully competed for raw materials and resources with state manufacture in the western provinces". At the same time, "a new decree granted political (and, therefore, certain civil) rights to many Jews".

The second communist assault on private enterprise, which eventually resulted in the dismantling of NEP, began at the end of 1926. "First, private grain trade was prohibited, followed by bans on raw skins, oil seeds and tobacco trade... Private mills, creameries, tanneries and tobacco houses were expropriated. Fixed prices on shop merchandise were introduced in the summer of 1927. Most craftsmen couldn't work because of shortage of raw materials".[2254]

The state of affairs in the shtetls of western Russia alarmed international Jewry. For instance, Pasmanik wrote in 1922 that Jews as people are doomed to disappear under Bolsheviks and that communists reduced all Russian Jewry into a crowd of paupers.[2255] However, the Western public (including Jews) did not want to hear all this. The West saw the USSR in good light partly because of general left-leaning of European intelligentsia but mainly because the world and American Jewry were now confident in bright future and security of Russian Jews and skillful Soviet propaganda only deepened this impression.

Benevolent public opinion was extremely instrumental for Soviet leaders in securing Western, and especially American, financial aid, which was indispensable for economical recovery after their brave "War Communism". As Lenin said at the Party Congress in 1921, "as the revolution didn't spread to other countries, we should do anything possible to secure assistance of big progressive capitalism and for that we are ready to pay hundreds of millions and even billions from our immense wealth, our vast resources, because otherwise our recovery would take

---

[2254] Б. Бруцкус. Еврейское население под коммунистической властью // Современные записки, 1928, кн. 36, с. 513-518.
[2255] Д.С. Пасманик. Русская революция и еврейство, с. 194, 195.

decades".[2256] And the business went smoothly as progressive capitalism showed no scruples about acquiring Russian wealth. The first Soviet international bank, Roskombank, was founded in 1922. It was headed by the already mentioned Olof Aschberg (who was reliably delivering aid to Lenin during entire revolutionary period) and by former Russian private bankers (Shlezinger, Kalashkin and Ternovsky). There was also Max May of Morgan Guaranty Trust in the US who was of great assistance to Soviets. Now they developed a scheme allowing Roskombank to directly purchase goods in US, despite the futile protests from the Secretary of State Charles Hughes, who asserted that this kind of relations meant a de-facto recognition of Soviet regime. A Roskombank Swedish adviser, professor G. Kassel, said that it is reckless to leave Russia with all her resources alone.[2257]

Concessioners flocked into USSR where they were very welcome. Here we see Lenin's favorite, Armand Hammer, who in 1921 decided "to help rebuild Ural industry" and procured a concession on asbestos mines at Alapayevsk.

Lenin mentioned in 1921 that Hammer's father will provide "two million stones of bread on very favorable terms (5%) in exchange for Ural jewelry to be sold in America".[2258] And Hammer shamelessly exported Russian art treasures in exchange for the development of pencil manufacturing. (Later, in the times of Stalin and Khrushchev, Hammer frequented Moscow, continuing to export Russian cultural treasures (e.g., church utensils, icons, paintings, china, etc. in huge volumes.)

However, in 1921-22 large sums were donated by American Jewry and distributed in Russia by the American Relief Administration (ARA) for assistance to the victims of "bloody pogroms, for the rescue of towns in the South of Russia and for the peasantry of Volga Region". Many ARA associates were Jews.[2259]

Another novel idea from the 20's – not so much an idea originating among Jews – as one dreamed up to appeal to them, was Jewish colonization of agricultural land. It is said their history of dispersion had denied them possibilities in agriculture and forced them to engage in money lending, commerce and trade.

[2256] В.И. Ленин. Доклад о замене развёрстки натуральным налогом. 15 марта 1921 // Сочинения: В 45 т. 4-е изд. Т. 32, с. 201.

[2257] Э. Саттон. Уолл-стрит и большевицкая революция / Пер. с англ. М., 1998, с. 64-66, 193.

[2258] В.И. Ленин. Полное собрание сочинений: В 55 т. 5-е изд. Т. 53, с. 267.

[2259] Б. Бруцкус. Еврейское население под коммунистической властью // Современные записки, 1928, кн.36, с. 525.

Now at last Jews could occupy the land and thereby renounce the harmful ways of the past to labor productively under Soviet skies, and thus putting to flight the unflattering myths which had grown up about them.

Soviet authorities turned to the idea of colonization partially to improve productivity, but mostly for political reasons. This was sure to bring a swell of sympathy, but more important, financial aid. Brutskus writes: "the Soviet government, needing credits, searched for support among the foreign bourgeoisie and highly valued its relations with the foreign Jewish bourgeoisie."

However, towards 1924 the donations stopped pouring in and even "the Jewish American Charity ('Joint Committee') was forced to halt its work in Europe. To again collect large amounts of money (as they had through the American Relief Administration in 1921), they needed to create, as they say in the U.S., a 'boom'. Colonization became the 'boom' for Jewish charities. The grandiose project for resettling 100,000 Jewish families on their own land was, apparently, mostly a public relations ploy.[2260] The committee for the "State Land Trust for Jewish Laborers" (KomZET) was founded In 1924, followed by the "all-Soviet Volunteer Land Society of Jewish Laborers (OZET). (I remember as school children we were made to join and pay membership dues – by bringing money from home, to ODD (Society of Friends of the Children) and OZET. In many countries sister organizations to OZET sprung up.

It was immediately clear that "the assistance of the Soviet government in the passage of poor Jews to the land" was "a matter of international significance... Through this the foreign proletariat could judge the "power and solidity of the Soviet government." This development had the active participation and financial support of the powerful America *Joint*. The *Jewish Chronicle of London*, Oct 16,1925: "The Crimea has been offered as replacement for Palestine. Why send Jews to Palestine which is so unproductive... and which will mean so much sacrifice and hard work... when the rich land of Ukraine and fruited fields of the Crimea are smiling upon suffering Jews. Moscow will be the benefactor and defender of Russian Jewry and will be able to seek moral support from Jews around the globe..." As well, "the plan will cost nothing, as American Jews are covering all expenses".[2261]

It didn't take the Russian émigré press long to recognize the Soviet maneuver. P. Struve in the Parisian journal *Renaissance* wrote: "this entire undertaking serves to bind Jewry – both Russian and international – to communist power and definitively mark Jews with the brand of

---

[2260] Там же, с. 524-526.
[2261] Ю. Ларин*, с. 293, 297-298.

communism".[2262] In a lead editorial from the Berlin *Rul*: "It's true... the world identifies the Bolsheviks with the Jews. There is a need to further connect them with shared responsibility for the fate of hundreds of thousands of poor. Then you can trick wealthy American Jews with a threat: the fall of Soviet power followed by a mass pogrom which sweeps away the Jewish societies they founded. Therefore they will support Soviet power at all costs".[2263]

In a fateful irony, the Bolshevik bluff met American enterprise and the Americans fell for it, not knowing what was going on in the USSR.[2264]

Actually, the world Jewish community was excited by hope in the rehabilitation of Jewish agriculture. In September, 1925 at the all-German session... the Jewish bourgeoisie under the leadership of the Director of the German National Bank, Hialmar Schacht decided to support the project. Leon Blum founded the "Jewish Construction Fund" in France which sent tractors to the settlers. The "Society for Aid for Jewish Land Colonization" was founded in New York. In countries around the globe, all the way to South Africa, money was collected for the colonization plan from Social Democrats, anarchists, and, so they say, ordinary workers.

The editors of the American magazine *Morning Journal*, posed the question – as did many others – "Is it ethical for Russian Jews to colonize land that was expropriated?" The *Jewish Chronicle* recalled that most of the former land owners were in prison, shot or exiled. They were answered by the leading American jurist Louis Marshall and chairman of the World Joint Committee who claimed the *beneficent right* of revolutionary expropriation.[2265] Indeed, during the years 1919-1923 "more than 23,000 Jews had settled in former estates near the towns and villages in the former Pale of Settlement". By spring 1923, no more of this land remained available and the first small groups of Jews started to form for resettlement to the free steppe land in Southern Ukraine.[2266] This movement picked up speed after 1925.

The international Jewish Agro-Joint was formed by Marshall with the banker Paul Warburg as the director. Here our chroniclers of the history of communism decline to issue a denunciation of class enemies, and instead, approve of their efforts.

[2262] П. Струве. Проект еврейской колонизации России // Возрождение, Париж, 1925, 25 октября (№ 145), с. 1.
[2263] Руль, Берлин, 1925, 1 октября (№ 1469), с. 1.
[2264] М. Бенедиктов. Еврейская колонизация в СССР // Последние новости, 1925, 6 ноября (№ 1699), с. 2.
[2265] Ю. Ларин, с. 295, 296, 300-302.
[2266] КЕЭ, т. 8, с. 184.

The Agro-Joint concluded an agreement with KomZET about the contribution of tractors, farm machinery, seed, the digging of artesian wells and professional training for Jewish youth. EKO assisted as well. At a 1926 session of OZET Kalinin spoke out forcefully against any plans for Jewish assimilation and, instead, proposed a wide-ranging program for Jewish autonomy known in the West as the "Kalinin Declaration."

The early plans called for resettlement to the south of Ukraine and northern Crimea of approximately 100,000 families or 20% of the entire Jewish population of the USSR. The plans contemplated separate Jewish national regions as well. ("Many remained jobless and nevertheless declined the opportunity to work" and "only half of all Jews who agreed to resettle actually took up residence in the villages they were supposed to resettle in".)[2267]

However, American Zionists objected to the OZET plan and saw in the "propaganda for the project of widespread Jewish agricultural colonization in the Soviet Union a challenge to Zionism and its idea for the settlement of Eretz Israel." OZET falsely claimed its plans did not contradict at all the idea of colonization of Palestine.[2268]

Great hope was placed on Crimea. There were 455,000 hectares given over to Jewish colonization in Ukraine and Byelorussia; 697,000 hectares set aside in Crimea for that purpose. According to the 10-Year Plan for the settlement of Jews in Crimea, the Jewish proportion of the population was to grow from 8% in 1929 to 25% in 1939. (It was assumed that the Jews would substantially outnumber the Tatars by that time.) "There shall be no obstacles to the creation in the Crimean ASSR a Northern Crimean Autonomous Jewish Republic or oblast".[2269]

The settlement of the Jews in the Crimea provoked the hostility of the Tatars ("Are they giving Crimea to the Jews?") and dissatisfaction of local landless peasants. Larin writes "evil and false rumors are circulating throughout the country about removal of land from non-Jews, the expulsion of non-Jews and the particularly strong support the authorities have given to the Jewish settlers". It went so far that the chairman of the CIK of the Crimean ASSR, Veli Ibraimov published an interview in the Simferopol paper *Red Crimea* (Sept 26, 1926) which Larin does not quote from, but which he claims was a manifestation of "evil bourgeois chauvinism" and a call for a pogrom.

[2267] КЕЭ, т. 8, с. 185, 188.
[2268] КЕЭ, т. 6, с. 139-140.
[2269] Ю. Ларин, с. 74, 174, 175, 308.

Ibraimov also promulgated a resolution and projects, which were *"not yet ready for publication"* (also not quoted by Larin). For this, Larin denounced Ibraimov to the Central Control Commission of CK of VKPb, recounting the incident with pride in his book. As a result Ibraimov was "removed and then shot", after which the Jewish colonization of Crimea gained strength.

As was typical for the communist regime, the closed trial of Ibraimov resulted in a political conviction for "connections with a Kulak bandit gang," officially, for "banditry".[2270] A certain Mustafa, the assistant to the chair of the CIK, was also shot with Ibraimov as a bandit.[2271]

Rumors of the effective assistance given to the Jewish settlers did not die down. The authorities tried to counter them. A government newspaper in 1927 wrote "the generous assistance to Jewish settlers" is coming from "Jewish community organizations" (without mentioning they were Western organizations), and not from the government as is rumored. To refute the rumors, Shlikhter (that young brawler from Kiev's Duma in October, 1905), now Narkom of Agriculture of Ukraine, toured over the South of Ukraine.

Rumors that the Jews were not working the land given to them but were renting it out or hiring farm laborers, were met with: "we haven't observed this behavior, but the Jewish settlers must be forbidden to rent out their land" and "the unhealthy atmosphere surrounding the Jewish resettlement must be countered with the widest possible education campaign".[2272]

The article allows one to judge about the scale of events. It states that 630 Jewish households moved into Kherson Province between the end of 1925 and July of 1927.[2273] In 1927, there were 48 Jewish agricultural settlements in Ukraine with a total population of 35,000. In Crimea, 4463 Jews lived in Jewish agricultural settlements in 1926.[2274] Other sources implausibly claimed that "by 1928, 220,000 Jews lived in Jewish agricultural colonies".[2275] Similarly, Larin mentioned 200,000 by the beginning of 1929. Where does this *order of magnitude* discrepancy come from? Larin here contradicts himself, saying that in 1929 the share of Jews in agriculture was negligible, less than 0.2% (and almost 20% among merchants and 2% in population in general).[2276]

[2270] Там же, с. 150-152, 233-234.
[2271] Известия, 1928, 1 мая, с. 4.
[2272] Известия, 1927, 13 июля, с. 4.
[2273] Там же.
[2274] КЕЭ, т. 2, с. 552, т. 4, с. 599.
[2275] Г. Аронсон. Еврейский вопрос в эпоху Сталина // КРЕ-2, с. 137.
[2276] Ю. Ларин, с. 97-98, 236.

Mayakovsky saw it differently:

"A hard toiling Jew

Tills the rocky land"

However, the program of Jewish land colonization, for all practical purposes, was a failure. For many of the settlers there was little motivation to stay. It didn't help that the resettlement and the building project had come from on high and the money from western organizations. A lot of government assistance for Jewish settlers didn't help. It is little known that tractors from neighboring collective farms were ordered to till Jewish land.[2277] Despite the flow of 2-3 thousand resettling Jewish families, by the end of five year work "Jewish settlements in Crimea" listed only around 5 thousand families" instead of pre-planned 10 to 15 thousand. The reason was that settlers frequently returned to their place of origin or moved to the cities of Crimea or other parts of the country.[2278] This mass departure of Jews from agriculture in the 1920's and 30's resembles similar Jewish withdrawal from agricultural colonies in the 19th century, albeit now there were many new occupations available in industry (and in administration, a prohibited field for Jews in Tsarist Russia).[2279]

Eventually, collectivization arrived. Suddenly in 1930 Semyon Dimanstein, for many years the head of the "Jewish Section of CK of VKPb," a staunch communist who bravely put up with all Soviet programs in the 20's, came out in the press against universal collectivization in the national regions.

He was attempting to protect the Jewish colony from collectivization which he had been "warned about".[2280] However, collectivization came, not sparing the "fresh shoots of Jewish land stewardship".[2281] At almost the same time, the Jewish and non-Jewish Kolkhozes were combined under the banner of "internationalism"[2282] and the program of Jewish settlement in Ukraine and Crimea was finally halted.

The principal Soviet project of Jewish colonization was at Birobidzhan, a territory "nearly the size of Switzerland" between the 2 branches of the Amur river near the Chinese border. It has been described variously. In 1956 Khrushchev bragged in conversations with Canadian communists that the soil was rich, the climate was southern, there was "much sun and

---

[2277] Там же, с. 206.
[2278] КЕЭ, т. 4, с. 600.
[2279] КЕЭ, т. 2, с. 554.
[2280] Там же, с. 354.
[2281] Г. Аронсон. Еврейский вопрос в эпоху Сталина // КРЕ-2, с. 137.
[2282] КЕЭ, т. 2, с. 554.

water" and "rivers filled with fish" and "vast forests." The *Socialist Vestnik* described it as covered with "wild taiga… swampland made up a significant portion" of the territory.[2283]

According the *Encyclopedia Britannica*: "a plain with swamps in places," but a "fertile land along the Amur".[2284]

The project came about in 1927 from the KomZET (a committee of the CIK) and was intended to: "turn a significant part of the Jewish population into a settled agricultural people in one location" (Kalinin). Also the Jewish Autonomous Republic was to serve as a counterweight to Zionism, creating a national homeland with at least half a million population.[2285] (One possible motive behind the plan which cannot be excluded: to wedge a loyal Soviet population into the hostile Cossack frontier.)

OZET sent a scientific expedition to Birobidzhan in 1927 and, before large settlements of Jews began arriving, in 1928 started preparations and building for the settlement using laborers from the local populace and wandering work crews of Chinese and Koreans.

Older residents of the area – Trans-Baikal Cossacks exiled there between the 1860's and the 1880's and already tested by the hardships of the frontier woods – remember being concerned about the Jewish settlement. The Cossacks needed vast tracts of land for their farming methods and feared they would be crowded out of lands they used for hunting and hay harvesting. The KomZET commission report was "a preliminary plan for the possible gradual resettlement of 35,000 families". But reality was different. The CIK of VKPb in 1928 assigned Birobidzhan for Jewish colonization and preparation of first settler trains began immediately. "For the first time ever, city dwellers (from Ukraine and Byelorussia) without any preparation for agricultural labor were sent to farm the land." (They were lured by the prospect of having the status of "lishenets" removed.).[2286]

The Komsomol published the "Monthly OZET" and Pioneer delegations traveled around the country collecting for the Birobidzhan resettlement.

The hastily dispatched Jewish families were horrified by the conditions they met upon arrival. They moved into barracks at the Tikhonkaya railroad station, in the future town of Birobidzhan. "Among the inhabitants… were some who never left the barracks for the land, living off the loans and

---

[2283] Хрущёв и миф о Биробиджане // Социалистический вестник, Нью-Йорк, 1958, № 7-8, с. 142-143.
[2284] Encyclopaedia Britannica, 15th ed., 1981, Vol. X., p. 817, clmn. 2.
[2285] КЕЭ*, Т. 1, с. 445-446. 159 Ю. Ларин, с. 183-184.
[2286] Larine, pp. 183-184.

credits they managed to obtain for making the move. Others less nimble, lived in abject poverty".[2287]

"During the first year of work at Birobidzhan only 25 huts were built, only 125 hectares were plowed and none were planted. Many did not remain in Birobidzhan; 1,000 workers arrived in the Spring of 1928 and by July, 25% of all those who arrived in 1928 had left. "By February 1929 more than half of the population had abandoned Birobidzhan".[2288] From 1928 to 1933 more than 18,000 arrived, yet the Jewish population grew only by 6,000. By some calculations "only 14% of those Jews who resettled remained in 1929".[2289] They returned either to their homes or moved to Khabarovsk and Vladivostok.

Larin, who devotes no small number of reasoned and impassioned pages to the building of Jewish agriculture sniffs that "an unhealthy fuss… has been raised around Birobidzhan… a utopian settlement of a million Jews…

Resettlement was practically presented as a national obligation of Soviet Jews, Zionism turned inside out… a kind of back-to-the-province movement". While international Jewish organizations provided no finances for Birobidzhan, from the beginning "considering it too expensive and risky for them".[2290] More likely the western Jewish organizations, Agro-Joint, ORT and EKO could not support the distant project beyond the Urals.[2291] It wasn't a "Jewish plan," but a scheme of Soviet authorities eager to tear down and build life anew in the country.

From the October revolution to the end of the 20's the lives of ordinary Jews were affected by the actions of Yevseks – members of the YevSek (The Jewish section of the CK of VKPb.) Besides the Jewish Commissariat, an active Jewish organization grew up in the VKPb. As well, from 1918, local organizations were formed in the guberniyas. They created an environment fanatically inspired with the idea and ideas of communism, even more so than was Soviet authority itself and at times these organizations even opposed Soviet projects. For example, "at the insistence of the YevSek, the Jewish Commissariat decreed Hebrew to be a language of 'reaction and counter-revolution' in early 1919, requiring Jewish schools to teach in Yiddish".[2292] The Central Bureau of the YevSek

---

[2287] Хрущёв и миф о Биробиджане // Социалистический вестник* 1958, №7-8, с. 144.
[2288] Ю. Ларин, с. 188, 189.
[2289] КЕЭ, т. 1, с. 448, т. 8, с. 188.
[2290] Ю. Ларин, с. 184, 186-189.
[2291] КЕЭ, т. 8, с. 188.
[2292] КЕЭ, т. 8, с. 146.

was part of the CK of VKPb and local YevSeks operated in the former Pale of Settlement.

"The purpose of the YevSek was communist education and Sovietization of the Jewish population in their native language of Yiddish."

From 1924 to 1928 responsibility for "all Jewish education and culture" was under the Jewish Bureaus of the republic-level administrative bodies, but these were abolished for "excesses in forced Yiddishization" and more power accrued to the YevSek.[2293]

The activities of the YevSek in the 20's were contradictory. "On one hand they carried out active agitprop work in communist education in Yiddish and mercilessly battled against Judaism, traditional Jewish education, Jewish social structures, independent Jewish organizations, political parties and movements, Zionism and Hebrew. On the other hand it opposed assimilation with its support of the Yiddish language and a Yiddish culture and organizations of Jewish education, Jewish scientific research and activity to improve the economic status of Soviet Jews. In this "the YevSek often held a more radical position than even the central party bodies".[2294]

The anti-Zionist YevSek was made up "to a large degree" of "former Bundists and socialist-territorialists"[2295] who were thought of as traitors or "neophyte communists" in VKPb. The purpose of the YevSek was to develop communist influence on Russian Jewry and to create a "Jewish Soviet nation"

isolated from world Jewry. But at the same time its actions paradoxically turned it from a technical apparatus urging the Jewish population to build socialism into a focal point for Jewish life in the USSR. A split arose in the YevSek between supporters of "forced assimilation" and those who thought its work was a "necessary means of preservation of the Jewish people".[2296]

The *Book of Russian Jewry* observes with sympathy that the activity of the YevSek "still carried a clear and expressly Jewish stamp under the banner of the Proletariat." For instance in 1926 using the slogan "to the countryside!," [meant to rouse interest in working in and propagandizing rural areas] the YevSek came up with "to the Shtetl!"

"… This activity resonated widely in Jewish circles in Poland and in the U.S." The author further calls it "a many-faceted Jewish nationalism in

---

[2293] Там же, с. 165-166.
[2294] Там же, с. 166.
[2295] КЕЭ, т. 7, с. 947.
[2296] КЕЭ, т. 2, с. 465.

communist form".²²⁹⁷ But in 1926 the CP halted the activity of the YevSek and turned it into the Jewish Bureau. In 1930 the Jewish Bureau was closed along with all national sections of VKPb²²⁹⁸. After that the activity of the YevSeks continued under the banner of communism. "Russian Jewry lost all forms of self-expression, including communistic forms".²²⁹⁹

The end of the YevSek symbolized the final dissolution of the Bund movement "to allow a separate nationalist existence, even if it went against strict social-democratic theory". ²³⁰⁰ However, after the YevSek was abolished, many of the former Yevseks and Jewish socialists did not come to their senses and put the "building of socialism" higher than the good of their own people or any other good, staying to serve the party-government apparatus. And that overflowing service was evident more than anything.

Whether statistically or using a wealth of singular examples, it is obvious that Jews pervaded the Soviet power structure in those years. And all this happened in the state that persecuted freedom of speech, freedom of commerce and religion, not to mention its denigration of human worth.

Bikerman and Pasmanik paint a very gloomy picture of the state of Jewish culture in the USSR in 1923: "all is torn up and trampled underfoot in the field of Jewish culture".²³⁰¹ "All foundations of a nationalist Jewish culture are shaken and all that is sacred is stomped into the mud".²³⁰² S. Dubnov saw something similar in 1922 and wrote about "rueful wreckage" and a picture "of ruin and the progress of dark savages, destroying the last remnants of a bygone culture".²³⁰³

However, Jewish historiography did not suffer destruction in the first 10 years after the revolution, as is attested to by the range of allowed publications.

Government archives, including those from the department of police, opened after the revolution have given Jewish scholars a view on Jewish participation in the revolutionary movement, pogroms, and "blood libel" trials. The Jewish Historical-Ethnographical Society was founded in 1920 and published the 2-volume Material on the *History of anti-Jewish Pogroms in Russia*. The Society later came under attack from the YevSek and it was abolished in 1929. The journals, *The Jewish News* and *The*

[2297] Г. Аронсон. Еврейский вопрос в эпоху Сталина // КРЕ-2, с. 137.
[2298] КЕЭ, т. 2, с. 465.
[2299] Б. Орлов. Россия без евреев // "22," 1988, № 60, с. 161.
[2300] Leonard Schapiro. The Role of the Jews in the Russian Revolutionary Movement // The Slavonic and East European Review, vol. 40, 1961-62, p. 167.
[2301] К евреям всех стран! // РиЕ, с. 5.
[2302] Д.С. Пасманик. Чего же мы добиваемся? // РиЕ, с. 214.
[2303] Он же. Русская революция и еврейство*, с. 195.

Jewish Chronicle were shut down in the mid-twenties. S. Dubnov's *Jewish Antiquity* remained in publication (even after he left the USSR in 1922) but was closed in 1930. The Jewish Ethnographical Museum functioned from 1916, but was closed in 1930.[2304]

In the 1920's, Jewish culture had two divergent fates — one in Hebrew and one in Yiddish. Hebrew was strongly repressed and forbidden as authorities saw it as a carrier of religion and Zionism. Before the consolidation of Soviet power in the years 1917-1919 "there were more than 180 books, brochures, and journals in Hebrew" (mostly in Odessa, but also in Kiev and Moscow). The feeling that the fate of Hebrew was connected with the fate of the victorious communist revolution held in the early 20's "among young people attempting to create a 'revolutionary literary tribune, under whose banner they hoped to unite the creative youthful strength of world Jewry'".[2305] However at the insistence of the YevSek, Hebrew was declared a "reactionary language" and already in 1919 the People's Commissariat of Education had "forbidden the teaching of Hebrew in all educational institutions. The removal of all Hebrew books from libraries had begun".[2306]

Yiddish culture fared much better. Yiddish was the language of the Jewish masses. According to the 1926 census, 73% of Jews listed Yiddish as their mother tongue[2307] (another source cites a figure of 66%[2308]) – that is the Jewish population could preserve its culture in Yiddish. Soviet authorities used this. If, in the early years of Soviet power and Bolshevism the opinion prevailed that Jews should discard their language and nationality, later the Jewish Commissariat at the Narkomat of Nationalities, the YevSek, and the Jewish sections of the republican narkomats of education began to build Soviet culture in Yiddish. In the 20's Yiddish was declared one of the *official* languages of Byelorussia; In Odessa of the 20's and even the 30's it was a language of many government institutions, with "Jewish hours" on the radio and court proceedings in Yiddish.[2309]

"A rapid growth in Yiddish schools began in 1923 throughout the Soviet Union." Beginning in 1923 and continuing through 1930 a program of systematic "Yiddishization" was carried out, even forced, upon Jewish

---

[2304] КЭЕ, т. 2, с. 439, РЭЕ, т. 2, с. 432, Б. Орлов. Россия без евреев // "22," 1988. № 60, с. 161.
[2305] И. Слуцкий. Судьба иврит в России // КРЕ-2, с. 241-242, 246.
[2306] КЭЕ, т. 2, с. 422.
[2307] С. Шварц. Евреи в Советском Союзе с начала Второй мировой войны (1939-1965). Нью-Йорк: Изд. Американского Еврейского Рабочего Комитета, 1966, с. 407.
[2308] Ю. Ларин, с. 56.
[2309] КЭЕ, т. 1, с. 326, т. 2, с. 465, т. 6, с. 125.

schools in the former Pale of Settlement. Many schools were switched to Yiddish without considering the wishes of parents. In 1923 there were 495 Yiddish schools with 70,000 Jewish children, by 1928 there were 900 schools and in 1930 they had 160,000 children. (This can be partially explained by the fact that Ukrainians and Byelorussians at this time received full cultural autonomy and saw Jewish children as potential agents of Russification; Jewish parents didn't want their children in Ukrainian or Byelorussian schools and there were no more Russian schools — they had no choice but to go to Yiddish schools. They did not study Jewish history in these schools; instead there was "class war and the Jews".[2310] (Just as in the Russian schools there was no study of Russian history, or of any history, only "social sciences".) Throughout the 20's "even those few elements of a specifically Jewish education were gradually driven out of Soviet Jewish schools." By the early 30's the autonomously functioning system of Soviet Jewish schools had been officially done away with.[2311]

From 1918 there were independent Jewish schools of higher education — ENU (Jewish People's University) until 1922 in Moscow; PENU in Petrograd which became Petrograd IVEZ (Institute of Higher Jewish Learning, one of whose founders and later Rector was Semyon Lozinsky) boasting "a number of distinguished scholars among faculty and large number of Jewish graduates".

Supported by Joint, IVEZ functioned until 1925. Jewish divisions were established at educational science departments at Byelorussian University (1922) and at Second Moscow State University (1926). Central Jewish CP School teaching in Yiddish was established in 1921. Jewish educational system included special educational science technical colleges and more than 40 industrial and agricultural training schools.[2312]

Jewish culture continued to exist and even received no small encouragement — but on the terms of Soviet authorities. The depths of Jewish history were closed. This took place on a background of the destruction of Russian historical and philosophical sciences complete with arrests of scholars.

Jewish culture of the 20's could more accurately be called a Soviet "proletarian" culture in Yiddish. And for that kind of Jewish culture the government was ready to provide newspapers and theatre. Forty years later the *Book of Russian Jewry* gives a less than gloomy assessment of the cultural situation of Jews in the USSR in the early Soviet years. In Moscow the worldwide Jewish Telegraphic agency (ETA) continued to exist into

---

[2310] Ю. Марк. Еврейская школа в Советском Союзе // КРЕ-2, с. 235-238.
[2311] КЕЭ, т. 8, с.175.
[2312] Там же, с. 177-179, РЕЭ, т. 2, с. 195-196.

the 40's as an independent unit — the only such agency in the Soviet nation that did not come under TASS, sending communications abroad (of course, subject to Soviet censorship). Newspapers were published in Yiddish, the main one being the house organ of the YevSek, The Moscow *Der Amos* from 1920 to 1938. According to Dimanstein there were 34 Yiddish publishers in 1928.

Yiddish literature was encouraged, but, naturally, with a purpose: to turn Jews away from an historical Jewish past; to show "before October" as a gloomy prologue to the epoch of happiness and a new dawn; to smear anything religious and find in the Soviet Jew the "new man." Even with all this, it was so attractive to some prominent Jewish writers who had left the country that they started to return to the USSR: poets David Gofstein ("always suspected of harboring nationalist sentiment") and Leib Kvitko ("easily accommodated to Soviet environment and become a prolific poet") returned in 1925; Perez Markish ("easily understands the needs of the party") — in 1926; Moses Kulbak and Der Nistor (the real name of the latter was Pinkhos Kaganovich, he later wrote novel *Mashber Family* characterized as the most "un-Soviet and liberal work of Jewish prose in Soviet Union") — returned in 1928. David Bergelson returned in 1929, he "paid tribute to those in power: 'the revolution has a right to cruelty'.[2313] (Which he, Markish and Kvitko were to experience themselves in 1952.)

The "bourgeois" Hebrew culture was suppressed. A group of writers headed by H.N. Byalik left for Palestine in 1921. Another group "of Hebrew writers existed until the mid-30's, occasionally publishing in foreign journals. Some of these authors were arrested and disappeared without a trace while others managed to escape the Soviet Union".[2314]

Regarding Jewish culture expressed in Russian language, Yevseks interpreted it as the "result of government-directed efforts to assimilate Jews in Tsarist Russia." Among those writing in Yiddish, a split between "proletarian" writers and "companions" developed in mid-20's, like in Soviet literature at large. Majority of mainstream authors then switched to Russian language.[2315]

The Jewish Chamber Theater in Yiddish in Moscow flowered since 1921 at a high artistic level with government aid (in 1925 it was transformed into the State Jewish Theater, GosET). It traveled through Europe and became an unexpected representative of Soviet power in the eyes of world Jewry.

[2313] Ю. Марк. Литература на идиш в Советской России // КРЕ-2, с. 224-229.
[2314] И. Слуцкий. Судьба иврит в России // КРЕ-2, с. 245, 247.
[2315] КЕЭ, т. 8, с. 174, 181-182.

It made fun of pre-revolutionary ways and religious life of the shtetl. Mikhoels excelled as an actor and in 1928 became the director.[2316]

The history of the Hebrews theater "Gabima," which began before the revolution was much more complicated. Originally supported by Lunacharsky, Gorky and Stanislavsky it was persecuted as a "Zionist nest" by the YevSek and it took a decision by Lenin to allow it to exist. "Gabima" became a government theatre. It remained the only outpost of Hebrew in the USSR, though it was clear it had no future.[2317] (The theatre critic A. Kugel said it had departed from Jewish daily life and lost its Jewish spirit.[2318]) In 1926 the troupe went on a European tour and did not return, disappearing from history soon after.[2319]

By contrast, the government Yiddish theatre "was a real boon for Jewish theater arts in the USSR." In the early 30's there were 19 professional Yiddish theater groups... with a training school at GosET in Moscow, and Jewish dramatic arts studios in Kiev, Minsk and Moscow.[2320]

Here it is worth remembering the posthumous treatment of the ill-fated "Jewish Gogol" Semen Ushkevitch. His book *Episodes*, published in 1926 "satirizes revolution-era Jewish bourgeois". He died in 1927 and in 1928 the Soviet censor banned his play *Simka, The Rabbit Hearted* based on his earlier book. As an anti- bourgeois work it should have been fine, but "taking place in a Jewish setting and making fun of the stupidity, cowardice and greed of its subjects, it was banned because of fears that it would cause Judeophobic feelings".[2321]

In the meantime what was the condition of Zionist organizations in the USSR?

They were fundamentally incompatible with communist authority and were accused of "international imperialism" and collaboration with the Entente.

Because of their international standing the Soviets had to deal carefully with them. In 1920 the YevSek declared a "civil war on the Jewish street" against the Zionist organizations. Repression of Zionism deepened with the ban on Hebrew.

However "anti-Zionist pressure did not exist everywhere and was not sufficiently severe" — that is "long-term imprisonment and exile were

---

[2316] Г. Свет. Еврейский театр в Советской России // КРЕ-2, с. 266-271.
[2317] КЕЭ, т. 9, с. 477.
[2318] КЕЭ, т. 4, с. 616.
[2319] Г. Свет. Еврейский театр... // КРЕ-2, с. 273-278.
[2320] КЕЭ, т. 8, с. 183.
[2321] В. Левитина. Стоило ли сжигать свой храм... // "22," 1984, № 34, с. 204.

relatively rare." In spring 1920 right-wing Zionists were frightened with arrests, but on May 1 were amnestied.

The dual policy of the Kremlin was apparent in its discussions with representatives of the World Zionist Organization. Chicherin did not dismiss out of hand it's the latter's solicitations as the Soviets were "not yet ready to denounce Zionism once and for all" as had the YevSek. The more so since "from the beginning of NEP, lessening government pressure gave Zionist groups a breathing space".[2322] Interestingly, Dzerzhinsky wrote in 1923 that "the program of the Zionists is not dangerous to us, on the contrary I consider it useful" and again in 1924 "principally, we can be friends with Zionists".[2323] The Central Zionist Bureau existed in Moscow from 1920 to 1924. In March of 1924 its members were arrested and only after much pleading from within the country and from overseas was exile to Central Asia replaced with exile abroad.[2324] In 1923 only two officially permitted Zionist organizations remained: Poale-Zion and the "legal" portion of the youth organization Gekhaluz, whose purpose was agricultural colonization of Palestine. They saw experience with collective farms in the USSR as preparation for this. They published a journal from 1924 to 1926.[2325] Even the left-wing of the Zionist socialist party Zirei-Zion ('Youth of Zion') adopted a sharper tone vis a vis the Bolsheviks, and when the arrests in 1924, though short in duration, became more widespread they went underground. This underground movement was finally dispersed only in the late 20's.

"Jewish blood will not oil the wheels of revolution," an organizational slogan of the movement, conveys the sense of the underground Zirei-Zion with its significant youth organizations in Kiev and Odessa. Regarding the government, "they formally recognized Soviet authority, but at the same time declared opposition to the dictatorship of the communist party." Much of its work was directed against the YevSek. "In particular, they agitated against the Crimean resettlement plan, seeing it as disturbing their 'national isolation'."

From 1926 the party weakened and then disappeared.[2326] There was a wave of arrests of Zionists from September to October of 1924. Some of those arrested were tried in secret and given sentences of 3 to 10 years in the camps. But in 1925 Zionist delegates were assured by the CIK of VKPb (Smidovitch) and the Sovnarkom (Rykov) and the GPU that they had

---

[2322] И.Б. Шехтман. Советская Россия, сионизм и Израиль // КРЕ-2. 321-323.
[2323] КЕЭ, т. 8, с. 200.
[2324] Там же, с. 201.
[2325] КЕЭ, т. 5, с. 476, т. 7, с. 948.
[2326] Михаил Хейфец. Воспоминаний грустный свиток. Иерусалим, 1996, с. 74-79.

nothing against Zionists as long as they "did not arouse the Jewish population against Soviet power".[2327]

D. Pasmanik suggested in 1924 that "Zionists, Orthodox and nationalist Jews should be in the front ranks of those fighting alongside Soviet power and the Bolshevik worldview".[2328] But there was no united front and no front rank.

In the second half of the 20's, persecution of the Zionists was renewed and the exchange of prison sentences for exile abroad was sharply curtailed. "In 1928 authorities dissolved, the until then quasi-legal Poale-Zion and liquated the legal Gekhaluz, closing its farms… Almost all underground Zionist organizations were destroyed at that time." Opportunities to leave declined sharply after 1926. Some of the Zionists remained in prison or were exiled.[2329]

The mass attraction of young urban Jews to communist and Soviet culture and programs was matched with a no less stubborn resistance from religious Jewry and older Jews from the former Pale. The party used the rock of the YevSek to crush and suppress this resistance.

"One only has to be in a Jewish city such as Minsk or Vitebsk to see how all that was once worthy in Judaism, respected and worthy of respect has been turned upside down, crushed with poverty, insult, and hopelessness and how those pushed into higher places are the dissolute, frivolous, arrogant and brazen".[2330] Bolshevik power "become the carrier of terrible ruin, material and moral… in our Jewish world".[2331] "The mass of Jewish Bolsheviks on one hand and of Jewish NEPmen on the other indicate the depth of the cultural collapse of Jewry. And if radical healing from Bolshevism among the Russian people is to come from a revival of religious, moral and nationalist life then the Jewish idea must work for that also in their lives".[2332]

And work they did, but indicators vary as to degree of intensity and success. A near contemporary considered "Jewish society turned out either to have no rudder and no sail or was confused and in this confusion spiritually turned away from its sources" in contrast to Russian society where there was still some resistance, albeit "clumsy and unsuccessful".[2333]

[2327] И.Б. Шехтман. Советская Россия, сионизм и Израиль // КРЕ-2, с. 324-325.
[2328] Д.С. Пасманик. Чего же мы добиваемся? // РиЕ, с, 214.
[2329] КЕЭ, т. 7, с. 948. И.Б. Шехтман. Советская Россия, сионизм и Израиль // КРЕ-2, с. 325-328.
[2330] И.М. Бикерман. Россия и русское еврейство // РиЕ, с. 92.
[2331] Там же, с, 53.
[2332] И.О.Левин. Евреи в революции // РиЕ, с. 138.
[2333] Г.А. Ландау. Революционные идеи в еврейской общественности // РиЕ, с. 118.

"From the end of the 20's to the beginning of the 30's the Jews abandoned their traditional way of life on a mass scale."[2334] "In the past 20 years Russian Jewry has gone further and further away from its historical past… killing the Jewish spirit and Jewish tradition".[2335] And a few years later on the very eve of WWII "with the ascension in Russia of the Bolshevik dictatorship, the fight between fathers and children in the Jewish street has taken a particularly bitter form".[2336]

Taking stock a half-century later, M. Agursky reminisces in Israel, that the misfortunes that befell Jews after the revolution to a large degree were brought on by the renunciation by Jewish youth of its religion and national culture, "the singular, exclusive influence of communist ideology…" "The mass penetration by Jews in all areas of Russian life" and of the Soviet leadership in the first 20 years after the revolution turned not to be constructive for Jews, but harmful.[2337]

Finally, an author in the 1990's writes: "Jews were the elite of the revolution and on the winning side. That's a peculiar fact of the Russian internationalist socialist revolution. In the course of modernizing, Jewry was politically Bolshevized and socially Sovietized: The Jewish community as an ethnic, religious and national structure disappeared without a trace".[2338] Jewish youth coming to Bolshevism were intoxicated by its new role and influence. For this, others too would have gladly given up their nationality. But this turning from the old ways to internationalism and atheism was not the same as assimilation into the surrounding majority, a centuries-old Jewish fear. This was leaving the old, along with all other youth, to come together and form a new *Soviet people*. "Only a small stream was truly assimilationalist in the old sense," like those people who converted to Orthodox Christianity and wished their own dissolution in the Russian culture. We find one such example in attorney Y. Gurevich, legal defender of metropolitan Venamin during his fatal trial in 1922.[2339]

The *Jewish Encyclopedia* writes of Jewish workers in the "party and government apparatus of economic, scientific and even military organizations and institutions, that most did not hide their Jewish origins,

---

[2334] КЕЭ, т. 8, с. 199.

[2335] Г.Б. Слиозберг. Дела минувших дней: Записки русского еврея. Париж, 1934. Т. 3, с. 376.

[2336] Ст. Иванович. Евреи и советская диктатура // ЕМ-1, с. 47.

[2337] Jerusalem Post, 1973, April 13, 1979, October 7.

[2338] Sonja Margolina. Das Ende der Lugen: Rufiland und die Juden im20. Jahrhundert. Berlin: Siedler Verlag. 1992, S. 106.

[2339] М. Агурский. Идеология национал-большевизма, с. 114.

but they and their families quickly absorbed Russian culture and language and being Jewish lost its cultural content".[2340]

Yes, the culture which sustained them suffered, "Soviet Man" was created, but the decades which followed showed that a remnant of Jewish self-awareness was preserved and remained. Even in the flood of the internationalism of the 20's, mixed marriages (between Jews and Russians or Jews and any non-Jew), as measured from 1924-1926, were only 6.3% of the total marriages for Jews in the USSR, including 16.8% in RSFSR, but only 2.8% in Byelorussia and 4.5% in Ukraine[2341] (according to another source, on average in USSR, 8.5%; in RSFSR, 21%; in Byelorussia, 3.2%; and in Ukraine, 5%[2342]). Assimilation had only begun.

And what was the status of the Jewish religion in the new conditions?

Bolshevik power was hostile to all religions. During the years of the hardest blows against the Orthodox Church, Jewish religious practice was treated with restraint. "In March, 1922 *Dar Amos* noted that the department of agitprop of the Central Committee would not offend religious feelings... In the 20's this tolerance did not extend to Russian Orthodoxy, which the authorities considered one of the main enemies of the Soviet order".[2343] Nevertheless, the confiscation of church valuables extended to synagogues as well. E. Yarolslavsky wrote in *Izvestia* an article titled "What Can be Taken from a Synagogue": Often Rabbis will say there is nothing of value in a synagogue. Usually that is the case... The walls are usually bare. But menorahs are often made of silver. These must be confiscated." Three weeks before that 16 silver objects were taken from Jewish preaching house on Spasso-Glinischevsky avenue and in the neighboring choral synagogue "57 silver objects and 2 of gold." Yaroslavsky further proposes a progressive tax on those who buy costly seats in the synagogue.[2344] (Apparently, this proposal went nowhere.)

However "functionaries from the YevSek demanded of authorities that the same policy applied towards Christianity be carried out towards Judaism".[2345] In the Jewish New Year, 1921 the YevSek orchestrated a "public trial of the Jewish religion" in Kiev. The *Book of Russian Jewry* describes this and other show trials in 1921-1922: there was a court proceeding against a Cheder (a traditional elementary school with

---

[2340] КЭЕ, т. 1, с. 235.
[2341] С. Познер. Советская Россия* // ЕМ-1, с. 271.
[2342] Ю. Ларин*, с. 304.
[2343] КЭЕ, т. 8, с. 194.
[2344] Поход на синагоги в Советской России* // Еврейская трибуна, 1922, 21 апреля (№ 120), с. 7.
[2345] КЭЕ, т. 8, с. 196.

instruction in Hebrew) in Vitebsk, against a Yeshiva (a Jewish school for study of the traditional, texts, the Talmud, the Torah, and the Rabbinical literature) in Rostov and even against Day of Atonement in Odessa.

They were intentionally conducted in Yiddish, as the YeSsek explained, so that Jewish Bolsheviks would "judge" Judaism.

Religious schools were closed by administrative order and in December 1920 the Jewish section of the Narkomat of Education issued a encyclical about the liquidation of Cheders and Yeshivas. "Nevertheless, large numbers of Cheders and Yeshivas continued teaching semi-legally or completely underground for a long time after that".[2346] "In spite of the ban on religious education, as a whole the 20's were rather a liberal period for Jewish religious life in the USSR".[2347]

"[A]t the request of Jewish laborers," of course, there were several attempts to close synagogues, but this met with "bitter opposition from believers." Still "during the 20's the central synagogues were closed in Vitebsk, Minsk, Gomel, Kharkov, Bobruisk".[2348] The central Moscow synagogue on Maroseika managed stay open thanks to the efforts of Rabbi Maze in the face of Dzerzhinsky and Kalinin.[2349] In 1926, the "choral synagogue in Kiev was closed" and children's Yiddish theatre opened in its place.[2350] But "the majority of synagogues continued to function. In 1927, 1034 synagogues and prayer halls were functioning in Ukraine and the number of synagogues towards the end of the 20s' exceeded the number in 1917".[2351]

Authorities attempted to institute "Living Synagogues" based on the model of the "Living Church" imposed upon the Russian Orthodox Church. A "portrait of Lenin was to be hung in a prominent place" of such a synagogue, the authorities brought in "red Rabbis" and "communized Rabbis." However they "failed to bring about a split among the believers"[2352] and the vast majority of religious Jews was decisively against the 'Living Synagogue', bringing the plan of Soviet authorities to naught.[2353]

At the end of 1930 a group of rabbis from Minsk was arrested. They were freed after two weeks and made to sign a document prepared by the GPU

[2346] Г. Свет. Еврейская религия в Советской России // КРЕ-2, с. 205-207.
[2347] КЕЭ, т. 8, с. 194.
[2348] Там же, с. 195.
[2349] Г. Свет. Еврейская религия... // КРЕ-2, с. 209.
[2350] КЕЭ, т. 4, с. 257.
[2351] КЕЭ, т. 8, с. 195.
[2352] Г. Свет. Еврейская религия... // КРЕ-2, с. 208.
[2353] КЕЭ, т. 8, с. 197.

agreeing that: (1) the Jewish religion was not persecuted in the USSR and, (2) during the entire Soviet era not one rabbi had been shot.[2354]

Authorities tried to declare the day of rest to be Sunday or Monday in Jewish areas. School studies were held on the Sabbath by order of the YevSek.

In 1929 authorities tried the five-day work week and the six-day work week with the day of rest upon the 5th or 6th day, respectively. Christians lost Sunday and Jews lost the Sabbath. Members of the YevSek rampaged in front of synagogues on holidays and "in Odessa broke into the Brodsky Synagogue and demonstratively ate bread in front of those fasting and praying." They instituted "community service" days during sacred holidays like Yom Kippur. "during holidays, especially when the synagogue was closed, they requisitioned Talles, Torah scrolls, prayer shawls and religious books... import of matzoh from abroad was sometimes allowed and sometimes forbidden [2355] ... in 1929 they started taxing matzoh preparation.[2356] Larin notes the "amazing permission" granted to bring matzoh from Königsberg to Moscow for Passover in 1929.[2357]

In the 20's private presses still published Jewish religious literature. "In Leningrad, Hasids managed to print prayer books in several runs, a few thousands copies each" while Katzenelson, a rabbi from Leningrad, was able to use the printing-house "Red Agitator." During 1920's, the Jewish calendars were printed and distributed in tens of thousand copies.[2358] The Jewish community was the only religious group in Moscow allowed to build religious buildings. A second synagogue was built on Visheslaviz alley nearby Sushchevsky Embankment and a third in Cherkizov. These three synagogues stayed open throughout the 30's.[2359]

But "young Jewish writers and poets... gleefully wrote about the empty synagogues, the lonely rabbi who had no one to teach and about the boys from the villages who grew up to become the terrible red commissars".[2360] And we saw the Russian members of Komsomol rampaging on Easter Sunday, knocking candles and holy bread out of worshippers' hands, tearing the crosses from the cupolas and we saw thousands of beautiful

---

[2354] Там же, с. 198.
[2355] Г. Свет. Еврейская религия... // КРЕ-2, с. 208-209.
[2356] КЕЭ, т. 8, с. 199.
[2357] Ю. Ларин, с. 285.
[2358] И. Слуцкий. Судьба иврит в России // КРЕ-2, с. 246.
[2359] Сорок сороков: Альбом-указатель всех московских церквей: В 4 т. / Сост. С. Звонарёв [П. Паламарчук]. Париж, YMCA-Press, 1988. Т. 1, с. 13. С. Познер. Советская Россия // ЕМ-1, с. 271.
[2360] М. Поповский. О нас — со всей искренностью // Новый американец, 1981, 20-26 сентября (№ 84), с. 7.

churches broken into a rubble of bricks and we remember the thousands of priests that were shot and the thousands of others who were sent to the camps.

In those years, we all drove God out. From the early Soviet years the path for Jewish intelligentsia and youth was open as wide as possible in science and culture, given Soviet restrictions. (Olga Kameneva, Trotsky's sister, patronized high culture in the very early Soviet years.)

Already in 1919 "a large number of Jewish youth" went into moviemaking — an art praised by Lenin for its ability to govern the psychology of the masses.

Many of them took charge of movie studios, film schools and film crews. For example, B. Shumyatsky, one of the founders of the Mongolian Republic, and S. Dukelsky were heads of the main department of the movie industry at different times.[2361] Impressive works of early Soviet motion cinematography were certainly a Jewish contribution. The *Jewish Encyclopedia* lists numerous administrators, producers, directors, actors, script writers and motion picture theorists. Producer Dziga Vertov is considered a classic figure in Soviet, cinema, mostly nonfiction. His works include *Lenin's Truth, Go Soviets, Symphony of Donbass* [the Donetsk Basin], and *The Three Songs about Lenin*.[2362] (It is less known that he also orchestrated desecration of the holy relics of St. Sergius of Radonezh.) In the documentary genre, Esther Shub, "by tendentious cutting and editing of fragments of old documentaries, produced full-length propaganda movies (*The Fall of Romanovs* (1927) and others), and later — glorifying ones." Other famous Soviet names include S. Yutkevitch, G. Kozintsev and L. Trauberg (*SVD, New Babel*). F. Ermler organized the Experimental Movie Studio. Among notable others are G. Roshal (*The Skotinins*), Y. Raizman (*Hard Labor Camps, Craving of Earth* among others.).

By far, the largest figure of Soviet cinematography was Sergei Eisenstein. He introduced "the epic spirit and grandeur of huge crowd scenes, tempo, new techniques of editing and emotionality" into the art of cinematography.[2363]

However he used his gifts as ordered. The worldwide fame of *Battleship Potemkin* was a battering ram for the purposes of the Soviets and in its irresponsibly falsified history encouraged the Soviet public to further curse Tsarist Russia. Made-up events, such as the "massacre on Odessa Steps" scene and the scene where a crowd of rebellious seamen is covered with

---

[2361] КЕЭ, т. 4, с. 275, РЕЭ, т. 3, с. 439.
[2362] КЕЭ, т. 1, с. 653.
[2363] КЕЭ, т. 4, с. 276-277.

tarpaulin for execution, entered the world's consciousness as if they were facts. First it was necessary to serve Stalin's totalitarian plans and then his nationalistic idea.

Eisenstein was there to help.

Though the *Jewish Encyclopedia* list names in the arts by nationality, I must repeat: not in the nationalism does one find the main key to the epoch of the early Soviet years, but in the destructive whirlwind of internationalism, estranged from any feeling of nationality or traditions. And here in theater but close to authorities we see the glorious figure of Meyerhold, who became the leading and most authoritarian star of the Soviet theater. He had numerous impassioned admirers but wasn't universally recognized. From late recollections of Tyrkova-Vyazemskaya, Meyerhold appears as a dictator subjugating both actors and playwrites alike to his will "by his dogmatism and dry formalism." Komissarzhevskaya sensed "that his novelty lacks creative simplicity and ethical and esthetical clarity." He "clipped actor's wings… paid more attention to frame than to portrait".[2364] He was a steady adversary of Mikhail Bulgakov.

Of course, the time was such that artists had to pay for their privileges. Many paid, including Kachalov, Nemirovitch-Danchenko and A. Tairov-Kornblit, the talented producer of the Chamber Theater and a star of that unique early Soviet period. (In 1930, Tairov "denounced" 'Prompartia' in the party newspapers.)

Artist Marc Chagall emigrated by 1923. The majority of artists in the 20's were required to contribute to Soviet mass propaganda. There some Jewish artists distinguished themselves, beginning with A. Lisitsky who greeted the revolution as "a new beginning for humanity." He joined a number of various committees and commissions, made first banner of all-Russian Central Executive Committee, which was displayed on the Red Square in 1918 by members of government." He made famous poster "Strike Whites with the Red Wedge," designed numerous Soviet expositions abroad (from 1927) and propaganda albums for the West ("USSR Builds Socialism" etc.).[2365] A favorite with the authorities was Isaac Brodsky who drew portraits of Lenin, Trotsky and others including Voroshilov, Frunze and Budenny. "After completing his portrait of Stalin he became the leading official portrait artist of the USSR" in 1928 and in 1934 was named director of the all-Russian Academy of Arts.[2366]

[2364] А. Тыркова-Вильямс. Тени минувшего // ВМ, Нью-Йорк, 1990, № 111, с. 214-215.
[2365] КЕЭ, т. 4, с. 860-862.
[2366] КЕЭ, т. 1, с. 547.

During early years after revolution, Jewish musical life was particularly rich. At the start of century the first in the world Jewish national school of music in the entire world, which combined both traditional Jewish and contemporary European approaches, was established. The 1920's saw a number of works inspired by traditional Jewish themes and stories, such as *Youth of Abraham* by M. Gnesin, *The Song of Songs* by A, Krein, and *Jewish Rhapsody* by his brother G. Krein. In that age of restrictions, the latter and his son Yulian were sent into eight-years studying trip to Vienna and Paris to "perfect Yulian's performance".[2367] Jews were traditionally talented in music and many names of future stars were for the first time heard during that period. Many "administrators from music" appeared also, such as Matias Sokolsky-Greenberg, who was "chief inspector of music at Department of Arts of Ministry of Education" and a senior editor of ideological *Music and Revolution*."Later in 1930's Moses Greenberg, "a prominent organizer of musical performances," was director of State Publishing House in music and chief editor of the Department of Music Broadcasting at the State Radio Studio.[2368] There was Jewish Conservatory in Odessa as well.[2369]

Leonid Utesov (Lazar Vaysbeyn) thundered from the stage. Many of his songs were written by A. d'Aktil. A. P. German and Y. Hayt wrote the March of Soviet Aviation.[2370] This was the origin of Soviet mass singing culture.

Year after year, the stream of Soviet culture fell more and more under the hand of the government. A number of various state organizations were created such as the State Academic Council, the monopolistic State Publishing House (which choked off many private publishing firms and even had its own political commissar, certain David Chernomordnikov in 1922-23,[2371] and the State Commission for Acquisition of Art Pieces (de facto power over artist livelihood). Political surveillance was established. (The case of A. K. Glazunov, Rector of the Leningrad Conservatory, will be reviewed below).

Of course, Jews were only a part of the forward triumphal march of proletarian culture. In the heady atmosphere of the early Soviet epoch no one noticed the loss of Russian culture and that Soviet culture was driving Russian culture out along with its strangled and might-have-been names.

[2367] КЕЭ, т. 5, с. 541-542; РЕЭ, т. 2, с. 86-87.
[2368] РЕЭ, т.1, с. 377.
[2369] РЕЭ, т. 2, с. 287.
[2370] РЕЭ, т.1, с. 288, 409.
[2371] РЕЭ, т. 3, с. 336.

A vicious battle for the dominance within the Party was waged between Trotsky and Stalin from 1923 to 1927. Later Zinoviev fought for first place equally confident of his chances. In 1926 Zinoviev and Kamenev, deceived by Stalin, united with Trotsky ("the United Opposition") — that is, three of the most visible Jewish leaders turned out on one side. Not surprisingly, many of the lower rank Trotskyites were Jewish. (Agursky cites A. Chiliga, exiled with Trotskyites in the Urals: "indeed the Trotskyites were young Jewish intellectuals and technicians," particularly from Left Bundists.[2372]

"The opposition was viewed as principally Jewish" and this greatly alarmed Trotsky. In March of 1924 he complained to Bukharin that among the workers it is openly stated: "The kikes are rebelling!" and he claimed to have received hundreds of letters on the topic. Bukharin dismissed it as trivial. Then "Trotsky tried to bring the question of anti-Semitism to a Politburo session but no one supported him." More than anything, Trotsky feared that Stalin would use popular anti-Semitism against him in their battle for power. And such was partially the case according to Uglanov, then secretary of the Moscow Committee of the CP. "Anti-Semitic cries were heard" during Uglanov's dispersal of a pro-Trotsky demonstration in Moscow November 7, 1927.[2373]

Maybe Stalin considered playing the anti-Jewish card against the "United Opposition," but his superior political instinct led him away from that. He understood that Jews were numerous in the party at that time and could be a powerful force against him if his actions were to unite them against him. They were also needed in order to maintain support from the West and would be of further use to him personally. He never parted from his beloved assistant Lev Mekhlis — and from the Civil War at Tsaritsyn, his faithful aid Moses Rukhimovitch.

But as Stalin's personal power grew towards the end of the 20's the number of Jews in the Soviet Apparatus began to fall off. It was no accident that he sent Enukidze to take photographs "among the Jewish delegates" at a "workers and peasants" conference during the height of the struggle for party dominance.[2374]

Yaroslavsky writes in *Pravda*: "Incidents of anti-Semitism are the same whether they are used against the opposition or used by the opposition in its fight against the party." They are an "attempt to use any weakness, any fissures in the dictatorship of the proletariat... there is "nothing more stupid or reactionary than to explain the roots of opposition to the dictatorship of the proletariat as related to the nationality of this or that opposition group

---

[2372] М. Агурский. Идеология национал-большевизма, с. 240.
[2373] Там же, с. 240-242, 244.
[2374] Известия, 1927, 13 октября, с. 2.

member".[2375] At the same Party Congress, the 25th, where the "united opposition" was decisively broken, Stalin directed Ordzhonikidze to specifically address the national question in his report to the Central Committee, as if in defense Jews. (Statistics from the report were discussed earlier in this chapter.)

"The majority of the apparatus is Russian, so any discussion of Jewish dominance has no basis whatever".[2376] At the 26th Party Congress in 1930 Stalin declared "Great Russian chauvinism" to be the "main danger of the national question." Thus, at the end of the 20's Stalin did not carry out his planned purge of the party and government apparatus of Jews, but encouraged their expansion in many fields, places and institutions.

At the 25th Congress in December 1927, the time had come to address the looming "peasant question" — what to do with the presumptuous peasantry which had the temerity to ask for manufactured goods in exchange for their grain. Molotov delivered the main report on this topic and among the debaters were the murderers of the peasantry — Schlikhter and Yakovlev-Epstein.[2377] A massive war against the peasantry lay ahead and Stalin could not afford to alienate any of his reliable allies and probably thought that in this campaign against a disproportionately Slavic population it would be better to rely on Jews than on Russians. He preserved the Jewish majority in the Gosplan. The commanding heights of collectivization and its theory included, of course, Larin. Lev Kritzman was director of the Agrarian Institute from 1928. As Assistant to the President of the Gosplan in 1931-33 he played a fateful role in the persecution of Kondratev and Chayanov. Yakov Yakovlev-Epstein took charge of People's Commissariat of Agriculture in 1929. (Before that he worked in propaganda field: he was in charge of Head Department of Political Education since 1921, later — in the agitprop division of Central Committee and in charge of press division of Central Committee. His career in agriculture began in 1923 when during the 13th Party Congress he drafted resolutions on agricultural affairs.[2378] And thus he led the "Great Change," the imposition of collectivization on millions of peasants with its zealous implementers on the ground. A contemporary writer reports: "for the first time ever a significant number of young Jewish communists arrived in rural communities as commanders and lords over life and death. Only during collectivization did the

---

[2375] Ем. Ярославский. Против антисемитизма // Правда, 1927, 12 ноября, с. 2.
[2376] Известия, 1927, 11 декабря, с. 1.
[2377] Там же, 22 декабря, с. 2-4, 23 декабря, с. 4, 5.
[2378] РЕЭ, т. 2, с. 93, т. 3, с. 497.

characterization of the Jew as the hated enemy of the peasant take hold — even in those places where Jews had never been seen before".[2379]

Of course regardless of the percentage of Jews in the party and Soviet apparatus, it would be a mistake to explain the ferocious anti-peasant plan of communism as due to Jewish participation. A Russian could have been found in the place of Yakovlev-Epstein — that's sufficiently clear from our post-October history.

The cause and consequences of de-Kulakization and collectivization were not only social and economic: The millions of victims of these programs were not a faceless mass, but real people with traditions and culture, cut off from their roots and spiritually killed. In its essence, de-Kulakization was not a socio-economic measure, but a measure taken against a nationality. The strategic blow against the Russian people, who were the main obstacle to the victory of communism, was conceived of by Lenin, but carried out after his death. In those years communism with all its cruelty was directed mostly against Russians. It is amazing that not everything has perished during those days. Collectivization, more than any other policy of the communists, gives the lie to the conception of Stalin's dictatorship as nationalist, i.e., "Russian."

Regarding Jewish role in collectivization, it is necessary to remember that Jewish communists participated efficiently and diligently. From a third-wave immigrant who grew up in Ukraine. "I remember my father, my mother, aunts, uncles all worked on collectivization with great relish, completing 5-year plans in 4 years and writing novels about life in factories"[2380] - a mainstream Soviet literary genre in the 20's.

In 1927 *Izvestia* declared "there is no Jewish question here. The October revolution gave a categorical answer long ago. All nationalities are equal – that was the answer".[2381] However when the dispossessors entering the peasant huts were not just commissars but Jewish commissars the question still glowered in the distance.

"At the end of the 20's" writes S. Ettinger, "in all the hardship of life in the USSR, to many it seemed that Jews were the only group which gained from the revolution. They were found in important government positions, they

---

[2379] Sonja Margolina. Das Ende der Lugen: Rufiland und die Juden im 20. Jahrhundert. S. 84.
[2380] М. Поповский. О нас — со всей искренностью // Новый американец, 1981, 20-26 сентября (№ 84), с. 7.
[2381] Н. Семашко. Евреи на земле // Известия, 1927, 20 августа, с. 3.

made up a large proportion of university students, it was rumored that they received the best land in the Crimea and have flooded into Moscow".[2382]

Half a century later, June 1980, at a Columbia University conference about the situation of Soviet Jewry, I heard scholars describe the marginalized status of Jews in the USSR and in particular how Jews were offered the choice of either emigration or denying their roots, beliefs and culture in order to become part of a denationalized society.

Bah! That was what was required of all peoples in the 20's under the threat of the Solovki prison camp – and emigration was not an alternative.

The "golden era" of the 20's cries out for a sober appraisal. Those years were filled with the cruelest persecution based upon class distinction, including persecution of children on account of the former life of their parents – a life which the children did not even see. But Jews were not among *these* children or parents.

The clergy, part of the Russian character, centuries in the making, was hounded to death in the 20's. Though not majority Jewish, too often the people saw Jews directing the special "ecclesiastical departments of the GPU" which worked in this area.

A wave of trials of engineers took place from the end of the 20's through the 30's. An entire class of older engineers was eliminated. This group was overwhelmingly Russian with a small number of Germans.

Study of Russian history, archeology, and folklore were suppressed — the Russians could not have a past. No one from the persecutors would be accused having their own national interest. (It must be noted that the commission which prepared the decree abolishing the history and the philology departments at Russian universities was made up Jews and non-Jews alike — Goykhbarg, Larin, Radek and Ropstein as well as Bukharin, M. Pokrovskii, Skvortsov-Stepanov and Fritche. It was signed into existence by Lenin in March, 1921.) The spirit of the decree was itself an example of nationalist hatred: It was the history and language of the Great Russians that was no longer needed. During the 20's the very understanding of Russian history was changed — there was none! And the understanding of what a Great Russian is changed — there was no such thing.

And what was most painful, we Russians ourselves walked along this suicidal path. The very period of the 20's was considered the dawn of liberated culture, liberated from Tsarism and capitalism! Even the word

---

[2382] S. Ettinger // Bulletin on Soviet and East European Jewish Affairs, 1970, № 5, p. 38-39.

"Russian," such as "I am Russian" sounded like a counter-revolutionary cry which I well remember from my childhood. But without hesitation everywhere was heard and printed "Russopyati"! - a disparaging term for ethnic Russians.

Pravda published the following in a prominent place in 1925 by V. Aleksandrovsky (not known for any other contribution):

Rus! Have you rotted, fallen and died?
Well... here's to your eternal memory...
... you shuffle, your crutches scraping along,
Your lips smeared with soot from icons,
over your vast expanses the raven caws,
You have guarded your grave dream.
Old woman — blind and stupid...[2383]

V. Bloom in *Moscow Evening* could brazenly demand the removal of "history's garbage from [city] squares": to remove Minin-Pozharsky monument from the Red Square, to remove the monument to Russia's thousand-year anniversary in Novgorod and a statue of St. Vladimir on the hill in Kiev. "Those tons of metal are needed for raw material." (The ethnic coloring of the new names has already been noted.)

Swept to glory by the political changes and distinguished by personal shamelessness, David Zaslavsky demanded the destruction of the studios of Igor Graybar used to restore ancient Russian art, finding that "reverend artist fathers were trying again to fuse the church and art".[2384]

Russia's self-mortification reflected in the Russian language with the depth, beauty and richness of meaning were replaced by an iron stamp of Soviet conformity.

We have not forgotten how it looked at the height of the decade: Russian patriotism was abolished forever. But the feelings of the people will not be forgotten. Not how it felt to see the Church of the Redeemer blown up by the engineer Dzhevalkin and that the main mover behind this was Kaganovich who wanted to destroy St. Basil's cathedral as well. Russian Orthodoxy was publicly harassed by "warrior atheists" led by Gubelman-Yaroslavsky. It is truthfully noted: "That Jewish communists took part in the destruction of churches was particularly offensive... No matter how offensive the participation of sons of Russian peasants in the persecution of the church, the part played by each non-Russian was even more

---

[2383] Правда, 1925, 13 августа, с. 3.
[2384] Сорок Сороков: Альбом-указатель всех московских церквей. Т. 1*, с. 15.

offensive".[2385] This went against the Russian saying: "*if you managed to snatch a room in the house, don't throw the God out*".

In the words of A. Voronel, "The 20's were perceived by the Jews as a positive opportunity while for the Russian people, it was a tragedy".[2386]

True, the Western leftist intellectuals regarded Soviet reality even higher; their admiration was not based on nationality but upon ideas of socialism. Who remembers the lightening crack of the firing squad executing 48 "food workers" for having "caused the Great Famine" (i.e., rather than Stalin): the wreckers in the meat, fish, conserves and produce trade? Among these unfortunates were not less than ten Jews.[2387] What would it take to end the world's enchantment with Soviet power? Dora Shturman attentively followed the efforts of B. Brutskus to raise a protest among Western intellectuals. He found some who would protest – Germans and "rightists." Albert Einstein hotheadedly signed a protest, but then withdrew his signature without embarrassment because the "Soviet Union has achieved a great accomplishment" and "Western Europe... will soon envy you."

The recent execution by firing squad was an "isolated incident." Also, "from this, one cannot exclude the possibility that they were guilty." Romain Rolland maintained a "noble" silence. Arnold Zweig barely stood up to the communist rampage. At least he didn't withdraw his signature, but said this settling of accounts was an "ancient Russian method." And, if true, what then should be asked of the academic Ioffe in Russia who was prompting Einstein to remove his signature?[2388]

No, the West never envied us and from those "isolated incidents" millions of innocents died. We'll never discover why this brutality was forgotten by Western opinion. It's not very readily remembered today.

Today a myth is being built about the past to the effect that under Soviet power Jews were always second class citizens. Or, one sometimes hears that "there was not the persecution in the 20's, that was to come later."[2389]

It's very rare to hear an admission that not only did they take part, but there was a certain enthusiasm among Jews as they carried out the business of the barbaric young government. "The mixture of ignorance and arrogance which Hannah calls a typical characteristic of the Jewish parvenu filled the

---

[2385] Sonja Margolina. Das Ende der Ltigen: Rufiland und die Juden im 20. Jahrhundert. S. 79.

[2386] А. Воронель. Трепет иудейских забот. 2-е изд. Рамат-Ган: Москва-Иерусалим, 1981, с. 120.

[2387] Известия, 1930, 22 сентября, с. 1, 3-4, 25 сентября, с. 1.

[2388] Д. Штурман. Они — ведали // "22," 1990, № 73, с. 126-144.

[2389] И. Зунделевич. Восхождение // "22," 1983, № 29, с. 54.

government, social and cultural elite. The brazenness and ardor with which all Bolshevik policies were carried out — whether confiscation of church property or persecution of 'bourgeois intellectuals' gave Bolshevik power in the 20's a certain Jewish stamp".[2390]

In the 90's another Jewish public intellectual, writing of the 20's said : "In university halls Jews often set the tone without noticing that their banquet was happening against the backdrop of the demise of the main nationality in the country... During the 20's Jews were proud of fellow Jews who had brilliant careers in the revolution, but did not think much about how that career was connected to the real suffering of the Russian people... Most striking today is the unanimity with which my fellow Jews deny any guilt in the history of 20th century Russia".[2391]

How healing it would be for both nations if such lonely voices were not drowned out... because it's true, in the 20's, Jews in many ways served the Bolshevik Moloch not thinking of the broken land and not foreseeing the eventual consequences for themselves. Many leading Soviet Jews lost all sense of moderation during that time, all sense of when it was time to stop.

[2390] Sonja Margolina. Das Ende der Lugen: Rufiland und die Juden im20. Jahrhundert. S. 144-145.

[2391] Г. Шурмак. Шульгин и его апологеты // Новый мир, 1994, № 11, с. 244.

Chapter 19

In the 1930s

The 1930s were years of an intense industrialized spurt, which crushed the peasantry and altered the life of the entire country. Mere existence demanded adaptation and development of new skills. But through crippling sacrifices, and despite the many absurdities of the Soviet organizational system, the horrible epic somehow led to the creation of an industrialized power.

Yet the first and second five-year plans came into existence and were carried out not through the miracle of spontaneous generation, nor as a result of the simple violent round-up of large masses of laborers. It demanded many technical provisions, advanced equipment, and the collaboration of specialists experienced in this technology. All this flowed plentifully from the capitalist West, and most of all from the United States; not in the form of a gift, of course, and not in the form of generous help. The Soviet communists paid for all of this abundantly with Russia's mineral wealth and timber, with concessions for raw materials markets, with trade areas promised to the West, and with plundered goods from the Empire of the tsars. Such deals flowed with the help and approval of international financial magnates, most of all those on Wall Street, in a persistent continuation of the first commercial ties that the Soviet communists developed on the American stock exchanges as early as during the Civil War.

The new partnership was strengthened by shiploads of tsarist gold and treasures from the Hermitage.

But wait a second, were we not thoroughly taught by Marx that capitalists are the fierce enemies of proletarian socialism and that we should not expect help from them, but rather a destructive, bloody war? Well, it's not that simple: despite the official diplomatic non-recognition, trade links were completely out in the open, and even written about in *Izvestiya*: "American merchants are interested in broadening of economic ties with the Soviet Union." [2392] American unions came out against such an

---

[2392] *Izvestiya*, January 22, 1928, p. 1.

expansion (defending their markets from the products of cheap and even slave Soviet labor). The "Russian-American Chamber of Commerce," created at that time, simply did not want to hear about any political opposition to communism, or "to mix politics with business relations."[2393]

Anthony Sutton, a modern American scholar, researched the recently-opened diplomatic and financial archives and followed the connections of Wall Street with the Bolsheviks; he pointed to the amoral logic of this long and consistent relationship. From as early as the "Marburg" plan at the beginning of the 20th century, which was based on the vast capital of Carnegie, the idea was to strengthen the authority of international finance, through global "socialization," "for control ... and for the forced appeasement." Sutton concluded that: "International financiers prefer to do business with central governments. The banking community least of all wants a free economy and de-centralized authority." "Revolution and international finance do not quite contradict each other, if the result of revolution should be to establish a more centralized authority," and, therefore, to make the markets of these countries manageable. And there was a second line of agreement: "Bolsheviks and bankers shared an essential common platform — internationalism."[2394]

In that light, the subsequent support of "collective enterprises and the mass destruction of individual rights by Morgan-Rockefeller" was not surprising. In justification of this support, they claimed in Senate hearings: "Why should a great industrial country, like America, desire the creation and subsequent competition of another great industrial rival?"[2395] Well, they rightly believed that with such an obviously uncompetitive, centralized and totalitarian regime, Soviet Russia could not rival America. Another thing is that Wall Street could not predict further development of the Bolshevik system, nor its extraordinary ability to control people, working them to the very bone, which eventually led to the creation of a powerful, if misshapen, industry.

But how does this tie in with our basic theme? Because as we have seen, American financiers completely refused loans to pre-revolutionary Russia due to the infringement of the rights of Jews there, even though Russia was always a profitable financial prospect. And clearly, if they were prepared to sacrifice profits at that time, then now, despite all their counting on the Soviet markets, the "Morgan-Rockefeller Empire" would not assist the Bolsheviks if the persecution of the Jews was looming on horizon in the USSR at the start of the 1930s.

[2393] *Izvestiya*, January 26, 1928, p. 3.
[2394] A. Sutton. *Wall Street and the Bolshevik Revolution*. Moscow, 1998; p. 210, 212.
[2395] Ibid, p. 214, 215.

That's just the point: for the West, the previously described Soviet oppression of the traditional Jewish culture and of Zionists easily disappeared under the contemporary general impression that the Soviet power would not oppress the Jews, but on the contrary, that many of them would remain at the levers of power.

Certain pictures of the past have the ability to conveniently rearrange in our mind in order to soothe our consciousness. And *today* a perception has formed that in the 1930s the Jews were already forced out of the Soviet ruling elite and had nothing to do with the administration of the country. In the 1980s we see assertions like this: in the Soviet times, the Jews in the USSR were "practically destroyed as a people; they had been turned into a social group, which was settled in the large cities "as a social stratum to serve the ruling class."[2396]

No. Not only far from "serving", the Jews were to the large extent members of the "ruling class." And the "large cities," the capitals of the constituent Soviet republics, were the very thing the authorities bought off through improved provisioning, furnishing and maintenance, while the rest of the country languished from oppression and poverty. And now, after the shock of the Civil War, after the War Communism, after the NEP and the first five-year plan, it was the *peace-time life* of the country that was increasingly managed by the government apparatus, in which the role of the Jews was quite conspicuous, at least until 1937-38.

In 1936, at the 8th Congress of Soviets of the Soviet Union, Molotov, on orders from Stalin (perhaps to differ from Hitler in the eyes of the West) delivered this tirade: "Our brotherly feelings toward the Jewish people are determined by the fact that they begat the genius and the creator of the ideas of the communist liberation of Mankind," Karl Marx; "that the Jewish people, alongside the most developed nations, brought forth countless prominent scientists, engineers, and artists [that undoubtedly had already manifested itself in the Soviet 1930s, and will be even more manifest in the post-war years], and gave many glorious heroes to the revolutionary struggle ... and in our country they gave and *are still giving new, remarkable, and talented leaders and managers in all areas of development and defense of the Cause of Socialism.*"[2397]

The italics are mine. No doubt, it was said for propaganda purposes. But Molotov's declaration was appropriate. And the "defense of the Cause of

---

[2396] A. Voronel // *"22"*: Obshchestvenno-politicheskiy i literaturniy zhurnal evreyskoy intelligentsii iz SSSR v Izraile [*Social, Political and Literary Journal of the Jewish Intelligentsia from the USSR in Israel* (henceforth – *"22"*)]. Tel-Aviv, 1986, (50), p. 160.

[2397] *Izvestiya*, November 30, 1936, p. 2.

Socialism" during all those years was in the hands of the GPU, the army, diplomacy, and the ideological front. The willing participation of so many Jews in these organs continued in the early and mid-1930s, until 1937-38.

Here we will briefly review – according to contemporary newspapers, later publications, and modern Jewish encyclopedias – the most important posts and names that had emerged mainly in the 1930s. Of course, such a review, complicated by the fact that we know nothing about how our characters identified themselves in regard to nationality, may contain mistakes in individual cases and can in no way be considered comprehensive.

After the destruction of the "Trotskyite opposition," the Jewish representation in the party apparatus became noticeably reduced. But that *purge* of the supreme party apparatus was absolutely not anti-Jewish. Lazar Kaganovich retained his extremely prominent position in the *Politburo*; he was an ominously merciless individual and, at the same time, a man of notoriously low professional level. (Nevertheless, from the mid-1930s he was the Secretary of the Central Committee, and *simultaneously* a member of the Organizational Bureau of the Central Committee — only Stalin himself held both these positions at the same time). And he placed three of his brothers in quite important posts. Mikhail Kaganovich was deputy chair of the Supreme Soviet of the National Economy beginning in 1931; from 1937 he was narkom (*nar* odny *kom* issar, that is, "people's commissar") of the defense industry; later he simultaneously headed the aviation industry. Yuli Kaganovich, passing through the leading party posts in Nizhniy Novgorod (as all the brothers did), became deputy narkom of the foreign trade.[2398] (Another, absolutely untalented brother, was a "big gun" in Rostov-on-Don. It reminds me of a story by Saltykov-Shchedrin, where one Vooz Oshmyanskiy tried to place his brother Lazar in a profitable post). However, both the ethnic Russian opposition factions, that of Rykov, Bukharin and Tomsky, and that of Syrtsov, Ryutin, and Uglanov, were destroyed by Stalin in the beginning of the 1930s with support of the Jewish Bolsheviks — he drew necessary replacements from their ranks.

Kaganovich was the principal and the most reliable of Stalin's supporters in the Politburo: he demanded the execution of Ryutin (October 1932-January 1933) but even Stalin wasn't able to manage it then.[2399] The purge of 1930-1933 dealt with the Russian elements in the party.

Out of 25 members in the Presidium of the Central Control Commission after the 16th Party Congress (1930), 10 were Jews: A. Solts, "the

---

[2398] Rossiyskaya Evreiskaya Entsiklopediya [The Russian Jewish Encyclopedia (henceforth — RJE)]. 2nd Ed. Moscow, 1994. v.1, p. 527-528.
[2399] Robert Conquest. *Bolshoy Terror* [The Great Terror]. Firenze: Edizioni Aurora, 1974, p. 70, 73.

conscience of the Party" (in the bloodiest years from 1934 to 1938 was assistant to Vyshinsky, the General Prosecutor of the USSR[2400]); Z. Belenky (one of the three abovementioned Belenky brothers); A. Goltsman (who supported Trotsky in the debate on trade unions); ferocious Rozaliya Zemlyachka (Zalkind); M. Kaganovich, another of the brothers; the *Chekist* Trilisser; the "militant atheist" Yaroslavsky; B. Roizenman; and A.P. Rozengolts, the surviving assistant of Trotsky. If one compares the composition of the party's Central Committee in the 1920s with that in the early 1930s, he would find that it was almost unchanged — both in 1925 as well as after the 16th Party Congress, Jews comprised around 1/6 of the membership.[2401]

In the upper echelons of the communist party after the 17th Congress ("the congress of the victors") in 1934, Jews remained at 1/6 of the membership of the Central Committee; in the Party Control Commission — around 1/3, and a similar proportion in the Revision Commission of the Central Committee. (It was headed for quite a while by M. Vladimirsky. From 1934 Lazar Kaganovich took the reins of the Central Control Commission). Jews made up the same proportion (1/3) of the members of the Commission of the Soviet Control.[2402]

For five years filled with upheaval (1934-1939) the deputy General Prosecutor of the USSR was Grigory Leplevsky.[2403]

Occupants of many crucial party posts were not even announced in *Pravda*. For instance, in autumn 1936 the Secretary of the Central Committee of Komsomol (the Union of Communist Youth) was E. Fainberg.[2404] The Department of the Press and Publishing of the Central Committee – the key ideological establishment – was managed by B. Tal. Previously, the department was headed by Lev Mekhlis, who had by then shifted to managing *Pravda* full-time; from 1937 Mekhlis became deputy narkom of defense and the head of Political Administration of the Red Army.

We see many Jews in the command posts in provinces: in the Central Asia Bureau, the Eastern Siberia Krai Party Committee (kraikom), in the posts of first secretaries of the *obkoms* [party committee of oblasts] of the Volga German Republic, the Tatar, Bashkir, Tomsk, Kalinin, and Voronezh oblasts and in many others. For example, Mendel Khatayevich (a member of the Central Committee from 1930) was consequently secretary of Gomel, Odessa, Tatar, and Dnepropetrovsk obkoms, secretary of the

---

[2400] RJE, v. 3, p. 95.
[2401] *Izvestiya*, July 14, 1930, p. 1.
[2402] *Izvestiya*, February 11, 1934, p. 1-2.
[2403] RJE, v. 2, p. 163.
[2404] RJE, v. 3, p. 189.

Middle Volga kraikom, and second secretary of the Communist Party of Ukraine. Yakov Chubin was secretary of the Chernigov and Akmolinsk obkoms and of the Shakhtinsk district party committee; later he served in several commissions of the Party Control in Moscow, Crimea, Kursk, and Turkmenia, and from 1937 he was the first secretary of the Central Committee of Turkmenia.[2405] There is no need to list all such names, but let's not overlook the real contribution of these *secretaries* into the Bolshevik cause; also note their striking geographical mobility, as in the 1920s. Reliable cadres were still in much demand and indispensable. And there was no concern that they lacked knowledge of each new locality of which they took charge.

Yet much more power was in the hands of the narkoms. In 1936 we see nine Jewish narkoms in the Government. Take the worldwide-famous narkom of foreign affairs Litvinov (in the friendly cartoons in *Izvestiya*, he was portrayed as a knight of peace with a spear and shield taking a stand against foreign filth); no less remarkable, but only within the limits of the USSR, was the narkom of internal affairs Yagoda; the ascending and all-glorious "Iron Narkom" of railroads, Lazar Kaganovich; foreign trade was headed by A. Rozengolts(before that we saw him in the Central Control Commission); I.Ya. Weitser was in charge of domestic trade; M. Kalmanovich was in charge of sovkhozes [state owned farms that paid wages] (he was the foods-commissar from the end of 1917); I.E. Lyubimov was narkom of light industry; G. Kaminskiy was narkom of healthcare, his instructive articles were often published in *Izvestiya*; and the above-mentioned Z. Belenky was the head of the Commission of the Soviet Control.[2406] In the same Government we can find many Jewish names among the deputy narkoms in various people's commissariats: finance, communications, railroad transport, water, agriculture, the timber industry, the foodstuffs industry, education, justice. Among the most important deputy narkoms were: Ya. Gamarnik (defense), A. Gurevich ("he made a significant contribution to the creation of the metallurgical industry in the country"[2407]); Semyon Ginzburg, he was deputy narkom of heavy industry, and later he became narkom of construction, and even later minister of construction of military enterprises.[2408]

The famous "Great Turning Point" took place place from the end of 1929 to the beginning of 1931. Murderous collectivization lay ahead, and at this decisive moment Stalin assigned Yakovlev-Epshtein as its sinister principal executive. His portraits and photos, and drawings by I. Brodsky,

---

[2405] Ibid., p. 283, 344.
[2406] *Izvestiya*, January 18, 1936, p. 1 and February 6, 1936, p. 3.
[2407] RJE, V. 1, p. 394.
[2408] Ibid., p. 313.

were prominently reproduced in newspapers then and later, from year to year.[2409]

Together with the already mentioned M. Kalmanovich, he was a member of the very top Soviet of Labor and Defense (there was hardly anyone apart from Stalin, Molotov, Mikoyan, Ordzhonikidze, Voroshilov in that organ).[2410] In March of 1931, at the 6th Session of Soviets, Yakovlev reported on the progress of collectivization – about the development of *sovkhozes and kolkhozes* (that is, the destruction of the way of life of the people).[2411] On this 'glorious' path to the ruination of Russia, among Yakovlev's collaborators, we can see deputy narkom V.G. Feigin, members of the Board of *the* people's commissariat of agriculture M.M. Volf, G.G. Roshal, and other 'experts'. The important organization, the Grain Trust, was attached to the people's commissariat of agriculture to pump out grain from peasants for the state; the chairman of the board of directors was M.G. Gerchikov, his portraits appeared in *Izvestiya*, and Stalin himself sent him a telegram of encouragement.[2412] From 1932 the People's Commissariat of Sovkhozes and Kolkhozes with M. Kalmanovich at the helm was separated from the people's commissariat of agriculture.[2413] From 1934 the chairman of the national Soviet of Kolkhozes was the same Yakovlev-Epshtein.[2414] The chairman of the Commission of Purveyance was I. Kleiner (who was awarded the Order of Lenin). During the most terrible months of collectivization, M. Kalmanovich was deputy narkom of agriculture. But at the end of 1930 he was transferred into the People's Commissariat of Finance as deputy narkom; he also became chairman of the board of the Gosbank [The State Bank], for in monetary matters a strong will was also much needed. In 1936, Lev Maryasin became chairman of the board of the Gosbank; he was replaced in that post by Solomon Krutikov in 1936.[2415]

In November 1930 the People's Commissariat of Foreign Trade was created, and A.P. Rozengolts served for seven years as its head. Jews comprised one-third of its board members. Among them was Sh. Dvoylatsky, who simultaneously served in the Central Commissions on Concessions; in 1934-1936 he became the Soviet trade representative in France.[2416] At the end of 1930 the People's Commissariat of Supply was

---

[2409] See, for example: *Izvestiya*, June 12, 1930; March 14 and 17, 1931; January 6, 1934; January 10 and February 21, 1936.
[2410] *Izvestiya*, December 25, 1930, p. 1.
[2411] *Izvestiya*, March 14, 1931, p. 3-4; March 17, p. 1-2.
[2412] *Izvestiya*, February 2, 1931, p. 4; May 30, p. 1.
[2413] *Izvestiya*, February 20, 1936, p. 4.
[2414] RJE, v. 3, p. 497.
[2415] RJE, v. 2, p. 98, 256.
[2416] RJE, v. 1, p. 418.

created with A. Mikoyan at the helm; on its board we see M. Belenky — that is another, actually the fifth, man with the surname "Belenky" encountered here; soon he himself became the narkom, replacing Mikoyan. In general, in the People's Commisariats of Trade and Supply, the Jewish component was higher than in the upper party echelons — from a quarter to a half. Still let's not overlook the Tsentrosoyuz (the bureaucratic center of Soviet pseudo-cooperation). After Lev Khichuk in the 1920s, it was managed from 1931 to 1937 by I.A. Zelensky, whom we met earlier as a member of the board of the people's commissariat of foodstuffs.[2417]

Let me point it out once more: all these examples are for illustrative purposes only. They should not be taken to create the impression that there were no members of other nationalities on all those boards and in the presidiums; of course there were. Moreover, all the above-mentioned people occupied their posts only for a while; they were routinely transferred between various important positions.

Let's look at transport and communications. First, railroads were managed by M. Rukhimovich (his portraits could be found in the major newspapers of the time[2418]); later he became narkom of defense industry (with M. Kaganovich as his deputy), while the command over railroads was given to L. Kaganovich.[2419] There were important changes in the Coal Trust: I. Schwartz was removed from the board and M. Deych was assigned to replace him.[2420] T. Rozenoer managed *Grozneft* [Grozny Oil]. Yakov Gugel headed the construction of the Magnitogorsk metallurgical giant; Yakov Vesnik was the director of the Krivoy Rog Metallurgical industrial complex; and the hell of the Kuznetsk industrial complex with its 200,000 hungry and ragged workers was supervised by S. Frankfurt, and after him by I. Epshtein (the latter was arrested in 1938 but landed on his feet because he was sent to take command over the construction of the Norilsk industrial complex).[2421]

The Supreme Soviet of the National Economy still existed, but its significance waned. After Unshlikht, it was headed by A. Rozengolts, and then by Ordzhonikidze, with Jews comprising the majority of its board.[2422]

[2417] Ibid., p. 483.
[2418] See, for example: *Izvestiya*, May 17, 1931, p. 3.
[2419] *Izvestiya*, December 9, 1936, p. 1.
[2420] *Izvestiya*, July 7, 1930, p. 2.
[2421] RJE, v.1, p. 222, 387; v. 3, p. 237, 464.
[2422] *Izvestiya*, November 14, 1930, p. 2; November 16, p. 4.

At that time, the Gosplan [state planning ministry] gathered strength. In 1931, under the chairmanship of Kuibyshev, Jews comprised more than half of its 18-member board.[2423]

Let's now examine the top posts in economy during the "last burgeoning year" of Stalin's era, 1936. In 1936 *Izvestiya* published[2424] the complete roster of the board of the people's commissariat of domestic trade. Those 135 individuals had essentially ruled over the entire domestic trade in the USSR (and they were hardly disinterested men). Jews comprised almost 40% of this list, including two deputies to the narkom, several trade inspectors, numerous heads of food and manufactured goods trades in the oblasts, heads of consumer unions, restaurant trusts, cafeterias, food supplies and storage, heads of train dining cars and railroad buffets; and of course, the head of Gastronom No.1 in Moscow ("Eliseyevsky") was also a Jew. Naturally, all this facilitated smooth running of the industry in those far from prosperous years.

In the pages of *Izvestiya* one could read headlines like this: "The management of the Union's Fishing Trust made major political mistakes." As a result, Moisei Frumkin was relieved of his post at the board of the People's Commissariat of Ddomestic Trade (we saw him in the 1920s as a deputy of the Narkom of Foreign Trade). Comrade Frumkin was punished with a stern reprimand and a warning; comrade Kleiman suffered the same punishment; and comrade Nepryakhin was expelled from the party.[2425]

Soon after that, *Izvestiya* published[2426] an addendum to the roster of the People's Commissariat of Heavy Industry with 215 names in it. Those wishing to can delve into it as well. A present-day author thus writes about those people: by the 1930s "the children of the déclassé Jewish petty bourgeois succeeded ... in becoming the 'commanders' of the "great construction projects." And so it appeared to those who, putting in 16 hours a day for weeks and months, never leaving the foundation pits, the swamps, the deserts, and taiga ..., that it was "their country."[2427] However, the author is wrong: it was the blackened hard-workers and yesterday's peasants, who had no respite from toiling in foundation pits and swamps, while the directors only occasionally promenaded there; they mainly spent time in offices enjoying their special provision services ("the bronze foremen"). But undoubtedly, their harsh and strong-willed decisions

---

[2423] *Izvestiya*, February 13, 1931, p. 3.
[2424] *Izvestiya*, April 9, 1936, p. 2.
[2425] *Izvestiya*, November 5, 1930, p. 2; November 11, p. 5.
[2426] *Izvestiya*, June 11, 1936, p. 2.
[2427] V. Boguslavskiy. *V zashchitu Kunyayeva* [In Defense of Kunyaev] // "22", 1980, (16), p. 174.

helped to bring these construction projects to completion, building up the industrial potential of the USSR.

Thus the Soviet Jews obtained a weighty share of state, industrial, and economic power at all levels of government in the USSR.

The personality of B. Roizenman merits particular attention. See for yourself: he received the Order of Lenin "in recognition of his exceptional services" in the adjustment of the state apparatus "to the objectives of the large-scale offensive for Socialism." What secrets, inscrutable to us, could be hidden behind this "offensive"? We can glance into some of them from the more direct wording: for carrying out "special missions of top state importance on the clean-up of state apparatus in the Soviet diplomatic missions abroad."[2428]

Now let's look at the state of affairs in diplomacy. The 1920s were examined in the preceding chapter. Now we encounter other important people.

For example, in spring of 1930, *Izvestiya* reported on page 1 and under a separate heading that "F.A. Rotshtein, the board member of the People's Commissariat of Internal Affairs, returned from vacation and resumed his duties."[2429] (Well, didn't they only write this way about Stalin? To the best of my knowledge, neither Ordzhonikidze, nor Mikoyan – other very top functionaries – was honored in such a way?) Yet very soon Rotshtein made a slip and his career ended just two months later, in July 1930. With the designation of Litvinov as narkom, Rotshtein was removed from the board (even though, we may remember, he claimed credit for the creation of the British Communist Party). In the 1930s, at the peak of Litvinov's power, a new generation appeared. *The Jewish Encyclopedia* writes: "there was a notion of 'the Litvinov school of diplomacy'" that included the outstanding personalities of K. Umansky, Ya. Surits, B. Shtein (he was already successful by the beginning of the 1920s) and E. Gnedin (son of Parvus).[2430] Ehrenburg added here the name of E. Rubinin. Just as in the 1920s diplomacy attracted a cadre of Jews, so it did through the early and mid-1930s. From the moment the USSR was accepted into the League of Nations, we see Litvinov, Shtein, Gnedin, and also Brenner, Stashevsky, Marcus, Rozenberg, and Svanidze (a Georgian) as the senior members of the Soviet delegation. It was these people who represented Soviet Russia at that forum of nations. There were Soviet plenipotentiaries in Europe of Jewish origin: in England — Maisky; in Germany (and later in France)—

[2428] *Izvestiya*, April 24, 1931, p. 2.

[2429] *Izvestiya*, May 18, 1930, p. 1.

[2430] Kratkaya Evreiskaya Entsiklopediya [The Short Jewish Encyclopedia (henceforth—SJE)]. Jerusalem, 1976-2001. v. 4, p. 879.

Ya. Surits; in Italy—B. Shtein (after Kamenev); we also see Jewish plenipotentiaries in Spain, Austria, Romania, Greece, Lithuania, Latvia, Belgium, Norway, and in Asia. For example, the above-mentioned Surits represented the Soviet Union in Afghanistan as early as the Russian Civil War; later, from 1936, B. Skvirsky served in Afghanistan; for many years he was the unofficial Soviet representative in Washington.[2431] In the early and mid-1930s, a great number of Jews successfully continued to work in Soviet trade delegations. (Here we find another Belenky, already the sixth individual of that name, B.S.Belenky, who was the trade representative in Italy from 1934 to 1937).[2432]

Concerning the Red Army, the aforementioned Israeli researcher, Aron Abramovich, writes that in the 1930s "a significant number of Jewish officers served" in the army. "There were many of them, in particular in the Revolutionary Military Soviet, in the central administrations of the people's commissariat of defense, in the general staff, and at lower levels – in the military districts, in the armies, corps, divisions, brigades, and all military units.

The Jews still played a prominent role in the political organs."[2433] The entire Central Political Administration of the Red Army came under command of the trustworthy Mekhlis after the suicide of the trustworthy Gamarnik. Here are several names from the cream of the Political Administration: Mordukh Khorosh was the deputy director of the Political Administration of the Red Army in the 1930s, and later, until his arrest, he was in charge of the Political Administration of the Kiev military district. From 1929 through to 1937, Lazar Aronshtam headed the political administration of the Belorussian military district, then of the Special Far Eastern Army, and later – of the Moscow military district. Isaak Grinberg was the Senior Inspector of the Political Administration of the Red Army, and later the deputy director of the Political Administration of the Leningrad district. Boris Ippo (he participated in the pacification of Central Asia during the Civil War as the head of the Political Administration of the Turkestan Front and later of the Central-Asian district) was the head of the political administration of the Caucasus Red Army; and later the director of the Military Political Academy. The already-mentioned Mikhail Landa from 1930 to 1937 was the chief editor of *Krasnaya Zvezda* (*The Red Star*, the official newspaper of the Soviet military).Naum Rozovsky was a

---

[2431] RJE, v. 3, p. 58.
[2432] RJE, v. 1, p. 101.
[2433] Aron Abramovich. *V reshayushchey voyne: Uchastie i rol evreyev SSSR v voyne protiv natsizma* [In the Deciding War: Participation and Role of Soviet Jews in the War against Nazism]. 2nd Edition. Tel-Aviv, 1982. v.1, p. 61.

military prosecutor since the Civil War; by 1936 he was the chief military prosecutor of the Red Army.[2434]

Gamarnik remained the deputy to Voroshilov, the chairman of the Revolutionary Military Soviet until 1934 (when the organization was disbanded). In the 1930s, in addition to those named in the previous chapter, among the heads of the central administrations of the Red Army, we encounter the following individuals: Abram Volp (the head of the Administrative Mobilization Administration; in the previous chapter he was identified as the chief of staff of the Moscow military district), Semyon Uritsky (of the Military Intelligence Administration, until 1937), Boris Feldman – the head of the Central Personnel Administration, and Leontiy Kotlyar — the head of the Central Military Engineering Administration in the pre-war years. Among the commanders of the branches of the military we find A. Goltsman, the head of military aviation from 1932 (we already saw him in the Central Control Commission, and as a union activist; he died in a plane crash). Among the commanders of the military districts we again see Iona Yakir (Crimean district, and later the important Kiev District), and Lev Gordon (Turkestan district).[2435]

Although we have no data on Jewish representation in the lower ranks, there is little doubt that when a structure (be it a political administration of the army, a supply service, or a party or a commissariat apparatus) was headed by a Jew, it was accompanied, as a rule, by a quite noticeable Jewish presence among its staff.

Yet service in the army is not a vice; it can be quite constructive. So what about our good old GPU-NKVD? A modern researcher, relying on archives, writes: "The first half of the 1930s was characterized by the increasingly important role of Jews in the state security apparatus." And "on the eve of the most massive repressions ... the ethnic composition of the supreme command of the NKVD ... [can be understood with the help of] the list of decorated Chekists on the occasion of the 20th anniversary of the Cheka-OGPU-NKVD.

The list of 407 senior officials published in the central press contained 56 Jews (13.8%), and 7 Latvians (1.7%)."[2436]

[2434] RJE, v. 1, p. 63, 376, 515; v. 2, p. 120, 491; v. 3, p. 300-301.
[2435] RJE, v. 1, p. 244, 350; v. 2, p. 78; v. 3, p. 179, 206-207, 493-494. See also Aron Abramovich. *V reshayushchey voyne.* [In the Deciding War], v. 1, p. 62.
[2436] *L.Yu. Krichevsky.* Evrei v apparate VChK-OGPU v 20-e gody *[The Jews in the apparatus of the Cheka-OGPU in the 1920s]* // Evrei i russkaya revolyutsia: Materiali i issledovaniya [Jews and the Russian Revolution: Materials and Research] Compiled by O.V. Budnitsky. Moscow; Jerusalem: Gesharim, 1999, p. 343-344; see also *Izvestiya*, December 20, 1937, p. 2.

When the GPU was reformed into the NKVD (1934) with Yagoda at the head, they twice published the names of the supreme commissars of the NKVD (what a rare chance to peek behind a usually impenetrable wall![2437]): commissars of State Security of the 1st Rank Ya.S. Agranov (the first deputy to Yagoda), V.A. Balitsky, T.D. Deribas, G.E. Prokovev, S.F. Redens, L.M. Zakovsky; of the 2nd Rank: L.N. Belskiy, K.V. Pauker (they were already decorated in 1927 on the decennial of the Cheka), M.I. Gay, S.A. Goglidze, L.B. Zalin, Z.B. Katsnelson, K.M. Karlson, I.M. Leplevsky, G.A. Molchanov, L.G. Mironov, A.A. Slutsky, A.M. Shanin, and R.A. Pillyar. Of course, not all of them were Jews but a good half were. So, the Jewish Chekists were still there; they didn't leave, nor were they forced out of the NKVD, the same NKVD which was devouring the country after the death of Kirov, and which later devoured itself.

A.A. Slutsky was the director of the NKVD's foreign section; that is, he was in charge of espionage abroad. "His deputies were Boris Berman and Sergey Shpigelglas." Pauker was a barber from Budapest, who connected with the communists while he was a Russian POW in 1916. Initially, he was in charge of the Kremlin security and later became the head of the operations section of the NKVD.[2438] Of course, due to secrecy and the non-approachability of these highly placed individuals, it is difficult to judge them conclusively.

Take, for instance, Naum (Leonid) Etingon, who orchestrated the murder of Trotsky and was the organizer of the "Cambridge Five" espionage ring and who oversaw the nuclear espionage after the war — a true ace of espionage.[2439]

Or take Lev Feldbin (he used a catchy pseudonym of 'Aleksandr Orlov'). A prominent and long-serving Chekist, he headed the economic section of the foreign department of GPU, that is, he supervised all foreign trade of the USSR.

He was a trusted agent, of those who were instructed in the shroud of full secrecy on how "to extract false confessions [from the victims]." "Many [of the NKVD investigators] ended up being subordinate to him."[2440] And yet he was completely hidden from the public and became famous only later, when he defected to the West. And how many such posts were there?

[2437] *Izvestiya*, November 27, 1935, p. 1; November 29, p. 1.
[2438] Robert Conquest. *Bolshoy terror* [The Great Terror], p. 187.
[2439] RJE, v. 3, p. 473.
[2440] Aleksandr Orlov. *From the introduction to the book* Taynaya istoriya stalinskikh prestupleniy [The Secret History of Stalin's Crimes] // Vremya i my: Mezhdunarodny zhurnal literatury i obshchestvennykh problem [*Epoch and We: International Journal of Literature and Social Problems* (henceforth – *EW*)]. New York, 1982, No.67, p. 202.

Or take Mikhail Koltsov-Fridlyand ("the political advisor" to the Republican government of Spain)[2441], who took part in some of the major GPU adventures.

M. Berman was assigned as deputy to the Narkom of Internal Affairs Ezhov within three days after the latter was installed on September 27, 1936. Still, Berman remained the director of the GULag.[2442] And along with Ezhov, came his handymen. Mikhail Litvin, his long-time associate in the Central Committee of the party, became the director of the personnel department of the NKVD; by May 1937 he rose to the unmatched rank of director of the Secret Political section of the Main Directorate of State Security of the NKVD. In 1931-36, Henrikh Lyushkov was the deputy director of that section; he deserted to Japan in 1938 and was then killed by a Japanese bullet in 1945 – by the end of the war the Japanese did not want to give him back and had no option but shoot him. In this way, we can extensively describe the careers of each of them. In the same section, Aleksandr Radzivilovsky was an "agent for special missions." Another long-time Ezhov colleague, Isaak Shapiro, was Ezhov's personal assistant from 1934, and then he became the director of the NKVD Secretariat, and later was the director of the infamous Special Section of the Main Directorate of State Security of the NKVD.[2443]

In December 1936, among the heads of ten sections (for secrecy, designated only by number) of the Main Directorate of State Security of the NKVD, we see seven Jews: the Security section (section #1)—K. Pauker; Counter-Intelligence (3) — L. Mironov; Special section (5)—I. Leplevsky; Transport (6)—A. Shanin; Foreign section (7) — A. Slutsky; Records and Registration (8)—V. Tsesarsky; Prisons (10)—Ya. Veinshtok. Over the course of the meat-grinding year of 1937 several other Jews occupied posts of directors of those sections: A. Zalpeter—Operations section (2); Ya. Agranov, followed by M. Litvin—Secret Political section (4); A Minaev-Tsikanovsky—Counter-Intelligence (3); and I. Shapiro – Special section (9).[2444]

I named the leadership of the GULag in my book, *GULag Archipelago*. Yes, there was a large proportion of Jews among its command. (Portraits of the directors of construction of the White Sea-Baltic Canal, which I reproduced from the Soviet commemorative corpus of 1936, caused outrage: they claimed that I have selected the Jews only on purpose. But I

[2441] RJE, v. 2, p. 62.
[2442] *Izvestiya*, September 27, 1936, p. 1; September 30, p. 3. See also RJE, v. 1, p. 124.
[2443] RJE, v. 2, p. 187, 218, 432; v. 3, p. 358.
[2444] A. Kokurin, N. Petrov. *NKVD: struktura, funktsii, kadry* [The NKVD: Organization, Functions, Cadres] // *Svobodnaya mysl* [Free Thought], 1997, (6), p. 113-116.

did not select them, I've just reproduced the photographs of *all the High Directors* of the *BelBaltlag* [White Sea – Baltic Canal camp administration] from that immortal book. Am I guilty that they had turned out to be Jews? Who had selected them for those posts?

Who is guilty?) I will now add information about three prominent men, whom I did not know then. Before the *BelBaltlag*, one Lazar Kogan worked as the head of the GULag; Zinovy Katsnelson was the deputy head of the GULag from 1934 onward; Izrail Pliner was the head of the GULag from 1936, and later he oversaw the completion of construction of the Moscow-Volga Canal (1937).[2445]

It can't be denied that History elevated many Soviet Jews into the ranks of the arbiters of the fate of all Russians.

Never publicized information about events of different times flows from different sources: about the regional *Plenipotentiaries of GPU-NKVD* in the 1930s (before 1937). The names of their offices fully deserved to be written in capital letters, for it was precisely them and not the secretaries of the *obkoms*, who were the supreme masters of their *oblasts*, masters of the life and death of any inhabitant, who reported directly only to the central NKVD in Moscow. The full names of some of them are known, while only initials remain from others; and still of others, we know only their last names. They moved from post to post, between different provinces. (If we could only find the dates and details of their service! Alas, all this was done in secret). And in all of the 1930s, many Jews remained among those provincial lords. According to the recently published data, in the regional organs of State Security, not counting the Main Directorate of State Security, there were 1,776 Jews (7.4% of the total members serving).[2446]

A few Jewish plenipotentiaries are listed here: in Belorussia – Izrail Leplevsky (brother of the deputy General Prosecutor Grigory Leplevsky, we already saw him in the Cheka; later, he worked in a senior post in the GPU as a Commissar of State Security of 2nd Rank; and now we see him as the Narkom of Internal Affairs of Belorussia from 1934 to 1936); in the Western Oblast – I.M. Blat, he later worked in Chelyabinsk; in the Ukraine – Z. Katsnelson, we saw him in the Civil War all around the country, from the Caspian Sea to the White Sea. Now he was the deputy head of the GULag; later we see him as Deputy Narkom of Internal Affairs of Ukraine; in 1937 he was replaced by Leplevsky. We see D.M. Sokolinsky first In Donetsk Oblast and later in Vinnitsa Oblast; L.Ya. Faivilovich and

---

[2445] RJE, v. 2, p. 22, 51-52, 389.
[2446] A. Kokurin, N. Petrov. *NKVD: struktura, funktsii, kadry* [The NKVD: Organization, Functions, Cadres] // *Svobodnaya mysl* [Free Thought], 1997, (6), p. 118.

Fridberg – in the Northern Caucasus; M.G. Raev-Kaminsky and Purnis – in Azerbaijan; G. Rappoport – in Stalingrad Oblast; P.Sh. Simanovsky – in Orlov Oblast; Livshits – in Tambov Oblast; G.Ya. Abrampolsky – in Gorkov Oblast; A.S. Shiyron, supervising the round-up of the dispossessed kulaks – in Arkhangel Oblast; I.Z. Ressin – in the German Volga Republic; Zelikman – in Bashkiriya; N. Raysky – in Orenburg Oblast; G.I. Shklyar – in Sverdlovsk Oblast; L.B. Zalin – in Kazakhstan; Krukovsky – in Central Asia; Trotsky – in Eastern Siberia, and Rutkovsky – in the Northern Krai.

All these high placed NKVD officials were tossed from one oblast to another in exactly the same manner as the secretaries of obkoms. Take, for instance, Vladimir Tsesarsky: was plenipotentiary of the GPU-NKVD in Odessa, Kiev and in the Far East. By 1937 he had risen to the head of the Special section of the Main Directorate of State Security of the NKVD (just before Shapiro). Or look at S. Mironov-Korol: in 1933-36 he was the head of the Dnepropetrovsk GPU-NKVD; in 1937 he was in charge of the Western Siberian NKVD; he also served in the central apparatus of the GPU-NKVD.[2447]

In the mid-1930s, we see L. Vul as the head of Moscow and later of Saratov Police. The plenipotentiary in Moscow was L. Belsky (after serving in Central Asia); later, he had risen to the head of the Internal Service Troops of the NKVD. In the 1930s we see many others: Foshan was in charge of the border troops; Meerson was the head of the Economic Planning section of the NKVD; L.I. Berenzon and later L.M. Abramson headed the finance department of the GULag; and Abram Flikser headed the personnel section of the GULag. All these are disconnected pieces of information, not amenable to methodical anal Moreover, there were special sections in each provincial office of the NKVD.

Here is another isolated bit of information: Yakov Broverman was the head of Secretariat of the Special Section of the NKVD in Kiev; he later worked in the same capacity in the central NKVD apparatus.[2448]

Later, in 1940, when the Soviets occupied the Baltic states of Lithuania, Latvia, and Estonia, the head of the Dvinsk NKVD was one Kaplan. He dealt so harshly with the people there, that in 1941, when the Red Army had hardly left and before the arrival of Germans, there was an explosion of public outrage against the Jews.

In the novel by D.P. Vitkovsky, *Half-life*, there is a phrase about the Jewish looks of investigator, Yakovlev (the action is set during Khrushchev's regime).

[2447] RJE, v. 2, p. 293; v. 3, p. 311.
[2448] RJE, v. 1, p. 170.

Vitovsky put it rather harshly so that Jews, who by the end of the 1960s were already on the way of breaking away from communism and in their new political orientation developed sympathy to any camp memoirs, were nonetheless repulsed by such a description. I remember V. Gershuni asked me how many *other* Jewish investigators did Vitovsky come across during his 30-year-long ordeal?

What an astonishing forgetfulness betrayed by that rather innocent slip!

Would not it have been more appropriate to mention not the "30 years" but 50 years, or, at least, 40 years? Indeed, Vitovsky might not have encountered many Jewish investigators during *his last thirty* years, from the end of the 1930s (though they could still be found around even in the 1960s). Yet Vitovsky was persecuted by the Organs for *forty* years; he survived the Solovki camp; and he apparently did not forget the time when a Russian investigator was a less frequent sight than a Jewish or a Latvian one.

Nevertheless, Gershuni was right in implying that all these outstanding and not so outstanding posts were fraught with death for their occupants; the more so, the closer it was to 1937-38.

Our arbiters confidently ruled from their heights and when they were suddenly delivered a blow, it must have seemed to them like the collapse of the universe, like the end of the world. Wasn't there anyone among them before the onslaught who reflected on the usual fate of revolutionaries?

Among the major communist functionaries who perished in 1937-38, the Jews comprise an enormous percentage. For example, a modern historian writes that if "from 1 January 1935 to 1 January 1938 the members of this nationality headed more than 50% of the main structural units of the central apparatus of the people's commissariat of internal affairs, then by 1 January 1939 they headed only 6%."[2449]

Using numerous "execution lists" that were published over the recent decades, and the biographical tomes of the modern *Russian Jewish Encyclopedia*, we are able to trace to some degree the fates of those outstanding and powerful Chekists, Red commanders, Soviet party officials, diplomats, and others, whom we mentioned in the previous chapters of this book.

Among the Chekists the destruction was particularly overwhelming (the names of those *executed* are italicized):

[2449] G.V. Kostirchenko. *Taynaya politika Stalina: Vlast i antisemitizm* [Stalin's Secret Policy: Power and Anti-semitism]. Moscow: Mezhdunarodnie otnosheniya [International Relations], 2001, p. 210.

G.Ya. Abrampolsky; L.M. Abramson, died in prison in 1939; Yakov Agranov, 1938; [2450] Abram Belenky, 1941; Lev Belsky-Levin, 1941; Matvey Berman, 1939; Boris Berman, 1939; Iosif Blat, 1937; Ya. Veinshtok, 1939; Leonid Vul, 1938, Mark Gai-Shtoklyand, 1937; Semyon Gendin, 1939; *Benjamin Gerson, 1941;* Lev Zadov-Zinkovsky, 1938; Lev Zalin-Levin, 1940; A. Zalpeter, 1939; Lev Zakharov-Meyer, 1937; N.Zelikman, 1937; Aleksandr Ioselevich, 1937, Zinovy Katsnelson, 1938; Lazar Kogan, 1939; Mikhail Koltsov-Fridlyand, 1940; Georg Krukovsky, 1938; Izrail Leplevsky, 1938; Natan Margolin, 1938; A. Minaev-Tsikanovsky, 1939; Lev Mironov-Kagan, 1938; Sergey Mironov-Korol, 1940; Karl Pauker, 1937; Izrail Pliner, 1939; Mikhail Raev-Kaminsky, 1939; Aleksandr Radzivilovsky, 1940; Naum Raysky-Lekhtman, 1939; Grigoriy Rappoport, 1938; Ilya Ressin, 1940; *A. Rutkovsky;* Pinkhus Simanovsky, 1940; *Abram Slutsky, poisoned in 1938;* David Sokolinsky, 1940; Mikhail Trilisser; Leonid Fayvilovich, 1936; Vladimir Tsesarsky, 1940; A. Shanin, 1937; Isaak Shapiro, 1940; *Evsey Shirvindt, 1938; Grigoriy Shklyar;* Sergey Shpigelglas, 1940; Genrikh Yagoda, 1938.

Nowadays entire directories, containing lists of the highest officials of the Central Apparatus of the Main Directorate of State Security of the NKVD who fell during the Ezhov's period of executions and repressions, are published. There we see many more Jewish names.[2451]

But only accidentally, thanks to the still unbridled *glasnost* that began in the beginning of the 1990s, we learn about several mysterious biographies formerly shrouded in secrecy. For example, from 1937, professor Grigory Mayranovsky, a specialist in poisons, headed the "Laboratory X" in the Special Section of Operations Technology of the NKVD, which carried out death sentences through injections with poisons by "the direct decision of the government in 1937-47 and in 1950"; the executions were performed in a special prisoner cell at "Laboratory X" as well as abroad even in the 1960s and 1970s.[2452]

Mayranovsky was arrested only in 1951; from his cell he wrote to Beria: "Dozens of sworn enemies of the Soviet Union, including all kinds of

---

[2450] The names of those executed and the year of execution are italicized throughout the text; in other instances the date indicates the year of arrest; those who committed suicide on the eve of arrest and those who died in custody are mentioned specifically.

[2451] See for example: NV. Petrov, K.V. Skorkin. *Kto rukovodil NKVD: 1934-1941:* Spravochnik [Who Ran the NKVD: 1934-1941. Information Book]. Moscow: Zvenya, 1999.

[2452] Pavel Sudoplatov. *Spetsoperatsii: Lubyanka i Kreml: 1930s-1950s* [Special Operations: Lubyanka [Prison] and the Kremlin: the 1930s through the 1950s]. Moscow: OLMA-Press, 1997, p. 440-441.

nationalists, were destroyed by my hand."[2453] And from the astonishing disclosure in 1990 we learned that the famous *mobile gas chambers* were invented, as it turns out, not by Hitler during the World War II, but in the Soviet NKVD in 1937 by Isai Davidovich Berg, the head of the administrative and maintenance section of the NKVD of Moscow Oblast (sure, he was not alone in that enterprise, but he organized the whole business). This is why it is also important to know who occupied middle-level posts. It turns out, that I.D. Berg was entrusted with carrying out the sentences of the "troika" of the NKVD of Moscow Oblast; he dutifully performed his mission, which involved shuttling prisoners to the execution place. But when three "troikas" began to work simultaneously in the Moscow Oblast, the executioners became unable to cope with the sheer number of executions. Then they invented a time-saving method: the victims were stripped naked, tied, mouths plugged, and thrown into a closed truck, outwardly disguised as a bread truck. On the road the exhaust fumes were redirected into the prisoner-carrying compartment, and by the time the van arrived to the burial ditch, the prisoners were "ready." (Well, Berg himself was shot in 1939, not for those evil deeds, of course, but for "the anti-Soviet conspiracy". In 1956 he was rehabilitated without any problem, though the story of his murderous invention was kept preserved and protected in the records of his case and only recently discovered by journalists)[2454]

There are so many individuals with outstanding lives and careers in the list above! Bela Kun, the Butcher of Crimea, himself fell at that time, and with him the lives of twelve Commissars of the communist government of Budapest ended.[2455]

However, it would be inappropriate to consider the expulsion of Jews from the *punitive organs* as a form of persecution. There was no anti-Jewish motif in those events. (Notwithstanding, that if Stalin's praetorians valued not only their present benefits and power but also the opinion of the people whom they governed, they should have left the NKVD and not have waited until they were kicked out. Still, this wouldn't have spared many of them death, but surely it would have spared them the stigma?) The notion of purposeful anti-Jewish purge doesn't hold water: "according to available data, at the end of the 1930s the Jews were one of the few national minorities, belonging to which did not constitute a "crime" for an NKVD official. There were still no regulations on national and personnel policy in

---

[2453] *Izvestiya*, May 16, 1992 p. 6.
[2454] E. Zhirnov. *"Protsedura kazni nosila omerzitelniy kharakter"* [A Horrible Execution] // *Komsomolskaya Pravda*, October 28, 1990, p. 2.
[2455] Robert Conquest. *Bolshoy Terror* [The Great Terror], p. 797-798.

the state security agencies that was enforced ... from the end of the 1940s to the early 1950s"[2456]

Many Party activists fell under the destructive wave of 1937-1938. From 1936-37 the composition of the Soviet of People's Commissars began to change noticeably as the purges during the pre-war years ran through the prominent figures in the people's commissariats. The main personage behind collectivization, Yakovlev, had met his bullet; the same happened to his comrades-in-arms, Kalmanovich and Rukhimovich, and many others. The meat-grinder devoured many old "honored" Bolsheviks, such as the long-retired Ryazanov or the organizer of the murder of the Tsar Goloshchekin, not to mention Kamenev and Zinovyev. (Lazar Kaganovich was spared although, he himself was the "iron broom" in several purges during 1937-38; for example, they called his swift purge of the city of Ivanov the "Black Tornado.")[2457]

They offer us the following interpretation: "This is a question about the victims of the Soviet dictatorship; they were used by it and then mercilessly discarded when their services became redundant." [2458] What a great argument! So for twenty years these powerful Jews were really *used*? Yet weren't they themselves the zealous cogs in the *mechanism of that very dictatorship* right up to the very time when their "services became redundant"? Did not they make the great contribution to the destruction of religion and culture, the intelligentsia, and the multi-million peasantry?

A great many Red Army commanders fell under the axe. "By the summer of 1938 without exception all... commanders of military districts ... who occupied these posts by June 1937 disappeared without a trace." The Political Administration of the Red Army "suffered the highest losses from the terror" during the massacre of 1937, after the suicide of Gamarnik. Of the highest political officers of the Red Army, death claimed all 17 army commissars, 25 out of 28 corps commissars, and 34 out of 36 brigade (divisional) commissars.[2459] We see a significant percentage of Jews in the now-published lists of military chiefs executed in 1937-38.[2460]

Grigory Shtern had a very special military career; he advanced along the political officer's path. During the Civil War he was military commissar at

---

[2456] L.Yu. Krichevsky. Evrei v apparate VChK-OGPU v 20-e gody *[The Jews in the apparatus of the Cheka-OGPU in the 1920s]* // Evrei i russkaya revolyutsia: Materiali i issledovaniya [Jews and the Russian Revolution], p. 343, 344.

[2457] Robert Conquest. *Bolshoy Terror* [The Great Terror], p. 459.

[2458] Yu. Margolin. *Tel-Avivskiy bloknot* [Tel-Aviv Notebook] // *Novoe Russkoe Slovo* [The New Russian Word], New York, August 5, 1968.

[2459] Robert Conquest. *Bolshoy Terror* [The Great Terror], p. 427-428, 430.

[2460] See for example: O.F. Suvenirov. *Tragediya RKKA: 1937-1938.* [The Tragedy of the Red Army: 1937-1938] Moscow, Terra, 1998.

regimental, brigade, and divisional levels. In 1923-25 he was the head of all special detachments in the Khorezm [a short-lived republic after the Bolshevik revolution] troops during the suppression of rebellions in Central Asia. Until 1926, he was the head of the political administration division. Later he studied at the military academy for senior military officers [and thus became eligible for proper *military* posts]; in 1929-34 he was a "military advisor to the Republican government in Spain" (not to be confused with Manfred Shtern, who also distinguished himself among the Red Spaniards under the alias of "General Kleber"). Later he was the Chief of Staff of the Far Eastern Front and conducted bloody battles at Lake Khasan in 1938 together with Mekhlis, at the same time conspiring against Marshall Blücher, whom he ruined and whose post of the front commander he took over after the arrest of the latter. In March 1939, at the 18th Party Congress, he made this speech: "Together we have destroyed a bunch of good-for-nothings— the Tukhachevskys, Gamarniks, Uborevichs [former Soviet Marshalls[and similar others." Well, he himself was shot later, in autumn 1941. [2461] Shtern's comrade-in-arms in aviation, Yakov Smushkevich, also had a head-spinning career. He too began as a political officer (until the mid-1930s); then he studied at the academy for top officers. In 1936-37 he had also fought in Spain, in aviation, and was known as "General Douglas". In 1939 he was commander of the aviation group at Khalkhin Gol [on the Manchurian-Mongolian border, site of Soviet-Japanese battles won by the Russians]. After that he rose to the commander of all air forces of the Red Army – the General Inspector of the Air Force; he was arrested in May 1941 and executed in the same year.[2462]

The wave of terror spared neither administrators, nor diplomats; almost all of the diplomats mentioned above were executed.

Let's name those party, military, diplomatic, and managerial figures whom we mentioned before on these pages who now were persecuted (the names of the *executed* are italicized):

Samuil Agursky, arrested in 1938; *Lazar Aronshtam, 1938; Boris Belenky, 1938;* Grigory Belenky, 1938; *Zakhar Belenky,1940; Mark Belenky, 1938; Moris Belotsky, 1938; German Bitker, 1937; Aron Vainshtein, 1938; Yakov Vesnik, 1938; Izrail Veitser, 1938; Abram Volpe, 1937;* Yan Gamarnik, committed suicide in 1937; *Mikhail Gerchikov, 1937;* Evgeny Gnedin, arrested in 1939; *Philip Goloshchekin, 1941; Ya. Goldin, 1938;* Lev

---

[2461] RJE, v. 3, p. 430. See also Aron Abramovich. V reshayushchey voyne. *[In the Deciding War], v. 1, p. 66. See also V. Katuntsev, I. Kots.* Intsident: Podopleyka Khasanskikh sobitiy [The Incident: the Causes of the Lake Khasan Conflict] // Rodina, 1991, (6), p. 17.

[2462] RJE, v. 3, p. 82. See also Aron Abramovich, *V reshayushchey voyne.* [In the Deciding War] v. 1, p. 64-66.

Gordon, arrested in 1939; *Isaak Grinberg, 1938; Yakov Gugel, 1937; Aleksandr Gurevich, 1937; Sholom Dvoilatsky, 1937; Maks Deych, 1937; Semyon Dimanshtein, 1938; Efim Dreitser, 1936; Semyon Zhukovsky, 1940; Samuil Zaks, 1937;* Zinovy Zangvil, *Isaak Zelensky, 1938;* Grigory Zinovyev, *1936; S. Zorin-Gomberg, 1937; Boris Ippo, 1937;* Mikhail Kaganovich, committed suicide in expectation of arrest, 1941; *Moisey Kalmanovich, 1937; Lev Kamenev, 1936; Abram Kamensky, 1938; Grigoriy Kaminsky, 1938;* Ilya Kit-Viytenko, arrested in 1937 and spent 20 years in camps; *I.M. Kleiner, 1937; Evgeniya Kogan, 1938; Aleksandr Krasnoshchyokov-Tobinson, 1937; Lev Kritsman, 1937; Solomon Kruglikov, 1938; Vladimir Lazarevich, 1938; Mikhail Landa, 1938; Ruvim Levin, 1937; Yakov Livshits, 1937;* Moisey Lisovsky, arrested in 1938; *Frid Markus, 1938; Lev Maryasin, 1938; Grigory Melnichansky, 1937;* Aleksandr Minkin-Menson, died in camp in 1955; *Nadezhda Ostrovskaya, 1937; Lev Pechersky, 1937; I. Pinson, 1936; Iosif Pyatnitsky-Tarshis, 1938; Izrail Razgon, 1937; Moisey Rafes, 1942;* Grigory Roginsky, 1939; *Marsel Rozenberg, 1938; Arkady Rozengolts, 1938; Naum Rozovsky, 1942; Boris Royzenman, 1938;* E. Rubinin, spent 15 years in camps; *Yakov Rubinov, 1937; Moisey Rukhimovich, 1938; Oskar Ryvkin, 1937; David Ryazanov, 1938; Veniamin Sverdlov, 1939; Boris Skvirsky, 1941; Iosif Slavin, 1938;* Grigoriy Sokolnikov-Brilliant, killed in prison, 1939; Isaak Solts, died in confinement in 1940; *Naum Sokrin, 1938; Lev Sosnovsky, 1937; Artur Stashevsky-Girshfeld, 1937; Yury Steklov-Nakhamkis, 1941; Nikolay Sukhanov-Gimmer, 1940; Boris Tal, 1938; Semyon Turovsky, 1936; Semyon Uritsky, 1937; Evgeny Fainberg, 1937; Vladimir Feigin, 1937; Boris Feldman, 1937;* Yakov Fishman, arrested in 1937; *Moisey Frumkin, 1938;* Maria Frumkina-Ester, died in camp, 1943; *Leon Khaikis, 1938;* Avenir Khanukaev; Moisey Kharitonov, died in camp, 1948; *Mendel Khataevich, 1937; Tikhon Khvesin, 1938; Iosif Khodorovsky, 1938; Mordukh Khorosh, 1937;* Isay Tsalkovich, arrested in 1937; *Efim Tsetlin, 1937;* Yakov Chubin; N. Chuzhak-Nasimovich; *Lazar Shatskin, 1937; Akhiy Shilman, 1937;* Ierokhim Epshtein, arrested in 1938; *Iona Yakir, 1937; Yakov Yakovlev-Epshtein, 1938; Grigory Shtern, 1941.*

This is indeed a commemoration roster of many top-placed Jews. Below are the fates of some prominent Russian Jewish socialists, who did not join the Bolsheviks or who even struggled against them.

Boris Osipovich Bogdanov (born 1884) was an Odessan, the grandson and son of lumber suppliers. He graduated from the best commerce school in Odessa. While studying, he joined Social Democrat societies. In June 1905, he was the first civilian who got on board the mutinous battleship, *Potemkin,* when she entered the port of Odessa; he gave a speech for her crew, urging sailors to join Odessa's labor strike; he delivered letters with appeals to consulates of the European powers in Russia. He avoided punishment by departing for St. Petersburg where he worked in the Social Democratic underground; he was a Menshevik. He was sentenced to two 2-year-long exiles, one after another, to Solvychegodsk and to Vologda. Before the war, he entered the elite of the Menshevik movement; he worked legally on labor questions. In 1915 he became the secretary of the Labor Group at the Military Industrial Committee, was arrested in January 1917 and freed by the February Revolution. He was a member of the Executive Committee of the Soviet of Workers' and Soldiers' Deputies of Petrograd, and regularly chaired its noisy sessions which attracted thousands of people. From June 1917 he was a member of the Bureau of the All-Russian Central Executive Committee and persistently opposed ongoing attempts of the Bolsheviks to seize power. After the failed Bolshevik rebellion in July 1917 he accepted the surrender of the squad of sailors besieged in the Petropavlovsk Fortress. After the October coup, in 1918 he was one of the organizers of anti-Bolshevik workers movement in Petrograd. During the Civil War he lived in Odessa. After the Civil War he tried to restart the Menshevik political activity, but at the end of 1920 he was arrested for one year. That was the beginning of many years of unceasing arrests and sentences, exiles and camps, and numerous transfers between different camps — the so-called "Great Road" of so many socialists in the USSR. And all that was just for being a Menshevik in the past and for having Menshevik convictions even though by that time he no longer engaged in politics and during brief respites simply worked on economic posts and just wanted a quiet life; however, he was suspected of economic "sabotage." In 1922 he requested permission to emigrate, but shortly before departure was arrested again. First he was sent to the Solovki prison camp and later exiled to the Pechora camp [in the Urals]; his sentences were repeatedly extended by three years; he experienced solitary confinement in the Suzdal camp and was repeatedly exiled. In 1931 they attempted to incriminate him in the case of the "All-Soviet Bureau of Mensheviks," but he was lucky and they left him alone. Yet he was hauled in again in 1937, imprisoned in the Omsk jail (together with already-imprisoned communists), where he survived non-stop interrogations which sometimes continued without a pause for weeks, at any time of the day or night (there were three shifts of investigators); he served out 7 years in the Kargopol camp (several other Mensheviks were shot there); later he was exiled to Syktyvkar; in 1948 he was again sentenced and exiled to Kazakhstan. In 1956 he was rehabilitated; he died in 1960, a worn-out old man.

Boris Davidovich Kamkov-Kats (born 1885) was the son of a country doctor. From adolescence, he was a member of the Socialist Revolutionary Party. Exiled in 1905 to the Turukhan Krai, he escaped. Abroad, he graduated from the Heidelberg University School of Law. He was a participant in the Zimmerwald [Switzerland] Conference of socialists (1915). After the February Revolution he returned to Russia. He was one of the founders of the Left Socialist Revolutionary Party; at the time of the October coup he entered into a coalition with the Bolsheviks. He took part in the dispersal of the Russian Constituent Assembly in January 1918. From April he urged breaking the alliance with the Bolsheviks; in June he already urged "a revolutionary uprising against them. After the failed rebellion of the Socialist Revolutionaries, he went underground. After a brief arrest in 1920, he was arrested again in 1921, and exiled in 1923. Between exiles he spent two years in prison and experienced the same "Great Road." In 1933 he was exiled to Archangel; he was arrested again in 1937 and executed in 1938.

Abram Rafailovich Gots (born 1882) was the grandson of a millionaire tea merchant, V.Ya. Visotsky. From the age of 14, he was in the Socialist Revolutionary movement from the very creation of the SR party in 1901 (his brother Mikhail was the party leader). From 1906, he was a terrorist, a member of the militant wing of the SRs. From 1907-1915 he was in hard labor camps; he spent some time sitting in the infamous Aleksandrovsky Central. He was a participant of the February Revolution in Irkutsk and later in Petrograd. He was a member of the executive committees of the Soviet of Workers' and Soldiers' Deputies of Petrograd and of the Soviet Peasant's Deputies and a member of the Presidium of the All-Russian Central Executive Committee. From 25 October 1917 he headed the anti-Bolshevik Committee for the Salvation of the Motherland and Revolution. During the Civil War he continued his struggle against Bolsheviks. In 1920 he was arrested; at the trial of the Socialist Revolutionaries in 1922 he was sentenced to death, commuted to 5 years of imprisonment. Later he experienced the "Great Road" of endless new prison terms and exiles. In 1939 he was sentenced to 25 years in the camps and died in one a year later.

Mikhail Yakovlevich Gendelman (born 1881) was an attorney-at-law and a Socialist Revolutionary from 1902. He participated in the February Revolution in Moscow, was a member of the Executive Committee of the Soviet of Soldiers' and Workers' Deputies, a member of the Presidium of the All-Russian Central Executive Committee, and a member of the Central Committee of the Socialist Revolutionary Party. On 25 October 1917, he left the meeting of the 2nd All-Russian Congress of the Soviets in protest against the Bolsheviks. He was elected to the Constituent Assembly and participated in its only session, on 5 January 1918. Later in Samara he participated in the Committee of Members of the Constituent Assemby. He was arrested in 1921; in 1922 he was sentenced to death at the trial of the Socialist Revolutionaries, commuted to 5 years in prison. After numerous prison terms and exiles, he was shot in 1938.

Mikhail Isaakovich Liber-Goldman (born 1880) was one of the founders of the Bund (1897), a member of the Central Committee of the [General Jewish Labor] Bund of Lithuania, Poland and Russia in Emigration; he represented the Bund at the congresses of the Russian Social Democratic Workers' Party. He participated in the revolution of 1905-06. In 1910 he was exiled for three years to Vologda Province, fled soon thereafter and emigrated again. He was a steady and uncompromising opponent of Lenin. He returned to Russia after 1914, and joined the Socialist "Defender" movement ("Defense of the Motherland in War"). After the February revolution, he was a member of the Executive Committee of the Petrograd Soviet of Soldiers' and Workers' Deputies, and later he was a member of the Presidium of the All-Russian Central Executive Committee. (He left the latter post after the October coup). Then he briefly participated in the Social Democratic Workers' Party of the Mensheviks. He worked on economic positions andwas one of the leaders of the Menshevik underground in the USSR. His "Great Road" arrests and exiles began in1923.

He was arrested again and executed in Alma-Ata in 1937. For many, there was a similar fate, with repeated sentences and exiles, right up to the climax of 1937-38.

Yet in those years purges swept all over the country, destroying the lives of countless ordinary people, including Jews, people who had nothing to do with politics or authority. Here are some of the Jews who perished:

Nathan Bernshtein (born 1876) a music scholar and critic; he taught the history of music and aesthetics and wrote a number of books; arrested in 1937, he died in prison.

Matvei Bronshtein (born 1906) a talented theoretical physicist, Doctor of Science, who achieved extraordinary results. He was the husband of Lyudmila K. Chukovskaya. Arrested in 1937, he was executed in 1938.

Sergey Ginter (born 1870) an architect and engineer; arrested in 1934, exiled to Siberia, arrested again in 1937 and executed.

Veniamin Zilbermints (born 1887) a mineralogist and geochemist; specialist on rare elements, he laid the foundation for semi-conductor science; he was persecuted in 1938.

Mikhail Kokin (born 1906) an Orientalist, Sinologist and historian, arrested in 1937 and executed.

Ilya Krichevsky (born 1885) a microbiologist, immunologist (also trained in physics and mathematics), Doctor of Medical Sciences, founder of a scientific school, chairman of the National Association of Microbiologists; arrested in 1938 and died in 1943.

Solomon Levit (born 1894), geneticist; he studied the role of heredity and environment in pathology. Arrested in 1938 and died in prison.

Iokhiel Ravrebe (born 1883), an Orientalist, Judaist, one of the founders of the reestablished Jewish Ethnographic Society in 1920. Accused of creating a Zionist organization, he was arrested in 1937 and died in prison.

Vladimir Finkelshtein (born 1896), a chemical physicist, professor, corresponding member of the Ukrainian Academy of Sciences; he had many works in applied electrical chemistry; persecuted in 1937.

Ilya Khetsrov (born 1887), a hygienist and epidemiologist; he studied environmental hygiene, protection of water resources, and community hygiene. Arrested in 1938 and executed.

Nakhum Schwartz (born 1888), a psychiatrist, studied Jewish psychology. In 1921-23 he taught Hebrew and wrote poetry in Hebrew. Accused of Zionist activity, he was arrested in 1937 and later died in prison.

Here are the fates of the three brothers *Shpilrein* from Rostov-on-Don. *Jan (born 1887)* was a mathematician; he applied mathematical methods in electrical and heat engineering, he was professor at the Bauman Moscow State Technical University and later the dean of its Electrical Engineering Department. He was persecuted and died in 1937. *Isaak (born 1891)* was a psychologist, Doctor of Philosophy. In 1927 he became the head of the All-Russian Society of Psychotechnology and Applied Psychophysiology; he performed extensive psychological analysis of professions and optimization of working environment. He was arrested in 1935 and later executed. *Emil (born 1899)* was a biologist, the dean of the Biology Department of Rostov University. He was shot in 1937.

Leonid Yurovsky (born 1884) Doctor of Political Economy, one of the authors of the monetary reform of 1922-24. A close friend to A.V. Chayanov and N.D. Kondratev [prominent Russian scientists], he was arrested in 1930, freed in 1935, then arrested again in 1937 and executed.

Despite the overwhelming percentage of high-placed, "aristocratic" Jews, who fell under Stalin's axe, the free Western press did not perceive the events as specifically the persecution of Jews: the Jews were massacred simply because of their abundance in the top tiers of the Soviet hierarchy. Indeed, we read such a stipulation in the collection of works *Evreysky Mir* [The Jewish World] (1939): "No doubt that the Jews in the USSR have numerous opportunities, which they did not have before the revolution, and which they do not have even now in some democratic countries. They can become generals, ministers, diplomats, professors, the most high-ranking and the most servile aristocrats."

Opportunities but "in no way rights", because of the absence of such rights, "Yakir, Garmanik, Yagoda, Zinovyev, Radek, Trotsky" and the rest fell from their heights and lost their very lives."[2463] Still, no nationality enjoyed such a right under the communist dictatorship; it was all about the ability to cling to power.

The long-time devoted socialist, emigrant S. Ivanovich (S.O. Portugeis), admitted: "Under the Tsars, the Jews were indeed restricted in their 'right of living'; yet their 'right to live' was incomparably greater then than under Bolshevism." Indeed. However, at the same time, despite being perfectly aware of collectivization, he writes that the "awkward attempts to establish 'socialism' in Russia took the heaviest toll from the Jews"; that "the scorpions of Bolshevism did not attack any other people with such brutal force as they attacked Jews."[2464]

Yet during the Great Plague of dekulakization, it was not thousands but millions of peasants who lost both their 'right of living' and the 'right to live'.

And yet all the Soviet pens (with so many Jews among them) kept complete silence about this cold-blooded destruction of the Russian peasantry. In unison with them, the entire West was silent. Could it be really out of the lack of knowledge? Or was it for the sake of protecting the Soviet regime? Or was it simply because of indifference? Why, this is almost inconceivable: 15 million peasants were not simply deprived of entering the institutes of higher learning or of the right to study in graduate school, or to occupy nice posts — no! They were dispossessed and driven like cattle out of their homes and sent to certain death in the taiga and tundra. And the Jews, among other passionate urban activists, enthusiastically took the reins of the collectivization into their hands, leaving behind them persistent evil memory. And who had raised their voices in defense of the peasants *then*? And now, in 1932-33, in Russia and Ukraine – on the very outskirts of Europe, five to six million people died from hunger! And the free press of the free world maintained utter silence... And even if we take into account the extreme Leftist bias of the contemporary Western press and its devotion to the socialist "experiment" in the USSR, it is still impossible not to be amazed at the degree to which they could go to be blind and insensitive to the sufferings of even tens of millions of fellow humans.

[2463] St. Ivanovich. *Evrei i sovetskaya diktatura* [The Jews and the Soviet Dictatorship] // *Evreyskiy Mir: Ezhegodnik na 1939* [Jewish World: Yearbook for 1939]. (henceforth — *JW-1*). Paris: Obedinenie russko-evreyskoy intelligentsii [Association of the Russo-Jewish Intelligentsia], p. 43.

[2464] Ibid., p. 44-46.

If you don't see it, your heart doesn't cry. During the 1920s, the Ukrainian Jews departed from their pro-Russian-statehood mood of 1917-1920, and by the end of the 1920s "the Jews are among Ukrainian chauvinists and separatists, wielding enormous influence there—but only in the cities."[2465] We can find such a conclusion: the destruction of Ukrainian-language culture in 1937 was in part aimed against Jews, who formed "a genuine union" with Ukrainians "for the development of local culture in Ukrainian language."[2466] Nevertheless, such a union in cultural circles could not soften the attitudes of the wider Ukrainian population toward Jews. We have already seen in the previous chapter how in the course of collectivization "a considerable number of Jewish communists functioned in rural locales as commanders and lords over life and death."[2467] This placed a new scar on Ukrainian-Jewish relations, already tense for centuries. And although the famine was a direct result of Stalin's policy, and not only in Ukraine (it brutally swept across the Volga Region and the Urals), the suspicion widely arose among Ukrainians that the entire Ukrainian famine was the work of the Jews. Such an interpretation has long existed (and the Ukrainian émigré press adhered to it until the 1980s). "Some Ukrainians are convinced that 1933 was the revenge of the Jews for the times of Khmelnitsky."[2468] [A 17th century Cossack leader who conducted bloody anti-Jewish pogroms in Ukraine].

Don't expect to reap wheat where the weed was sewn. The supreme authority of so many Jews along with only a small number of Jews being touched by the grievances which afflicted the rest of population could lead to all sorts of interpretations.

Jewish authors who nervously kept an eye on anti-Semitism in the USSR did not notice this trampled ash, however, and made rather optimistic conclusions. For instance, Solomon Schwartz writes: "From the start of the 1930s, anti-Semitism in the Soviet Union quickly abated", and "in the mid-1930s it lost the character of a mass phenomenon ...anti-Semitism reached the all-time low point." He explains this, in part, as the result of the end of the NEP (the New Economic Policy) and thereby the disappearance of Jewish businessmen and petty Jewish merchants. Later, "forced industrialization and lightning-fast collectivization," which he favorably

---

[2465] *Pismo V.I. Vernadskogo I.I. Petrunkevichu ot 14 Iyunya 1927* [A letter from V.I. Vernadsky to I.I. Petrunkevich of June 14, 1927] // *Novy Mir* [New World], 1989, (12), p. 220.

[2466] Mikhail Kheyfetz. *Uroki proshlogo* [Lessons of the Past] // *"22"*, 1989, (63), p. 202.

[2467] Sonja Margolina. Das Ende der Lügen: Russland und die Juden im 20. Jahrhundert. Berlin: Siedler Verlag, 1992, S. 84.

[2468] M. Tsarinnik. *Ukrainsko-evreyskiy dialog* [Ukraino-Jewish Dialogue] // *"22"*, 1984, (37), p. 160.

compares with a kind of "shock therapy, i.e., treatment of mental disorders with electric shocks," was of much help. In addition he considers that in those years the ruling communist circles began to struggle with Great-Russian "chauvinism." (Well, they did not begin; they just continued the policy of Lenin's intolerance). Schwartz soundly notes that the authorities were "persistently silent about anti-Semitism", "in order to avoid the impression that the struggle against Great-Russian chauvinism is a struggle for the Jews."[2469]

In January 1931, first the *New York Times*,[2470] and later the entire world press published a sudden and ostentatious announcement by Stalin to the Jewish Telegraph Agency: "The Communists, as consistent internationalists, cannot help but be an irreconcilable and sworn enemy of anti-Semitism. In the USSR, anti-Semitism is strictly prosecuted by law as a phenomenon deeply hostile to the Soviet order. Active anti-Semites are punished, according to the laws of the USSR, with the death penalty."[2471] See, he addressed the democratic West and did not mind specifying the punishment. And it was only one nationality in the USSR that was set apart by being granted such a protection. And world opinion was completely satisfied with that.

But characteristically, the announcement by the Leader *was not printed* in the Soviet press (because of his cunning reservations); it was produced for export and he hid this position from his own citizens; in the USSR it was only printed at the end of 1936.[2472] Then Stalin sent Molotov to make a similar announcement at the Congress of Soviets.

A contemporary Jewish author, erroneously interpreting Molotov's speech, suggests that speaking on behalf of the government he threatened to punish "anti-Semitic feelings" with death.[2473] *Feelings!* No, Molotov did not mention anything like that; he did not depart from Stalin's policy of persecuting "active anti-Semites." We are not aware of any instance of death penalty in the 1930s for anti-Semitism, but people *were* sentenced for it according to the Penal Code. (People whispered that *before* the revolution the authorities did not punish as harshly even for libels against the Tsar.)

[2469] S.M. Schwartz. *Antisemitizm v Sovetskom Soyuze* [Anti-Semitism in the Soviet Union]. New York: Chekov's Publishing House, 1952, p. 8, 98-99, 107-108.
[2470] New York Times, January 15, 1931, p. 9.
[2471] I.V. Stalin. *Sochineniya* (v 13 tomakh) [Written Works (in 13 volumes)]. M.: Gospolitizdat, 1946-1951. v. 13, p. 28.
[2472] *Izvestiya*, November 30, 1936, p. 2.
[2473] S. Pozner. *Sovetskaya Rossiya* [The Soviet Russia] // *JW-1*, p. 260.

But now S. Schwartz observes a change: "In the second half of the 1930s, these sentiments [people's hostility toward Jews] became much more prevalent... particularly in the major centers, where the Jewish intelligentsia and semi-intelligentsia were concentrated.... Here again the legend about "Jewish domination" gradually began to come back to life, and they began to spread exaggerated notions about the role of Jews in the middle and top ranks of government." Well, whether or not it was really a legend, he immediately attempted to explain it, though in a quite naïve manner, suggesting the same old excuse that the Jewish intelligentsia and semi-intelligentsia simply had almost no other source of livelihood under Soviet conditions except the government service."[2474]

This is so shameful to read. What oppression and despair! See, they had almost no other sources of livelihood, only privileged ones. And the rest of population was absolutely free to toil on kolkhoz fields, to dig pits, and to roll barrows at the great construction projects of the 5-year plans...

In official policy, nothing had changed in the 1930s in the Jewish Question from the time of the revolution; no official hostility toward Jews existed.

Indeed, they used to dream and proclaim about the impending end of all national conflicts.

And the foreign Jewish circles did not and could not sense any oppression of the Jews in the USSR. In the article *The Jews and the Soviet Dictatorship*, S. Ivanovich wrote: "Abroad, many believe that there is no anti-Semitism in Russia, and on that basis they are favorably disposed toward the Soviet authorities. But in Russia they know that this is not true." However, Jews "pray for the long-life of the Soviet regime ... and are strongly afraid of its demise," for "Stalin protects them from pogroms and hopefully would protect them in future." The author sympathizes with such an opinion, although he considers it flawed: "If the Bolshevik dictatorship falls, no doubt there will be wild anti-Semitic ravages and violence ...The fall of the Soviet regime would be a catastrophe for the Jews, and any friend of the Jewish people should reject such a prospect with horror"; yet at the same time he remarks that "the Soviet dictatorship is already embarrassed by the Judeophilia and Jewish dominance attributed to it."[2475]

The resolution on Stalin's report at the 16th Party Congress provided the general political direction for the 1930s, calling for an energetic struggle against chauvinism, and primarily against the *Great Russian chauvinism*. The Party language was easily understood by all. And for several more

---

[2474] S.M. Schwartz. *Antisemitizm v Sovetskom Soyuze* [Anti-Semitism in the Soviet Union]. New York: Chekov's Publishing House, 1952, p. 118.
[2475] St. Ivanovich. *Evrei i Sovetskaya diktatura* [The Jews and the Soviet Dictatorship] // *JW-1*, p. 50, 51, 52.

years this struggle was enthusiastically carried on. Yet what kind of Stalinist madness was it? By that time there was no trace left of the Great Russian chauvinism. Stalin was not able to envision the immediate future [of WWII] – when only Russian patriotism would save him from imminent doom.

Then they have already started to sound the alarm about the danger of any rebirth of Russian patriotism. In 1939, S. Ivanovich claimed to notice a trend "of this dictatorship returning to some national traditions of Moscovite Russ and Imperial Russia"; he caustically cited several stamps that entered popular discourse around that time such as the "'love for the Motherland', 'national pride' etc."[2476]

See, this is where the mortal danger for Russia lurked then, immediately before Hitler's assault – in that ugly Russian patriotism!

This alarm did not leave the minds of Jewish publicists for the next half century, even when they looked back at that war, when mass patriotism blazed up, at the war which saved Soviet Jewry. So in 1988 we read in an Israeli magazine: "Vivid traditions of the Black Hundreds ... were the foundation of 'vivifying Soviet patriotism', which blossomed later, during the Great Patriotic War" [2477] [the official Russian designation for the Eastern front in WWII].

Looking back at that war of 1941-1945, let's admit that this is a highly ungrateful judgment.

So, even the purest and most immaculate Russian patriotism has no right to exist – not now, not ever?

Why is it so? And why it is that Russian patriotism is thus singled out?

An important event in Jewish life in the USSR was the closing of the YevSek at the Central Committee of the All-Russian Communist Party of Bolsheviks in 1930. Though in accord with the Soviet blueprint, this act blocked any separate development of a Jewish society having "national, cultural, and individual Jewish autonomy." From now on Jewish cultural development lay within the Soviet mainstream. In 1937-38 the leading Yevseks – Dimanshtein, Litvakov, Frumkina-Ester and their associates Motl Kiper, Itskhok Sudarsky, Aleksandr Chemerissky – who, in words of Yu. Margolina, "in the service of the authorities carried out the greatest pogrom against Jewish culture,"[2478] were arrested and soon executed. Many Yevseks, "occupying governing positions in the central and local

---

[2476] Ibid., p. 51-52.
[2477] B. Orlov. *Rossiya bez evreyev* [Russia without Jews] // *"22"*, 1988, (60), p. 160.
[2478] Yu. Margolin. *Tel-Avivskiy bloknot* [Tel-Aviv Notebook] // *Novoe Russkoe Slovo* [The New Russian Word], New York, August 5, 1968.

departments of the Society for Settling Toiling Jews on the Land (OZET) and in the Jewish community, Jewish cultural and educational structures," also fell under the juggernaut. In 1936-39, the majority of them were persecuted."[2479] The poisonous atmosphere of 1930s now reached these levels too. During open public meetings they began to accuse and expose prominent Jewish communists, who at some time before were members either of the Bund or of the Zionist Socialist Party, or even of Poale-Zion, all of which were crippled under the Soviet regime. Was there anyone, whose past the Bolsheviks did not try to criminalize? "Who have you been before...?" In 1938 *Der Emes* was closed also.

What about education? "Right up to 1933 the number of Jewish schools and Jewish students in them increased despite the early (1920s) critique "of nationalistic over-zealousness"' in the actions of the *Yevseks* on the 'forced transition of Jewish education into Yiddish.'"[2480] From 1936 to 1939 a "period of accelerated decline and even more accelerated inner impoverishment" of the schools in Yiddish was noted.[2481] After 1936-37 "the number of Jewish schools began to decline quickly even in Ukraine and Belorussia"; the desire of parents to send their children to such schools had diminished. "Education in Yiddish was seen as less and less prestigious; there was an effort to give children an education in the Russian language." Also, from the second half of the 1930s the number of institutions of higher education lecturing in Yiddish began to decline rapidly"; "almost all Jewish institutions of higher education and technical schools were closed by 1937-38."[2482]

At the start of 1930s the Jewish scientific institutes at the academies of science of Ukraine and Belorussia were closed; in Kiev 'The Institute of Jewish Proletarian Culture' fell into desolation." And soon after this arrests followed (Mikhail Kokin of the Leningrad Institute of Philosophy, literature and History was executed; Iokhiel Rabrebe, formerly of the Petrograd Institute of Higher Jewish Studies, who in the 1930s headed the Jewish Section of the Public Library, was sentenced to 8 years and died in the transit camp).[2483]

Persecutions spread to writers in Yiddish: Moyshe Kulbak was persecuted in 1937; Zelik Akselrod, in 1940; Abram Abchuk, a teacher of Yiddish and

---

[2479] SJE, v. 8, p. 167.
[2480] Ibid., p. 176.
[2481] Yu. Mark. *Evreyskaya shkola v Sovetskom Soyuze* [The Jewish School in the Soviet Union] // *Kniga o russkom evreystve: 1917-1967* [The Book of Russian Jewry: 1917-1967 (henceforth — BRJ)]. New York: Association of Russian Jews, 1968, p. 239.
[2482] SJE, v. 8, p. 176, 177, 179.
[2483] RJE, v. 2, p. 58, 432.

a critic, in 1937; writer Gertsl Bazov, was persecuted in 1938. Writer I. Kharik and critic Kh. Dunets were persecuted also.

Still, "literature in Yiddish was actively published until the end of the 1930s. Jewish publishers were working in Moscow, Kiev, and Minsk." Yet what kind of literature was it? In the 1930s "the overwhelming majority of works were written stereotypically, in accordance with the unshakable principles of 'socialist realism.'"[2484] Literature in Yiddish "from the 1930s up to June 1941 ... was marked by the cult of Stalin. Unbridled flattery for Stalin flowed from the bosom of Jewish poetry..." [2485] Itsik Feder "managed to light up even official propaganda with lyrical notes. These monstrous sayings are ascribed to his pen: 'You betrayed your father — this is great!', and 'I say 'Stalin' but envision the sun.'"[2486] Most of these writers, who zealously tried to please Stalin, were arrested ten years later. But some of them, as mentioned above, had already drawn this lot.

Similarly, "the ideological press of official communist doctrine signified for many Jewish artists and sculptors a complete break up, quite often tragic, with the national Jewish traditions." (Still, what culture in the USSR was not touched by this?) So it comes as little surprise that "the overwhelming majority... of Jewish theaters devoted much attention to propaganda performances."

This included all 19 aforementioned professional Yiddish theaters and "numerous independent collectives, studios, and circles."[2487]

Concerning Hebrew culture which preserved the national traditions: it was by now conclusively banished and went underground.

It has already been mentioned that the Zionist underground was crushed by the beginning of the 1930s. Many Zionists were already rounded up, but still many others were accused of "the Zionist conspiracy." Take Pinkhas Dashevsky (from Chapter 8) – in 1933 he was arrested as a Zionist. Pinkhas Krasny was not a Zionist but was listed as such in his death sentence. He was former Minister of Petliura's Directorate, emigrated but later returned into the USSR.

He was executed in 1939. Volf Averbukh, a Poale-Zionist from his youth, left for Israel in 1922, where "he collaborated with the communist press." In 1930, he was sent back to the USSR, where he was arrested.[2488]

[2484] SJE, v. 8, p. 179, 181.
[2485] Yu. Mark. *Literatura na idish v Sovetskoy Rossii* [Literature in Yiddish in Soviet Russia] // BRJ, p. 216.
[2486] Ibid., p. 230.
[2487] SJE, v. 8, p. 182-183.
[2488] RJE, v. 1, p. 15, 417; v. 2, p. 84.

"Most of the semi-legal cheder schools and yeshivas were shut down" around that time. Arrests rolled on from the late 1920s in the Hasidic underground. Yakov-Zakharia Maskalik was arrested in 1937, Abrom-Levik Slavin was arrested in 1939. By the end of 1933, "237 synagogues were closed, that is, 57% of all existing in the first years of Soviet authority … In the mid-1930s, the closure of synagogues accelerated." From 1929, "the authorities began to impose excessive tax on matzo baking." In 1937, "the Commission on the Questions of Religions at the Central Executive Committee of the USSR prohibited baking matzo in Jewish religious communities." In 1937-38 "the majority of clergy of the Jewish religious cult were persecuted. There were no rabbis in the majority of still-functioning synagogues."[2489] "In 1938 a 'hostile rabbinical nest' was discovered in the Moscow Central Synagogue; the rabbis and a number of parishioners were arrested."[2490] The Rabbi of Moscow, Shmuel-Leib Medalia, was arrested and executed in 1938. (His son, Moishe Medalia, was arrested at the same time). In 1937, the Rabbi of Saratov, Iosif Bogatin, was arrested.[2491]

In the early 1930s, when the Jewish religion was restricted in the USSR, the closing of thousands of Orthodox Christian temples and the destruction of many of them rolled along throughout the entire country. They especially hurried to "liberate" Soviet Moscow from the church; Boris Iofan was in charge of that "reconstruction." In that bitter and hungry year of devastating breakdown of the country, they promoted projects for a grand Palace of Soviets in place of the Cathedral of Christ the Savior. *Izvestiya* reports: "So far, eleven projects are presented at the exhibition. Particularly interesting among them are the works of architects Fridman, B. Iofan, Bronshtein, and Ladovsky."[2492] Later, the arrests reached the architects as well.

The move toward "settling the toiling Jews on the land" gradually became irrelevant for Soviet Jews. "The percentage of Jewish settlers abandoning lands given to them remained high." In 1930-32, the activity of foreign Jewish philanthropic organizations such as Agro-Joint, OKG, and EKO in the USSR, had noticeably decreased." And although in 1933-38 it had still continued within the frameworks of new restrictive agreements, "in 1938 the activity ceased completely." "In the first half of 1938, first the OZET and then the Committee for Settling the Toiling Jews on the Land (KomZET) were dissolved. The overwhelming majority of remaining

---

[2489] SJE, v. 8, p. 198-199.
[2490] Gershon Svet. *Evreiskaya religiya v Sovetskoy Rossii* [The Jewish Religion in Soviet Russia] // BRJ, p. 209.
[2491] RJE, v. 1, p. 145; v. 2, p. 260.
[2492] *Izvestiya*, July 19, 1931, p. 2.

associates of these organizations, who were still at liberty, were persecuted." By 1939, "the Central Committee of the Communist Party of Ukraine decided to liquidate ...'the artificially' created national Jewish districts and boroughs."[2493]

Nonetheless, the idea of a Jewish colony in Birobidzhan was not abandoned in the 1930s and was even actively advanced by government. In order to put spirit into the masses, the authorities staged the Second All-Union Congress of the OZET in Moscow in December 1930.[2494] By the end of 1931, the general population of that oblast was 45,000 with only 5,000 Jews among them, although whole villages with homes were built for their settlement and access roads were laid (sometimes by inmates from the camps nearby; for example, the train station of Birobidzhan was constructed in this manner).[2495] Yet non-Jewish colonization of the region went faster than Jewish colonization.

In order to set matters right, in autumn of 1931 the Presidium of the Central Executive Committee of the RSFSR decreed that another 25,000 Jews should be settled in Birobidzhan during the next two years, after which it would be possible to declare it the Jewish Autonomous Republic. However, in the following years the number of Jews who left exceeded the number of Jews arriving, and by the end of 1933, after six years of colonization, the number of settled Jews amounted only to 8,000; of them only 1,500 lived in rural areas, i.e. worked in kolkhozes; that is, the Jews comprised less than 1/5 of all kolkhoz workers there. (There is also information that the land in the Jewish kolkhozes was fairly often tilled by hired Cossacks and Koreans). The oblast could not even provide enough agricultural products for its own needs.[2496]

Nevertheless, in May 1934, when the non-Jewish population had already reached 50,000, Birobidzhan was loudly declared a Jewish Autonomous Oblast. (It still did not qualify for the status of a "republic.")

Thus, there was no "national enthusiasm among the Jewish masses, which would ease the overcoming of the enormous difficulties inherent in such colonization." There was no industry in Birobidzhan, and "the economic and social structure" of the settlers "resembled that of contemporary Jewish towns and shtetls in Ukraine and Belorussia" This was particularly true for the city of Birobidzhan, especially considering "the increased role of the Jews in the local administrative apparatus."[2497]

[2493] SJE, v. 8, p. 173, 190, 193.
[2494] *Izvestiya*. December 12, 1930, p. 2.
[2495] S.M. Schwartz, *Birobidjan* // BRJ, p. 170-171, 200.
[2496] Ibid., p. 177-78.
[2497] S.M. Schwartz, *Birobidjan* // BRJ, p. 173, 180.

Culture in Yiddish had certainly developed in the autonomous oblast – there were Jewish newspapers, radio, schools, a theater named after Kaganovich (its director was the future author E. Kazakevich), a library named after Sholem Aleichem, a museum of Jewish culture, and public reading facilities. Perets Markish had published the exultant article, *A People Reborn*, in the central press."[2498] (In connection with Birobidzhan, let's note the fate of the demographer Ilya Veitsblit. His position was that "the policy of recruitment of poor urban Jews in order to settle them in rural areas should end"; "there are no declassé individuals among the Jews, who could be suitable for Birobidzhan."

He was arrested in 1933 and likely died in prison).[2499] Yet the central authorities believed that that the colonization should be stimulated even further; and from 1934 they began a near compulsory recruitment among Jewish artisans and workers in the western regions, that is, among the urban population without a slightest knowledge of agriculture. The slogan rang out: "The entire USSR builds the Jewish Autonomous Oblast!" – meaning that recruitment of non-Jewish cadres is needed for quicker development. The ardent Yevsek Dimanshtein wrote that "we do not aim to create a Jewish majority in the Jewish Autonomous Oblast as soon as possible; ... this would contradict to the principles of internationalism."[2500]

But despite all these measures, during the next three years only another 11,000 to eight or nine thousand Jews were added to those already living there; still, most of newcomers preferred to stay in the oblast capital closer to its railroad station and looked for opportunities to escape). Yet as we know, the Bolsheviks may not be defeated or dispirited. So, because of dissatisfaction with the KomZET, in 1936 the "Central Executive Committee of the USSR decided to partially delegate the overseeing of Jewish resettlement in the Jewish Autonomous Oblast to the resettlement department of the NKVD."[2501] In August of 1936, the Presidium of the Central Executive Committee of the USSR proclaimed that "for the first time in the history of the Jewish people, their ardent desire to have their own homeland has been realized and their own national statehood has been established."[2502] And now they began planning resettlement of 150,000 more Jews to Birobidzhan.

Looking back at it, the Soviet efforts to convert the Jews to agriculture suffered the same defeat as the Tsarist efforts a century before.

[2498] *Izvestiya*, October 26, 1936, p. 3.
[2499] RJE, v. 1, p. 214.
[2500] S.M. Schwartz. *Birobidjan* // BRJ, p. 176.
[2501] SJE, v. 8, p. 190.
[2502] S.M. Schwartz. *Birobidjan* // BRJ, p. 177.

In the meantime, the year 1938 approached. KomZET was closed, OZET was disbanded, and the main Yevseks in Moscow and the administrators of the Jewish Autonomous Oblast were arrested. Those Birobidzhan Jews who could left for the cities of the Far East or for Moscow. According to the 1939 Census, the general population of the Jewish Autonomous Oblast consisted of 108,000 people; however, "the number of Jews there remained secret ... the Jewish population of Birobidzhan was still low." Presumably, eighteen Jewish kolkhozes still existed, of 40-50 families each,[2503] but in those kolkhozes ... they conversed and corresponded with the authorities in Russian.

Yet what could Birobidzhan have become for Jews? Just forty-five years later, the Israeli General Beni Peled emphatically explained why neither Birobidzhan nor Uganda could give the Jewish people a sense of connection with the land: "I simply feel that I am not ready to die for a piece of land in Russia, Uganda, or New Jersey! ..."[2504]

This sense of connection, after thousands of years of estrangement, was restored by Israel.

The migration of Jews to the major cities did not slow down in the 1930s. *The Jewish Encyclopedia* reports that, according to the Census of 1926, there were 131,000 Jews in Moscow; in 1933, there were 226,500; and in 1939, there were 250,000 Jews. "As a result of the massive resettlement of Ukrainian Jews, their share among Moscow Jewry increased to 80%."[2505] In the *Book on the Russian Jewry* (1968), we find that in the 1930s up to a half-million Jews "were counted among government workers, sometimes occupying prominent posts, primarily in the economy."[2506] (The author also reports, that in the 1930s "up to a half-million Jews became involved in industry, mainly in manual labor." On the other hand, Larin provides another figure, that among the industrial workers there were only 2.7% Jews or 200,000[2507] or 2.5 times less than the first estimate). "The flow of Jews into the ranks of office workers grew constantly.

The reason for this was the mass migration to cities, and also the sharp increase of the educational level, especially of Jewish youth."[2508] The Jews predominantly lived in the major cities, did not experience artificial social

---

[2503] Ibid., p. 178, 179.
[2504] Beni Peled. *Mi ne mozhem zhdat eshcho dve tisyachi let!* [We Cannot Wait Two Thousand Years More!] [Interview] // *"22"*, 1981, (17), p. 116.
[2505] SJE, v. 5, p. 477-478.
[2506] G. Aronson. *Evreyskiy vopros v epokhu Stalina* [The Jewish Question in the Stalin's Era] // BRJ, p. 137.
[2507] Yu. Larin. *Evrei i anti-Semitism v SSSR* [The Jews and Anti-Semitism in the USSR]. M.; L.: GIZ, 1929, p. 245.
[2508] SJE, v. 8, p. 190.

restrictions, so familiar to their Russian peers, and, it needs to be said, they studied devotedly, thus preparing masses of technical cadres for the Soviet future.

Let's glance into statistical data: "in 1929 the Jews comprised 13.5% of all students in the higher educational institutions in the USSR; in 1933—12.2%; in 1936—13.3% of all students, and 18% of graduate students" (with their share of the total population being only 1.8%);[2509] from 1928 to 1935, "the number of Jewish students per 1,000 of the Jewish population rose from 8.4 to 20.4 [while] per 1,000 Belorussians there were 2.4 students, and per 1,000 Ukrainians – 2.0"; and by 1935 "the percentage of Jewish students exceeded the percentage of Jews in the general population of the country by almost seven times, thus standing out from all other peoples of the Soviet Union."[2510] G.V. Kostirchenko, who researched Stalin's policies on Jews, comments on the results of the 1939 census: "After all, Stalin could not disregard the fact that at the start of 1939 out of every 1,000 Jews, 268 had a high school education, and 57 out of 1,000 had higher education" (among Russians the figures were, respectively, 81 and 6 per 1,000).[2511] It is no secret that "highly successful completion of higher education or doctoral studies allowed individuals to occupy socially-prestigious positions in the robustly developing Soviet economy of the 1930s."[2512]

However, in *The Book on Russian Jewry* we find that "without exaggeration, after Ezhov's purges, not a single prominent Jewish figure remained at liberty in Soviet Jewish society, journalism, culture, or even in the science."[2513] Well, it was absolutely not like that, and it is indeed a gross exaggeration. (Still, the same author, Grigory Aronson, in the same book, only two pages later says summarily about the 1930s, that "the Jews were not deprived of general civil rights ... they continued to occupy posts in the state and party apparatus", and "there were quite a few Jews ... in the diplomatic corps, in the general staff of the army, and among the professors in the institutions of higher learning...Thus we enter into the year 1939."[2514]

The voice of Moscow was that of the People's Artist, Yury Levitan – "the voice of the USSR", that incorruptible prophet of our Truth, the main host of the radio station of the Comintern and a favorite of Stalin. Entire

---

[2509] Ibid.
[2510] S. Pozner. *Sovetskaya Rossiya* [The Soviet Russia] // *JW-1*, p. 264.
[2511] G. Kostirchenko. *Taynaya politika Stalina* [The Secret Policy of Stalin], p. 198.
[2512] SJE, v. 8, p. 190.
[2513] G. Aronson. *Evreyskiy vopros v epokhu Stalina* [The Jewish Question in the Stalin's Era] // BRJ, p. 138.
[2514] Ibid., p. 140-141.

generations grew up, listening to his voice: he read Stalin's speeches and summaries of Sovinformburo [the Soviet Information Bureau], and the famous announcements about the beginning and the end of the war.[2515]

In 1936 Samuil Samosud became the main conductor of the Bolshoi Theatre and served on that post for many years. Mikhail Gnesin continued to produce music "in the style of modern European music and in the style of the so-called 'New Jewish music'"; Gnesin's sisters successfully ran the music school, which developed into the outstanding Musical Institute. The ballet of Aleksandr Krein was performed in the Mariinsky and Bolshoi theatres. Well, Krein distinguished himself by his symphony, *Rhapsody*, that is, a Stalin's speech set to music. Krein's brother and nephew flourished also.[2516] A number of brilliant musicians rose to national and later to international fame: Grigory Ginzburg, Emil Gilels, Yakov Zak, Lev Oborin, David Oistrakh, Yakov Flier and many others. Many established theatre directors, theatre and literary critics, and music scholars continued to work without hindrance.

Examining the culture of the 1930s, it is impossible to miss the extraordinary achievements of the songwriter composers. Isaak Dunaevsky, "a founder of genres of operetta and mass song in Soviet music", "composed easily digestible songs ... routinely glorifying the Soviet way of life (*The March of Merry Lads*, 1933; *The Song of Kakhovka*, 1935; *The Song about Homeland*, 1936; *The Song of Stalin*, 1936, etc.). Official propaganda on the arts declared these songs ... the embodiment of the thoughts and feelings of millions of Soviet people."[2517] Dunaevsky's tunes were used as the identifying melody of Moscow Radio. He was heavily decorated for his service: he was the first of all composers to be awarded the Order of the Red Banner of Labour and elected to the Supreme Soviet of the USSR in the notorious year 1937. Later he was also awarded the Order of Lenin. He used to preach to composers that the Soviet people do not need symphonies.[2518]

Matvey Blanter and the brothers Daniil and Dmitry Pokrass were famous for their complacent hit song *If War Strikes Tomorrow* ("we will instantly crush the enemy") and for their earlier hit the *Budyonny March*. There were many other famous Jewish songwriters and composers in 1930s and later: Oskar Feltsman, Solovyev-Sedoy, Ilya Frenkel, Mikhail Tanich, Igor Shaferan, Yan Frenkel and Vladimir Shainsky, etc. They enjoyed copy

---

[2515] RJE, v. 2, p. 150.
[2516] Gershon Svet. *Evrei v russkoy muzikalnoy culture v sovetskiy period* [The Jews in Russian Musical Culture in the Soviet Period] // BRJ, p. 256-262.
[2517] SJE, v. 2, p. 393-394.
[2518] Yuriy Elagin. *Ukroshchenie iskusstv* [Conquest of the Arts] / Introduction by M. Rostropovich. New York: Ermitazh, 1988, p. 340-345.

numbers in the millions, fame, royalties — come on, who dares to name those celebrities among the oppressed? And after all, alongside the skillfully written songs, how much blaring Soviet propaganda did they churn out, confusing, brainwashing, and deceiving the public and crippling good taste and feelings?

What about movie industry? The modern Israeli *Jewish Encyclopedia* states that in the 1930s "the main role of movies was to glorify the successes of socialism; a movie's entertainment value was minimal. Numerous Jewish filmmakers participated in the development of standards of a unified and openly ideological film industry, conservative in form and obsessively didactic. Many of them were already listed in the previous chapter; take, for example, D. Vertov's *Symphony of the Donbass*, 1931, released immediately after the Industrial Party Trial. Here are a few of the then-celebrated names: F. Ermler (*The Coming, The Great Citizen, Virgin Soil Upturned*), S. Yutkevich (*The Coming, The Miners*), the famous Mikhail Romm (*Lenin in October, Lenin in 1918*), L. Arnshtam (*Girlfriends, Friends*), I. Trauberg (*The Son of Mongolia, The Year 1919*), A. Zarkhi and I. Kheifits (*Hot Days, Ambassador of the Baltic*).[2519] Obviously, filmmakers were not persecuted in the 1930s, though many cinematography, production and film distribution managers were arrested; two high-ranking bosses of the central management of the cinema industry, B. Shumyatsky and S. Dukelsky, were even shot.[2520]

In the 1930s, Jews clearly comprised a majority among filmmakers. So, who was really the victim – deceived viewers, whose souls were steamrolled with lies and rude didactics, or the filmmakers, who "forged documentaries, biographies and produced pseudo-historical and essentially unimportant propaganda films," characterized by "phony monumentality and inner emptiness"? *The Jewish Encyclopedia* adds sternly: "Huge numbers of Jewish operators and directors were engaged in making popular science, educational, and documentary films, in the most official sphere of the Soviet cinematography, where adroit editing helped to produce a "genuine documentary" out of a fraud. For example, R. Karmen, did it regularly without scruples." [2521] (He was a glorified Soviet director, producer of many documentaries about the civil war in Spain and the Nuremberg Trials; he made "the anniversary-glorifying film *The Great Patriotic War*", *Vietnam,* and a film about Cuba; he was a recipient of three USSR State Prizes (the Stalin Prize) and the Lenin Prize; he held the titles of the People's Artist of the USSR and the Hero of the Socialist Labor).[2522]

[2519] SJE, v. 4, p. 277.
[2520] Ibid., p. 275.
[2521] Ibid., p. 277-278.
[2522] SJE, v. 4, p. 116.

Let's not forget filmmaker Konrad Wolf, the brother of the famous Soviet spy, Marcus Wolf.[2523]

No, the official Soviet atmosphere of 1930s was absolutely free of ill will toward Jews. And until the war, the overwhelming majority of Soviet Jewry sympathized with the Soviet ideology and sided with the Soviet regime. "There was no *Jewish Question* indeed in the USSR before the war – or almost none"; then the "open anti-Semites were not yet in charge of newspapers and journals… they did not control personnel departments"[2524] (quite the opposite – many such positions were occupied by Jews).

Sure, then Soviet "culture" consisted of "Soviet patriotism," i.e., of producing art in accordance with directives from above. Unfortunately, many Jews were engaged in that pseudo-cultural sphere and some of them even rose to supervise the Russian language culture. In the early 1930s we see B.M. Volin-Fradkin at the head of the Main Administration for Literary and Publishing Affairs (GlavLit), the organ of official censorship, directing the development of the culture. Many of the GlavLit personnel were Jewish. For example, in GlavLit, from 1932 to 1941 we see A.I. Bendik, who would become the Director of the Book Palace during the war.[2525] Emma Kaganova, the spouse of Chekist Pavel Sudoplatov was "trusted to manage the activities of informants among the Ukrainian intelligentsia."[2526] After private publishers were abolished, "a significant contribution to the organization and management of Soviet government publishers was made by S. Alyansky, M. Volfson, I. Ionov (Bernshtein), A. Kantorovich, B. Malkin, I. Berite, B. Feldman, and many others."[2527] Soon all book publishing was centralized in the State Publishing House and there was no other place for an author to get his work published.

The Jewish presence was also apparent in all branches of the printed propaganda Works of the clumsy caricaturist Boris Efimov could be found in the press everyday (he produced extremely filthy images of Western leaders; for instance, he had portrayed Nicholas II in a crown carrying a rifle, trampling corpses). Every two to three days, sketches of other dirty satirists, like G. Riklin, the piercingly caustic D. Zaslavsky, the adroit Radek, the persistent Sheinin and the brothers Tur, appeared in press. A future writer L. Kassil wrote essays for *Izvestiya*. There were many others:

[2523] RJE, v. 1, p. 245-246.
[2524] Lev Kopelev. *O pravde i terpimosti* [Of Truth and Tolerance]. New York: Khronika Press, 1982, p. 56-57.
[2525] RJE, v. 1, p. 108, 238-239.
[2526] Pavel Sudoplatov. *Spetsoperatsii: Lubyanka i Kreml: 1930s-1950s* [Special Operations: Lubyanka [Prison] and the Kremlin: the 1930s through the 1950s]. Moscow: OLMA-Press, 1997, p. 19.
[2527] SJE, v. 4, p. 397.

R. Karmen, T. Tess, Kh. Rappoport, D. Chernomordikov, B. Levin, A. Kantorovich, and Ya. Perelman.

These names I found in *Izvestiya* only, and there were two dozen more major newspapers feeding the public with blatant lies. In addition, there existed a whole sea of ignoble mass propaganda brochures saturated with lies. When they urgently needed a mass propaganda brochure devoted to the Industrial Party Trial (such things were in acute demand for all of the 1930s), one B. Izakson knocked it out under the title: "Crush the viper of intervention!" Diplomat E. Gnedin, the son of Parvus, wrote lying articles about the "incurable wounds of Europe" and the imminent death of the West. He also wrote a rebuttal article, *Socialist Labor in the Forests of the Soviet North*, in response to Western "slanders" about the *allegedly* forced labor of camp inmates felling timber.

When in the 1950s Gnedin returned from a camp after a long term (though, it appears, not having experienced tree felling himself), he was accepted as a venerable sufferer and no one reminded him of his lies in the past.

In 1929-31 Russian historical science was destroyed; the Archaeological Commission, the Northern Commission, Pushkin House, the Library of the Academy of Sciences were all abolished, traditions were smashed, and prominent Russian historians were sent to rot in camps. (How much did we hear about *that* destruction?) Third and fourth-rate *Russian historians* then surged in to occupy the vacant posts and brainwash us for the next half a century. Sure, quite a few Russian slackers made their careers then, but Jewish ones did not miss their chance.

Already in the 1930s, Jews played a prominent role in Soviet science, especially in the most important and technologically-demanding frontiers, and their role was bound to become even more important in the future. "By the end of 1920s, Jews comprised 13.6% of all scientists in the country; by 1937 their share increased to 17.6%"; in 1939 there were more than 15,000 or 15.7% Jewish scientists and lecturers in the institutions of higher learning."[2528]

In physics, member of the Academy A. F. Ioffe nurtured a highly successful school. As early as 1918, he founded the Physical-Technical Institute in Petrograd. Later, "fifteen affiliated scientific centers were created"; they were headed by Ioffe's disciples. "His former students worked in many other institutes, in many ways determining the scientific and technological potential of the Soviet Union." [2529] (However,

---

[2528] SJE, v. 8, p. 190-191.
[2529] L.L. Mininberg. *Sovetskie evrei v nauke i promishlennosti SSSR v period Vtoroi mirovoi voyny (1941-1945)* [Soviet Jews in the Soviet Science and Industry during the Second World War (1941-1945)]. Moscow, 1995, p. 16.

repressions did not bypass them. In 1938, in the Kharkov Physics-Technological Institute, six out of eight heads of departments were arrested: Vaisberg, Gorsky, Landau, Leipunsky, Obreimov, Shubnikov; a seventh—Rueman—was exiled; only Slutskin remained).[2530] The name of Semyon Aisikovich, the constructor of *Lavochkin* fighter aircraft, was long unknown to the public.[2531] Names of many other personalities in military industry were kept secret as well. Even now we do not know all of them. For instance, M. Shkud "oversaw development of powerful radio stations,"[2532] yet there were surely others, whom we do not know, working on the development of no less powerful jammers.)

Numerous Jewish names in technology, science and its applications prove that the flower of several Jewish generations went into these fields. Flipping through the pages of biographical tomes of the *Russian Jewish Encyclopedia*, which only lists the Jews who were born or lived in Russia, we see an abundance of successful and gifted people with real accomplishments (which also means the absence of obstacles to career entry and advancement in general).

Of course, scientists had to pay political tribute too. Take, for example, "the First National Conference for the Planning of Science" in 1931. Academician Ioffe stated that "modern capitalism is no longer capable of a technological revolution," it is only possible as a result of a social revolution, which has "transformed the once barbaric and backward Russia into the Socialist Union of Republics." He praised the leadership of the proletariat in science and said that science can be free only under Soviet stewardship. "Militant philosopher" E. Ya. Kolman ("one of main ideologists of Soviet science in the 1930s"; he fulminated against the Moscow school of mathematics) asserted that "we should… introduce labor discipline in the sciences, adopt collective methods, socialist competition, and shock labor methods; he said that science advances "thanks to the proletarian dictatorship," and that each scientist should study Lenin's *Materialism and Empirico-criticism*. Academician A.G. Goldman (Ukraine) enthusiastically chimed in: "The academy now became the leading force in the struggle for the Marxist dialectic in science!"[2533]

The Jewish Encyclopedia summarizes: "At the end of 1930s, the role of the Jews in the various spheres of the Soviet life reached its apogee for the entire history of the Soviet regime." According to the 1939 census, 40% of all economically active Jews were state employees. Around 364,000 were

---

[2530] Alexander Weissberg. *Conspiracy of Silence*. London, 1952, p. 359-360.
[2531] SJE, v. 4, p. 660.
[2532] RJE, v. 3, p. 401.
[2533] *Izvestiya*, April 7, 1931, p. 2; April 11, p. 3; April 12, p. 4. See also RJE, v. 2, p. 61-62.

categorized among the intelligentsia. Of them, 106,000 were engineers or technologists, representing 14% of all professionals of this category countrywide; 139,000 were managers at various levels, 7% of all administrators in the USSR; "39,000 doctors, or slightly less than 27% of all doctors; 38,000 teachers, or more than 3% of all teachers; "more than 6,500 writers, journalists, and editors; more than 5,000 actors and filmmakers; more than 6,000 musicians; a little less than 3,000 artists and sculptors; and more than 5,000 lawyers."[2534]

In the opinion of the *Encyclopedia*, such impressive representation by a national minority, even in the context of official internationalism and brotherhood of the peoples of the USSR, created the prerequisites for the backlash by the state."[2535]

During his political career, Stalin often allied with Jewish leaders of the communist party and relied on many Jewish back-benchers. By the mid-1930s he saw in the example of Hitler all the disadvantages of being a self-declared enemy of the Jews. Yet he likely harbored hostility toward them (his daughter's memoirs support this), though even his closest circle was probably unaware of it. However, struggling against the Trotskyites, he, of course, realized this aspect as well — his need to further get rid of the Jewish influence in the party. And, sensing the war, he perhaps was also grasping that "proletarian internationalism" alone would not be sufficient and that the notion of the "homeland," and even the "Homeland", would be much needed.

S. Schwartz lamented about anti-revolutionary transformation of the party as the "unprecedented 'purge' of the ruling party, the virtual destruction of the old party and the establishment of a new communist party under the same name in its place – new in social composition and ideology." From 1937 he also noted a "gradual displacement of Jews from the positions of power in all spheres of public life." "Among the old Bolsheviks who were involved in the activity before the party came to power and especially among those with the pre-revolutionary involvement, the percentage of Jews was noticeably higher than in the party on average; in younger generations, the Jewish representation became even smaller... As a result of the purge, almost all important Jewish communists left the scene."[2536] Lazar Kaganovich was the exception. Still, in 1939, after all the massacres, the faithful communist Zemlyachka was made the deputy head of the Soviet of People's Commissars, and S. Dridzo-Lozovsky was assigned the

---

[2534] SJE, v. 8, p. 191.
[2535] SJE, v. 8, p. 191.
[2536] S.M. Schwartz. *Antisemitizm v Sovetskom Soyuze* [Anti-Semitism in the Soviet Union]. New York: Chekov's Publishing House, 1952, p. 111-112, 114, 121-122.

position of Deputy to the Narkom of Foreign Affairs.[2537] And yet, in the wider picture, Schwartz's observations are reasonable as was demonstrated above.

S. Schwartz adds that in the second half of 1930s Jews were gradually barred from entering "institutions of higher learning, which were preparing specialists for foreign relations and foreign trade, and were barred from military educational institutions."[2538] The famous defector from the USSR, I.S. Guzenko, shared rumors about a secret percentage quota on Jewish admissions to the institutions of higher learning which was enforced from 1939.

In the 1990s they even wrote that Molotov, taking over the People's Commissariat of Foreign Affairs in the spring of 1939, publicly announced during the general meeting with the personnel that he "will deal with the synagogue here," and that he began firing Jews on the very same day. (Still, Litvinov was quite useful during the war in his role as Soviet ambassador to the U.S. They say that upon his departure from the U.S. in 1943 he even dared to pass a personal letter to Roosevelt suggesting that Stalin had unleashed an anti-Semitic campaign in the USSR).[2539]

By the mid-1930s the sympathy of European Jewry toward the USSR had further increased. Trotsky explained it in 1937 on his way to Mexico: "The Jewish intelligentsia ... turns to the Comintern not because they are interested in Marxism or Communism, but in search of support against aggressive [German] anti-Semitism."[2540] Yet it was *this same* Comintern that approved the Molotov-Ribbentrop Pact, the pact that dealt a mortal blow to the East European Jewry!

"In September 1939, hundreds of thousands of Polish Jews fled from the advancing German armies, fleeing further and further east and trying to head for the territory occupied by the Red Army.... For the first two months they succeeded because of the favorable attitude of the Soviet authorities.

[2537] RJE, v. 1, p. 486; v. 2, p. 196.
[2538] *S.M. Schwartz*. Evrei v Sovetskom Soyuze s nachala Vtoroi mirovoi voyny (1939-1965) [Jews in the Soviet Union after the Beginning of the Second World War (1939-1965)]. New York: Publication of the American Jewish Workers Committee, 1966, p. 410.
[2539] Z. Sheinis, M.M. Litvinov. *Poslednie dni* [The Last Days] // *Sovershenno Sekretno* [Top Secret]. Moscow, 1992, (4), p. 15.
[2540] Lev Trotsky. *Pochemu oni kayalis* [Why They Repented] // *EW*, New York, 1985, (87), p. 226.

The Germans quite often encouraged this flight." But "at the end of November the Soviet government closed the border."[2541]

In different areas of the front things took shape differently: in some areas, the Soviets would not admit Jewish refugees at all; in other places they were welcomed but later sometimes sent back to the Germans. Overall, it is believed that around 300,000 Jews managed to migrate from the Western to the Eastern Poland in the first months of the war, and later the Soviets evacuated them deeper into the USSR. They demanded that Polish Jews register as Soviet citizens, but many of them did not rush to accept Soviet citizenship: after all, they thought, the war would soon be over, and they would return home, or go to America, or to Palestine. (Yet in the eyes of the Soviet regime they thereby immediately fell under the category of "suspected of espionage," especially if they tried to correspond with relatives in Poland).[2542] Still, we read in the Chicago *Sentinel* that the Soviet Union gave refuge to 90% of all European Jewish refugees fleeing from Hitler."[2543]

According to the January 1939 census, 3,020,000 Jews lived in the USSR. Now, after occupation of the Baltics, annexation of a part of Poland, and taking in Jewish refugees, approximately two million more Jews were added, giving a total of around 5 million.[2544] Before 1939, the Jews were the seventh largest people in the USSR number-wise; now, after annexation of all Western areas, they became the *fourth* largest people of the USSR, after the three Slavic peoples, Russian, Ukrainian, and Belorussian. "The mutual non-Aggression Pact of 23 August 1939 between the Third Reich and the Soviet Union evoked serious fear about the future of Soviet Jewry, though the policy of the Soviet Union toward its Jewish citizens was not changed." And although there were some reverse deportations, overall, "the legal status of Jewish population remained unchanged during the 20 months of the Soviet-German collaboration."[2545]

With the start of war in Poland, Jewish sympathies finally crystallized and Polish Jews, and the Jewish youth in particular, met the advancing Red

---

[2541] E. Kulisher. *Izgnanie i deportatsiya evreev* [The Expulsion and Deportation of the Jews] // *Evreiskiy mir* [The Jewish World], v. 2 (henceforth— *JW-2*). New York: Soyuz russkikh evreyev v New Yorke [The Union of Russian Jews in New York], 1944, p. 259.
[2542] S.M. Schwartz. *Evrei v Sovetskom Soyuze s nachala Vtoroi mirovoi voyny (1939-1965)* [Jews in the Soviet Union after the Beginning of the Second World War (1939-1965)]. New York: Publication of the American Jewish Workers Committee, 1966, p. 33-34.
[2543] *The Sentinel*, Chicago, Vol. XXXXIII, (13), 1946, 27 June, p.5.
[2544] G. Aronson. *Evreyskiy vopros v epokhu Stalina* [The Jewish Question in the Stalin's Era] // BRJ, p. 141.
[2545] I. Shekhman. *Sovetskoe evreystvo v germano-sovetskoy voyne* [Soviet Jewry in the Russo-German War] // *JW-2*, p. 221-222.

Army with exulting enthusiasm. Thus, according to many testimonies (including M. Agursky's one), Polish Jews, like their co-ethnics in Bessarabia, Bukovina and Lithuania, became the main pillar of the Soviet regime, supporting it tooth and nail.

Yet how much did these East European Jews know about what was going on in the USSR?

They unerringly sensed that a catastrophe was rolling at them from Germany, though still not fully or clearly recognized, but undoubtedly a catastrophe. And so the Soviet welcome appeared to them to embody certain salvation.

Chapter 20

In the camps of GULag

If I haven't been there, it wouldn't be possible for me to compose this chapter. Before the camps I thought that "one should not notice nationalities", that there are no nationalities, there is only humankind.

But when you are sent into the camp, you find it out: if you are of a lucky nationality then you are a fortunate man. You are provided for. You have survived! But if you are of a *common* nationality – well then, no offence...

Because nationality is perhaps the most important trait that gives a prisoner a chance to be picked into the life-saving corps of *"Idiots"* - from Russian "придурок" – a fool or idiot. This is an inmate slang term to denote other inmates who didn't do common labor but managed to obtain positions with easy duties, usually pretending to be incapable of doing hard work because of poor health. Every experienced camp inmate can confirm that ethnic proportions among *Idiots* were very different from those in the general camp population. Indeed, there were virtually no Pribalts among Idiots, regardless of their actual number in the camp (and there were many of them); there were always Russians, of course, but in incomparably smaller proportion than in the camp on average (and those were often selected from *orthodox* members of the Party); on the other hand, some others were noticeably concentrated – Jews, Georgians, Armenians; and Azeris also ended there in higher proportions, and, to some extent, Caucasian mountaineers also.

Certainly, none of them can be blamed for that. Every nation in the Gulag did its best crawling to survival, and the smaller and nimbler it was, the easier it was to accomplish. And again, Russians were the very last nation in "their own Russian camps", like they were in the German *Kriegsgefangenenlagers*.

Yet it is not us who could have blamed them, but it is they – Armenians, Georgians, highlanders, who would have been in their right to ask us: "Why did you establish these camps? Why do you force us to live in your state? Do not hold us and we will not land here and occupy these such attractive

Idiotic positions! But while we are your prisoners – *à la guerre comme à la guerre.*"

But what about Jews? For Fate interwove Russian and Jews, perhaps forever, which is why this book is being written.

Before that, before this very line, there will be readers who have been in the camps and who haven't been, who will be quick to contest the truth of what I say here. They will claim that many Jews were forced to take part in *common* labor activities. They will deny that there were camps where Jews were the majority among *Idiots*. They will indignantly reject that nations in the camps were helping each other selectively, and, therefore, at the expense of others.

Some others will not consider themselves as distinct *"Jews"* at all, perceiving themselves as Russians in everything. Besides, even if there *was* overrepresentation of Jews on key camp positions, it was absolutely unpremeditated, wasn't it? The selection was exclusively based on merit and personal talents and abilities to do business. Well, who is to blame if Russians lack business talents?

There will be also those who will passionately assert directly opposite: that it was Jews who suffered worst in the camps. This is exactly how it is understood in the West: in Soviet camps nobody suffered as badly as Jews.

Among the letters from readers of *Ivan Denisovich* there was one from an anonymous Jew: "You have met innocent Jews who languished in camps with you, and you obviously not at once witnessed their suffering and persecution.

They endured double oppression: imprisonment and enmity from the rest of inmates. Tell us about these people!"

And if I wished to *generalize* and state that the life of Jews in camps was especially difficult, then I would be allowed to do so and wouldn't be peppered with admonitions for unjust ethnic generalizations. But in the camps, where I was imprisoned, it was the other way around – the life of Jews, to the extent of possible generalization, *was* easier.

Semen Badash, my campmate from Ekibastuz, recounts in his memoirs how he had managed to settle – later, in a camp at Norilsk – in the medical unit: Max Minz asked a radiologist Laslo Newsbaum to solicit for Badash before a free head of the unit. He was accepted.[2546] But Badash at least finished three years of medical school before imprisonment. Compare that with other nurses – Genkin, Gorelik, Gurevich (like one of my pals, L.

[2546] Семён Бадаш. Колыма ты моя, Колыма... New York: Effect Publishing Inc.. 1986, с. 65-66.

Kopelev from Unzlag) – who never before in their lives had anything to do with medicine.

Some people absolutely seriously write like this: A. Belinkov "was thrown into the most despicable category of *Idiots*..." (and I am tempted to inappropriately add "and languishers" here, though the *"Languishers"* were the social antipodes of *Idiots* and Belinkov never was among the *Languishers*). – "To be thrown into the group of *Idiots*"! – what's an expression! "To be diminished by being accepted into the ranks of gentlemen"? And here goes the justification: "To dig soil? But at the age of 23 he not only never did it – he never saw a shovel in his life".[2547] Well then he had no other choice but to become an *Idiot*.

Or read what Levitin-Krasnov wrote about one Pinsky, a literature expert, that he was a nurse in the camp. Which means that he, on the camp scale, has adhered well. However, Levitin presents this as an example of the greatest humiliation possible for a professor of the humanities.

Or take prisoner who survived, Lev Razgon, a journalist and not a medic at all, who was heavily published afterwards. But from his story in "Ogonek" (1988) we find that he used to be a medic in the camp's medical unit, and, moreover, an *unescorted* medic. (From other his stories we can figure out that he also worked as a senior controller at a horrible timber logging station. But there is not a single story from which we can conclude that he ever participated in *common* labor.)

Or a story of Frank Dikler, a Jew from faraway Brazil: he was imprisoned and couldn't speak Russian, of course, and guess what? He had pull in the camp, and he has became a chief of the medical unit's kitchen – a truly magnificent treasure!

Or Alexandr Voronel, who was a "political youngster" when he landed in the camps, says that immediately after getting in the camp, he was "readily assisted... by other Jewish inmates, who had not a slightest idea about my political views". A Jewish inmate, responsible for running the bathhouse (a very important *Idiot* as well), has spotted him instantly and "ordered him to come if he needs any help"; a Jew from prisoner security (also an *Idiot*) told another Jew, a brigadier: "There are two Jewish guys, Hakim, don't allow them to get in trouble". And the brigadier gave them strong protection. "Other thieves, especially "elders", approved him: You are so

---

[2547] В. Лемпорт. Эллипсы судьбы // Время и мы: Международный журнал литературы и общественных проблем. Нью-Йорк, 1991, № 113. с. 168.

right, Hakim! You support your own kin! Yet we, Russians, are like wolves to each other"".[2548]

And let's not forget that even during camp imprisonment, by virtue of a common stereotype regarding all Jews as businessmen, many of them were getting commercial offers, sometimes even when they didn't actively look for such enterprises. Take, for instance, M. Hafez. He emphatically notes: "What a pity that I can't describe you those camp situations. There are so many rich, beautiful stories! However, the ethical code of a "reliable Jew" seals my mouth.

You know even the smallest commercial secret should be kept forever. That's the law of the Tribe".[2549]

A Lett Ane Bernstein, one of my witnesses from *Archipelago*, thinks that he managed to survive in the camps only because in times of hardship he asked the Jews for help and that the Jews, judging by his last name and nimble manners, mistook him for their tribesman – and always provided assistance. He says that in all his camps Jews always constituted the upper crust, and that the most important free employees were also Jews (Shulman – head of special department, Greenberg – head of camp station, Kegels – chief mechanic of the factory), and, according to his recollections, they also preferred to select Jewish inmates to staff their units.

This particular Jewish national contract between free bosses and inmates is impossible to overlook. A free Jew was not so stupid to actually see an "Enemy of the People" or an evil character preying on "the people's property" in an imprisoned Jew (unlike what a dumb-headed Russian saw in another Russian).

He in the first place saw a suffering tribesman – and I praise them for this sobriety! Those who know about terrific Jewish mutual supportiveness (especially exacerbated by mass deaths of Jews under Hitler) would understand that a free Jewish boss simply could not indifferently watch Jewish prisoners flounder in starvation and die, and not help. But I am unable to imagine a free Russian employee who would save and promote his fellow Russian prisoners to the privileged positions only because of their nationality. Though we have lost 15 millions during collectivization, we are still numerous. You can't care about everyone, and nobody would even think about it.

[2548] Л. Воронель. Трепет иудейских забот. 2-е изд. Рамат-Ган: Москва-Иерусалим, 1981, с. 28-29.
[2549] Михаил Хейфец. Место и время (еврейские заметки). Париж: Третья волна, 1978, с. 93.

Sometimes, when such a team of Jewish inmates smoothly bands together and, being no longer impeded by the ferocious struggle for survival, they can engage in extraordinary activities. An engineer named Abram Zisman tells us:

"In Novo-Archangelsk camp, in our spare time, [we] decided to count how many Jewish pogroms occurred over the course of Russian history. We managed to excite the curiosity of our camp command on this question (they had a peaceful attitude toward us). The *Nachlag* [camp commander] was captain Gremin (N. Gershel, a Jew, son of a tailor from Zhlobin). He sent an inquiry to the archives of the former Interior Department requesting the necessary information, and after eight months we received an official reply that ... 76 Jewish pogroms occurred from 1811 to 1917 on the territory of Russia with the number of victims estimated at approximately 3,000" (That is, the total number of those who suffered in any way.) The author reminds us that during one six-month period in medieval Spain more than twenty thousand Jews were killed.[2550]

A plot-like atmosphere emanates from the recollections of Josef Berger, a communist, about a highly-placed snitch Lev Ilyich Inzhir. A former Menshevik, arrested in 1930, he immediately began collaborating with the GPU, fearing reprisals against his family and the loss of his apartment in the center of Moscow. He "helped to prepare the Menshevik trial" of 1931, falsely testified against his best friends, was absolved and immediately appointed as a chief accountant of Belomorstroi. During the *Yezhovschina* he was a chief accountant of the GULag "enjoying the complete trust of his superiors and with connections to the very top NKVD officials". (Inzhir recalled one "Jewish NKVD veteran who interlarded his words with aphorisms from Talmud".) He was arrested later again, this time on the wave of anti-Yezhov purges. However, Inzhir's former colleagues from the GULag favorably arranged his imprisonment. However, at this point he turned into an explicit "snitch and provocateur", and other inmates suspected that the plentiful parcels he was receiving were not from his relatives but directly from the Third Department.

Nevertheless, later in 1953 in the Tayshet camp, he was sentenced to an additional jail term, this time being accused of Trotskyism and of concealing his "sympathies for the State of Israel" from the Third Department.[2551]

[2550] А. Зисман. «Книга о русском еврействе» // Новая Заря, Сан-Франциско, 1960, 7 мая, с. 3.
[2551] Иосиф Бергер. Крушение поколения: Воспоминания / Пер. с англ. Firenze: Edizioni Aurora. 1973, с. 148-164.

Of worldwide infamy, BelBallag absorbed hundreds of thousands of Russian, Ukrainian and Middle Asian peasants between 1931 and 1932.

Opening a newspaper issue from August, 1933, dedicated to the completion of the canal [between White and Baltic seas], we find a list of awardees. Lower ranking orders and medals were awarded to concreters, steelfixers, etc, but the highest degree of decoration, the Order of Lenin, was awarded to eight men only, and we can see large photographs of each. Only two of them were actual engineers, the rest were the chief commanders of the canal (according to Stalin's understanding of personal contribution). And whom do we see here?

Genrikh Yagoda, head of NKVD. Matvei Berman, head of GULag. Semen Firin, commander of BelBaltlag (by that time he was already the commander of Dmitlag, where the story will later repeat itself). Lazar Kogan, head of construction (later he will serve the same function at Volgocanal). Jacob Rapoport, deputy head of construction. Naftaly Frenkel, chief manager of the labor force of Belomorstroi (and the evil demon of the whole Archipelago).[2552]

And all their portraits were enlarged and reprinted again in the solemnly shameful book *Belomorcanal*[2553] – a book of huge Scriptural size, like some revelation anticipating advent of the Millenarian Kingdom.

And then I reproduced these six portraits of villains in *Archipelago*, borrowing them from their own exhibition and without any prior editing, showing everybody who was originally displayed. Oh my God, what a worldwide rage has surged! *How dared I?! This is anti-Semitism!* I am a branded and screwed anti-Semite. At best, to reproduce these portraits was "national egotism" – i.e. Russian egotism! And they dared to say it despite what follows immediately on the next pages of *Archipelago*: how docilely "Kulak" lads were freezing to death under their barrows.

One wonders, where were their eyes in 1933 when it was printed for the very first time? Why weren't they so indignant then?

Let me repeat what I professed once to the Bolsheviks: one should be ashamed of hideosity not when it is disclosed to public but when it is done.

A particular conundrum exists with respect to the personality of Naftaly Frenkel, that tireless demon of *Archipelago*: how to explain his strange return from Turkey in 1920's? He successfully got away from Russia with all his capitals after the first harbingers of revolution. In Turkey, he attained

---

[2552] Известия, 1933. 5 августа, с. 1-2.
[2553] Беломорско-Балтийский Канал имени Сталина: История строительства / Под ред. М. Горького, Л.Л. Авербаха. С.Г. Фирина. [М.]: История Фабрик и Заводов, 1934.

a secure, rich and unconstrained social standing, and he never harbored any Communist ideas. And yet he returned? To come back and become a toy for the GPU and for Stalin, to spend several years in imprisonment himself, but in return to accomplish the most ruthless oppression of imprisoned engineers and the extermination of hundreds of thousands of the "de-Kulakized"? What could have motivated his insatiable evil heart? I am unable to imagine any possible reason except vengeance toward Russia. If anyone can provide an alternative explanation, please do so.[2554]

What else could be revealed by someone with a thorough understanding of the structure of the camp command? The head of 1st Department of Belomorstroi was one Wolf; the head of the Dmitrov section of Volgocanal was Bovshover. The finance division of Belomorstroi was headed by L. Berenzon, his deputies were A. Dorfman, the already mentioned Inzhir, Loevetsky, Kagner, Angert. And how many of the other humbler posts remain unmentioned? Is it really reasonable to suppose that Jews were digging soil with shovels and racing their hand-barrows and dying under those barrows from exhaustion and emaciation? Well, view it as you wish. A. P. Skripnikova and D. P. Vitkovsky, who were there, told me that Jews were overrepresented among *Idiots* during construction of Belomorcanal, and they did not roll barrows and did not die under them.

And you could find highly-placed Jewish commanders not only at BelBaltlag. Construction of the Kotlas-Vorkuta railroad was headed by Moroz (his son married Svetlana Stalina); the special officer-in-charge of GULag in the Far East was Grach. These are only a few of the names, which resurfaced accidentally. If a former inmate Thomas Sgovio, an American national, didn't write to me, I wouldn't be aware about the head of the Chai-Uryinsk Mining Administration on Kolyma between 1943-44 (at the depths of the Patriotic War): "Half-colonel Arm was a tall black-haired Jew with a terrible reputation... His orderly man was selling ethanol to everybody, 50 grams for 50 rubles. Arm had his own personal tutor of English – a young American, arrested in Karelia. His wife was paid a salary for an accountant's position, but she didn't work – her job was actually performed by an inmate in the office" (a common practice revealing how families of GULag commanders used to have additional incomes).

Or take another case: during the age of *glasnost*, one Soviet newspaper published a story about the dreadful GULag administration that built a tunnel between Sakhalin and the mainland. It was called the "Trust of

---

[2554] Подробнее о Френкеле — в «Архипелаге ГУЛаге».

Arais".[2555] Who was that comrade Arais? I have no idea. But how many perished in his mines and in the unfinished tunnel?

Sure, I knew a number of Jews (they were my friends) who carried all the hardships of common labor. In *Archipelago*, I described a young man, Boris Gammerov, who quickly found his death in the camp. (While his friend, the writer Ingal, was made an accountant from the very first day in the camp, although his knowledge of arithmetic was very poor.) I knew Volodya Gershuni, an irreconcilable and incorruptible man. I knew Jog Masamed, who did common labor in the hard labor camp at Ekibastuz *on principle*, though he was called upon to join the *Idiots*. Besides, I would like to list here a teacher Tatyana Moiseevna Falike, who spent 10 years drudging, she said, like a beast of burden. And I also would like to name here a geneticist Vladimir Efroimson, who spent 13 out of his 36 months of imprisonment (one out of his two terms) doing common labor. He also did it on principle, though he also had better options. Relying on parcels from home (one cannot blame him for that), he picked the hand-barrow precisely because there were many Jews from Moscow in that Jezkazgan camp, and they were used to settling well, while Efroimson wanted to dispel any grudge toward Jews, which was naturally emerging among inmates. And what did his brigade think about his behavior? – "He is a black sheep among Jews; would a real Jew roll a barrow?" He was similarly ridiculed by Jewish *Idiots* who felt annoyed that he "flaunted himself" to reproach them.

In the same vein, another Jew, Jacov Davydovich Grodzensky, who also *beavered in the common* category, was judged by others: "Is he really a Jew?" It is so symbolic! Both Efroimson and Grodzenskiy did those right and best things, which could be only motivated by the noblest of Jewish appeals, to honestly share the common lot, and they were not understood by either side!

They are always difficult and derided – the paths of austerity and dedication, the only ones that can save humanity.

I try not to overlook such examples, because all my hopes depend on them.

Let's add here a valiant Gersh Keller, one of the leaders of Kengir uprising in 1954 (he was 30 years old when executed). I also read about Yitzhak Kaganov, commander of an artillery squadron during the Soviet-German war. In 1948, he was sentenced to 25 years for Zionism. During 7 years of

---

[2555] Г. Миронова. Туннель в прошлое // Комсомольская правда, 1989, 18 апреля, с. 1.

imprisonment he wrote 480 pieces of poetry in Hebrew, which he memorized without writing them down.[2556]

During his third trial (July 10, 1978), after already serving two terms, Alexander Ginsburg, was asked a question "What is your nationality?" and replied: "Inmate!" That was a worthy and serious response, and it angered the tribunal. But he deserved it for his work for the Russian Public Relief Fund, which provided assistance to families of political prisoners of *all nationalities*, and by his manly vocation. This is what we are – a genuine breed of prisoners, regardless of nationality.

However, my camps were different, – spanning from the "great" Belomor to the tiny 121st camp district of the 15th OLP of Moscow's UITLK (which left behind a not inconspicuous semi-circular building at Kaluga's gate in Moscow).

Out there, our entire life was directed and trampled by three leading *Idiots*: Solomon Solomonov, a chief accountant; David Burstein, first an "educator" and later a work-assigning clerk; and Isaac Bershader. (Earlier, in exactly the same way, Solomonov and Bershader ruled over the camp at the Moscow Highway Institute, MHI.) Note that all this happened under auspices of a Russian camp commander, one ensign Mironov.

All three of them came up before my eyes, and to get positions for them, in each case their Russian predecessors were instantly removed from the posts.

Solomonov was sent in first; he confidently seized a proper position and quickly got on the right side of the ensign. (I think, using food and money from outside.) Soon after that the wretched Bershader was sent in from MHI with an accompanying note "to use him only in the common labor category" (a quite unusual situation for a domestic criminal, which probably meant substantial delinquency). He was about fifty years old, short, fat, with a baleful glare. He walked around condescendingly inspecting our living quarters, with the look of a general from the head department.

The senior proctor asked him: "What is your specialty?" – "Storekeeper". – "There is no such specialty" – "Well, I am a storekeeper". – "Anyway, you are going to work in the common labor brigade".

For two days he was sent there. Shrugging his shoulders, he went out, and, upon entering the work zone, he used to seat himself on a stone and rest respectably.

[2556] Российская Еврейская Энциклопедия. 2-е изд., испр. и доп. М.. 1994. Т. 1, с. 526-527; 1995. Т. 2. с. 27.

The brigadier would have hit him, but he quailed – the newcomer was so self-confident, that anyone could sense power behind him. The camp's storekeeper, Sevastyanov, was depressed as well. For two years he was in charge of the combined provision and sundry store. He was firmly established and lived on good terms with the brass, but now he was chilled: everything is already settled! Bershader is a "storekeeper by specialty"!

Then the medical unit discharged Bershader from the labor duties on grounds of "poor health" and after that he rested in the living quarters.

Meanwhile, he probably got something from outside. And within less than a week Sevastyanov was removed from his post, and Bershader was made a storekeeper (with the assistance of Solomonov). However, at this point it was found that the physical labor of pouring grain and rearranging boots, which was done by Sevastyanov single-handedly, was also contraindicated for Bershader.

So he was given a henchman, and Solomonov's bookkeeping office enlisted the latter as service personnel. But it was still not a sufficiently abundant life. The best looking proudest woman of the camp, the swan-like lieutenant-sniper M. was bent to his will and forced to visit him in his storeroom in the evenings.

After Burstein showed himself in the camp, he arranged to have another camp beauty, A. S., to come to his cubicle.

Is it difficult to read this? But they were by no means troubled how it looked from outside. It even seemed as if they thickened the impression on purpose. And how many such little camps with similar establishments were there all across the Archipelago?

And did Russian *Idiots* behave in the same way, unrestrained and insanely!? Yes. But within every other nation it was perceived socially, like an eternal strain between rich and poor, lord and servant. However, when an alien emerges as a "master over life and death" it further adds to the heavy resentment. It might appear strange – isn't it all the same for a worthless negligible, crushed, and doomed camp dweller surviving at one of his dying stages? isn't it all the same who exactly seizes the power inside the camp and celebrates crow's picnics over his trench-grave? As it turns out, it is not.

These things have been etched into my memory inerasably. In my play *Republic of Labor*, I presented some of the events that happened in that camp on Bolshaya Kaluzhskaya 30. Understanding the impossibility of depicting everything like it was in reality, because it would be inevitably considered as incitement of anti-Jewish sentiment (as if that trio of Jews was not inflaming it in real life, caring little about consequences) I withheld the abominably greedy Bershader. I concealed Burstein. I recomposed the profiteer Rosa Kalikman into an amorphous Bella of eastern origin, and retained the only Jew, accountant Solomonov, exactly like he was in life.

So, what about my loyal Jewish friends after they perused the play? The play aroused extraordinarily passionate protests from V. L. Teush. He read it not immediately but when Sovremennik had already decided to stage it in 1962, so the question was far from scholarly. The Teushes were deeply injured by the figure of Solomonov. They thought it was dishonest and unjust to show such a Jew (despite that in the real life, in the camp, he was exactly as I showed him) in the age of oppression of Jews. (But then, it appears to me that such age is *everlasting*? When have our Jews *not* been oppressed?) Teush was alarmed and extremely agitated, and put forward an ultimatum that if I did not remove or at least soften up the image of Solomonov, then all our friendship will be ruined and he and his wife will no longer be able to keep my manuscripts. Moreover, they prophesized that my very name will be irretrievably lost and blemished if I leave Solomonov in the play. Why not to make him a Russian? They were astonished. Is it so important that he be a Jew? (But if it doesn't matter, why did Solomonov select Jews to be *Idiots*?)

I took a chill pill: a sudden censorial ban, no less weighty than the official Soviet prohibition, had emerged from an unanticipated direction. However, the situation was soon resolved by the official prohibition forbidding Sovremennik to stage the piece.

And there was another objection from Teush: "Your Solomonov has anything but Jewish personality. A Jew always behaves discreetly, cautiously, suppliantly, and even cunningly, but from where comes this pushy impudence of jubilant force? This is not true, it cannot happen like this!"

However, I remember not this Solomonov alone, and it was exactly like that! I saw many things in the 1920's and 1930's in Rostov-on-Don. And Frenkel acted similarly, according to the recollections of surviving engineers.

Such a slip of a triumphant power into insolence and arrogance is the most repelling thing for those around. Sure, it is usually behavior of the worst and rudest – but this is what becomes imprinted in memory. (Likewise the Russian image is soiled by the obscenities of our villains.)

All these blandishments and appeals to avoid writing about the things like they were – are undistinguishable from what we heard from the highest Soviet tribunes: about anti-defamation, about socialist realism – to write like it should be, not like it was.

As if a creator is capable of forgetting or creating his past anew! As if the full truth can be written in parts, including only what is pleasing, secure and popular.

And how meticulously all the Jewish characters in my books were analyzed with every personal feature weighted on apothecary scales. But the astonishing story of Grigory M., who did not deliver the order to retreat to a dying regiment because he was frightened (*Archipelago GULag*, v. 6, Ch. 6) – was not noticed.

It was passed over without a single word! And *Ivan Denisovich* added insult to injury: there were such sophisticated sufferers but I put forward a boor!

For instance, during Gorbachev's *glasnost*, emboldened Asir Sandler published his camp memoirs. "After first perusal, I emphatically rejected *One Day In The Life Of Ivan Denisovich*... the main personage was Ivan Denisovich, a man with minimal spiritual needs, focused only on his mundane troubles" – and Solzhenitsyn turned him into the national image... (Exactly like all well-meaning communists were grumbling at that time!) While "[Solzhenitsyn] preferred not to notice the true intelligentsia, the determinant of domestic culture and science". Sandler was discussing this with Miron Markovich Etlis (both used to be *Idiots* in medical unit). And Etlis added: "The story is significantly distorted, placed upside down". "Solzhenitsyn failed to emphasize ...the intelligent part of our contingent"... Self-centered reflections [of Ivan Denisovich] about himself... that patience... that pseudo-Christian attitude toward others". And in 1964 Sandler was lucky to relieve his feelings in conversation with Ehrenburg himself. And the latter affirmatively nodded when Sandler mentioned his "extremely negative" feeling toward my novelette.[2557]

However, not a single Jew reproached me that Ivan Denisovich, in essence, attends to Cesar Markovich as a servant, albeit with good feelings.

[2557] Асир Сандлер. Узелки на память: Записки реабилитированного. Магаданское книжн. изд-во. 1988, с. 22. 62-64.

Chapter 21

During the Soviet-German War

After Kristallnacht (November 1938) the German Jews lost their last illusions about the mortal danger they were facing. With Hitler's campaign in Poland, the deadly storm headed East. Yet nobody expected that the beginning of the Soviet-German War would move Nazi politics to a new level, toward total physical extermination of Jews.

While they naturally expected all kinds of hardship from the German conquest, Soviet Jews could not envision the indiscriminate mass killings of men and women of all ages – one cannot foresee such things. Thus the terrible and inescapable fate befell those who remained in the German-occupied territories without a chance to resist. Lives ended abruptly. But before their death, they had to pass through either initial forced relocation to a Jewish ghetto, or a forced labor camp, or to gas vans, or through digging one's own grave and stripping before execution.

The Russian Jewish Encyclopedia gives many names of the Russian Jews who fell victims to the Jewish Catastrophe; it names those who perished in Rostov, Simferopol, Odessa, Minsk, Belostok, Kaunas, and Narva. There were prominent people among them. The famous historian S.M. Dubnov spent the entire inter-war period in exile. He left Berlin for Riga after Hitler took power.

He was arrested during the German occupation and placed in a ghetto; "in December 1941 he was included into a column of those to be executed"."From Vilna, historian Dina Joffe and director of the Jewish Gymnasium Joseph Yashunskiy were sent to concentration camps (both were killed in Treblinka in 1943). Rabbi Shmuel Bespalov, head of the Hasidim movement in Bobruisk, was shot in 1941 when the city was captured by the Germans. Cantor Gershon Sirota, whose performance had once "caught the attention of Nicholas II" and who performed yearly in St. Petersburg and Moscow, died in 1941 in Warsaw.

There were two brothers Paul and Vladimir Mintz: Paul, the elder, was a prominent Latvian politician, "the only Jew in the government of Latvia".

Vladimir was a surgeon, who had been entrusted with the treatment of Lenin in 1918 after the assassination attempt. From 1920 he lived in Latvia. In 1940 the Soviet occupation authorities arrested Paul Mintz and placed him in a camp in Krasnoyarsk Krai, where he died early on. The younger brother lived in Riga and was not touched. He died in 1945 at Büchenwald. Sabina Shpilreyn, a doctor of medicine, psychoanalyst and a close colleague of Carl Jung, returned to Russia in 1923 after working in clinics in Zurich, Munich, Berlin and Geneva; in 1942 she was shot along with other Jews by Germans in her native Rostov-on-Don. (In Chapter 19, we wrote about the deaths of her three scientist brothers during Stalin's terror.)

Yet many were saved from death by evacuation in 1941 and 1942. Various Jewish wartime and postwar sources do not doubt the dynamism of this evacuation. For example, in *The Jewish World*, a book written in 1944, one can read: "The Soviet authorities were fully aware that the Jews were the most endangered part of the population, and despite the acute military needs in transport, thousands of trains were provided for their evacuation. ... In many cities ... Jews were evacuated first", although the author believes that the statement of the Jewish writer David Bergelson that "approximately 80% of Jews were successfully evacuated" [2558] is an exaggeration. Bergelson wrote: "In Chernigov, the pre-war Jewish population was estimated at 70,000 people and only 10,000 of them remained by the time the Germans arrived. ... In Dnepropetrovsk, out of the original Jewish population of 100,000 only 30,000 remained when the Germans took the city. In Zhitomir, out of 50,000 Jews, no less than 44,000 left."[2559] In the Summer 1946 issue of the bulletin, *Hayasa* E.M. Kulisher wrote: "There is no doubt that the Soviet authorities took special measures to evacuate the Jewish population or to facilitate its unassisted flight.

Along with the state personnel and industrial workers, Jews were given priority [in the evacuation] ... The Soviet authorities provided thousands of trains specifically for the evacuation of Jews." [2560] Also, as a safer measure to avoid bombing raids, Jews were evacuated by thousands of haywagons, taken from kolkhozes and sovkhozes [collective farms] and driven over to railway junctions in the rear. B.T. Goldberg, a son-in-law of

---

[2558] И. Шехтман. Советское еврейство в германо-советской войне // Еврейский мир: Сб. 2 (далее — ЕМ-2). Нью-Йорк: Союз русских евреев в Нью-Йорке, 1944. с. 225-226.

[2559] А.А. Гольдштейн. Судьба евреев в оккупированной немцами Советской России // Книга о русском еврействе. 1917-1967 (далее — КРЕ-2). Нью-Йорк: Союз Русских Евреев, 1968, с. 89, 92.

[2560] Rescue: Information Bulletin of the Hebrew Sheltering and Immigrant Aid Society (HIAS), July-August 1946 (Vol. Ill, № 7-8), p. 2. — Цит. по: С. Шварц. Евреи в Советском Союзе с начала Второй мировой войны (1939-1965). Нью-Йорк: Изд. Американского Еврейского Рабочего Комитета, 1966, с. 45.

Sholem Aleichem and then a correspondent for the Jewish newspaper *Der Tog* from New York, after a 1946-1947 winter trip to the Soviet Union wrote an article about the wartime evacuation of Jews (*Der Tog*, February 21, 1947). His sources in Ukraine, "Jews and Christians, the military and evacuees, all stated that the policy of the authorities was to give the Jews a preference during evacuation, to save as many of them as possible so that the Nazis would not destroy them."[2561] And Moshe Kaganovich, a former Soviet partisan, in his by then foreign memoirs (1948) confirms that the Soviet government provided for the evacuation of Jews all available vehicles in addition to trains, including trains of haywagons – and the orders were to evacuate "first and foremost the citizens of Jewish nationality from the areas threatened by the enemy".(Note that S. Schwartz and later researchers dispute the existence of such orders, as well as the general policy of Soviet authorities to evacuate Jews "as such."[2562])

Nevertheless, both earlier and later sources provide fairly consistent estimates of the number of Jews who were evacuated or fled without assistance from the German-occupied territories. Official Soviet figures are not available; all researchers complain that the contemporaneous statistics are at best approximate. Let us rely then on the works of the last decade. A demographer M. Kupovetskiy, who used formerly unavailable archival materials and novel techniques of analysis, offers the following assessment. According to the 1939 census, 3,028,538 Jews lived in the USSR within its old (that is, pre-1939-1940) boundaries. With some corrections to this figure and taking into account the rate of natural increase of the Jewish population from September 1939 to June 1941 (he analyzed each territory separately), this researcher suggests that at the outbreak of the war approximately 3,080,000 Jews resided within the old USSR borders. Of these, 900,000 resided in the territories which would not be occupied by Germans, and at the beginning of the war 2,180, 000 Jews ("Eastern Jews")[2563] resided in the territories later occupied by the Germans.

"There is no exact data regarding the number of Jews who fled or were evacuated to the East before the German occupation. Though based on some studies ..., we know that approximately 1,000,000 -1,100,000 Jews

---

[2561] *С. Шварц.* Евреи в Советском Союзе...*, с. 55.
[2562] *Моше Каганович.* Дер идишер онтайл ин партизанербавегунг фун Совет-Руссланд. Рим, 1948, с. 188. — Цит. по: *С. Шварц.* Советском Союзе..., с. 45-46.
[2563] *М. Куповецкий.* Людские потери еврейского населения в послевоенных границах СССР в годы Великой Отечественной войны // Вестник Еврейского Университета в Москве. 1995, № 2(9), с. 137, 145, 151.

managed to escape from the Eastern regions later occupied by Germans".[2564]

There was a different situation in the territories incorporated into the Soviet Union only in 1939-1940, and which were rapidly captured by the Germans at the start of the "Blitzkreig". The lightning-speed German attack allowed almost no chance for escape; meanwhile the Jewish population of these "buffer" zones numbered 1,885,000 ("Western Jews") in June 1941.[2565] And "only a small number of these Jews managed to escape or were evacuated. It is believed that the number is ... about 10-12 percent."[2566]

Thus, within the new borders of the USSR, by the most optimistic assessments, approximately 2,226,000 Jews (2,000,000 Eastern, 226,000 Western Jews) escaped the German occupation and 2,739,000 Jews (1,080,000 Easterners and 1,659,000 Westerners) remained in the occupied territories.

Evacuees and refugees from the occupied and threatened territories were sent deep into the rear, "with the majority of Jews resettled beyond the Ural Mountains, in particular in Western Siberia and also in Kazakhstan, Uzbekistan and Turkmenistan".[2567] The materials of the Jewish Anti-Fascist Committee (EAK) contain the following statement: "At the beginning of the Patriotic War about one and half million Jews were evacuated to Uzbekistan, Kazakhstan and other Central Asian Republics."[2568] This figure does not include the Volga, the Ural and the Siberian regions. (However, the *Jewish Encyclopedia* argues that "a 1,500,000 figure" is a great exaggeration."[2569]) Still, there was no organized evacuation into Birobidzhan, and no individual refugees relocated there, although, because of the collapse of Jewish kolkhozes, the vacated housing there could accommodate up to 11,000 families.[2570] At the same time, "the Jewish colonists in the Crimea were evacuated so much ahead of time that they were able to take with them all livestock and farm implements"; moreover, "it is well-known that in the spring of 1942, Jewish colonists from Ukraine established kolkhozes in the Volga region"

[2564] *Ицхак Арад.* Холокауст: Катастрофа европейского еврейства (1933-1945): Сб. статей. Иерусалим: Яд Ва-Шем, 1990 (далее — И. Арад. Холокауст), с. 62.
[2565] М. *Куповецкий.* Людские потери еврейского населения... // Вестник Еврейского Ун-та..., 1995, № 2(9), с. 145.
[2566] *И. Арад.* Холокауст, с. 61.
[2567] *С. Шварц.* Евреи в Советском Союзе..., с. 181.
[2568] *Г.В. Костырченко.* Тайная политика Сталина: Власть и антисемитизм*. М.: Международные отношения, 2001, с. 431.
[2569] Краткая Еврейская Энциклопедия (далее — КЕЭ). Иерусалим: Общество по исследованию еврейских общин, 1988. Т. 4, с. 167.
[2570] *С.М. Шварц.* Биробиджан // КРЕ-2, с. 187.

How? Well, the author calls it the "irony of Nemesis": they were installed in place of German colonists who were exiled from the German Republic of the Volga by Soviet government order starting on August 28, 1941.[2571]

As already noted, all the cited wartime and postwar sources agree in recognizing the energy and the scale of the organized evacuation of Jews from the advancing German army. But the later sources, from the end of the 1940s, began to challenge this. For example, we read in a 1960s source: "*a planned evacuation of Jews as the most endangered part of the population did not take place anywhere in Russia*" (italicized as in the source).[2572] And twenty years later we read this: after the German invasion of the Soviet Union, "contrary to the rumors that the government allegedly evacuated Jews from the areas under imminent threat of German occupation, no such measures had ever taken place… the Jews were abandoned to their fate. When applied to the citizen of Jewish nationality, the celebrated 'proletarian internationalism' was a dead letter".[2573]

This statement is completely unfair. Still, even those Jewish writers, who deny the "beneficence" of the government with respect to Jewish evacuation, do recognize its magnitude.

"Due to the specific social structure of the Jewish population, the percentage of Jews among the evacuees should have been much higher than the percentage of Jews in the urban population".[2574] And indeed it was. The Evacuation Council was established on June 24, 1941, just two days after the German invasion (Shvernik was the chairman and Kosygin and Pervukhin were his deputies).Its priorities were announced as the following: to evacuate first and foremost the state and party agencies with personnel, industries, and raw materials along with the workers of evacuated plants and their families, and young people of conscription age. Between the beginning of the war and November 1941, around 12 million people were evacuated from the threatened areas to the rear.[2575] This number included, as we have seen, 1,000,000 to 1,100,000 Eastern Jews and more than 200,000 Western Jews from the soon-to-be-occupied areas.

In addition, we must add to this figure a substantial number of Jews among the people evacuated from the cities and regions of the Russian Soviet Federated Socialist Republic (RSFSR, that is, Russia proper) that never fell

---

[2571] *И. Шехтман*. Советское еврейство в германо-советской войне // ЕМ-2, с. 226, 227.
[2572] *Г. Аронсон*. Еврейский вопрос в эпоху Сталина // КРЕ-2, с. 144.
[2573] *С. Цирюльников*. СССР, евреи и Израиль // Время и мы: Международный журнал литературы и общественных проблем. Нью-Йорк, 1987, № 96, с. 151-152.
[2574] *И. Шехтман*. Советское еврейство в германо-советской войне // ЕМ-2, с. 224.
[2575] Советский тыл в первый период Великой Отечественной войны: [Сб.]. М., 1988, с. 139.

to the Germans (in particular, those from Moscow and Leningrad). Solomon Schwartz states: "The general evacuation of state agencies and industrial enterprises with a significant portion of their staff (often with families) was in many places very extensive. Thanks to the social structure of Ukrainian Jewry with a significant percentages of Jews among the middle and top civil servants, including the academic and technical intelligentsia and the substantial proportion of Jewish workers in Ukrainian heavy industry, the share of Jews among the evacuees was larger than their share in the urban (and even more than in the total) population."[2576]

The same was true for Byelorussia. In the 1920s and early 1930s it was almost exclusively Jews, both young and old, who studied at "various courses, literacy classes, in day schools, evening schools and shift schools. ... This enabled the poor from Jewish villages to join the ranks of industrial workers.

Constituting only 8.9% of the population of Byelorussia, Jews accounted for 36% of the industrial workers of the republic in 1930."[2577]

"The rise of the percentage of Jews among the evacuees", continues S. Schwartz, "was also facilitated by the fact that for many employees and workers the evacuation was not mandatory. ... Therefore, many, mostly non-Jews, remained were they were." Thus, even the Jews, "who did not fit the criteria for mandatory evacuation ... had better chances to evacuate".[2578] However, the author also notes that "no government orders or instructions on the evacuation specifically of Jews or reports about it ever appeared in the Soviet press".

"There simply were no orders regarding the evacuation of Jews specifically. It means that there was no purposeful evacuation of Jews."[2579]

Keeping in mind the Soviet reality, this conclusion seems ill grounded and, in any case, formalistic. Indeed, reports about mass evacuation of the Jews did not appear in the Soviet press. It is easy to understand why. First, after the pact with Germany, the Soviet Union suppressed information about Hitler's policies towards Jews, and when the war broke out, the bulk of the Soviet population did not know about the mortal danger the German invasion posed for Jews.

Second, and this was probably the more-important factor – German propaganda vigorously denounced "Judeo-Bolshevism" and the Soviet

---

[2576] *С. Шварц*. Евреи в Советском Союзе..., с. 53.
[2577] *Л.Л. Мининберг*. Советские евреи в науке и промышленности СССР в период Второй мировой войны (1941 -1945). М., 1995, с. 13.
[2578] *С. Шварц*. Евреи в Советском Союзе..., с. 53.
[2579] Там же, с. 46, 53.

leadership undoubtedly realized that they gave a solid foundation to this propaganda during the 1920s and 1930s, so how could they now declare openly and loudly that the *foremost* government priority must be to save Jews? This could only have been seen as playing into Hitler's hands.

Therefore, there were no public announcements that among the evacuees "Jews were over-represented". "The evacuation orders did not mention Jews", yet "during the evacuation the Jews were not discriminated" against;[2580] on the contrary they were evacuated by all available means, but in silence, without press coverage inside the USSR. However, propaganda for foreign consumption was a different matter. For example, in December 1941, after repulsing the German onslaught on Moscow, Radio Moscow – not in the Russian language, of course, but "in Polish", and on "the next day, five more times in German, compared the successful Russian winter counteroffensive with the Maccabean miracle" and told the German-speaking listeners repeatedly that "precisely during Hanukkah week", the 134th Nuremberg Division, named after the city "where the racial legislation originated" was destroyed.[2581] In 1941- 42 the Soviet authorities readily permitted worshippers to overfill synagogues in Moscow, Leningrad, and Kharkov and to openly celebrate the Jewish Passover of 1942.[2582]

We cannot say that the domestic Soviet press treated German atrocities with silence. Ilya Ehrenburg and others (like the journalist Kriger) got the go-ahead to maintain and inflame hatred towards Germans throughout the entire war and not without mentioning the burning topic of Jewish suffering, yet without a special stress on it. Throughout the war Ehrenburg thundered, that "the German is a beast by his nature", calling for "not sparing even unborn Fascists" (meaning the murder of pregnant German women), and he was checked only at the very end, when the war reached the territory of Germany and it became clear that the Army had embraced only too well the party line of unbridled revenge against all Germans.

However these is no doubt that the Nazi policy of extermination of the Jews, its predetermination and scope, was not sufficiently covered by the Soviet press, so that even the Jewish masses in the Soviet Union could hardly realize the extent of their danger. Indeed, during the entire war, there were few public statements about the fate of Jews under German occupation. Stalin in his speech on Nov. 6, 1941 (the 24th anniversary of the October Revolution) said: "The Nazis are ... as eager to organize

---

[2580] *Н. Арад*. Отношение советского руководства к Холокосту // Вестник Еврейского Ун-та..., 1995, № 2(9), с. 23.
[2581] *И. Шехтман*. Советское еврейство в германо-советской войне // ЕМ-2, с. 238.
[2582] Там же, с. 237.

medieval Jewish pogroms as the Tsarist regime was. The Nazi Party is the party ... of medieval reaction and the Black-Hundred pogroms."[2583] "As far as we know", an Israeli historian writes, "it was the only case during the entire war when Stalin publicly mentioned the Jews".[2584] On January 6, 1942, in a note of the Narkomindel [People's Commissariat of Foreign Affairs] composed by Molotov and addressed to all states that maintained diplomatic relations with the Soviet Union, the Jews are mentioned as one of many suffering Soviet nationalities, and shootings of Jews in Kiev, Lvov, Odessa, Kamenetz-Podolsk, Dnepropetrovsk, Mariupol, Kerch were highlighted and the numbers of victims listed. "The terrible massacre and pogroms were inflicted by German invaders in Kiev, the capital of Ukraine. A significant number of Jews, including women and children, were rounded up; before the execution all of them were stripped naked and beaten and then ... shot by sub-machine guns. Many mass murders occurred ... in other Ukrainian cities, and these bloody executions were directed in particular against unarmed and defenseless Jews from the working class."[2585] On December 19, 1942, the Soviet government issued a declaration that mentioned Hitler's "special plan for total extermination of the Jewish population in the occupied territories of Europe" and in Germany itself; "although relatively small, the Jewish minority of the Soviet population ... suffered particularly hard from the savage bloodthirstiness of the Nazi monsters". But some sources point out that this declaration was somewhat forced; it came out two days after a similar declaration was made by the western Allies, and it was not republished in the Soviet press as was always done during newspaper campaigns. In 1943, out of seven reports of the Extraordinary State Commission for investigation of Nazi atrocities (such as extermination of Soviet prisoners of war and the destruction of cultural artifacts of our country), only one report referred to murders of Jews – in the Stavropol region, near Mineralnye Vody.[2586] And in March 1944 in Kiev, while making a speech about the suffering endured by Ukrainians under occupation, Khrushchev *"did not mention Jews at all"*.[2587]

Probably this is true. Indeed, the Soviet masses did not realize the scale of the Jewish Catastrophe. Overall, this was our common fate – to live under the impenetrable shell of the USSR and be ignorant of what was happening

---

[2583] Доклад Председателя Государственного Комитета Обороны тов. И.В. Сталина на торжественном заседании Московского Совета депутатов трудящихся 6 ноября 1941 года // Правда, 1941, 7 ноября, с. 1-2.
[2584] *И. Арад.* Отношение советского руководства к Холокосту // Вестник Еврейского Ун-та..., 1995, № 2(9), с. 17.
[2585] Известия, 1942, 7 января, с. 1-2.
[2586] *С. Шварц.* Евреи в Советском Союзе...*, с. 138-145.
[2587] *Г. Аронсон.* Еврейский вопрос в эпоху Сталина // КРЕ-2, с. 146.

in the outside world. However, Soviet Jews could not be all that unaware about the events in Germany. "In the mid-thirties the Soviet Press wrote a lot about German anti-Semitism... A novel by Leon Feichtwanger *The Oppenheim Family* and the movie based on the book, as well as another movie, *Professor Mamlock,* clearly demonstrated the dangers that Jews were facing."[2588]

Following the pogroms of Kristallnacht, *Pravda* published an editorial "The Fascist Butchers and Cannibals" in which it strongly condemned the Nazis: "The whole civilized world watches with disgust and indignation the vicious massacre of the defenseless Jewish population by German fascists. ... [With the same feelings] the Soviet people watch the dirty and bloody events in Germany.

... In the Soviet Union, along with the capitalists and landowners, all sources of anti-Semitism had been wiped out."[2589] Then, throughout the whole November, *Pravda* printed daily on its front pages reports such as "Jewish pogroms in Germany", "Beastly vengeance on Jews", "The wave of protests around the world against the atrocities of the fascist thugs". Protest rallies against anti-Jewish policies of Hitler were held in Moscow, Leningrad, Kiev, Tbilisi, Minsk, Sverdlovsk, and Stalin. *Pravda* published a detailed account of the town hall meeting of the Moscow intelligentsia in the Great Hall of the Conservatory, with speeches given by A.N. Tolstoy, A. Korneychuk, L. Sobolev; People's Artists [a Soviet title signifying prominence in the Arts] A.B. Goldenweiser and S.M. Mikhoels, and also the text of a resolution adopted at the meeting: "We, the representatives of the Moscow intelligentsia ... raise our voice in outrage and condemnation against the Nazi atrocities and inhuman acts of violence against the defenseless Jewish population of Germany. The fascists beat up, maim, rape, kill and burn alive in broad daylight people who are guilty only of belonging to the Jewish nation."[2590] The next day, on November 29, under the headline "Soviet intelligentsia is outraged by Jewish pogroms in Germany", *Pravda* produced the full coverage of rallies in other Soviet cities.

However, from the moment of the signing of the Ribbentrop-Molotov Pact in August of 1939, not only criticism of Nazi policies but also any information about persecution of the Jews in European countries under German control vanished from the Soviet press. "A lot of messages ... were

---

[2588] *С. Швейбиш*. Эвакуация и советские евреи в годы Катастрофы // Вестник Еврейского Ун-та..., 1995, № 2(9), с. 47.
[2589] Правда, 1938, 18 ноября, с. 1.
[2590] Правда, 1938, 28 ноября, с. 2-3.

reaching the Soviet Union through various channels – intelligence, embassies, Soviet journalists. ...

An important source of information... was Jewish refugees who managed to cross the Soviet border. However, the Soviet media, including the Jewish press, maintained silence."[2591]

"When the Soviet-German War started and the topic of Nazi anti-Semitism was raised again, many Jews considered it to be propaganda", argues a modern scholar, relying on the testimonies of the Catastrophe survivors, gathered over a half of century. "Many Jews relied on their own life experience rather than on radio, books and newspapers. The image of Germans did not change in the minds of most Jews since WWI. And back then the Jews considered the German regime to be one of the most tolerant to them."[2592] "Many Jews remembered, that during the German occupation in 1918, the Germans treated Jews better than they treated the rest of the local population, and so the Jews were reassured."[2593] As a result, "in 1941, a significant number of Jews remained in the occupied territories voluntarily". And even in 1942, "according to the stories of witnesses... the Jews in Voronezh, Rostov, Krasnodar, and other cities waited for the front to roll through their city and hoped to continue their work as doctors and teachers, tailors and cobblers, which they believed were always needed.... The Jews could not or would not evacuate for purely material reasons as well."[2594]

While the Soviet press and radio censored the information about the atrocities committed by the occupiers against the Jews, the Yiddish newspaper *Einigkeit* ("Unity"), the official publication of the Jewish Anti-Fascist Committee (EAK), was allowed to write about it openly from the summer of 1942. Apparently, the first step in the establishment of EAK was a radio-meeting in August 1941 of "representatives of the Jewish people" (S. Mikhoels, P. Marques, J. Ohrenburg, S. Marshak, S. Eisenstein and other celebrities participated.) For propaganda purposes, it was broadcast to the US and other Allied countries. "The effect on the Western public surpassed the most optimistic expectations of Moscow. ... In the Allied countries the Jewish organizations sprang up to raise funds for the needs of the Red Army." Their success prompted the Kremlin to establish a permanent Jewish Committee in the Soviet Union. "Thus began the

---

[2591] И. Арад. Отношение советского руководства к Холокосту // Вестник Еврейского Ун-та..., 1995, № 2(9), с. 15-16.
[2592] С. Швейбиш. Эвакуация и советские евреи в годы Катастрофы // Вестник Еврейского Ун-та..., 1995, № 2(9), с. 47-48.
[2593] КЕЭ, т. 8, с. 223.
[2594] Там же, с. 49.

seven-year-long cooperation of the Soviet authorities with global Zionism."[2595]

The development of the Committee was a difficult process, heavily dependent on the attitudes of government. In September 1941, an influential former member of the Bund, Henryk Ehrlich, was released from the prison to lead that organization. In 1917, Ehrlich had been a member of the notorious and then omnipotent Executive Committee of the Petrosoviet. Later, he emigrated to Poland where he was captured by the Soviets in 1939. He and his comrade, Alter, who also used to be a member of the Bund and was also a native of Poland, began preparing a project that aimed to mobilize international Jewish opinion, with heavier participation of foreign rather than Soviet Jews. "Polish Bund members were intoxicated by their freedom... and increasingly acted audaciously. Evacuated to Kuibyshev [Samara] along with the metropolitan bureaucracy, they contacted Western diplomatic representatives, who were relocated there as well,... suggesting, in particular, to form a Jewish Legion in the USA to fight on the Soviet-German front". "The things have gone so far that the members of the Polish Bund ... began planning a trip to the West on their own". In addition, both Bund activists "presumptuously assumed (and did not hide it) that they could liberally reform the Soviet political system". In December 1941, both overreaching leaders of the Committee were arrested (Ehrlich hanged himself in prison; Alter was shot).[2596]

Yet during the spring of 1942, the project of the Jewish Anti-Fascist Committee was revived, and a meeting "of the representatives of Jewish people" was called forth again. A Committee was elected, although this time exclusively from Soviet Jews. Solomon Mikhoels became its Chairman and Shakhno Epstein, "Stalin's eye in Jewish affairsánd a former fanatical Bundist and later a fanatical Chekist, became its Executive Secretary". Among others, its members were authors David Bergelson, Peretz Markish, Leib Kvitko, and Der Nistor; scientists Lina Shtern and Frumkin, a member of the Academy. Poet Itzik Fefer became the Vice President.[2597] (The latter was a former Trotskyite who was pardoned because he composed odes dedicated to Stalin; he was "an important NKVD agent", and, as a "proven secret agent", he was entrusted with a trip to the West.[2598]) The task of this Committee was the same: to influence international public opinion, and "to appeal to the 'Jews all over the world'

[2595] *В. Костырченко*. Тайная политика Сталина, с. 231.
[2596] *Г.В. Костырченко*. Тайная политика Сталина, с. 233-235.
[2597] *Г. Аронсон*. Еврейский вопрос в эпоху Сталина // КРЕ-2, с. 148.
[2598] *Павел Судоплатов*. Спецоперации: Лубянка и Кремль: 1930-1950 годы. М.: ОЛМА-Пресс, 1997, с. 465, 470.

but in practice it appealed primarily to the American Jews", [2599] building up sympathy and raising financial aid for the Soviet Union. (And it was the main reason for Mikhoels' and Fefer's trip to the United States in summer 1943, which coincided with the dissolution of Comintern. It was a roaring success, triggering rallies in 14 cities across the US: 50,000 people rallied in New York City alone. Mikhoels and Fefer were received by former Zionist leader Chaim Weizmann and by Albert Einstein.[2600]) Yet behind the scenes the Committee was managed by Lozovskiy-Dridzo, the Deputy Head of the Soviet Information Bureau (Sovinformbureau); the Committee did not have offices in the Soviet Union and could not act independently; in fact, it was "not so much a fundraising tool for the Red Army as an arm of ... pro-Soviet propaganda abroad."[2601]

Some Jewish authors argue that from the late 1930s there was a covert but persistent removal of Jews from the highest ranks of Soviet leadership in all spheres of administration. For instance, D. Shub writes that by 1943 not a single Jew remained among the top leadership of the NKVD, though "there were still many Jews in the Commissariat of Trade, Industry and Foods. There were also quite a few Jews in the Commissariat of Public Education and in the Foreign Office."[2602] A modern researcher reaches a different conclusion based on archival materials that became available in 1990s: "During the 1940s, the role of Jews in punitive organs remained highly visible, coming to the end only in the postwar years during the campaign against cosmopolitanism."[2603]

However, there are no differences of opinion regarding the relatively large numbers of Jews in the top command positions in the Army. The *Jewish World* reported that "in the Red Army now [during the war], there are over a hundred Jewish generals" and it provided a "small randomly picked list of such generals", not including "generals from the infantry". There were 17 names (ironically, "Major-General of Engineering Service Frenkel Naftaliy Aronovich" of GULag was also included).[2604] A quarter of a century later, another collection of documents confirmed that there were no less than a hundred Jewish generals in the middle of the war and provided additional names.[2605] (However, the volume unfortunately omitted the "Super-General" Lev Mekhlis – the closest and most trusted of

---

[2599] *С. Шварц.* Евреи в Советском Союзе..., с. 239.
[2600] *Г.В. Костырченко.* Тайная политика Сталина, с. 237-239.
[2601] *С. Шварц.* Евреи в Советском Союзе..., с. 166-170.
[2602] *Д. Шуб.* Евреи в русской революции // ЕМ-2, с. 145.
[2603] *Л.Ю. Кричевский.* Евреи в аппарате ВЧК-ОГПУ в 20-е годы // Евреи и русская революция: Материалы и исследования / Ред.-сост. О.В. Будницкий. Москва; Иерусалим: Гешарим, 1999, с. 344.
[2604] *Е. Сталинский.* Евреи в Красной армии // ЕМ-2, с. 243-245.
[2605] *Г. Аронсон.* Еврейский вопрос в эпоху Сталина //КРЕ-2, с. 143.

Stalin's henchmen from 1937 to 1940; from 1941 he was the Head of Political Administration of the Red Army. Ten days after the start of the war, Mekhlis arrested a dozen of the highest generals of the Western Front.[2606] He is also infamous for his punitive measures during the Soviet-Finnish War and then later at Kerch in the Crimea.)

The Short Jewish Encyclopedia provides an additional list of fifteen Jewish generals. Recently, an Israeli researcher has published a list of Jewish generals and admirals (including those who obtained the rank during the war).

Altogether, there were 270 generals and admirals! This is not only "not a few" – this is an immense number indeed. He also notes four wartime narkoms (people's commissars): in addition to Kaganovich, these were Boris Vannikov (ammunition), Semien Ginzburg (construction), Isaac Zaltzman (tank industry) and several heads of main military administrations of the Red Army; the list also contains the names of four Jewish army commanders, commanders of 23 corps, 72 divisions, and 103 brigades.[2607]

"In no army of the Allies, not even in the USA's, did Jews occupy such high positions, as in the Soviet Army", Dr. I. Arad writes.[2608] No, "the displacement of Jews from the top posts" during the war did not happen. Nor had any supplanting yet manifested itself in general aspects of Soviet life. In 1944 (in the USA) a famous Socialist Mark Vishnyak stated that "not even hardcore enemies of the USSR can say that its government cultivates anti-Semitism".[2609] *Back then* – it was undoubtedly true.

According to *Einigkeit* (from February 24, 1945, almost at the end of the war), "for courage and heroism in combat"... 63,374 Jews were awarded orders and medals", and 59 Jews became the Heroes of the Soviet Union. According to the Warsaw Yiddish language newspaper *Volksstimme* in 1963 the number of the Jews awarded military decorations in WWII was 160,772, with 108 Heroes of the Soviet Union among them.[2610] In the early 1990s, an Israeli author provided a list of names with dates of confirmation, in which 135 Jews are listed as Heroes of the Soviet Union and 12 Jews are listed as the full chevaliers of the Order of Glory.[2611] We find similar

---

[2606] В. Анфилов. Как «оправдался» Сталин // Родина, 1991, № 6-7, с. 31; Российская Еврейская Энциклопедия (далее — РЕЭ). 2-е изд., испр. и доп. М., 1995. Т. 2, с. 276-277.

[2607] Арон Абрамович. В решающей войне: Участие и роль евреев СССР в войне против нацизма. Тель-Авив, 1992. Т. 2, с. 536-578.

[2608] И. Арад. Холокауст, с. 93.

[2609] М. Вишняк. Международная конвенция против антисемитизма // ЕМ-2, с. 98.

[2610] Г. Аронсон. Еврейский вопрос в эпоху Сталина // КРЕ-2, с. 143.

[2611] А. Абрамович. В решающей войне. Т. 2, с. 548-555.

information in the three-volume *Essays on Jewish Heroism*.[2612] And finally, the latest archival research (2001) provides the following figures: "throughout the war 123,822 Jews were awarded military decorations";[2613] thus, among all nationalities of the Soviet Union, the Jews are in fifth place among the recipients of decorations, after Russians, Ukrainians, Byelorussians and Tatars.

I. Arad states that "anti-Semitism as an obstacle for Jews in their military careers, in promotion to higher military ranks and insignia did not exist in the Soviet Army during the war".[2614] Production on the home front for the needs of the war was also highly rewarded. A huge influx of Soviet Jews into science and technology during the 1930s had borne its fruit during the war. Many Jews worked on the design of new types of armaments and instrumentation, in the manufacturing of warplanes, tanks, and ships, in scientific research, construction and development of industrial enterprises, in power engineering, metallurgy, and transport. For their work from 1941 to 1945 in support of the front, 180,000 Jews were awarded decorations. Among them were scientists, engineers, administrators of various managerial levels and workers, including more than two hundred who were awarded the Order of Lenin; nearly three hundred Jews were awarded the Stalin Prize in science and technology. During the war, 12 Jews became Heroes of Socialist Labor, eight Jews became full members of the Academy of Science in physics and mathematics, chemistry and technology, and thirteen became Member-Correspondents of the Academy.[2615]

Many authors, including S. Schwartz, note that "the role of Jews in the war was systematically concealed" along with a deliberate policy of "silence about the role of Jews in the war". He cites as a proof the works of prominent Soviet writers such as K. Simonov (*Days and Nights*) and V. Grossman (*The People Is Immortal*) where "among a vast number of surnames of soldiers, officers, political officers and others, there is not a single Jewish name."[2616] Of course, this was due to censoring restrictions, especially in case of Grossman. (Later, military personnel with Jewish names re-appeared in Grossman's essays.) Another author notes that postcards depicting a distinguished submarine commander, Israel

---

[2612] Очерки еврейского героизма: В 3 т. / Сост. Г.С. Шапиро, С.Л. Авербух. Киев; Тель-Авив, 1994-1997.

[2613] Г.В. *Костырченко*. Тайная политика Сталина, с. 245 (со ссылкой на бывш. Центральный партийный архив при ЦК КПСС, ныне РГАСПИ. Ф. 17, оп. 125, ед. хр. 127, л. 220).

[2614] И. Арад. Холокауст, с. 128.

[2615] Л.Л. *Мининберг*. Советские евреи в науке и промышленности..., с. 18, 444-445, 452, 474-475.

[2616] С. *Шварц*. Евреи в Советском Союзе..., с. 154-156.

Fisanovich, were sold widely throughout the Soviet Union.[2617] Later, such publications were extended; and an Israeli researcher lists another 12 Jews, Heroes of the Soviet Union, whose portraits were mass reproduced on postal envelopes.[2618]

Even through I'm a veteran of that war, I have not researched it through books much, nor was I collecting materials or have written anything about it.

But I saw Jews on the front. I knew brave men among them. For instance, I especially want to mention two fearless antitank fighters: one of them was my university friend Lieutenant Emanuel Mazin; another was young ex-student soldier Borya Gammerov (both were wounded in action). In my battery among 60 people two were Jews – Sergeant Ilya Solomin, who fought very well through the whole war, and Private Pugatch, who soon slipped away to the Political Department. Among twenty officers of our division one was a Jew – Major Arzon, the head of the supply department. Poet Boris Slutsky was a real soldier, he used to say: "I'm full of bullet holes". Major Lev Kopelev, even though he served in the Political Department of the Army (responsible for counter-propaganda aimed at enemy troops), he fearlessly threw himself in every possible fighting melee. A former "Mifliyetz" Semyon Freylih, a brave officer, remembers: "The war began .... So I was off to the draft board and joined the army" without graduating from the University, as "we felt ashamed not to share the hardships of millions".[2619] Or take Lazar Lazarev, later a well-known literary critic, who as a young man fought at the front for two years until both his hands were mauled: "It was our duty and we would have been ashamed to evade it. ... it was life – the only possible one under the circumstances, the only decent choice for the people of my age and education".[2620] Boris Izrailevich Feinerman wrote in 1989 in response to an article in *Book Review,* that as a 17-year-old, he volunteered in July 1941 for an infantry regiment; in October, his both legs were wounded and he was taken prisoner of war; he escaped and walked out of the enemy's encirclement on crutches – then of course he was imprisoned for 'treason'" – but in 1943 he managed to get out of the camp by joining a penal platoon; he fought there and later became a machine gunner of the assault infantry unit in a tank regiment and was wounded two more times.

[2617] *Е. Сталинский.* Евреи в Красной армии // ЕМ-2, с. 250.
[2618] *А. Абрамович.* В решающей войне. Т. 2, с. 562.
[2619] S. Freilikh, Istoriia odnogo boia... [Histoire d'un combat], Kinostsenarii [Scénarios de films]. M., 1990, n° 3. p. 132.
[2620] L. Lazarev, Zapiski pojilogo tcheloveka [Notes d'un homme âgé], in Znamia, 2001, n"6, p. 167.

We can find many examples of combat sacrifice in the biographical volumes of the most recent *Russian Jewish Encyclopedia*. Shik Kordonskiy, a commander of a mine and torpedo regiment, "smashed his burning plane into the enemy cargo ship"; he was posthumously made a Hero of the Soviet Union.

Wolf Korsunsky, "navigator of the air regiment", became a Hero of the Soviet Union too. Victor Hasin, "a Hero of the Soviet Union ... squadron commander... participated in 257 air skirmishes, personally shot down a number of the enemy's airplanes", destroyed another 10 on the ground; he was shot down over "the enemy occupied territory, and spent several days reaching and crossing the front lines. He died in hospital from his wounds". One cannot express it better!

The *Encyclopedia* contains several dozens names of Jews who died in combat.

Yet, despite these examples of unquestioned courage, a Jewish scholar bitterly notes "the widespread belief in the army and in the rear that Jews avoided the combat units".[2621] This is a noxious and painful spot. But, if you wish to ignore the painful spots, do not attempt to write a book about ordeals that were endured together.

In history, mutual national perceptions do count. "During the last war, antiSemitism in Russia increased significantly. Jews were unjustly accused of evasion of military service and in particular, of evasion of front line service."[2622]

"It was often said about Jews that instead of fighting, they stormed the cities of Alma-Ata and Tashkent."[2623] Here is a testimony of a Polish Jew who fought in the Red Army: "In the army, young and old had been trying to convince me that... there was not a single Jew on the front. 'We've got to fight for them. I was told in a friendly' manner: 'You're crazy. All your people are safely sitting at home. How come you are here on the front?'"[2624] I. Arad writes: "Expressions such as 'we are at the front, and the Jews are in Tashkent', one never sees a Jew at the front linećould be heard among soldiers and civilians alike."[2625] I testify: Yes, one could hear this among

---

[2621] S. Schwartz, Les Juifs en Union soviétique..., p. 154.
[2622] Dr. Jerzy Gliksman. Jewish Exiles in Soviet Russia (1939-1943). part 2, July 1947, p. 17, in Archives du Comité juif américain de New York, cité d'après S. Schwartz, p. 157.
[2623] PEJ. t. 8. p. 223.
[2624] Rachel Erlich. Summary Report on Eighteen Intensive Interviews with Jewish DP's from Poland and the Soviet Union, October 1948. p. 27 [Archives du Comité juif américain de New York], cité d'après S. Schwartz. p. 192.
[2625] И. Арад. Холокауст, с. 128.

the soldiers on the front. And right after the war – who has not experienced that? – a painful feeling remained among our Slavs that *our* Jews could have acted in that war in a more self-sacrificing manner, that among the lower ranks on the front the Jews could have been more represent.

These feelings are easy to blame (and they are blamed indeed) on unwarranted Russian anti-Semitism.(However, many sources blame that on the "German propaganda" digested by our public. What a people! They are good only to absorb propaganda – be it Stalin's or Hitler's – and they are good for nothing else!) Now that it is half a century passed since then. Isn't it time to unscramble the issue?

There are no official data available on the ethnic composition of the Soviet Army during the Second World War. Therefore, most studies on Jewish participation in the war provide only estimates, often without citation of sources or explanation of the methods of calculation. However, we can say that the 500,000 figure had been firmly established by 1990s: "The Jewish people supplied the Red Army with nearly 500,000 soldiers."[2626] "During World War II, 550,000 Jews served in the Red Army."[2627] The *Short Jewish Encyclopedia* notes that "only in the field force of the Soviet Army alone there were over 500,000 Jews", and "these figures do not include Jewish partisans who fought against Nazi Germany".[2628] The same figures are cited in *Essays on Jewish heroism*, in Abramovich's book *In the Deciding War* and in other sources.

We came across only one author who attempted to justify his assessment by providing readers with details of his reasoning. It was an Israeli researcher, I. Arad, in his the above cited book on the Catastrophe.

Arad concludes that "the total number of Jews who fought in the ranks of the Soviet Army against the German Nazis was no less than 420,000-430,000".[2629] He includes in this number "the thousands of Jewish partisans who fought against the German invaders in the woods" (they were later incorporated into the regular army in 1944 after the liberation of Western Byelorussia and Western Ukraine. At the same time, Arad believes that during the war "approximately 25,000-30,000 Jewish partisans operated in the occupied areas of the Soviet Union".[2630] (The

---

[2626] Е. *Сталинский.* Евреи в Красной армии // ЕМ-2, с. 240.

[2627] А. *Воронель.* Люди на войне, или ещё раз об уникальности Израиля // "22": Общественно-политический и литературный журнал еврейской интеллигенции из СССР в Израиле. Тель-Авив, 1984, № 34, с. 146.

[2628] КЕЭ, т. 1, статья «Военная служба», с. 690; т. 4, ст. «Катастрофа», с. 159. В ст. «Советский Союз» (т. 8, с. 224) КЕЭ даёт цифру 450 тыс. евреев в составе Советской армии, и ещё 25-30 тыс. в партизанских отрядах.

[2629] *И. Арад.* Холокост, с. 102.

[2630] *И. Арад.* Холокост, с. 86.

Israeli *Encyclopedia* in the article "Anti-Nazi Resistance" provides a lower estimate: "In the Soviet Union, more than 15,000 Jews fought against the Nazis in the underground organizations and partisan units."[2631]) In his calculations, Arad assumes that the proportion of mobilized Jews was the same as the average percentage of mobilized for the entire population of USSR during the war, i.e., 13.0-13.5%. This would yield 390,000-405,000 Eastern Jews (out of the total of slightly more than 3 million), save for the fact that "in certain areas of Ukraine and Byelorussia, the percentage of Jewish population was very high; these people were not mobilized because the region was quickly captured by the Germans". However, the author assumes that in general the mobilization "shortfall" of the Eastern Jews was small and that before the Germans came, the majority of males of military age were still mobilized – and thus he settles on the number of 370,000-380,000 Eastern Jews who served in the army. Regarding Western Jews, Arad reminds us that in 1940 in Western Byelorussia and Western Ukraine, during the mobilization of conscripts whose year of birth fell between of 1919 and 1922, approximately 30,000 Jewish youths were enlisted, but the Soviet government considered the soldiers from the newly annexed western regions as "unreliable"; therefore, almost all of them were transferred to the Labor Army after the war began. "By the end of 1943, the process of re-mobilization of those who were previously transferred into the Labor Army began ... and there were Jews among them." The author mentions that 6,000 to 7,000 Western Jewish refugees fought in the national Baltic divisions. By adding the Jewish partisans incorporated into the army in 1944, the author concludes: "we can establish that at least 50,000 Jews from the territories annexed to the USSR, including those mobilized before the war, served in the Red Army". Thus I. Arad comes to the overall number of 420,000-430,000 Jews in military service between 1941 and 1944.[2632]

According to Arad, the number of 500,000 soldiers commonly used in the sources would imply a *general base* (500,000 conscripts taken out of the entire Jewish population) of 3,700,000-3,850,000 people. According to the abovementioned sources, the maximum estimate for the total number of Eastern and Western Jews who escaped the German occupation was 2,226,000, and even if we were to add to this *base all* 1,080,000 Eastern Jews who remained under the occupation, as though they had had time to supply the army with all the people of military age right before the arrival of the Germans – which was not the case – the base would still lack a half-million people. It would have also meant that the success of the evacuation, discussed above, was strongly underestimated.

[2631] КЕЭ, т. 8, с. 441.
[2632] *И. Арад*. Холокауст, с. 98-102.

There is no such contradiction in Arad's assessment. And though its individual components may require correction,[2633] overall, it surprisingly well matches with the hitherto unpublished data of the Institute of the Military History, derived from the sources of the Central Archive of the Ministry of Defense. According to that data, the numbers of mobilized personnel during the Great Patriotic War were as follows:

- Russians – 19,650,000
- Ukrainians – 5,320,000
- Byelorussians – 964,000
- Tartars – 511,000
- Jews – 434,000
- Kazakhs – 341,000
- Uzbeks – 330,000
- Others – 2,500,000[2634]

Thus, contrary to the popular belief, the number of Jews in the Red Army in WWII was proportional to the size of mobilization base of the Jewish population. The fraction of Jews that participated in the war in general matches their proportion in the population.

So then, were the people's impressions of the war really prompted by anti-Semitic prejudice? Of course, by the beginning of the war, a certain part of the older and middle-aged population still bore scars from the 1920s and 1930s. But a huge part of the soldiers were young men who were born at the turn of the revolution or after it; their perception of the world differed from that of their elders dramatically. Compare: during the First World War, in spite of the spy mania of the military authorities in 1915 against the Jews who resided near the front lines, there was no evidence of anti-Semitism in the Russian army. In 1914, out of 5 million Russian Jews,[2635] "by the beginning of WWI, about 400,000 Jews were inducted into the Russian Imperial Army, and by the end of war in 1917 this number reached 500,000".[2636] This means that at the outbreak of the war *every twelfth* Russian Jew fought in the war, while by the end, one out of ten. And in World War II, every *eighth or seventh*.

[2633] Скажем, нам представляется, что число «восточников», которых успели мобилизовать до прихода немцев, было несколько меньше, зато средний процент армейцев от всего населения СССР, был, возможно, несколько выше, чем рассчитанный И. Арадом.

[2634] В ныне выходящей Военной энциклопедии едва ли не впервые приведены сведения об общем числе мобилизованных в годы Великой Отечественной Войны — 30 миллионов. См.: Военная энциклопедия: В 8 т. М.: Воениздат, 2001. Т. 5. с. 182.

[2635] КЕЭ, т. 7, с. 385.

[2636] КЕЭ, т. 1, с. 686.

So, what was the matter? It can be assumed that the new disparities inside the army played their role with their influences growing stronger and sharper as one moved closer to the deadly frontline.

In 1874 Jews were granted equal rights with other Russian subjects regarding universal conscription, yet during WWI until the February Revolution, Tsar Alexander II's law which stipulated that Jews could not advance above the rank of petty officer (though it did not apply to military medics) was still enforced. Under the Bolsheviks, the situation had changed radically, and during the WWII, as the Israeli *Encyclopedia* summarizes, "compared to other nationalities of the Soviet Union, Jews were disproportionately represented among the senior officers, mainly because of the higher percentage of college graduates among them".[2637] According to I. Arad's evaluation, "the number of Jews-commissars and political officers in various units during the war was relatively higher than number of Jews on other Army positions"; "at the very least, the percentage of Jews in the political leadership of the army" was "three times higher than the overall percentage of Jews among the population of the USSR during that period".[2638] In addition, of course, Jews were "among the head professionals of military medicine ... among the heads of health departments on several fronts. ... Twenty-six Jewish generals of the Medical Corps and nine generals of the Veterinary Corps were listed in the Red Army." Thirty-three Jewish generals served in the Engineering Corps.[2639] Of course, Jewish doctors and military engineers occupied not only high offices: "among the military medical staff... there were many Jews (doctors, nurses, orderlies)."[2640] Let us recall that in 1926 the proportion of Jews among military doctors was 18.6% while their proportion in the male population was 1.7%,[2641] and this percentage could only increase during the war because of the large number of female Jewish military doctors: "traditionally, a high percentage of Jews in the Soviet medicine and engineering professions naturally contributed to their large number in the military units."[2642]

However undeniably important and necessary for *final* victory these services were, what mattered is that not everybody could survive to see it.

Meanwhile an ordinary soldier, glancing back from the frontline, saw all too clearly that even the second and third echelons behind the front were also considered participants in the war: all those deep-rear headquarters,

---

[2637] Там же, с. 686-687.
[2638] *И. Арад.* Холокауст, с. 118.
[2639] *А. Абрамович.* В решающей войне. Т. 2, с 531-532.
[2640] КЕЭ, т. 8, с. 232.
[2641] *И. Арад.* Холокауст, с. 96.
[2642] Там же, с. 126.

suppliers, the whole Medical Corps from medical battalion to higher levels, numerous behind-the-lines technical units and, of course, all kinds of service personnel there, and, in addition, the entire army propaganda machine, including touring ensembles, entertainment troupes – they all were considered war veterans and, indeed, it was apparent to everyone that the concentration of Jews was much higher there than at the front lines. Some write that "among Leningrad's veteran-writers", the Jews comprised "by most cautious and perhaps understated assessment... 31%"[2643] – that is, probably more. Yet how many of them were editorial staff? As a rule, editorial offices were situated 10-15 kilometers behind the frontline, and even if a correspondent happened to be at the front during hostilities, nobody would have forced him "to hold the position", he could leave immediately, which is a completely different psychology. Many trumpeted their status as "front-liners", but writers and journalists are guilty of it the most. Stories of prominent ones deserve a separate dedicated analysis. Yet how many others – not prominent and not famous – *front-liners* settled in various newspaper publishing offices at all levels – at fronts, armies, corps and divisions? Here is one episode. After graduating from the machine gun school, Second Lieutenant Alexander Gershkowitz was sent to the front. But, after a spell at the hospital, while "catching up with his unit, at a minor railroad station he sensed the familiar smell of printing ink, followed it – and arrived at the office of a division-level newspaper, which serendipitously was in need of a front-line correspondent". And his fate had changed. (But what about catching up with his infantry unit?) "In this new position, he traveled thousands of kilometers of the war roads.".[2644] Of course, military journalists perished in the war as well.

Musician Michael Goldstein, who got "the white ticket" ("not fit") because of poor vision, writes of himself: "I always strived to be at the front, where I gave thousands of concerts, where I wrote a number of military songs and where I often dug trenches."[2645] Often? Really? A visiting musician – and with a shovel in his hands? As a war veteran, I say – an absolutely incredible picture.

Or here is another amazing biography. Eugeniy Gershuni "in the summer of 1941... volunteered for a militia unit, where he soon organized a small pop ensemble". Those, who know about these unarmed and even non-uniformed columns marching to certain death, would be chilled. Ensemble,

---

[2643] Ю. *Колкер*. [Рецензия на справочник «Ленинградские писатели-фронтовики. 1941-1945» / Сост. В. Бахтин. Л.: Сов. писатель, [1985] // Страна и мир: Обществ.-политический, экономический и культурно-философский журнал. Мюнхен, 1987, № 5, с. 138.
[2644] *С. Черток* // Русская мысль, 1992, 1 мая, с. 18.
[2645] *М. Гольдштейн* // Русская мысль, 1968, 1 августа, с. 10.

indeed! In September 1941, "Gershuni with his group of artists from the militia was posted to Leningrad's Red Army Palace, where he organized and headed a troop-entertainment circus". The story ends "on May 9, 1945, when Gershuni's circus threw a show on the steps of the Reichstag in Berlin".[2646]

Of course, the Jews fought in the infantry and on the frontline. In the middle of the 1970s, a Soviet source provides data on the ethnic composition of two hundred infantry divisions between January 1, 1943 and January 1, 1944 and compares it to the population share of each nationality within the pre-September 1939 borders of the USSR.. During that period, Jews comprised respectively 1.5% and 1.28% in those divisions, while their proportion in the population in 1939 was 1.78%,[2647] Only by the middle of 1944, when mobilization began in the liberated areas, did the percentage of Jews fall to 1.14% because almost all Jews in those areas were exterminated.

It should be noted here that some audacious Jews took an even more fruitful and energetic part in the war outside of the front. For example, the famous "Red Orchestra" of Trepper and Gurevich spied on Hitler's regime from within until the fall of 1942, passing to the Soviets extremely important strategic and tactical information. (Both spies were arrested and held by the Gestapo until the end of the war; then, after liberation, they were arrested and imprisoned in the USSR – Trepper for 10 years and Gurevich for 15 years.[2648])

Here is another example: a Soviet spy, Lev Manevich, was ex-commander of a special detachment during the Civil War and later a long-term spy in Germany, Austria, and Italy. In 1936, he was arrested in Italy, but he managed to communicate with Soviet intelligence even from the prison. In 1943, while imprisoned in the Nazi camps under the name of Colonel Starostin, he participated in the anti-fascist underground. In 1945, he was liberated by the Americans but died before returning to the USSR (where he could have easily faced imprisonment). Only 20 years later, in 1965, was he awarded the title of Hero of the Soviet Union posthumously.[2649] (One can also find very strange biographies, such as Mikhail Scheinman's. Since the 1920s he served as a provincial secretary of the Komsomol; during the most rampant years of the Union of Militant Atheists he was employed at its headquarters; then he graduated from the Institute of Red Professors and worked in the press department of the Central Committee

---

[2646] РЭЭ, т. 1, с. 296-297.
[2647] А.П. Артемьев. Братский боевой союз народов СССР в Великой Отечественной войне. М.: Мысль, 1975, с. 58-59.
[2648] КЕЭ, т. 8, с. 1051; П. Судоплатов. Спецоперации, с. 217-228.
[2649] КЕЭ, т. 5, с. 83; Очерки еврейского героизма. Т. 1, с. 405-430.

of the VKPb. In 1941, he was captured by the Germans and survived the entire war in captivity – a Jew and a high-level commissar at that! And despite categorical evidence of his culpability from SMERSH's [Translator's note: a frontline counter-intelligence organization, literally, "Death to Spies"] point of view, how could he possibly survive if he was not a traitor? Others were imprisoned for a long time for lesser "crimes". Yet nothing happened, and in 1946 he was already safely employed in the Museum of the History of Religion and then in the Institute of History at the Academy of Science.[2650])

Yet such anecdotal evidence cannot make up a convincing argument for either side and there are no reliable and specific statistics nor are they likely to surface in the future.

Recently, an Israeli periodical has published some interesting testimony.

When a certain Jonas Degen decided to volunteer for a Komsomol platoon at the beginning of the war, another Jewish youth, Shulim Dain, whom Jonas invited to come and join him, replied "that it would be really fortunate if the Jews could just watch the battle from afar since this is not their war, though namely this war may inspire Jews and help them to rebuild Israel. When I am conscripted to the army, I'll go to war. But to volunteer? Not a chance."[2651] And Dain was not the only one who thought like this; in particular, older and more experienced Jews may have had similar thoughts. And this attitude, especially among the Jews devoted to the eternal idea of Israel, is fully understandable.

And yet it is baffling, because the advancing enemy was the arch enemy of the Jews, seeking above all else to annihilate them. How could Dain and like-minded individuals remain neutral? Did they think that the Russians had no other choice but to fight for their land anyway?

One modern commentator (I know him personally – he is a veteran and a former camp inmate) concludes: "Even among the older veterans these days I have not come across people with such clarity of thought and depth of understanding" as Shulim Dain (who perished at Stalingrad) possessed: "two fascist monsters interlocked in deadly embrace". Why should we participate in that?[2652]

Of course, Stalin's regime was not any better than Hitler's. But for the *wartime Jews*, these two monsters could not be equal! If *that other* monster

---

[2650] РЕЭ, т. 3, с. 383.
[2651] В. *Каган*. Правильное решение* // "22". Ноябрь 1990-Январь 1991, № 74, с. 252. (Это — рецензия на книгу: И. *Деген*. Из дома рабства. Тель-Авив: Мория, 1986.)
[2652] Там же, с. 252.

won, what could then have happened to the Soviet Jews? Wasn't *this* war the personal Jewish war? wasn't it their *own Patriotic War* – to cross arms with the deadliest enemy in the entire Jewish history? And those Jews who perceived the war as their own and who did not separate their fate from that of Russians, those like Freylikh, Lazarev and Fainerman, whose thinking was opposite to Shulim Dain's, they fought selflessly.

God forbid, I do not explain the Dain's position as "Jewish cowardice". Yes, the Jews demonstrated survivalist prudence and caution throughout the entire history of the Diaspora, yet it is this history that explains these qualities.

And during the Six-Day War and other Israeli wars, the Jews have proven their outstanding military courage.

Taking all that into consideration, Dain's position can only be explained by a relaxed feeling of dual citizenship – the very same that back in 1922, Professor Solomon Lurie from Petrograd considered as one of the main sources of anti-Semitism (and its explanation) – a Jew living in a particular country belongs *not only to that* country, and his loyalties become inevitably split in two. The Jews have "always harbored nationalist attitudes, but the object of their nationalism was Jewry, not the country in which they lived".[2653] Their interest in *this* country is partial. After all, they – even if many of them only unconsciously – saw ahead looming in the future *their very own* nation of Israel.

And what about the rear? Researchers are certain about the "growth of antiSemitism ... during the war."[2654] "The curve of anti-Semitism in those years rose sharply again, and anti-Semitic manifestations ... by their intensity and prevalence dwarfed the anti-Semitism of the second half of the 1920s."[2655]

"During the war, anti-Semitism become commonplace in the domestic life in the Soviet deep hinterland."[2656]

During evacuation, "so-called domestic anti-Semitism, which had been dormant since the establishment of the Stalinist dictatorship in the early 1930s, was revived against the background of general insecurity and breakdown and other hardships and deprivations, engendered by the war."[2657] This statement refers mainly to Central Asia, Uzbekistan, and

---

[2653] *С.Я. Лурье.* Антисемитизм в древнем мире. Тель-Авив: Сова, 1976, с. 77 [1-е изд. — Пг.: Былое, 1922].
[2654] *В. Александрова.* Евреи в советской литературе // КРЕ-2, с. 297.
[2655] *С.М. Шварц.* Антисемитизм..., с. 197.
[2656] *С. Шварц.* Евреи в Советском Союзе..., с. 6.
[2657] *Г.В. Костырченко.* Тайная политика Сталина, с. 242.

Kazakhstan, "especially when the masses of wounded and disabled veterans rushed there from the front",[2658] and exactly there the masses of the evacuated Jews lived, including Polish Jews, who were "torn from their traditional environment" by deportation and who had no experience of Soviet kolkhozes. Here are the testimonies of Jewish evacuees to Central Asia recorded soon after the war: "The low labor productivity among evacuated Jews ... served in the eyes of the locals as a proof of allegedly characteristic Jewish reluctance to engage in physical labor."[2659] "The intensification of [anti-Semitic] attitudes was fueled by the Polish refugees' activity on the commodity markets."[2660] "Soon they realized that their regular incomes from the employment in industrial enterprises, kolkhozes, and cooperatives ... would not save them from starvation and death. To survive, there was only one way – trading on the market or 'speculation'"; therefore, it was the Soviet reality that drove "Polish Jews to resort to market transactions whether they liked it or not."[2661] "The non-Jewish population of Tashkent was ill-disposed toward the Jewish evacuees from Ukraine. Some said, 'Look at these Jews. They always have a lot of money.'"[2662] "Then there were incidents of harassment and insults of Jews, threats against them, throwing them out of bread queues."[2663] "Another group of Russian Jews, mostly bureaucrats with a considerable amount of cash, inspired the hostility of the locals for inflating the already high market prices."[2664]

The author proceeds confidently to explain these facts thus: "Hitler's propaganda reaches even here",[2665] and he is not alone in reaching such conclusions.

What a staggering revelation! How could Hitler's propaganda victoriously reach and permeate all of Central Asia when it was barely noticeable at the front with all those rare and dangerous-to-touch leaflets thrown from airplanes, and when all private radio receiver sets were confiscated throughout the USSR?

[2658] С. Шварц. Евреи в Советском Союзе..., с. 157.
[2659] Dr. Jerzy Gliksman. Jewish Exiles in Soviet Russia (1939-1943). Part 2, July 1947, p. 6 // Архив Американского Еврейского Комитета в Нью-Йорке. — Цит. по: С. Шварц. Евреи в Советском Союзе..., с. 157.
[2660] С.М. Шварц. Антисемитизм..., с. 191.
[2661] Rachel Erlich. Summary Report on Eighteen Intensive Interviews with Jewish DP's from Poland and the Soviet Union. October 1948, p. 9f // Архив Американского Еврейского Комитета в Нью-Йорк — Цит. по: С. Шварц. Антисемитизм..., с. 192.
[2662] Там же, р. 26. — Цит. по: С.М. Шварц. Антисемитизм..., с. 194.
[2663] Dr. Jerzy Gliksman. Jewish Exiles..., p. 17. — Цит. по: С.Шварц. Евреи в Советском Союзе..., с. 159.
[2664] Там же, р. 15. — Цит. по: С.Шварц. Евреи в Советском Союзе..., с. 159.
[2665] С. Шварц. Евреи в Советском Союзе..., с. 157.

No, the author realizes that there "was yet another reason for the growth of anti-Semitic attitudes in the districts that absorbed evacuees *en masse*. There, the antagonism between the general mass of the provincial population and the privileged bureaucrats from the country's central cities manifested itself in a subtle form. Evacuation of organizations from those centers into the hinterland provided the local population with an opportunity to fully appreciate the depth of social contrast."[2666]

Then there were those populations that experienced the German invasion and occupation, for instance, the Ukrainians. Here is testimony published in March 1945 in the bulletin of the Jewish Agency for Palestine: "The Ukrainians meet returning Jews with hostility. In Kharkov, a few weeks after the liberation, Jews do not dare to walk alone on the streets at night. ... There have been many cases of beating up Jews on the local markets. ... Upon returning to their homes, Jews often found only a portion of their property, but when they complained in courts, Ukrainians often perjured themselves against them."[2667] (The same thing happened everywhere; besides it was useless to complain in court anyway: many of the returning non-Jewish evacuees found their old places looted as well.) "There are many testimonies about hostile attitudes towards Jews in Ukraine after its liberation from the Germans."[2668] "As a result of the German occupation, anti-Semitism in all its forms has significantly increased in all social strata of Ukraine, Moldova and Lithuania."[2669]

Indeed, *here*, in these territories, Hitler's anti-Jewish propaganda did work well during the years of occupation, and yet the main point was the same: that under the Soviet regime the Jews had merged with the ruling class – and so a secret German report from the occupied territories in October 1941 states that the "animosity of the Ukrainian population against Jews is enormous.... they view the Jews ... as informants and agents of the NKVD, which organized the terror against the Ukrainian people."[2670]

Generally speaking, early in the war, the "German's plan was to create an impression that it was not Germans but the local population that began extermination of the Jews"; S. Schwartz believes that, unlike the reports of the German propaganda press, "the German reports not intended for

---

[2666] Там же, с. 158.
[2667] Bulletin of the Rescue Committee of the Jewish Agency for Palestine. March 1945, p. 2-3. — Цит. по: *С.Шварц*. Евреи в Советском Союзе..., с. 160.
[2668] *С. Шварц*. Евреи в Советском Союзе..., с. 184.
[2669] *Л. Шапиро*. Евреи в Советской России после Сталина // КРБ-2, с. 359.
[2670] Trial of the Major War Criminals before the International Military Tribunal, Nuremberg. 14 November 1945-1 October 1946. — Nuremberg, 1949, Vol. 38, p. 292-293, Doc. 102-R. — Цит. по: *С.Шварц*. Евреи в Советском Союзе..., с. 101.

publication are reliable."²⁶⁷¹ He profusely quotes a report by SS Standartenführer F. Shtoleker to Berlin on the activities of the SS units under his command (operating in the Baltic states, Byelorussia and in some parts of the RSFSR) for the period between the beginning of the war in the East and October 15, 1941: "Despite facing considerable difficulties, we were able to direct local anti-Semitic forces toward organization of anti-Jewish pogroms within several hours after arrival [of German troops]. ... It was necessary to show that ... it was a natural reaction to the years of oppression by Jews and communist terror. ... It was equally important to establish for the future as an undisputed and provable fact that ... the local people have resorted to the most severe measures against Bolsheviks and Jews on their own initiative, without demonstrable evidence for any guidance from the German authorities."²⁶⁷²

The willingness of the local population for such initiatives varied greatly in different occupied regions. "In the tense atmosphere of the Baltics, the hatred of Jews reached a boiling point at the very moment of Hitler's onslaught against Soviet Russia on June 22, 1941."²⁶⁷³ The Jews were accused of collaboration with the NKVD in the deportation of Baltic citizens. The *Israeli Encyclopedia* quotes an entry from the diary of Lithuanian physician E. Budvidayte-Kutorgene: "All Lithuanians, with few exceptions, are unanimous in their hatred of Jews."²⁶⁷⁴ Yet, the Standartenführer reports that "to our surprise, it was not an easy task ... to induce a pogrom there". This was achieved with the help of Lithuanian partisans, who exterminated 1,500 Jews in Kaunas during the night of June 26 and 2,300 more in the next few days; they also burned the Jewish quarter and several synagogues.²⁶⁷⁵ "Mass executions of the Jews were conducted by the SS and the Lithuanian police on October 29 and November 25, 1941." About 19,000 of the 36,000 Jews of Kaunas were shot in the Ninth Fort.²⁶⁷⁶ "In many Lithuanian cities and towns, all of the Jewish population was exterminated by local Lithuanian police under German control in the autumn of 1941."²⁶⁷⁷ "It was much harder to induce the same self-cleaning operations and pogroms in Latvia", reports the Standartenführer, because there "the entire national leadership, especially in Riga, was destroyed or

---

²⁶⁷¹ *С. Шварц*. Евреи в Советском Союзе..., с. 88.
²⁶⁷² Trial of the Major War Criminals... Vol. 37, p. 672-683, Doc. 180-L. — Цит. по: *С. Шварц*. Евреи в Советском Союзе..., с. 89.
²⁶⁷³ *И. Гар*. Евреи в Прибалтийских странах под немецкой оккупацией // КРЕ-2, с. 97.
²⁶⁷⁴ КЕЭ, т. 8, с. 218.
²⁶⁷⁵ Trial of the Major War Criminals... Vol. 37, p. 672-683, Doc. 180-L. Цит. по: *С.Шварц*. Евреи в Советском Союзе..., с. 89-90.
²⁶⁷⁶ КЕЭ, т. 8, с. 218.
²⁶⁷⁷ КЕЭ, т. 8, с. 218.

deported by the Bolsheviks."²⁶⁷⁸ Still, on July 4, 1941, Latvian activists in Riga "set fire to several synagogues into which the Jews had been herded. ... About 2,000 died"; in the first days of occupation, locals assisted in executions by the Germans of several thousand Jews in the Bikernieki forest near Riga, and in late October and in early November in the shootings of about 27,000 Jews at a nearby railway station Rumbula.²⁶⁷⁹ In Estonia, "with a small number of Jews in the country, it was not possible to induce pogroms", reports the officer.²⁶⁸⁰ (Estonian Jews were destroyed without pogroms: "In Estonia, about 2,000 Jews remained.

Almost all male Jews were executed in the first weeks of the occupation by the Germans and their Estonian collaborators. ... The rest were interned in the concentration camp Harku near Tallinn", and by the end of 1941 all of them were killed.²⁶⁸¹

But the German leadership was disappointed in Byelorussia. S. Schwartz: "the failure of the Germans to draw sympathy from the broad masses of locals to the cause of extermination of Jews... is completely clear from secret German documents ... The population invariably and consistently refrains from any independent action against the Jews."²⁶⁸² Still, according to eyewitnesses in Gorodok in the Vitebsk oblast, when the ghetto was liquidated on Oct. 14, 1941, the "*Polizei* were worse than the Germans";²⁶⁸³ and in Borisov, the "Russian police" (it follows in the report that they were actually imported from Berlin) "destroyed within two days [October 20 and 21, 1941] 6,500 Jews. Importantly, the author of the report notes that the killings of Jews were not met with sympathy from the local population: 'Who ordered that... How is it possible...? Now they kill the Jews, and when will be our turn? What have these poor Jews done? They were just workers. The really guilty ones are, of course, long gone.'"²⁶⁸⁴ And here is a report by a German "trustee", a native Byelorussian from Latvia: "In Byelorussia, there is no Jewish question. For them, it's a purely German business, not Byelorussian... Everybody sympathizes with and pities the Jews, and they look at Germans as barbarians and murderers of the Jews

---

²⁶⁷⁸ Trial of the Major War Criminals... Vol. 37, p. 672-683, Doc. 180-L. — Цит. по: *С. Шварц*. Евреи в Советском Союзе..., с. 90.
²⁶⁷⁹ КЕЭ, т. 8, с. 218.
²⁶⁸⁰ Trial of the Major War Criminals... Vol.37, p. 672-683, Doc. 180-L. — Цит. по: *С. Шварц*. Евреи в Советском Союзе..., с. 89-90.
²⁶⁸¹ Уничтожение евреев СССР в годы немецкой оккупации (1941-1944): Сб. документов и материалов / Под ред. И. Арада. Иерусалим: Яд Ва-Шем, 1991, с. 12.
²⁶⁸² Trial of the Major War Criminals... Vol. 37, p. 672-683, Doc. 180-L. — Цит. по: *С. Шварц*. Евреи в Советском Союзе..., с. 91-92.
²⁶⁸³ КЕЭ, т. 8, с. 218.
²⁶⁸⁴ *С.М. Шварц*. Антисемитизм...*, с. 134-135.

[Judenhenker]: a Jew, they say, is a human being just like a Byelorussian."[2685] In any case, S. Schwartz writes that "there were no national Byelorussian squads affiliated with the German punitive units, though there were Latvian, Lithuanian, and mixed squads; the latter enlisted some Byelorussians as well."[2686]

The project was more successful in Ukraine. From the beginning of the war, Hitler's propaganda incited the Ukrainian nationalists ("Bandera?s Fighters") to take revenge on the Jews for the murder of Petliura by Schwartzbard.[2687] The organization of Ukrainian Nationalists of Bandera-Melnik (OUN) did not need to be persuaded: even before the Soviet-German War, in April 1941, it adopted a resolution at its Second Congress in Krakow, in which paragraph 17 states: "The Yids in the Soviet Union are the most loyal supporters of the ruling Bolshevik regime and the vanguard of Moscow imperialism in Ukraine... The Organization of Ukrainian Nationalists considers the Yids as the pillar of the Moscow-Bolshevik regime, while educating the masses that Moscow is the main enemy."[2688] Initially, the "Bandera Fighters" allied with the Germans against the Bolsheviks. During the whole of 1940 and the first half of 1941, the OUN leadership was preparing for a possible war between Germany and the USSR. "Then the main base of the OUN was the Generalgouvernement, i. e., the Nazi-occupied Poland. ... Ukrainian militias were being created there, and lists of suspicious persons, with Jews among them, were compiled. Later these lists were used by Ukrainian nationalists to exterminate Jews. ... 'Mobile units' for the East Ukraine were created and battalions of Ukrainian Nationalists, 'Rolandánd 'Nakhtigal', were formed in the German Army." The OUN arrived in the East [of Ukraine] together with the frontline German troops.

During the summer of 1941 "a wave of Jewish pogroms rolled over Western Ukraine. ... with participation of both Melnyk's and of Bandera's troops. As a result of these pogroms, around 28,000 Jews were killed."[2689] Among OUN documents, there is a declaration by J. Stetzko (who in July 1941 was named the head of the Ukrainian government): "The Jews help Moscow to keep Ukraine in slavery, and therefore, I support extermination

---

[2685] Там же*, с. 132.
[2686] Там же*, с. 93.
[2687] *И. Шехтман*. Советское еврейство в германо-советской войне // ЕМ-2, с. 235-236.
[2688] *А. Вайс*. Отношение некоторых кругов украинского национального движения к евреям в период Второй мировой войны* // Вестник Еврейского Ун-та..., 1995, № 2(9), с. 106.
[2689] *А. Вайс*. Отношение некоторых кругов украинского национального движения к евреям в период Второй мировой войны* // Вестник Еврейского Ун-та..., 1995, № 2(9), с. 105-106, 107.

of the Yids and the need to adopt in Ukraine the German methods of extermination of Jewry." In July, a meeting of Bandera's OUN leaders was held in Lvov, where, among other topics, policies toward Jews were discussed. There were various proposals: to build the policy "on the principles of Nazi policy before 1939. ...

There were proposals to isolate Jews in ghettoes. ... But the most radical proposal was made by Stepan Lenkavskiy, who stated: 'Concerning the Jews we will adopt all the measures that will lead to their eradication.'"[2690] And until the relations between the OUN and the Germans deteriorated (because Germany did not recognize the self-proclaimed Ukrainian independence), there were "many cases, especially in the first year ... when Ukrainians directly assisted the Germans in the extermination of Jews." "Ukrainian auxiliary police, recruited by the Germans mainly in Galicia and Volhynia,"[2691] played a special role. "In Uman in September 1941, Ukrainian city police under command of several officers and sergeants of the SS shot nearly 6,000 Jews"; and in early November 6 km outside Rovno, "the SS and Ukrainian police slaughtered 21,000 Jews from the ghetto."[2692] However, S. Schwartz writes: "It is impossible to figure out which part of the Ukrainian population shared an active anti-Semitism with a predisposition toward pogroms. Probably quite a large part, particularly the more cultured strata, did not share these sentiments." As for the original part of the Soviet Ukraine [within the pre-September 1939 Soviet borders], "no evidence for the spontaneous' pogroms by Ukrainians could be found in the secret German reports from those areas."[2693] In addition, "Tatar militia squads in the Crimea were exterminating Jews also."[2694]

Regarding indigenous Russian regions occupied by the Germans, the Germans "could not exploit anti-Russian sentiments and the argument about Moscow's imperialism was unsustainable; and the argument for any Judeo-Bolshevism, devoid of support in local nationalism, largely lost its appeal"; among the local Russian population "only relatively few people actively supported the Germans in their anti-Jewish policies of extermination."[2695]

A researcher on the fate of Soviet Jewry concludes: the Germans in Lithuania and Latvia "had a tendency to mask their pogromist activities, bringing to the fore extermination squads made up of pogromists emerging

---

[2690] Там же, с. 106-107.
[2691] *С. Шварц*. Евреи в Советском Союзе..., с. 98, 101.
[2692] КЕЭ, т. 8, с. 218.
[2693] *С. Шварц*. Евреи в Советском Союзе..., с. 99.
[2694] *А.А. Гольдштейн*. Судьба евреев в оккупированной немцами Советской России // КРЕ-2, с. 74.
[2695] *С. Шварц*. Евреи в Советском Союзе..., с. 102.

under German patronage from the local population"; but "in Byelorussia, and to a considerable extent even in Ukraine and especially in the occupied areas of the RSFSR", the Germans did not succeed as "the local population had mostly disappointed the hopes pinned on it" – and there "the Nazi exterminators had to proceed openly."[2696]

Hitler's plan for the military campaign against the Soviet Union (Operation Barbarossa) included "*special tasks* to prepare the ground for political rule, with the character of these tasks stemming from the all-out struggle between the two opposing political systems." In May and June 1941, the Supreme Command of the Wehrmacht issued more specific directives, ordering execution without trial of persons suspected of hostile action against Germany (and of political commissars, partisans, saboteurs and Jews in any case) in the theater of Barbarossa.[2697]

To carry out *special tasks* in the territory of the USSR, four special groups (*Einsatzgruppen*) were established within the Security Service (SS) and the Secret Police (Gestapo), that had operational units (*Einsatzkommando*) numerically equal to companies. The *Einsatzgruppen* advanced along with the front units of the German Army, but reported directly to the Chief of Security of the Third Reich, Reinhard Heydrich.

Einsatzgruppe A (about 1000 soldiers and SS officers under the command of SS Standartenführer Dr. F. Shtoleker) of Army Group "North" operated in Lithuania, Latvia, Estonia, and the Leningrad and Pskov oblasts. Group B (655 men, under the command of Brigadenführer A. Neveu) was attached to Army Group "Centre", which was advancing through Byelorussia and the Smolensk Oblast toward Moscow. Group C (600, Standartenführer E. Rush) was attached to Army Group "South" and operated in the Western and Eastern Ukraine.

Group D (600 men under the command of SS Standartenführer Prof. O. Ohlendorf) was attached to the 11th Army and operated in Southern Ukraine, the Crimea, and in the Krasnodar and Stavropol regions.

Extermination of Jews and commissars ("carriers of the Judeo-Bolshevik ideology") by the Germans began from the first days of the June 1941invasion, though they did so "somewhat chaotically and with an extremely broad scope."[2698] "In other German-occupied countries, elimination of the Jewish population proceeded gradually and thoroughly. It usually started with legal restrictions, continued with the creation of ghettos and introduction of forced labor and culminated in deportation and

---

[2696] Там же, с. 74, 90.
[2697] Уничтожение евреев СССР в годы немецкой оккупации*, с. 4.
[2698] *С. Шварц*. Евреи в Советском Союзе..., с. 65.

mass extermination. In Soviet Russia, all these elements were strangely intermingled in time and place. In each region, sometimes even within one city, various methods of harassment were used... there was no uniform or standardized system." [2699] Shooting of Jewish prisoners of war could happen sometimes right upon capture and sometimes later in the concentration camps; civilian Jews were sometimes first confined in ghettoes, sometimes in forced-labor camps, and in other places they were shot outright on the spot, and still in other places the "gas vans" were used. "As a rule, the place of execution was an anti-tank ditch, or just a pit."[2700]

The numbers of those exterminated in the cities of the Western USSR by the winter of 1941 (the first period of extermination) are striking: according to the documents, in Vilnius out of 57,000 Jews who had lived there about 40,000 were killed; in Riga out of 33,000 – 27,000; in Minsk out of the 100,000-strong ghetto – 24,000 were killed (there the extermination continued until the end of occupation); in Rovno out of 27,000 Jews – 21,000 were killed; in Mogilev about 10,000 Jews were shot; in Vitebsk – up to 20,000; and near Kiselevich village nearly 20,000 Jews from Bobruisk were killed; in Berdichev – 15,000.[2701]

By late September, the Nazis staged a mass extermination of Jews in Kiev.

On September 26 they distributed announcements around the city requiring all Jews, under the penalty of death, to report to various assembly points. And Jews, having no other option but to submit, gathered obediently, if not trustingly, altogether about 34,000; and on September 29 and 30, they were methodically shot at Babi Yar, putting layer upon layers of corpses in a large ravine. Hence there was no need to dig any graves – a giant hecatomb!

According to the official German announcement, not questioned later, 33,771 Jews were shot over the course of two days. During the next two years of the Kiev occupation, the Germans continued shootings in their favorite and so *convenient* ravine. It is believed that the number of the executed – not only Jews – had reached, perhaps, 100,000.[2702]

The executions at Babi Yar have become a symbol in world history. People shrug at the cold-blooded calculation, the business-like organization, so typical for the 20th century that crowns humanistic civilization: during the

---

[2699] И. *Шехтман*. Советское еврейство в германо-советской войне // ЕМ-2, с. 229.
[2700] КЕЭ*, т. 8, с. 218.
[2701] От источника к источнику цифры несколько разнятся. Статистику этих истреблений, вероятно, невозможно установить точно. См. уже цитированную статью А.А. Гольдштейна в «Книге о Русском Еврействе» (1968); сборник И. Арада «Уничтожение евреев СССР в годы немецкой оккупации» (1991); статью «Советский Союз» в КЕЭ, т. 8 (1996).
[2702] КЕЭ, т. 1, с. 275.

"savage" Middle Ages people killed each other *en masse* only in a fit of rage or in the heat of battle.

It should be recalled that within a few kilometers from Babi Yar, in the enormous Darnitskiy camp, tens of thousands Soviet prisoners of war, soldiers and officers, died during the same months: yet we do not commemorate it properly, and many are not even aware of it. The same is true about the more than two million Soviet prisoners of war who perished during the first years of the war.

The Catastrophe persistently raked its victims from all the occupied Soviet territories. In Odessa on October 17, 1941, on the second day of occupation by German and Romanian troops, several thousand Jewish males were killed, and later, after the bombing of the Romanian Military Office, the total terror was unleashed: about 5,000 people, most of them Jews and thousands of others, were herded into a suburban village and executed there. In November, there was a mass deportation of people into the Domanevskiy District, where "about 55,000 Jews" were shot in December and January of 1942.[2703] In the first months of occupation, by the end of 1941, 22,464 Jews were killed in Kherson and Nikolayev; 11,000 in Dnepropetrovsk; 8,000 in Mariupol' and almost as many in Kremenchug; about 15,000 in Kharkov's Drobytsky Yar; and more than 20,000 in Simferopol' and Western Crimea.[2704]

By the end of 1941, the German High Command had realized that the "blitz" had failed and that a long war loomed ahead. The needs of the war economy demanded a different organization of the home front. In some places, the German administration slowed down the extermination of Jews in order to exploit their manpower and skills. "As the result, ghettoes survived in large cities like Riga, Vilnius, Kaunas, Baranovichi, Minsk, and in other, smaller ones, where many Jews worked for the needs of the German war economy."[2705]

Yet the demand for labor that prolonged the existence of these large ghettoes did not prevent resumption of mass killings in other places in the spring of 1942: in Western Byelorussia, Western Ukraine, Southern Russia and the Crimea, 30,000 Jews were deported from the Grodno region to Treblinka and Auschwitz; Jews of Polesia, Pinsk, Brest-Litovsk, and Smolensk were eradicated. During the 1942 summer offensive, the Germans killed local Jews immediately upon arrival: the Jews of Kislovodsk, Pyatigorsk and Essentuki were killed in antitank ditches near Mineralni'ye Vody; thus died evacuees to Essentuki from Leningrad and

---

[2703] КЕЭ, т. 6, с. 125-126.
[2704] Уничтожение евреев СССР в годы немецкой оккупации, с. 16.
[2705] Там же, с. 17.

Kishinev. Jews of Kerch and Stavropol were exterminated as well. In Rostov-on-Don, recaptured by the Germans in late July 1942, all the remaining Jewish population was eradicated by August 11.

In 1943, after the battles of Stalingrad and Kursk, the outcome of the war became clear. During their retreat, the Germans decided to exterminate all remaining Jews. On June 21, 1943 Himmler ordered the liquidation of the remaining ghettoes. In June 1943, the ghettoes of Lvov, Ternopol, and Drohobych were liquidated. After the liberation of Eastern Galicia in 1944, "only 10,000 to 12,000 Jews were still alive, which constituted about 2% of all Jews who had remained under occupation." Able-bodied Jews from ghettoes in Minsk, Lida, and Vilnius were transferred to concentration camps in Poland, Estonia, and Latvia, while the rest were shot. Later, during the summer, 1944 retreat from the Baltics, some of the Jews in those camps were shot, and some were moved into camps in Germany (Stutthof et al.).[2706]

Destined for extermination, Jews fought for survival: underground groups sprang up in many ghettoes to organize escapes. Yet after a successful breakout, a lot depended on the local residents – that they not betray the Jews, provide them with non-Jewish papers, shelter and food. In the occupied areas, Germans sentenced those helping Jews to death.[2707] "But everywhere, in all occupied territories, there were people who helped the Jews. ... Yet there were few of them. They risked their lives and the lives of their families. ... There were hundreds, maybe thousands of such people. But the majority of local populations just watched from a distance."[2708] In Byelorussia and the occupied territories of the RSFSR, where local populations were not hostile to the remaining Jews and where no pogroms ever occurred, the local population provided still less assistance to Jews than in Europe or even "in Poland, the country ... of widespread, traditional, folk anti-Semitism." [2709] (Summaries of many similar testimonies can be found in books by S. Schwartz and I. Arad.) They plausibly attribute this not only to the fear of execution but also to the habit of obedience to authorities (developed over the years of Soviet rule) and to not meddling in the affairs of others.

Yes, we have been so downtrodden, so many millions have been torn away from our midst in previous decades, that any attempt at resistance to government power was foredoomed, so now Jews as well could not get the support of the population.

[2706] Там же, с. 26-27.
[2707] КЕЭ, т. 8, с. 222.
[2708] Уничтожение евреев СССР в годы немецкой оккупации, с. 24.
[2709] *С. Шварц.* Евреи в Советском Союзе..., с. 108.

But even well-organized Soviet underground and guerrillas directed from Moscow did little to save the doomed Jews. Relations with the Soviet guerrillas were a specially acute problem for the Jews in the occupied territories. Going into the woods, i.e., joining up with a partisan unit, was a better lot for Jewish men than waiting to be exterminated by the Germans. Yet hostility to the Jews was widespread and often acute among partisans, and "there were some Russian detachments that did not accept Jews on principle. They alleged that Jews cannot and do not want to fight", writes a former Jewish partisan Moshe Kaganovich. A non-Jewish guerilla recruit was supplied with weapons, but a Jew was required to provide his own, and sometimes it was traded down.

"There is pervasive enmity to Jews among partisans. ... in some detachments anti-Semitism was so strong that the Jews felt compelled to flee from such units."[2710]

For instance, in 1942 some two hundred Jewish boys and girls fled into the woods from the ghetto in the shtetl of Mir in Grodno oblast, and "there they encountered anti-Semitism among Soviet guerrillas, which led to the death of many who fled; only some of them were able to join guerrilla squads."[2711] Or another case: A guerrilla squad under the command of Ganzenko operated near Minsk. It was replenished "mainly with fugitives from the Minsk ghetto", but the "growing number of Jews in the unit triggered anti-Semitic clashes" – and then the Jewish part of the detachment broke away.[2712] Such actions on the part of the guerrillas were apparently spontaneous, not directed from the center.

According to Moshe Kaganovich, from the end of 1943 "the influence of more-disciplined personnel arriving from the Soviet Union" had increased "and the general situation for [the Jews had] somewhat improved."[2713] However, he complains that when a territory was liberated by the advancing regular Soviet troops and the partisans were sent to the front (which is true, and everybody was sent indiscriminately), it was primarily Jews who were sent[2714] – and that is incredible.

However, Kaganovich writes that Jews were sometimes directly assisted by the partisans. There were even "partisan attacks on small towns in order to save Jews" from ghettoes and [concentration] camps, and that "Russian partisan movement helped fleeing Jews to cross the front lines. ... [And in this way they] smuggled across the frontline many thousands of Jews who

---

[2710] Там же*, с. 121-124.
[2711] КЕЭ, т. 5, с. 366.
[2712] РЕЭ, т. 1, с. 499.
[2713] С. Шварц. Евреи в Советском Союзе...*, с. 127.
[2714] Там же*, с. 129.

were hiding in the forests of Western Byelorussia escaping the carnage." A partisan force in the Chernigov region accepted "more than five hundred children from Jewish family camps in the woods, protected them and took care of them... After the Red Army liberated Sarny (on Volyn), several squads broke the front and sent Jewish children to Moscow." (S. Schwartz believes that "these reports are greatly exaggerated. [But] they are based on real facts, [and they] merit attention."[2715])

Jewish family camps originated among the Jewish masses fleeing into the woods and there "were many thousands of such fugitives." Purely Jewish armed squads were formed specifically for the protection of these camps. (Weapons were purchased through third parties from German soldiers or policemen.) Yet how to feed them all? The only way was to take food as well as shoes and clothing, both male and female, by force from the peasants of surrounding villages. "The peasant was placed between the hammer and the anvil. If he did not carry out his assigned production minimum, the Germans burned his household and killed him as a partisan'. On the other hand, guerrillas took from him by force all they needed"[2716] – and this naturally caused spite among the peasants: they are robbed by Germans and robbed by guerrillas – and now in addition even the Jews rob them? And the Jews even take away clothes from their women?

In the spring of 1943, partisan Baruch Levin came to one such family camp, hoping to get medicines for his sick comrades. He remembers: Tuvia Belsky "seemed like a legendary hero to me. ... Coming from the people, he managed to organize a 1,200-strong unit in the woods. ... In the worst days when a Jew could not even feed himself, he cared for the sick, elderly and for the babies born in the woods." Levin told Tuvia about Jewish partisans: "We, the few survivors, no longer value life. Now the only meaning of our lives is revenge. It is our duty – to fight the Germans, wipe out all of them to the last one." I talked for a long time; ... offered to teach Belsky's people how to work with explosives, and all other things I have myself learned. But my words, of course, could not change Tuvia's mindset... 'Baruch, I would like you to understand one thing. It is precisely because there are so few of us left, it is so important for me that the Jews survive. And I see this as my purpose; it is the most important thing for me.'"[2717]

And the very same Moshe Kaganovich, as late as in 1956, wrotein a book published in Buenos Aires, "in peacetime, years after the devastating defeat of Nazism" – shows, according to S. Schwartz, "a really bloodthirsty

---

[2715] С. Шварц. Евреи в Советском Союзе...*, с. 125-126.
[2716] Там же*, с. 121, 128.
[2717] Уничтожение евреев СССР в годы немецкой оккупации, с. 386-387.

attitude toward the Germans, an attitude that seems to be influenced by the Hitler plague.... he glorifies putting German prisoners to Jewish death' by Jewish partisans according to the horrible Nazi' examples or excitedly recalls the speech by a commander of a [Jewish] guerrilla unit given before the villagers of a Lithuanian village who were gathered and forced to kneel by partisans in the square after a punitive raid against that village whose population had actively assisted the Germans in the extermination of Jews (several dozen villagers were executed during that raid)."[2718] S. Schwartz writes about this with a restrained but clear condemnation.

Yes, a lot of things happened. Predatory killings call for revenge, but each act of revenge, tragically, plants the seeds of new retribution in the future.

The different Jewish sources variously estimate the total losses among Soviet Jews during the Second World War (within the post-war borders). "How many Soviet Jews survived the war?", asks S. Schwartz and offers this calculation: 1,810,000-1,910,000 (excluding former refugees from the Western Poland and Romania, now repatriated). "The calculations imply that the number of Jews by the end of the war was markedly lower than two million and much lower than the almost universally accepted number of three million."[2719] So, the *total* number of losses according to Schwarz was 2,800,000-2,900,000.

In 1990 I. Arad provided his estimate: "During the liberation of German-occupied territories ... the Soviet Army met almost no Jews. Out of the 2,750,000-2,900,000 Jews who remained under the Nazi rule [in 1941] in the occupied Soviet territories, almost all died." To this figure Arad suggests adding "about 120,000 Jews – Soviet Army soldiers who died on the front, and about 80,000 shot in the POW camps", and "tens of thousands of Jews [who died] during the siege of Leningrad, Odessa and other cities, and in the deep rear ... because of harsh living conditions in the evacuation."[2720]

Demographer M. Kupovetskiy published several studies in the 1990s, where he used newly available archival materials, made some corrections to older data and employed an improved technique for ethnodemographic analysis.

His result was that the general losses of Jewish population within the postwar USSR borders in 1941-1945 amounted to 2,733,000 (1,112,000 Eastern and 1,621,000 Western Jews), or 55% of 4,965,000 – the total number of Jews in the USSR in June 1941. This figure, apart from the

---

[2718] *С. Шварц.* Евреи в Советском Союзе...*, с. 132.
[2719] Там же, с. 171-173.
[2720] *И. Арад.* Холокауст, с. 91.

victims of Nazi extermination, includes the losses among the military and the guerrillas, among civilians near the front line, during evacuation and deportation, as well as the victims of Stalin's camps during the war. (However, the author notes, that quantitative evaluation of each of these categories within the overall casualty figure is yet to be done. [2721]) Apparently, the *Short Jewish Encyclopedia* agrees with this assessment as it provides the same number.[2722]

The currently accepted figure for the total losses of the Soviet population during the Great Patriotic War is 27,000,000 (if the "method of demographic balance" is used, it is 26,600,000[2723]) and this may still be underestimated.

We must not overlook what that war was for the Russians. The war rescued not only their country, not only Soviet Jewry, but also the entire social system of the Western world from Hitler. This war exacted such sacrifice from the Russian people that its strength and health have never since fully recovered. That war overstrained the Russian people. It was yet another disaster on top of those of the Civil War and de-kulakization – and from which the Russian people have almost run dry.

The ruthless and unrelenting Catastrophe, which was gradually devouring Soviet Jewry in a multitude of exterminating events all over the occupied lands, was part of a greater Catastrophe designed to eradicate the entire European Jewry.

As we examine only the events in Russia, the Catastrophe as a whole is not covered in this book. Yet the countless miseries having befallen on both our peoples, the Jewish and the Russian, in the 20th century, and the unbearable weight of the lessons of history and gnawing anxiety about the future, make it impossible not to share, if only briefly, some reflections about it, reflections of mine and others, and impossible not to examine how the high Jewish minds look at the Catastrophe from the historical perspective and how they attempt to encompass and comprehend it.

It is for a reason that the "Catastrophe" is always written with a capital letter. It was an epic event for such an ancient and historical people. It could not fail to arouse the strongest feelings and a wide variety of reflections and conclusions among the Jews.

[2721] *М. Куповецкий*. Людские потери еврейского населения… // Вестник Еврейского Ун-та…, 1995, № 2(9), с. 134-155.

[2722] КЕЭ, т. 8, с. 299.

[2723] *Е.М. Андреев, Л.Е. Царский, Т.Л. Харькова*. Население Советского Союза, 1922-1991. М., 1993, с. 78.

In many Jews, long ago assimilated and distanced from their own people, the Catastrophe reignited a more distinct and intense sense of their Jewishness.

Yet "for many, the Catastrophe became a proof that God is dead. If He had existed, He certainly would never have allowed Auschwitz."[2724] Then there is an opposite reflection: "Recently, a former Auschwitz inmate said: "In the camps, we were given a new Torah, though we have not been able to read it yet."[2725]

An Israeli author states with conviction: "The Catastrophe happened because we did not follow the Covenant and did not return to our land. We had to return to our land to rebuild the Temple."[2726]

Still, such an understanding is achieved only by a very few, although it does permeate the entire Old Testament.

Some have developed and still harbor a bitter feeling: "Once, humanity turned away from us. We weren't a part of the West at the time of the Catastrophe. The West rejected us, cast us away."[2727] "We are as upset by the nearly absolute indifference of the world and even of non-European Jewry to the plight of the Jews in the fascist countries as by the Catastrophe in Europe itself.

... What a great guilt lies on the democracies of the world in general and especially on the Jews in the democratic countries! ... The pogrom in Kishinev was an insignificant crime compared to the German atrocities, to ... the methodically implemented plan of extermination of millions of Jewish lives; and yet Kishinev pogrom triggered a bigger protest... Even the Beilis Trial in Kiev attracted more worldwide attention."[2728]

But this is unfair. After the world realized the essence and the scale of the destruction, the Jews experienced consistent and energetic support and passionate compassion from many nations.

Some contemporary Israelis recognize this and even warn their compatriots against any such excesses: "Gradually, the memory of the Catastrophe ceased to be just a memory. It has become the ideology of the Jewish state. ... The memory of the Catastrophe turned into a religious devotion, into the state cult.

[2724] КЭЕ, т. 4, с. 175.
[2725] *М. Каганская*. Миф против реальности // "22", 1988, № 58, с. 144.
[2726] *Н. Гутина*. Ориентация на Храм // Там же, с. 191.
[2727] *М. Каганская*. Миф против реальности // Там же, с. 141 -142.
[2728] *А. Менес*. Катастрофа и возрождение // ЕМ-2, с. 111.

... The State of Israel has assumed the role of an apostle of the cult of the Catastrophe, the role of a priest who collects routine tithes from other nations. And woe to those who refuse to pay that tithe!" And in conclusion: "The worst legacy of Nazism for Jews is the Jews role of a super-victim."[2729]

Here is a similar excerpt from yet another author: the cult of the Catastrophe has filled "a void in the souls of secular Jews," "from being a reaction to an event of the past, the trauma of the Catastrophe has evolved into a new national symbol, replacing all other symbols." And "this 'mentality of the Catastrophe is growing with each passing year"; "if we do not recover from the trauma of Auschwitz, we will never become a normal nation."[2730]

Among the Jews, the sometimes painful work of re-examining the Catastrophe never ceases. Here is the opinion of an Israeli historian, a former inmate of a Soviet camp: "I do not belong to those Jews who are inclined to blame the evil 'goyim' for our national misfortunes while casting ourselves as... poor lambs or toys in the hands of others. Anyway not in the 20th century!

On the contrary, I fully agree with Hannah Arendt that the Jews of our century were equal participants in the historical games of the nations and the monstrous Catastrophe that befell them was the result of not only evil plots of the enemies of mankind, but also of the huge fatal miscalculations on the part of the Jewish people themselves, their leaders and activists."[2731]

Indeed, Hannah Arendt was "searching for the causes of the Catastrophe [also] in Jewry itself. ... Her main argument is that modern anti-Semitism was one of the consequences of the particular attitudes of the Jews towards the state and society in Europe"; the Jews "turned out to be unable to evaluate power shifts in a nation state and growing social contradictions."[2732]

In the late 1970s, we read in Dan Levin's book: "On this issue, I agree with Prof. Branover who believes that the Catastrophe was largely a punishment for our sins, including the sin of leading the communist movement. There is something in it."[2733]

[2729] *Бен-Барух.* Тень // "22", 1988, № 58, с. 197-198, 200.
[2730] *Ури Авнери.* Последняя месть Адольфа Гитлера // "22", 1993, № 85, с. 132, 134, 139.
[2731] *М. Хейфец.* Что надо выяснить во времени // "22", 1989, № 64, с. 218-219.
[2732] *Sonja Margolina.* Das Ende der Lügen: Rußland und die Juden im 20. Jahrhundert. Berlin: Siedler Verlag, 1992, pp. 137-138.
[2733] *Дан Левин.* На краю соблазна: [Интервью] // "22", 1978, № 1, с. 55.

Yet no such *noticeable* movement can be observed among world Jewry. To a great many contemporary Jews such conclusions appear insulting and blasphemous.

To the contrary: "The very fact of the Catastrophe served as a moral justification for Jewish chauvinism. Lessons of the Second World War have been learned exactly contrariwise. ... The ideology of Jewish Nationalism has grown and strengthened on this soil. This is terribly sad. A feeling of guilt and compassion towards the nation-victim has become an indulgence, absolving the sin unforgivable for all others. It is hence comes the moral permissibility of public appeals not to mix one's own ancient blood with the alien blood."[2734]

In the late 1980s, a Jewish publicist from Germany wrote: "Today, the moral capital of Auschwitz is already spent."[2735] One year later, she stated: "Solid moral capital gained by the Jews because of Auschwitz seems to be depleted"; the Jews "can no longer proceed along the old way by raising pretensions to the world. Today, the world already has the right to converse with the Jews as it does with all others"; "the struggle for the rights of Jews is no more progressive than a struggle for the rights of all other nations. It is high time to break the mirror and look around – we are not alone in this world."[2736]

It would have been equally great for Russian minds to elevate themselves to similarly decent and benevolent self-criticism, especially in making judgments about Russian history of the 20th century – the brutality of the Revolutionary period, the cowed indifference of the Soviet times and the abominable plundering of the post-Soviet age. And to do it despite the unbearable burden of realization that it was we Russians who ruined our history – through our useless rulers but also through our own worthlessness – and despite the gnawing anxiety that this may be irredeemable – to perceive the Russian experience as possibly a punishment from the Supreme Power.

[2734] Д. *Хмельницкий*. Под звонкий голос крови, или с самосознанием наперевес // "22", 1992, № 80, с. 175.

[2735] С. *Марголина*. Германия и евреи: вторая попытка // Страна и мир, 1991, № 3, с. 142.

[2736] Sonja Margolina. *Das Ende der Lügen*..., pp. 150-151.

Chapter 22

From the end of the war to Stalin's death

At the beginning of the 1920s the authors of a collection of articles titled *Russia and the Jews* foresaw that "all these bright perspectives" (for the Jews in the USSR) looked so bright only "if one supposes that the Bolsheviks would want to protect us. But would they? Can we assume that the people who in their struggle for power betrayed everything, from the Motherland to Communism, would remain faithful to us even when it stops benefiting them?"[2737]

However, during so favorable a time to them as the 1920s and 1930s the great majority of Soviet Jews chose to ignore this sober warning or simply did not hear it.

Yet the Jews with their contribution to the Russian Revolution should have expected that one day the inevitable recoil of revolution would hit even them, at least during its ebb.

The postwar period became "the years of deep disappointments"[2738] and adversity for Soviet Jews. During Stalin's last eight years, Soviet Jewry was tested by persecutions of the "cosmopolitans," the loss of positions in science, arts and press, the crushing of the Jewish Anti-Fascist Committee (EAK) with the execution of its leadership and, finally, by the "Doctors' Plot."

By the nature of a totalitarian regime, only Stalin himself could initiate the campaign aimed at weakening the Jewish presence and influence in the Soviet system. Only he could make the first move.

Yet because of the rigidity of Soviet propaganda and Stalin's craftiness, not a single sound could be uttered nor a single step made in the open. We have seen already that Soviet propaganda did not raise any alarm about the

---

[2737] И.М. Бикерман. Россия и русское еврейство // Россия и евреи: Сб. 1 / Отечественное объединение русских евреев за границей. Париж: YMCA-Press, 1978, с. 80 [1-е изд. — Берлин: Основа, 1924].

[2738] С. Шварц. Евреи в Советском Союзе с начала Второй мировой войны (1939-1965). Нью-Йорк: Изд. Американского Еврейского Рабочего Комитета, 1966, с. 198.

annihilation of Jews in Germany during the war; indeed it covered up those things, obviously being afraid of appearing pro-Jewish in the eyes of its own citizens.

The disposition of the Soviet authorities towards Jews could evolve for years without ever really surfacing at the level of official propaganda. The first changes and shuffles in the bureaucracy began quite inconspicuously at the time of growing rapprochement between Stalin and Hitler in 1939. By then Litvinov, a Jewish Minister of Foreign Affairs, was replaced by Molotov (an ethnic Russian) and a 'cleansing' of the Ministry of Foreign Affairs (NKID) was underway. Simultaneously, Jews were barred from entrance into diplomatic schools and military academies. Still, it took many more years before the disappearance of Jews from the NKID and the sharp decline of their influence in the Ministry of Foreign Trade became apparent.

Because of the intrinsic secrecy of all Soviet inner party moves, only very few were aware of the presence of the subtle anti-Jewish undercurrents in the Agitprop apparatus by the end of 1942 that aimed to push out Jews from the major art centers such as the Bolshoi Theatre, the Moscow Conservatory, and the Moscow Philarmonic, where, according to the note which Alexandrov, Head of Agitprop, presented to the Central Committee in the summer of 1942, 'everything was almost completely in the hands of non-Russians' and 'Russians had become an ethnic minority' (accompanied by a detailed table to convey particulars).[2739] Later, there had been attempts to "begin national regulation of cadres... from the top down, which essentially meant primarily pushing out Jews from the managerial positions".[2740] By and large, Stalin regulated this process by either supporting or checking such efforts depending on the circumstances.

The wartime tension in the attitudes toward Jews was also manifested during post-war re-evacuation. In Siberia and Central Asia, wartime Jewish refugees were not welcomed by the local populace, so after the war they mostly settled in the capitals of Central Asian republics, except for those who moved back, not to their old shtetls and towns, but into the larger cities.[2741]

The largest returning stream of refugees fled to Ukraine where they were met with hostility by the local population, especially because of the return of Soviet officials and the owners of desirable residential property. This reaction in the formerly occupied territories was also fueled by Hitler's

---

[2739] Г.В. Костырченко. Тайная политика Сталина: Власть и антисемитизм. М.: Международные отношения, 2001, с. 259-260.
[2740] Там же, с. 310.
[2741] С. Шварц. Евреи в Советском Союзе..., с. 181-182, 195.

incendiary propaganda during the Nazi occupation. Khrushchev, the Head of Ukraine from 1943 (when he was First Secretary of the Communist Party and at the same time Chairman of the Council of People's Commissars of Ukraine), not only said nothing on this topic in his public speeches, treating the fate of Jews during the occupation with silence, but he also upheld the secret instruction throughout Ukraine not to employ Jews in positions of authority.

According to the tale of an old Jewish Communist Ruzha-Godes, who survived the entire Nazi occupation under a guise of being a Pole named Khelminskaya and was later denied employment by the long-awaited Communists because of her Jewishness, Khrushchev stated clearly and with his peculiar frankness: "In the past, the Jews committed many sins against the Ukrainian people. People hate them for that. We don't need Jews in our Ukraine. It would be better if they didn't return here. They would better go to Birobidzhan. This is Ukraine. And, we don't want Ukrainian people to infer that the return of Soviet authority means the return of Jews".[2742]

"In the early September 1945 a Jewish major of the NKVD was brutally beaten in Kiev by two members of the military. He shot both of them dead. This incident caused a large-scale massacre of Jews with five fatalities".[2743] There are documented sources of other similar cases.[2744]

Sotsialistichesky Vestnik wrote that the Jewish "national feelings (which were exacerbated during the war) overreacted to the numerous manifestations of anti-Semitism and to the even more common indifference to anti-Semitism".[2745]

This motif is so typical — almost as much as anti-Semitism itself: the indifference to anti-Semitism was likely to cause outrage. Yes, preoccupied by their own miseries, people and nations often lose compassion for the troubles of others. And the Jews are not an exception here. A modern author justly notes: "I hope that I, as a Jew who found her roots and place in Israel, would not be accused of apostasy if I point out that in the years

---

[2742] Хрущёв и еврейский вопрос // Социалистический вестник*, Нью-Йорк, 1961, № 1, с. 19.

[2743] Краткая Еврейская Энциклопедия (далее — КЕЭ). Иерусалим: Общество по исследованию еврейских общин, 1996. Т. 8, с. 236.

[2744] Социалистический вестник, 1961, № 1, с. 19-20; Книга о русском еврействе, 1917-1967 (далее — КРЕ-2). Нью-Йорк: Союз Русских Евреев, 1968, с. 146.

[2745] Хрущёв и миф о Биробиджане // Социалистический вестник, 1958, № 7-8, с. 145.

of our terrible disasters, the Jewish intellectuals did not raise their voices in defense of the deported nations of Crimea and the Caucasus".[2746]

After the liberation of Crimea by the Red Army in 1943, "talks started among circles of the Jewish elite in Moscow about a rebirth of the Crimean project of 1920s," i.e., about resettling Jews in Crimea. The Soviet government did not discourage these aspirations, hoping that "American Jews would be more generous in their donations for the Red Army." It is quite possible that Mikhoels and Feffer [heads of the Jewish Anti-Fascist Committee, EAK], based on a verbal agreement with Molotov, negotiated with American Zionists about financial support of the project for Jewish relocation to Crimea during their triumphal tour of the USA in summer of 1943. The idea of a Crimean Jewish Republic was also backed by Lozovsky, the then-powerful Assistant Minister of Foreign Affairs.[2747]

The EAK had yet another project for a Jewish Republic — to establish it in the place of the former Volga German Autonomous Soviet Socialist Republic (where, as we have seen in previous chapters, Jewish settlements were established in the wake of the exile of the Germans). Ester Markish, widow of EAK member Perets Markish, confirms that he presented a letter "concerning transferring the former German Republic to the Jews".[2748]

In the Politburo, "Molotov, Kaganovich and Voroshilov were the most positively disposed to the EAK".[2749] And, "according to rumors, some members of the Politburo... were inclined to support this [Crimean] idea".[2750] On February 15, 1944, Stalin was forwarded a memorandum about that plan which was signed by Mikhoels, Feffer and Epshtein. (According to P. Sudoplatov, although the decision to expel the Tatars from Crimea had been made by Stalin earlier, the order to carry it out reached Beria on February 14,[2751] so the memorandum was quite timely.)

That was the high point of Jewish hopes. G. V. Kostirenko, a researcher of this period, writes: the leaders of the EAK "plunged into euphoria. They imagined (especially after Mikhoels' and Feffer's trip to the West) that with the necessary pressure, they could influence and steer their

---

[2746] М. Блинкова. Знание и мнение // Стрелец, Jersey City, 1988, № 12, с. 12.
[2747] Г.В. Костырченко. Тайная политика Сталина, с. 428-429.
[2748] Э. Маркиш. Как их убивали // "22": Общественно-политический и литературный журнал еврейской интеллигенции из СССР в Израиле. Тель-Авив, 1982, № 25, с. 203.
[2749] Г.В. Костырченко. Тайная политика Сталина, с. 430.
[2750] КЕЭ, т. 4, с. 602.
[2751] Павел Судоплатов. Спецоперации: Лубянка и Кремль: 1930-1950 годы. М.: ОЛМА-Пресс, 1997, с. 466-467.

government's policy in the interests of the Soviet Jews, just like the American Jewish elite does it".[2752]

But Stalin did not approve the Crimean project – it did not appeal to him because of the strategic importance of the Crimea. The Soviet leaders expected a war with America and probably thought that in such case the entire Jewish population of Crimea would sympathize with the enemy. (It is reported that at the beginning of the 1950s some Jews were arrested and told by their MGB [Ministry for State Security, a predecessor of KGB] investigators: "You are not going to stand against America, are you? So you are our enemies.") Khrushchev shared those doubts and 10 years later he stated to a delegation of the Canadian Communist party that was expressing particular interest in the Jewish question in the USSR: Crimea "should not be a center of Jewish colonization, because in case of war it will become the enemy's bridgehead".[2753] Indeed, the petitions about Jewish settlement in Crimea were very soon used as a proof of the "state treason" on the part of the members of the EAK.

By the end of WWII the authorities again revived the idea of Jewish resettlement in Birobidzhan, particularly Ukrainian Jews. From 1946 to 1947 several organized echelons and a number of independent families were sent there, totaling up to 5-6 thousand persons.[2754] However, quite a few returned disillusioned. This relocation movement withered by 1948. Later, with a general turn of Stalin's politics, arrests among the few Birobidjan Jewish activists started. (They were accused of artificial inculcation of Jewish culture into the non-Jewish population and, of course, espionage and of having planned Birobidzhan's secession in order to ally with Japan). This was the de facto end of the history of Jewish colonization in Birobidzhan. At the end of the 1920s there were plans to re-settle 60,000 Jews there by the end of the first 5-year planning period. By 1959 there were only 14,000 Jews in Birobidzhan, less than 9% of the population of the region.[2755] However, in Ukraine the situation had markedly changed in favor of Jews.

The government was engaged in the fierce struggle with Bandera's separatist fighters and no longer catered to the national feelings of Ukrainians. At the end of 1946, the Communist Party "started a covert campaign against antiSemitism, gradually conditioning the population to the presence of Jews among authorities in different spheres of the national economy." At the same time, in the beginning of 1947, Kaganovich took

---

[2752] Г.В. Костырченко. Тайная политика Сталина, с. 435.
[2753] Крымское дело // Социалистический вестник, 1957, № 5, с. 98.
[2754] С.М. Шварц. Биробиджан // КРЕ-2, с. 189.
[2755] Там же, с. 192, 195-196.

over for Khrushchev as the official leader of Ukrainian Communist Party. The Jews were promoted in the party as well, "of which a particular example was the appointment of a Jew ... the Secretary... of Zhitomir Obkom".[2756]

However, the attitudes of many Jews towards this government and its new policies were justifiably cautious. Soon after the end of the war, when the former Polish citizens began returning to Poland, many non-Polish Jews "hastily seized this opportunity" and relocated there.[2757] (What happened after that in Poland is yet another story: a great overrepresentation of Jews occurred in the post-war puppet Polish government, among managerial elites and in the Polish KGB, which would again result in miserable consequences for the Jews of Poland. After the war, other countries of Eastern Europe saw similar conflicts: "the Jews had played a huge role in economic life of all these countries," and though they lost their possessions under Hitler, after the war, when "the restitution laws were introduced... (they) affected very large numbers of new owners." Upon their return Jews demanded the restoration of their property and enterprises that were not nationalized by Communists and this created a new wave of hostility towards them.[2758])

Meanwhile, during these very years the biggest event in world Jewish history was happening — the state of Israel was coming into existence. In 1946-47, when the Zionists were at odds with Britain, Stalin, perhaps out of anti-British calculation and or opportunistically hoping to get a foothold there, took the side of the former. During all of 1947 Stalin, acting through Gromyko in the UN, actively supported the idea of the creation of an independent Jewish state in Palestine and supplied the Zionists with a critical supply of Czechoslovak-made weapons. In May 1948, only two days after the Israeli declaration of nationhood, the USSR officially recognized that country and condemned hostile actions of Arabs.

However, Stalin miscalculated to what extent this support would reinvigorate the national spirit of Soviet Jews. Some of them implored the EAK to organize a fundraiser for the Israeli military, others wished to enlist as volunteers, while still others wanted to form a special Jewish military division.[2759]

Amid this burgeoning enthusiasm, Golda Meir arrived to Moscow in September of 1948 as the first ambassador of Israel and was met with unprecedented joy in Moscow's synagogues and by Moscow's Jewish

---

[2756] С. Шварц. Евреи в Советском Союзе..., с. 185-186.
[2757] Там же, с. 130.
[2758] Там же, с. 217-218.
[2759] Г.В. Костырченко. Тайная политика Сталина, с. 403-404.

population in general. Immediately, as the national spirit of Soviet Jews rose and grew tremendously because of the Catastrophe, many of them began applying for relocation to Israel. Apparently, Stalin had expected that. Yet it turned out that many of his citizens wished to run away en masse into, by all accounts, the pro-Western State of Israel. There, the influence and prestige of the United States grew, while the USSR was at the same time losing support of Arab countries. (Nevertheless, "the cooling of relations [with Israel] was mutual. Israel more and more often turned towards American Jewry which became its main support".[2760])

Probably because he was frightened by such a schism in the Jewish national feelings, Stalin drastically changed policies regarding Jews from the end of 1948 and for the rest of his remaining years. He began acting in his typical style — quietly but with determination, he struck to the core, but with only tiny movements visible on the surface.

Nevertheless, while the visible tiny ripples hardly mattered, Jewish leaders had many reasons to be concerned, as they felt the fear hanging in the air. The then editor of the Polish-Jewish newspaper Folkshtimme, Girsh Smolyar, recalled the "panic that seized Soviet communist Jews after the war."

Emmanuel Kazakevitch and other Jewish writers were distressed. Smolyar had seen on Ehrenburg's table "a mountain of letters — literally scream of pain about current anti-Jewish attitudes throughout the country".[2761]

Yet Ehrenburg knew his job very well and carried it out. (As became known much later, it was exactly then that the pre-publication copy of the Black Book compiled by I. Ehrenburg and B. Grossman, which described the mass killings and suffering of the Soviet Jews during the Soviet-German war, was destroyed.) In addition, on September 21, 1948, as a counterbalance to Golda Meir's triumphal arrival, Pravda published a large article commissioned by Ehrenburg which stated that the Jews are not a nation at all and that they are doomed to assimilate.[2762] This article created dismay not only among Soviet Jews, but also in America. With the start of the Cold War, "the discrimination against the Jews in the Soviet Union "became one of the main anti-Soviet trump cards of the West. (As was the inclination in the West towards various ethnic separatist movements in the USSR, a sympathy that had never previously gained support among Soviet Jews).

[2760] С. Цирюльников. СССР, евреи и Израиль // Время и мы (далее — ВМ): Международный журнал литературы и общественных проблем. Нью-Йорк, 1987, № 96, с. 156.
[2761] С. Цирюльников. СССР, евреи и Израиль // ВМ, Нью-Йорк, 1987, № 96, с. 150.
[2762] И. Эренбург. По поводу одного письма // Правда, 1948, 21 сентября, с. 3.

However, the EAK, which had been created to address war-time issues, continued gaining influence. By that time it listed approximately 70 members, had its own administrative apparatus, a newspaper and a publishing house. It functioned as a kind of spiritual and physical agent of all Soviet Jews before the CK (Central Committee) of the VKPb (all-Russian Communist Party of Bolsheviks), as well as before the West. "EAK executives were allowed to do and to have a lot — a decent salary, an opportunity to publish and collect royalties abroad, to receive and to redistribute gifts from abroad and, finally, to travel abroad." EAK became the crystallization center of an initially elitist and upper-echelon and then of a broadly growing Jewish national movement",[2763] a burgeoning symbol of Jewish national autonomy. For Stalin, the EAK become a problem which had to be dealt with.

He started with the most important figure, the Head of the Soviet Information Bureau (Sovinformburo), Lozovsky, who, according to Feffer (who was vice-chairman of EAK since July 1945), was "the spiritual leader of the EAK... knew all about its activities and was its head for all practical purposes."

In the summer of 1946, a special auditing commission from Agitprop of the CK [of the VKPb] inspected Sovinformburo and found that "the apparatus is polluted ... [there is] an intolerable concentration of Jews." Lozovsky was ejected from his post of Assistant Minister of Foreign Affairs (just as Litvinov and Maisky had been) and in summer of 1947 he also lost his post as of Head of the Sovinformburo.[2764]

After that, the fate of the EAK was sealed. In September of 1946, the auditing commission from the Central Committee concluded that the EAK, instead of "leading a rigorous offensive ideological war against the Western and above all Zionist propaganda... supports the position of bourgeois Zionists and the Bund and in reality... it fights for the reactionary idea of a United Jewish nation." In 1947, the Central Committee stated, that "the work among the Jewish population of the Soviet Union is not a responsibility" of the EAK. "The EAK's job was to focus on the "decisive struggle against aggression by international reactionaries and their Zionist agents".[2765]

However, these events coincided with the pro-Israel stance of the USSR and the EAK was not dissolved. On the other hand, EAK Chairman Mikhoels who was "the informal leader of Soviet Jewry, had to shed his illusions about the possibility of influencing the Kremlin's national policy

---

[2763] Г.В. Костырченко. Тайная политика Сталина, с. 353, 398.
[2764] Там же*, с. 361, 363-364.
[2765] Там же, с. 366, 369.

via influencing the Dictator's relatives." Here, the suspicion fell mostly on Stalin's son—in-law Grigory Morozov. However, the most active help to the EAK was provided by Molotov's wife, P.S. Zhemchyzhina, who was arrested in the beginning of 1949, and Voroshilov's wife, "Ekaterina Davidovna (Golda Gorbman), a fanatic Bolshevik, who had been expelled from the synagogue in her youth."

Abakumov reported that Mikhoels was suspected of "gathering private information about the Leader".[2766] Overall, according to the MGB he "demonstrated excessive interest in the private life of the Head of the Soviet Government," while leaders of the EAK "gathered materials about the personal life of J. Stalin and his family at the behest of US Intelligence".[2767] However, Stalin could not risk an open trial of the tremendously influential Mikhoels, so Mikhoels was murdered in January 1948 under the guise of an accident. Soviet Jewry was shocked and terrified by the demise of their spiritual leader.

The EAK was gradually dismantled after that. By the end of 1948 its premises were locked up, all documents were taken to Lubyanka, and its newspaper and the publishing house were closed. Feffer and Zuskin, the key EAK figures, were secretly arrested soon afterwards and these arrests were denied for a long time. In January 1949 Lozovsky was arrested, followed by the arrests of a number of other notable members of the EAK in February. They were intensively interrogated during 1949, but in 1950 the investigation stalled.

(All this coincided [in accord with Stalin's understanding of balance] with the annihilation of the Russian nationalist tendencies in the leadership of the Leningrad government — the so-called "anti-party group of Kuznetsov-Rodionov-Popkov," but those developments, their repression and the significance of those events were largely overlooked by historians even though "about two thousand party functionaries were arrested and subsequently executed"[2768] in 1950 in connection with the "Leningrad Affair").

In January 1948, Stalin ordered Jews to be pushed out of Soviet culture. In his usual subtle and devious manner, the "order" came through a prominent editorial in *Pravda*, seemingly dealing with a petty issue, "about one anti-Party group of theatrical critics".[2769] (A more assertive article in *Kultura i*

[2766] Г.В. Костырченко. Тайная политика Сталина, с. 376, 379, 404.
[2767] КЕЭ, т. 8, с. 243.
[2768] Там же, с. 248.
[2769] Правда, 1949, 28 января, с. 3.

Zhizn followed on the next day[2770]). The key point was the "decoding" of Russian the Russian pen-names of Jewish celebrities. In the USSR, "many Jews camouflage their Jewish origins with such artifice," so that "it is impossible to figure out their real names" explains the editor of a modern Jewish journal.[2771]

This article in *Pravda* had a long but obscure pre-history. In 1946 reports of the Central Committee it was already noted "that out of twenty-eight highly publicized theatrical critics, only six are Russians. It implied that the majority of the rest were Jews." Smelling trouble, but still "supposing themselves to be vested with the highest trust of the Party, some theatrical critics, confident of victory, openly confronted Fadeev" in November 1946.[2772] Fadeev was the all-powerful Head of the Union of Soviet Writers and Stalin's favorite. And so they suffered a defeat. Then the case stalled for a long time and only resurfaced in 1949.

The campaign rolled on through the newspapers and party meetings. G. Aronson, researching Jewish life "in Stalin's era" writes: "The goal of this campaign was to displace Jewish intellectuals from all niches of Soviet life.

Informers were gloatingly revealing their pen-names. It turned out that E. Kholodov is actually Meyerovich, Jakovlev is Kholtsman, Melnikov is Millman, Jasny is Finkelstein, Vickorov is Zlochevsky, Svetov is Sheidman and so on. *Literaturnaya Gazeta* worked diligently on these disclosures".[2773]

Undeniably, Stalin hit the worst-offending spot, the one that highly annoyed the public. However, Stalin was not so simple as to just blurt out "the Jews."

From the first push at the "groups of theatrical critics" flowed a broad and sustained campaign against the "cosmopolitans" (with their Soviet inertial dim-wittedness they overused this innocent term and spoiled it). "Without exception, all 'cosmopolitans' under attack were Jews. They were being discovered everywhere. Because all of them were loyal Soviet citizens never suspected of anything anti-Soviet, they survived the great purges by Yezhov and Yagoda.

Some were very experienced and influential people, sometimes eminent in their fields of expertise".[2774] The exposure of "cosmopolitans" then turned

---

[2770] На чуждых позициях: (О происках антипатриотической группы театральных критиков) // Культура и жизнь, 1949, 30 января, с. 2-3.
[2771] В. Перельман. ...Виноваты сами евреи // ВМ, Тель-Авив, 1977, № 23, с. 216.
[2772] Г.В. Костырченко. Тайная политика Сталина, с. 321, 323.
[2773] Г. Аронсон. Еврейский вопрос в эпоху Сталина // КРЕ-2, с. 150.
[2774] Г. Аронсон. Еврейский вопрос в эпоху Сталина // КРЕ-2, с. 150.

into a ridiculous, even idiotic glorification of Russian "primacy" in all and every area of science, technology and culture.

Yet the "cosmopolitans" usually were not being arrested but instead were publicly humiliated, fired from publishing houses, ideological and cultural organizations, from TASS, from Glavlit, from literature schools, theaters, orchestras; some were expelled from the party and publication of their works was often discouraged.

And the public campaign was expanding, spreading into new fields and compromising new names. Anti-Jewish cleansing of "cosmopolitans" was conducted in the research institutes of the Academy of Science: Institute of Philosophy (with its long history of internecine feuding between different cliques), the institutes of Economy, Law, in the Academy of Social Sciences at the CK of the VKPb, in the School of Law (and then spread to the office of Public Prosecutor).

Thus, in the Department of History at MGU (Moscow State University), even a long-standing faithful communist and falsifier, I. I. Minz, member of the Academy, who enjoyed Stalin's personal trust and was awarded with Stalin Prizes and concurrently chaired historical departments in several universities, was labeled "the head of cosmopolitans in Historical Science." After that numerous scientific posts at MGU were 'liberated' from his former students and other Jewish professors.[2775]

Purges of Jews from technical fields and the natural sciences were gradually gaining momentum. "The end of 1945 and all of 1946 were relatively peaceful for the Jews of this particular social group." L. Mininberg studied Jewish contributions in Soviet science and industry during the war: "In 1946, the first serious blow since the end of the war was dealt to the administration and a big 'case' was fabricated. Its principal victims were mainly Russians... there were no Jews among them," though "investigation reports contained testaments against Israel Solomonovitch Levin, director of the Saratov Aviation Plant. He was accused on the charge that during the Battle for Stalingrad, two aviation regiments were not able to take off because of manufacturing defects in the planes produced by the plant. The charge was real, not made-up by the investigators. However, Levin was neither fired nor arrested." In 1946, "B.L. Vannikov, L.M. Kaganovich, S.Z. Ginzburg, L.Z. Mekhlis all kept their Ministry posts in the newly formed government... Almost all Jewish former deputy

---

[2775] А. Некрич. Поход против "космополитов" в МГУ // Континент: Литературный, обществ.-политический и религиозный журнал. Париж, 1981, № 28, с. 301-320.

ministers also retained their positions as assistants to ministers." The first victims among the Jewish technical elite appeared only in 1947.[2776]

In 1950, academic A. F. Ioffe "was forced to retire from the post of Director of the Physical-Engineering Institute, which he organized and headed since its inception in 1918." In 1951, 34 directors and 31 principal engineers of aviation plants had been fired. "This list contained mostly Jews." If in 1942 there were nearly forty Jewish directors and principal engineers in the Ministry of General Machine-Building (Ministry of Mortar Artillery) then only three remained by 1953. In the Soviet Army, "the Soviet authorities persecuted not only Jewish generals, but lower ranking officers working on the development of military technology and weaponry were also removed".[2777]

Thus, the "purging campaigns" spread over to the defense, airplane construction, and automobile industries (though they did not affect the nuclear branch), primarily removing Jews from administrative, directorial and principal engineering positions; later purging was expanded onto various bureaucracies.

Yet the genuine, ethnic denominator was never mentioned in the formal paperwork. Instead, the sacked officials faced charges of economic crimes or having relatives abroad at a time when conflict with the USA was expected, or other excuses were used. The purging campaigns rolled over the central cities and across the provinces. The methods of these campaigns were notoriously Soviet, in the spirit of 1930s: a victim was inundated in a vicious atmosphere of terror and as a result often tried to deflect the threat to himself by accusing others.

By repeating the tide of 1937, albeit in a milder form, the display of Soviet Power reminded the Jews that they had never become truly integrated and could be pushed aside at any moment. "We do not have indispensable people!"

(However, "Lavrentiy Beria was tolerant of Jews. At least, in appointments to positions in government".[2778])

"'Pushing' Jews out of prestigious occupations that were crucial for the ruling elite in the spheres of manufacturing, administration, cultural and ideological activities, as well as limiting or completely barring the entrance of Jews into certain institutions of higher education gained enormous momentum in 1948-1953. ... Positions of any importance in the KGB,

---

[2776] Л.Л. Мининберг. Советские евреи в науке и промышленности СССР в период Второй мировой войны (1941-1945). М., 1995, с. 413, 414, 415.
[2777] Там же, с. 416, 417, 427, 430.
[2778] Л.Л. Мининберг. Советские евреи в науке и промышленности... с. 442.

party apparatus, and military were closed to the Jews, and quotas were in place for admission into certain educational institutions and cultural and scientific establishments".[2779]

Through its "fifth item" [i.e., the question about nationality] Soviet Jews were oppressed by the very same method used in the Proletarian Questionnaire, other items of which were so instrumental in crushing the Russian nobility, clergy, intellectuals and all the rest of the "former people" since the 1920s.

"Although the highest echelon of the Jewish political elite suffered from administrative perturbations, surprisingly it was not as bad as it seemed," — concludes G. V. Kostyrchenko. "The main blow fell on the middle and the most numerous stratum of the Jewish elite — officials... and also journalists, professors and other members of the creative intelligentsia. ... It was these, so to say, nominal Jews — the individuals with nearly complete lack of ethnic ties — who suffered the brunt of the cleansing of bureaucracies after the war".[2780]

However, speaking of scientific cadres, the statistics are these: "at the end of the 1920s there were 13.6% Jews among scientific researchers in the country, in 1937 — 17.5%",[2781] and by 1950 their proportion slightly decreased to 15.4% (25,125 Jews among 162,508 Soviet researchers).[2782] S. Margolina, looking back from the end of the 1980s concludes that, despite the scale of the campaign, after the war, "the number of highly educated Jews in high positions always remained disproportionally high. But, in contrast with the former "times of happiness," it certainly had decreased".[2783] A.M. Kheifetz recalls "a memoir article of a member of the Academy, Budker, one of the fathers of the Soviet A-bomb" where he described how they were building the first Soviet A-bomb — being exhausted from the lack of sleep and fainting from stress and overwork — and it is precisely those days of persecution of "cosmopolitans" that were "the most inspired and the happiest" in his life.[2784]

In 1949 "among Stalin Prize laureates no less than 13% were Jews, just like in the previous years." By 1952 there were only 6%.[2785] Data on the

---

[2779] КЕЭ, т. 6, с. 855.
[2780] Г.В. Костырченко. Тайная политика Сталина, с. 515, 518.
[2781] КЕЭ, т. 8, с. 190.
[2782] И. Домальский. Технология ненависти* // ВМ, Тель-Авив, 1978, № 25, с. 120.
[2783] Sonja Margolina. Das Ende der LAgen: Rulland und die Juden im 20. Jahrhundert. Berlin: Siedler Verlag, 1992, S. 86.
[2784] Михаил Хейфец. Место и время (еврейские заметки). Париж: Третья волна, 1978, с. 68-69.
[2785] С.М. Шварц. Антисемитизм в Советском Союзе. Нью-Йорк: Изд-во им. Чехова, 1952, 225-226. 229.

number of Jewish students in USSR were not published for nearly a quarter of century, from the pre-war years until 1963. We will examine those in the next chapter.

The genuine Jewish culture that had been slowly reviving after the war was curtailed and suppressed in 1948-1951. Jewish theatres were no longer subsidized and the few remaining ones were closed, along with book publishing houses, newspapers and bookstores. [2786] In 1949, the international radio broadcasting in Yiddish was also discontinued.[2787]

In the military, "by 1953 almost all Jewish generals" and "approximately 300 colonels and lieutenant colonels were forced to resign from their positions".[2788]

As the incarcerated Jewish leaders remained jailed in Lubyanka for over three years, Stalin slowly and with great caution proceeded in dismantling the EAK.

He was very well aware what kind of international storm would be triggered by using force. (Luckily, though, he acquired his first H-bomb in 1949.) On the other hand, he fully appreciated the significance of unbreakable ties between world Jewry and America, his enemy since his rejection of the Marshall Plan.

Investigation of EAK activities was reopened in January 1952. The accused were charged with connections to the "Jewish nationalist organizations in America," with providing "information regarding the economy of the USSR" to those organizations... and also with "plans of repopulating Crimea and creating a Jewish Republic there".[2789] Thirteen defendants were found guilty and sentenced to death: S. A. Lozovsky, I. S. Ysefovich, B. A. Shimeliovich, V. L. Zuskin, leading Jewish writers D.R. Bergelson, P. D. Marshik, L. M. Kvitko, I. S. Feffer, D. N. Gofshtein, and also L. Y. Talmi, I. S. Vatenberg, C. S. Vatenberg — Ostrovsky, and E. I. Teumin.[2790] They were secretly executed in August.

(Ehrenburg, who was also a member of the EAK, was not even arrested. (He assumed it was pure luck.) Similarly, the crafty David Zaslavsky survived also.

[2786] С. Шварц. Евреи в Советском Союзе..., с. 161-163; Л. Шапиро. Евреи в Советской России после Сталина // КРЕ-2, с. 373.
[2787] КЕЭ, т. 8, с. 245.
[2788] КЕЭ, т. 1, с. 687.
[2789] КЕЭ, т. 8, с. 251.
[2790] Г.В. Костырченко. Тайная политика Сталина, с. 473.

And even after the execution of the Jewish writers, Ehrenburg continued to reassure the West that those writers were still alive and writing.[2791] The annihilation of the Jewish Antifascist Committee went along with similar secret "daughter" cases; 110 people were arrested, 10 of them were executed and 5 died during the investigation.[2792]

In autumn of 1952 Stalin went into the open as arrests among Jews began, such as arrests of Jewish professors of medicine and among members of literary circles in Kiev in October 1952. This information immediately spread among Soviet Jews and throughout the entire world. On October 17th, *Voice of America* broadcast about "mass repressions" among Soviet Jews.[2793] Soviet "Jews were frozen by mortal fear".[2794]

Soon afterwards in November in Prague, a show trial of Slansky, the Jewish First Secretary of the Czechoslovak Communist Party, and several other top state and party leaders took place in a typically loud and populist Stalinist-type entourage. The trial was openly anti-Jewish with naming "world leading" Jews such as Ben Gurion and Morgenthau, and placing them in league with American leaders Truman and Acheson. The outcome was that eleven were hanged, eight Jews among them. Summing up the official version, K. Gotwald said: "This investigation and court trial ... disclosed a new channel through which treason and espionage permeated the Communist Party. This is Zionism".[2795]

At the same time, since summer of 1951, the development of the "Doctors' Plot" was gaining momentum. The case included the accusation of prominent physicians, doctors to the Soviet leadership, for the criminal treatment of state leaders. For the secret services such an accusation was nothing new, as similar accusations had been made against Professor D. D. Pletnev and physicians L. G. Levin and I. N. Kazakov already during the "Bukharin trial" in 1937. At that time, the gullible Soviet public gasped at such utterly evil plots. No one had any qualms about repeating the same old scenario.

Now we know much more about the "Doctors' Plot." Initially it was not entirely an anti-Jewish action; the prosecution list contained the names of several prominent Russian physicians as well. In essence, the affair was fueled by Stalin's generally psychotic state of mind, with his fear of plots and mistrust of the doctors, especially as his health deteriorated. By September 1952 prominent doctors were arrested in groups. Investigations

---

[2791] Г. Аронсон. Еврейский вопрос в эпоху Сталина //КРЕ-2, с. 155-156.
[2792] Г.В. Костырченко. Тайная политика Сталина, с. 507.
[2793] Г. Аронсон. Еврейский вопрос в эпоху Сталина // КРЕ-2, с. 152.
[2794] В. Богуславский. У истоков // "22," 1986, № 47, с. 102.
[2795] Г.В. Костырченко. Тайная политика Сталина*, с. 504.

unfolded with cruel beatings of suspects and wild accusations; slowly it turned into a version of "spying-terroristic plot connected with foreign intelligence organizations," "American hirelings," "saboteurs in white coats," "bourgeois nationalism" — all indicating that it was primary aimed at Jews. (Robert Conquest in *The Great Terror* follows this particular tragic line of involvement of highly placed doctors. In 1935, the false death certificate of Kuibyshev was signed by doctors G. Kaminsky, I. Khodorovsky, and L. Levin. In 1937 they signed a similarly false death certificate of Ordzhonikidze. They knew so many deadly secrets — could they expect anything but their own death? Conquest writes that Dr. Levin had cooperated with the Cheka since 1920. "Working with Dzerzhinsky, Menzhinsky, and Yagoda. ... [he] was trusted by the head of such an organization. ... It is factually correct to consider Levin... a member of Yagoda's circle in the NKVD." Further, we read something sententious:

"Among those outstanding doctors who [in 1937] moved against [Professor of Medicine] Pletnev and who had signed fierce accusative resolutions against him, we find the names of M. Vovsi, B. Kogan and V. Zelenin, who in their turn... were subjected to torture by the MGB in 1952-53 in connection with "the case of doctor-saboteurs," "as well as two other doctors, N. Shereshevky and V. Vinogradov who provided a pre-specified death certificate of Menzhinsky".[2796])

On January 3, 1953 *Pravda* and *Izvestiya* published an announcement by TASS about the arrest of a "group of doctors-saboteurs." The accusation sounded like a grave threat for Soviet Jewry, and, at the same time, by a degrading Soviet custom, prominent Soviet Jews were forced to sign a letter to *Pravda* with the most severe condemnation of the wiles of the Jewish "bourgeois nationalists" and their approval of Stalin's government. Several dozen signed the letter. (Among them were Mikhail Romm, D. Oistrakh, S. Marshak, L. Landau, B. Grossman, E. Gilels, I. Dunayevsky and others. Initially Ehrenburg did not sign it — he found the courage to write a letter to Stalin: "to ask your advice." His resourcefulness was unsurpassed indeed. To Ehrenburg, it was clear that "there is no such thing as the Jewish nation" and that assimilation is the only way and that Jewish nationalism "inevitably leads to betrayal." Yet that the letter that was offered to him to sign could be invidiously inferred by the "enemies of our country." He concluded that "I myself cannot resolve these questions," but if "leading comrades will let me know ... [that my signature] is desired ...

[2796] Роберт Конквест. Большой террор / Пер. с англ. Firenze: Edizioni Aurora, 1974, с. 168, 353, 738-739, 754, 756-757.

[and] useful for protecting our homeland and for peace in the world, I will sign it immediately".[2797])

The draft of that statement of loyalty was painstakingly prepared in the administration of the Central Committee and eventually its style became softer and more respectful. However, this letter never appeared in the press. Possibly because of the international outrage, the "Doctors' Plot" apparently began to slow down in the last days of Stalin.[2798]

After the public announcement, the "'Doctors' Plot' created a huge wave of repression of Jewish physicians all over the country. In many cities and towns, the offices of State Security began fabricating criminal cases against Jewish doctors. They were afraid to even go to work, and their patients were afraid to be treated by them".[2799]

After the "cosmopolitan" campaign, the menacing growl of "people's anger" in reaction to the "Doctors' Plot" utterly terrified many Soviet Jews, and a rumor arose (and then got rooted in the popular mind) that Stalin was planning a mass eviction of Jews to the remote parts of Siberia and North — a fear reinforced by the examples of postwar deportation of entire peoples. In his latest work G. Kostyrchenko, a historian and a scrupulous researcher of Stalin's "Jewish" policies, very thoroughly refutes this "myth of deportation," proving that it had never been confirmed, either then or subsequently by any facts, and even in principle such a deportation would not have been possible.[2800]

But it is amazing how bewildered were those circles of Soviet Jews, who were unfailingly loyal to the Soviet-Communist ideology. Many years later, S. K. told me: "There is no single action in my life that I am as ashamed of as my belief in the genuineness of the "Doctors' Plot" of 1953! — that they, perhaps involuntarily, were involved a foreign conspiracy..."

An article from the 1960s states that "in spite of a pronounced antiSemitism of Stalin's rule ... many [Jews] prayed that Stalin stayed alive, as they knew through experience that any period of weak power means a slaughter of Jews. We were well aware of the quite rowdy mood of the 'fraternal nations' toward us".[2801]

[2797] «Против попыток воскресить еврейский национализм.» Обращение И.Г. Эренбурга к И.В. Сталину // Источник: Документы русской истории. М., 1997, № 1, с. 141-146.
[2798] Г.В. Костырченко. Тайная политика Сталина, с. 682, 693.
[2799] КЕЭ, т. 8, с. 254, 255.
[2800] Г.В. Костырченко. Тайная политика Сталина, с. 671-685.
[2801] Н. Шапиро. Слово рядового советского еврея // Русский антисемитизм и евреи. Сб. Лондон, 1968, с, 50.

On February 9th a bomb exploded at the Soviet embassy in Tel Aviv. On February 11, 1953 the USSR broke off diplomatic relations with Israel. The conflict surrounding the "Doctors' Plot" intensified due to these events.

And then Stalin went wrong, and not for the first time, right? He did not understand how the thickening of the plot could threaten him personally, even within the secure quarters of his inaccessible political Olympus. The explosion of international anger coincided with the rapid action of internal forces, which could possibly have done away with Stalin. It could have happened through Beria (for example, according to Avtorhanov's version.[2802])

After a public communiqué about the "Doctors' Plot" Stalin lived only 51 days. "The release from custody and the acquittal of the doctors without trial were perceived by the older generation of Soviet Jews as a repetition of the Purim miracle": Stalin had perished on the day of Purim, when Esther saved the Jews of Persia from Haman.[2803]

On April 3 all the surviving accused in the "Doctors' Plot" were released. It was publicly announced the next day. And yet again it was the Jews who pushed the frozen history forward.

[2802] А. Авторханов. Загадка смерти Сталина: (Заговор Берия). Франкфурт-на-Майне: Посев, 1976, с. 231-239.
[2803] Д. Штурман. Ни мне мёда твоего, ни укуса твоего // "22," 1985, № 42, с. 140-141.

Chapter 23

Before the Six-Day War

On the next day after Stalin's death, on March 6, the MGB (Ministry of State Security) "ceased to exist", albeit only formally, as Beria had incorporated it into his own Ministry of Interior Affairs (MVD). This move allowed him "to disclose the abuses" by the MGB, including those of the still publicly unannounced MGB Minister, Ignatiev (who secretly replaced Abakumov). It seems that after 1952 Beria was losing Stalin's trust and had been gradually pushed out by Ignatiev-Ryumin during the Doctors' Plot'. Thus, by force of circumstances, Beria became a magnet for the new anti-Stalin opposition. And now, on April 4, just a month after Stalin's death, he enjoyed enough power to dismiss the "Doctors' Plot" and accuse Ryumin of its fabrication. Then three months later the diplomatic relations with Israel were restored.

All this reinvigorated hope among the Soviet Jews, as the rise of Beria could be very promising for them. However, Beria was soon ousted.

Yet because of the usual Soviet inertia, "with the death of Stalin ... many previously fired Jews were reinstalled in their former positions"; "during the period called the "thaw", many old Zionists ... were released from the camps"; "during the post-Stalin period, the first Zionist groups started to emerge – initially at local levels."[2804]

Yet once again the things began to turn unfavorably for the Jews. In March 1954, the Soviet Union vetoed the UN Security Council attempt to open the Suez Canal to Israeli ships. At the end of 1955, Khrushchev declared a pro-Arab, anti-Israel turn of Soviet foreign policy. In February 1956, in his famous report at the 20th Party Congress, Khrushchev, while speaking profusely about the massacres of 1937-1938, did not point any attention to the fact that there were so many Jews among the victims; he did not name Jewish leaders executed in 1952; and when speaking of the "Doctors' Plot," he did not stress that it was specifically directed against the Jews. "It is easy to imagine the bitter feelings this aroused among the Jews," they "swept

---

[2804] Краткая Еврейская Энциклопедия (далее — КЕЭ). Иерусалим: Общество по исследованию еврейских общин, 1996. Т. 8, с. 256.

the Jewish communist circles abroad and even the leadership of those Communist parties, where Jews constituted a significant percentage of members (such as in the Canadian and US Communist parties)."[2805] In April 1956 in Warsaw, under the communist regime (though with heavy Jewish influence), the Jewish newspaper *Volksstimme* published a sensational article, listing the names of Jewish cultural and social celebrities who perished from 1937-1938 and from 1948-1952. Yet at the same time the article also condemned the "capitalist enemies", "Beria's period" and welcomed the return of "Leninist national policy." "The article in *Volksstimme* had unleashed a storm."[2806]

International communist organizations and Jewish social circles loudly began to demand an explanation from the Soviet leaders. "Throughout 1956, foreign visitors to the Soviet Union openly asked about Jewish situation there, and particularly why the Soviet government has not yet abandoned the dark legacy of Stalinism on the Jewish question?"[2807] It became a recurrent theme for the foreign correspondents and visiting delegations of "fraternal communist parties". (Actually, that could be the reason for the loud denouncement in the Soviet press of the "betrayal" of Communism by Howard Fast, an American writer and former enthusiastic champion of Communism. Meanwhile, "hundreds of Soviet Jews from different cities in one form or another participated in meetings of resurgent Zionist groups and coteries"; "old Zionists with connections to relatives or friends in Israel were active in those groups."[2808]

In May 1956, a delegation from the French Socialist Party arrived in Moscow. "Particular attention was paid to the situation of Jews in the Soviet Union."[2809] Khrushchev found himself in a hot corner – now he could not afford to ignore the questions, yet he knew, especially after experiencing postwar Ukraine, that the Jews are not likely to be returned to their [high] social standing like in 1920s and 1930s. He replied: "In the beginning of the revolution, we had many Jews in executive bodies of party and government ....

After that, we have developed new cadres .... If Jews wanted to occupy positions of leadership in our republics today, it would obviously cause discontent among the local people .... If a Jew, appointed to a high office,

---

[2805] С. Шварц. Евреи в Советском Союзе с начала Второй мировой войны (1939-1965). Нью-Йорк: Изд. Американского Еврейского Рабочего Комитета, 1966, с. 247.
[2806] Там же, с. 247-248.
[2807] Хрущёв и еврейский вопрос // Социалистический вестник, Нью-Йорк, 1961, № 1, с. 20.
[2808] КЕЭ, т. 8, с. 257.
[2809] Хрущёв и еврейский вопрос // Социалистический вестник, 1961, № 1, с. 20.

surrounds himself with Jewish colleagues, it naturally provokes envy and hostility toward all Jews." (The French publication *Socialist Herald* calls "strange" and "false" the Khrushchev's point about "surrounding himself with Jewish colleagues".) In the same discussion, when Jewish culture and schools were addressed, Khrushchev explained that "if Jewish schools were established, there probably would not be many prospective students. The Jews are scattered all over the country .... If the Jews were required to attend a Jewish school, it certainly would cause outrage. It would be understood as a kind of a ghetto."[2810]

Three months later, in August 1956, a delegation of the Canadian Communist Party visited the USSR – and it stated outright that it had "a special mission to achieve clarity on the Jewish question". Thus, in the postwar years, the Jewish question was becoming a central concern of the western communists.

"Khrushchev rejected all accusations of anti-Semitism as a slander against him and the party." He named a number of Soviet Jews to important posts, "he even mentioned his Jewish daughter-in-law," but then he "quite suddenly ... switched to the issue of "good and bad features of each nation" and pointed out "several negative features of Jews", among which he mentioned "their political unreliability." Yet he neither mentioned any of their positive traits, nor did he talk about other nations.[2811]

In the same conversation, Khrushchev expressed his agreement with Stalin's decision against establishing a Crimean Jewish Republic, stating that such [Jewish] colonization of the Crimea would be a strategic military risk for the Soviet Union. This statement was particularly hurtful to the Jewish community. The Canadian delegation insisted on publication of a specific statement by the Central Committee of Communist Party of the Soviet Union about the sufferings of Jews, "but it was met with firm refusal" as "other nations and republics, which also suffered from Beria's crimes against their culture and intelligentsia, would ask with astonishment why this statement covers only Jews?" (S. Schwartz dismissively comments: "The pettiness of this argumentation is striking."[2812])

Yet it did not end at that. "Secretly, influential foreign Jewish communists tried" to obtain "explanations about the fate of the Jewish cultural elite", and in October of the same year, twenty-six Western "progressive Jewish

---

[2810] Слова Н.С. Хрущёва приведены в отчёте переводчика французской делегации Пьера Лошака: Realites, Paris, Mai 1957, p. 64-67, 101-104. — Мы цитируем их в обратном переводе «Социалистического вестника» (1961, № 1, с. 21).

[2811] *J.B. Salsberg*, Talks with Soviet Leaders on the Jewish Question // Jewish Life, Febr. 1957. — Цит. в переводе «Соц. вестника» (1961, № 1, с. 20).

[2812] *С. Шварц*. Евреи в Советском Союзе...*, с. 250.

leaders and writers" appealed publicly to Prime-Minister Bulganin and "President" Voroshilov, asking them to issue "a public statement about injustices committed [against Jews] and the measures the government had designed to restore the Jewish cultural institutions."[2813]

Yet during both the "interregnum" of 1953-1957 and then in Khrushchev's period, the Soviet policies toward Jews were inconsistent, wary, circumspect and ambivalent, thus sending signals in all directions.

In particular, the summer of 1956, which was filled with all kinds of social expectations in general, had also became the apogee of Jewish hopes. One Surkov, the head of the Union of Writers, in a conversation with a communist publisher from New York City mentioned plans to establish a new Jewish publishing house, theater, newspaper and quarterly literary magazine; there were also plans to organize a countrywide conference of Jewish writers and cultural celebrities. It also noted that a commission for reviving the Jewish literature in Yiddish had been already established. In 1956, "many Jewish writers and journalists gathered in Moscow again."[2814] The Jewish activists later recalled that "the optimism inspired in all of us by the events of 1956 did not quickly fade away."[2815]

Yet the Soviet government continued with its meaningless and aimless policies, discouraging any development of an independent Jewish culture. It is likely that Khrushchev himself was strongly opposed to it.

And then came new developments – the Suez Crisis, where Israel, Britain and France allied in attacking Egypt ("Israel is heading to suicide," formidably warned the Soviet press), and the Hungarian Uprising, with its anti-Jewish streak, nearly completely concealed by history,[2816] (resulting, perhaps, from the overrepresentation of Jews in the Hungarian KGB). (Could this be also one of the reasons, even if a minor one, for the complete absence of Western support for the rebellion? Of course, at this time the West was preoccupied with the Suez Crisis. And yet wasn't it a signal to the Soviets suggesting that it would be better if the Jewish theme be kept hushed?)

Then, a year later, Khrushchev finally overpowered his highly placed enemies within the party and, among others, Kaganovitch was cast down.

[2813] Там же*, с. 249-251.
[2814] Там же, с. 241, 272.
[2815] Ю. *Штерн*. Ситуация неустойчива и потому опасна: [Интервью] // "22": Общественно-политический и литературный журнал еврейской интеллигенции из СССР в Израиле. Тель-Авив, 1984, № 38, с. 132.
[2816] Andrew Handler. Where Familiarity with Jews Breeds Contempt // Red Star, Blue Star: The Lives and Times of Jewish Students in Communist Hungary (1948-1956). New-York: Columbia University Press, 1997, p. 36-37.

Could it really be such a big deal? The latter was not the only one ousted and even then, he was not the principal figure among the dethroned; and he was definitely not thrown out because of his Jewishness. Yet "from the Jewish point of view, his departure symbolized the end of an era". Some looked around and counted – "the Jews disappeared not only from the ruling sections of the party, but also from the leading governmental circles."[2817]

It was time to pause and ponder thoroughly – what did the Jews really think about *such* new authorities?

David Burg, who emigrated from the USSR in 1956, came upon a formula on how the Jews should treat the Soviet rule. (It proved quite useful for the authorities): "To some, the danger of anti-Semitism 'from below' seems greater than the danger of anti-Semitism 'from above'"; "though the government oppresses us, it nevertherless allows us to exist. If, however, a revolutionary change comes, then during the inevitable anarchy of the transition period we will simply be exterminated. Therefore, let's hold on to the government no matter how bad it is."[2818]

We repeatedly encountered similar concerns in the 1930s – that the Jews should support the Bolshevik power in the USSR because without it their fate would be even worse. And now, even though the Soviet power had further deteriorated, the Jews had no other choice but hold on to it as before.

The Western world and particularly the United States always heeded such recommendations, even during the most strained years of the Cold War. In addition, socialist Israel was still full of communist sympathizers and could forgive the Soviet Union a lot for its role in the defeat of Hitler. Yet how then could Soviet anti-Semitism be interpreted? In this aspect, the recommendation of D. Burg stood up to the acute "social demand" – to move emphasis from the anti-Semitism of the Soviet government to the "anti-Semitism of the Russian people" – that ever-present curse.

So now some Jews have even fondly recalled the long-disbanded YevSek [the "Jewish Section" of the Central Committee, dismantled in 1930 when Dimanshtein and its other leaders were shot]. Even though back in the 1920s it seemed overly pro-Communist, the YevSek was "to certain extent

---

[2817] Л. Шапиро. Евреи в Советской России после Сталина // Книга о русском еврействе, 1917-1967 (далее — КРЕ-2). Нью-Йорк: Союз Русских Евреев, 1968, с. 360-361.

[2818] *David Burg.* Die Judenfrage in Der Sowjetunion // Der Anti-kommunist, München, Juli-August 1957, № 12, S.35.

a guardian of Jewish national interests ... an organ that produced some positive work as well."[2819]

In the meantime, Khrushchev's policy remained equivocal; it is reasonable to assume that though Khrushchev himself did not like Jews, he did not want to fight against them, realizing the international political counter-productivity of such an effort. In 1957-1958, Jewish musical performances and public literary clubs were authorized and appeared in many cities countrywide. (For example, "in 1961, Jewish literary soirees and Jewish song performances were attended by about 300,000 people."[2820]) Yet at the same time, the circulation of Warsaw's *Volksstimme* was discontinued in the Soviet Union, thus cutting the Soviet Jews off from an outside source of Jewish information.[2821] In 1954, after a long break, Sholom Aleichem's *The Adventures of Mottel* was again published in Russian, followed by several editions of his other books and their translations into other languages; in 1959 a large edition of his collected works was produced as well.

In 1961 in Moscow, the Yiddish magazine *Sovetish Heymland* was established (though it strictly followed the official policy line). Publications of books by Jewish authors, who were executed in Stalin's times, were resumed in Yiddish and Russian, and one even could hear Jewish tunes on the broadcasts of the All-Soviet Union radio.[2822] By 1966, "about one hundred Jewish authors were writing in Yiddish in the Soviet Union," and "almost all of the named authors simultaneously worked as Russian language journalists and translators," and "many of them worked as teachers in the Russian schools."[2823] However, the Jewish theater did not re-open until 1966. In 1966, S. Schwartz defined the Jewish situation [in the USSR] as "cultural orphanhood." [2824] Yet another author bitterly remarks: "The general lack of enthusiasm and interest ... from the wider Jewish population ... toward those cultural undertakings ... cannot be explained solely by official policies ...." "With rare exceptions, during those years the Jewish actors performed in half-empty halls. Books of Jewish writers were not selling well."[2825]

[2819] *С. Шварц*. Евреи в Советском Союзе...*, с. 238.
[2820] Там же, с. 283-287; КЕЭ, т. 8, с. 258.
[2821] *С. Шварц*. Евреи в Советском Союзе..., с. 281.
[2822] *Э. Финкелъштейн*. Евреи в СССР: Путь в Двадцать первый век // Страна и мир: Обществ.-политический, экономический и культурно-философский журнал. Мюнхен, 1989, № 1, с. 65-66.
[2823] *Л. Шапиро*. Евреи в Советской России после Сталина // КРЕ-2, с. 379-380.
[2824] *С. Шварц*. Евреи в Советском Союзе..., с. 280, 288.
[2825] *Э. Финкелъштейн*. Евреи в СССР: Путь в Двадцать первый век // Страна и мир, 1989, № 1, с. 66.

Similarly ambivalent, but more hostile policies of the Soviet authorities in Khrushchev's period were implemented against the Jewish religion. It was a part of Khrushchev's general anti-religious assault; it is well known how devastating it was for the Russian Orthodox Church. Since the 1930s, not a single theological school functioned in the USSR. In 1957 a yeshiva – a school for training rabbis – opened in Moscow. It accommodated only 35 students, and even those were being consistently pushed out under various pretexts such as withdrawal of residence registration in Moscow. Printing of prayer books and manufacturing of religious accessories was hindered. Up to 1956, before the Jewish Passover matzah was baked by state-owned bakeries and then sold in stores. Beginning in 1957, however, baking of matzah was obstructed and since 1961 it was banned outright almost everywhere. One day, the authorities would not interfere with receiving parcels with matzah from abroad, another day, they stopped the parcels at the customs, and even demanded recipients to express in the press their outrage against the senders.[2826] In many places, synagogues were closed down. "In 1966, only 62 synagogues were functioning in the entire Soviet Union."[2827] Yet the authorities did not dare to shut down the synagogues in Moscow, Leningrad, Kiev and in the capitals of the republics. In the 1960s, there used to be extensive worship services on holidays with large crowds of 10,000 to 15,000 on the streets around synagogues.[2828] C. Schwartz notes that in the 1960s Jewish religious life was in severe decline, yet he large-mindedly reminds us that it was the result of the long process of secularization that began in Russian Jewry in the late 19th Century. (The process, which, he adds, has also succeeded in extremely non-communist Poland between the First and Second World Wars.[2829]) Judaism in the Soviet Union lacked a united control center; yet when the Soviet authorities wanted to squeeze out a political show from the leading rabbis for foreign policy purposes, be it about the well-being of Judaism in the USSR or outrage against the nuclear war, the government was perfectly able to stage it.[2830] "The Soviet authorities had repeatedly used Jewish religious leaders for foreign policy goals." For example, "in November 1956 a group of rabbis issued a protest against" the actions of Israel during the Suez War.[2831]

Another factor, which aggravated the status of Judaism in the USSR after the Suez War, was the growing fashionability of what was termed the "struggle against Zionism." Zionism, being, strictly speaking, a form of

---

[2826] С. Шварц. Евреи в Советском Союзе..., с. 304-308.
[2827] КЕЭ, т. 8, с. 259.
[2828] Л. Шапиро. Евреи в Советской России после Сталина // КРЕ-2, с. 358.
[2829] С. Шварц. Евреи в Советском Союзе..., с. 290.
[2830] Там же, с. 294-296.
[2831] КЕЭ, т. 8, с. 258.

socialism, should naturally had been seen as a true brother to the party of Marx and Lenin. Yet after the mid-1950s, the decision to secure the friendship of the Arabs drove the Soviet leaders toward persecution of Zionism. However, for the Soviet masses Zionism was a distant, unfamiliar and abstract phenomenon. Therefore, to flesh out this struggle, to give it a distinct embodiment, the Soviet government presented Zionism as a caricature composed of the characteristic and eternal Jewish images. The books and pamphlets allegedly aimed against Zionism also contained explicit anti-Judaic and anti-Jewish messages. If in the Soviet Union of 1920-1930s Judaism was not as brutally persecuted as the Russian Orthodox Christianity, then in 1957 a foreign socialist commentator noted how that year signified "a decisive intensification of the struggle against Judaism," the "turning point in the struggle against the Jewish religion," and that "the character of struggle betrays that it is directed not only against Judaism, but against the Jews in general."[2832] There was one stirring episode: in 1963 in Kiev, the Ukrainian Academy of Sciences published 12,000 copies of a brochure *Unadorned Judaism* in Ukrainian, yet it was filled with such blatant anti-Jewish caricatures that it provoked a large-scale international outcry, joined even by the communist "friends" (who were financially supported by Moscow), such as the leaders of the American and British communist parties, newspapers *L'Humanite*, *L'Unita*, as well as a pro-Chinese communist newspaper from Brussels, and many others. The UN Human Rights Commission demanded an explanation from its Ukrainian representative. The World Jewish Cultural Association called for the prosecution of the author and the cartoonist. The Soviet side held on for awhile, insisting that except for the drawings, "the book deserves a generally positive assessment."[2833] Finally, even *Pravda* had to admit that it was indeed "an ill-prepared ... brochure" with "erroneous statements ... and illustrations that may offend feelings of religious people or be interpreted as anti-Semitic," a phenomenon that, "as is universally known, does not and cannot exist in our country."[2834] Yet at the same time *Izvestia* stated that although there were certain drawbacks to the brochure, "its main idea ... is no doubt right."[2835]

There were even several arrests of religious Jews from Moscow and Leningrad – accused of "espionage [conversations during personal meetings in synagogues] for a capitalistic state [Israel]" with synagogues

---

[2832] Антисемитский памфлет в Советском Союзе // Социалистический вестник, 1965, № 4, с. 67.
[2833] Антисемитский памфлет в Советском Союзе // Социалистический вестник*, 1965, № 4, с. 68-73.
[2834] В Идеологической комиссии при ЦК КПСС // Правда, 1964, 4 апреля, с. 4.
[2835] Об одной непонятной шумихе // Известия, 1964, 4 апреля, с. 4.

allegedly used as "fronts for various criminal activities"[2836] – to scare others more effectively.

Although there were already no longer any Jews in the most prominent positions, many still occupied influential and important second-tier posts (though there were exceptions: for example, Veniamin Dymshits smoothly ran Gosplan (the State Planning Committee) from 1962, while being at the same time the Deputy Chairman of the Council of Ministers of USSR and a member of Central Committee from 1961 to 1986[2837]). Why, at one time the Jews were joining "NKVD and the MVD ... in such numbers that even now, after all purges of the very Jewish spirit, a few individuals miraculously remained, such as the famous Captain Joffe in a camp in Mordovia."[2838]

According to the USSR Census of 1959, 2,268,000 Jews lived in the Soviet Union. (Yet there were caveats regarding this figure: "Everybody knows ... that there are more Jews in the Soviet Union than the Census showed," as on the Census day, a Jew states his nationality not according to his passport, but any nationality he wishes.[2839]) Of those, 2,162,000 Jews lived in the cities, i.e., 95,3% of total population – much more than 82% in 1926 or 87% in 1939.[2840]

And if we glance forward into the 1970 Census, the observed "increase in the number of Jews in Moscow and Leningrad is apparently caused not by natural growth but by migration from other cities (in spite of all the residential restrictions)." Over these 11 years, "at least several thousand Jews relocated to Kiev. The concentration of Jews in the large cities had been increasing for many decades."[2841]

These figures are very telling for those who know about the differences in living standards between the urban and the rural populations in the Soviet Union. G. Rosenblum, the editor of the prominent Israeli newspaper, *Yedioth Ahronoth*, recalls an almost anecdotal story by Israeli Ambassador to Moscow Dr. Harel about his tour of the USSR in the mid-1960s. In a large kolkhoz near Kishinev he was told that "the Jews who work here want to meet [him]. [The Israeli] was very happy that there were Jews in the

---

[2836] *С. Шварц*. Евреи в Советском Союзе..., с. 303.
[2837] Российская Еврейская Энциклопедия. 2-е изд., испр. и доп. М., 1994. Т. 1, с. 448.
[2838] *Р. Рутман*. Кольцо обид // Новый журнал, Нью-Йорк. 1974. № 117, с. 185.
[2839] *И. Домальский*. Технология ненависти // Время и мы (далее — ВМ): Международный журнал литературы и общественных проблем. Тель-Авив. 1978, № 26, с. 113-114.
[2840] КЕЭ, т. 8, с. 298, 300.
[2841] *И. Ляст*. Алия из СССР — демографические прогнозы // "22", 1981, № 21, с. 112-113.

kolkhoz" (love of agriculture – a good sign for Israel). He recounts: "Three Jews came to meet me ... one was a cashier, another – editor of the kolkhoz's wall newspaper and the third one was a kind of economic manager. I couldn't find any other. So, what the Jews used to do [i.e. before], they are still doing." G. Rosenblum confirms this: "Indeed, the Soviet Jews in their masses did not take to the physical work."[2842] L. Shapiro concludes, "Conversion of Jews to agriculture ended in failure despite all the efforts ... of public Jewish organizations and ... the assistance of the state."[2843]

In Moscow, Leningrad and Kiev – the cities enjoying the highest living and cultural standards in the country, the Jews, according to the 1959 Census, constituted 3.9%, 5.8%, and 13.9 % of the population, respectively, which is quite a lot, considering that they accounted only for 1.1% of the entire population of the USSR.[2844]

So it was that this extremely high concentration of Jews in urban areas – 95% of all Soviet Jews lived in the cities – that made "the system of prohibitions and restrictions" particularly painful for them. (As we mentioned in the previous chapter, this system was outlined back in the early 1940s.) And "although the restrictive rules have never been officially acknowledged and officials stoutly denied their existence, these rules and restrictions very effectively barred the Jews from many spheres of action, professions and positions."[2845]

Some recall a disturbing rumor circulating then among the Jews: allegedly, Khrushchev said in one of his unpublished speeches that "as many Jews will be accepted into the institutions of higher education as work in the coal mines."[2846]

Perhaps, he really just blurted it out in his usual manner, because such "balancing" was never carried out. Yet by the beginning of 1960s, while the absolute number of Jewish students increased, their relative share decreased substantially when compared to the pre-war period: if in 1936 the share of Jews among students was 7.5 times higher than that in the total population,[2847] then by 1960s it was only 2.7 times higher. These new data on the distribution of students in higher and secondary education by nationality were published for the first time (in the post-war period) in 1963

[2842] *Г. Розенблюм, В. Перельман*. Крушение Чуда: причины и следствия*: [Беседа] // ВМ, Тель-Авив, 1977, № 24, с. 120.
[2843] *Л. Шапиро*. Евреи в Советской России после Сталина // КРЕ-2, с. 346.
[2844] КЕЭ, т. 8, с. 300.
[2845] *Э. Финкельштейн*. Евреи в СССР... // Страна и мир, 1989, № 1, с. 65.
[2846] *Н. Шапиро*. Слово рядового советского еврея // Русский антисемитизм и евреи: Сборник. Лондон, 1968, с. 55.
[2847] КЕЭ, т. 8, с. 190.

in the statistical annual report, *The National Economy of the USSR*,[2848] and a similar table was annually produced up to 1972. In terms of the absolute number of students in institutions of higher education and technical schools in the 1962-1963 academic year, Jews were fourth after the three Slavic nations (Russians, Ukrainians, Byelorussians), with 79,300 Jewish students in institutions of higher education out of a total 2,943,700 students (2.69%). In the next academic year 1963-1964, the number of Jewish students increased to 82,600, while the total number of students in the USSR reached 3,260,700 (2.53%). This share remained almost constant until the 1969-1970 academic year; 101,000 Jewish students out of total 4,549,900.

Then the Jewish share began to decline and in 1972-1973 it was 1.91%: 88,500 Jewish students out of total 4,630,246.[2849] (This decline coincided with the beginning of the Jewish immigration to Israel.)

The relative number of Jewish scientists also declined in 1960s, from 9.5% in 1960 to 6.1% in 1973.[2850] During those same years, "there were tens of thousands Jewish names in the Soviet art and literature,"[2851] including 8.5% of writers and journalists, 7.7% of actors and artists, more than 10% of judges and attorneys, and about 15% doctors.[2852] Traditionally, there were always many Jews in medicine, yet consider the accursed "Soviet psychiatry," which in those years began locking up healthy people in mental institutions. And who were those psychiatrists? Listing the "Jewish occupations," M.I. Heifets writes: "Psychiatry is a Jewish monopoly, a friend, a Jewish psychiatrist, told me, just before [my] arrest; 'we began to get Russians only recently and even then as the result of an order'" [translator's note: admission into medical residency training was regulated at local and central levels; here author indicates that admission of ethnically Russian doctors into advanced psychiatry training was mandated from the higher levels]. He provides examples: the Head Psychiatrist of Leningrad, Professor Averbukh, provides his expertise for the KGB in the "Big House"; in Moscow there was famous Luntz; in the Kaluga Hospital there was Lifshitz and "his Jewish gang." When Heifetz was arrested, and his wife began looking for a lawyer with a "clearance," that is, with a

---

[2848] Народное хозяйство СССР в 1963 году: Статистический ежегодник. М.: Статистика, 1965, с. 579.
[2849] Народное хозяйство СССР в 1969 году. М., 1970, с. 690; Народное хозяйство СССР в 1972 году. М., 1972, с. 651.
[2850] *И. Домальский*. Технология ненависти // ВМ, Тель-Авив, 1978, №25, с. 120.
[2851] *Э. Финкелъштейн*. Евреи в СССР... // Страна и мир, 1989, № 1, с. 66.
[2852] *А. Нов, Жд. Ньют*. Еврейское население СССР: демографическое развитие и профессиональная занятость // Евреи в Советской России (1917-1967). Израиль: Библиотека «Алия», 1975, с. 180.

permission from the KGB to work on political cases, she "did not find a single Russian" among them as all such lawyers were Jews²⁸⁵³).

In 1956, Furtseva, then the First Secretary of Moscow Gorkom (the City's Party Committee), complained that in some offices Jews constitute more than half of the staff.²⁸⁵⁴ (I have to note for balance that *in those* years the presence of Jews in the Soviet apparatus was not detrimental. The Soviet legal machinery was in its essence stubbornly and hardheartedly anti-human, skewed against any man in need, be it a petitioner or just a visitor. So it often happened that the Russian officials in Soviet offices, petrified by their power, looked for any excuse to triumphantly turn away a visitor; in contrast, one could find much more understanding in a Jewish official and resolve an issue in a more humane way). L. Shapiro provides examples of complaints that in the national republics, the Jews were pushed out and displaced from the bureaucratic apparatus by native intelligentsia²⁸⁵⁵ – yet it was a common and officially-mandated system of preferences in the ethnic republics [to affirm the local cadres], and Russians were displaced just as well.

This reminds me of an example from contemporary American life. In 1965, the New York Division of the American Jewish Committee had conducted a four-months-long unofficial interview of more than a thousand top officials in New York City banks. Based on its results, the American Jewish Committee mounted a protest because less than 3% of those surveyed were Jews, though they constituted one quarter of the population of – that is, the Committee demanded *proportional representation*. Then the chairman of the Association of Banks of New York responded that banks, according to law, do not hire on the basis of "race, creed, color or national origin" and do not keep records of such categories (that would be our accursed "fifth article" [the requirement in the Soviet internal passport – "nationality"]!). (Interestingly, the same American Jewish Committee had conducted a similar study about the ethnic composition of management of the fifty largest U.S. public utility services two years before, and in 1964 it in similar vein it studied industrial enterprises in the Philadelphia region.)²⁸⁵⁶

Yet let us return to the Soviet Jews. Many Jewish emigrants loudly advertised their former activity in the periodical-publishing and film-making industries back in the USSR. In particular, we learn from a Jewish

---

²⁸⁵³ *Михаил Хейфец*. Место и время (еврейские заметки)*. Париж: Третья волна, 1978, с. 63-65, 67, 70.
²⁸⁵⁴ *Л. Шапиро*. Евреи в Советской России после Сталина // КРЕ-2, с. 363.
²⁸⁵⁵ Там же.
²⁸⁵⁶ *New York Times*, 1965, October 21, p. 47.

author that "it was due to his [Syrokomskiy's] support that all top positions in *Literaturnaya Gazeta* became occupied by Jews."[2857]

Yet twenty years later we read a different assessment of the time: "The new anti-Semitism grew stronger ... and by the second half of the 1960s it already amounted to a developed system of discreditation, humiliation and isolation of the entire people."[2858]

So how can we reconcile such conflicting views? How can we reach a calm and balanced assessment?

Then from the high spheres inhabited by economic barons there came alarming signals, signals that made the Jews nervous. "To a certain extent, Jewish activity in the Soviet Union concentrated in the specific fields of economy along a characteristic pattern, well-known to Jewish sociologists."[2859]

By then, at the end of 1950s, Nikita [Khrushchev] suddenly realized that the key spheres of the Soviet economy are plagued by rampant theft and fraud.

"In 1961, an explicitly anti-Semitic campaign was initiated against the theft of socialist property."[2860] Beginning in 1961, a number of punitive decrees of the Supreme Soviet of the USSR were passed. The first one dealt with "foreign currency speculations," another – with bribes, and still another later introduced capital punishment for the aforementioned crimes, at the same time lawlessly applying the death penalty retroactively, for the crimes committed before those decrees were issued (as, for example, the case of J. Rokotov and B. Faybishenko). Executions started in the very first year. During the first nine trials, eleven individuals were sentenced to death – among them were "perhaps, six Jews."[2861] *The Jewish Encyclopedia* states it more specifically, "In 1961-1964, thirty-nine Jews were executed for economic crimes in the RSFSR and seventy-nine – in Ukraine," and forty-three Jews in other republics.[2862] In these trials, "the vast majority of defendants were Jews." (The publicity was such that the court reports indicated the names and patronymics of the defendants, which was the

---

[2857] В. Перельман. О либералах в советских верхах // ВМ, Нью-Йорк, 1985, № 87, с. 147.
[2858] Э. Финкелъштейн. Евреи в СССР... // Страна и мир, 1989, № 1, с. 66.
[2859] Л. Шапиро. Евреи в Советской России после Сталина // КРЕ-2, с. 362.
[2860] КЕЭ, т. 8, с. 261.
[2861] С. Шварц. Евреи в Советском Союзе..., с. 326-327, 329.
[2862] КЕЭ, т. 8, с. 261.

normal order of pleadings, yet it was getting "absolutely clear from that that they were Jews."[2863])

Next, in a large court trial in Frunze in 1962, nineteen out of forty-six defendants were apparently Jewish. "There is no reason to think that this new policy was conceived as a system of anti-Jewish measures. Yet immediately upon enforcement, the new laws acquired distinct anti-Jewish flavor," – the author of the quote obviously points out to the publication of the full names of defendants, including Jewish ones; other than that, neither the courts, nor the government, nor the media made any generalizations or direct accusations against the Jews. And even when *Sovetskaya Kyrgizia* wrote that "they occupied different posts, but they were closely linked to each other," it never clarified the begged question "how were they linked?" The newspaper treated this issue with silence, thus pushing the reader to the thought that the nucleus of the criminal organization was composed of the "closely linked" individuals. Yet "closely linked by" what? By their Jewishness. So the newspaper "emphasized the Jews in this case."[2864] ... Yet people can be "closely linked" by any illegal transaction, greed, swindling or fraud. And, amazingly, nobody argued that those individuals could be innocent (though they could have been innocent). Yet to *name* them was equal to Jew-baiting.

Next, in January 1962, came the Vilnius case of speculators in foreign currency. *All* eight defendants were Jews (during the trial, non-Jewish members of the political establishment involved in the case escaped public naming – a usual Soviet trick). This time, there was an explicit anti-Jewish sentiment from the prosecution: "The deals were struck in a synagogue, and the arguments were settled with the help of wine."[2865]

S. Schwartz is absolutely convinced that this legal and economic harassment was nothing else but rampant anti-Semitism, yet he completely disregards "the tendency of Jews to concentrate their activity in the specific spheres of economy." Similarly, the entire Western media interpreted this as a brutal campaign against Jews, the *humiliation and isolation of the entire people*; Bertrand Russell sent a letter of protest to Khrushchev and got a personal response from the Soviet leader.[2866] However, after that, the Soviet authorities apparently had second thoughts when they handled the Jews.

[2863] *Н. Шапиро.* Слово рядового советского еврея // Русский антисемитизм и евреи, с. 55.
[2864] *С. Шварц.* Евреи в Советском Союзе..., с. 330-333.
[2865] Там же, с. 333-334.
[2866] Обмен письмами между Б. Расселом и Н.С. Хрущёвым // Правда, 1963, 1 марта, с. 1.

In the West, the official Soviet anti-Semitism began to be referred to as "the most pressing issue" in the USSR (ignoring any more acute issues) and "the most proscribed subject." (Though there were numerous other proscribed issues such as forced collectivization or the surrender of three million Red Army soldiers in the year of 1941 alone, or the murderous nuclear "experimentation" on our own Soviet troops on the Totskoye range in 1954.) Of course, after Stalin's death, the Communist Party avoided explicit anti-Jewish statements.

Perhaps, they practiced incendiary "invitation-only meetings" and "briefings" – that would have been very much in the Soviet style. Solomon Schwartz rightly concludes: "Soviet anti-Jewish policy does not have any sound or rational foundation," the strangulation of the Jewish cultural life "appears puzzling.

How can such bizarre policy be explained?"[2867]

Still, when all living things in the country were being choked, could one really expect that such vigorous and agile people would escape a similar lot? To that, the Soviet foreign policy agendas of 1960s added their weight: the USSR was designing an anti-Israel campaign. Thus, they came up with a convenient, ambiguous and indefinite term of "anti-Zionism," which became "a sword of Damocles hanging above the entire Jewish population of the country."[2868]

Campaigning against "Zionism" in the press became a sort of impenetrable shield as its obvious anti-Semitic nature became unprovable. Moreover, it sounded menacing and dangerous – "Zionism is the instrument of the American imperialism." So the "Jews had to prove their loyalty in one way or other, to somehow convince the people around them that they had no connection to their own Jewishness, especially to Zionism."[2869]

The feelings of ordinary Jews in the Soviet Union became the feelings of the oppressed as vividly expressed by one of them: "Over the years of persecutions and vilifications, the Jews developed a certain psychological complex of suspicion to any contact coming from non-Jews. In everything they are ready to see implicit or explicit hints on their nationality .... The Jews can never publicly declare their Jewishness, and it is formally accepted that this should be kept silent, as if it was a vice, or a past crime."[2870]

[2867] С. Шварц. Евреи в Советском Союзе..., с. 421-422.
[2868] Э. Финкельштейн. Евреи в СССР... // Страна и мир, 1989, № 1, с. 65.
[2869] Э. Финкельштейн. Евреи в СССР... // Страна и мир, 1989, № 1, с. 66-67.
[2870] Н. Шапиро. Слово рядового советского еврея // Русский антисемитизм и евреи, с. 48, 55.

An incident in Malakhovka in October 1959 added substantially to that atmosphere. On the night of October 4, in Malakhovka, a settlement "half an hour from Moscow ... with 30,000 inhabitants, about 10% of whom are Jews ..., the roof of the synagogue caught fire along with ... the house of the Jewish cemetery keeper ... [and] the wife of the keeper died in the fire. On the same night, leaflets were scattered and posted across Malakhovka: Away with the Jews in commerce! ... We saved them from the Germans ... yet they became arrogant so fast that the Russian people do not understand any longer... who's living on whose land.'"[2871]

Growing depression drove some Jews to such an extreme state of mind as that described by D. Shturman: some "Jewish philistines developed a hatred toward Israel, believing it to be the generator of anti-Semitism in the Soviet politics. I remember the words of one successful Jewish teacher: One good bomb dropped on Israel would make our life much easier.'"[2872]

Yet that was an ugly exception indeed. In general, the rampant anti-Zionist campaign triggered a "consolidation of the sense of Jewishness in people and the growth of sympathy towards Israel as the outpost of the Jewish nation."[2873]

There is yet another explanation of the social situation in those years: yes, under Khrushchev, "fears for their lives had become the things of the past for the Soviet Jews," but "the foundations of new anti-Semitism had been laid," as the young generation of political establishment fought for caste privileges, "seeking to occupy the leading positions in arts, science, commerce, finance, etc. There the new Soviet aristocracy encountered Jews, whose share in those fields was traditionally high." The "social structure of the Jewish population, which was mainly concentrated in the major centers of the country, reminded the ruling elite of their own class structure."[2874]

Doubtless, such encounter did take place; it was an epic "crew change" in the Soviet ruling establishment, switching from the Jewish elite to the Russian one. It had clearly resulted in antagonism and I remember those conversations among the Jews during Khrushchev's era – they were full of not only ridicule, but also of bad insults with the ex-villagers, "muzhiks," who have infiltrated the establishment.

Yet altogether all the various social influences combined with the great prudence of the Soviet authorities led to dramatic alleviation of "prevalence

---

[2871] Социалистический вестник, 1959, № 12, с. 240-241.
[2872] Д. *Штурман*. Советский антисемитизм — причины и прогнозы: [Семинар] // "22", 1978, № 3, с. 180.
[2873] *С. Шварц*. Евреи в Советском Союзе..., с. 395.
[2874] Э. *Финкельштейн*. Евреи в СССР... // Страна и мир, 1989, № 1, с. 64-65.

and acuteness of modern Soviet anti-Semitism" by 1965, which became far inferior to what had been observed "during the war and the first post-war years," and it appears that "a marked attenuation, maybe even a complete dying out of 'the percentage quote is happening."[2875] Overall, in the 1960s the Jewish worldview was rather positive. This is what we consistently hear from different authors.

(Contrast this to what we just read, that "the new anti-Semitism grew in strength in the 1960s.") The same opinion was expressed again twenty years later – "Khrushchev's era was one of the most peaceful periods of the Soviet history for the Jews."[2876]

"In 1956-1957, many new Zionist societies sprang up in the USSR, bringing together young Jews who previously did not show much interest in Jewish national problems or Zionism. An important impetus for the awakening of national consciousness among Soviet Jews and for the development of a sense of solidarity with the State of Israel was the Suez Crisis [1956]." Later, "The International Youth Festival [Moscow, 1957] became a catalyst for the revival of the Zionist movement in the USSR among a certain portion of Soviet Jews ... Between the festival and the Six-Day War [1967], Zionist activity in the Soviet Union was gradually expanding. Contacts of Soviet Jews with the Israeli Embassy became more frequent and less dangerous." Also, "the importance of Jewish Samizdat increased dramatically."[2877]

During the so-called Khrushchev's "thaw" period (the end of 1950s to the beginning of the 1960s), Soviet Jews were spiritually re-energized; they shook off the fears and distress of the previous age of the "Doctors' Plot" and the persecution of "cosmopolitan." It "even became fashionable" in the metropolitan society "to be a Jew"; the Jewish motif entered Samizdat and poetic soirees then so popular among the young. Rimma Kazakova even ventured to declare her Jewish identity from the stage. Yevtushenko quickly caught the air and expressed it in 1961 in his *Babi Yar*[2878], proclaiming himself a Jew in spirit. His poem (and the courage of *Literaturnaya Gazeta*) was a literary trumpet call for all of Soviet and world Jewry. Yevtushenko recited his poem during a huge number of poetic soirees, always accompanied by a roar of applause. After a while, Shostakovich, who often ventured into Jewish themes, set Yevtushenko's poem into his 13th Symphony. Yet its public performance was limited by

---

[2875] С. Шварц. Евреи в Советском Союзе..., с. 372, 409.
[2876] Михаил Хейфец. Новая «аристократия»? // Грани: Журнал литературы, искусства, науки и общ.-политической мысли. Франкфурт-на-Майне, 1987, № 146, с. 189.
[2877] КЕЭ, т. 8, с. 262-263.
[2878] R. Rutman // Soviet Jewish Affairs, London, 1974, Vol. 4, № 2, p. 11.

the authorities. *Babi Yar* spread among Soviet and foreign Jewries as a reinvigorating and healing blast of air, a truly "revolutionary act ...

in the development of the social consciousness in the Soviet Union"; "it became the most significant event since the dismissal of the Doctors' Plot.'"[2879]

In 1964-65 Jewish themes returned into popular literature; take, for example, *Summer in Sosnyaki* by Anatoliy Rybakov or the diary of Masha Rolnik[2880] ("written apparently under heavy influence of *Diary of Anne Frank*"[2881]).

"After the ousting of Khrushchev from all his posts, the official policy towards Jews was softened somewhat. The struggle against Judaism abated and nearly all restrictions on baking matzah were abolished .... Gradually, the campaign against economic crimes faded away too ...." Yet "the Soviet press unleashed a propaganda campaign against Zionist activities among the Soviet Jews and their connections to the Israeli Embassy."[2882]

All these political fluctuations and changes in the Jewish policies in the Soviet Union did not pass unnoticed but served to awaken the Jews.

In the 1959 Census, only 21% Jews named Yiddish as their first language (in 1926 -72%).[2883] Even in 1970s they used to say that "Russian Jewry, which was [in the past] the most Jewish Jewry in the world, became the least Jewish."[2884] "The current state of Soviet society is fraught with destruction of Jewish spiritual and intellectual potential."[2885] Or as another author put it: the Jews in the Soviet Union were neither "allowed to assimilate," nor were they "allowed to be Jews."[2886]

Yet Jewish identity was never subdued during the entire Soviet period.

In 1966 the official mouthpiece *Sovetish Heymland* claimed that "even assimilated Russian-speaking Jews still retain their unique character, distinct from that of any other segment of population."[2887] Not to mention the Jews of Odessa, Kiev, and Kharkov, who "sometimes were even snooty

---

[2879] *С. Шварц.* Евреи в Советском Союзе..., с. 371.
[2880] Соответственно: Новый мир, 1964, № 12; *Мария Рольникайте.* Я должна рассказать // Звезда, 1965, № 2 и № 3.
[2881] *С. Шварц.* Евреи в Советском Союзе..., с. 373.
[2882] КЕЭ, т. 8, с. 262, 264.
[2883] Там же, с. 295, 302.
[2884] *Г. Розенблюм.* Крушение Чуда...: [Беседа с В. Перелъманом] // ВМ, Тель-Авив, 1977, №24, с. 120.
[2885] *Л. Цигельман-Дымерская.* Советский антисемитизм — причины и прогнозы: [Семинар] // "22", 1978, №3, с. 175.
[2886] *Ю. Штерн.* Ситуация неустойчива...: [Интервью] // "22", 1984, № 38, с. 135.
[2887] *Л. Шапиро.* Евреи в Советской России после Сталина // КРЕ-2, с. 379.

about their Jewishness – to the extent that they did not want to befriend a goy."[2888]

Scientist Leo Tumerman (already in Israel in 1977) recalls the early Soviet period, when he used to "reject any nationalism." Yet now, looking back at those years: "I am surprised to notice what I had overlooked then: despite what appeared to be my full assimilation into the Russian life, the entire circle of my close and intimate friends at that time was Jewish."[2889]

The sincerity of his statement is certain – the picture is clear. Such things were widespread and I witnessed similar situations quite a few times, and Russians people did not mind such behavior at all.

Another Jewish author notes: in the USSR "non-religious Jews of all walks of life hand in hand defended the principle of 'racial purity.'" He adds: "Nothing could be more natural. People for whom the Jewishness is just an empty word are very rare, especially among the unassimilated [Jews]."[2890]

Natan Sharansky's testimonial, given shortly after his immigration to Israel, is also typical: "Much of my Jewishness was instilled into me by my family.

Although our family was an assimilated one, it nevertheless was Jewish." "My father, an ordinary Soviet journalist, was so fascinated with the revolutionary ideas of 'happiness for allánd not just for the Jews, that he became an absolutely loyal Soviet citizen." Yet in 1967 after the Six-Day War and later in 1968 after Czechoslovakia, "I suddenly realized an obvious difference between myself and non-Jews around me ... a kind of a sense of the fundamental difference between my Jewish consciousness and the national consciousness of the Russians."[2891]

And here is another very thoughtful testimonial (1975): "The efforts spent over the last hundred years by Jewish intellectuals to reincarnate themselves into the Russian national form were truly titanic. Yet it did not give them balance of mind; on the contrary, it rather made them to feel the bitterness of their bi-national existence more acutely." And "they have an answer to the tragic question of Aleksandr Blok: 'My Russia, my life, are we to drudge through life together?' To that question, to which a Russian as a rule gives an unambiguous answer, a member of Russian-Jewish intelligentsia used to reply (sometimes after self-reflection): 'No, not together. For the time being, yes, side by side, but not together'... A duty

---

[2888] Ю. Штерн. Двойная ответственность: [Интервью] // "22", 1981, № 21, с. 127.
[2889] "22"*, 1978, № 1, с. 204.
[2890] А. Этерман. Истина с близкого расстояния // "22", 1987, № 52, с. 112.
[2891] А. Щаранский. [Интервью] // "22", 1986, № 49. с. 111-112.

is no substitute for Motherland." And so "the Jews felt free from obligations at all sharp turns of Russian history."[2892]

Fair enough. One can only hope for all Russian Jews to get such clarity and acknowledge this dilemma.

Yet usually the problem in its entirety is blamed on "anti-Semitism": "Excluding us from everything genuinely Russian, their anti-Semitism simultaneously barred us from all things Jewish .... Anti-Semitism is terrible not because of what it *does to the Jews* (by imposing restrictions on them), but because of what it *does with the Jews* by turning them into neurotic, depressed, stressed, and defective human beings."[2893]

Still, those Jews, who had fully woken up to their identity, were very quickly, completely, and reliably cured from such a morbid condition.

Jewish identity in the Soviet Union grew stronger as they went through the historical ordeals predestined for Jewry by the 20th Century. First, it was the Jewish Catastrophe during the Second World War. (Through the efforts of official Soviet muffling and obscuring, Soviet Jewry only comprehended its full scope later.)

Another push was given by the campaign against "cosmopolitans" in 1949-1950. Then there was a very serious threat of a massacre by Stalin, eliminated by his timely death. And with Khrushchev's "thaw" and after it, later in the 1960s, Soviet Jewry quickly awoke spiritually, already sensing its unique identity.

During the second half of the 1950s, "the growing sense of bitterness, spread over large segments of Soviet Jewry", lead to "consolidation of the sense of national solidarity."[2894]

But "only in the late 1960s did a very small but committed group of scientists (note, they were not humanitarians; the most colorful figure among them was Alexander Voronel) begin rebuilding of Jewish national consciousness in Russia."[2895]

And then against the nascent national consciousness of Soviet Jews, the Six-Day War suddenly broke out and instantly ended in what might have seemed a miraculous victory. Israel has ascended in their minds and Soviet Jews awoke to their spiritual and consanguineous kinship [with Israel].

[2892] Б. *Орлов.* Не те вы учили алфавиты // ВМ, Тель-Авив, 1975, № 1, с. 129, 132-133.
[2893] В. *Богуславский.* Галуту — с надеждой // "22", 1985, № 40, с. 133, 134.
[2894] С. *Шварц.* Евреи в Советском Союзе..., с. 415.
[2895] Г. *Файн.* В роли высокооплачиваемых швейцаров // ВМ, Тель-Авив. 1976, № 12. с. 133-134.

But the Soviet authorities, furious at Nasser's disgraceful defeat, immediately attacked Soviet Jews with the thundering campaign against the "Judeo-Zionist-Fascism," insinuating that all the Jews were "Zionists" and claiming that the "global conspiracy" of Zionism "is the expected and *inevitable product of the entirety of Jewish history, Jewish religion, and the resultant Jewish national character"* and "because of the consistent pursuit of the ideology of racial supremacy and apartheid, Judaism turned out to be a very convenient religion for securing world dominance."[2896]

The campaign on TV and in the press was accompanied by a dramatic break of diplomatic relations with Israel. The Soviet Jews had many reasons to fear: "It looked like it was going to come to calls for a pogrom."[2897]

But underneath this scare a new and already unstoppable explosion of Jewish national consciousness was growing and developing.

"Bitterness, resentment, anger, and the sense of social insecurity were accruing for a final break up which would lead to complete severing of all ties with [this] country and [this] society – to emigration."[2898]

"The victory of the Israeli Army contributed to the awakening of national consciousness among the many thousands of almost completely assimilated Soviet Jews .... The process of national revival has began .... The activity of Zionist groups in cities all across the country surged .... In 1969, there were attempts to create a united Zionist Organization [in the USSR] .... An increasing number of Jews applied to emigrate to Israel."[2899]

And the numerous refusals to grant exit visas led to the failed attempt to hijack an airplane on June 15, 1970. The following "Dymshits-Kuznetsov hijacking affair" can be considered a historic landmark in the fate of Soviet Jewry.

[2896] *Р. Нудельман.* Советский антисемитизм — причины и прогнозы: [Семинар] // "22", 1978, № 3, с. 144.
[2897] *Э. Финкельштейн.* Евреи в СССР... // Страна и мир, 1989, № 1, с. 67.
[2898] Там же.
[2899] КЕЭ, т. 8. с. 267.

Chapter 24

Breaking away from Bolshevism

At the beginning of the 20th century, Europe imagined itself to be on the threshold of worldwide enlightenment. No one could have predicted the strength with which nationalism would explode in that very century among all nations of the world. One hundred years later it seems nationalist feelings are not about to die soon (the very message that international socialists have been trying to drum into our heads for the whole century), but instead are gaining strength.

Yet, does not the multi-national nature of humanity provide variety and wealth? Erosion of nations surely would be an impoverishment for humanity, the entropy of the spirit. (And centuries of the histories of national cultures would then turn into irredeemably dead and useless antics.) The logic that it would be easier to manage such a uniform mankind fails by its petty reductionism.

However, the propaganda in the Soviet empire harped non-stop in an importunately-triumphant manner about the imminent withering away and amalgamation of nations, proclaiming that no "national question" exists in our country, and that there is certainly no "Jewish question."

Yet why should not the Jewish question exist — the question of the unprecedented three-thousand-year-old existence of the nation, scattered all over the Earth, yet spiritually soldered together despite all notions of the state and territoriality, and at the same time influencing the entire world history in the most lively and powerful way? Why should there not be a "Jewish question" given that all national questions come up at one time or other, even the "Gagauz question" [a small Christian Turkic people, who live in the Balkans and Eastern Europe]?

Of course, no such silly doubt could ever arise, if the Jewish question were not the focus of many different political games.

The same was true for Russia too. In pre-revolutionary Russian society, as we saw, it was the *omission* of the Jewish question that was considered "anti-Semitic." In fact, in the mind of the Russian public the Jewish question — understood as the question of civil rights or civil equality —

developed into perhaps the central question of the whole Russian public life of that period, and certainly into the central node of the conscience of every individual, its acid test.

With the growth of European socialism, all national issues were increasingly recognized as merely regrettable obstacles to that great doctrine; all the more was the Jewish question (directly attributed to capitalism by Marx) considered a bloated hindrance. Mommsen wrote that in the circles of "Western-Russian socialist Jewry," as he put it, even the slightest attempt to discuss the Jewish question was branded as "reactionary" and "anti-Semitic" (this was even before the Bund).

Such was the iron standard of socialism inherited by the USSR. From 1918 the communists forbade (under threat of imprisonment or death) any separate treatment or consideration of the Jewish question (except sympathy for their suffering under the Tsars and positive attitudes for their active role in communism). The intellectual class voluntarily and willingly adhered to the new canon while others were required to follow it.

This cast of thought persisted even through the Soviet-German war as if, even then, there was not any particular Jewish question. And even up to the demise of the USSR under Gorbachev, the authorities used to repeat hard-headedly: no, there is no Jewish question, no, no, no! (It was replaced by the "Zionist question.")

Yet already by the end of the World War II, when the extent of the destruction of the Jews under Hitler had dawned on the Soviet Jews, and then through Stalin's "anti-cosmopolitan" campaign of the late 1940s, the Soviet intelligentsia realized that the Jewish question in the USSR does exist! And the pre-revolutionary understanding — that it is central to Russian society and to the conscience of every individual and that it is the "true measure of humanity"[2900] — was also restored.

In the West it was only the leaders of Zionism who confidently talked from the late 19th century about the historical uniqueness and everlasting relevance of the Jewish question (and some of them at the same time maintained robust links with diehard European socialism).

And then the emergence of the state of Israel and the consequent storms around it added to the confusion of naive socialist minds of Europeans.

Here I offer two small but at the time quite stirring and typical examples. In one episode of so-called "the dialogue between the East and the West" show (a clever Cold-War-period programme, where Western debaters were

---

[2900] В. *Левитина*. Русский театр и евреи. Иерусалим: Библиотека – Алия, 1988. Т. 1, с. 24.

opposed by Eastern-European officials or novices who played off official nonsense for their own sincere convictions) in the beginning of 1967, a Slovak writer, Ladislav Mnacko, properly representing the socialist East, wittily noted that he never in his life had any conflict with the Communist authorities, except one case when his driver's license was suspended for a traffic violation. His French opponent angrily said that at least in one other case, surely Mnacko should be in the opposition: when the uprising in neighboring Hungary was drowned in blood.

But no, the suppression of Hungarian Uprising neither violated the peace of Mnacko's mind, nor did it force him to say anything sharp or impudent. Then, a few months passed after the "dialogue" and the Six-Day War broke out. At that point the Czechoslovak Government of Novotny, all loyal Communists, accused Israel of aggression and severed diplomatic relations with it. And what happened next? Mnacko — a Slovak married to a Jew — who had calmly disregarded the suppression of Hungary before, now was so outraged and agitated that he left his homeland and as a protest went to live in Israel.

The second example comes from the same year. A famous French socialist, Daniel Meyer, at the moment of the Six-Day War had written in *Le Monde*, that henceforth he is: 1) ashamed to be a *socialist* — because of the fact that the Soviet Union calls itself a socialist country (well, when the Soviet Union was exterminating not only its own people but also other *socialists* — he was not ashamed); 2) ashamed of being a French (obviously due to the wrong political position of de Gaulle); and, 3) ashamed to be a *human* (wasn't that too much?), and ashamed of all except being a Jew.[2901]

We are ready to accept both Mnacko's outrage and Meyer's anger, yet we would like to point out at the extreme intensity of their feelings — given the long history of their obsequious condoning of communism. Surely, the intensity of their feelings is also an aspect of the Jewish question in the 20th century.

So in what way "did the Jewish question not exist"?

If one listened to American radio broadcasts aimed at the Soviet Union from 1950 to the 1980s, one might conclude that there was no other issue in the Soviet Union as important as the Jewish question. (At the same time in the United States, where the Jews "can be described as ... the most privileged minority" and where they "gained an unprecedented status, the majority of [American Jews] still claimed that hatred and discrimination by their Christian compatriots was a grim fact of the modern life";[2902] yet

---

[2901] *Daniel Mayer.* J'ai honte d'être socialiste // Le Monde, 1967, 6 Juin, p. 3.

[2902] *Michael Medved.* The Jewish Question // National Review, 1997, July 28, p. 53.

because it would sound incredible if stated aloud, then the Jewish question does not exist, and to notice it and talk about it is unnecessary and improper.)

We have to get used to talking about Jewish question not in a hush and fearfully, but clearly, articulately and firmly. We should do so not overflowing with passion, but sympathetically aware of both the unusual and difficult Jewish world history and centuries of our Russian history that are also full of significant suffering. Then the mutual prejudices, sometimes very intense, would disappear and calm reason would reign.

Working on this book, I can't help but notice that the Jewish question has been omnipresent in world history and it never was a national question in the narrow sense like all other national questions, but was always — maybe because of the nature of Judaism? — interwoven into something much bigger.

When in the late 1960s I mused about the fate of the communist regime and felt that yes, it is doomed, my impression was strongly supported by the observation that so many Jews had already abandoned it.

There was a period when they persistently and in unison supported the Soviet regime, and at that time the future definitely belonged to it. Yet now the Jews started to defect from it, first the thinking individuals and later the Jewish masses. Was this not a sure sign that the years of the Soviet rule are numbered?

Yes, it was.

So when exactly did it happen that the Jews, once such a reliable backbone of the regime, turned into almost its greatest adversary?

Can we say that the Jews always struggled for freedom? No, for too many of them were the most zealous communists. Yet now they turned their backs on it. And without them, the ageing Bolshevist fanaticism had not only lost some of its fervor, it actually ceased to be fanatical at all, rather it became lazy in the Russian way.

After the Soviet-German War, the Jews became disappointed by Communist power: it turned out that they were worse off than before. We saw the main stages of this split. Initially, the support of the newborn state of Israel by the USSR had inspired the Soviet Jews. Then came the persecution of the "cosmopolitans" and the mainly Jewish intelligentsia (not the philistine masses yet) began to worry: communism pushes the Jews aside? oppresses them? The terrible threat of massacre by Stalin overwhelmed them as well — but it was short-lived and miraculously disappeared very soon. During the "interregnum," [following Stalin's death] and then under Khrushchev, Jewish hopes were replaced by dissatisfaction and the promised stable improvement failed to materialize.

And then the Six-Day War broke out with truly biblical force, rocking both Soviet and world Jewry, and the Jewish national consciousness began to grow like an avalanche. After the Six-Day War, "much was changed ... the action acquired momentum. Letters and petitions began to flood Soviet and international organizations. National life was revived: during the holidays it became difficult to get into a synagogue, underground societies sprang up to study Jewish history, culture and Hebrew."[2903]

And then there was that rising campaign against "Zionism," already linked to "imperialism," and so the resentment grew among the Jews toward that increasingly alien and abominable and dull Bolshevism — *where did such a monster come from*?

Indeed, for many educated Jews the departure from communism was painful as it is always difficult to part with an ideal — after all, was not it a "great, and perhaps inevitable, planetary experiment initiated in Russia in 1917; an experiment, based on ancient attractive and obviously high ideas, not all of which were faulty and many still retain their beneficial effect to this day....

Marxism requires educated minds."[2904]

Many Jewish political writers strongly favored the term "Stalinism" — a convenient form to justify the earlier Soviet regime. It is difficult to part with the old familiar and sweet things, if it is really possible at all.

There have been attempts to increase the influence of intellectuals on the ruling elite. Such was the *Letter to the XXIII Congress* (of the Communist Party) by G. Pomerants (1966). The letter asked the Communist Party to trust the "scientific and creative intelligentsia," that "desires not anarchy but the rule of law ... that wants not to destroy the existing system but to make it more flexible, more rational, more humane" and proposed to establish an advisory think tank, which would *generally* consult the executive leadership of the country.[2905]

The offer remained unanswered.

And many souls long ached for such a wasted opportunity with such a "glorious" past.

[2903] *Михаил Хейфец*. Место и время (еврейские заметки). Париж: Третья волна, 1978, с. 174.
[2904] *Ю. Колкер* // Русская мысль, 24 апреля 1987, с. 12.
[2905] *Г. Померанц*. Проект письма XXIII съезду // Неопубликованное. Frankfurt/Main: Посев, 1972, с. 269-276.

But there was no longer any choice. And so the Soviet Jews split away from communism. And now, while deserting it, they turned against it. And that was such a perfect opportunity — they could themselves, with expurgatory repentance, acknowledge their formerly active and cruel role in the triumph of communism in Russia.

Yet almost none of them did (I discuss the few exceptions below). The above-mentioned collection of essays, *Russia and the Jews*, so heartfelt, so much needed and so timely when published in 1924 was fiercely denounced by Jewry. And even today, according to the opinion of the erudite scholar, Shimon Markish: "these days, nobody dares to defend those hook-nosed and burry commissars because of fear of being branded pro-Soviet, a Chekist, a God-knows-what else…. Yet let me say in no uncertain terms: the behavior of those Jewish youths who joined the Reds is a thousand times more understandable than the reasons of the authors of that collection of works."[2906]

Still, some Jewish authors began to recognize certain things of the past as they really were, though in the most cautious terms: "It was the end of the role of the Russian-Jewish intelligentsia' that developed in the prewar and early postwar years and that was — to some degree sincerely — a bearer of Marxist ideology and that professed, however timidly and implicitly and contrary to actual practice, the ideals of liberalism, internationalism and humanism."[2907] A bearer of Marxist ideology? — Yes, of course. The ideals of internationalism? — Sure. Yet liberalism and humanism? — True, but only after Stalin's death, while coming to senses.

However, very different things can be inferred from the writings of the majority of Jewish publicists in the late Soviet Union. Looking back to the very year of 1917, they find that under communism there was nothing but Jewish suffering! "Among the many nationalities of the Soviet Union, the Jews have *always* been stigmatized as the least 'reliable element.'"[2908]

What incredibly short memory one should have to state such things in 1983? *Always*! And what about the 1920s? And the 1930s? To assert that they were *then* considered the *least reliable*?! Is it really possible to forget everything so completely?

[2906] Ш. Маркиш. Ещё раз о ненависти к самому себе // "22": Общественно-политический и литературный журнал еврейской интеллигенции из СССР в Израиле. Тель-Авив, 1980, № 16, с. 188.
[2907] Р. Нудельман. Советский антисемитизм — причины и прогнозы: [Семинар] // "22", 1978, № 3, с. 147.
[2908] Ф. Колкер. Новый план помощи советскому еврейству // "22". 1983, № 31, с. 145.

"If ... one takes a bird's-eye view of the entire history of the Soviet era, then the latter appears as one gradual process of destruction of the Jews." Note — the *entire* history! We investigated this in the previous chapters and saw that even without taking into account Jewish over-representation in the top Soviet circles, there had been a period of well-being for many Jews with mass migration to cities, open access to higher education and the blossoming of Jewish culture. The author proceeds with a reservation: "Although there were... certain 'fluctuations', the overall trend continued ... Soviet power, destroying all nationalities, generally dealt with the Jews in the most brutal way."[2909]

Another author considers a disaster even the early period when Lenin and the Communist Party called upon the Jews to help with state governance, and the call was heard, and the great masses of Jews from the shtetls of the hated Pale moved into the capital and the big cities, closer to the avant-garde [of the Revolution]"; he states that the "... formation of the Bolshevik regime that had turned the greater part of Jews into déclassé', impoverished and exiled them and destroyed their families" was a catastrophe for the "majority of the Jewish population." (Well, that depends on one's point of view. And the author himself later notes: in the 1920s and 1930s, the "children of déclassé Jewish petty bourgeois were able to graduate from ... the technical institutes and metropolitan universities and to become commanders of the great developments.'") Then his reasoning becomes vague: "in the beginning of the century the main feature of Jewish activity was ... a fascination ... with the idea of building a new fair society"– yet the army of revolution "consisted of plain rabble — all those who were nothing,' [a quote from *The Internationale*]."

Then, "after the consolidation of the regime" that rabble "decided to implement their motto and tò become all' [also a quote from *The Internationale*], and finished off their own leaders.... And so the kingdom of rabble — unlimited totalitarianism — was established." (And, in this context, the Jews had nothing to do with it, except that they were among the victimized leaders.) And the purge continued "for four decades" until the "mid-1950s"; then the last "bitter pill ... according to the scenario of disappointments" was prescribed to the remaining "'charmed' Jews."[2910] Again we see the same angle: the entire Soviet history was one of unending oppression and exclusion of the Jews.

[2909] *Ю. Штерн.* Ситуация неустойчива и потому опасна: [Интервью] // "22", 1984, № 38, с. 130.
[2910] *В. Богуславский.* В защиту Куняева // "22", 1980. № 16, с. 169-174.

Yet now they wail in protest in unison: "We did not elect this regime!" Or even "it is not possible to cultivate a loyal Soviet elite among them [the Jews]."[2911]

Oh my God, was not this method working flawlessly for 30 years, and only later coming undone? So where did all those glorious and famous names — whom we've seen in such numbers — came from? And why were their eyes kept so tightly shut that they couldn't see the essence of Soviet rule for thirty to forty years? How is that that their eyes were opened only now? And what opened them?

Well, it was mostly because of the fact that now that power had suddenly turned around and began pushing the Jews not only out of its ruling and administrative circles, but out of cultural and scientific establishments also.

"The disappointment was so fresh and sore, that we did not have the strength, nor the courage to tell even our children about it. And what about the children? ... For the great majority of them the main motivation was the same — graduate school, career, and so on."[2912]

Yet soon they would have to examine their situation more closely.

In the 1970s we see examples of rather amazing agreement of opinions, unthinkable for the past half a century.

For instance, Shulgin wrote in 1929: "We must acknowledge our past. The flat denial ... claiming that the Jews are to blame for nothing — neither for the Russian Revolution, nor for the consolidation of Bolshevism, nor for the horrors of the communism — is the worst way possible.... It would be a great step forward if this groundless tendency to blame all the troubles of Russia on the Jews could be somewhat differentiated. It would be already great if any 'contrasts could be found."[2913]

Fortunately, such contrasts, and even more — comprehension, and even remorse — were voiced by some Jews. And, combined with the honest mind and rich life experience, they were quite clear. And this brings hope.

Here's Dan Levin, an American intellectual who immigrated to Israel: "It is no accident, that none of the American writers who attempted to describe and explain what happened to Soviet Jewry, has touched this important issue — the [Jewish] responsibility for the communism.... In Russia, the people's anti-Semitism is largely due to the fact that the Russians perceive the Jews as the cause of all the evil of the revolution. Yet American writers

---

[2911] Ю. Штерн. Ситуация неустойчива... // "22", 1984, № 38, с. 130.
[2912] В. Богуславский. В защиту Куняева // "22", 1980. № 16. с. 175.
[2913] В.В. Шульгин. «Что нам в них не нравится...»: Об Антисемитизме в России. Париж, 1929, с.49-50.

— Jews and ex-Communists ... do not want to resurrect the ghosts of the past. However, oblivion is a terrible thing."[2914]

Simultaneously, another Jewish writer, an émigré from the Soviet Union, published: the experience of the Russian (Soviet) Jewry, in contrast to that of the European Jewry, whose historical background "is the experience of a collision with the forces of *outer* evil ... requires a look not from inside out but rather of introspection and ... inner self-examination." "In this reality we saw only one Jewish spirituality — that of the Commissar — and its name was Marxism." Or he writes about "our young Zionists who demonstrate so much contempt toward Russia, her rudeness and savagery, contrasting all this with [the worthiness of] the ancient Jewish nation." "I saw pretty clearly, that those who today sing hosanna to Jewry, glorifying it in its entirety (without the slightest sense of guilt or the slightest potential to look inside), yesterday were saying: 'I wouldn't be against the Soviet regime, if it was not anti-Semitic,ánd two days ago they beat their breasts in ecstasy: 'Long live the great brotherhood of nations! Eternal Glory to the Father and Friend, the genius Comrade Stalin!'"[2915]

But today, when it is clear how many Jews were in the iron Bolshevik leadership, and how many more took part in the ideological guidance of a great country to the wrong track — should the question not arise [among modern Jews] as to some sense of responsibility for the actions of *those* [Jews]? It should be asked in general: shouldn't there be a kind of moral responsibility — not a joint liability, yet the responsibility *to remember and to acknowledge*? For example, modern Germans accept liability to Jews directly, both morally and materially, as perpetrators are liable to the victims: for many years they have paid compensation to Israel and personal compensation to surviving victims.

So what about Jews? When Mikhail Kheifets, whom I repeatedly cite in this work, after having been through labor camps, expressed the grandeur of his character by repenting on behalf of his people for the evil committed by the Jews in the Soviet Union in the name of communism — he was bitterly ridiculed.

The whole educated society, *the cultured circle*, had genuinely failed to notice any *Russian* grievances in the 1920s and 1930s; they didn't even assume that *such* could exist — yet they instantly recognized the Jewish grievances as soon as those emerged. Take, for example, Victor Perelman, who after emigrating published an anti-Soviet Jewish journal *Epoch and We* and who served the regime in the filthiest place, in Chakovsky's

---

[2914] *Дан Левин*. На краю соблазна: [Интервью] // "22", 1978, № 1, с. 55.
[2915] *А. Суконик*. О религиозном и атеистическом сознании // Вестник Русского Христианского Движения. Париж-Нью-Йорк-Москва, 1977, № 123, с. 43-46.

Literaturnaya Gazeta — until the Jewish question had entered his life. Then he opted out....

At a higher level, they generalized it as "the crash of ... illusions about the integration [of Jewry] into the Russian social movements, about making any change in Russia."[2916]

Thus, as soon as the Jews recognized their explicit antagonism to the Soviet regime, they turned into its intellectual opposition — in accord to their social role. Of course, it was not them who rioted in Novocherkassk, or created unrest in Krasnodar, Alexandrov, Murom, or Kostroma. Yet the filmmaker Mikhail Romm plucked up his heart and, during a public speech, unambiguously denounced the "anti-cosmopolitan" campaign — and that became one of the first Samizdat documents (and Romm himself, who in so timely a manner rid himself of his ideological impediments, became a kind of spiritual leader for the Soviet Jewry, despite his films *Lenin in October* (1937), *Lenin in 1918* (1939), and despite being a fivefold winner of the Stalin Prize).

And after that the Jews had become reliable supporters and intrepid members of the "democratic" and "dissident" movements.

Looking back from Israel at the din of Moscow, another witness reflected: "A large part of Russian democrats (if not the majority) are of Jewish origin.... Yet they do not identify [themselves] as Jews and do not realize that their audience is also mostly Jewish."[2917]

And so the Jews had once again become the Russian revolutionaries, shouldering the social duty of the Russian intelligentsia, which the Jewish Bolsheviks so zealously helped to exterminate during the first decade after the revolution; they had become the true and genuine nucleus of the new public opposition. And so yet again no progressive movement was possible without Jews.

Who had halted the torrent of false political (and often semi-closed) court trials? Alexander Ginzburg, and then Pavel Litvinov and Larisa Bogoraz did. I would not exaggerate if I claim that their appeal "To world public opinion" in January 1968, delivered not through unreliable Samizdat, but handed fearlessly to the West in front of Cheka cameras, had been a milestone of Soviet ideological history. Who were those seven brave souls who dragged their leaden feet to Lobnoye Mesto [a stone platform in Red Square] on Aug. 25, 1968?

[2916] Р. Нудельман. Оглянись в раздумье...: [Круглый стол] // "22. 1982, № 24, с. 112.

[2917] А. Воронель. Будущее русской алии // "22", 1978, № 2, с. 186.

They did it not for the greater success of their protest, but to wash the name of Russia from the Czechoslovak disgrace by their sacrifice. Four out of the seven were Jews. (Remember, that the percentage of Jews in the population of the country then was less than 1%) We should also remember Semyon Gluzman, who sacrificed his freedom in the struggle against the "nuthouses" [dissidents were sometimes incarcerated in psychiatric clinics]. Many Jewish intellectuals from Moscow were among the first punished by the Soviet regime.

Yet very few dissidents ever regretted the past of their Jewish fathers. P. Litvinov never mentioned his grandfather's role in Soviet propaganda. Neither would we hear from V. Belotserkovsky how many innocents were slaughtered by his Mauser-toting father. Communist Raisa Lert, who became a dissident late in life, was proud of her membership in *that* party even after *The Gulag Archipelago*; the party "she had joined in good faith and enthusiastically" in her youth; the party to which she had "wholly devoted herself" and from which she herself had suffered, yet nowadays it is "not the same" party anymore.[2918]

Apparenty she did not realize how appealing the early Soviet terror was for her. After the events of 1968, Sakharov joined the dissident movement without a backward glance. Among his new dissident preoccupations were many individual cases; in particular, personal cases of Jewish refuseniks [those, overwhelming Jewish, dissidents who requested, but were refused the right to emigrate from the Soviet Union]. Yet when he tried to expand the business (as he had innocently confided to me, not realizing all the glaring significance of what he said), Gelfand, a member of the Academy of Science, told him that "we are tired of helping these people to resolve their problems," while another member, Zeldovich, said: "I'm not going to sign any petition on behalf of victims of any injustice — I want to retain the ability to protect those who suffer for their nationality." Which means — to protect the Jews only.

There was also a purely Jewish dissident movement, which was concerned only with the oppression of the Jews and Jewish emigration from the Soviet Union (more about it — later).

A transformation in public consciousness often pushes forward outstanding individuals as representatives, symbols and spokesmen of the age. So in the 1960s Alexander Galich became such a typical and accurate representative of the processes and attitudes in the Soviet intellectual circles. ("'Galich is a pen name, explains N. Rubinstein. It is made of

---

[2918] Р. Лерт. Поздний опыт // Синтаксис: Публицистика, критика, полемика. Париж, 1980, № 6, с. 5-6.

syllables of his real name — Ginsburg Alexander Arkadievich. Choosing a pen name is a serious thing."[2919]

Actually, I assume that the author was aware that, apart from being "just a combination of syllables," "Galich" is also the name of the ancient Russian city from the very heart of Slavic history.) Galich enjoyed the general support of Soviet intelligentsia; tape recordings of his guitar performances were widely disseminated; and they have almost become the symbol of the social revival of the 1960s expressing it powerfully and vehemently. The opinion of the *cultural circle* was unanimous: "the most popular people's poet," the "bard of modern Russia."

Galich was 22 when the Soviet-German War broke out. He says that he was exempt from military service because of poor health; he then moved to Grozny, where he "unexpectedly easily became the head of the literature section of the local Drama Theatre"; he also "organized a theater of political satire"; then he evacuated through Krasnovodsk to Chirchik near Tashkent; in 1942, he moved from there to Moscow with a front-line theatrical company under formation and spent the rest of the war with that company.

He recalled how he worked on hospital trains, composing and performing couplets for wounded soldiers; how they were drinking spirits with a trainmaster.... "All of us, each in his own way, worked for the great common cause: we were defending our Motherland."[2920] After the war he became a well-known Soviet scriptwriter (he worked on many movies) and a playwright (ten of his plays were staged by "many theaters in the Soviet Union and abroad" [216] [references in square brackets refer to the page number in the source 21]. All that was in 1940s and 1950s, in the age of general spiritual stagnation — well, he could not step out of the line, could he? He even made a movie about Chekists, and was awarded for his work.

Yet in the early 1960s, Galich abruptly changed his life. He found courage to forsake his successful and well-off life and "walk into the square." [98] It was after that that he began performing guitar-accompanied songs to people gathering in private Moscow apartments. He gave up open publishing, though it was, of course, not easy: "[it was great] to read a name on the cover, not just someone else's, but mine!" [216]

[2919] Н. Рубинштейн. Выключите магнитофон — поговорим о поэте // Время и мы (далее — ВМ): Международный журнал литературы и общественных проблем. Тель-Авив, 1975, № 2, с. 164.
[2920] *Александр Галич*. Песни. Стихи. Поэмы. Киноповесть. Пьеса. Статьи. Екатеринбург: У-Фактория, 1998 (далее — Галич), с. 552, 556, 561-562. Страницы в тексте в квадратных скобках; Указаны также по этому изданию.

Surely, his anti-regime songs, keen, acidic, and and morally demanding, were of benefit to the society, further destabilizing public attitudes.

In his songs he mainly addressed Stalin's later years and beyond; he usually did not deplore the radiant past of the age of Lenin (except one instance: "The carts with bloody cargo / squeak by Nikitsky Gate" [224]). At his best, he calls the society to moral cleansing, to resistance ("Gold-digger's waltz" [26], "I choose liberty" [226], "Ballad of the clean hands" [181], "Our fingers blotted from the questionnaires" [90], "Every day silent trumpets glorify thoughtful vacuity" [92]). Sometimes he sang the hard truth about the past ("In vain had our infantry perished in 1943, to no avail" [21]), sometimes — "Red myths," singing about poor persecuted communists ("There was a time — almost a third of the inmates came from the Central Committee, / There was a time when for the red color / they added ten years [to the sentence]!"[69]). Once he touched dekulakization ("Disenfranchised ones were summoned in first" [115]). Yet his main blow was against the current establishment ("There are fences in the country; behind fences live the leaders" [13]). He was justly harsh there; however, he oversimplified the charge by attacking their privileged way of life only: here they eat, drink, rejoice [151-152]. The songs were embittering, but in a narrow-minded way, almost like the primitive "Red proletarian" propaganda of the past. Yet when he was switching his focus from the leaders to "the people", his characters were almost entirely boobies, fastidious men, rabble and rascals — a very limited selection.

He had found a precise point of perspective for himself, perfectly in accord with the spirit of the time: he impersonalized himself with all those people who were suffering, persecuted and killed ("I was a GI and as a GI I'll die" [248], "We, GIs, are dying in battle"). Yet with his many songs narrated from the first person of a former camp inmate, he made a strong impression that he was an inmate himself ("And that other inmate was me myself" [87]; "I froze like a horseshoe in a sleigh trail / Into ice that I picked with a hammer pick / After all, wasn't it me who spent twenty years / In those camps" [24]; "as the numbers

[personal inmate number tattooed on the arm] / we died, we died"; "from the camp we were sent right to the front!"[69]). Many believed that he was a former camp inmate and "they have tried to find from Galich when and where he had been in camps."[2921]

So how did he address his past, his longstanding participation in the stupefying official Soviet lies? That's what had struck me the most: singing with such accusatory pathos, he had never expressed *a single word of his personal remorse, not a word of personal repentance, nowhere*! Didn't he

---

[2921] В. *Волин*. Он вышел на площадь // *Галич*, с. 632.

realize that when he sang: "Oh Party's Iliad! What a giftwrapped groveling!" [216], he sang about himself? And when he crooned: "If you sell the unction" [40], as though referring to somebody else, did it occur to him that he himself was "selling unction" for half of his life. Why on earth would he not renounce his pro-official plays and films? No! "We did not sing glory to executioners!" [119] Yet, as the matter of fact, they did. Perhaps he did realize it or he gradually came to the realization, because later, no longer in Russia, he said: "I was a well-off screenwriter and playwright and a well-off Soviet flunky. And I have realized that I could no longer go on like that. Finally, I have to speak loudly, speak the truth ..." [639].

But then, in the sixties, he intrepidly turned the pathos of the civil rage, for instance, to the refutation of the Gospel commandments ("do not judge, lest ye be judged"): "No, I have contempt for the very essence / Of this formula of existence!" And then, relying on the sung miseries, he confidently tried on a prosecutor's robe: "I was not elected. But I am the judge!" [100] And so he grew so confident, that in the lengthy *Poem about Stalin (The Legend of Christmas*), where he in bad taste imagined Stalin as Christ, and presented the key formula of his agnostic mindset — his really famous, the clichéd -quotes, and so harmful lines: "Don't be afraid of fire and hell, / And fear only him / Who says: I know the right way!'" [325].

But Christ did teach us *the right way*.... What we see here in Galich's words is just boundless intellectual anarchism that muzzles any clear idea, any resolute offer. Well, we can always run as a thoughtless (but *pluralistic*) herd, and probably we'll get somewhere.

Yet the most heartrending and ubiquitous keynote in his lyrics was the sense of Jewish identity and Jewish pain ("Our train leaves for Auschwitz today and daily"). Other good examples include the poems *By the rivers of Babylon* and *Kadish*. (Or take this: "My six-pointed star, burn it on my sleeve and on my chest." Similar lyrical and passionate tones can be found in the *The memory of Odessa* ("I wanted to unite Mandelstam and Chagall). "Your kinsman and your cast-off / Your last singer of the Exodus" — as he addressed the departing Jews.)

The Jewish memory imbued him so deeply that even in his non-Jewish lyrics he casually added expressions such as: "Not a hook-nosed"; "not a Tatar, not a Yid" [115, 117]"; "you are still not in Israel, dodderer?" [294]; and even Arina Rodionovna [Pushkin's nanny, immortalized by the poet in his works] lulls him in Yiddish [101]. Yet he doesn't mention a single prosperous or non-oppressed Jew, a well-off Jew on a good position, for instance, in a research institute, editorial board, or in commerce — such characters didn't even make a passing appearance in his poems. A Jew is always either humiliated, or suffering, or imprisoned and dying in a camp. Take his famous lines: "You are not to be chamberlains, the Jews ... / Neither the Synod, nor the Senate is for you / You belong in Solovki and Butyrki" [the latter two being political prisons] [40].

What a short memory they have — not only Galich, but his whole audience who were sincerely, heartily taking in these sentimental lines! What about those twenty years, when Soviet Jewry was not nearly in the Solovki, when so many of them did parade as chamberlains and in the Senate!?

They have forgotten it. They have sincerely and completely forgotten it. Indeed, it is so difficult to remember bad things about yourself.

And inasmuch as among the successful people milking the regime there were supposedly no Jews left, but only Russians, Galich's satire, unconsciously or consciously, hit the Russians, all those Klim Petroviches and Paramonovs; all that social anger invoked by his songs targeted them, through the stressed "russopyaty" [derogatory term for Russians] images and details, presenting them as informers, prison guards, profligates, fools or drunks. Sometimes it was more like a caricature, sometimes more of a contemptuous pity (which we often indeed deserve, unfortunately): "Greasy long hair hanging down, / The guest started "Yermak" [a song about the cossack leader and Russian folk hero] ... he cackles like a cock / Enough to make a preacher swear / And he wants to chat / About the salvation of Russia" [117-118]. Thus he pictured the Russians as always drunk, not distinguishing kerosene from vodka, not interested in anything except drinking, idle, or simply lost, or foolish individuals. Yet he was considered a *folk* poet.... And he didn't image a single Russian hero-soldier, workman, or intellectual, not even a single decent camp inmate (he assigned the role of the main camp inmate to himself), because, you know, all those "prison-guard seed" [118] camp bosses are Russians. And here he wrote about Russia directly: "Every liar is a Messiah! / <...> And just dare you to ask — / Brothers, had there even been / Any Rus in Russia?" — "It is abrim with filth." — And then, desperately: "But somewhere, perhaps, / She does exist!?" That invisible Russia, where "under the tender skies / Everyone shares / God's word and bread." "I pray thee: / Hold on! / Be alive in decay, / So in the heart, as in Kitezh, / I could hear your bells!" [280-281]

So, with the new opportunity and the lure of emigration, Galich was torn between the submerged legendary Kitezh [legendary Russian invisble city] and today's filth: "It's the same vicious circle, the same old story, the ring, which cannot be either closed, or open!" [599]. He left with the words: "I, a Russian poet, cannot be separated from Russia by 'the fifth article' [the requirement in the Soviet internal passport – "nationality"]!" [588]

Yet some other departing Jews drew from his songs a seed of aversion and contempt for Russia, or at least, the confidence that it is right to break away from her. Heed a voice from Israel: "We said goodbye to Russia. Not without pain, but forever... Russia still holds us tenaciously. But ... in a year, ten years, a hundred years — we'll escape from her and find our own home. Listening to Galich, we once again recognize that it is the right way."[2922]

[2922] *Н. Рубинштейн.* Выключите магнитофон — поговорим о поэте // ВМ, Тель-Авив, 1975, № 2, с. 177.

Chapter 25

Accusing Russia

The Jewish break from the Soviet communism was doubtless a movement of historical significance.

In the 1920s and 1930s, the fusion of the Soviet Jewry and Bolshevism seemed permanent. Then suddenly, they diverge? What a joy!

Of course, as is always true for both individuals and nations, it is unreasonable to expect words of remorse from Jews regarding their past involvement. But I absolutely could not expect that the Jews, while deserting Bolshevism, rather than expressing even a sign of repentance or at least some embarrassment, instead angrily turned on the Russian people: it is the *Russians* who had ruined democracy in Russia (i.e., in February 1917), it is the *Russians* who are guilty of support of this regime from 1918 on.

Sure, they claim, it is we (the Russian people) who are the guilty! Actually, it was earlier than 1918 – the dirty scenes of the *radiant* February Revolution were tale-telling. Yet the neophyte anti-communists were uncompromising – from now on everyone must accept that they have always fought against this regime, and no one should recall that it used to be their favorite and should not mention how well they had once served this tyranny. Because it was the "natives" who created, nurtured and cared for it:

"The leaders of the October Coup ... were the followers rather than the leaders. [Really? The New Iron Party was made up of the "followers"?] They simply voiced the dormant wishes of the masses and worked to implement them. They did not break with the grassroots." "The October coup was a disaster for Russia. The country could evolve differently.... Then [in the stormy anarchy of the February Revolution] Russia saw the signs of law, freedom and respect for human dignity by the state, but they all were swept away by the people's wrath."[2923]

[2923] B. Shragin. *Protivostoyanie dukha* [Standoff of the Spirit (hereinafter — B. Shragin)]. London: Overseas Publications, 1977, p. 160, 188-189.

Here is a more recent dazzling treatment of Jewish participation in Bolshevism: "The Bolshevism of Lenin and Russian Social Democratic Workers' Party of Bolsheviks was just an intellectual and civilized form of 'plebian' Bolshevism. Should the former fail, the latter, much more dreadful, would prevail." Therefore, "by widely participating in the Bolshevik Revolution, providing it with cadres of intellectuals and organizers, the Jews saved Russia from total mob rule. They came out with the most humane of possible forms of Bolshevism."[2924] Alas, "just as the rebellious people had used the Party of Lenin to overthrow the democracy of intellectuals [when did that exist?], the pacified people used Stalin's bureaucracy to get rid of ... everything still harboring free intellectual spirit."[2925] Sure, sure: "the guilt of the intelligentsia for the subsequent dismal events of Russian history is greatly exaggerated." And in the first place, "the intelligentsia is liable to itself,"[2926] and by no means to the people. On the contrary, "it would be nice if the people realized their guilt before the intelligentsia."[2927]

Indeed, "the totalitarian rule ... in its essence and origin is that of the people."[2928] "This is a totalitarian country ... because such was the choice of Russian people."[2929]

It is all because the "Tatar's wild spirit captured the soul of Orthodox Russia,"[2930] that is, the "Asian social and spiritual structure, inherited by the Russians from the Mongols ... is stagnant and incapable of

---

[2924] Nik. Shulgin. *Novoe russkoe samosoznanie* [The New Russian Mind]. // Vek 20 i mir [The 20th Century and the World]. Moscow, 1990, (3), p. 27.
[2925] M. Meyerson-Aksenov. *Rozhdeniye novoi intelligentsii* [The Birth of New Intelligentsia]. // Samosoznanie: Sb. statei. [Self-consciousness: The Collection of Articles]. New York: Chronicles, 1976, p. 102.
[2926] B. Shragin, p, 246, 249.
[2927] O. Altaev. *Dvoinoe soznanie intelligentsii i psevdo-kultura* [Dual Mind of Intelligentsia and Pseudo-Culture]. // Vestnik Russkogo Studencheskogo Khristianskogo Dvizheniya [Herald of Russian Student Christian Movement]. Paris – New York, 1970, (97), p. 11.
[2928] M. Meyerson-Aksenov. *Rozhdeniye novoi intelligentsii* [The Birth of New Intelligentsia]. // Samosoznanie: Sb. statei. [Self-consciousness: The Collection of Articles]. New York: Chronicles, 1976, p. 102.
[2929] Beni Peled. *My ne smozhem zhdat escho dve tysyachi let!* [We cannot wait for another two thousand years!]. [Interview] // *"22"*: Obshchestvenno-politicheskiy i literaturniy zhurnal evreyskoy intelligentsii iz SSSR v Izraile [*Social, Political and Literary Journal of the Jewish Intelligentsia from the USSR in Israel*]. Tel-Aviv, 1981, (17), p. 114.
[2930] N. Prat. *Emigrantskie kompleksy v istoricheskom aspekte* [Emigrant's Fixations in the Historical Perspective]. // *Vremya i my*: Mezhdunarodny zhurnal literatury i obshchestvennykh problem [*Epoch and We* (hereinafter – EW) : International Journal of Literature and Social Problems]. New York, 1980, (56), p. 191.

development and progress."²⁹³¹ (Well, Lev Gumilev also developed a theory that instead of the Tatar yoke, there was a friendly alliance of Russians and Tatars. However, Russian folklore, in its many proverbs referring to Tatars as to enemies and oppressors, provided an unambiguous answer to that question. Folklore does not lie; it is not pliant like a scientific theory.) Therefore, "the October coup was an unprecedented breakthrough of the Asian essence [of Russians]."²⁹³²

For those who want to tear and trample Russian history, Chaadayev is the favorite theoretician (although he is undoubtedly an outstanding thinker). First Samizdat and later émigré publications carefully selected and passionately quoted his published and unpublished texts which suited their purposes. As to the unsuitable quotations and to the fact that the main opponents of Chaadayev among his contemporaries were not Nicholas I and Benckendorff, but his friends – Pushkin, Vyazemsky, Karamzin, and Yazikov – these facts were ignored. In the early 1970s, the hate against all things Russian was gathering steam.

Derogatory expressions about Russian culture entered Samizdat and contemporary slang. "Human pigsty" – so much contempt for Russia as being spoiled material was expressed in the anonymous Samizdat article signed by "S. Telegin" (G. Kopylov)! Regarding the forest fires of 1972, the same "Telegin" cursed Russia in a Samizdat leaflet: "So, the Russian forests burn? It serves Russia right for all her evil-doing!! "The entire people consolidate into the reactionary mass" (G. Pomerants). Take another sincere confession: "The sound of an accordion [the popular Russian national instrument] drives me berserk; the very contact with these masses irritates me."²⁹³³ Indeed, love cannot be forced. "'Jews,'' Jewish destiny' is just the rehash of the destiny of intelligentsia in this country, the destiny of her culture; the Jewish orphanage symbolizes loneliness because of the collapse of the traditional faith in 'the people.'"²⁹³⁴

(What a transformation happened between the 19th and mid-20th century with the eternal Russian problem of "the people"! By now they view "the people" as an indigenous mass, apathetically satisfied with its existence and its leaders.

And by the inscrutable providence of Fate, the Jews were forced to live and suffer in the cities of their country. To love these *masses* is impossible; to care about them – unnatural.) The same Khazanov (by then still in the

---

²⁹³¹ B. Shragin, p, 304.
²⁹³² Ibid., p. 305.
²⁹³³ M. Deich. *Zapiski postoronnego* [Commentaries of an Outsider]. // *"22"*, 1982, (26), p. 156.
²⁹³⁴ B. Khazanov. *Novaya Rossiya* [new Russia]. // *EW*, Tel-Aviv, 1976, (8), p. 143.

USSR) reasoned: The Russia which I love is a Platonic idea that does not exist in reality. The Russia which I see around is abhorrent"; "she is a unique kind of Augean stables"; "her mangy inhabitants"; "there'll be a day of shattering reckoning for all she is today."[2935]

Indeed, there will be a day of reckoning, though not for the state of adversity that had fallen on Russia much earlier.

In the 1960s, many among intelligentsia began to think and talk about the situation in the USSR, about its future and about Russia itself. Due to strict government censorship these arguments and ideas were mentioned only in private or in mostly pseudonymous Samizdat articles. But when Jewish emigration began, the criticisms of Russia openly and venomously spilled across the free Western world, as it formed one of the favorite topics among the émigrés and was voiced so loudly that often nothing else could be heard.

In 1968, Arkady Belinkov fled abroad. He was supposedly a fierce enemy of the Soviet regime and not at all of the Russian people. Wasn't he? Well, consider his article *The Land of Slaves, the Land of Masters* in *The New Bell*, a collection he edited himself. And *at what* did he direct his wrath? (It is worth considering that the article was written back in the USSR and the author did not have enough courage to accuse *the regime* itself.) Belinkov does not use the word "Soviet" even once, instead preferring a familiar theme: eternally enslaved Russia, freedom "for our homeland is worse than gobbling broken glass" and in Russia "they sometimes hang the wrong people, sometimes the wrong way, and never enough." Even in the 1820s "it was much evident that in the process of evolution, the population of [Russia] ...would turn into a herd of traitors, informers, and torturers"; "it was the "Russian fear" – to prepare warm clothes and to wait for a knock at the door" – note that even here it was not the "*Soviet* fear." (Yet who before the Bolshevik revolution had ever waited for a knock on the door in the middle of the night?) "The court in Russia does not judge, it already knows everything. Therefore, in Russia, it only condemns."[2936]

(Was it like that even during the Alexandrine reforms?.... And what about juries and magistrates? Hardly a responsible, balanced judgment!)

Indeed, so overwhelming is the author's hate and so bitter his bile that he vilifies such great Russian writers as Karamzin, Zhukovsky, Tyutchev and even Pushkin, not to mention Russian society in general for its insufficient revolutionary spirit: "a pathetic society of slaves, descendants of slaves and

---

[2935] Ibid., p. 141, 142, 144.
[2936] A. Belinkov. *Strana rabov, strana gospod* [The land of slaves, the land of masters]. // *The New Bell: The Collection of Literary and Opinion Writings*. London, 1972, p. 323, 339, 346, 350.

ancestors of slaves," "the cattle trembling from fear and anger," "rectum-pipers, shuddering at the thought of possible consequences," "the Russian intelligentsia always been willing to help stifle freedom."[2937]

Well, if, for Belinkov, it was all "masked anti-Soviet sentiments," a sly wink, then why did he not rewrite it abroad? If Belinkov actually thought *differently*, then why print it in this form?

No, that is *the way* he thought and *what* he hated. So was *this* how dissident Jews repudiated Bolshevism?

Around the same time, at the end of the 1960s, a Jewish collection about the USSR was published in London. It included a letter from the USSR: "In the depths of the inner labyrinths of the Russian soul, there is always a pogromist.... A slave and a thug dwell there too."[2938] Belotserkovsky happily repeats someone else's joke: "the Russians are a strong nation, except for their heads."[2939] "Let all these Russians, Ukrainians ... growl drunkenly with their wives, gobble vodka and get happily misled by communist lies ... without us ...

They were crawling on all fours worshipping wood and stone when we gave them the God of Abraham, Isaac and Jacob."[2940]

(Let us note that any insulting judgment about the "Russian soul" *in general* or about the "Russian character" *generally* does not give rise to the slightest protest or doubt among civilized people. The question "of daring to judge nations as one uniform and faceless whole" does not arise. If someone does not like all things Russian or feels contempt for them, or even expresses in progressive circles the belief that "Russia is a cesspool," this is no sin in Russia and it does not appear reactionary or backward. And no one immediately appeals to presidents, prime ministers, senators, or members of Congress with a reverent cry, "What do you think of such incitement of ethnic hatred?" We've said worse of ourselves since the 19th century and right up to the revolution. We have a rich tradition of this.)

Then we learn of "semi-literate preachers of their religion," and that "Russian Orthodoxy hasn't earned the credence of intellectuals" (from "Telegin"). The Russians "so easily abandoned the faith of their

---

[2937] Ibid., p. 325-328, 337, 347, 355.
[2938] N. Shapiro. *Slovo ryadovogo sovetskogo evreya* [The Word of an Ordinary Soviet Jew]. // The Russian Anti-Semitism and Jews. Collection of essays. London, 1968, p. 50-51.
[2939] *The New American*, New York, 1982, March 23-29, (110), p. 11.
[2940] Jakob Yakir. *Ya pishu Viktoru Krasinu* [I Write to Viktor Krasin]. // *Our Country*, Tel Aviv, 1973, December 12. Cited from the *New Journal*, 1974, (117), p. 190. "Oh, if only you would have held your peace! This would have been regarded as your wisdom." (Job 13:5).

forefathers, indifferently watched how their temples were destroyed in front of their eyes."

Oh, here is a guess: "Perhaps, the Russian people only temporarily submitted to the power of Christianity?" That is for 950 years! "And they only waited for the moment to get rid of it,"[2941] that is, for the revolution? How much ill will must accumulate in someone's heart to utter something like that! (Even Russian publicists often slipped into this trap of distorted consciousness. The eminent early emigrant journalist S. Rafalsky, perhaps even a priest's son, wrote that "Orthodox Holy Russia allowed its holy sites to be easily crushed."[2942] Of course, the groans of those mowed down by Chekists' machine guns during Church riots in 1918 were not heard in Paris. There have been no uprisings since. I would like to have seen this priest's son try to save the sacred sites in the 1920s himself.)

Sometimes it is stated bluntly: "Russian Orthodoxy is a Hottentot religion" (Grobman). Or, "idiocy perfumed by Rublev, Dionysius and Berdyaev"; the idea of the "restoration" of traditional Russian historical orthodoxy "scares many.... This is the darkest future possible for the country and for Christianity."[2943] Or, as novelist F. Gorenshtein said: "Jesus Christ was the Honorary Chairman of the Union of the Russian People [pre-revolutionary Russian Nationalist organization], whom they perceived as a kind of universal ataman [Cossack chieftain]."[2944]

Don't make it too sharp – you might chip the blade!

However, one must distinguish from such open rudeness that velvet soft Samizdat philosopher-essayist Grigory Pomerants who worked in those years.

Presumably, he rose above all controversies – he wrote about the fates of *nations in general*, about the fate of the intelligentsia *generally*; he suggested that nowadays no such thing as *people* exists, save, perhaps, Bushmen. I read him in 1960s Samizdat saying: "The people are becoming more and more vapid broth and only we, the intelligentsia, remain the salt of the earth." "Solidarity of the intelligentsia across the borders is a more real thing than the solidarity of the intelligentsia and its people."

[2941] Amram. *Reaktsiya ottorzheniya* [The Reaction of Rejection]. // *"22"*, 1979, (5), p. 201.
[2942] *The New Russian Word*, New York, 1975, November 30, p. 3.
[2943] M. Ortov. *Pravoslavnoe gosudarstvo I tserkov* [The orthodox State and the Church]. *The Way: The Orthodox Almanac.* New York, 1984, May-June, (3), p. 12, 15.
[2944] F. Gorenshtein. *Shestoi konets krasnoi zvezdy* [The Sixs Point of the Red Star]. // *EW*, New York, 1982, (65), p. 125.

It sounded very modern and wise. And yet, in Czechoslovakia in 1968 it was precisely the unity of the intelligentsia with the "vapid broth" of its nonexistent people that created a spiritual stronghold long unheard of in Europe.

The presence of two-thirds of a million Soviet troops couldn't break their spirit; it was their communist leaders who eventually gave in. (And 12 years later, the same thing happened in Poland.)

In his typically ambiguous manner of constructing endless parallel arguments that never merge into a clear logical construct, Pomerants never explicitly addressed the national question. He extensively dwelt on the Diaspora question, in the most abstract and general manner, not specifying any nation, hovering aloft in relativism and agnosticism. He glorified the Diaspora: "Everywhere, we are not exactly strangers. Everywhere, we are not exactly natives."... "An appeal to one faith, tradition and nation flies in the face of another." He complained: "According to the rules established for the Warsaw students, one can love only one nation" but "what if I am related by blood to this country, but love others as well?"[2945]

This is a sophisticated bait-and-switch. Of course, you can love not only one, but ten or more countries and nations. However, you can belong to and be *a son* of only one motherland, just as you can only have one mother.

To make the subject clearer, I want to describe the letter exchange I had with the Pomerants couple in 1967. By that year, my banned novel *The First Circle* circulated among the Samizdat – and among the first who had sent me their objections were G. S. Pomerants and his wife, Z. A. Mirkin. They said that I hurt them by my inept and faulty handling of the Jewish question, and that I had irreparably damaged the image of Jews in the novel – and thus my own image. How did I damage it? I thought I had managed to avoid showing those cruel Jews who reached the heights of power during the early Soviet years. But Pomerants' letters abounded with undertones and nuances, and they accused me of insensitivity to Jewish pain.

I replied to them, and they replied to me. In these letters we also discussed the right to judge entire nations, even though I had done no such thing in my novel.

Pomerants suggested to me then – and to every writer in general as well as to anyone who offers any personal, psychological or social judgment – to behave and *to reason* as if no nation has ever existed in the world – not

---

[2945] G. Pomerants. *Chelovek niotkuda* [The Man from Nowhere]. From G. Pomerants, *Unpublished*. Frankfurt, Posev, 1972, p. 143, 145, 161-162.

only to abstain from judging them as a whole but to ignore every man's nationality.

"What is natural and excusable for Ivan Denisovich (to see Cesar Markovich as a non-Russian) – is a disgrace for an intellectual, and for a Christian (not a *baptized person* but a Christian) is a great sin: 'There is no Hellene and no Jew for me.'"

What an elevated point of view. May God help us all reach it one day. After all, without it, would not the meaning of *united humanity,* and so Christianity, have been useless?

Yet we have already been aggressively convinced once that there are no nations, and were instructed to quickly destroy our own, and we madly did it back then.

In addition, regardless of the argument, how can we portray specific people without referring to their nationality? And if there are no nations, are there no languages? But no writer can write in any language other than his native one. If nations would wither away, languages would die also.

One cannot eat from an empty bowl.

I noticed that it was more often Jews than any others who insisted that we pay no attention to nationality! What does "nationality" have to do with anything? What "national characteristics," what "national character" are you talking about?

And I was ready to shake hands on that: "I agree! Let's ignore it from now on...." But we live in our unfortunate century, when perhaps the first feature people notice in others for some reason is exactly their nationality. And, I swear, Jews are the ones who distinguish and closely monitor it most jealously and carefully. Their *own* nation....

Then, what should we do with the fact – you have read about it above – that Jews so often judge Russians precisely in *generalized terms*, and almost always to condemn? The same Pomerants writes about "the pathological features of the Russian character," including their "internal instability." (And he is not concerned that he judges the entire nation. Imagine if someone spoke of "pathological features of the Jewish character"... What would happen then?) The Russian "masses *allowed* all the horrors of Oprichnina to happen just as they later *allowed* Stalin's death camps."[2946] (See, the Soviet internationalist bureaucratic elite would have stopped them – if not for this dull mass....) More sharply still, "Russian

---

[2946] G. Pomerants. *Sny zemli* [Nightdreams of Earth]. // *"22"*, 1980, (12), p. 129.

Nationalism will inevitably end in an aggressive pogrom,"[2947] meaning that every Russian who loves his nation already has the potential for being pogromist.

We can but repeat the words of that Chekhov's character: "Too early!" Most remarkable was how Pomerants's second letter to me ended. Despite his previously having so insistently demanded that it is not proper to distinguish between nations, in that large and emotionally charged letter, (written in a very angry, heavy hand), he delivered an ultimatum on how I could still save my disgusting *The First Circle*. The offered remedy was this: *to turn Gerasimovich*

[the hero] *into a Jew*! So a Jew would commit the novel's greatest act of spiritual heroism! "*It is absolutely not important* that Gerasimovich had been drawn from a Russian prototype," says our indifferent-to-nations author (italics added). In truth, he did give me an alternative: if I still insisted on leaving Gerasimovich Russian, then I must *add* an equally powerful image of a noble, self-sacrificing Jew to my story. And if I would not follow any of his advice, Pomerants threatened to open a public campaign against me. (I ignored it at this point.)

Notably, he conducted this one-sided battle, calling it "our polemic," first in foreign journals and, when it became possible, in the Soviet magazines, often repeating and reprinting the same articles, although taking care each time to exorcise the blemishes his critics had picked up the last time. In the course of this he uttered another pearl of wisdom: there was only *one* Absolute Evil in the world and it was Hitlerism – in this regard, our philosopher was not a relativist, not at all. But as to communism, this former prisoner of the camps and by no means a Communist himself, suddenly proclaims that communism – *is not an unquestionable evil* (and even "some spirit of democracy surrounded the early Cheka"), and he does so harder and harder over the years (reacting to my intransigence towards communism). [2948] On the other hand, hard core anti-communism is undoubtedly evil, especially if it builds upon the Russian Nationalism (which, as he had reminded us earlier, *cannot be separated from pogroms*).

That is where Pomerants's smooth high-minded and "non-national" principles led.

Given *such* a skewed bias, can mutual understanding between Russians and Jews be achieved?

[2947] G. Pomerants. *Chelovek niotkuda* [The Man from Nowhere]. From G. Pomerants, *Unpublished*. Frankfurt, Posev, 1972, p. 157.
[2948] G. Pomerants. *Son o spravedlivom vozmezdii* [A Dream about Recompense]. // *Syntaksis: Journalism, Critique, Polemic*. Paris, 1980, (6), p. 21.

"You mark the speck in your brother's eye, but ignore the plank in your own."

In those same months when I corresponded with Pomerants, some liberal hand in the Leningrad Regional Party Committee copied a secret memorandum signed by Shcherbakov, Smirnov, and Utekhin on the matter of alleged "destructive Zionist activity in the city" with "subtle forms of ideological subversion." My Jewish friends asked me "How should we deal with this?" "It is clear, how," – I replied before even reading the paper – "Openness! Publish it in Samizdat! Our strength is transparency and publicity!" But my friends hesitated: "We cannot do it just like that because it would be misunderstood."

After reading the documents, I understood their anxiety. From the reports, it was clear that the youth's literary evening at the Writers' House on January 30, 1968 had been politically honest and brave – the government with its politics and ideology had been both openly and covertly ridiculed. On the other hand, the speeches had clear *national* emphases (perhaps, the youth there were mostly Jewish); they contained explicit resentment and hostility, and even, perhaps, contempt for Russians, and longing for Jewish spirituality. It was because of this that my friends were wary of publishing the document in Samizdat.

I was suddenly struck by how *true* these Jewish sentiments were. "Russia is reflected in the window glass of a beer stand," – the poet Ufland had supposedly said there. How horrifyingly true! It seemed that the speakers accused the Russians, not directly, but by allusions, of crawling under counters of beer pubs and of being dragged from the mud by their wives; that they drink vodka until unconscious, they squabble and steal....

We *must see* ourselves objectively, see our fatal shortcomings. Suddenly, I grasped the Jewish point of view; I looked around and I was horrified as well: Dear God, where *we, the Jews*? Cards, dominoes, gaping at TV.... What cattle, what animals surround us! They have neither God nor spiritual interests. And so much feeling of hurt from past oppression rises in your soul.

Only it is forgotten, that the real Russians were killed, slaughtered and suppressed, and the rest were stupefied, embittered, and driven to the extremes by Bolshevik thugs and not without the zealous participation of the fathers of today's young Jewish intellectuals. Modern day Jews are irritated by those mugs who have become the Soviet leadership since the 1940s – but they irritate us as well. However, the best among us were killed, not spared.

"Do not look back!" – Pomerants lectured us later in his Samizdat essays; do not look back like Orpheus who lost Eurydice this way. Yet we have *already* lost more than Eurydice. We were taught since the 1920s to throw away the past and jump on board modernity. But the old Russian proverb advises – go ahead but always look back.

We must look back. Otherwise, we would never understand anything. Even if we had tried not to look back, we would always be reminded that the "core [Russian issue] is in fact *the inferiority complex of the spiritless leaders of the people* that has persisted throughout its long history," and this very complex "pushed the Russian Tsarist government towards military conquests....

An inferiority complex is disease of mediocrity."[2949] Do you want to know why the Revolution of 1917 happened in Russia? Can you guess? Yes, "the same inferiority complex caused a revolution in Russia."[2950] (Oh, immortal Freud, is there nothing he hasn't explained?)

They even stated that "Russian socialism was a direct heir of Russian autocracy"[2951] – precisely a direct one, it goes without saying. And, almost in unison, "there is direct continuity between the Tsarist government and communism ... there is qualitative similarity."[2952] What else could you expect from "Russian history, founded on blood and provocations?"[2953] In a review of Agursky's interesting book, *Ideology of National Bolshevism*, we find that "in reality, traditional, fundamental ideas of the Russian national consciousness began to penetrate into the practice and ideology of the ruling party very early"; "the party ideology was transformed as early as the mid-1920s." Really?

Already in the mid-1920s? How come we missed it at the time? Wasn't it the same mid-1920s when the very words "Russian," "I am Russian" had been considered counter-revolutionary? I remember it well. But, you see, even back then, in the midst of persecution against all that was Russian and Orthodox, the party ideology "began in practice to be persistently guided by the national idea"; "outwardly preserving its internationalist disguise, Soviet authorities actually engaged in the consolidation of the Russian state."[2954] Of course! "Contrary to its internationalist declarations, the

---

[2949] L. Frank. *Eshche raz o "russkom voprose"* [The "Russian Question" Once Again]. // *Russkaya mysl* [The Russian Thinker], 1989, May 19, p. 13.

[2950] Amrozh. *Sovetskii antisemitism – prichiny i prognozy* [Soviet Anti-Semitism: Causes and Prospects]. Seminar. // *"22"*, 1978, (3), p. 153.

[2951] V. Gusman. *Perestroika: mify i realnost* [Perestroika: Myths and the Reality]. // *"22"*, 1990, (70), p. 139, 142.

[2952] B. Shragin, p, 99.

[2953] M. Amusin. *Peterburgskie strasti* [Passions of St. Petersburg]. // *"22"*, 1995, (96), p. 191.

[2954] I. Serman. Review. // *"22"*, 1982, (26), p. 210-212.

revolution in Russia has remained a national affair."[2955] This "Russia, upturned by revolution, continued to build the people's state."[2956]

People's state? How dare they say that, knowing of the Red Terror, of the *millions* of peasants killed during collectivization, and of the insatiable Gulag?

No, Russia is irrevocably condemned for all her history and in all her forms. Russia is always under suspicion, the "Russian idea" without antiSemitism "seems to be no longer an idea and not even the Russian one." Indeed, "hostility towards culture is a specific Russian phenomenon"; "how many times have we heard that they are supposedly the only ones in the whole world who have preserved purity and chastity, respecting God in the middle of their native wilderness";[2957] "the greatest soulful sincerity has supposedly found shelter in this crippled land. This soulful sincerity is being presented to us as a kind of national treasure, a unique product like caviar."[2958]

Yes, make fun of us Russians; it is for our own good. Unfortunately, there is some truth to these words. But, while expressing them, do not lapse into such hatred. Having long been aware of the terrifying decline of our nation under the communists, it was precisely during those 1970s that we gingerly wrote about a hope of revival of our morals and culture. But strangely enough, the contemporary Jewish authors attacked the idea of Russian revival with a relentless fury, as if (or because?) they feared that Soviet culture would be replaced by the Russian one. "I am afraid that the new 'dawn' of this doomed country would be even more repugnant than its current [1970-1980s] decline."[2959]

Looking back from the "democratic" 1990s, we can agree that it was a prophetic declaration. Still, was it said with compassion or with malice?

And here is even more: "Beware, when someone tells you to love your homeland: such love is charged with hatred.... Beware of stories that tell you that in Russia, Russians are the worst off, that Russians suffered the most, and that the Russian population is dwindling" – sure, as we all know, this is a lie!

[2955] B. Shragin, p, 158.
[2956] M. Meyerson-Aksenov. *Rozhdeniye novoi intelligentsii* [The Birth of New Intelligentsia]. // Samosoznanie: Sb. statei. [Self-consciousness: The Collection of Articles] New York: Chronicles, 1976, p. 102.
[2957] B. Khazanov. *Pisma bez stempelya* [The Letters without Postmark]. // *EW*, New York, 1982, (69), p. 156, 158, 163.
[2958] B. Khazanov. *Novaya Rossiya* [New Russia]. // *EW*, Tel Aviv, 1976, (8), p. 142.
[2959] M. Vaiskopf. *Sobstvenny Platon* [Our Own Platon]. // *"22"*, 1981, (22), p. 168.

"Be careful when someone tells you about that great statesman ... who was assassinated" (i.e., Stolypin) – is that also a deception? No, it is not a deception: "Not because the facts are incorrect" – nevertheless, do not accept even these true facts: "Be careful, be aware!"[2960]

There is something extraordinary in this stream of passionate accusations. Who would have guessed during the fiery 1920s that after the enfeeblement and downfall of that "beautiful" (i.e., Communist) regime in Russia, those Jews, who themselves had suffered much from communism, who seemingly cursed it and ran away from it, would curse and kick not communism, but Russia itself – blast her from Israel and from Europe, and from across the ocean!? There are so many, such confident voices ready to judge Russia's many crimes and failings, her inexhaustible guilt towards the Jews – and they so sincerely believe this guilt to be inexhaustible – almost all of them believe it! Meanwhile, their own people are coyly cleared of any responsibility for their participation in Cheka shootings, for sinking the barges and their doomed human cargo in the White and Caspian seas, for their role in collectivization, the Ukrainian famine and in all the abominations of the Soviet administration, for their talented zeal in brainwashing the "natives." This is not contrition.

We, brothers or strangers, need to share that responsibility. It would have been cleanest and healthiest to exchange contrition for *everything committed*. I will not stop calling the Russians to do that.

And I am inviting the Jews to do the same. To repent not for Trotsky, Kamenev and Zinoviev; they are known and anyway can be brushed aside, "they were not real Jews!" Instead, I invite Jews to look honestly into the oppressive depths of the early Soviet system, at all those "invisible" characters such as Isai Davidovich Berg, who created the infamous "gas wagon"[2961] which later brought so much affliction on the Jews themselves, and I call on them to look honestly on those many much more obscure bureaucrats who had pushed papers in the Soviet apparatus, and who had never appeared in light.

However, the Jews would not be Jews if they all behaved the same. So other voices were heard. As soon as the great exodus of Jews from the USSR began there were Jews who – fortunately for all, and to their honor – while remaining faithful to Judaism, went above their own feelings and

---

[2960] B. Khazanov. *Po kom zvonit zatonuvshy kolokol* [For Whom the Sunken Bell Tolls]. // Strana i mir: Obshchestvenno-politichesky, economichesky i kulturno-filosofsky zhurnal [Country and World: Social, Political, Economic and Cultural-Philosophical Journal (henceforth – *Country and World*]. Munich, 1986, (12), p. 93-94.
[2961] E. Zhirnov. *"Protsedura kazni nosila omerzitelny kharakter"* [The Execution was Abominable]. // Komsomolskaya Pravda, 1990, October 28, p. 2.

looked at history from that vantage point. It was a joy to hear them, and we hear them still. What hope for the future it gives! Their understanding and support are especially valuable in the face of the violently thinned and drastically depleted ranks of Russian intelligentsia.

A melancholy view, expressed at end of 19th century, comes to mind: "Every country deserves the Jews it has."[2962]

It depends where you look. If it were not for voices from the third wave of emigration and from Israel, one would despair of dialogue and of possibility for mutual understanding between Russians and Jews.

Roman Rutman, a cybernetics worker, had his first article published in the émigré Samizdat in 1973. It was a bright, warm story of how he first decided to emigrate and how it turned out – and even then he showed distinct warmth towards Russia. The title was illustrative: "A bow to those who has gone and my brotherhood to those who remain."[2963] Among his very first thoughts during his awakening was "Are we Jews or Russians?"; and among his thoughts on departure there was "Russia, crucified for mankind."

Next year, in 1974, in an article *The Ring of Grievances*, he proposed to revise "some established ideas on the 'Jewish question'" and "to recognize the risk of overemphasizing these ideas." There were three: (1) "The unusual fate of the Jewish people made them a symbol of human suffering"; (2) "A Jew in Russia has always been a victim of unilateral persecution"; and (3) "Russian society is indebted to the Jewish people." He quoted a phrase from *The Gulag Archipelago*: "During this war we discovered that the worst thing on earth is to be a Russian" and recognized that the phrase is not artificial or empty, that it is based on war losses, on the revolutionary terror before that, on hunger, on "the wanton destruction of both the nation's head – its cognitive elite, and its feet, the peasantry." Although modern Russian literature and democratic movements preach about the guilt of Russian society before Jews, the author himself prefers to see the "circle of grievances" instead of "the saccharine sentimentality

---

[2962] M. Morgulis. *Evreisky vopros v ego osnovaniyakh i chastnostyakh* [The Basics and Details of the Jewish Question]. // Voskhod, St. Petersburg, January 1881, Book 1, p. 18.

[2963] R. Rutman. *Ukhodyashchemu – poklon, ostayushchemusya – bratstvo* [A bow to those who has gone and my brotherhood to those who remain]. // New Journal, New York, 1973, (112), p. 284-297.

about the troubles and talents of the Jewish people." "To break this "'circle of grievances' one must pull at it from both sides."²⁹⁶⁴

Here it is – a thoughtful, friendly and calm voice. And over these years, we many times heard the firm voice of Michael Kheifetz, a recent GULag prisoner. "A champion of my people, I cannot but sympathize with the nationalists of other peoples."²⁹⁶⁵ He had the courage to call for Jewish repentance: "The experience of the German people, who have not turned away from their horrifying and criminal past, and who never tried to lay the blame for Nazism on some other culprits, on strangers, etc. but, instead constantly cleansed itself in the fire of national repentance, and thus created a German state that for the first time was admired and respected by all mankind; this experience should, in my opinion, become a paragon for the peoples that participated in the crimes of Bolshevism, including the Jews." "We, Jews, must honestly analyze the role we played in other nations' affairs, the role so extraordinarily foretold by Z. Jabotinsky."²⁹⁶⁶

M. Kheifetz demonstrated a truly noble soul when he spoke of "the genuine guilt of assimilated Jews before the native peoples of those countries where they live, the guilt, which cannot and must not allow them to live comfortably in the Diaspora." About Soviet Jewry of the 1920s and 1930s he said: "Who if not us, their bitterly remorseful descendants, has the right to condemn them for this historic mistake [zealous participation in building communism] and the settling of historical scores with Russia for the Pale of Settlement and the pogroms?"²⁹⁶⁷

(Kheifetz also mentioned that B. Penson and M. Korenblit, who had served labor camp terms along with him, shared his views.)

Almost simultaneously with the words of Kheifetz, by then already an emigrant, Feliks Svetov vividly called out for Jewish repentance from inside the Soviet Union in a Samizdat novel *Open the doors to me*.²⁹⁶⁸ (It was no accident that F. Svetov, due to his Jewish perceptivity and intelligence, was one of the first to recognize the beginning of Russian

---

²⁹⁶⁴ R. Rutman. *Koltso obid* [Circle of Grievances]. // *New Journal*, New York, 1974, (117), p. 178-189; and in English: Soviet Jewish Affairs, London, 1974, Vol. 4, No. 2, p. 3-11.

²⁹⁶⁵ M. Kheifetz. *Russkii patriot Vladimir Osipov* [Russian Patriot Vladimir Osipov]. // *Kontinent: Literaturny, obshchestvenno-politichesky i religiozny zhurnal* [Continent: Literary, Social, Political and Religious Journal (henceforth – *Continent*]. Paris, 1981, (27), p. 209.

²⁹⁶⁶ M. Kheifetz. *Nashi obshchie uroki* [The Lessons We Shared]. // *"22"*, 1980, (14), p. 162-163.

²⁹⁶⁷ M. Kheifetz. *Evreiskie zametki* [The Jewish Notes]. Paris. Tretya volna [The Third Wave], 1978, p. 42, 45.

²⁹⁶⁸ Feliks Svetov. *Open the doors to me*. Paris: Éditeurs Réunis, 1978.

religious revival.) Later, during a passionate discourse surrounding the dispute between Astafiev and Edelman, Yuri Shtein described "our Ashkenazi-specific personality traits, formed on the basis of our belief of belonging to the chosen people and an insular, small town mentality. Hence, there is a belief in the infallibility of our nation and our claim to a monopoly on suffering.... It is time for us to see ourselves as a normal nation, worthy but not faultless, like all the other peoples of the world. Especially now, that we have our own independent state and have already proved to the world that Jews can fight and plow better than some more populous ethnic groups."[2969]

During the left liberal campaign against V. Astafiev, V. Belov, and V. Rasputin, literary historian Maria Shneyerson, who, after emigrating, continued to love Russia dearly and appreciate Russian problems, offered these writers her enthusiastic support.[2970]

In the 1970s, a serious, competent, and forewarning book on the destruction of the environment in the USSR under communism was published in the West. Written by a Soviet author, it was naturally published under a pseudonym, B. Komarov. After some time, the author emigrated and we learned his name – Zeev Wolfson. We discovered even more: that he was among the compilers of the album of destroyed and desecrated churches in Central Russia.[2971]

Few active intellectuals remained in the defeated Russia, but friendly, sympathetic Jewish forces supported them. With this shortage of people and under the most severe persecution by the authorities, our Russian Public Foundation was established to help victims of persecution; I donated all my royalties for *The Gulag Archipelago* to this fund; and, starting with its first talented and dedicated manager, Alexander Ginzburg, there were many Jews and half-Jews among the Fund's volunteers. (This gave certain intellectually blind extreme Russian nationalists sufficient reason *to brand* our Foundation as being "Jewish.") Similarly, M. Bernshtam, then Y. Felshtinsky and D.Shturman were involved in our study of modern Russian history.

[2969] Yu. Shtein. Letter to Editor. // *Country and World*, 1987, (2), p. 112.
[2970] M. Shneyerson. *Razreshennaya pravda* [Allowable Truth]. // *Continent*, 1981, (28); see also: M. Shneyerson. *Khudozhestvenny mir pisatelya i pisatel v miru* [The Artistic World of an Author and the Author in the World]. // *Continent*, 1990, (62).
[2971] B. Komarov. *Unichtozhenie prirody* [Destruction of the Nature]. Frankfurt: Posev, 1978; *Razrushennye i oskvernennye khramy: Moskva i Srednyaya Rossia* [Destroyed and Desecrated Churches: Moscow and Central Russia]. Afterword: *Predely vandalizma* [The Limits of Vandalism]. Frankfurt: Posev, 1980.

In the fight against communist lies, M. Agursky, D.Shturman, A. Nekrich, M. Geller, and A. Serebrennikov distinguished themselves by their brilliant, fresh, and fair-minded journalism.

We can also recall the heroism of the American professor Julius Epstein and his service to Russia. In self-centered, always self-righteous, and never regretful of any wrongdoings America, he single-handedly revealed the mystery of *Operation Keelhaul,* how after the end of the war and from *their own continent,* Americans handed over to Stalinist agents and therefore certain death, hundreds and thousands of Russian Cossacks, who had naively believed that since they reached the 'land of free' they had been saved.[2972]

All these examples should encourage sincere and mutual understanding between Russians and Jews, if only we would not shut it out by intolerance and anger.

Alas, even the mildest remembrance, repentance, and talk of justice elicits severe outcries from the self-appointed guardians of extreme nationalism, both Russian and Jewish. "As soon as Solzhenitsyn had called for national repentance" – meaning among Russians, and the author didn't mind that – "here we are! Our own people are right there in the front line." He did not mention any name specifically but he probably referred to M. Kheifetz. "See, it turns out that we are more to blame, we helped ... to install ... no, not helped, but simply established the Soviet regime ourselves ... were disproportionately present in various organs."[2973]

Those who began to speak in a voice of remorse were furiously attacked in an instant. "They prefer to extract from their hurrah-patriotic gut a mouthful of saliva" – what a style and nobility of expression! – "and to thoroughly spit on all 'ancestors,' to curse Trotsky and Bagritsky, Kogan, and Dunaevsky"; "M. Kheifetz invites us to 'purge ourselves in the fire of national repentance.'"[2974]

And what a thrashing F. Svetov received for the autobiographical hero of his novel: "A book about conversion to Christianity ... will contribute not to an abstract search for repentance, but to a very specific anti-Semitism.... This book is anti-Semitic." Yes, and what is there to repent? –The indefatigable David Markish angrily exclaims. Svetov's hero sees a "betrayal" in the fact that "we desert the country, leaving behind a

---

[2972] *Julius Epstein.* Operation Keelhaul: The Story of Forced Repatriation from 1944 to the Present. *Old Greenwich, Connecticut: Devin-Adair, 1973.*
[2973] V. Zeev. *Demonstratsiya objektivnosti* [Pretending to be Evenhanded]. // New American, 1982, June 1-7, (120), p. 37.
[2974] V. Boguslavsky. *V zashchitu Kunyaeva* [In Defence of Kunyaev]. // *"22"*, 1980, (16), p. 166-167, 170.

deplorable condition which is entirely our handiwork: it is we, as it turns out, who staged a bloody revolution, shot the father-tsar, befouled and raped the Orthodox Church and in addition, founded the GULag Archipelago," isn't that right? First, these "comrades" Trotsky, Sverdlov, Berman, and Frenkel are not at all related to the Jews. Second, the very question about someone's *collective* guilt is wrong.[2975] (As to blaming Russians, you see, it is a different thing altogether: it was always acceptable to blame them en masse, from the times of the elder Philotheus.)

David's brother, Sh. Markish reasons as follows, "as to the latest wave of immigrants from Russia ... whether in Israel or in the U.S., they do not exhibit real Russophobia ... but a self-hatred that grows into direct anti-Semitism is obvious in them only too often."[2976]

See, if Jews repent – it is anti-Semitism. (This is yet another new manifestation of that prejudice.)

The Russians should realize their national guilt, "the idea of national repentance cannot be implemented without a clear understanding of national guilt.... The guilt is enormous, and there is no way to shift it on to others. This guilt is not only about the things of past, it is also about the vile things Russia commits now, and will probably continue committing in the future," as Shragin wrote in the early 1970s.[2977]

Well, we too tirelessly call the Russians to repent; without penitence, we will not have a future. After all, only those who were directly affected by communism recognized its evils. Those who were not affected tried not to notice the atrocities and later on to forget and forgive them, to the extent that now they do not even understand what to repent of. (Even more so those who themselves committed the crimes.)

Every day we are burning with shame for our unsettled people. And we love it too. And we do not envision our lives without it. And yet, for some reason, we have not lost all faith in it. Still, is it absolutely certain that you had no part in our great guilt, in our unsuccessful history?

Here, Shimon Markish referred to Jabotinsky's 1920s article. "Jabotinsky several times (on different occasions) observed that Russia is a foreign country to us, our interest in her should be detached, cool, though sympathetic; her anxiety, grief and joy are not ours, and our feelings are foreign to her too."

[2975] D. Markish. *Vykrest* [Convert to Christianity]. // *"22"*, 1981, (18), p. 210.

[2976] Sh. Markish. *O evreiskoi nenavisti k Rossii* [On the Jewish Hatred towards Russia]. // *"22"*, 1984, (38), p. 218.

[2977] B. Shragin, p, 159.

Markish added: "That's also my attitude towards Russian worries." And he invites us to "call a spade a spade. However, regarding this delicate point even free western Russians are not awesomely courageous.... I prefer to deal with enemies."[2978]

Yet this sentence should be divided into two: is it the case that to "call a spade a spade" and to speak *frankly* mean being an *enemy*? Well, there is a Russian proverb: do not love the agreeable; love the disputers.

I invite all, including Jews, to abandon this fear of bluntness, to stop perceiving honesty as hostility. We must abandon it historically! Abandon it forever!

In this book, I "call a spade a spade". And at no time do I feel that in doing so it is being hostile to the Jews. I have written more sympathetically than many Jews write about Russians.

The purpose of this book, reflected even in its title, is this: we should *understand each other*, we should recognize *each other's standpoint and feelings*. With this book, I want to extend a handshake of understanding – for all our future.

But we must do so mutually!

This interweaving of Jewish and Russian destinies since the 18th century which has so explosively manifested itself in the 20th century, has a profound historical meaning, and we should not lose it in the future. Here, perhaps, lies the Divine Intent which we must strive to unravel – to discern its mystery and to do what must be done.

And it seems obvious that to know the truth about our shared past is *a moral imperative* for Jews and Russians alike.

[2978] Sh. Markish. *Eshche raz o nenavisti k samomu sebe* [Once Again on Self-Hatred]. *"22"*, 1980, (16), p. 178-179, 180.

Chapter 26

The beginning of Exodus

The Age of Exodus, as Jews themselves would soon name it, began rather silently: its start can be traced to a December 1966 article in *Izvestiya*, where the Soviet authorities magnanimously approved "family reunification," and under this "banner the Jews were given the right to leave the USSR"[2979]. And then, half a year later, the historic Six-Day War broke out. "Like any epic, this Exodus began with a miracle. And as it should be in an epic, three miracles were revealed to the Jews of Russia – to the Exodus generation": the miracle of the foundation of Israel, "the miracle of the Purim 1953" (that is, Stalin's death), and "the miracle of the joyous, brilliant, intoxicating victory of 1967."[2980]

The Six-Day War gave a strong and irreversible push to the ethnic consciousness of the Soviet Jews and delivered a blow to the desire of many to assimilate. It created among Jews a powerful motivation for national self-education and the study of Hebrew (within a framework of makeshift centers) and gave rise to pro-emigration attitudes.

How did the majority of Soviet Jews perceive themselves by the end of the 1960s, on the eve of Exodus? No, those who retrospectively write of a constant feeling of oppression and stress do not distort their memories: "Hearing the word 'Jew,' they cringe, as if expecting a blow.... They themselves use this sacramental word as rarely as possible, and when they do have to say it, they force the word out as quickly as possible and in a suppressed voice, as if they were seized by the throat.... Among such people there are those who are gripped by the eternal incurable fear

---

[2979] F. Kolker. *Novyi plan pomoshchi sovetskomu evreistvu* [A New Plan for Assistance to the Soviet Jewry]. // *"22"*: Obshchestvenno-politicheskiy i literaturniy zhurnal evreyskoy intelligentsii iz SSSR v Izraile [*Social, Political and Literary Journal of the Jewish Intelligentsia from the USSR in Israel* (henceforth – *"22"*)]. Tel-Aviv, 1983, (31), p. 145.
[2980] V. Boguslavsky. *Otsy i deti russkoi alii* [Fathers and Children of Russian Aliyah]. // *"22"*, 1978, (2), p. 176.

ingrained in their mentality."²⁹⁸¹ Or take a Jewish author who wrote of spending her entire professional life worrying that her work would be rejected only because of her nationality [ethnicity in American terminology].²⁹⁸² Despite having an apparently higher standard of living than the general population, many Jews still harbored this sense of oppression.

Indeed, cultivated Jews complained more of cultural rather than economic oppression. "The Soviet Jews are trying ... to retain their presence in the Russian culture. They struggle to retain the Russian culture in their inner selves."²⁹⁸³ Dora Shturman recalls: "When the Russian Jews, whose interests are chained to Russia, are suddenly deprived – even if only on paper or in words – of their right to engage in the Russian life, to participate in the Russian history, as if they were interlopers or strangers, they feel offended and bewildered. With the appearance of Tamizdat [a Russian neologism for dissident self-published (Samizdat) literature, published outside the USSR (from the Russian word, 'tam', meaning 'there' or 'out there')] and Samizdat, the xenophobia felt by some Russian authors toward Jews who sincerely identified themselves as Russians manifested itself for the first time in many years, not only on the street level and on the level of state bureaucracy, but appeared on the elite intellectual level, even among dissidents. Naturally, this surprised Jews who identified with Russians."²⁹⁸⁴ Galich: "Many people brought up in the 1920s, 1930s and 1940s used to regard themselves as Russians from their earliest years, in fact from birth, and indeed ... they share all their values and thoughts with the Russian culture."²⁹⁸⁵

Another author drew the portrait of "the average modern Russian Jew," who "would serve this country with good faith and fidelity. He ... had carefully examined and identified his own flaws. He had become aware of them.... And now he tries to get rid of them ... he has stopped arms flourishing. He has gotten rid of his national peculiarities of speech which were carried over into Russian.... At some point he would aspire to become

---

[2981] I. Domalsky. *Tekhnologiya nenavisti* [The Technology of Hate]. // Vremya i my: Mezhdunarodny zhurnal literatury i obshchestvennykh problem [*Epoch and We: International Journal of Literature and Social Problems* (henceforth – *EW*)]. Tel Aviv, 1978, (25), p. 106-107.
[2982] Ya. Voronel. *U kazhdogo svoi dom* [Everyone Has a Home]. // "22", 1978, (2), p. 150-151.
[2983] I. Domalsky. *Tekhnologiya nenavisti* [The Technology of Hate]. // *EW*. Tel Aviv, 1978, (25), p. 129.
[2984] D. Shturman. *Razmyshleniya nad rukopisyu* [Mulling over the Manuscript]. // "22", 1980, 812), p. 133.
[2985] *Aleksandr Galich*. Pesni. Stikhi. Poemy. Kinopovest. Piesa. Statii [*Songs. Verses. Poems*. Movie-essay. Piece. Essays]. Ekaterinburg, U-Faktoriya, 1998, p.586.

equal with the Russians, to be indistinguishable from them." And so: "You might not hear the word 'Jew' for years on end. Perhaps, many have even forgotten that you are a Jew. Yet you can never forget it yourself. It is this silence that always reminds you who you are. It creates such an explosive tension inside you, that when you do hear the word 'Jew,' it sounds like fate's blow." This is a very telling account. The same author describes the cost of this transformation into a Russian. "He had left behind too much" and become spiritually impoverished. "Now, when he needs those capacious, rich and flexible words, he can't find them....When he looks for but can't find the right word, something dies inside him," he had lost "the melodic intonation of Jewish speech" with all its "gaiety, playfulness, mirth, tenacity, and irony."[2986]

Of course, these exquisite feelings did not worry each Soviet Jew; it was the lot of the tiniest minority among them, the top cultural stratum, those who genuinely and persistently tried to *identify* with Russians. It was them who G. Pomeranz spoke about (though he made a generalization for the whole intelligentsia): "Everywhere, we are not quite out of place. Everywhere, we are not quite in our place"; we "have become something like non-Israeli Jews, the people of the air, who lost all their roots in their mundane existence."[2987]

Very well put.

A. Voronel develops the same theme: "I clearly see all the sham of their [Jews'] existence in Russia today."[2988]

If there's no merging, there will always be alienation.

Nathan Sharansky often mentioned that from a certain point he started to feel being different from the others in Russia.

During the Dymshits–Kuznetsov hijacking affair trial in December 1970, L. Hnoh openly stated what he had apparently nurtured for quite a while: "It became unbearable for me to live in a country I don't regard as my own."

What integrity of mind and courage of word!

So it was *this* feeling that grew among the Soviet Jews, and now increasingly among the broad Jewish masses.

[2986] Rani Aren. *V russkom galute* [In the Russian Galuth]. // *"22"*, 1981, (19), p. 133-135, 137.
[2987] G. Pomerantz. *Chelovek niotkuda* [A Man from Nowhere]. From G. Pomerantz, *Unpublished*. Frankfurt: Posev, 1972, p. 161, 166.
[2988] A. Voronel. *Trepet iudeiskikh zabot* [The Thrills of Jewish Worries]. 2nd Edition, Ramat-Gahn: Moscow-Jerusalem, 1981, p. 122.

Later, in 1982, another Jewish journalist put it like thus: "I am a stranger. I am a stranger in my own country which I love abstractly but fear in reality."[2989]

In the beginning of the 1970s, in a conversation with L.K. Chukovskaya she told me (I made a note at the time): "This Exodus was forced on Jewry. I pity those whom the Russians made feel Jewish. The Soviet Jews have already lost their sense of Jewishness and I consider this artificial awakening of their national sense to be specious."

This was far from the truth. Despite the fact that she socialized with many Jews from both capitals, Chukovskaya was mistaken. This Jewish national awakening was not artificial or forced; it was an absolutely natural and even necessary milestone of Jewish history. It was the sudden realization that "one can say 'Jew' proudly!"[2990]

Another Jewish publicist reflected on the experience of his generation of young people in the USSR: "So what are we – the 'grandchildren' and heirs of that cruel experiment, who broke through the shell and hatched here in Israel – what are we to say about our fathers and grandfathers? Should we blame them that they didn't raise us in Jewish way? Yet our very sense of Jewishness was in great part the result of their (as well as our) failures, catastrophes and despair.

So let us appreciate this past.... Is it up to us to throw stones at the shattered skulls of the romantics of yesterday?"[2991]

This sincerely and honestly expressed intergenerational connection to the fathers and grandfathers, who were so enthusiastic in the early Soviet years, greatly supplements the whole picture. (You can read between the lines the author's rejection of the benefits and advantages of the 'new class' that has replaced those 'romantics.')

A Samizdat article properly pointed out: "The opinion that the current rise in Jewish ethnic consciousness among assimilated Soviet Jews is just a reaction to the re-emergence of anti-Semitism seems deeply mistaken. What we have here is more likely a coincidence."[2992]

[2989] M. Deich. *Zapiski postoronnego* [Notes of an outsider] // *"22,"* 1982, (26), p. 156.
[2990] R. Rutman. *Ukhodyashchemu – poklon, ostayushchemusya – bratstvo* [Farewell to those who leaves, brotherhood to those who stay]. // *The New Journal*, 1973, (112), p. 286.
[2991] V. Boguslavsky. *V zashchitu Kunyaeva* [In Defence of Kunyaev]. // *"22"*, 1980, (16), p. 176.
[2992] N. Ilsky. *Istoriya i samosoznanie* [The History and Consciousness]. // *The Jews in the USSR*, 1977, (15): citation from *"22"*, 1978, (1), p. 202.

Different contemporaries described the development of their Jewish self-identification somewhat differently. Some wrote that "nearly everyone agreed that nothing was happening in the 1960s" in the sense of national revival, though "after the war of 1967 things began to change." Yet it was the plane hijacking incident that led to the breakthrough.[2993] Others suggest that "Jewish groups were already forming in the mid-1960s in Leningrad, Moscow, and Riga," and that by the end of the decade a Jewish "underground center" was established in Leningrad. Yet what kind of conspiracy could it be? "Makeshift centers to study Hebrew and Jewish history were formed ... and not really for study of Hebrew, but rather for the socialization of people who wished to study it. Actual language usually was learnt not beyond two to three hundred words....

As a rule, all participants were state functionaries, and, like their entire milieu, far removed from the Jewish religion and national traditions alike." "The Jews of the 1960s had only a vague conception of Zionism." And yet, "we felt ourselves to be sufficiently Jewish, and saw no need whatsoever for any sort of additional 'Jewish educational remedy.'" In response to the barrage of anti-Israeli propaganda, "the inner sympathy towards Jewry and to Israel" grew.

"Even if we were told then that Israel had abandoned Judaism, it would make no difference for us." And then the movement "began to transform from an underground to a mass, open ... 'parlour' phenomenon." Still, "then nobody believed in the possibility of emigration, at least in our time, yet everyone considered a quite real possibility of ending up in a camp."[2994] (The interviewer comments: "Alas, it is too short a step from conspiracy to 'devilry'. I saw this in the Jewish movement of the 1970s, after the trials in Leningrad.")[2995]

Thus, the return to Jewish culture started and continued without counting on emigration and initially did not affect the everyday life of the participants.

"I'm not sure that Aliyah [return to Israel] began because of Zionists," as those first Zionist groups were too weak for this. "To a certain extent, it was the Soviet government that triggered the process by raising a tremendous noise around the Six-Day War. The Soviet press painted the

---

[2993] A. Eterman. *Tretye pokolenie* [The Third Generation]. Interview. // *"22"*, 1986, (47), p. 124.
[2994] V. Boguslavsky. *U istokov* [At the Origins]. Interview. // *"22"*, 1986, (47), p. 102, 105-108.
[2995] Ibid., p. 109.

image of a warlike invincible Jew, and this image successfully offset the inferiority complex of the Soviet Jews."[2996]

But "hide your 'Judaic terror' from your co-workers' eyes, from your neighbors' ears!" At first, there was a deep fear: "these scraps of paper, bearing your contact details, were as if you were signing a sentence for yourself, for your children, for your relatives." Yet soon "we ceased whispering, we began to speak aloud," "to prepare and celebrate" the Jewish holidays and "study history and Hebrew." And already from the end of 1969 "the Jews by the tens and hundreds began signing open letters to the 'public abroad.' They demanded to be 'released' to Israel."[2997] Soviet Jewry, "separated from world Jewry, trapped in the melting pot of the despotic Stalinist empire ... was seemingly irredeemably lost for Jewry – and yet suddenly the Zionist movement was reborn and the ancient Moses' appeal trumpeted again: 'Let my people go!'"[2998]

"In 1970 the whole world began to talk about Russian Jews." They "rose, they became determined....There is only one barrier separating them from their dream – the barrier of governmental prohibition. To break through, to breech it, to fly through it was their only wish.... 'Flee from Northern Babylon!'" was the behest of the arrested plane hijackers, the group led by E. Kuznetsov and M. Dymshits.[2999] In December 1970 during their trial in Leningrad "they weren't silent, they didn't evade, they openly declared that they wanted to steal a plane to fly it across the border to Israel. Remember, they faced the death sentence!

Their 'confessions' were in essence the declarations of Zionism."[3000] A few months later in May 1971, there was a trial of the 'Zionist organizations of Leningrad,' soon followed by similar trials in Riga and Kishinev.

These trials, especially the two Leningrad trials, became the new powerful stimulus for the development of the Jewish ethnic consciousness. A new Samizdat journal, *The Jews in the USSR*, began to circulate soon afterwards, in October 1972. It vividly reported on the struggle for the legalization of emigration to Israel and covered the struggle for the right to freely develop Jewish culture in the USSR.

[2996] V. Boguslavsky. *Oglyanis v razdumye* [Look Behind and Think]. Panel discussion. // *"22"*, 1982, (24), p. 113.
[2997] V. Boguslavsky. *Otsy i deti russkoi alii* [Fathers and Children of Russian Aliyah]. // *"22"*, 1978, (2), p. 176-177.
[2998] I. Oren. *Ispoved* [Confession] // *"22"*, 1979, (7), p. 140.
[2999] V. Boguslavsky. *Otsy i deti russkoi alii* [Fathers and Children of Russian Aliyah]. // *"22"*, 1978, (2), p. 177-178.
[3000] V. Boguslavsky. *U istokov* [At the Origins]. Interview. // *"22"*, 1986, (47), p. 121.

But even at this point only a minority of Jews were involved in the nascent emigration movement. "It seems that the life was easier for the Soviet Jews when they knew that they had no choice, that they only could persevere and adapt, than now, when they've got a choice of where to live and what to do....

The first wave that fled from Russia at the end of the 1960s was motivated only by the goal of spending the rest of their lives in the only country without antiSemitism, Israel."[3001] (As the author noted, this does not include those who emigrated for personal enrichment.)

And "a part of Soviet Jewry would happily repudiate their national identity, if they were allowed to do so."[3002] – so scared they were. This section included those Jews who cursed 'that Israel,' claiming that *it is because of Israel* that law-abiding Jews are often being prevented from career advancement: "because of those leaving, we too will suffer."

The Soviet government could not but be alarmed by this unexpected (for them as for the whole world) awakening of ethnic consciousness among Soviet Jews. It stepped up propaganda efforts against Israel and Zionism, to scare away the newly conscious. In March 1970 it made use of that well-worn Soviet trick, to get the denunciation from the mouths of the "people themselves," in this case from the people of "Jewish nationality." So the authorities staged a denunciatory public press-conference and it was dutifully attended not only by the most hypocritical "official Jews" such as Vergelis, Dragunsky, Chakovsky, Bezymensky, Dolmatovsky, the film director Donsky, the propagandists Mitin and Mintz, but also by prominent people who could easily refuse to participate in the spectacle and in signing the "Declaration" without significant repercussions for themselves. Among the latter were: Byalik: the members of Academy, Frumkin and Kassirsky: the internationally renowned musicians, Fliyer and Zak; the actors, Plisetskaya, Bystritskaya, and Pluchek. But sign it they did. The "Declaration" "heaped scorn on the aggression carried by the Israeli ruling circles ... which resurrects the barbarism of the Hitlerites"; "Zionism has always been an expression of the chauvinist views of the Jewish bourgeois and its Jewish raving"; and the signatories intend "to open the eyes of the gullible victims of Zionist propaganda": "under the guidance of the Leninist party, working Jews have gained full freedom from the hated Tsarism." Amazing, see who was the real oppressor? The one already dead for half a century!

[3001] G. Fain. *V roli vysokooplachivaemykh shveitzarov* [In the Role of Highly Paid Doorkeepers]. // *EW*, Tel Aviv, 1976, (12), p. 135.

[3002] I. Domalsky. *Tekhnologiya nenavisti* [The Technology of Hate]. // *EW*. Tel Aviv, 1978, (25), p. 106.

But times had changed by this point. The "official Jews" were publicly rebuked by I. Zilberberg, a young engineer who had decided to irrevocably cut ties with this country and leave. He circulated an open letter in response to the "Declaration" in Samizdat, calling its signatories "lackey souls", and repudiated his former faith in communism: "we naively placed our hopes in 'our' Jews – the Kaganovichs, the Erenburgs, etc." (So, after all, they had once indeed placed their hopes there?) At the same time he criticised Russians: after the 1950s, did

"Russians repent and were they contrite ... and, after spilling a meagre few tears about the past ... did they swear love and commitment to their new-found brothers?" In his mind there was no doubt that Russian guilt Jews was entirely one-sided.

Such events continued. Another Samizdat open letter became famous a year later, this one by the hitherto successful film director Mikhail Kalik, who had now been expelled from the Union of Soviet film-makers because he declared his intention to leave for Israel. Kalik unexpectedly addressed a letter about his loyalty to Jewish culture "to the Russian intelligentsia." It looked as if he had spent his life in the USSR not among the successful, but had suffered for years among the oppressed, striving for freedom. And now, leaving, he lectured this sluggish Russian intelligentsia from the moral high ground of his victimhood.

"So you will stay ... with your silence, with your 'obedient enthusiasm?' Who then will take care for the moral health of the nation, the country, the society?"

Six months later there was another open letter, this time from the Soviet writer Grigory Svirsky. He was driven to this by the fact that he hadn't been published for several years and even his name had been removed from the *Encyclopaedia of Literature* in punishment for speaking out against antiSemitism at the Central Literary House in 1968. This punishment he termed "murder," with understandable fire, though he forgot to glance back and to see how many others suffered in this regard. "I do not know how to live from now on," he wrote to the Union of Writers. (This was a sentiment common to all 6,000 members of the union: they all believed that the government was bound to feed them for their literary work). These were "the reasons which made me, a man of Russian culture, what is more a Russian writer and an expert on Russian literature, feel myself to be a Jew and to come to the irrevocable decision to leave with my family to Israel"; "I wish to become an Israeli writer." (But he achieved no such transformation of his profession from one nation to another.

Svirsky, like many previous emigrants, had not realized how difficult he would find adjusting to Israel, and chose to leave there too.)

The hostile anti-Russian feelings and claims we find in so many voices of the awakened Jewish consciousness surprise and bewilder us, making our hearts bleed. Yet in these feelings of the "mature ferocity" we do not hear any apology proffered by our Jewish brothers for at least the events of 1920s. There isn't a shadow of appreciation that Russians too are a wronged people. However, we heard some other voices among the "ferocious" in the previous chapter. Looking back on those times when they were already in Israel, they sometimes gave a more sober account: "we spent too much time settling debts with Russia in *Jews in the USSR*" at the expense even of devoting "too little to Israel and our life there ... and thinking too little about the future."[3003]

For the ordinary mundane and unarmed living, the prospect of breaking the steel shell that had enveloped the USSR seemed an impossible and hopeless task. But then they despaired – and had to try – and something gave! The struggle for the right to emigrate to Israel was characterised throughout by both determination and inventiveness: issuing complaints to the Supreme Soviet, demonstrations and hunger strikes by the "refuseniks" (as Jews who had been refused exit to Israel called themselves); seminars by fired Jewish professors on the pretext of wanting "to maintain their professional qualifications"; the organization in Moscow of an international symposium of scientists (at the end of 1976); finally, refusal to undergo national service.

Of course, this struggle could only be successful with strong support from Jewish communities abroad. "For us the existence in the world of Jewish solidarity was a startling discovery and the only glimmer of hope in that dark time" remembers one of the first refuseniks.[3004] There was also substantial material assistance: "among refuseniks in Moscow there was born a particular sort of independence, founded on powerful economic support from Jews abroad."[3005] And so they attached even more hopes to assistance from the West, now expecting similarly powerful public and even political help.

This support had its first test in 1972. Somebody in the higher echelons of the Soviet government reasoned as follows: here we have the Jewish intelligentsia, educated for free in the Soviet system and then provided with opportunities to pursue their academic careers, and now they just leave for abroad to work there with all these benefits subsidized by the Soviet state.

[3003] R. Nudelman. *Oglyanis v razdumye* [Look Behind and Think]. Panel discussion. // *"22"*, 1982, (24), p. 141.
[3004] N. Rubinshtein. Kto chitatel? [Who is the Reader?] // *EW*, Tel Aviv, 1976, (7), p. 131.
[3005] E. Manevich. Letter to the editor. // *EW*, New York, 1985, (85), p. 230-231.

Would it not be just to institute a tax on this? Why should the country prepare for free educated specialists, taking up the places loyal citizens might have had, only to have them use their skills in other countries? And so they started to prepare a law to institute this tax. This plan was no secret, and quickly became known and widely discussed in Jewish circles. It became law on August 3, 1972 in the Order of the Presidium of the Supreme Soviet of the USSR "On the compensation by citizens of the USSR, who are leaving to permanently live abroad, of the government expenditure on their education." The amount proscribed was between 3,600 and 9,800 roubles, depending on the rank of the university (3,600 was in those days the yearly salary of an ordinary senior researcher without a doctorate).

A storm of international indignation erupted. During the 55 years of its existence, none of the monstrous list of the USSR's crimes had caused as united an international protest as this tax on educated emigrants. American academics, 5,000 in number, signed a protest (Autumn 1972); and two thirds of American senators worked together to stop an expected favorable trade agreement with the USSR. European parliamentarians behaved similarly. For their part, 500 Soviet Jews sent an open letter to UN General Secretary Kurt Waldheim (nobody yet suspected that he too would soon be damned) describing: "serfdom for those with a higher education." (In reaching for a phrase they failed to realize how this would sound in a country which had genuine kolkhoz serfdom). The Soviet government buckled, and consigned the order to the scrapheap.

As to the agreement on trade? In April 1973, union leader George Meany argued that the agreement was neither in the interest of the USA nor would it ease international tensions, but the senators were concerned only about Soviet Jews and ignored these arguments. They passed the agreement but adding the "Jackson amendment," which stated that it would only be agreed to once Jews were allowed to leave the USSR *freely*. And so the whole world heard the message coming from the American capital: we will help the Soviet government if they release from their country, not everyone, but specifically and only Jews.

Nobody declared loud and clear: gentlemen, for 55 years it has been but a dream to escape from under the hated Soviet regime, not for hundreds of thousands but for millions of our fellow citizens; but nobody, ever had the right to leave. And yet the political and social leaders of the West never showed surprise, never protested, never moved to punish the Soviet government with trade restrictions. (There was one unsuccessful attempt in 1931 to organise a campaign against Soviet dumping of lumber, a practise made possible only by the use of cheap convict labour, but even this campaign was apparently motivated by commercial competition). 15

million peasants were destroyed in the "dekulakisation," 6 million peasants were starved to death in 1932, not even to mention the mass executions and millions who died in the camps; and at the same time it was fine to politely sign agreements with Soviet leaders, to lend them money, to shake their "honest hands", to seek their support, and to boast of all this in front of your parliaments. But once it was specifically Jews that became the target, then a spark of sympathy ran through the West and it became clear just *what* sort of regime this was. (In 1972 I made a note on a scrap of paper: "You've realized [what's going on], thank God. But for how long will your realisation last? All it takes is for the problems Jews had with emigrating to be resolved, and you'll become deaf, blind and uncomprehending again to the entirety of what is going on, to the problems of Russia and of communism.")

"You cannot imagine the enthusiasm with which it [the Jackson amendment] was met by Jews in Russia.... 'Finally a lever strong enough to shift the powers in the USSR is discovered.'"[3006] Yet suddenly in 1975 the Jackson amendment became an irrelevance, as the Soviet government unexpectedly turned down the offer of the trade agreement with the US. (Or it rather calculated that it could get more advantages from other competing countries).

The Soviet refusal made an impression on Jewish activists in the USSR and abroad, but not for long. Both in America and Europe support for Jewish emigration out of the USSR became louder. "The National Conference in Defence of Soviet Jews." "The Union on Solidarity with Soviet Jewry." "The Student Committee of Struggle for Soviet Jewry." On the "Day of National Solidarity with Soviet Jews" more than 100,000 demonstrated in Manhattan, including senators Jackson and Humphrey (both were running for the Democratic nomination for President.) "Hundreds different protests took place.... The largest of these were the yearly 'Solidarity Sundays' – demonstrations and rallies in New York which were attended by up to 250,000 people (these ran from 1974-1987)."[3007] A three day meeting of 18 Nobel laureates in support of the Corresponding Member of Academy Levich took place in Oxford. Another 650 academics from across the world gave their support – and Levich was allowed to emigrate. In January 1978 more than a hundred American academics sent a telegram to Brezhnev demanding that he allow professor Meiman to go abroad. Another worldwide campaign ended in another success: the mathematician

---

[3006] V. Perelman. Krushenie chuda: prichiny i sledstviya. Beseda s G. Rosenblyumom [Collapse of the Miracle: Causes and Consequences. Conversation with G. Rosenblum]. // *EW*, Tel Aviv, 1977, (24), p. 128.

[3007] *Kratkaya Evreiskaya Entsiklopediya* [*The Short Jewish Encyclopedia* (henceforth—SJE)]. Jerusalem, 1996. v. 8, p. 380.

Chudnovsky received permission to leave for a medical procedure unavailable in the USSR. It was not just the famous: often a name until then unheard of would be trumpeted across the world and then returned to obscurity. For example, we heard it especially loudly in May 1978, when the world press told us a heart-rending story: a seven year old Moscow girl Jessica Katz had an incurable illness, and her parents were not allowed to go to the States! A personal intervention from Senator Edward Kennedy followed, and presto! Success! The press rejoiced. The main news on every television channel broadcast the meeting at the airport, the tears of happiness, the girl held aloft. The Russian Voice of America devoted a whole broadcast to how Jessica Katz was saved (failing to notice that Russian families with sick children still faced the same impenetrable wall). A medical examination later showed that Jessica wasn't ill at all, and that her cunning parents had fooled the whole world to ensure her leaving. (A fact acknowledged through gritted teeth on the radio, and then buried. Who else would be forgiven such a lie?) Similarly, the hunger strike of V. Borisov (December 1976) who had already spent nine years in a 'mental asylum' was reported by the Voice of America no differently from the 15 days of imprisonment of Ilya Levin, and if anything, more attention was given to the latter. All a few refuseniks had to do was sign a declaration about their inability to leave the USSR and it was immediately reported by the Freedom, Voice of America, the BBC and by the other most important sources of mass information, so much so that it is hard now to believe how loudly they were trumpeted.

Of course it has to be noted that all the pomp surrounding the appearance of a Soviet Jewish movement served to awaken among worldwide Jewry, including those in America, an exciting conception of themselves as a nation.

"Prophetic obsession of the first Zionists" in the USSR "induced exulting sympathy among the Western Jews." "The Western Jews saw their own ideals in action. They began to believe in Russian Jews ... that meant for them believing in their own best qualities.... All that which Western Jews wanted to see around themselves and ... didn't see."[3008] Others said, with a penetrating irony: "The offered product (an insurrectionary *Jewish spirit*) found a delighted buyer (American Jews). Neither America, nor American Jews are at all interested in Jews from the USSR in themselves. The product bought was precisely the spirit of Jewish revolt. The Jews of America (and with them the Jews of London, Amsterdam, Paris, etc.), whose sense of Jewishness had been excited by the Six-Day War triumph ... saw the

---

[3008] A. Voronel. *Vmesto poslesloviya* [Instead of Afterword]. // *"22"*, 1983, (31), p. 140.

chance to *participate*.... It was a comfortable 'struggle'... that moreover did not involve any great exertion."[3009]

However, it cannot be denied that these inspirations both here and there merged, and worked together to destabilise the walls of the steel shell of the old Soviet Union.

It is the general opinion that mass Jewish emigration from the USSR began in 1971, when 13,000 people left (98% to Israel). It was 32,000 in 1972, 35,000 in 1973 (the proportion going to Israel varying from 85% to 100%).[3010] However these were for the most part not from the ethnically Russian areas, but from Georgia and the Baltic. (A Jewish delegate to an international congress declared that "Georgia is a country without anti-Semitism"; many Georgian Jews later became disappointed with their move to Israel and wanted to go back). There was no mass movement from the central part of the USSR. Later, when leaving was made more difficult, some expressed a serious regret (R. Nudelman): the "tardy courage of future refuseniks might have, perhaps, been unnecessary if they had taken advantage of the breech made when they'd had the chance."

Someone disagrees: "But people need time to mature! ... See how long it took before we understood that we must not stay, that it is simply a crime against your own children."[3011]

"Ho, ho, [come forth], and flee from the land of the north, saith the LORD." (Zech 2:6)

Nonetheless, the excitement of Jewish emigration took root in Russian and Ukrainian towns too. By March 1973, 700,000 requests to emigrate had been registered. However, autumn 1973 saw the Yom Kippur War, and the desire of many to emigrate suddenly diminished. "Israel's image changed sharply after the Yom Kippur War. Instead of a secure and brave rich country, with confidence in tomorrow and a united leadership, Israel unexpectedly appeared before the world as confused, flabby, ripped apart by internal contradictions. The standard of living of the population fell sharply."[3012]

As a result only 20,000 Jews left the USSR in 1974. In 1975-76, "up to 50% of emigrating Soviet Jews" once in the stopover point of Vienna "went

---

[3009] V. Boguslavsky. *Oni nichego ne ponyali* [They still don't get it]. // *"22"*, 1984, (38), p. 156.
[3010] F. Kolker. *Novy plan pomoshchi sovetskomu evreistvu* [A New Plan for Assistance to the Soviet Jewry]. // *"22"*, 1983, (31), p. 144.
[3011] Yu. Shtern. *Situatsia neustoichiva i potomu opasna* [The Situation is Unstable and Therefore Dangerous]. Interview. // *"22"*, 1984, (38), p. 132, 133.
[3012] E. Manevich. *Novaya emigratsiya: slukhi i realnost* [New Emigration: the Rumors and Reality]. // *EW*, New York, 1985, (87), p. 107-108.

... past Israel. This period saw the birth of the term 'directists'" – that is to say those who went *directly* to the United States.[3013] After 1977, their numbers "varied from 70 to 98 percent."[3014]

"Frankly, this is understandable. The Jewish state had been conceived as a national refuge for Jews of the whole world, the refuge which, to begin with, guarantees them a safe existence. But this did not transpire. The country was in the line of fire for many years."[3015]

What is more "it soon became clear that Israel needed not intellectual Soviet Jews ... but a national Jewish intelligentsia." At this point "thinking Jews ... realised with a horror that in the way they had defined themselves their whole life they had no place in Israel," because as it turned out for Israel you had to be immersed in Jewish national culture – and so only then "the arrivals realised their tragic mistake: there had been no point to leaving Russia".[3016] (although this was also due to the loss of social position) – and letters back warned those who hadn't left yet of this. "Their tone and content at that time was almost universally negative. Israel was presented as a country where the government intervenes in and seeks to act paternally in all aspects of a citizen's life."[3017] "A prejudice against emigration to Israel began to form among many as early as the mid-1970s."[3018] "The firm opinion of Israel that the Moscow and Leningrad intelligentsia began to acquire was of a closed, spiritually impoverished society, buried in its own narrow national problems and letting today's ideological demands have control over the culture.... At best ... it is a cultural backwater, at worst ... yet another totalitarian government, lacking only a coercive apparatus."[3019] "Many Soviet Jews gained the impression, not without reason, that in leaving the USSR for Israel they were exchanging one authoritarian regime for another."[3020]

[3013] F. Kolker. *Novy plan pomoshchi sovetskomu evreistvu* [A New Plan for Assistance to the Soviet Jewry]. // *"22"*, 1983, (31), p. 144.

[3014] V. Perelman. *Oglyanis v somnenii* [Look Back in Doubt]. // *EW*, New York, 1982, (66), p. 152.

[3015] S. Tsirulnikov. *Izrail – god 1986* [Israel, the Year of 1986]. // *EW*, New York, 1986, (88), p. 135.

[3016] G. Fain. *V roli vysokooplachivaemykh shveitzarov* [In the Role of Highly Paid Doorkeepers]. // *EW*, Tel Aviv, 1976, (12), p. 135-136.

[3017] E. Manevich. *Novaya emigratsiya: slukhi i realnost* [New Emigration: the Rumors and Reality]. // *EW*, New York, 1985, (87), p. 111.

[3018] E. Finkelshtein. *Most, kotory rukhnul...* [The Bridge that Had Collapsed]. // *"22"*, 1984, (38), p. 148.

[3019] E. Sotnikova. Letter to Editor. // *EW*, Tel Aviv, 1978, (25), p. 214.

[3020] M. Nudler. *Oglyanis v razdumye* [Look Behind and Think]. Panel discussion. // *"22"*, 1982, (24), p. 138.

When in 1972-73 more than 30,000 Soviet Jews had left for Israel per year, Golda Meir used to meet them personally at the airport and wept, and the Israeli press called their mass arrivals "the Miracle of the 20th century." Back then "everyone left for Israel. Those who took the road to Rome," that is to say not to Israel, "were pointed out. But then the number of arrivals started to fall from year to year. It decreased from tens of thousands to thousands, from thousands to hundreds, from hundreds to a few lone individuals. In Vienna, it was no longer those taking the road to Rome [the next stop on the road to the final desired destination, usually the U.S.] who were pointed out, it was those 'loners,' those 'clowns,' those 'nuts,' who still left for Israel."[3021] "Back then Israel used to be the 'norm' and you had to explain why you were going 'past' it, but it was the other way round now: it was those planning to leave for Israel that often had to explain their decision."[3022]

"Only the first wave was idealistic"; "starting with 1974, so to speak the second echelon of Jews began to leave the USSR, and for those Israel might have been attractive, but mainly from a distance." [3023] Another's consideration:

"Perhaps the phenomenon of neshira [*neshira* – dispersal on the way to Israel; *noshrim* – the dispersed ones] is somehow connected to the fact that initial emigration used to be from the hinterlands [of the USSR], where [Jewish] traditions were strong, and now it's more from the centre, where Jews have substantially sundered themselves from their traditions."[3024]

Anyway, "the more open were the doors into Israel, the less Jewish was the efflux," the majority of activists barely knowing the Hebrew alphabet.[3025] "Not to find their Jewishness, but to get rid of it ... was now the main reason for emigration."[3026] They joked in Israel that "the world has not been filled with the clatter of Jewish feet running to settle in their own home.... Subsequent waves quickly took into account the mistake of the vanguard, and instead enthusiastically leapt en masse to where others' hands had already built their own life. En masse, it should be noted, for

---

[3021] V. Perelman. Letter to Editor. // *EW*, Tel Aviv, 1977, (23), p. 217.
[3022] Yu. Shtern. *Dvoinaya otvetstvennost* [Dual Liability]. Interview // *"22"*, 1981, (21), p. 126.
[3023] E. Manevich. *Novaya emigratsiya: slukhi i realnost* [New Emigration: the Rumors and Reality]. // *EW*, New York, 1985, (87), p. 109-110.
[3024] G. Freiman. *Dialog ob alie i emigratsii* [The Dialog (with Voronel) on Aliyah and Emigration]. // *"22"*, 1983, (31), p. 119.
[3025] A. Eterman. *Tretye pokolenie* [The Third Generation] Interview // *"22"*, 1986, (47), p. 126.
[3026] B. Orlov. *Puti-dorogi "rimskikh piligrimov"* [The Ways and Roads of "Roman Pilgrims"] // *EW*, Tel Aviv, 1977, (14), p. 126.

here finally was that much spoken of 'Jewish unity.'"[3027] But of course these people "left the USSR in search of 'intellectual freedom,' and so must live in Germany or England" or more simply in the United States.[3028] And a popular excuse was that the Diaspora is needed as "somebody has to give money to resource-less Israel and to make noise when it is being bullied! But on the other hand, the Diaspora perpetuates antiSemitism."[3029]

A. Voronel made a broader point here: ""The situation of Russian Jews and the problem of their liberation is a reflection of the all-Jewish crisis.... The problems of Soviet Jews help us to see the disarray in our own ranks"; "the cynicism of Soviet Jews" in using calls from made up relatives in Israel instead of "accepting their fate, the Way of Honour, is nothing more than a reflection of the cynicism and the rot affecting the whole Jewish (and non-Jewish) world"; "questions of conscience move further and further into background under the influence of the business, the competition and the unlimited possibilities of the Free World."[3030]

So it's all quite simple – it was just a mass escape from the harsh Soviet life to the easy Western one, quite understandable on a human level. But then what's about "repatriation?" And what is the "spiritual superiority" of those who dared to leave over those who stayed in the "country of slaves"? In fighting in those days for emigration Soviet Jews loudly demanded: "Let my people go!" But that was a truncated quote. The Bible said: "Let my people go, that they may hold a feast unto me in the wilderness." (Ex. 5:1) Yet somehow too many of those released went not into the desert, but to the abundance of America.

Can we nonetheless say that in the early years of sudden and successful emigration to Israel, it was the Zionists beliefs and ambitions that acted as the prime stimulus for Jews to leave? The testimony of various Jewish writers would suggest not.

"The Soviet situation of the end of the 1960s was one of Aliyah, not of a Zionist movement. There were many people psychologically ready to flee the USSR. What can be called a Zionist movement was entirely subsidiary to this group of people."[3031] Those who joined makeshift centres dedicated to the actual study of Jewish history and culture "were mostly characterised

---

[3027] A. Voronel. *Oglyanis v razdumye* [Look Behind and Think]. Panel discussion. // *"22"*, 1982, (24), p. 117-118.
[3028] E. Levin. *Oglyanis v razdumye* [Look Behind and Think]. Panel discussion. // *"22"*, 1982, (24), p. 127.
[3029] A. Dobrovich. Letter to Editor. // *"22"*, 1989, (67), p. 218.
[3030] A. Voronel. *Vmesto poslesloviya* [Instead of Afterword]. // *"22"*, 1983, (31), p. 139-141.
[3031] V. Boguslavsky. *Oglyanis v razdumye* [Look Behind and Think]. Panel discussion. // *"22"*, 1982, (24), p. 139.

by a complete lack of the careerism so common among the Soviet-Jewish intelligentsia. This was why they dedicated the entirety of their free time to Jewish affairs."[3032] For them the "era of the Hebrew teachers" had started even as early as the end of the 1970s, and by the beginning of the 1980s these "Torah teachers were the only ones who still influenced the minds."[3033]

The motives of many others who emigrated are explained as follows: "The Soviet government has placed obstacles in the way of achieving the most important things – professional advancement," and so "Jewry is in danger of degradation."[3034] "They were driven into Jewishness, and then into Zionism …

by their faceless bureaucratic nemesis." [3035] "Many … had never encountered anti-Semitism or political persecution. What burdened them was the dead end that their lives as Soviet Jews had become – as bearers of a contradiction from which they could free themselves neither by 'assimilation' nor by their 'Jewishness'"[3036] "There was a growing sense of incompatibility and sorrow"; "dozens and dozens of dolts … are dragging you into insignificance … are pushing you to the bottom."[3037] So came the longing to escape the Soviet Union.

"This bright hope, when a man under the complete control of the Soviet government could in three months become free … was genuinely exhilarating."[3038]

Of course, a complex emotional environment developed around the act of departure. A writer says: the majority of Soviet Jews are "using the same 'Zionist' door … they sadly leave that familiar, that tolerant Russia" (a slip, but one that is closer to the truth, as the author had meant to say "tolerated by" Jews).[3039] Or said thusly: "The vast majority decided to emigrate with their heads, while their insides," that is to say concern with being part of a

---

[3032] V. Boguslavsky. *U istokov* [At the Origins]. Interview. // *"22"*, 1986, (47), p. 105.
[3033] A. Eterman. *Tretye pokolenie* [The Third Generation]. Interview // *"22"*, 1986, (47), p. 136-140.
[3034] A. Voronel. *Dialog ob alie i emigratsii* [The Dialog (with G. Freiman) on Aliyah and Emigration]. // *"22"*, 1983, (31), p. 119.
[3035] Lev Kopelev. *O pravde i terpimosti* [On Truth and Tolerance]. New York: Khronika Press, 1982, c. 61.
[3036] Editorial. (R. Nudelman] // *"22"*, 1979, (7), p. 97.
[3037] E. Angenits. *Spusk v bezdnu* [Descend into Abyss]. // *"22"*, 1980, (15), p. 166, 167.
[3038] A. Eterman. *Tretye pokolenie* [The Third Generation] Interview // *"22"*, 1986, (47), p. 125.
[3039] V. Boguslavsky. *V zashchitu Kunyaeva* [In Defence of Kunyaev]. // *"22"*, 1980, (16), p. 175.

country and its traditions, "were against."³⁰⁴⁰ No one can judge to what extent this was a "majority." But as we've seen the mood varied from the good poetry of Liya Vladimorova: But for you my beloved, for you the proud, I bequest the memories and the departure to the then-popular joke: "Could the last person to leave please turn off the lights."

This growing desire to emigrate among Soviet Jews coincided with the beginning of the "dissident" movement in the USSR. These developments were not entirely independent: "for some of them [Jewish intellectuals] 'Jewish ethnic consciousness in the USSR' was a new vector of intellectual development ... a new form of heterodoxy,"³⁰⁴¹ and they regarded their own impatient escape from the country as also a desperately important political cause. In essence, the dilemma facing the Zionists at the start of the 20th century was repeated: if it is your aim to leave Russia, should you at the same time maintain a political struggle within it? Back then, most had answered "yes" to the struggle; now, most answered "no." But an increasingly daredevil attitude to emigration could not but feed a similarly daredevil attitude to politics, and sometimes the daredevils were one and the same. So for example (in 1976) several activists in the Jewish movement — V. Rubin, A. Sharansky, V. Slepak — together made an independent decision to support the "Helsinki Group" of dissidents, "but this was regarded in Jewish circles as an unjustifiable and unreasonable risk," as it would lead "to the immediate and total escalation of the government's repression of Jewish activism," and would moreover turn the Jewish movement "into the property of dissidents."³⁰⁴²

On the other side, many dissidents took advantage of the synchronicity of the two movements, and used emigration as a means of escape from their political battlefield for their own safety. They found theoretical justifications for this: "Any honest man in the USSR is an eternal debtor to Israel, and here is why.... The emigration breech was made in the iron curtain thanks to Israel ...it protects the rear of those few people willing to oppose the tyranny of the Communist Party of the Soviet Union [CPSU] and to fight for human rights in the USSR. The absence of this 'emergency exit' would be deadly to the current democratic movement."³⁰⁴³

It has to be admitted that this is a very cynical justification, and that it says little good of the dissident movement as a whole. A hostile critic then noted: "these 'opponents' [of the CPSU] are playing an odd game: they

---

[3040] V. Lyubarsky. *Chto delat, a ne kto vinovat* [The Question Is Not Who Is Guilty, But What to Do]. // *EW*, New York, 1990, (109), p. 129.

[3041] B. Khazanov. *Novaya Rossiya* [The New Russia]. // *EW*, Tel Aviv, 1976, (8), p. 143.

[3042] V. Lazaris. *Ironicheskaya pesenka* [Ironic Song]. // *"22"*, 1978, (2), p. 207.

[3043] I. Melchuk. Letter to Editor // *EW*, Tel Aviv, 1977, (23), p. 213-214.

become involved in the democratic movement, already sure of an 'emergency exit' for themselves. But by this they demonstrate the temporary and inconsequential character of their activity. Do potential emigrants have the right to speak of changing Russia, or especially on behalf of Russia?"[3044]

One dissident science fiction author (and later, after emigration, a Russian Orthodox priest) suggested this formulation, that Jewish emigration creates "a revolution in the mind of Soviet man"; "the Jews, in fighting for the right to leave, become transformed into fighters for freedom" in general...."The Jewish movement serves as a social gland that begins to secrete the hormones of rights awareness;" it has become "a sort of ferment perpetuating dissidence." "Russia is becoming 'deserted,'" "that 'abroad,' so mythical before, is becoming populated by our own people," "the Jewish Exodus ... is gradually leading totalitarian Soviet Moscow to the plains of freedom."[3045]

This view was readily accepted and in the coming years came to be loudly trumpeted: "the right to emigrate is the primary human right." It was repeated often and in unison that this was an "enforced escape," and "talk about the privileged position Jews occupy with regards to emigration is slander."[3046]

Yes, taking a lifeboat from a sinking ship is indeed an act of necessity. But to *own a lifeboat* is a great privilege, and after the gruelling ordeals of half a century in the USSR Jews owned one, while the rest did not. Those more perceptive expressed a more conscientious feeling: "It is fine to fight for the repatriation of Jews, it is understandable, and it is fine to fight for the right to emigrate for everyone – that too is understandable; but you cannot fight for the right to emigrate but, for some reason, *only for Jews.*"[3047] Contrary to the self-satisfied theoreticians of emigration, and their belief that it brought all Soviet people closer to emigrating abroad and so partly freed them, in reality those unable to emigrate came to feel more hopeless, to an even greater extent fooled and enslaved. There were emigrants who understood this: "What is cruellest about this situation is that it is Jews who are leaving. It has bizarrely become a question of something akin to a certificate of authenticity."[3048]

[3044] V. Lazaris. *Ironicheskaya pesenka* [Ironic Song]. // *"22"*, 1978, (2), p. 200.
[3045] M. Aksenov-Meerson. *Evreiskii iskhod v rossiiskoi perspective* [The Jewish Exodus from Russian Point of View]. // *EW*, Tel Aviv, 1979, (41).
[3046] G. Sukharevskaya. Letter to Editor. // Seven Days, New York, 1984, (51).
[3047] I. Shlomovich. *Oglyanis v razdumye* [Look Behind and Think]. Panel discussion. // *"22"*, 1982, (24), p. 138.
[3048] B. Khazanov. *Novaya Rossiya* [The New Russia] // *EW*, Tel Aviv, 1976, (8), p. 143.

Precisely. But they chose to blind themselves to this. What could the remaining residents of "totalitarian Moscow" think? There was a great variety of responses, from grievance ("You, Jews, are allowed to leave and we aren't...") to the despair of intellectuals. L.K Chukovksaya expressed it in conversation to me: "Dozens of valuable people are leaving, and as a result human bonds vital for the country are ripped apart. The knots that hold together the fabric of culture are being undone." To repeat the lesson: "Russia is becoming deserted."

We can read the thoughtful comments of an emigrant Jewish author about this Departure: "Russian Jewry were pathfinders in their experiment to merge with the Russian people and Russian culture, they became involved in Russia's fate and history, and, repulsed away as if by a similarly charged body, left."

(What an accurate and penetrating comparison!) "What is most stunning about this Departure is how, at the moment of greatest assimilation, voluntary it was.... The pathetic character of the Russian Aliyah of the 1970s ... was that we were not exiled from the country on a king's order or by the decision of party and parliament, and we were not fleeing to save ourselves from the whips of an enraged popular pogrom ... this fact is not immediately obvious to the participants in this historical event."[3049]

No doubt, the Jewish emigration from the USSR ushered in a great historical shift. The beginning of the Exodus drew a line under an epoch lasting two centuries of coerced co-existence between Jews and Russians. From that point every Soviet Jew was free to choose for himself — to live in Russia or outside it. By the second half of the 1980s each was entirely free to leave for Israel without struggle.

The events that took place over two centuries of Jewish life in Russia – the Pale of Settlement, the escape from its stultifying confines, the flowering, the ascension to the ruling circles of Russia, then the new constraints, and finally the Exodus – none of these are random streams on the outskirts of history.

Jewry had completed its spread from its origin on the Mediterranean Sea to as far away as Eastern Europe, and it was now returning back to its point of origin. We can see in both this spread and in its reversal a supra-human design.

Perhaps those that come after us will have the opportunity to see it more clearly and to solve its mystery.

[3049] B. Orlov. *Ne te vy uchili alfavity* [You Have Studied Wrong Alphabets]. // *EW*, Tel Aviv, 1975, (1), p. 127-128.

Chapter 27

About the assimilation

When and how did this extraordinary Jewish status of "guests everywhere" begin? The conventional wisdom suggests that the centuries-old Jewish diaspora should be dated from the destruction of Jerusalem by Titus in AD70; and that, after being thrown out of their native land, the Jews began wandering around the world. However, it is not true because "the great majority of the Jews were already dispersed by that time; hardly more than one-eighth of the nation lived in Palestine."[3050] The Jewish Diaspora had begun much earlier: "The Jews were mainly a dispersed nation by the time of the Babylonian captivity [6th century B.C.] and, possibly, even earlier; Palestine was only a religious and, to certain extent, a cultural center."[3051]

Scattering of the Jews was already foretold in the Pentateuch. "I will scatter you among the nations" (Leviticus 26:33). "Yahweh will scatter you among the peoples, and you shall be left few in number among the nations" (Deuteronomy 4:27).

"Only a small part of the Jews had returned from the [Babylonian] captivity; many had remained in Babylon as they did not want to abandon their property." Large settlements were established outside of Palestine; "large numbers of Jews concentrated ... in major trade and industrial centers of the ancient world." (For example, in Alexandria under Ptolemaic dynasty, Jews accounted for two-fifth of the population.) "They were, mainly, traders and craftsmen."[3052] The Jewish-Hellenistic philosopher Philo Judaeus (who died in the middle of the 1st century, 20 years before the destruction of the Temple) states: "[The Jews] regard the Holy City as their metropolis because the Holy Temple of Almighty God is situated there, and they call "homeland" the countries where they live, and where

---

[3050] *I.M. Bikerman*. K samopoznaniyu evreya: Chem my byli, chem my stali, chem my dolzhny byt [To the Self-Knowledge of a Jew: What We Were, What We Became, What We Must Be]. Paris, 1939, p. 17.
[3051] *S.Ya. Lurye*. Antisemitizm v drevnem mire [Anti-Semitism in the Ancient World]. Tel-Aviv: Sova, 1976, p. 160 [1st ed. – Petrograd: Byloye, 1922].
[3052] Ibid.*, p. 64, 122, 159.

their fathers, grandfathers, great-grandfathers and ancient forebears lived, and where they were born and brought up."³⁰⁵³

Mikhail Gershenzon mused on the fates of the Jewish nation after the Babylonian captivity: "[The Jews] took roots in foreign lands and, contrary to expectations, didn't aspire to return to their old homeland." "Just recall: the Kingdom of Judah was still there, yet most of the Jews were already scattered across the whole Middle East; the Second Temple still stood in all its splendor, but the Language of the Bible was no longer heard on the streets and in the houses of Jerusalem; everybody spoke either Syrian or Greek there." Even back then the Jews were inclined to think: "We should not hold dear our national independence, we should learn to live without it, under foreign rule; we should not become attached to a land or to a single language."³⁰⁵⁴

Modern Jewish authors agree: "The Jews in the ancient world were scattered and established large centers in the Diaspora even before the collapse of Jewish nationhood."³⁰⁵⁵ "The nation which was given the Law did not want to return to its native country. There is some very profound and still not understood meaning in it. It is much easier to chat about Jewish values and about the preservation of Jewry than to explain the true reasons for such a long Galut."³⁰⁵⁶ (Even in the mid-20th century the Hebrew language still had no word for "Diaspora" as for the living in the voluntary scattering, there was only "Galut," referring to the forced exile.)

From the historical evidence we see that the scattering of the Jews was not solely their unfortunate fate, but also a *voluntary quest*. Indeed, it was a bemoaned disaster, but could it also be a method of making life easier? This is an important question in attempting to understand the Diaspora.

The Jews still do not have a generally accepted view on the Diaspora, whether it has been blessing for them or a bane.

Zionism, from the very moment of its birth, responded to this question firmly (and fully in line with its essence): "Our scattering is our biggest curse; it brings us no good, and no advantages and no peace to others as

---

³⁰⁵³ *S.Ya. Lurye.* Antisemitizm v drevnem mire* [Anti-Semitism in the Ancient World], p. 160.
³⁰⁵⁴ *M. Gershenzon.* Sudby evreyskogo naroda [The Destinies of the Jewish Nation] // "22": Obshchestvenno-politicheskiy i literaturniy zhurnal evreyskoy intelligentsii iz SSSR v Izraile [*Social, Political and Literary Journal of the Jewish Intelligentsia from the USSR in Israel*]. Tel-Aviv, 1981, (19), p. 109-110.
³⁰⁵⁵ *S. Tsiryulnikov.* Filosofiya evreyskoy anomalii [Philosophy of the Jewish Anomaly] // Vremya i my (daleye – VM): Mezhdunarodny zhurnal literatury i obshchestvennykh problem [*Epoch and We* (hereinafter – *EW*): *International Journal of Literature and Social Problems*]. New York, 1984, (77), p. 148.
³⁰⁵⁶ *A.-B. Yoshua.* Golos pisatelya [*Voice of the Writer*] // "22", 1982, (27), p. 158.

well.... We are guests everywhere ... and we are still unwanted, everybody wants to get rid of us."[3057] "To be a homeless man, feeling as a guest everywhere — this is the true curse of exile, its real bitterness!"[3058] "Some say that having several 'homes' improves chances to survive for the Jews. In my view, a nation staying in many other's homes and not caring about its own cannot expect security. The availability of many homes corrupts."[3059]

Yet the opposite opinion is even more prevalent, and it seems to be more credible. "Perhaps, the Jewish nation had survived and persevered not in spite of its exile, but because of it; the Jewish Diaspora is not an episode, but the organic 'ingredient' of Jewish history."[3060]

"Was the Jewish nation preserved in all its uniqueness in spite of the exile and scattering or because of it? The tragedy of Jerusalem in AD70 destroyed the state, yet it was necessary to save the people"; "the extraordinarily intensified instinct of national self-preservation" prompted Jews toward salvation through Diaspora."[3061] "Jewry was never able to fully comprehend its situation and the causes for it. They saw exile as the punishment for their sins, yet time and time again it turned out to be the dispensation by which the Lord has distinguished his nation. Through the Diaspora, the Jew worked out the mark of the Chosen he foresaw on his brow.... The scattered state of the nation is not unnatural for him.... Already in the periods of the most comfortable existence in their own state, Jewry was stationing garrisons on its route and spearheading vanguards in all directions, as if sensing its future dispersion and getting ready to retreat to the positions it had prepared in advance." "Thus, the Diaspora is a special form of Jewish existence in space and time of this world."[3062] And look how awesomely mobile are the Jews in Diaspora. "The Jewish people never strike root in one place, even after several generations."[3063]

But after they were so widely scattered and had become small minorities among other nations, the Jews had to develop a clear position toward those

---

[3057] *Max Brod*. Lyubov na rasstoyanii [Love at the Distance] // TW, Tel-Aviv, 1976, (11), p. 197-198.
[3058] *Amos Oz*. O vremeni i o sebe [On Time and on Me] // Kontinent: Literaturny, obshchestvenno-politicheskiy i religiozny zhurnal [*Continent: Literary, Social, Political and Religious Journal*]. Moscow, 1991, (66), p. 260.
[3059] *A.-B. Yoshua*. Golos pisatelya [*Voice of the Writer*] // "22", 1982, (27), p. 159.
[3060] *S. Tsiryulnikov*. Filosofiya evreyskoy anomalii [Philosophy of the Jewish Anomaly] // *EW*, New York, 1984, (77), p. 149-150.
[3061] *P. Samorodnitskiy*. Stranny narodets [Strange Little Nation] // "22", 1980, (15), p. 153, 154.
[3062] *E. Fishteyn*. Iz galuta s lyubovyu [From the Galut with Love] // "22", 1985, (40), p. 112-114.
[3063] *M. Shamir*. Sto let voyny [One Hundred Years of War] // "22", 1982, (27), p. 167.

nations — how to behave among them and how to relate to them, to seek ultimate bonding and merging with those nations, or to reject them and separate from them? The Holy Scripture contains quite a few covenants of isolation. The Jews avoided even their closest kindred neighbors, the Samaritans and Israelites, so irreconcilably that it was not permitted to even take a piece of bread from them. Mixed marriages were very strictly forbidden. "We will not give our daughters to the peoples of the land or take their daughters for our sons." (Nehemiah 10:30) And Ezra had ordered them to dissolve even the existing marriages, even those with children.

Thus, living in Diaspora for thousands of years, the Jews did not mix with other nations, just as butter does not mix with water, but comes to the surface and floats. During all those long centuries, they perceived themselves as something distinct, and until the 18th century "the Jews as a nation have never shown any inclination for assimilation." The pre-revolutionary *Jewish Encyclopedia*, while quoting Marx's assertion that "the Jews had not assimilated, because they represented the highest economic class, that is the class of capitalists amidst the agricultural and petty bourgeois nations," objects, saying that the economy was secondary: "the Jews of the Diaspora have consciously established their own economy which protected them from assimilation. They did it because they were conscious of their cultural superiority," which, for its part, was created by "the spiritual meaning of Judaism in its most complete form. The latter protected them from imitation."[3064]

But "from the mid-18th century the Jews started to believe in assimilation, and that becomes … the ferment of decomposition of the Jewish nation in Western Europe of the 19th century." Assimilation begins when "the surrounding culture reaches the height held by the Jewish culture, or when the Jewry ceases to create new values." The national will of the European Jews was weakened by the end of the 18th century; it had lost ground because of extremely long waiting. Other nations began creating brilliant cultures that eclipsed Jewish culture."[3065] And exactly then Napoleon launched the Pan-European emancipation; in one country after another, the roads to social equality were opening before the Jews, and that facilitated assimilation. (There is an important caveat here: "There is no unilateral assimilation," and "the assimilating Jews supplemented the host cultures with Jewish national traits."

[3064] Evreyskaya Entsiklopediya (daleye – EE) [*The Jewish Encyclopedia* (hereinafter – *TJE*)]: 16 volumes. Sankt-Petersburg.: Obshchestvo dlya Nauchnykh Evreyskikh Izdaniy i Izd-vo Brokgauz-Efron [St. Petersburg: Society for Scientific Jewish Publications and Publisher Brokgauz-Efron], 1906-1913. V. 3, p. 312.
[3065] Ibid., p. 313.

Heine and Börne, Ricardo and Marx, Beaconsfield-Disraeli and Lassalle, Meyerbeer and Mendelssohn — "during their assimilation into the host cultures, they added Jewish elements to them."[3066])

In some cases, assimilation leads to a brighter creative personal self-fulfillment. But, overall, "assimilation was the price paid by the Jews for the benefit of having access to the European culture. Educated Jews convinced themselves that "the Jews are not a nation, but only a religious group."[3067] "The Jewish nation, after it joined the realm of European nations, began to lose its national uniqueness ... only the Jew from the ghetto retained pronounced national traits ... while the intelligent Jew tried with all his strength to look unlike a typical Jew." Thus spread "the theory that there is no Jewish nation, but only 'the Poles, Frenchmen and Germans of Mosaic Law.'"[3068]

Marx, and then Lenin saw the solution of Jewish question in the *full* assimilation of the Jews in the countries of their residence.

In contrast to the clumsiness of those ideologues, the ideas of M.O. Gershenzon are much more interesting. He put them forward late in life, in 1920, and they are all the more interesting because the lofty thinker Gershenzon was a completely assimilated Russian Jew. Nevertheless, the Jewish question was alive and well in his mind. He explored it in his article *The Destinies of the Jewish Nation*.

Unlike the contemporary *Jewish Encyclopedia*, Gershenzon believes that Jewish assimilation is the ancient phenomenon, from time immemorial. One voice constantly "tempted him [the Jew] to blend with the environment — hence comes this ineradicable and ancient Jewish aspiration to assimilate." Yet another voice "demanded above all things to preserve his national uniqueness.

The whole story of scattering is the never-ending struggle of two wills within Jewry: the human will against the superhuman one, the individual against the collective.... The requirements of the national will towards the individual were so ruthless and almost beyond human power, that without

---

[3066] Ibid.

[3067] M. *Krol.* Natsionalizm i assimilyatsiya v evreyskoy istorii [Nationalism and Assimilation in the Jewish History] // Evreyskiy mir: Ezhegodnik na 1939 g. (daleye – EM-1) [The Jewish World: Yearbook for 1939 (hereinafter – JW-1)]. Paris: Obyedineniye russko-evreyskoy intelligentsii [Association of Russian-Jewish Intelligentsia], p. 187.

[3068] *I.L. Klauzner*. Literatura na ivrite v Rossii [Literature in Hebrew in Russia] // Kniga o russkom evreystve: Ot 1860-kh godov do Revolyutsii 1917 g. [Book on the Russian Jewry: From the 1860s until the 1917 Revolution]. New York: Soyuz Russkikh Evreyev [The Union of Russian Jews], 1960, p. 506.

having a great hope common to all Jewry, the Jew would succumb to despair every now and then, and would be tempted to fall away from his brethren and desert that strange and painful common cause." Contrary to the view that it is not difficult to explain why assimilation began precisely at the end of the 18th century, Gershenzon is rather surprised: "Is it not strange that assimilation so unexpectedly accelerated exactly during the last one hundred years and it continues to intensify with each passing hour? Shouldn't the temptation to fall apart be diminished greatly nowadays, when the Jews obtained equal rights everywhere?" No, he replies: "It is not the external force that splits the Jews; Jewry disintegrates from the inside.

The main pillar of Jewry, the religious unity of the Jewish nation, is decayed and rotten." So, what about assimilation, where does it lead to? "At first sight, it appears that ... [the Jews] are imbued, to the marrow of their bones, with the cosmopolitan spirit or, at least, with the spirit of the local culture; they share beliefs and fixations of the people around them." Yet it is not exactly like that: "They love the same things, but not in the same way.... They indeed crave to embrace the alien gods... They strive to accept the way of life of modern culture.... They pretend that they already love all that — truly love, and they are even able to convince themselves of that." Alas! One can only love his own faith, "the one born in the throes from the depths of the soul."[3069]

Jewish authors genuinely express the spiritual torment experienced by the assimilating Jew. "If you decided to pretend that you are not a Jew, or to change your religion, you are doomed to unending internal struggle with your Jewish identity.... You live in terrible tension.... In a way, this is immoral, a sort of spiritual self-violation."[3070] (This inner conflict was amazingly described by Chekhov in his essay *Tumbleweed*.) "This evil stepmother — assimilation ...

forced the individual to adapt to everything: to the meaning of life and human relations, to demands and needs, to the way of life and habits. It crippled the psychology of the nation in general and ... that of the national intelligentsia in particular." It compelled people "to renounce their own identity, and, ultimately, led to self-destruction."[3071] "It is a painful and humiliating search of identity."[3072]

[3069] *M. Gershenzon*. Sudby evreyskogo naroda [The Destinies of the Jewish Nation] // *"22"*, 1981, (19), p. 111-115.
[3070] *N. Podgorets*. Evreyi v sovremennom mire [The Jews in the Modern World]: [Interview] // *EM*, New York, 1985, (86), p. 117.
[3071] *V. Levitina*. Stoilo li szhigat' svoy khram.... [Should We Really Burn Our Temple....] // *"22"*, 1984, (34), p. 194.
[3072] *Boguslavskiy*. Zametki na polyakh [Marginal Notes] // *"22"*, 1984, (35), p. 125.

But even "the most complete assimilation is ephemeral: it never becomes natural," it does not liberate "from the need to be on guard" all the time.[3073]

In addition to the lack of trust on the part of surrounding native people, assimilating Jews come under fire from their fellow Jews; they are accused of "consumerism and conformism," of "the desire to desert their people, to dispose of their Jewish identity," and of "the national defection."[3074]

Nevertheless, during the 19th century everything indicated that assimilation was feasible and necessary, that it was predetermined and even inevitable. Yet the emergence of *Zionism* cast a completely new light on this problem. Before Zionism, "every Jew suffered from painful duality,"[3075] the dissonance between the religious tradition and the surrounding external world.

In the early 20th century Jabotinsky wrote: "When the Jew adopts a foreign culture ... one should not trust the depth and strength of such conversion. The assimilated Jew cannot withstand a single onslaught, he abandons the 'adopted' culture without any resistance whatsoever, as soon as he sees that the power of that culture is over ... he cannot be the pillar for such a culture." He provided a shining example of the Germanized Austria-Hungary, when, with the growth of Czech, Hungarian and Polish cultures, Germanized Jews actively conformed to new ways of life. "It is all about certain hard realities of the natural relationship between a man and *his* culture, the culture created by his ancestors."[3076] This observation is true, of course, though "hard realities" sounds somewhat dry.

(Jabotinsky not only objected to assimilation fiercely, he also insistently warned the Jews to avoid Russian politics, literature and art, cautioning that after a while the Russians would inevitably turn down such service.[3077])

Many individual and collective examples, both in Europe and Russia, in the past and nowadays, illustrate the fragility of Jewish assimilation.

[3073] O. Rapoport. Simptomy odnoy bolezni [Symptoms of One Disease] // *"22"*, 1978, (1), p. 122.

[3074] L. Tsigel'man-Dymerskaya. Sovetskiy antisemitizm – prichiny i prognozy [Soviet AntiSemitism – Causes and Forecasts]: [Seminar] // *"22"*, 1978, (3), p. 173-174.

[3075] G. Shaked. Trudno li sokhranit' izrail'skuyu kul'turu v konfrontatsii s drugimi kul'turami [Is It Difficult to Preserve Jewish Culture in Confrontation with Other Cultures] // *"22"*, 1982, (23), p. 135.

[3076] Vl. Jabotinsky. Na lozhnom puti [On a False Road] // Vl. Jabotinsky. Felyetony [Feuilletons]. Sankt-Peterburg: Tipografiya "Gerold" [St. Petersburg: Gerold Printing Establishment], 1913, p. 251, 260-263.

[3077] Vl. Jabotinsky. Chetyre statyi o "chirikovskom intsidente" [Four Articles on the "Chirikov Incident"] (1909) // Ibid., p. 76.

Consider Benjamin Disraeli, the son of a non-religious father; he was baptized in adolescence and he did not just display the English way of life, he became no less than the symbol of the British Empire. So, what did he dream about at leisure, while riding his novel-writing hobby-horse? He wrote about exceptional merits and Messianism of the Jews, expressed his ardent love to Palestine, and dreamt of restoring the Israeli homeland![3078]

And what's about Gershenzon? He was a prominent historian of Russian culture and an expert on Pushkin. He was even criticized for his "Slavophilism." But, nevertheless, at the end of his life, he wrote: "Accustomed to European culture from a tender age, I deeply imbibed its spirit ... and I truly love many things in it.... But deep in my mind I live differently. For many years a secret voice from within appeals to me persistently and incessantly: This is not yours! This is not yours! A strange will inside me sorrowfully turns away from [Russian] culture, from everything happening and spoken around me.... I live like a stranger who has adapted to a foreign country; the natives love me, and I love them too; I zealously work for their benefit ... yet I feel I am a stranger, and I secretly yearn for the fields of my homeland."[3079]

After this confession of Gershenzon, it is appropriate to formulate the key thesis of this chapter. There are different types of assimilation: civil and domestic assimilation, when the assimilated individual is completely immersed in the surrounding life and accepts the interests of the native nation (in that sense, the overwhelming majority of Russian, European and American Jews would perhaps consider themselves assimilated); cultural assimilation; and, at the extreme, spiritual assimilation, which also happens, albeit rarely. The latter is more complex and does not result from the former two types of assimilation.

(In the opinion of a critic, *The Correspondence between Two Corners* by Vyacheslav Ivanov and M.O. Gershenzon, that "small book of tremendous importance", serves as "a proof of the inadequacy of Jewish assimilation, even in the case of apparently complete cultural assimilation."[3080])

Or take another individual, [M. Krol], a revolutionary in his youth and a "converted" émigré after the revolution, he marvels that the Russian Jews even in their new countries of emigration demonstrated "a huge amount of national energy" and were building an "original Jewish culture" there. Even in London the Jews had their own Yiddish schools, their own social

---

[3078] *TJE*, V. 4, p. 560, 566-568.
[3079] *Vyacheslav Ivanov, M.O. Gershenzon. Perepiska iz dvukh uglov* [The Correspondence Between The Two Corners]. Petrograd: Alkonost, 1921, p. 60, 61.
[3080] *O. Rapoport. Simptomy odnoy bolezni* [The Symptoms of One Disease] // *"22"*, 1978, (1), p. 123.

organizations, and their own solid economics; they did not merge with the English way of life, but only accommodated to its demands and reinforced the original English Jewry.

(The latter even had their own British Council of Jews, and called themselves the "Jewish community of the Great Britain" — note that all this was in England, where Jewish assimilation was considered all but complete.) He witnessed the same thing in France, and was particularly impressed by the similar "feat" in the United States.[3081]

And there is also that unfailing and reliable Jewish mutual support, that truly outstanding ability that preserves the Jewish people. Yet it further weakens the stability of assimilation.

It was not only the rise of Zionism that prompted the Jews to reject assimilation. The very course of the 20th century was not conductive to assimilation.

On the eve of World War II in 1939, a true Zionist, Max Brod, wrote: "It was possible to argue in support of the theory of assimilation in the days of far less advanced statehood of the 19th century," but "this theory lost any meaning in the era when the peoples increasingly consolidate"; "we, the Jews, will be inevitably crushed by bellicose nationalistic peoples, unless we take our fate into our hands and retreat in time."[3082]

Martin Buber had a very stern opinion on this in 1941: "So far, our existence had served only to shake the thrones of idols, but not to erect the throne of God. This is exactly why our existence among other nations is so mysterious. We purport to teach others about the absolute, but in reality we just say 'no' to other nations, or, perhaps, we are actually nothing more than just the embodiment of such negation. This is why we have turned into the nightmare of the nations."[3083]

Then, two deep furrows, the Catastrophe and the emergence of Israel soon afterwards, crossed the course of Jewish history, shedding new and very bright light on the problem of assimilation.

Arthur Koestler clearly formulated and expressed his thoughts on the significance of the state of Israel for world Jewry in his book *Promise and*

[3081] *M. Krol*. Natsionalizm i assimilyatsiya v evreyskoy istorii [Nationalism and Assimilation in the Jewish History] // JW-1, p. 191-193.
[3082] *Max Brod*. Lyubov' na rasstoyanii [Love at a Distance] // *EW*, Tel-Aviv, 1976, (11), p. 198-199.
[3083] *Martin Buber*. Natsionalnye bogi i Bog Izrailya [The National Gods and the God of Israel] // *EW*, Tel-Aviv, 1976, (4), p. 117.

Fulfillment: Palestine 1917-1949 and in an article, *Judah at the Crossroads*.

An ardent Zionist in his youth, Koestler left Vienna for a Palestinian kibbutz in 1926; he worked for a few years in Jerusalem as a Hebrew-writing columnist for Jabotinsky's newspaper; he also reported for several German newspapers. And then he wrote: "If we exclude from the Jewish religion the mystical craving for the Promised Land, then the very basis and essence of this religion would disappear." And further, "after the restoration of the Jewish state, most of the Jewish prayers, rites and symbols lost their meaning.... The God of Israel has abided by the treaty; he had returned the land of Canaan to Abraham's seed.... If, however, [the religious Jew] defies the order to return to the land of his ancestors and thus violates the treaty, he consequently ... anathematizes himself and loses his Jewishness." On the other hand, it may be difficult for not very religious Jews to understand why they should make sacrifices to preserve "Jewish values" not included in the religious doctrine. "The [Jewish] religion loses any sense if you continue to pray about the return to Zion even after you have grimly determined not to go there." A painful choice, yes, but "the choice that must be made immediately, for the sake of the next generation.... Do I want to move to Israel? If I do not, then what right do I have to continue calling myself a Jew and thus to mark my children with the stigma of isolation? The whole world would sincerely welcome the assimilation of the Jews," and after three generations or so, "the Jewish question would fade away."[3084]

The London newspaper *Jewish Chronicle* objected to Koestler: perhaps, "it is much better, much more reasonable and proper for a Jew from the Diaspora to live as before, at the same time helping to build the State of Israel?" Yet Koestler remained adamant: "They want both to have their cake and eat it. This is the route to disaster."[3085]

Yet all previous attempts at assimilation ended in failure; so why it should be different this time? — argued the newspaper. Koestler replied: "Because all previous attempts of assimilation were based on the wrong assumption that the Jews could be adequate sons of the host nation, while at the same time preserving their religion and remaining 'the Chosen people.'" But *"ethnic assimilation is impossible if Judaism is preserved; and conversely Judaism collapses in case of ethnic assimilation.* Jewish religion perpetuates the national isolation — there is nothing you can do about this fact." Therefore, "before the restoration of Israel, the renunciation of one's

---

[3084] *Artur Koestler.* Iuda na pereputye [Judah at the Crossroads] // *EW*, Tel-Aviv, 1978, (33), p. 104-107, 110.
[3085] Ibid., p. 112.

Jewish identity was equivalent to refusal to support the persecuted and could be regarded as a cowardly surrender." But "now, we are talking not about surrender, but about a free choice."[3086]

Thus, Koestler offered a tough choice to the Diaspora Jews: "to become Israelis or to stop being Jews. He himself took the latter path." [3087] (Needless to say, Jews in the Diaspora met Koestler's conclusions mainly with angry criticism.)

Yet those who had chosen the first option, the citizens of the State of Israel, obtained a new support and, from that, a new view at this eternal problem. For instance, a modern Israeli author writes sharply: "The Galut Jew is an immoral creature. He uses all the benefits of his host country but at the same time he does not fully identify with it. These people demand the status which no other nation in the world has — to be allowed to have two homelands: the one, where they currently live, and another one, where 'their heart lives.' And after that they still wonder why they are hated!"[3088]

And they do wonder a lot: "Why, why are the Jews so disliked (true, the Jews are disliked, this is fact; otherwise, why strive for liberation?)? And from what? Apparently, not from our Jewishness...." "We know very well that we should liberate ourselves, it is absolutely necessary, though ... we still cannot tell exactly what from."[3089]

A natural question — what should we do to be loved — is seldom asked. Jewish authors usually see the whole world as hostile to them, and so they give way to grief: "The world is now split into those who sympathize with the Jewish people, and those seeking to destroy the Jewish people."[3090] Sometimes, there is proud despair: "It is humiliating to rely on the authorities for the protection from the nation which dislikes you; it is humiliating to thank ingratiatingly the best and worthiest of this nation, who put in a good word for you."[3091]

Another Israeli disagrees: "In reality, this world is not solely divided on the grounds of one's attitude toward Jews, as we sometimes think owing to our

---

[3086] Ibid., p. 117, 126.
[3087] V. Boguslavskiy. Galutu – s nadezhdoy [To the Galuth with Hope] // *"22"*, 1985, (40), p. 135.
[3088] A.-B. Yoshua. Golos pisatelya [Voice of the Writer] // *"22"*, 1982, (27), p. 159.
[3089] Yu. Viner. Khochetsya osvoboditsya [I Want to Become Free] // *"22"*, 1983, (32), p. 204-205.
[3090] M. Goldshteyn. Mysli vslukh [Thoughts Aloud] // Russkaya mysl [Russian Thinker], 1968, February 29, p. 5.
[3091] M. Kaganskaya. Nashe gostepriimstvo... [Our Hospitality...] // *"22"*, 1990, (70), p. 111.

excessive sensitivity." A. Voronel agrees: "The Jews pay too much attention to anti-Semites, and too little — to themselves."[3092]

Israel, the Jewish state, must become the center that secures the future of world Jewry. As early as in the 1920s no other than Albert Einstein wrote to no other than Pyotr Rutenberg, a former Social Revolutionary and possibly the main author of the revolutionary demands of January 9, 1905 (he accompanied Orthodox Father Gapon during the workers' procession on that date but was later one of his executioners; still later, Rutenberg left Russia to rebuild Palestine): "First of all, your [Palestinian settlers'] lives must be protected, because you sacrifice yourselves for the sake of the Spirit and in the name the entire Jewish nation. We must demonstrate that we are a nation with the will to live and that we are strong enough for the great accomplishment that would consolidate our people and protect our future generations. For us and for our posterity, the State must become as precious as the Temple was for our ancestors."[3093]

Jewish authors support this conviction in many ways: "The Jewish problem, apparently, has no reliable solution without the Jewish state."[3094]

"Israel is the center that guarantees the future of the Jews of the whole world."[3095] Israel is the only correct place for Jews, one where their "historical activity does not result in historical fiasco."[3096]

And only a rumble coming from that tiny and endlessly beleaguered country betrays "the phantom of the Catastrophe, permanently imprinted in the collective unconscious of the Israelis."[3097]

And what is the status of assimilation, the Diaspora, and Israel today? By the 1990s, assimilation had advanced very far. For example, "for 80-90% of the American Jews, the modern tendencies of the Jewish life promise gradual assimilation." This holds true not only for the United States: "Jewish life gradually disappears from most of the Diaspora communities." Most modern-day Jews "do not have painful memories of the Catastrophe.... They identify with Israel much less than their parents."

[3092] *A. Voronel'*. Oglyanis' v razdumye... [Look Back in Reflection]: [Round Table] // *"22"*, 1982, (24), p. 131.

[3093] *A. Chernyak*. Neizvestnoye pismo Einshteyna [The Unknown Letter of Einstein] // *"22"*, 1994, (92), p. 212.

[3094] *A. Katsenelenboygen*. Antisemitizm i evreyskoye gosudarstvo [Anti-Semitism and the Jewish State] // *"22"*, 1989, (64), p. 180.

[3095] *I. Libler*. Izrail — diaspora: Krizis identifikatsii [Israel — the Diaspora: The Crisis of Identification] // *"22"*, 1995, (95), p. 168.

[3096] *N. Gutina*. Dvusmyslennaya svyaz [An Ambiguous Connection] // *"22"*, 1981, (19), p. 124.

[3097] *M. Kaganskaya*. Mif protiv realnosti [Myth Against Reality] // *"22"*, 1988, (58), p. 141.

Doubtlessly, "the role of the Diaspora is shrinking disastrously, and this is fraught with inevitable loss of its essential characteristics." "Will our grandchildren remain Jews...? Will the Diaspora survive the end of this millennium and, if so, for how long? Rabbi Adin Steinsaltz, one of the greatest teachers of our time ... warns that the Jews of the Diaspora are no longer a group, 'whose survival is guaranteed by being in jeopardy.'" And because of that, they, paradoxically, "are already on the road to extinction, participating in the 'Catastrophe of self-destruction.'" Moreover, "anti-Semitism in Western countries cannot be anymore considered as the element that strengthens Jewish identity. Anti-Semitic discrimination in politics, business, universities, private clubs, etc. is for all practical purposes eliminated."[3098] In present-day Europe "there are many Jews who do not identify as Jews and who react idiosyncratically to any attempt to connect them with that artificial community." "The assimilated Jew does not want to feel like a Jew; he casts away the traits of his race (according to Sartre)."[3099] The same author offers a scorching assessment: "European Jews reject their Jewishness; they think it is anti-Semitism that compels them to be the Jews. Yet that is a contradiction: A Jew identifies as a Jew only when he is in danger. Then he escapes as a Jew. But when he himself becomes the source of danger, he is not a Jew."[3100]

Thus, "the contours of the collapse of the Diaspora take shape exactly when the Western Jews enjoy freedom and wealth unprecedented in Jewish history, and when they are, or appear to be, stronger than ever." And "if the current trends do not change, most of the Diaspora will simply disappear. We have to admit a real possibility of the humiliating, though voluntary, gradual degradation of the Diaspora.... Arthur Koestler, the advocate of assimilation, who in the 1950s predicted the death of the Diaspora, might prove to be right after all."[3101]

Meanwhile, "the Jews of the world, sometimes even to their own surprise, feel like they are personally involved in the destiny of Israel." "If, God forbid, Israel is destroyed, then the Jews in other countries will disappear too. I cannot explain why, but the Jews will not survive the second Catastrophe in this century."[3102] Another author attributes the "Jewish

---

[3098] *I. Libler.* Izrail — diaspora... [Israel — the Diaspora...] // *"22"*, 1995, (95), p. 149-150, 154, 157.

[3099] *Sonja Margolina.* Das Ende der Lügen: Rußland und die Juden im 20. Jahrhundert. Berlin: Siedler Verlag, 1992, S. 95, 99.

[3100] *S. Margolina.* Germaniya i evrei: vtoraya popytka [Germany and the Jews: The Second Attempt] // Strana i mir [*The Country and the World*], 1991, (3), p. 143.

[3101] *I. Libler.* Izrail — diaspora... [Israel – the Diaspora...] // *"22"*, 1995, (95), p. 150, 155.

[3102] *N. Podgorets.* Evreyi v sovremennom mire [The Jews in the Modern World]: [Interview] // *EW*, New York, 1985, (86), p. 113, 120.

mythology of the imminent Catastrophe" precisely to life in the Diaspora, and this is why "American (and Soviet) Jews often express such opinions." They prepare for the Catastrophe: should Israel fall, it will be they who will carry on the Jewish nation.[3103] Thus, "almost all of many hypotheses attempting to explain the purpose of Jewish Diaspora ... recognize that it makes Jewry nearly indestructible; it guarantees Jewry eternal life within the limits of the existence of mankind."[3104]

We also encounter quite a bellicose defense of the principle of Diaspora. American professor Leonard Fayne said: "We oppose the historical demand to make *aliyah*. We do not feel like we are in exile." In June 1994 "the President of the World Jewish Congress, Shoshana S. Cardin, aggressively announced to the Israelis: 'We are not going to become the forage for *aliyah* to Israel, and we doubt you have any idea about the richness and harmony of American Jewish life.'"[3105] Others state: "We are interesting for the peoples of the world not because of peculiarities of our statehood, but because of our Diaspora which is widely recognized as one of the greatest wonders of world history."[3106] Others are rather ironic: "One rogue came up with ... the elegant excuse that the "choseness" of the Jews is allegedly nothing else but to be eternally scattered."[3107] "The miracle of the restoration of Israel post factum gave new meaning to the Diaspora; simultaneously, it had brilliantly concluded the story that could otherwise drag on. In short, it had crowned the miracle of the Diaspora. It crowned it, but did not abolish it."[3108] Yet "it is ironic too, as the goals for which we struggled so hard and which filled us with such pride and feeling of difference, are already achieved."[3109]

Understanding the fate of the Diaspora and any successful prediction of its future largely depends on the issue of *mixed marriages*. Intermarriage is the most powerful and irreversible mechanism of assimilation. (It is no accident that such unions are so absolutely forbidden in the Old Testament: "They have dealt faithlessly with the Lord; for they have borne alien children." (Hosea 5:7)) When Arnold J. Toynbee proposed intermarriage

---

[3103] Z. *Bar-Sella*. Islamskiy fundamentalizm i evreyskoye gosudarstvo [Islamic Fundamentalism and the Jewish State] // *"22"*, 1988, (58), p. 182-184.
[3104] E. *Fishteyn*. Iz galuta s lyubovyu [From the Galuth with Love] // *"22"*, 1985, (40), p. 112.
[3105] I. *Libler*. Izrail – diaspora... [Israel — the Diaspora...] // *"22"*, 1995, (95), p. 152.
[3106] E. *Fishteyn*. Glyadim nazad my bez boyazni... [We Are Looking Back with No Fear] // *"22"*, 1984, No. 39, p. 135.
[3107] A. *Voronel*. Oglyanis' v razdumye... [Look Back in Reflection]: [Round Table] // *"22"*, 1982, (24), p. 118.
[3108] E. *Fishteyn*. Iz galuta s lyubovyu [From the Galuth with Love] // *"22"*, 1985, (40), p. 114.
[3109] I. *Libler*. Izrail — diaspora... [Israel –the Diaspora...] // *"22"*, 1995, (95), p. 156.

as a means to fight antiSemitism, hundreds of rabbis opposed him: "Mass mixed marriage means the end of Jewry."[3110]

A dramatic growth of mixed marriages is observed in the Western countries: "Data documenting the statistics of 'dissolution' are chilling. In the 1960s 'mixed marriages' accounted for approximately 6% of Jewish marriages in the United States, the home of the largest Jewish community in the world.

Today [in 1990s], only one generation later, this number reached 60% — a tenfold increase. The share of 'mixed marriages' in Europe and Latin America is approximately the same.... Moreover, apart from the orthodox Jews, almost all Jewish families in Western countries have an extremely low birth rate." In addition, "only a small minority of children from 'mixed families' are willing to adopt a distinctly Jewish way of life."[3111]

And what about Russia? *The Shorter Jewish Encyclopedia* provides the following statistics: in 1988 [still under the Soviet regime], in the RSFSR (Russian Soviet Federated Socialist Republic), 73% of married Jewish men, and 63% of married Jewish women had non-Jewish spouses (in 1978 these numbers were lower: 13% for men, and 20% for women.). "Actually, Jews in such marriages tend to lose their Jewish self-consciousness much faster; they more often identify themselves with other nationalities during census."[3112]

Thus, almost everywhere, to a greater or lesser degree, we have the "erosion of Jewish life," "dilution of racial, religious and ethnic borders that, until recently, served as the barriers for assimilation and intermarriage.'"

Today, "when common anti-Semitism declined so abruptly, ... the Jews have lost a many great principles that in past used to be strong pillars of self-identification."[3113]

The Jews of the Diaspora are often attacked by the Israelis. Thirty and forty years after the creation of the State of Israel, the Israelis ask Diaspora Jews mockingly and sometimes angrily: "So, what about modern Jews? Most likely, they will always remain in their true historical home, in the

---

[3110] *Ed Norden*. Pereschityvaya evreyev* [Recounting the Jews] // *"22"*, 1991, (79), p. 126.

[3111] *I. Libler*. Izrail — diaspora... [Israel — the Diaspora...] // *"22"*, 1995, (95), p. 151, 152.

[3112] Kratkaya Evreyskaya Entsiklopediya [*The Shorter Jewish Encyclopedia*]: Jerusalem: Obshchestvo po issledovaniyu evreyskikh obshchin [Society for Study of Jewish Communities], 1996, V. 8, p. 303, Table 15.

[3113] *I. Libler*. Izrail — diaspora... [Israel — the Diaspora...] // *"22"*, 1995, (95), p. 156.

Galuth."[3114] "The Algerian Jews had preferred France to Israel, and then the majority of the Iranian Jews, who left Khomeini's rule, gave a wide berth to Israel." "By pulling up stakes, they search for countries with higher standards of living, and a higher level of civilization. The love of Zion is not sufficient in itself."[3115] "The eternal image of a classical 'imminent catastrophe' does not attract the Jews to Israel anymore."[3116] "The Jews are a nation corrupted by their stateless and ahistoric existence."[3117] "The Jews did not pass the test. They still do not want to return to their homeland. They prefer to stay in Galut and complain about anti-Semitism every time they are criticized.... And nobody may say a bad word about Israel, because to criticize Israel is 'anti-Semitism!' If they are so concerned about Israel, why do they not move here to live? But no, this is exactly what they try to avoid!"[3118] "Most of the Jews of the world have already decided that they do not want to be independent.... Look at the Russian Jews. Some of them wanted independence, while others preferred to continue the life of a mite on the Russian dog. And when the Russian dog had become somewhat sick and angry, they have turned to the American dog. After all, the Jews lived that way for two thousand years."[3119]

And now, the Diaspora Jew "is often nervous when confronted by an Israeli; he would rather feel guilty than ... share his fate with Israel. This sense of inferiority is compensated by intensely maintaining his Jewish identity ... through deliberate over-emphasizing of petty Jewish symbolism." At the same time, "the Jew from the Diaspora alone shoulders the specific risk of confronting surrounding anti-Semitism." Yet, "no matter how the Israel behaves, the Diaspora has no choice: it will quietly stand behind the Israelis like an unloved but faithful wife."[3120]

It was forecasted that "by 2021, the Diaspora will probably shrink by another million souls." "The interior workings of Jewish history... indicate that, most likely, the size of world Jewry will further decrease with the

---

[3114] *N. Gutina*. Dvusmyslennaya svyaz [An Ambiguous Connection] // *"22"*, 1981, (19), p. 125.
[3115] *S. Tsiryulnikov*. Filosofiya evreyskoy anomalii [Philosophy of Jewish Anomaly] // *EW*, New York, 1984, (77), p. 148.
[3116] *I. Libler*. Izrail — diaspora... [Israel — the Diaspora...] // *"22"*, 1995, (95), p. 165.
[3117] *Z. Bar-Sella*. Islamskiy fundamentalizm i evreyskoye gosudarstvo [Islamic Fundamentalism and the Jewish State] // *"22"*, 1988, (58), p. 184.
[3118] *A.-B. Yoshua*. Golos pisatelya [Voice of the Writer] // *"22"*, 1982, (27), p. 158.
[3119] *Beni Peled*. Soglasheniye ne s tem partnyorom [Agreement with the Wrong Partner] // *"22"*, 1983, (30), p. 125.
[3120] *E. Fishteyn*. Iz galuta s lyubovyu [From the Galuth with Love] // *"22"*, 1985, (40), p. 115, 116.

gradual concentration of a Jewish majority in Zion and not in the Diaspora."[3121]

Yet couldn't it be the other way around? Maybe, after all, the Russian Jew Josef Bikerman was right when he confidently claimed that the Diaspora is indestructible? "I accept Galut, where we have lived for two thousand years, where we have developed strong cohesion, and where we must live henceforth, to live and prove ourselves."[3122] Could it be that those two voices which, according to Gershenzon, always sound in Jewish ears — one calling to mix with the surroundings, and another demanding to preserve Jewish national uniqueness, — will sound forever?

A reputable historian noted (after World War II) "a paradox in the life of modern Jewry: ever-growing immersion of Jews in the life of other nations does not diminish their national identity and sometimes even intensifies it."[3123]

Below are few testimonies made by Russian Jews during the Soviet ("internationalist") period.

"I always had an acute perception of my Jewishness.... From the age of 17, when I left the cradle of high school, I mixed in circles where the Jewish question was central." "My father had a very strong Jewish spirit; despite that, he never observed traditions, Mitzvoth, did not know the language, and yet ... everything, that he, a Jew, knew, was somehow subordinated to his Jewish identity."[3124]

A writer from Odessa, Arkady Lvov, remembers: "When I was a 10-year old boy, I searched for the Jews among scientists, writers, politicians, and first of all, as a Young Pioneer [a communist youth group in the former Soviet Union], I looked for them among the members of government." Lazar Kaganovich was in third place, ahead of Voroshilov and Kalinin, "and I was proud of Stalin's minister Kaganovich... I was proud of Sverdlov, I was proud of Uritsky... And I was proud of Trotsky — yes, yes, of Trotsky!" He thought that Ostermann (the adviser of Peter the Great) was a Jew, and when he found that Ostermann actually was German,

---

[3121] *Ed Norden*. Pereschityvaya evreyev [Recounting the Jews] // *"22"*, 1991, (79), p. 120, 130-131.
[3122] *I.M. Bikerman*. K samopoznaniyu evreya [To the Self-Knowledge of a Jew]. Ibid., p. 62.
[3123] *Sh. Ettinger*. Noveyshiy period [Modern Period] // Istoriya evreyskogo naroda [History of the Jewish Nation] / Sh. Ettinger (Ed.). Jerusalem: Gesharim; Moscow: Mosty kultury [Bridges of Culture], 2001, p. 587.
[3124] *A. Eterman*. Tretye pokoleniye [The Third Generation] [Interview] // *"22"*, 1986, (47), p. 123-124.

he had "a feeling of disappointment, a feeling of loss," but he "was openly proud that Shafirov was a Jew."³¹²⁵

Yet there were many Jews in Russia who were not afraid "to merge with the bulk of the assimilating body,"³¹²⁶ who devotedly espoused Russian culture:

"In the old days, only a handful of Jews experienced this: Antokolsky, Levitan, Rubinstein, and a few others. Later there were more of them. Oh, they've fathomed Russia so deeply with their ancient and refined intuition of heart and mind! They've perceived her shimmering, her enigmatic play of light and darkness, her struggles and sufferings. Russia attracted their hearts with her dramatic fight between good and evil, with her thunderstorms and weaknesses, with her strengths and charms. But several decades ago, not a mere handful, but thousands Jews entered Russian culture.... And many of them began to identify sincerely as Russians in their souls, thoughts, tastes and habits.... Yet there is still something in the Jewish soul ... a sound, a dissonance, a small crack — something very small, but through it, eventually, distrust, mockery and hostility leaks from the outside, while from the inside some ancient memory works away.

So who am I? Who am I? Am I Russian? No, no. I am a Russian Jew."³¹²⁷ Indeed, assimilation apparently has some insurmountable limits. That explains the difference between full spiritual assimilation and cultural assimilation, and all the more so, between the former and widespread civic and social assimilation. Jews — fatefully for Jewry — preserve their identity despite all outward signs of successful assimilation, they preserve "the inner Jewish character" (Solomon Lurie).

The wish to fully merge with the rest of mankind, in spite of all strict barriers of the Law seems natural and vivid. But is it possible? Even in the 20ᵗʰ century some Jews believed that "the unification of the mankind is the ideal of Judaic Messianism."³¹²⁸ But is it really so? Did such an ideal ever exist?

Far more often, we hear vigorous objections to it: "Nobody will convince or compel me to renounce my Jewish point of view, or to sacrifice my

---

[3125] *A. Lvov*. Vedi za soboy otsa svoyego [Lead the Way to Your Father] // *EW*, New York, 1980, (52), p. 183-184.
[3126] *Vl. Jabotinsky*. Na lozhnom puti [On the Wrong Road] // Vl. Jabotinsky. Felyetony [Feuilletons]. Ibid., p. 251.
[3127] *Rani Aren*. V russkom galute [In the Russian Galuth] // *"22"*, 1981, (19), p. 135-136.
[3128] *G.B. Sliozberg*. Dela minuvshikh dney: Zapiski russkogo evreya [The Things of Days Bygone: The Memoirs of a Russian Jew]: 3 volumes. Paris, 1933-1934, V. 1, p. 4.

Jewish interests for the sake of some universal idea, be it 'proletarian internationalism,' (the one we idiots believed in the 1920s) or 'Great Russia,' or 'the triumph of Christianity,' or 'the benefit of all mankind,' and so on."[3129]

Nearly assimilated non-Zionist and non-religious Jewish intellectuals often demonstrate a totally different attitude. For instance, one highly educated woman with broad political interests, T.M.L., imparted to me in Moscow in 1967 that "it would be horrible to live in an entirely Jewish milieu. The most precious trait of our nation is cosmopolitanism. It would be horrible if all Jews would gather in one militarist state. It is totally incomprehensible for assimilated Jews." I objected timidly: "But it cannot be a problem for the assimilated Jews as they are not Jews anymore." She replied: "No, we still have some [Jewish] genes in us."

Yet it is not about the fatality of origin, blood or genes, it is about which pain — Jewish pain or that of the host nation — is closer to one's heart. "Alas, nationality is more than just knowledge of language, or an introduction to the culture, or even an attachment to the nature and way of life of the country. There is another dimension in it — that of the commonality of historic destiny, determined for each individual by his involvement in the history and destiny of his own people. While for others this involvement is predetermined by birth, for the Jew it is largely a question of personal choice, that of a hard choice."[3130]

So far, assimilation has not been very convincing. All those who proposed various ways for *universal* assimilation have failed. The difficult problem of assimilation persists. And though on a global scale the process of assimilation has advanced very far, it by no means foredooms the Diaspora.

"Even Soviet life could not produce a fully assimilated Jew, the one who would be assimilated at the deepest, psychological level."[3131] And, as a Jewish author concludes, "Wherever you look, you will find insoluble Jewish residue in the assimilated liquid."[3132]

Yet individual cases of deep assimilation with bright life histories do occur.

And we in Russia welcome them wholeheartedly.

[3129] *Sh. Markish*. Eshchyo raz o nenavisti k samomu sebe [Once Again on the Hate to Yourself] // *"22"*, 1980, (16), p. 189.

[3130] *L. Tsigelman-Dymerskaya*. Sovetskiy antisemitizm — prichiny i prognozy [Soviet AntiSemitism — Causes and Forecasts]: [Seminar] // *"22"*, 1978, (3), p. 175.

[3131] *Yu. Shtern*. Dvoynaya otvetstvennost [Double Responsibility] // *"22"*, 1981, (21), p. 127.

[3132] *O. Rapoport*. Simptomy odnoy bolezni [Symptoms of One Disease] // *"22"*, 1978, (1), p. 123.

"A Russian Jew ... A Jew, a Russian.... So much blood and tears have been shed around this boundary, so much unspeakable torment with no end in sight piled up. Yet, at the same time, we have also witnessed much joy of spiritual and cultural growth.... There were and still are numerous Jews who decide to shoulder that heavy cross: to be a Russian Jew, and at the same time, a Russian.

Two affections, two passions, two struggles.... Isn't it too much for one heart? Yes, it is too much. But this is exactly where the fatal tragedy of this dual identity is. Dual identity is not really an identity. The balance here is not an innate but rather an acquired entity."[3133] That reflection on the pre-revolutionary Russia was written in 1927 in the Paris emigration.

Some fifty years later, another Jew, who lived in Soviet Russia and later emigrated to Israel, looked back and wrote: "We, the Jews who grew up in Russia, are a weird cross — the Russian Jews.... Others say that we are Jews by nationality and Russians by culture. Yet is it possible to change your culture and nationality like a garment...? When an enormous press drives one metal into another, they cannot be separated, not even by cutting. For decades we were pressed together under a huge pressure. My national identity is expressed in my culture. My culture coalesced with my nationality. Please separate one from another. I am also curious which cells of my soul are of the Russian color and which are of the Jewish one. Yet there was not only pressure, not only a forced fusion. There was also an unexpected affinity between these intercrossing origins, at some deep spiritual layers. It was as if they supplemented each other to a new completeness: like space supplements time, the spiritual breadth supplements the spiritual depth, and the acceptance supplements the negation; and there was a mutual jealousy about 'choseness'. Therefore, I do not have two souls, which quarrel with each other, weaken each other, and split me in two. I have one soul ... and it is not two-faced, not divided in two, and not mixed. It is just one."[3134]

And the response from Russia: "I believe that the contact of the Jewish and Slavic souls in Russia was not a coincidence; there was some purpose in it."[3135]

[3133] *St. Ivanovich.* Semyon Yushkevich i evreyi [Semyon Yushkevich and the Jews] / Publikatsiya Ed. Kapitaykina [Publication of Ed. Kapitaykin] // Evrei v kul'ture Russkogo Zarubezhya [The Jews in the Russian-Language Culture]. Jerusalem, 1992, V. 1, p. 29.

[3134] [*R. Nudelman*] Kolonka redaktora [Editor's Column] // *"22"*, 1979, (7), p. 95-96.

[3135] *L-skiy.* Pisma iz Rossii [Letters from Russia] // *"22"*, 1981, (21), p. 150.

Author's afterword

In 1990, while finishing *April 1917* and sorting out the enormous amount of material not included in *The Red Wheel*, I decided to present some of that material in the form of a historical essay about Jews in the Russian revolution.

Yet it became clear almost immediately that in order to understand those events the essay must step back in time. Thus, it stepped back to the very first incorporation of the Jews into the Russian Empire in 1772. On the other hand, the revolution of 1917 provided a powerful impetus to Russian Jewry, so the essay naturally stretched into the post-revolutionary period. Thus, the title *Two Hundred Years Together* was born.

However, it took time for me to realize the importance of that distinct historical boundary drawn by mass emigration of the Jews from the Soviet Union that had begun in the 1970s (exactly 200 years after the Jews appeared in Russia) and which had become unrestricted by 1987. This boundary had been abolished, so that for the first time, the non-voluntary status of the Russian Jews no longer a fact: they ought not to live here anymore; Israel waits for them; all countries of the world are open to them. This clear boundary changed my intention to keep the narrative up to the mid-1990s, because the message of the book was already played out: the uniqueness of Russian-Jewish entwinement disappeared at the moment of the new Exodus.

Now, a totally new period in the history of the by-now-free Russian Jewry and its relations with the new Russia began. This period started with swift and essential changes, but it is still too early to predict its long-term outcomes and judge whether its peculiar *Russian-Jewish* character will persevere or it will be supplanted with the universal laws of the Jewish Diaspora. To follow the evolution of this new development is beyond the lifespan of this author.

Other titles

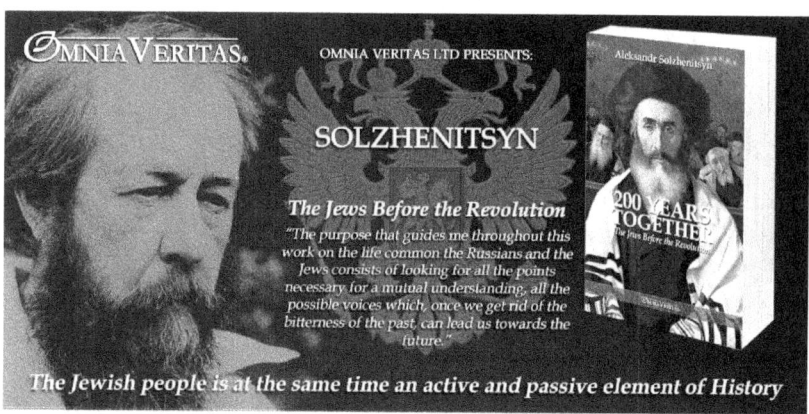

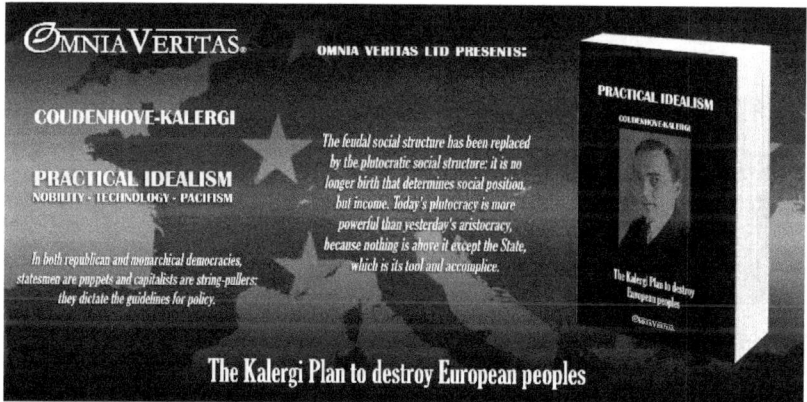

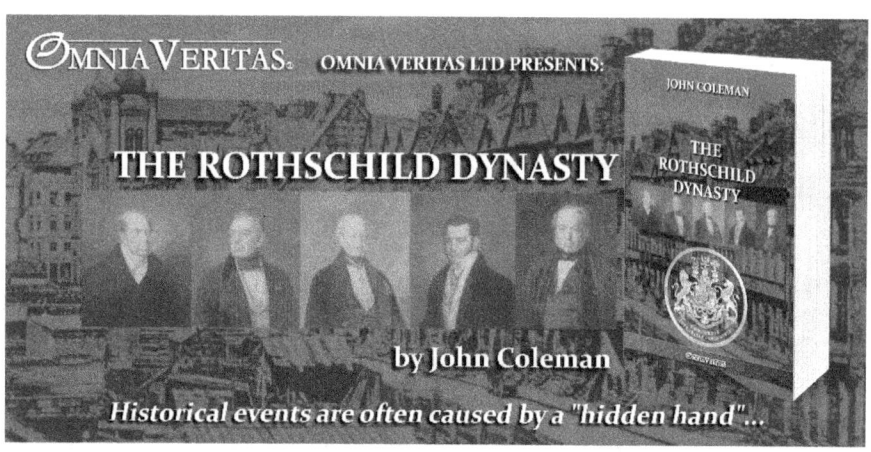

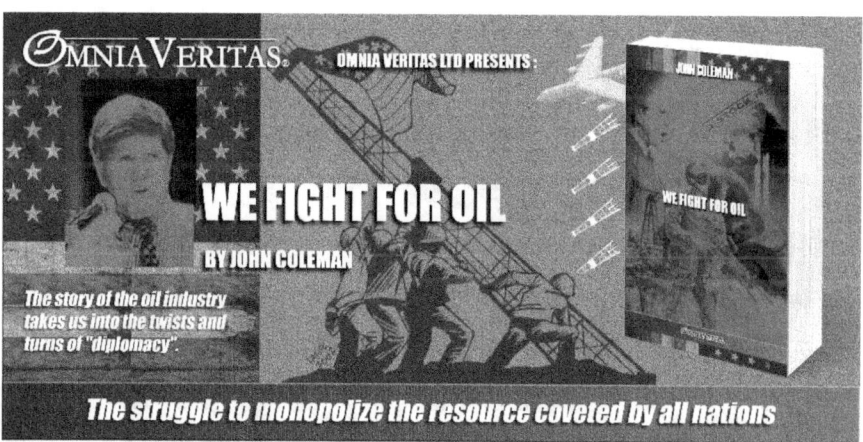

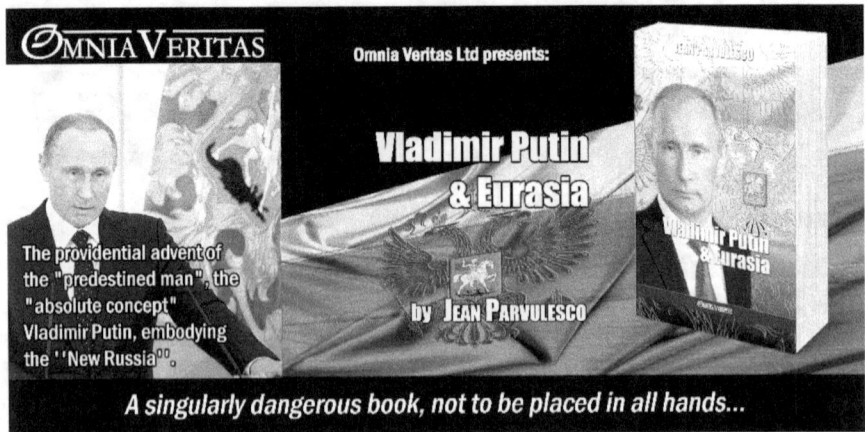

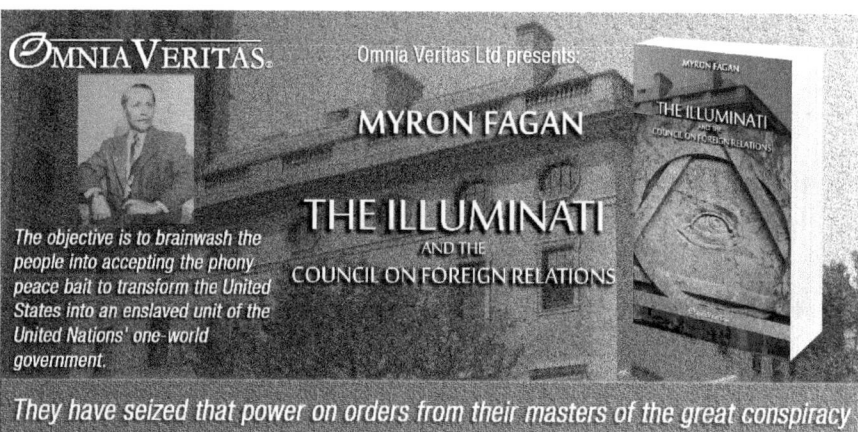
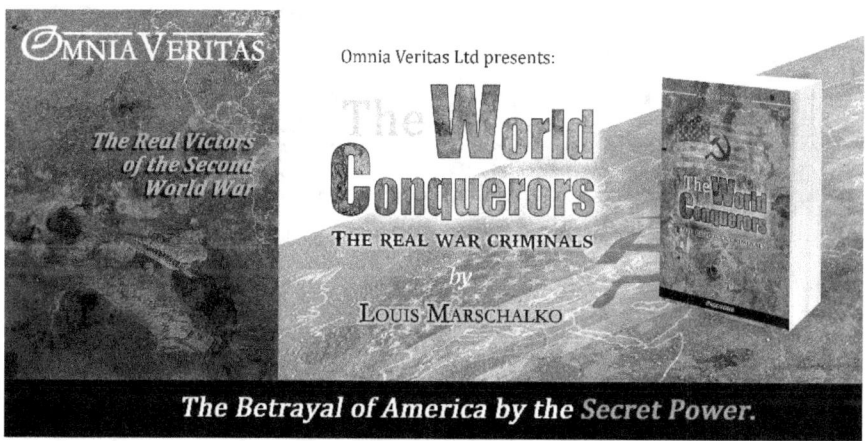

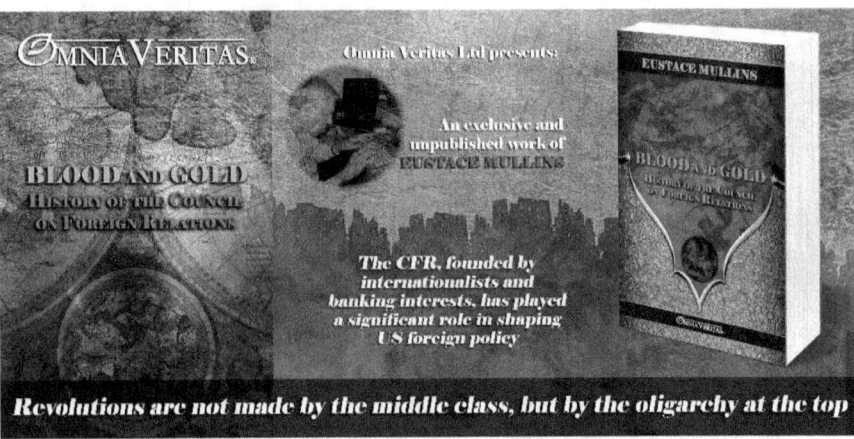

www.ingramcontent.com/pod-product-compliance
Lightning Source LLC
Chambersburg PA
CBHW050324230426
43663CB00010B/1732